SOCIAL AND STRUCTURAL CHANGE - CONSEQUENCES FOR BUSINESS CYCLE SURVEYS

Social and Structural Change - Consequences for Business Cycle Surveys

Selected papers presented at the 23rd Ciret conference, Helsinki 1997

Edited by
KARL HEINRICH OPPENLÄNDER
GÜNTER POSER

Routledge
Taylor & Francis Group
LONDON AND NEW YORK

First published 1998 by Ashgate Publishing

Reissued 2018 by Routledge
2 Park Square, Milton Park, Abingdon, Oxon, OX14 4RN
711 Third Avenue, New York, NY 10017, USA

Routledge is an imprint of the Taylor & Francis Group, an informa business

Copyright © Karl Heinrich Oppenländer and Günter Poser 1998

All rights reserved. No part of this book may be reprinted or reproduced or utilised in any form or by any electronic, mechanical, or other means, now known or hereafter invented, including photocopying and recording, or in any information storage or retrieval system, without permission in writing from the publishers.

Notice:
Product or corporate names may be trademarks or registered trademarks, and are used only for identification and explanation without intent to infringe.

Publisher's Note
The publisher has gone to great lengths to ensure the quality of this reprint but points out that some imperfections in the original copies may be apparent.

Disclaimer
The publisher has made every effort to trace copyright holders and welcomes correspondence from those they have been unable to contact.

A Library of Congress record exists under LC control number: 98072622

ISBN 13: 978-1-138-34471-6 (hbk)
ISBN 13: 978-1-138-34473-0 (pbk)
ISBN 13: 978-0-429-43831-8 (ebk)

Contents

	List of Contributors	ix
	Preface	xv
I	**Leading Indicators**	
	1 A Leading Indicator of Equipment Investment Demand in the Italian Economy *Paolo Carnazza*	3
	2 A New Look at Promptly Available Leading Indicators *John P. Cullity / Philip A. Klein*	21
	3 Use of Leading Indicators in a Model-based Forecast *Henk C. Kranendonk / Cees L. Jansen*	37
	4 An Update of OECD Leading Indicators *Gerald Petit / Gerard Salou / Pierre Beziz / Christophe Degain*	53
II	**Timing of Cyclical Turning Points**	
	5 Confidence and the Macroeconomy: A Markov Switching Model *Roy Batchelor*	77
	6 An Alternative Method to Predict the Business Cycle *Georg Goldrian / Birgit Lehne*	95
	7 The Timing of M-shaped Growth Cycles of the German Economy *Ernst Helmstädter*	105
	8 Survey on the Timing of Cyclical Turning Points *Rudolf Marty / Bernd Schips*	117

III Firm Behaviour

9 Inflation and Asymmetric Output Adjustments:
Tests Using Business Survey Data
Robert A. Buckle / John A. Carlson 131

10 Production and Price Flexibility with Stock Adjustment:
South African Evidence from Survey Data
Daniël Marais / Eon Smit / Willie J. Conradie 147

11 Productivity and Prices - Testing the Relationship
Using Micro Data
Julian Peters 175

12 Forecasting Models for Demand Series of Private Firms -
Using Survey Results and Dynamic Methods of Econometrics
Kurt Stock 203

13 Survey Results Relating to Changes in the International
Competitiveness of Belgian Manufacturing Enterprises
Jean-Jacques Vanhaelen / Chantal Winter 225

IV Financial Indicators

14 The Use of the Interest-Rate-Investment Relationship for Business
Cycle Forecast: The Case of the South African Economy
Lorraine Greyling / Gerhardus van Zyl 241

15 Economic Policies and Business Cycles in Germany
Willi Leibfritz / Alexander Juchems 259

16 An Index of Leading Indicators on Inflationary Trends
and the Business Cycle
Franz Seitz 269

17 Term Structure or Money Growth as Leading Indicator
of Inflation: An Empirical Analysis for Germany
Jürgen Wolters 285

V Economic Policy Recommendations

18 Aggregate Demand and Economic Growth:
    Empirical Evidence from Business Survey Data
    Marcella Corsi 301

19 Post-Unemployment Wages: Findings Based on the
    Swiss Labour Force Survey
    Monica Curti 321

20 A Time Series and Cross Sectional Analysis of
    Consumer Sentiment and its Components
    Detelina Ivanova / Kajal Lahiri 337

21 A Microsimulation Approach for Tax and Social Policy
    Recommendations in the Federal Republic of Germany
    Gerhard Wagenhals 363

VI Transition Economies

22 Why do the Russian Enterprises Hoard Labour?
    Sergei Aukutsionėk / Rostislav Kapeliushnikov 385

23 Business Cycles in Poland
    Zbigniew Matkowski 407

VII Surveys Covering the Service Sector

24 First Results of the Ifo Business Survey in the Data Processing
    Services Sector in Western and Eastern Germany
    Joachim Gürtler 431

25 Construction of a Confidence Indicator for Retail Trade
    by the European Commission
    Franz-Josef Klein / Guy Lejeune / Anne Roy 447

VIII Social and Structural Change

26 Understanding and Measuring the Intangible Economy:
   Current Status and Suggestions for Further Research
   Charles Goldfinger 465

27 Analysing the Information Society through Statistics -
   Problems, Weaknesses and Advantages
   Timo Relander 487

28 Social and Structural Change: Challenge and Consequences
   for Official Statistics
   Erich Bader 495

29 The European Monetary Union: Challenges and Opportunities
   for the European Statistical System
   Alberto De Michelis / Frank Schönborn 505

List of Contributors

Sergei Aukutsionek, Director of the Centre for Research in Transitional Economics, Institute of World Economy and International Relations (IMEMO), Moscow. Fields of interest: Survey of enterprises and banks, transition economy, economic fluctuations and crises, enterprise and bank behaviour.

Erich Bader, President of the Austrian Central Bureau of Statistics in Vienna.

Roy Batchelor, Midland Bank Professor of Banking and Finance at City University Business School in London. His current research and teaching is focussed on forecasting and risk management in financial markets. He has acted as consultant to a number of financial institutions, to the World Gold Council, the UK Treasury, the Bank of England, and the European Commission.

Pierre Beziz, Administrator at the OECD, Statistics Directorate, Paris. He is currently completing a Ph.D. on Statistical Methods for Cyclical Analysis at the University Paris IX Dauphin.

Robert A. Buckle, Associate Professor of Economics, Faculty of Commerce and Administration, Victoria University of Wellington, New Zealand. Research fields include macroeconomic theory and policy, business cycle theory and analysis, and the application of survey data for analysing output, employment, pricing and expectations of firms.

John A. Carlson, Loeb Professor of Economics at Purdue University, West Lafayette, USA. His research interests include studies of influences on exchange rates and using survey data to analyze firm pricing behavior.

Paolo Carnazza, degree in Economics at the University of Siena and Master of Science in Economics at the University of York (Great Britain) and Head of Unit "Business and Consumer Surveys" at ISCO (Istituto Nazionale per lo Studio della Congiuntura, Rome). His main scientific interests: business cycle analysis; business and consumer surveys; industrial economics.

Willie J. Conradie, Associate Professor at the Department of Statistics and Actuarial Science at the University of Stellenbosch. His field of interest is the analysis of categorical data (ordinal and nominal).

Marcella Corsi, Associate Professor of Economics at LUISS "G. Carli" in Rome, where she teaches Political Economy (Microeconomics and Macroeconomics). Her research activity focuses on both theoretical and empirical subjects concerning economic growth and business cycles.

John P. Cullity, Professor of Economics (em.), Rutgers - The State University, New York at Newark, and Senior Research Scholar, Economic Cycle Research Institute, New York.

Monica Curti, Researcher at the Federal Office for Economics and Labour of the Swiss Federal Department (Ministry) for Economics. She supervises Research Projects, principally when concerning Unemployment and Labour Market Policy.

Christophe Degain, Statistical Officer at the WTO, Merchandise Trade Section. He was Principal Statistical Assistant at the OECD, Statistics Directorate, Paris, at the time of drafting the paper.

Richard Etter, Head of Unit "Business Surveys" at the Centre for the Research of Economic Activity (KOF/ETH) Zurich. Activities: Development of new and revision of existing business surveys. Research on business survey data.

Charles Goldfinger received his Ph.D. in Economics from the University of California at Berkeley. Since 1987 he is heading Global Electronic Finance (GEF), an international consultancy firm, located in Brussels.

Georg Goldrian, Head of the department Business Surveys, Investment Analysis and Entrepreneurial Behaviour at the ifo Institute for Economic Research, Munich. His main research includes time series analysis and in the development of leading indicators on the basis of business surveys.

Lorraine Greyling, Professor in Economics at Rand Afrikaans University, Johannesburg, South Africa. Research Activities: Economic modelling and forecasting, applied macroeconomics and quantitative economic and statistical analysis.

Joachim Gürtler, Senior Researcher in the department Business Surveys, Investment Analysis and Entrepreneurial Behaviour at the ifo Institute for Economic Research, Munich. Activities: Business survey New Länder, Development of new business surveys in the service sector.

Ernst Helmstädter, Professor em. at the University of Münster, Germany. Research Professor at the Institute for Work and Technology of the Science Center of North-Rhine-Westphalia Gelsenkirchen, Germany. 1983-1988 member of the German Council of Economic Experts for the Economic Development; 1983-1987 President of the German Economic Association - Verein für Socialpolitik; 1992-1994 President of the International J.A. Schumpeter Society.

Detelina Ivanova, Ph. D. student in economics and a Presidential Fellow at the State University of New York, Albany. She is specializing in econometrics, forecasting and financial economics.

Cees L. Jansen is presently employed at the Ministry of Economic Affairs, Directorate-General for for Energy in The Hague, The Netherlands. He was a senior economist in CPB, Netherlands Bureau for Economic Policy Analysis, The Hague, at the time of drafting the paper.

Alexander Juchems, Senior Researcher in the department for macro-economics at the ifo Institute, Munich. His special interest is in the field of monetary policy and politics of European monetary integration.

Rostislav Kapeliushnikov, Senior Researcher at the Institute of World Economy and International Relations (IMEMO) and member of the , "Russian Economic Barometer" Group, Moscow.

Franz-Josef Klein, Head of Unit "Business Surveys and Publications", European Commission, Directorate general "Economic and Financial Affairs", Brussels. Tasks: macroeconomic analysis of member countries and of the European Community; business surveys.

Philip A. Klein, Professor of Economics, Penn State University, and Senior Research Scholar, Economic Cycle Research Institute, New York.

Henk C. Kranendonk, Senior Economist at the Cyclical Analysis Division of the CPB Netherlands Bureau for Economic Policy Analysis in The Hague. His main task is monitoring short-term developments of the Dutch economy. Research activities concern especially leading indicators.

Kajal Lahiri, Professor of Economics and Director, Econometric Research Institute at the State University of New York in Albany. He holds a Ph. D. (1975) in Economics from the University of Rochester. Special interests: analyzing establishment tendency surveys, leading indicators, household survey data on expectations and perceptions, and on sentiment measures.

Birgit Lehne, Research Fellow at the ifo Institute for Economic Research, Munich. Her research interests comprise statistics and business cycle analysis.

Willi Leibfritz, Head of the department Macroeconomic Analysis and Public Finance at the ifo Institute for Economic Research, Munich. Between 1993 and 1997 he was Head of the Public Economics Division in the Economics Department of the OECD in Paris.

Guy Lejeune, degree in Economics at the Free University in Brussels. Administrator at the European Commission, Directorate General for Economic and Financial Affairs, Brussels.

Daniel Marais, Business Information Manager at SASOL (South African petrochemical company), Johannesburg, with the aim of facilitating SASOL to become a global player in the field of petrochemicals.

Rudolf Marty graduated at the University of Zurich in economics. He then obtained a Ph.D. at the same University with a Doctoral Thesis on an empirical study of real interest rate movements. At the Swiss Institute for Business Cycle Research, Zurich, he is mainly involved in the analysis of survey data and the construction of leading indicators.

Zbigniew Matkowski. Senior lecturer at Warsaw School of Economics and Professor of Economics, B. Janski School of Management and Business, Warsaw. Major fields of interest: macroeconomics, business cycles, economics forecasts, international trade, world economy. Since 1994 project leader "Composite Leading Indicators for Polish Economy".

Alberto De Michelis, Director at Eurostat, Brussels and Luxembourg, responsible for statistics on National Accounts, Prices, Balance of Payments, Monetary and Financial Statistics. Main recent activity concerned the excessive deficit procedure in the context of the Maastricht criteria.

Lars-Erik Öller received his Ph.D. in Statistics from the University of Helsinki in 1978. He has worked in economic forecasting since 1970 and is now Director of Research at the National Institute of Economic Research, Sweden, and Professor of Econometrics at the Stockholm School of Economics.

Julian Peters, Economist, New Zealand Institute of Economic Research, Wellington, New Zealand.

Gerald Petit, Administrator at the European Commission, Directorate-General for Industry. He was Administrator at the OECD, Statistics Directorate, Paris, at the time of drafting the paper.

Timo Relander, Director General of Statistics Finland in Helsinki.

Anne Roy worked for the European Commission (DG II), Brussels, as a consultant.

Gerard Salou, Principal Administrator at the OECD, Head of the Statistical Technology Section, Statistics Directorate, Paris.

Bernd Schips, Professor of Economics, ETH, Zurich; Director of the Centre for Research of Economic Activity (KOF/ETH), Zurich. Main fields of research: econometric methods, economic theory.

Frank Schönborn, Adviser at Eurostat, Brussels and Luxembourg, for Economic Statistics, Economic and Monetary Convergence and Accession Negotiations.

Franz Seitz, Professor of Economics at the University of Applied Sciences Amberg-Weiden, Germany. His main field of research is empirical macroeconomics, especially monetary theory, monetary policy and international economics.

List of Contributors

Eon Smit, Professor and Director of the Graduate School of Business at the University of Stellenbosch, Republic of South Africa. His fields of speciality are Business Forecasting and Derivate Instruments. He is also editor of the Journal for Studies in Economics and Econometrics and The Investment Analysts Journal.

Johan Snyman received his Ph.D. from the University of Cape Town and is Director of Medium-Term Forecasting Associates, Building Economists, Stellenbosch, Republic of South Africa. The firm specializes in forecasting of building activity and building costs.

Kurt Stock, Research Fellow at the ifo Institute for Economic Research in Munich. Fields of activity: econometrics, statistics and operations research. In recent years he used survey results for developing indicators and analyzing as well as forecasting firm demand.

Jean-Jacques Vanhaelen, Advisor with the Research Department, National accounts and business surveys cell, National Bank of Belgium, Brussels.

Gerhard Wagenhals, Professor of Statistics and Econometrics at the Department of Economics, Unversity of Hohenheim, Germany. His main fields of interest are Statistics and Econometrics, Labour Supply and Taxes, and Natural Ressources.

Chantal Winter, Assistant Advisor, National accounts and business surveys cell, National Bank of Belgium, Brussels.

Jürgen Wolters, Professor of Econometrics at the Freie Universität Berlin. His research specialities are: time series analysis, econometrics and applied macroeconomics.

Gerhardus van Zyl, Associate Professor in Microeconomics and Head of the Motor Vehicle Research Unit at the Rand Afrikaans University, Auckland Park, Republic of South Africa.

Preface

The Centre for International Research on Economic Tendency Surveys (CIRET) held its 23rd Conference at the invitation of ETLA, The Research Institute of the Finnish Economy, in Helsinki from July 30 to August 1, 1997.

In her welcoming speech Dr. Sirkka Hämäläinen, Governor of the Central Bank of Finland forecasted for the Finnish Economy a continuing high growth of GDP in 1997 and in 1998, and made it clear, that Finland was preparing to comply with the Maastricht criteria to be able to join the European Monetary Union in the first round.

The conference papers selected for this volume are grouped into seven chapters: Leading Indicators, Timing of Cyclical Turning Points, Firm Behaviour, Financial Indicators, Economic Policy Recommendations, Transition Economies, and Service Sector. Given the limited space of this volume only a selection of the papers presented at the conference could be included. Others will be published as a special edition in the series CIRET Studies.

In addition to the main topics of the conference, one session dealt with the question of what consequences are to be expected from the ongoing social and structural change and how these changes could be reflected in official statistics and in business cycle indicators. Charles Goldfinger from the Global Electronic Finance Management S.A. in Brussels gave an introduction to this topic and Frank Schönborn from Eurostat, Director Erich Bader from the Austrian Central Office of Statistics and Timo Relander, President of Statistics Finland, gave answers from the Statistical Offices point of view.

The editors of this volume thank all persons who contributed to the success of the conference.

Our special thanks go to Dr. Pentti Vartia, Managing Director of ETLA, and his staff, particularly Caroline Mamia, who were competent organizers and wonderful hosts, and to the other members of the Local Organizing Committee: Erkki Hellsten, Director of the Confederation of Finnish Industry and Employers; Jorma Hilpinen, Head of Office in the Bank of Finland; and Markku Suur-Kujala, Director of Statistics Finland.

Finally we would like to thank the Ciret Co-ordinator, Sandra Waller, for her efforts in organizing the conference and Christiane Beckhäuser at the Ciret Office, especially for her work in compiling the papers and turning them into camera-ready-copy for publication.

Munich/Darmstadt Karl Heinrich Oppenländer
March 1998 Günter Poser

Part I
Leading Indicators

1 A Leading Indicator of Equipment Investment Demand in the Italian Economy

Paolo Carnazza

This paper aims at defining a leading indicator for the equipment investment demand in Italy based on information mainly drawn from ISCO's monthly survey on manufacturing firms. Qualitative series will be analysed in order to assess their ability to lead the annual percentage changes of equipment investment (assumed as reference series). The choice of the candidate series to be aggregated into a single synthetic indicator will be carried out through different tools: the traditional NBER methodology devoted to analyse the turning points and the cyclical evolution of each series and of the reference series; the cross-correlation analysis; some econometric tests. Two slightly different leading indicators will be scrutinized in order to assess their predictive ability and one of them will be, finally, chosen.

Among the various qualitative indicators, the paper will focus its attention on uncertainty which seems to play a relevant role in influencing investment decisions; in particular, the analysis will try to develop different uncertainty indicators, drawn from ISCO's survey on manufacturing firms.

1 Introduction

The aim of this paper is to build up a leading indicator of equipment investment in Italy.[1] The analysis will focus mainly on the qualitative replies derived from ISCO's monthly survey on manufacturing firms which have the advantage of being immediately available and not subject to revision; on the other hand quantitative economic data are often released with a delay of three to four months or more and are also subject to revisions.

The paper will be organized as follows. In the next section a reference series representing the evolution of equipment investment will be chosen while in the third section a set of candidate indicators will be scrutinized to assess their predictive power through different tools: the traditional NBER methodology, the cross-correlation analysis and some econometric tests. In the fourth section, the paper will focus on uncertainty which

---

[1] A previous attempt (Carnazza-Oneto, 1996) has been developed aimed at defining a leading indicator of private consumption in the Italian economy. Another study devoted to assess the empirical relationships between the business confidence indicator and some economic variables (such as GDP, industrial production, business investment) has been carried out recently (Santero - Westerlund, 1996).

seems to play a relevant role in influencing investment demand; in particular, the analysis will try to develop different uncertainty indicators, drawn form ISCO's survey on manufacturing firms. The chosen uncertainty indicator will then be aggregated with the other series (section 5) into a single synthetic indicator whose predictive performance will result much better than the performance of each separate component. The final section will summarize the main conclusions of the paper, outlining some limits of the leading indicator approach.

2 The Equipment Investment Demand as the Reference Series

The choice of the reference series represents the first and crucial step of the whole analysis. In this study, the quarterly National Account series of equipment investment at 1990 constant prices (seasonally adjusted) has been considered.[1]

This analysis is developed by considering the "growth cycles" which refer to the positive and negative variations of the rate of growth of the economy. Consequently, the cyclical profile of the reference series is defined after having eliminated the long-term component. The cyclical evolution of investment has been identified getting the annual percent changes of the equipment investment series. As a check, the cyclical component has been estimated applying the Hodrick-Prescott procedure (chart. 1). The cyclical behaviour looks quite similar: the turning points of the two series seem, in fact, to coincide with the exception of the last two. More specifically, the turning points of the difference cycle anticipate the last trough and peak of the de-trended series which occurred, respectively, in the third quarter of 1993 and in the fourth quarter of 1995.

Finally, the series referring to the annual percent changes of equipment investment has been chosen as reference series eliminating in this way - with a very simple and neutral procedure - the trend from the original series. On the other hand, the Hodrick-Prescott method should have changed significantly the cyclical characteristics of the series modifying the volatility and the correlation of the same series with the other variables (Canova, 1994).

3 The Search for the Candidate Series for the Leading Indicator of Equipment Investment

The choice of the more appropriate series to be analysed and included into a leading composite indicator of equipment investment has been developed carrying out a statistical and an econometric analysis.[2]

---

[1] The "single-series approach" is the only which can be adopted in this case as it is impossible to gather a set of coincident indicators related to equipment investment. For some considerations about the main features of the two different approaches in choosing the reference series ("single-series approach"; "multi-series approach") see Schlitzer (1993).

[2] Our analysis has, indeed, paid more attention to the statistical and econometric approach rather than to the theoretical framework which characterizes the investment decisions. For surveys of the main investment theories see Chirinko (1993) and Bond-Jenkinson (1996).

This study has focused its attention mainly on qualitative indicators drawn from ISCO's monthly survey on manufacturing referring to the whole industrial sector and to investment goods firms. The structure of the manufacturing survey is quite well known. The monthly section is designed to gather the entrepreneurs' opinions on some variables such as orders (domestic, external, general); production and stocks of finished products. In addition, entrepreneurs are asked to formulate short-term expectations (three-four months ahead) on the evolution of demand; production; selling prices; economy.

Firms can choose between three qualitative answers: positive (increase), neutral (no change), negative (decrease); the net balance of relative frequencies - expressed as the difference between the positive and negative responses - is considered in this analysis. The series are assumed to represent the cyclical evolution of each specific economic phenomenon.[1]

The series drawn from ISCO's industry survey considered as potential leading variables of equipment investment are the following:
- assessment of domestic order-books levels (investment goods firms);
- short-term expectations on demand (investment goods firms);
- general economy expectations in the industry as a whole;
- degree of capacity utilization in the industry as a whole;
- degree of capacity utilization (investment goods firms);
- assessment of current production capacity with respect to the expected demand in the next 12 months.

Besides the qualitative indicators drawn from ISCO's survey on manufacturing firms, a small set of other variables has been considered: ex ante real interest rate;[2] changes on annual basis of investment goods' import and ex post real interest rate.[3]

It is important to underline that the above mentioned series - which seem to explain quite well the recent evolution of equipment investment (chart.2) - derive by a quite long process of selection which has eliminated a lot of other series characterized by a very modest predictive performance.

Different approaches can be utilized in order to choose the more appropriate leading indicators. The first one, based on the NBER methodology, tries to evaluate the capacity of each series to anticipate systematically the turning points of the reference series. Having defined the various peaks and troughs of each candidate series on the basis of a graphical inspection we have to point out, first of all, a quite low degree of conformity of the cyclical evolution of each candidate series to the cyclical behaviour of equipment investment demand. In fact, the candidate series are generally characterized by a high number of turning points; moreover, no indicator seems to show a satisfactory ability in an-

---

[1] Systematic testing has ruled out the presence of seasonality. Only two series - the level of capacity utilization (for industry as a whole and for investment goods firms) - have been seasonally adjusted through the X-11 procedure.

[2] This series is given by the difference between lending interest rates and the expectations on producer prices derived from the quarterly survey carried out by Forum-Mondo Economico with a group of Italian experts for different sectors. For a more detailed analysis of the construction of this variable see Gaiotti, Nicoletti-Altimari (1996). The quantification procedure of inflation expectations has been developed in Visco (1984).

[3] This variable is expressed as the difference between lending interest rates and annual percent changes of producer prices.

ticipating the turning points and, more specifically, the recessionary phases of the reference series.[1]

The second approach, based on the cross - correlation analysis, has evidenced a fairly good degree of correlation between the candidate series and investment cycle: some series show the highest correlation with the reference series at one quarter lead (tab.1) (e.g. short-term expectations on demand; the assessment of current production capacity; ex ante real interest rate; the degree of uncertainty.[2] The remaining series present no lead as the highest linear correlation with the equipment investment is found at the same time, while the short-term expectations on the economy series reveals the highest correlation at two quarters lead (tab.1).[3]

Finally, some econometric tests - finalized to evaluate the overall ability of indicators in predicting equipment investment - have been carried out. More specifically, the test of causality has been implemented, including the reference series (ΔI_t=changes on annual basis of equipment investment) and the specific indicator (Z_t) in the following equation:

$$\Delta I_t = K + A(L) \Delta I_{t-1} + \beta(L) Z_{t-1} + \varepsilon_t \qquad (1)$$

where the $A(L)$ and $\beta(L)$ polynomials are truncated to four lags and ε_t is a white noise process. The null hypothesis that Z does not cause ΔI_t is then tested with a conventional F test on the restriction $\beta(L) = 0$

The second forecasting exercise is based on out - of - sample predictions, comparing the previous equation with the pure autoregressive one:

$$\Delta I_t = K + A(L) \Delta I_{t-1} + u_t \qquad (2)$$

For both equations, one and two - step-ahead forecasts are produced, using a rolling-regression technique (with a 9 year fixed-length sample) starting from the period 1979.1-1987.4. The forecasting performance has been evaluated - on the remaining period (1988.1-1996.4) - analysing the ratio between the root mean square error (RMSE) of the predictions generated by equation (2) and the RMSE derived from the predictions generated by equation (1).

---

[1] The various charts are contained in a previous analysis (Carnazza, 1997). The determination of the turning points, based on a graphical inspection, may be considered excessively arbitrary and subjective since it does not follow strict rules as those developed, e.g., in the Bry-Boschan procedure. In addition, it is not very easy to define exactly the position of turning points when the series are not characterized by well defined cycles. However, we believe that a graphical analysis can be quite useful in order to have an immediate information on the different cyclical patterns of the reference series and of each candidate series.

[2] In the next section this "variable" will be analysed very carefully.

[3] It is worth noting that in the tables 1 and 4, only the cross - correlations up to a lead of three quarters are considered while the cross - correlations between the lagged values of the candidate series and the reference series - which are not economically significant (being characterized by very low values) - are not, here, reported. The series characterized by the highest correlation with the equipment investment at a lead of one and two quarters are defined leading while the series which reveal the highest correlation at the same time are defined coincident. For a well detailed analysis on the "leading - coincident - lagging" features of a variable see Fiorito-Kollintzas (1994) and Schlitzer (1995).

A third forecast exercise has been carried out by comparing pairwise the predictions based on each indicator in order to test the independence of their information content through the following equation estimated over the period 1988.1-1996.4:

$$\Delta I_t = a\, P^i_t + (1-a)\, P^j_t + U_t$$

where P^i_t and P^j_t are the ex-post one-step-ahead forecasts derived from equation (1), including respectively indicator Z^i and Z^j. If both coefficients and (1-a) are significant on the basis of a t test, more efficient predictions are obtained utilizing both of them (their information content is considered "independent"). If - on the other hand - only one of the two coefficients is significant, the relative indicator dominates on the other and, consequently, more efficient predictions are carried out considering only this one.[1]

The econometric tests have evidenced that only some of them contribute to "cause" investment and show a quite satisfactory predictive power (tab.2).

In addition, the test concerning the independent information content of each variable seems to indicate that only the series expressing the annual percent changes of investment goods' import prevails systematically over the others (tab.3). Moreover, the ex ante real interest rate series - dominated by the above mentioned variable - prevails on the remaining series.

To summarize, at this stage of the analysis, the series which can be chosen to enter a synthetic indicator are:
- the assessment of domestic order-books levels expressed by investment goods firms;
- the assessment of current production capacity with respect to expected demand in the next 12 months;
- ex ante real interest rate;
- annual percent changes of investment goods' import.

4 The Degree of Uncertainty: A Further Series for the Leading Indicator of Equipment Investment Demand?

The aim of this section is to build up an uncertainty indicator and to ascertain if this series can play an important role in influencing investment decisions. In reality, the effects of uncertainty (in particular concerning the evolution of demand) on investment have long been the subject of controversy either on theoretical or empirical ground.

According to the literature on the irreversibility of investment,[2] it is assumed that the capital stock can be increased by investment, but cannot be adjusted downwards other than through depreciation. When investment is irreversible, the acquisition of new capital goods today may leave the firm with an excess of capital stock over quite a long period. Conversely, not investing today leaves the firm with an option to expand later. The value

---

[1] For a more detailed analysis of the econometric tests utilized in this paper, see Schlitzer (1993).
[2] An excellent analysis is contained in Dixit-Pindyck (1994). A well detailed analysis of irreversibility investment literature is also developed in Guiso-Parigi (1995). Previous works on irreversible investment have been developed in Arrow (1968) and Nickell (1978).

of this option - which has to be included in the cost of investing - has a certain cost which will increase with uncertainty, the main consequence being the reduction of current investment.

In the empirical field, recent works have evidenced the presence of a negative correlation between uncertainty and investment.[1]

For the Italian economy, three recent papers have confirmed the negative effects of uncertainty on investment decisions: the first one developed by Guiso-Parigi (1995) confirms the main conclusions of models of irreversible investment. Particularly, the study - utilizing the microeconomic data drawn by the annual survey on investment carried out by the Bank of Italy - has pointed out that "... the negative effect of uncertainty on investment is considerably smaller (in absolute terms) for firms that can more easily dispose of installed capital in second - hand markets and for firms with low market power" (p.10).

The other two papers (Calcagnini-Saltari, 1997 and Travaglini, 1997), referring to macroeconomic data, have estimated investment demand on the basis of different uncertainty indicators. Both of them have confirmed the negative influence of uncertainty on investment.

A quite relevant difficulty in analysing the link between uncertainty and investment decisions is related to the definition of an appropriate measure of uncertainty.[2] In this paper, some qualitative replies derived from the monthly survey on manufacturing firms carried out by ISCO are considered as a proxy of uncertainty. In particular, the replies concerning entrepreneurs' expectations on orders, production, general economy are utilized.[3]

Three different indicators of uncertainty have been constructed, respectively, as the inverse of the share of firms which have indicated a stability on the evolution of orders, production, general economy.

Inside the irreversible investment models, "bad news" seem to have a quite significant role in postponing the realization of an investment project; in particular, it is possible to argue as in Bernanke (1983) "... that of possible future outcomes, only the unfavourable ones have a bearing on the current propensity to undertake a given project" (p.91). In other words, only predicted positive states of nature would lead to investment decisions.

On the basis of this approach, other three uncertainty indicators have been defined as the inverse of the percentage of firms which have expressed stable and favourable expectations on the short-term evolution of demand, production, economy.[4]

---

[1] See Pindyck-Solimano (1993); Caballero-Pindyck (1993); Ferderer (1993a; 1993b); Leahy-Whited (1995).

[2] A general overview of different uncertainty indicators is developed in Leahy-Whited (1995) and Travaglini (1997).

[3] These uncertainty indicators (on orders and production) have been analysed in Calcagnini-Saltari (1997). Another uncertainty proxy derived from expectations about the state of the economy is considered in Parigi-Schlitzer (1995) in estimating the equipment investment demand. In this paper, the quantification of survey replies is based on the assumption of a logistic probability distribution function.

[4] The interpretation of these indicators is quite intuitive: e.g., the increase of the percentage of firms which have formulated stable and favourable expectations indicates a decrease of uncertainty; on the other hand, the decrease of the percentage of firms which have indicated stable and favourable expectations is equivalent to an increase of uncertainty. This type of uncertainty indicators may be considered more properly as a „pessimism indicator" but, however, an increasing degree of pessimism perceived by entrepreneurs may reflect an increase of uncertainty and viceversa.

The choice of the best uncertainty indicator - among the various uncertainty indicators - has been based on the cross - correlation analysis and on the econometric tests applied in the previous section. More specifically, the cross - correlation analysis - extended over quite a long period - seems to support the "Bernanke principle" (tab.4); moreover, the production uncertainty indicator reveals the highest correlation (-0.67) at a lead of one quarter. In addition, the Granger causality test confirms the satisfactory behaviour pointed out by the cross - correlation analysis while the predictive performance can be considered quite good, at two step-ahead (tab.5). Finally, the test of independence of the information content indicates that production uncertainty indicator prevails over the others (tab.6).

After having chosen the best uncertainty indicator, we have utilized the same statistical and econometric tools, just applied, to verify if this series can be aggregated, with the other candidate variables, in a leading indicator of the equipment investment demand.

The results have been quite satisfactory, on the basis of the cross - correlation analysis (the production uncertainty presents a quite high correlation at one quarter lead, tab.1) and of the Granger causality test and of the predictive performance (tab. 2); in addition, the test concerning the independent information content puts on evidence that production uncertainty - with the series expressing the changes on annual basis of investment good's import - prevails on the remaining series (tab. 3). Moreover, the graphical analysis shows that production uncertainty has been able to anticipate quite systematically the turning points of the reference series (chart.3). Consequently, given these satisfactory results, the production uncertainty indicator has been taken into account as an important variable in influencing the investment decisions.

5 The Leading Indicator for the Equipment Investment Demand

After having chosen, on the basis of different methodologies, the more appropriate leading series for the equipment investment demand we have to aggregate them into a single composite indicator. The aggregation of the various series, which is useful in order to minimize the "false signal" problem, has followed the OECD procedure based on an unweighted average of the normalized component series.[1]

Two slightly different leading indicators are considered here: the first one (Leadinve4) is given by the aggregation of four series; the second one (Leadinve5) is expressed as the aggregation of the five final chosen series (tab.7).[2]

Referring to the cyclical evolution of the two leading indicators, the modest performance of both of them is quite evident in anticipating the turning points of the reference series (charts. 4-5). However, the performance of the two leading indicators seems to be much better than the predictive ability of each single series; more specifically Leadinve4 (chart. 4) has been able to anticipate the last two turning points of the equipment investment demand with a lead, respectively, of two and one quarters.

---

[1] Oecd (1987). On the other hand, the approach developed by NBER applies specific weights linked to some general features of the various series. For a further analysis on the two different approaches see Carnazza-Oneto (1996).

[2] It is worth noting that the series labelled with X6, X7, X8 have been considered with an inverted sign, since they are countercyclical.

Moreover, the cross-correlation analysis and the various econometric tests confirm the better performance of the composite indicators with respect to the individual ones (tab.7). The Granger F-test strongly rejects the hypothesis of no causality between the two leading indicators and the equipment investment demand; furthermore, the out-of sample prediction tests indicate a significant reduction of the root mean square error in relation to one and two - step ahead.

Among the two leading indicators, our final choice has regarded Leadinve4 since the series expressing the changes on annual basis of investment goods' imports is generally available only with a significant delay which would make the predictive ability of the leading indicator useless. In addition, Leadinve4 seems to be characterized by a higher correlation at one quarter lead and by a more satisfactory performance in predicting the last two turning points of equipment investment demand.

6 Conclusion

In this paper we have tried to build up a composite leading indicator for the equipment investment demand in the Italian economy, utilizing different methodologies. As a final result of the analysis, two quite similar leading indicators have been presented and one of them chosen.

The final results can be considered satisfactory on the basis of the cross-correlation analysis and econometric tests of predictive performance. However, the comparison between the cyclical evolution of the two leading indicators and that of the reference series is quite unsatisfactory even if it is worth noting that the chosen leading indicator (Leadinve4) has been able to anticipate the last peak and trough of equipment investment with, respectively, a lead of two and one quarters.

Some limits of the analysis must be pointed out. A limit - which characterizes the whole leading indicator literature - is related to the modest theoretical basis on which the choice of leading indicators is generally based.[1]

Another limit appertains to the choice of the reference series. Other approaches could be carried out in order to find other reference series (e.g. monthly production of investment goods),[2] or different detrending procedures.[3]

Another aspect which deserves further investigation is the choice of a more appropriate and complex uncertainty indicator, based on both quantitative and qualitative indicators (drawn from other ISCO's surveys). The results presented in this paper are quite interesting: uncertainty - which is, here, related exclusively to the manufacturing firms - seems to play a quite important role in anticipating the evolution of equipment investment, but a further analysis should be developed in order to define an aggregate global

---

[1] Some attempts in reinforcing the theoretical framework of leading indicators have been recently carried out (Zarnowitz, 1992).
[2] A recent analysis (Nucci, 1997) has tried to build, for the 1990s, a monthly series of equipment investment.
[3] See Canova (1994) for a detailed analysis on the different detrending procedures and on their influence in affecting the cyclical chronology.

uncertainty indicator, based on the assumption that uncertainty has to be attributed to a lot of different factors.[1]

Finally, the most relevant difficulty in the definition of a leading indicator of equipment investment is related - in our opinion - to a general weakness of investment theories. None of them, in fact, has been able to understand completely the "source" of entrepreneurs' decisions in realizing long-term projects. This difficulty may derive - at least partially - from the fact that most human decisions " ... can only be taken as a result of animal spirits - of a spontaneous urge to action rather than inaction, and not as the outcome of a weighted average of quantitative benefits multiplied by quantitative probabilities" (Keynes, p.161).

Anyway, despite these limits, this paper has tried to offer a contribution in filling the „information gap" which often characterizes relevant economic phenomena. More specifically, the construction of a leading indicator for the equipment investment can be useful for, at least, two reasons: it can be utilized in order to anticipate the peaks and troughs of this high volatile[2] and often quite difficult to predict component of demand; in addition it can lead policy-makers, by allowing them to follow more carefully the evolution of investment, to adopt appropriate counter-cyclical economic measures.

---

[1] Some preliminary attempts have been carried out but the results have not been encouraging (Carnazza, 1997).

[2] From the beginning of 1970s up to now the standard deviation of equipment investment demand has been equal to 9.9 against a value of standard deviation of construction investment and GDP equal, respectively, to 3.5 and 2.5.

Table 1 Correlation analysis between the equipment investment (changes on annual basis) and some candidate series for leading indicator at quarter t-3, t-2, t-1, t (range: 1978.1 - 1996.4)

	t-3	t-2	t-1	t
x1	0.29	0.46	0.60	0.67
x2	0.30	0.36	0.38	0.34
x3	0.45	0.48	0.47	0.39
x4	0.14	0.27	0.38	0.44
x5	0.08	0.18	0.28	0.37
x6	-0.40	-0.52	-0.59	-0.57
x7	-0.29	-0.37	-0.39	-0.38
x8	-0.50	-0.59	-0.61	-0.53
x9	0.39	0.63	0.83	0.93
x10	-0.32	-0.44	-0.51	-0.52

x1 = Assessment of domestic order-books levels (investment goods firms).
x2 = Short-term expectations on demand (investment goods firms).
x3 = Short-term expectations on the economy (industry as a whole).
x4 = Level of capacity utilization (as percentage; industry as a whole).
x5 = Level of capacity utilization (as percentage; investment goods firms).
x6 = Assessment of current production capacity (industry as a whole).
x7 = Ex ante real interest rate.
x8 = Degree of uncertainty (inverse of the percentage of total manufacturing firms which have indicated stable and favourable expectations on production).
x9 = Changes on annual basis of investment goods' import.
X10 = Ex post real interest rate.

Source: ISCO, ISTAT.

Table 2 Test of the predictive performance of candidate indicators

Series	F(value) (1)	RMSE Ratio 1-step-ahead	RMSE Ratio 2-step-ahead	Synthesis of the performance of each series *: it stands the test 0: it does not stand the test		
x1	3.79	0.97	1.09	*	0	*
x2	1.26	0.39	1.00	0	0	0
x3	0.94	0.99	1.05	0	0	*
x4	0.55	0.96	1.00	0	0	0
x5	0.23	0.91	0.95	0	0	0
x6	2.01	0.92	0.97	*	0	0
x7	3.87	1.03	1.00	*	*	0
x8	2.91	1.06	1.11	*	*	*
x9	8.53	1.53	2.23	*	*	*
x10	2.69	0.94	0.90	*	0	0

(1) Testing the restriction B(L) = 0 in equation (1) in the text; the relative critical value at 0.05 confidence level is 1.91.

Table 3   Test of independence of the information content (*)
(Range: 1988.1 - 1996.4)

	x1	x2	x3	x4	x5	x6	x7	x8	x9	x10
x1	-	0.91	1.56	1.66	2.54	1.97	1.93	0.64	-2.05	2.34
x2	1.40	-	1.49	1.77	2.67	2.23	1.89	0.44	-1.42	2.28
x3	1.31	0.66	-	1.28	2.28	1.78	1.63	-0.18	-1.47	2.27
x4	0.93	0.38	0.28	-	2.04	1.40	1.49	-0.76	-1.80	1.61
x5	0.74	0.11	0.72	0.55	-	0.88	1.22	-0.57	-1.95	1.69
x6	0.31	0.01	0.30	0.31	1.64	-	1.28	-0.84	-2.68	1.62
x7	2.26	1.93	2.18	2.37	3.01	2.65	-	1.53	-1.44	2.69
x8	2.41	2.08	2.49	2.87	3.58	3.28	2.56	-	-0.98	3.11
x9	7.26	6.73	7.05	7.41	8.18	8.35	6.71	5.90	-	7.60
x10	1.45	0.84	1.58	1.64	2.36	1.81	1.52	0.65	-1.74	-

(*) Given the regression $i_t = aP_i + (1-a)P_j$, the t-value of the coefficient a is the entry at the intersection between row i and column j; the t-value of the coefficient $(1-a)$ is the entry at the intersection between row j and column i; P_n is the vector of one-step-ahead predictions generated by equation (1) in the text using indicator Y_n.

Table 4   Correlation analysis between the equipment investment (changes on an annual basis) and the degree of uncertainty at quarter t-3, t-2, t-1, t
(Range: 1971.1 - 1996.4)

	t-3	t-2	t-1	t
y1	-0.46	-0.49	-0.40	-0.23
y2	-0.32	-0.36	-0.38	-0.30
y3	-0.47	-0.51	-0.47	-0.33
y4	-0.44	-0.54	-0.52	-0.38
y5	-0.45	-0.62	-0.67	-0.59
y6	-0.49	-0.56	-0.53	-0.41

y1 = Inverse of the percentage of total manufacturing firms which have indicated stable expectations on the future evolution of demand.
y2 = Inverse of the percentage of total manufacturing firms which have indicated stable expectations on the future evolution of production.
y3 = Inverse of the percentage of total manufacturing firms which have indicated stable expectations on the future evolution of economy.
y4 = Inverse of the percentage of total manufacturing firms which have indicated stable and favourable expectations on the future evolution of production.
y5 = Inverse of the percentage of total manufacturing firms which have indicated stable and favourable expectations on the future evolution of production.
y6 = Inverse of the percentage of total manufacturing firms which have indicated stable and favourable expectations on the future evolution of economy.

Source: ISCO's monthly survey on manufacturing firms.

Table 5 Test of the predictive performance of uncertainty indicators

Series	F(value) (1)	RMSE Ratio		Synthesis of the perform-
		1-step-ahead	2-step-ahead	ance of each series
				*: it stands the test
				0: it does not stand the test
y1	1.29	0.91	0.92	0 0 0
y2	1.60	0.97	0.99	0 0 0
y3	1.20	0.87	0.93	0 0 0
y4	2.07	0.90	0.96	* 0 0
y5	2.40	0.94	1.03	* 0 *
y6	1.87	0.90	0.98	* 0 0

(1) Testing the restriction B(L) = 0 in equation (1) in the text; the critical value at 0.05 confidence level is 1.86.

Table 6 Test of independence of the information content (*)
(Range: 1988.1 - 1996.4)

	y1	y2	y3	y4	y5	y6
y1	-	0.91	2.86	0.75	1.10	2.04
y2	2.94	-	3.78	2.18	2.43	2.96
y3	1.68	1.05	-	1.35	1.28	0.44
y4	2.86	2.23	3.40	-	0.25	2.34
y5	3.39	2.94	4.17	2.33	-	3.20
y6	2.45	1.75	2.42	1.39	1.37	-

(*) Given the regression $i_t = aP_i + (1-a)P_j$, the t-value of the coefficient a is the entry at the intersection between row i and column j; the t-value of the coefficient $(1-a)$ is the entry at the intersection between row j and column i; P_n is the vector of one-step-ahead predictions generated by equation (1) in the text using indicator Y_n.

Table 7 The general predictive performance of the chosen series and of the two leading indicators

	Correlations with the reference series		Casuality test	Predictive Performance RMSE RATIO	
	Lead (Quarters)	Correlation coefficients	F value	1-step-ahead	2-step-ahead
x1	0	0.67	3.79	0.97	1.09
x6	-1	-0.59	2.01	0.92	0.97
x7	-1	-0.39	3.87	1.03	1.00
x8	-1	-0.61	2.91	1.06	1.11
x9	0	0.93	8.53	1.53	2.23
Leadinve4*	-1	0.74	5.76	1.07	1.15
Leadinve6**	0	0.81	7.71	1.13	1.27

x1 = Assessment of internal order-books levels (investment goods firms).
x6 = Assessment of current production capacity (industry as a whole).
x7 = Ex ante real interest rate.
x8 = Degree of uncertainty (inverse of the percentage of total manufacturing firms which have indicated stable
x9 = Changes on annual basis of investment goods' import.
*Leadinve4 = x1; x6, x7, x8 (with the inverted sign).
**Leadinve5 = x1; x6, x7, x8 (with the inverted sign); x9.

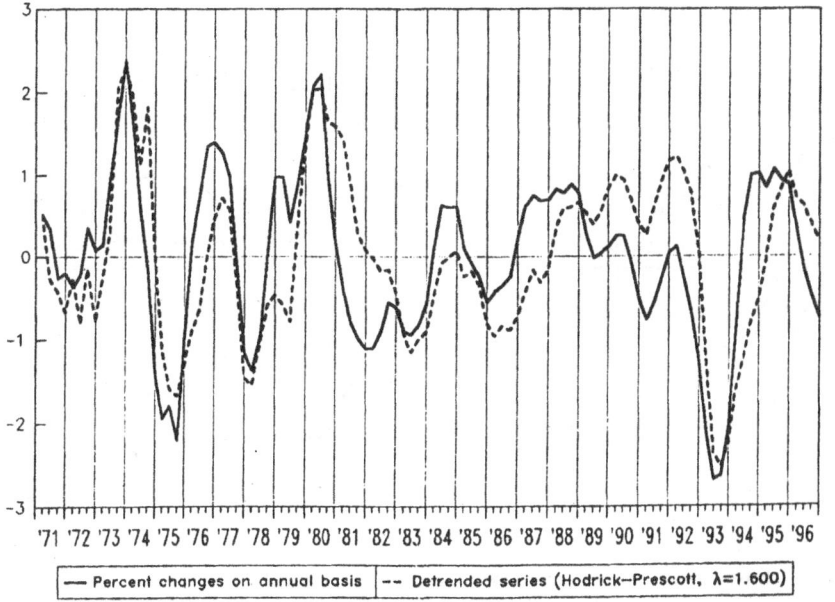

Chart 1 Equipment investment demand

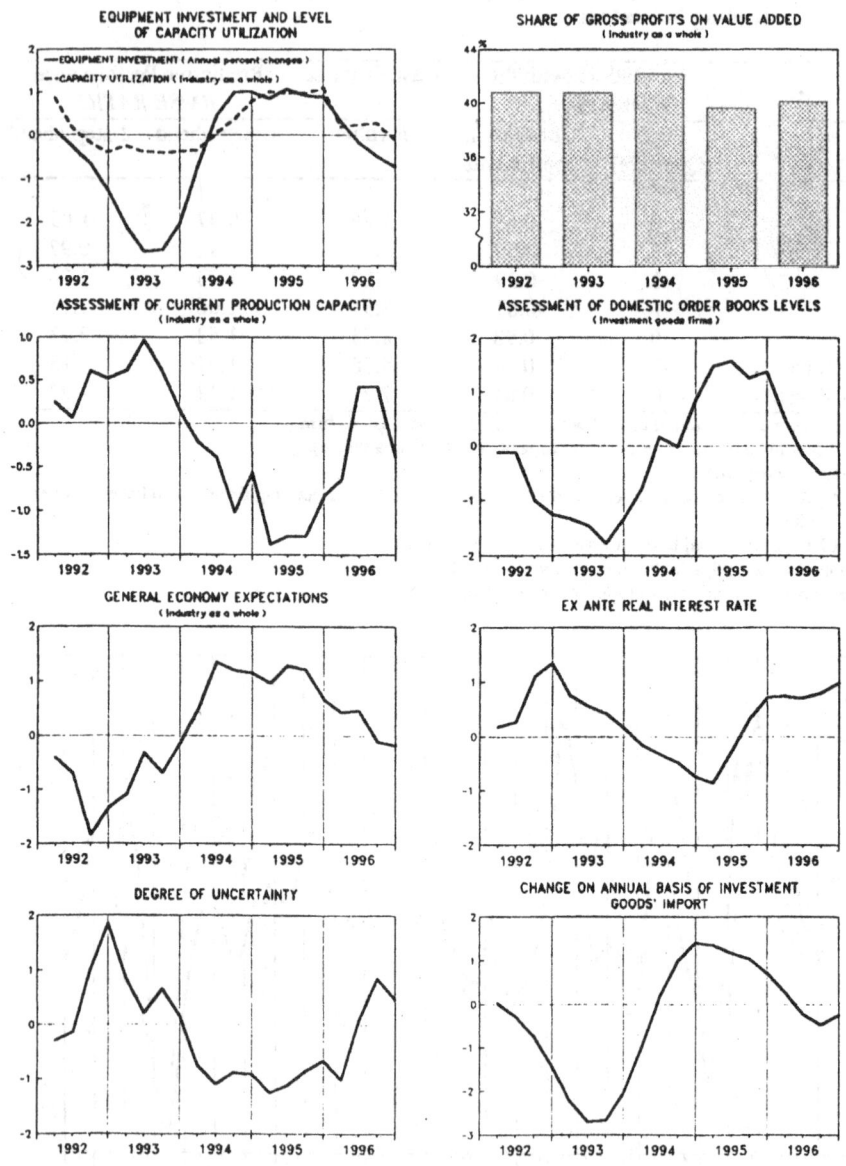

Chart 2 Equipment investment and its main determinants
The series - except that one referred to the share of gross profits on value added - have been standardized.
Source: ISTAT, ISCO, Bank of Italy.

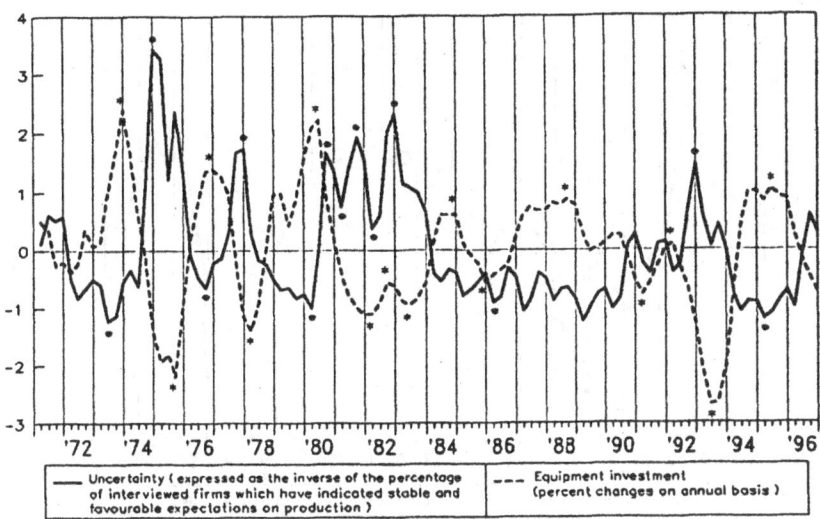

Chart 3 Equipment investment and uncertainty on short-term perspectives of production (normalized series)

(*) and (•) indicate the turning points obtained through a graphical inspection.

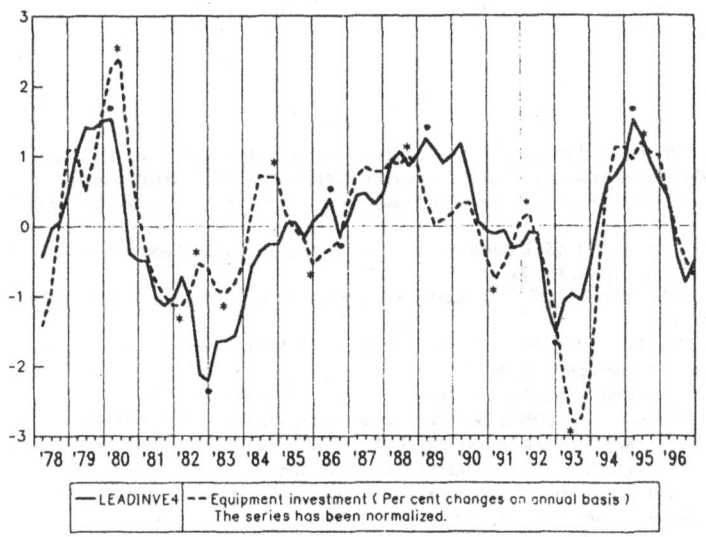

Chart 4 Leading indicator (Leadinve4) and equipment investment demand

(•) and (*) indicate the turning points of the two series obtained through a graphical inspection. Leadinve4 includes X1, X6, X7, X8 (X6, X7, X8 are considered with inverted sign).

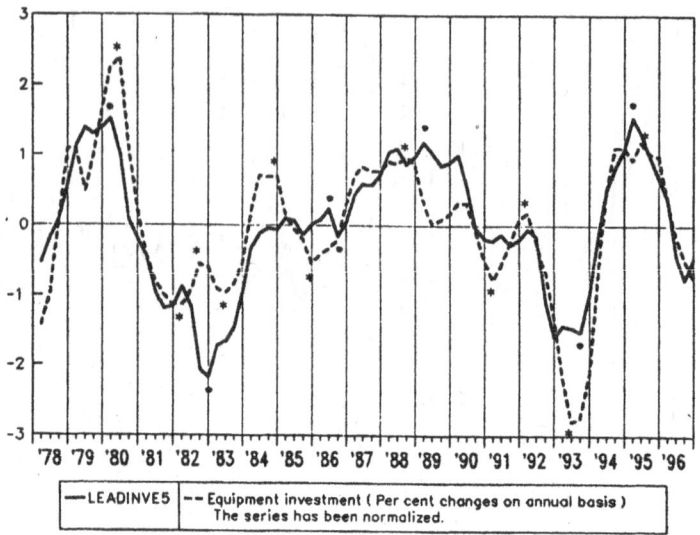

Chart 5   Leading indicator (Leadinve5) and equipment investment demand
(•) and (*) indicate the turning points of the two series obtained through a graphical inspection. Leadinve5 includes X1, X6, X7, X8, X9 (X6, X7, X8 are considered with inverted sign).

References

Arrow K.J. (1968), Optimal capital policy with irreversible investment, in J.N. Wolfe (ed), *Value, Capital and Growth. Papers in honour of Sir J. Hicks*, Edinburgh, Edinburgh University Press.

Bernanke B.S. (1983), Irreversibility, uncertainty and cyclical investment, *Quarterly Journal of Economics*, February.

Bond, J. and Jenkinson, T. (1996), The assessment: investment performance and policy, *Oxford Review of Economic Policy*, Vol.12, No. 2.

Caballero, R. and Pindick, J. (1993), Uncertainty, investment, and industry evolution, NBER, Working Paper No. 4160.

Calcagnini, G. and Saltari, E. (1997), Un'analisi del principio dell'acceleratore in condizioni di incertezza, in *Rassegna di Lavori dell'ISCO*, No. 1.

Canova, F. (1994), Detrending and turning points, *European Economic Review*, No. 38.

Carnazza, P. and Oneto, G.P. (1996), Searching for a leading indicator of household consumption in the Italian economy, in K.H. Oppenländer and G. Poser, *Business Cycle Surveys: Forecasting Issues and Methodological Aspects*, Avebury Ashgate Publishing Limited.

Chirinko, R.S. (1993), Business fixed investment spending: a critical survey of modelling strategies, empirical results, and policy, *Journal of Economic Literature*, No. 4.

Dixit, A. and Pindyck, R. (1994), *Investment under uncertainty*, Princeton University Press.

Ferderer, J.P. (1993a), The impact of uncertainty on aggregate investment spending: an empirical analysis, *Journal of Money, Credit and Banking*, Vol.25, No. 1, February.

Ferderer, J.P. (1993b), Does uncertainty affect investment spending?, *Journal of Post Keynesian Economics*, Vol.16, No.1, Fall.

Fiorito, R. and Kollintzas, T. (1994), Stylized facts of business cycles in the G7 from a real business cycles perspective, *European Economic Review*, No. 38.

Gaiotti, E. and Nicoletti-Altinari, S. (1996), Monetary policy transmission, the exchange rate and long-term yields under different hypotheses or expectations, *Temi di Discussione del Servizio Studi della Banca d'Italia*, No. 276, August.

Guiso, L. and Parigi, G. (1996), Investment and demand uncertainty, *Temi di Discussione del Servizio Studi della Banca d'Italia*, No. 289, November.

Holmes, R.A. and Shamsuddin, A. (1993), Evaluation of alternative leading indicators of British Columbia industrial employment, *International Journal of forecasting*, No. 9.

Keynes, J.M. (1936), *The General theory of employment, interest and money*, Macmillan Cambridge University Press.

Leahy, J. and Whited, T. (1995), The effects of uncertainty on investment: some stylized facts, NBER, Working Paper No. 4986.

Nickell, S.J. (1978), *The investment decisions of firms*, Cambridge University Press.

Nucci, F. (1997), Misurazione e previsione degli investimenti con il "metodo della disponibilità": analisi ed evidenze, Temi di Discussione del Servizio Studi della Banca d'Italia, No. 295, February.

OECD (1987), Oecd leading indicators and business cycles in member countries: 1960-1985, Oecd Main Economic Indicators Source and Methods, No. 39.

Parigi, G. and Schlitzer, G. (1995), Quarterly forecasts of the Italian business cycle by means of monthly economic indicators, *Journal of Forecasting*, Vol.14.

Pindyck, R. and Solimano, A. (1993), Economic instability and aggregate investment, NBER, Working Paper No. 4380.

Santero, T. and Westerlund, N. (1996), Confidence indicators and their relationship to changes in economic activity' OECD Economic Department, Working Papers No. 170.

Schlitzer, G. (1993), Nuovi strumenti per la valutazione e la previsione del ciclo economico in Italia, *Temi di Discussione del Servizio Studi della Banca d'Italia*, No. 200.

Schlitzer, G. (1995), Business cycles in Italy: a statistical investigation, *European of Political Economy*, Vol. II.

Travaglini, G. (1997), Componenti stocastiche e fluttuazioni cicliche: può l'incertezza influenzare l'investimento fisso?, in *Rassegna di Lavori dell'ISCO*, No. 1.

Visco I. (1984), *Price expectations and rising inflation*, Amsterdam, North Holland.

Zarnowitz, V. (1992), *Business cycles: theory, history, indicators and forecasting*, Chicago, University of Chicago press.

2 A New Look at Promptly Available Leading Indicators

John P. Cullity / Philip A. Klein

In our work in the United States on leading indicators we have long been interested not only in the possibilities for improving indicator systems by including survey indexes, but most particularly we have been much interested in developing promptly available indexes. It is well known that historically one of the major advantages has been that the results are often available significantly before comparable quantitative measures covering the same types of economic activity. We have reported at past CIRET conferences on various aspects of this work, and have shown that inclusion of survey data in leading indexes had two major advantages; it enabled us to cover types of activity for which quantitative data were not available at all in many countries, and it enabled us to lengthen the forecasts by including qualitative data available significantly earlier than a comparable quantitative series to which the survey pertained.

In recent years we have turned our attention to the development of leading indexes incorporating promptly available data. A major development of the past twenty years has been the availability in the United States of many series, both quantitative and qualitative, before the end of the month after the month to which the data pertain. This is our working definition of "promptly available" and the present paper is devoted to assessing the performance of indexes composed of such series in the United States in recent years.

In 1990, Geoffrey H. Moore and John P. Cullity wrote a report, "Promptly Available Economic Indicators", (Moore and Cullity, 1990) which dealt with their initial work on the development of a new promptly available leading index for the United States. The present paper updates that work by applying it to two new promptly available indexes at the Economic Cycle Research Institute (ECRI) and to the revised leading index maintained now by the Conference Board (a private organization representing a group of major corporate enterprises).[1] It is a revision of the leading composite index published by the U.S. Department of Commerce from the early 1960s until late 1995.

Such an effort is particularly timely now because the ECRI indexes are new and the Conference Board Index has been revised. An integral part of the work on monitoring the U.S. Leading Index from its inception at the National Bureau of Economic Research through the Commerce Department years has always included reconsidering periodically which series ought to be included in the index in light of newly available series, changes in coverage or calculation, etc. Not only has this benchmark leading index been revised since the 1990 study, but the promptly available leading indexes calculated at the Eco-

---

[1] For a description of the methodology used to construct the ECRI indexes, see Cullity and Banerji (1996).

nomic Cycle Research Institute have also undergone some revisions. It is to the record of these indexes that we now turn.

1 Release Schedules for Components of U.S. Leading Indexes

The Economic Cycle Research Institute has recently developed two leading economic indexes for the U.S. The first is called a long-range gauge (LRG) and it is designed to anticipate macroeconomic changes a year or so in the future. Table 1, Part A shows it consists of seven components. We classify the index as "promptly available" because five of its components are available before the end of the month following the month to which the data pertain. This is the requirement for classification as a promptly available indicator. Table 1, Part B provides the same information about the components of ECRI's short-range gauge (SRG).

The table introduces a pattern which we shall follow here of not only giving the release policy currently in effect for each indicator, but showing when according to this policy data for November 1997 might be available. The table makes clear that most of the indicators are available near the beginning of the following month.

The preliminary long range gauge composed of five of the seven components is available in the third week of the following month. The LRG contains survey data. Specifically, one of its components is an average of the University of Michigan and the Conference Board's indexes of consumer expectations.

Table 1 shows that all of the components of the short range gauge (SRG) are available promptly and all but one are available within a week of the month to which they pertain. Two survey series (Vendor Performance and Inventory Change) are available within the same week as the other six components. Note that the short range gauge is available within the first ten days of the month following the month to which the data pertain. This compares favourably with the leads for survey series found previously in our work.

Table 2 shows the same information for the components of the Conference Board's revised leading index. It is evident that this is also a promptly available index as all components are available within a month of the month to which the data pertain and indeed most are available one or two weeks into the following month.

Before we consider the timing of these components vis-à-vis the business cycle turning points it is well to note the initial relationship these release schedules produce in the availability of the three leading indexes under review here. Tables 3 and 4 show the release dates which apply for each month in 1997 (they are the actual dates through May and the scheduled dates, based on the rules governing release, scheduled for the rest of the year). This information suggests that the ECRI short range gauge is available on average each month by more than three weeks before the Conference Board index.[1] In addition, the ECRI long range gauge is available on average by about two weeks before the Conference Board index. These are significant leads and they need to be factored in ultimately, along with any differences in the average lead time at business cycle turning

---

[1] The Conference Board could release its index earlier but it delays publication until all the components are available.

points revealed by the analysis, in assessing the relative usefulness for forecasting of the leading indexes produced by the two agencies. Both can affect the relative usefulness for forecasting of the indexes from each agency.

Table 1   Release schedules of properly available leading indicators, United States

Part A   Long Leading Gauge (ECRI)

	Release Date in Following Month	Release Date for November 1997 Date
New Building Permits	12th business day except if Monday then 13th bus. day	December 16
Productivity Growth Rate (Hourly Manufacturing Output)	About 2 weeks after Real GDP for same quarter, or, about 6-weeks after end of quarter	Beginning of January
CPI for Services Growth Rate (Inverted)	Around the middle of month	December 16
Average of U of Michigan and Conference Board Series a. U of M Survey b. Conference Board Expectations	a. Prelim (or, 10th day est) = second Friday of month Final for month = final Friday of month b. Last Thursday of month	Middle of December (Prelim) November 25
Moody's yields on BAA (inverted)	Available daily, full month available immediately	December 1
Real M2 plus money in long term Mutual Funds	M2 weekly with 10 day lag ICI makes an early estimate of previous month, then reports full-month data late in month	December 1
Price to Unit Labor Cost (Q) Non Farm Business	Same as productivity above	March 10
Long-Range Gauge	Third week of following month[1]	December 16

[1] When building permits and CPI services are available.

Part B   Short Leading Gauge (ECRI)

	Release Date in Following Month	Release Date for November 1997 Date
Jobless Claims	Weekly with 5 day lag	December 4
Vendor Performance	First Business Day of Next Month	December 1
Inventory Chg. NAPM	Same as Above	December 1
S&P 500	Daily	November 29 (Sat)
Risk Spread	Daily	November 29
Weekly Hours	First Friday of Next Month	December 5
JOC	Daily	November 29
New Orders	Calculated from Durable Goods	December 23
Short Range Gauge	Tuesday after first Friday of following month	December 9

Table 2   Release schedule for components of conference board's promptly available leading index[1]

	Component	Typical Release	For Nov 1997
1	Average Weekly Hours, Mfg.	Generally the first Friday following the month	Dec 5
2	Initial Claims	Thursday of the first full week of the new month	Dec 4
3	Mfg. New Orders Consumer	Based on durable goods orders - out around 18th business day	Dec 23
4	New Orders Nondefense Capital	Based on durable goods orders - out around 18th business day	Dec 23
5	Building Permits	12th business day except if Monday, then 13th business day	Dec 16
6	Stock Prices	Daily	Nov 29
7	REAL M2	M2 weekly with 10 day lag= CPI around middle of month	Dec 11 for M2 Dec 16 for CPI
8	Supplier Delivery Time	First business day	Dec 1
9	Interest Rate Spread, 10 Yr-FF	Daily	Dec 1
10	Consumer Expectations	Prelim. (10th day est) = second Friday of month final est = final Friday	Nov 14 Nov 28
11	Leading Index	First or second working day of second month	Dec 29, 1997

[1] While all components fit the definition of „promptly available" one half are available only after the middle of the following month.

Table 3 Announced release schedule, 1997 Conference Board
U.S. leading economic index & Economic Cycle Research Institute
short range gauge

Month for Which Series Pertains	Conference Board Release Dates[1]	ECRI-SRG Release Dates	Lead in Months ECRI over Conf. Board
December 1996	February 4, 1997 (Tuesday)	January 14, 1997	(21 days)
January 1997	March 4, 1997 (Tuesday)	February 11, 1997	(21 days)
February 1997	April 4, 1997 (Friday)	March 11, 1997	(24 days)
March 1997	May 2, 1997 (Friday)	April 8, 1997	(24 days)
April 1997	June 2, 1997 (Monday)	May 6, 1997	(27 days)
May 1997	July 1, 1997 (Tuesday)	June 10, 1997	(21 days)
June 1997	August 4, 1997 (Monday)	July 8, 1997	(27 days)
July 1997	September 2, 1997 (Tuesday)	August 5, 1997	(28 days)
August 1997	September 30, 1997 (Tuesday)	September 9, 1997	(21 days)
September 1997	November 4, 1997 (Tuesday)	October 7, 1997	(28 days)
October 1997	December 1, 1997 (Monday)	November 11, 1997	(20 days)
November 1997	December 31, 1997 (Monday)	December 9, 1997	(22 days)
	Average Lead (days)		(24 days)

[1] During 1996-May 1997-Conference Board release dates are taken from their record. The rest of the year is based on the announced dates for the releases of the data on Personal Income. The announcement policy is to release the leading index the day after personal income is released. For the ECRI series the last half of the year is based on the announced plan to release the short leading gauge on the Tuesday after the first Friday of the month.

Table 4 Announced release schedule, 1997 Conference Board U.S. leading economic indicators & Economic Cycle Research Institute long leading gauge

Month for Which Series Pertains	Conference Board Release Dates[1]	ECRI-LRG Release Dates	Lead in Months ECRI over Conf. Board
December 1996	February 4, 1997 (Tuesday)	January 23, 1997	(12 days)
January 1997	March 4, 1997 (Tuesday)	February 21, 1997	(11 days)
February 1997	April 4, 1997 (Friday)	March 19, 1997	(16 days)
March 1997	May 2, 1997 (Friday)	April 18, 1997	(14 days)
April 1997	June 2, 1997 (Monday)	May 19, 1997	(14 days)
May 1997	July 1, 1997 (Tuesday)	June 18, 1997	(13 days)
June 1997	August 4, 1997 (Monday)	July 18, 1997	(17 days)
July 1997	September 2, 1997 (Tuesday)	August 20, 1997	(13 days)
August 1997	September 30, 1997 (Tuesday)	September 18, 1997	(12 days)
September 1997	November 4, 1997 (Tuesday)	October 20, 1997	(15 days)
October 1997	December 1, 1997 (Monday)	November 20, 1997	(11 days)
November 1997	December 31, 1997 (Monday)	December 17, 1997	(14 days)
	Average Lead (days)		(14 days)

[1] During 1996-May 1997-Conference Board release dates are taken from their record. The rest of the year is based on the announced dates for the releases of the data on personal income. The announcement policy is to release the leading index the day after personal income is released. For the ECRI series the last half of the year is based on the announced plan to release the short leading gauge on the Tuesday after the first Friday of the month.

2 Timing at Business Cycle Turning Points, Components of Three Leading Indexes

How well do the individual components of the three leading indexes anticipate turns in the U.S. business cycle? We are able to answer this question for the period 1948-1991 in some detail for the two ECRI indexes and in rather less detail for the Conference Board's revised index.

Table 5 shows the average lead at U.S. business cycle peaks of the seven components in the ECRI long range gauge. The leads at business cycle peaks are particularly impressive, the shortest (the money supply) leading by an average of fourteen months and the longest (Moody's FBAA) leading by over two years. The leads are observed at all the peaks for four of the series and at most of the peaks for the remainder. At troughs, as is almost always the case, the leads are shorter, but still usually at least several months in length and they occur fairly consistently as well. Overall the components of the long range gauge turn by close to a year on average before the business cycle peaks but at troughs the leads are much shorter. We submit that this gauge is, therefore, doubly useful - not only are the leads quite long and consistent, but the series are, as we have seen, available very promptly. The ECRI gauge, accordingly, can be regarded as a reasonable reliable, therefore useful forecasting measure.

Table 6 shows at business cycle peaks the components of the short range gauge show leads ranging from an average of eight months for the Standard and Poor's index of 500 stocks to fourteen months for initial claims for jobless benefits. The indicators are not so impressive at troughs. Although they all show a lead on average except for industrial materials prices, these leads are mostly very short. Moreover, the consistency with which the components lead is also far smaller than at peaks (and far smaller than was the case with the components of the long range gauge). Despite these reservations it is clear that on average the short range gauge and its components could be classified as leading indicators of turning points in U.S. business cycles.

Table 7 compares the distribution of leads and lags in the 15 components of the SRG and LRG with those of the ten components of the Conference Board leading index from 1959-91. The turns in the LRG components led the business cycle turns about 81 percent of the time. The SRG components led only 71 percent of the time. The Conference Board components led 77 percent of the turning points. Although the LRG components recorded the highest percent of leads, they also had a larger number of episodes for which no timing comparisons were disclosed.

Using a new ECRI methodology, promptly available long range and short range gauges have been constructed for the U.S. The components for the SRG group, as noted above, are statistics for which the data for a given month are released within the first seven days of the following month. A majority of the components of the LRG also meet this standard. Table 8 provides comparisons between the LRG and the Conference Board's leading index. We find that the LRG led ten of the twelve business cycle peaks and troughs during the thirty-one year period from 1960-91. Its average lead was 15 months at peaks, seven months at troughs, and eleven months at peaks and troughs. The average lead of the Conference Board's leading index was nine months at peaks, four months at troughs, and six months at all business cycle turning points. Thus, the ECRI gauge led the Conference Board series by five months at peaks, three months at troughs, and four months at all turns. However, the variability of the leads was somewhat greater for the ECRI leads, compared to the Conference Board leads.

Table 9 provides comparisons between the SRG and the Conference Board's leading index. Both of them led all of the business cycle turns from 1960-91. The average lead of both the SRG and the Conference Board's index was nine months at peaks. The Conference Board's index led the SRG by two months at troughs. The average leads of both indexes was six months at peaks and troughs. Once again the ECRI variability was greater than that of the Conference Board at peaks, but this time this was not the case at troughs.

Charts 1 and 2 show the movements of the Conference Board leading index and the ECRI long range and short range gauges from 1959-97. The shaded areas mark off the periods of business cycle contractions during that period.

Table 5   **Average leads at business cycles turning points, 1948-91 components of ECRI promptly available long run gauge**

Series	AVERAGE LEAD (-) OR LAG (+) IN MONTHS					
	PEAKS		TROUGHS		PEAKS AND TROUGHS	
	Average (Mos)	% Leads	Average (Mos)	% Leads	Average (Mos)	% Leads
New Building Permits	-17	100%	-5	89%	-11	94%
Productivity Growth Rate[1]	-10	75	-5	67	-7	
CPI for Services Growth Rate (Inverted)	-28	100	-10	100	-18	100
Average U. of M. & Conf. Bd. Consumer Expectations	-18 (-14)[2]	100 (100)	-4 (-4)[2]	100 (88)	-11 (-9)[2]	100 (93)
Moody's FBAA (Inverted)	-26	100	-8	100	-16	100
M2 Plus Money the Long term	-14	100	-7	100	-10	100
Price to Unit Labor[1] Cost (Q)	-18	78	-2	67	-11	72
Average (7 Indicators)	-19		-6		-12	
Average (5 Indicators)	-21		-7		-13	

Notes: [1]All components are available Apromptly@ except the two marked with an asterisk: The seven indicator average includes all components; the five component average excludes the two not available promptly.
[2]The average listed first pertains to the comparable measures for the two components. The second average (without parenthesis) includes for the University of Michigan Surveys the turns for additional cycles available prior to 1948-1961.

Table 6 Average leads at business cycle turning points, 1948-91 components of ECRI short range gauge

SERIES	AVERAGE LEAD (-) OR LAG (+), IN MONTHS					
	PEAKS		TROUGHS		PEAKS & TROUGHS	
	Average (Mos)	% Lead	Average (Mos)	% Lead	Average	% Leads
Initial Claims for Jobless Benefits (Inverted)	-14	100	-1	56	-7	78
Vendor Performance (NAPM)	-11	75	-4	78	-7	76
Change in Inventories (NAPM)	-12	100	-1	44	-6	72
S&P 500	-8	100	-5	100	-6	100
Risk Differential (Moody's AAA-BAA)	-9	75	-2	78	-5	76
Average Weekly Hours, Mfg.	-12	100	-2	56	-7	78
JOC Industrial Materials, Six-month Smoothed	-12	83	+4	71	-4	77
New Orders, Consumer Gds. & Contracts & Orders for Plant & Equip.	-9	89	-3	67	-6	78
Average Lead (-) Months	-11		-2		-6	

Table 7 Lead/lag records, 1959-91
Conference Board revised indicators and components of two ECRI indexes

Timing at Five Business Cycle Peaks	NUMBER OF OBSERVATIONS			PERCENT OF TOTAL		
	Conf. Board (Revised) (11 Indicators)	ECRI LRG (7 Indicators)	ECRI SRG (8 Indicators)	Conf. Board (Revised)	ECRI LRG	ECRI SRG
Leads	58	34	40	88	81	83
Coincidences	4	1	2	6	2	4
Lags	1	2	4	2	5	8
No Timing Comparison	3	5	2	4	12	4
TOTAL	66	42	48	100	100	99[1]
Timing at Six Business Cycle troughs						
Leads	52	34	28	68	81	58
Coincidences	18	3	10	23	7	21
Lags	5	1	8	6	2	17
No Timing Comparison	2	4	2	3	10	4
TOTAL	77	42	48	100	100	100
Timing at Peaks & Troughs						
Leads	110	68	68	77	81	71
Coincidences	22	4	12	15	5	12
Lags	6	3	12	4	4	12
No Timing Comparison	5	9	4	4	11	4
TOTAL	143	84	96	100	101[1]	101[1]

[1] Totals do not add to 100 because of rounding errors.

Table 8   Lead/lag record of Conference Board revised leading and ECRI indexes at U.S. business cycle turning points, 1960-1991

U.S. Business Cycles		PEAKS & TROUGHS DATES				LEAD (-) OR LAG (+) IN MONTHS					
		ECRI Promptly Available LRG		Conference Board Rev. Leading Index		ECRI vs Business Cycle		Conference. Board vs Business Cycle		ECRI LRG vs Conference Board	
P	T	P	T	P	T	P	T	P	T	P	T
4/60		11/58		5/59		-17		-11		-6	
	2/61		6/60		11/60		-8		-3		-5
12/69		2/69		4/69		-10		-8		-2	
	11/70		2/70		4/70		-9		-7		-2
11/73		12/72		2/73		-11		-9		-2	
	3/75		1/75		2/75		-2		-1		-
1/80		8/77		10/78		-29		-15		-14	
	7/80		NTC		4/80		NTC		-3		--
7/81		NTC		4/81		NTC		-3		--	
	11/82		10/81		3/82		-13		-8		-5
7/90		1/90		1/90		-6		-6		0	
	3/91		1/91		1/91		-2		-2		0
Average Lead				P		-15		-9		-5	
					T		-7		-4		-3
				P & T		-11		-6		-4	
Standard Deviation				P		9		4		6	
					T		5		3		5
				P & T		8		4		5	

Note: The ECRI long range gauge (LRG) includes five promptly available (See Table 1 note).

Table 9 Lead/lag record of Conference Board leading index and ECRI short promptly available index: 1960-91

U.S. Business Cycles		PEAK & TROUGH DATES				LEAD (-) OR LAG (+), IN MONTHS					
		ECRI SRG Promptly Available		Conference Board		ECRI SRG vs Business Cycles		Conference Board vs Business Cycles		ECRI SRG vs Conference Board	
P	T	P	T	P	T	P	T	P	T	P	T
4/60		5/59		5/59		-11		-11		0	
	2/61		12/60		11/60		-2		-3		+1
12/69		4/69		4/69		-8		-8		0	
	11/70		10/70		4/70		-1		-7		+6
11/73		10/73		2/73		-1		-9		+8	
	3/75		2/75		2/75		-1		-1		0
1/80		10/78		10/78		-15		-15		0	
	7/80		5/80		4/80		-2		-3		+1
7/81		4/81		4/81		-3		-3		0	
	11/82		8/82		3/82		-3		-8		+5
7/90		4/89		1/90		-15		-6		-9	
	3/91		1/91		1/91		-2		-2		0
Average Lead				P		-9		-9		0	
					T		-2		-4		+2
				P & T		-6		-6		+1	
Standard Deviation				P		6		4		5	
					T		1		3		3
				P & T		5		4		4	

Note: The ECRI long range gauge (LRG) includes five promptly available (See Table 1 note).

A New Look at Promptly Available Leading Indicators

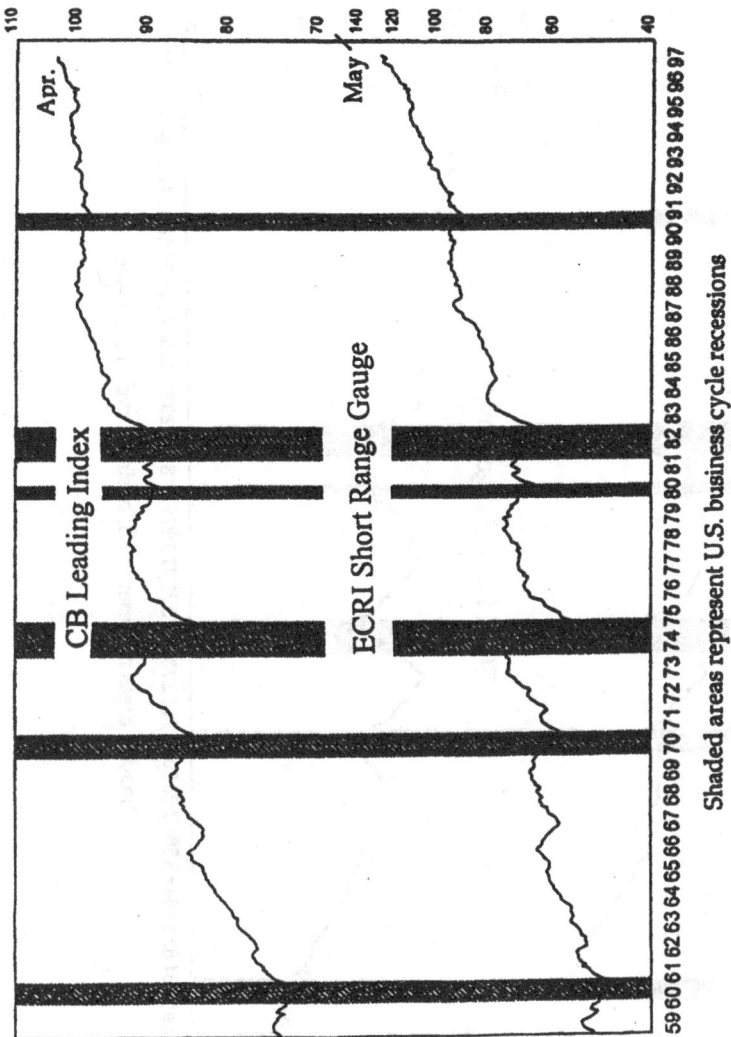

Chart 1 Timing at U.S. business cycles: Conference Board revised leading index and ECRI promptly available long range gauge

Social and Structural Change - Consequences for Business Cycle Surveys

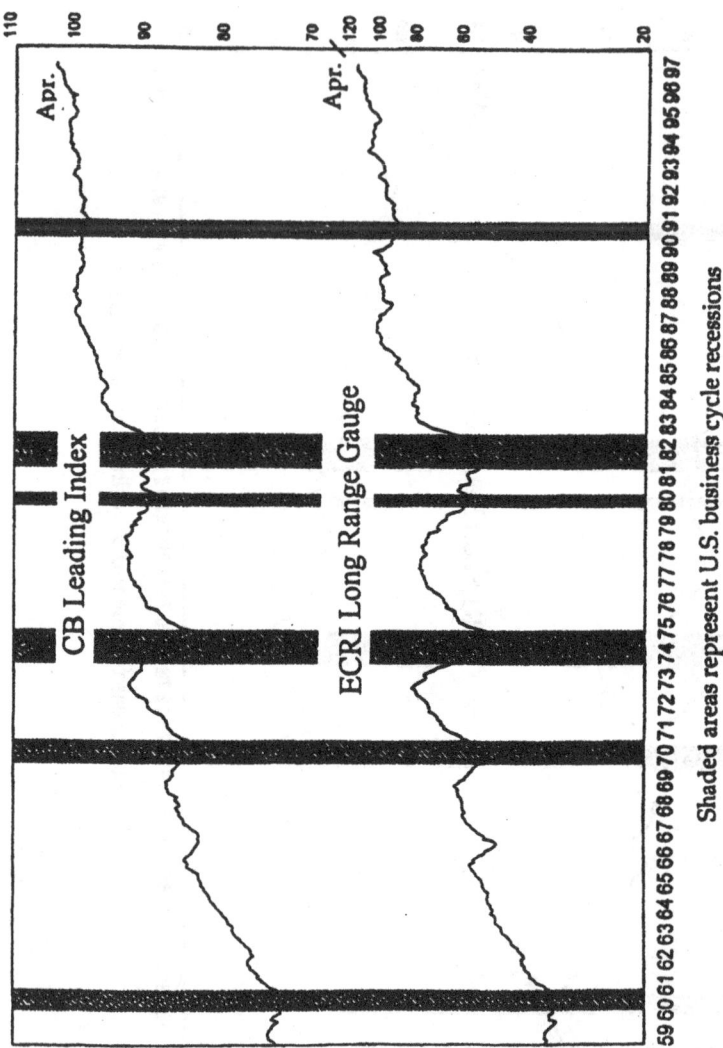

Chart 2 Conference Board revised leading index and ECRI promptly available short range gauge

3 Conclusion

1. We have examined three indexes of leading indicators useful in forecasting: the Conference Board's leading index, and the Economic Cycle Research Institute's short range and long range gauges. Our first finding is that on average the ECRI short range gauge is available 24 days before the Conference Board series. The range varies from one month in which the lead is only 20 days to two months in which the lead is 28 days.[1]
2. The Conference Board leading index leads the ECRI short range gauge by two months at troughs. The two series lead by virtually the same time period at business cycle peaks so that overall the Conference Board has an advantage in availability of one month.
3. On the other hand, the Conference Board leading index lags the ECRI long range gauge by five months at peaks, three months at troughs, for a four month disadvantage in availability overall. A four month advantage is significant in terms of the leads under review here.
4. Because ECRI shows that both its short range and long range gauges have valuable leading properties, it is clear that both can add to our ability to forecast, particularly at peaks. The lead in the long range gauge is so long that the lead in the short range gauge can be regarded as confirmatory.
5. Of all of the fifteen components of the ECRI short range and long range only one - the Journal of Commerce index of sensitive materials prices lags (by four months) but only at troughs (it, too leads at peaks). Thus all of the components on average are leaders at business cycle turning points.

4 Recommendation

We recommend that work on promptly available U.S. indicators be extended to include the construction of a promptly available coincident index. Among the components which could be included in this index are nonfarm employee hours, the NAPM production survey, and the *Business Week* production index. All of these are available in the first seven days of the subsequent month.

This work points to a potentially fruitful direction in which progress in successful forecasting could be extended to other market economies.

We wish to thank Michael P. Niemira for supplying necessary information for this paper and Eric Robinson for statistical assistance. In addition, we wish to thank Nancy Cole, my Research Secretary at Penn State, Anirvan Banerji, Dimitra Visviki, and Jean Maltz at ECRI for their comments and valuable assistance on this paper.

References

Cullity, J. and Banerji, A. (1996), Procedures for Constructing Composite Indexes: A Reassessment, Paper presented at the October meeting of the OECD, Paris, October.

Moore, G. H. and Cullity, J. P. (1990), Promptly Available Economic Indicators, in G.H. Moore (ed), *Leading Indicators for the 1990s*, Dow Jones, Irwin: Homewood, pp. 67-81.

---

[1] All of the components of the short range gauge are promptly available.

3 Use of Leading Indicators in a Model-based Forecast

Henk C. Kranendonk / Cees L. Jansen

Abstract

CPB uses a macroeconometric model as the core of its forecasting process. Moreover, we maintain a system of leading indicators, as it has proved to be a useful instrument in spotting turning points in economic activity. Our system of leading indicators has a similar kind of disaggregation as our macroeconometric model. This facilitates the incorporation of information from the indicators in the model-based-forecasts by means of add-factors in specific behavioral equations. Moreover, this approach has the advantage that we can analyze the Dutch business cycle in more detail.

1 Introduction

A number of leading indicators has been developed for the Dutch economy.[1] These leading indicators have little to say about either the prospects for individual sectors of the economy or the cyclical development of different expenditure categories. This is a serious drawback when leading indicators are used by an organization like CPB,[2] which uses a macroeconometric model as the core of its forecasting process. Therefore, we developed a system of leading indicators which can be combined easily with the model-based forecast, as it has essentially the same disaggregation. This paper first describes how the leading indicator is used in our forecasting process. Next, we discuss our system of leading indicators in more detail.

2 Forecasting Process

Once every quarter CPB prepares a short-term forecast. The so-called FKSEC quarterly macroeconometric model for the Netherlands (CPB, 1992) plays a central role in the

---

[1] Business cycles chronologies have been published by Van Duijn (1978) and Fase (1985). Examples of leading indicators are Klene (1983) and Bikker and De Haan (1988).
[2] CPB Netherlands Bureau for Economic Policy Analysis was established in 1945 by the Dutch government. The Bureau's mission is to undertake independent forecasts and analyses that are up-to-date, scientifically sound and relevant for policymaking – for the government, parliament, and other interested parties including political parties and industry.

forecasting process. The production of a forecast proceeds in several stages, as indicated in figure 1.[1]

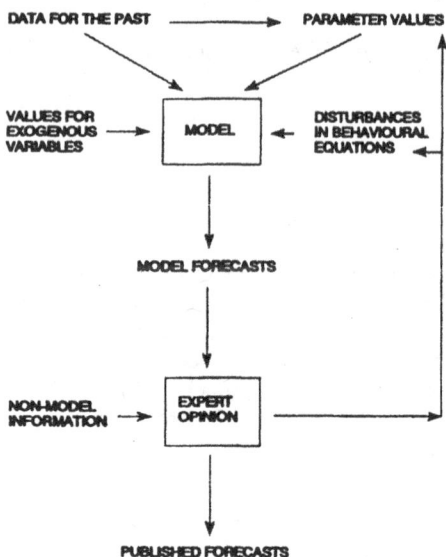

Figure 1   The forecasting process

With projections for the exogenous variables and for the disturbances we can make a forecast with the model. These disturbances are usually set at zero, but autocorrelation processes or non-model information may lead to nonzero values. In other words it is sometimes decided to introduce so-called add-factors. In fact, expert opinion is an important ingredient of any forecasting exercise with an econometric model. It brings in non-model information, for instance on variables or relations that were neglected at the modelling stage, but are considered to be relevant in the forecasting period. Add-factors may also be based on expert opinion, recent realizations, special events like strikes and information from surveys.

In figure 1 expert opinion is pictured as a filter for the model forecasts. Feed-back into the model results in a new forecast. In this way, the adjustment of some endogenous variables has consequences for all endogenous variables. Of course this is an iterative process which continues until it converges.

How can information from leading indicators be incorporated in the model-based forecasts? One possibility would be to include such variables in our macroeconometric

---

[1] This figure is taken from Don (1994). CPB forecasting practice is described in Van den Berg, Gelauff and Okker (1988).

model. Some large US-models use anticipatory (i.e. leading) variables in this way. A major disadvantage of this approach is the short forecasting horizon of these variables, so that endogenous estimates for the anticipations have to be used for later periods. Therefore, we do not include them in our model itself, but instead we use leading indicators to modify the model-based forecasts by means of add-factors. However, if the model and the leading indicator 'disagree', the implications for specific variables, and hence for the residuals of specific equations are by no means clear. For instance, if the leading indicator points to a cyclical slowdown, should we adjust consumption, investment or exports? That's why we have developed a system of leading indicators which can be combined easily with the model-based forecast, as it has a similar kind of disaggregation. In this way it gives implications for specific variables and hence for the residuals of specific equations.

All practising forecasters make judgemental adjustments[1], but little is published on the processes involved and the effects on the quality of the forecasts. McNees (1990) finds that these adjustments generally improve the accuracy of forecasts. This is especially true for short horizons, as forecasters have more non-model information then. But McNees also finds a slight overadjustment. Therefore we are careful with these adjustments and always have a clear reasoning behind them. In this respect a disaggregated leading indicator can be very useful to incorporate qualitative information in a model-based forecast.

3 CPB System of Leading Indicators

3.1 Methodology

We use the OECD/NBER methodology of constructing leading indicators (OECD, 1987; Nilsson, 1987). The first step is the selection of a reference series, that is to say the series whose future movement the leading indicator is intended to predict, and the identification of its past cyclical behavior. The cycle is calculated by elimination of the seasonal component, the trend and random factors and is expressed as deviation from trend[2].

The next step is to select economic time series whose cyclical movements typically predate those of the reference series. We use three criteria to evaluate these series: economic plausibility, cyclical behavior and practical considerations. The first criterion means that there should be some kind of economic reason for a series to be accepted as an indicator. Second, the cyclical behavior is tested both with regard to consistent timing (peak-and-trough analysis) and cyclical conformity (cross-correlation analysis). With regard to the last criterion, practical considerations are the availability of long time series without breaks and timeliness of publication.

The final step is to combine the selected indicators in one single indicator, which

---

[1] See e.g. Llewellyn, Potter and Samuelson (1985) and Surrey and Ormerod (1977).
[2] To eliminate the seasonal component we use the CPB seasonal correction programme which resembles the well-known CENSUS-X11 method (Den Butter and Fase, 1991). The Phase Average Trend method removes the trend (Boschan and Ebanks, 1978). The CPB smooth-filter is comparable to a 23-term Henderson. We convert some quarterly series to monthly frequency and smooth all time series before detrending them.

summarizes their behavior in a compact way. This is done in order to reduce the risk of false signals and to provide a leading indicator that has better qualities than any of its individual components.

3.2 Reference Series

The leading indicator technique is applied to different expenditure components (private consumption, investment and exports) and to different sectors of the economy (manufacturing industry, construction and commercial services). In this way the cyclical pattern of domestic production can be analyzed from two perspectives. In the demand approach the different reference series for the expenditure components are aggregated. The supply approach also produces a cyclical profile for domestic production. Finally, by combining these two aggregates, all information is summarized in one single series, which represents 'the' business cycle. In fact, this series excludes some components that are typically non-cyclical or less-cyclical, i.e. public sector production, medical and non-commercial services, energy and operation of real estate.

This set of disaggregated leading indicators not only has advantages when it is used in the forecasting process with our macroeconometric model, but also in analyzing the Dutch business cycle. Most leading indicators use industrial production as the reference series. In contrast, we also consider the production of the construction sector and the commercial services sector. Although the construction sector has only a small weight (5 per cent of GDP), it has a significant cyclical pattern (figure 2). The Dutch economy features a relatively small industrial base and a relatively large commercial services sector compared to other OECD countries. The trade and transport sector is particularly prominent. The share of the commercial services sector in total GDP is almost 50 per cent and this percentage is still increasing. From figure 2 it becomes clear that this sector acts as a stabilizing factor in the GDP cycle. Figure 2 not only shows that the cyclical pattern of these three sectors can differ with regard to the intensity of peaks and troughs, but also with regard to the dating of turning points. Analysis of the cyclical behavior of expenditure components of GDP also offers additional insights (figure 3). The development of demand categories is not the same in all cyclical episodes. For instance, in the 1993 downturn, private consumption growth was considerably stronger than in the early 1980s.

Use of Leading Indicators in a Model-based Forecast

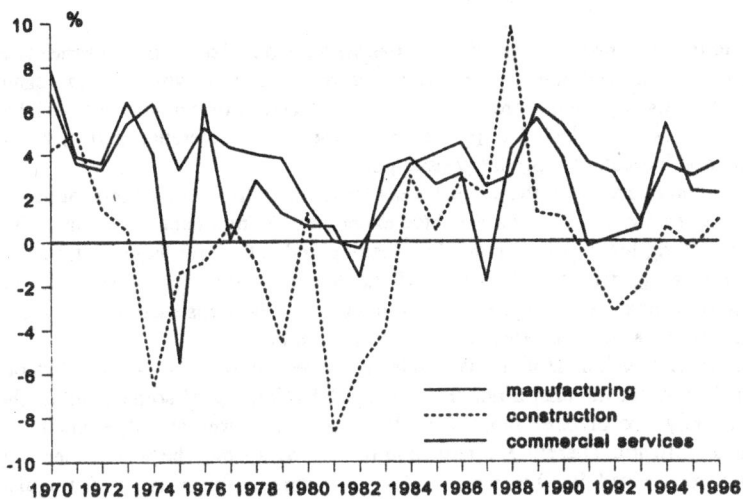

Figure 2   Sectoral growth rates

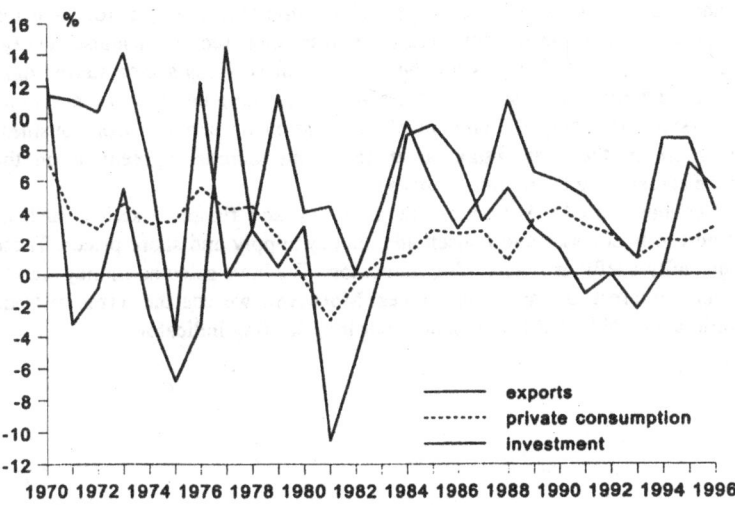

Figure 3   Growth rates of expenditure components

3.3 Selected Indicators

To select indicators we compare the candidate series with the detailed reference series (i.e. expenditure components and the production by sector) and not with the aggregate reference series. In this approach more time series are selected. For example the variable 'willingness to buy' is not selected if (total) production is the reference series, but it appears to be a good indicator for private consumption.

Table 1 gives an overview of the subject areas from which the selected indicators are chosen. The variables are divided over the three expenditure components, manufacturing production and a long-leading indicator. The leading indicators for construction and commercial services are weighted averages of the leading indicators of the relevant expenditures components[1]. This implies that production of the construction sector and production of commercial services are not included in this table.

For our short-leading indicator we have selected sixteen indicators. Most indicators have a lead of four to six months. Since there is a publication lag of some months, the effective lead is only two or three months. It also takes some time to judge whether a cyclical turn is significant. Therefore, a recession or a recovery may be well under way before we have recognized it. One way to deal with this problem is to distinguish indicators with long leads from others with short leads[2]. Five of the twenty-one indicators have a lead of one year or more and make up the long-leading indicator. The appendix gives a more detailed description of our system of leading indicators

Business and consumer surveys are the most important sources for selected indicators. For the manufacturing industry and the construction sector, business surveys are available for a long period. Surveys for the commercial services sector started only some years ago in the Netherlands, so these series are not yet long enough to incorporate in the indicator system. Probably the amount of information on services from business surveys will increase in the near future, as there is international agreement on the necessity for more statistical information on this sector.

The most frequently used other series are monetary and financial series, such as interest rates, credit to businesses and households, money supply and share prices. These variables are especially useful as long-leading indicators. We have selected money supply (M1), the long-term interest rate and share prices. Moreover, we use the terms of trade and cancelled orders on residential investment in our long-leading indicator.

---

[1] These weights are derived from a cumulated production structure matrix. This matrix is the reduced form of a standard input-output table, in which the matrix of domestic intermediaries has been removed by substitution. This matrix connects sectoral production with components of final demand (see CPB(1992), appendix 1).

[2] See Moore (1991) for a discussion on the usefulness of the differentiation between short-leading and long-leading indicators.

Use of Leading Indicators in a Model-based Forecast

Table 1 Summary of selected leading indicators

Indicator series by subject area	short-leading indicator			manufacturing production	total	long-leading indicator	total	OECD Netherlands[a]	OECD total[b]
	exports	consumption	investment						
							%	%	%
Production, stocks and orders									9
Construction, sales and trade			2		2	1	14	9	10
Labor force									3
Prices, costs and profits								9	6
Monetary and financial[c]		1			1	3	19	27	27
Foreign trade		1	1		2	1	14	9	6
External	3			1	3[d]		14	9	5
Business and consumer surveys	1	1	3	3	8		38	36	34
Total number of indicators	4	3	6	4	16	5	100	100	100

[a] 11 indicators.
[b] 190 indicators for 22 countries; Nilsson (1987), table 2.
[c] Including interest rates.
[d] IFO business climate indicator Germany is used twice.

Compared with other indicator-systems, like the OECD system (OECD,1987 and Nilsson,1987), we use more external and foreign trade series. We use three external series as indicators for Dutch exports: the IFO business climate indicator for Germany and the OECD leading indicators for Europe and the United States. Our experience is in line with research of Berk and Bikker (1995). They conclude that the forecasting power of national composite indicators in many OECD countries can be enhanced when indicators of well-known leading economies (notably USA, Japan and Germany) are included.

From other sources we select three indicators (two types of building permits granted and cancelled orders on residential investment). In the Netherlands labor-market indicators generally do not lead production. However, we use these indicators for our leading indicator of employment (see section 3.6).

3.4 Composite Indicators

The final step is to combine the selected time series in a so-called composite indicator. For this, we normalize all time series to ensure that their cyclical movements have the same amplitude. If this were not done, a series with a particularly marked cyclical amplitude would have undue weight in the cyclical indicator.

Like Berk and Bikker (1995), we adjust for the different leads of the selected indicators. This synchronisation with the reference series causes the turning points of the indicators to coincide on average, making the cyclical pattern of the composite indicator clearer than it would be without synchronization.

Finally, these adjusted time series are aggregated. In contrast with many other leading indicators, like the OECD-system, we use for our short-leading indicator in some cases non-equal weights (see appendix). The weights for the expenditure components and manufacturing industry are based on the quality of the indicators (the score in the peak-and-trough analysis and the cross-correlation coefficients). The expenditure components and sectoral production are aggregated, with the nominal shares as weights[1], to total demand and total supply respectively. The unweighted average of these two approaches of production gives the CPB short-leading indicator of economic activity.

3.5 Performance

Figure 4[2] illustrates the historical performance of the indicators for the expenditure components and manufacturing production. Exports and manufacturing production show the most dynamic pattern. The performance of the exports indicator was more accurate in the seventies than in the eighties. Possible explanations for the weaker 'fit' during the last

---

[1] Time series are first normalized and subsequently aggregated. Therefore the nominal shares must be corrected for the different variances of the components. For instance the weight of the construction industry is larger than the nominal share, because the cyclical pattern is more dynamic than that of (total) production.

[2] The composite leading indicators are presented as deviations from trend, as the focus is on the assessment of turning points. In figure 4 and 5 an ascending (declining) line indicates that growth is above (below) the average achieved during the previous business cycle.

decade are the increasing importance of re-exports[1] and the absence of an indicator of competitiveness. The dating of the turning points of manufacturing production is better than the description of the intensities of the peaks and troughs. The indicators for private consumption and investment closely correspond with their reference series. This applies both to the turning points and to the cyclical profile.

Figure 5 presents the composite leading indicators of economic activity. The short-leading indicator performs better than the long-leading indicator, both in predicting turning points and in 'general fit'. The fit of our long-leading indicator is especially weak in the eighties, partly because of the false signal of share prices in 1987.

We use the indicator system since 1989, so by now we have some experience with respect to the ex ante forecasting performance. The downturn in 1992/1993 and the upturn in 1994 were 'forecasted' by our system of leading indicators, although the intensity sometimes was underestimated. The indicators for exports, investment and manufacturing production showed a significant decline after the peak in 1990/1991. Also the turnaround in exports and manufacturing production in 1995 was predicted by the indicators. Figure 4 makes clear that the 1995 downturn was caused by exports: both the upturn of investment and of private consumption continued.

The usefulness of a separate short-leading and long-leading indicator was confirmed in recent years. The long-leading indicator gave early notice of both the cyclical upswing in 1993/1994 and the shallow and brief downturn in 1995. In the first months of 1996 the long-leading indicator pointed already to a cyclical recovery. The cyclical upturn was first confirmed by our short-leading indicator in September 1996: six months later than the first signal of the long-leading indicator.

---

[1] Re-exports are imported goods to which relatively little value is added before they are exported again. Re-exports account for around 25% of Dutch export value in 1995 (up from 17% in 1985).

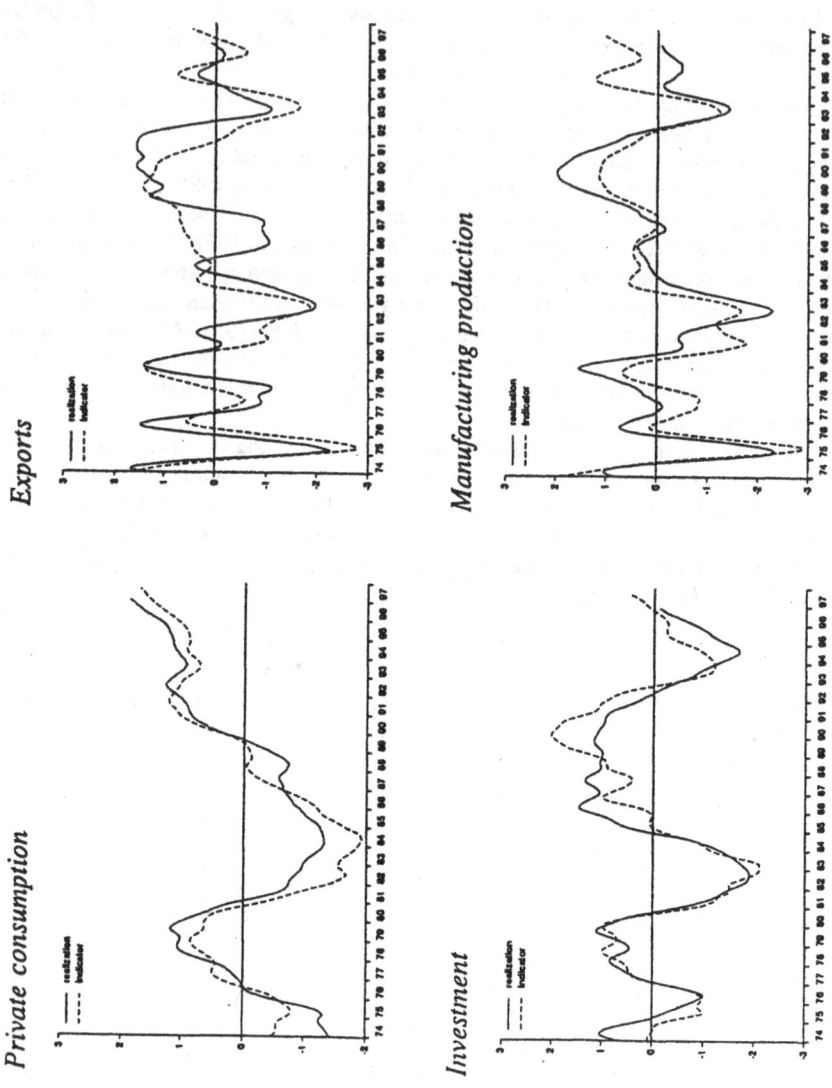

Figure 4 Leading indicators for expenditure components and manufacturing production

Use of Leading Indicators in a Model-based Forecast

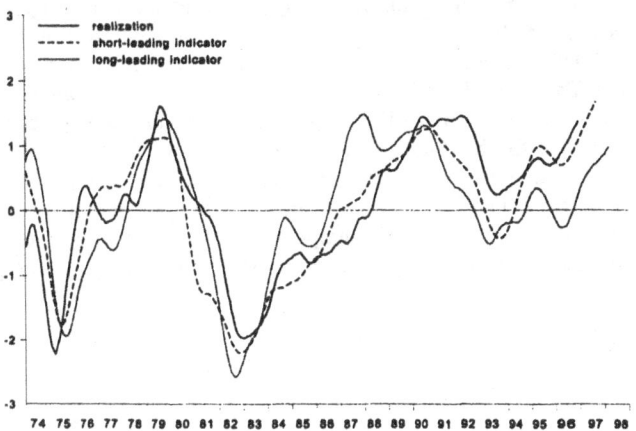

Figure 5   CPB leading indicators of economic activity

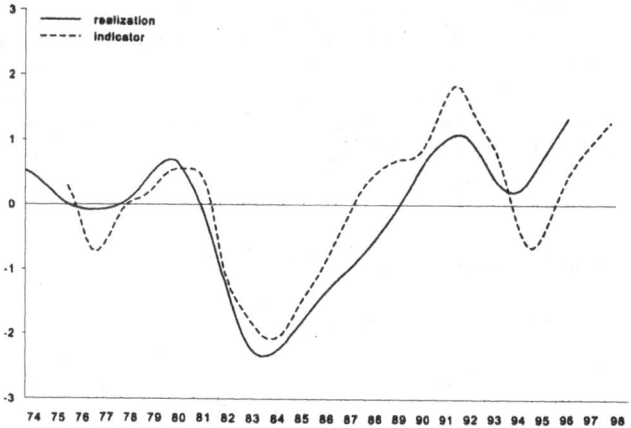

Figure 6   Leading indicator of employment

3.6 Leading Indicator of Employment

We have also constructed a leading indicator of employment in enterprises. Employment data are published on a quarterly basis in the Netherlands, with a publication lag of a quarter to half a year. A leading indicator is thus a very useful instrument in overcoming this lack of information. The cyclical profile of employment appears to be quite similar to that of production, but for a shift in time. Therefore, our leading indicator of economic activity is a suitable indicator for the (future) development of employment. In addition to this indicator, three labor-market indicators were selected: job vacancies, applications for layoffs (a requirement under Dutch law) and bankruptcies. The lead time of these series is more than one year. The leading indicator of employment, based on these four series, provides a good approximation of the actual demand for labor and possible turning points in the near future.

4 Conclusion

Experience in many countries has shown that leading indicators are a useful instrument in spotting turning points in economic activity. But leading indicators only give limited quantification, so that we primarily use the indicators as an overall check on the 'shape' of our forecast. It seems wise to do so, as the principal challenge for short-term forecasting is to improve the methods for predicting turning points (see Zarnowitz, 1991, p. 27). If the model and the indicators 'agree', confidence in the forecast increases. If the two methods give different results, it is a question of judgement which weight should be given to each of them. In our opinion this cannot be solved by means of a mechanical rule as the information content of both forecasts has to be judged. In this respect our disaggregated leading indicator has the advantage that a more detailed analysis of differences is possible. Information from indicators can be incorporated in the forecast by means of add-factors. If model and indicators 'disagree', this may also lead to the preparation of a simulation in which a different cyclical development is sketched. If used this way, leading indicators and macroeconometric models are not conflicting instruments, as both have merits in business cycle analysis and forecasting.

Appendix: CPB System of Leading Indicators

A lead of n months is indicated by (–n) behind the variable.

short-leading indicator of economic activity:

$$E = 0.35 * EUR(-5) + 0.25 * IFO(-5) + 0.15 * US(-5) + 0.25 * OIME(-4)$$
$$C = [\,WTB(-9) + MC(-2) + CC(-2)\,] / 3$$
$$IR = 0.4 * BPR(-6) + 0.6 * YTR(-8)$$
$$IB = 0.6 * BPN(-6) + 0.4 * YTN(-8)$$
$$IE = 0.7 * MI(-2) + 0.3 * OIMI(-4)$$
$$IT = 0.35 * IR + 0.2 * IB + 0.45 * IE$$

M   = 0.25 * C + 0.15 * IE + 0.6 * E
YEXP   = 0.7 * C + 0.3 * IT + 0.5 * E − 0.5 * M

YMI   = [2 * IFO(−5) + 2 * YEM(−5) + YTM(−5) + OIM(−6)] / 6
YCI   = 0.55 * IR + 0.25 * IB + 0.1 * C + 0.1 * E
YS   = 0.55 * C + 0.3 * E + 0.15 * IT
YSEC   = 0.35 * YMI + 0.10 * YCI + 0.55 * YS

SHORT = 0.5 * YEXP + 0.5 * YSEC

where

BPN	Building permits granted, private non-residential
BPR	Building permits granted, residential
C	Private consumption
CC	Consumer credit
E	Exports of goods, excluding energy
EUR	OECD leading indicator for Europe
IB	Private non-residential investment in buildings
IE	Private non-residential investment in equipment
IFO	IFO business climate indicator for Germany
IR	Private residential investment
IT	Total investment
M	Imports
MC	Imports of consumer goods
MI	Imports of investment goods
OIM	Orders inflow manufacturing industry
OIME	Orders inflow manufacturing exports
OIMI	Orders inflow inland manufacturing investment goods
SHORT	Short-leading indicator of economic activity
YCI	Production of construction industry
YEM	Expected production manufacturing industry
YEXP	Production in enterprises, expenditure approach
YMI	Production of manufacturing industry
YS	Production of commercial services
YSEC	Production in enterprises, sectoral approach
YTM	Production tendency manufacturing industry
YTN	Production tendency non-residential buildings
YTR	Production tendency residential buildings
US	OECD leading indicator for the United States
WTB	Willingness to buy

long-leading indicator of economic activity:

LONG = [RL(−16) + M1(−14) + SP(−11) + TT(−15) + AN(−28)] / 5 where

AN	Cancelled orders residential investment (inverse)
LONG	Long-leading indicator of economic activity
M1	Money supply (M1, real)
RL	Long-term interest rate (inverse)
SP	Share prices (real)
TT	Terms of trade

leading indicator of employment: (lead in quarters)

$$\text{EMPL} = [\text{SHORT}(-5) + \text{VAC}(-6) + \text{LAY}(-7) + \text{BR}(-6)]/4$$

where

BR	Bankruptcies (inverse)
EMPL	Leading indicator of employment in enterprises (excluding self-employed)
LAY	Applications for lay-off (inverse)
SHORT	Short-leading indicator of economic activity
VAC	Job vacancies

References

Berg, P.J.C.M., van den, G.M.M Gelauff and Okker, V.R. (1988), The Freia-Kompas model for the Netherlands: A quarterly macroeconomic model for the short and medium term, *Economic Modelling*, Vol. 5, pp. 170-236.

Berk, J.M. and Bikker, J.A. (1995), International Interdependence of Business Cycles in the Manufacturing Industry: The Use of Leading Indicators for Forecasting and Analysis, *Journal of Forecasting*, Vol. 14, pp. 1-23.

Bikker, J.A. and de Haan, L. (1988), Forecasting business cycles: a leading indicator for the Netherlands, De Nederlandsche Bank, Reprint 216.

Boschan, C. and Ebanks, W.W. (1987), The phase-average trend: A new way of measuring economic growth, *Proceedings of the Business and Economic Statistics section*, American Statistical Association, pp.332-335.

Butter, F.A.G den and Fase, M.M.G. (1991), *Seasonal Adjustment as a practical Problem*, North-Holland, Amsterdam.

CPB, 1992, *FKSEC, a macro-econometric model for the Netherlands*, Stenfert Kroese, Leiden/Antwerpen.

Don, F.J.H. (1994), Forecast uncertainty in economics, in: J. Grasman and G. van Straten (eds), *Predictability and Nonlinear Modelling in Natural Sciences and Economics*, Kluwer Academic Publishers.

Duijn, J.J. van (1978), Dating postwar business cycles in the Netherlands, 1948-1976, *De Economist 126*, No. 4., pp. 474-504.

Fase, M.M.G. and Bikker, J.A. (1985), De datering van economische fluctuaties: proeve van een conjunctuurspiegel voor Nederland 1965-1984, *Maandschrift Economie*, jaargang 49, pp. 299-332.

Klene, N. and Lenselink, R. (1983), New ABN business barometer for the Dutch economy, *ABN-review*, No. 96.

Llewellyn, J., Potter, S. and Samuelson, L. (1985), *Economic forecasting and policy, the international dimension*, Routledge and Kegan Paul.

McNees, S.K. (1990), Man vs. Model? The Role of Judgement in Forecasting, *New England Economic Review*, pp. 41-52.

Nilsson, R. (1987), OECD leading indicators, *OECD Economic studies*, No. 9, pp. 105-146.

OECD (1987), OECD Leading indicators and business cycles in member countries 1960-1985, *Main Economic Indicators*, Sources and Methods, No. 39, Paris.

Surrey, M.J.C. and Ormerod, P.A. (1977), Formal and informal aspects of forecasting with an econometric model, *National Institute Economic Review*, No. 81., pp. 67-71.

Zarnowitz, V. (1991), Has macro-forecasting failed?, *NBER Working Paper Series*, No. 3867.

4 An Update of OECD Leading Indicators[*]

Gerald Petit / Gerard Salou / Pierre Beziz / Christophe Degain

The partial study being presented here is a first step towards a more comprehensive update of the system of OECD leading indicators. While the system has worked relatively well since it was set up in its current form (see in particular Artis, Bladen-Howell, Zhang, 1995, and Nilsson, 1987), it would be useful to examine its actual performance and, where necessary, take a fresh look at its methodological foundations.

The OECD leading indicators were developed by a working party composed of Secretariat staff and national experts and were based on work by the National Bureau of Economic Research (NBER) of the United States (see OECD, 1987, Introduction and Part A). The working party's dissolution in 1981 did not end the contacts, however, since the principle of ad hoc meetings was adopted thereafter. Following the last such meeting, which was held in September 1984, the OECD leading indicators were published in their present form in late 1987, in the *Main Economic Indicators* series, preceded by a publication on Sources and Methods (OECD, 1987).[1]

A monthly newsletter on the leading indicators computed by the OECD was also distributed in the 1980s for in-house use by the Secretariat and Member country governments.

Since then, nearly ten years have gone by without major changes, primarily because the system has been operating fairly smoothly, but also because the Secretariat's programme of work and resource constraints have until now precluded the idea of major work. Enough time has elapsed to look at how the OECD leading indicators have actually evolved and to review any relevant innovations by the Member countries.

The purpose of this study is to provide a basis for discussion of the first of these items. It has been prepared entirely on the basis of data available in June 1996 and updated in the Main Economic Indicators database.

Over the past three years, the OECD has welcomed new countries. We have formulated a leading indicator of industrial production in Mexico, in particular to ascertain whether it would have been possible, and how far in advance, to predict the sudden economic reversal that took place in late 1994. This indicator is presented below and could ultimately be published in *Main Economic Indicators*, providing that the data

---

[*] The authors would like to express their appreciation, in particular, to Martine Durand and Paul van den Noord, of the OECD Economics Department, and to Béatrice du Boys, of the OECD Statistics Directorate, for their comments.

[1] Since late 1981, a set of charts (ratio to trend and trend restored) had already been published for three areas (OECD-Total, OECD-Europe and North America) and for Japan.

used to compute it are updated regularly by the national statistics agencies. The indicator's performance over a ten-year period is satisfactory.

To provide useful signals, quality updates and regular contacts with the Secretariat's statistics correspondents in the Member countries are essential. Over the past ten years, supply of some components of the leading indicators has been interrupted. Components can also become outdated, either because they have grown less relevant to the cycles of the reference series or because, over time, their updates have become less satisfactory for the computation of a composite index. Such cases, examples of which are cited in the following study, point to a deterioration of quality.

In this study, the component series of the leading indicators of three countries have been updated or overhauled: new composite indicators were introduced for the United States, in a relatively minor update, while German indicators were substantially simplified and the components of Norwegian indicators were revised. Norway posed an additional problem with regard to the choice of a reference series. Generally the industrial production is used as the reference series, and manufacturing output has so far been used for Norway.

Given the interest of outside users in the OECD leading indicators, the Statistics Directorate has added the corresponding monthly newsletter, which had previously been available in-house only, to its list of electronic publications available on the Internet. This recent initiative considerably expands the number of potential users of the indicators.

It must be stressed that, while the resources available to the Main Economic Indicators Division during publication production periods have been adequate to make the replacements needed to compute the indicators, production priorities have rarely made it possible to carry out the extensive research such replacements warrant. Moreover, the formulation of leading indicators by means of the method presented in OECD, 1987, is a statistical exercise that has often proved useful, but it is also costly and time-consuming. This study was carried out on a short deadline, with no additional resources and within the priorities of the Statistics Directorate's programme of work[1]. It makes no claims to be either perfect or complete, and is open to all your comments. We hope it will be of use in the substantive discussions of this first ad hoc meeting since 1984.

1 Mexico

The leading indicator of industrial production in Mexico that is presented herein is the first to be compiled by the OECD Secretariat. Previously, the Mexican National Statistics Institute (*Instituto Nacional de Estadística, Geografía e Informática, INEGI*) had carried out a study on the topic, the findings of which were published in 1992 (INEGI, 1992).

The composite leading indicator computed by the OECD anticipates cycles of the Mexican economy since 1985 by giving reliable signals of economic turning points. It therefore constitutes a practical tool for forecasting shifting economic trends.

---

[1] One of the top priorities is to update information about the data ("metadata") published in *Main Economic Indicators*, the importance of which was voiced during the meeting for the publication's thirtieth anniversary in October 1995.

In particular, the Mexican economy was recently marked by the severe recession that followed the devaluation of the peso in December 1994. Examination of the leading indicator shows that a signal of recession first appeared in February 1994. A simulation of the indicator as it would have been computed in October 1994 revealed that, at the time, its ratio to trend had been dropping for five months and that its relative amplitude was greater than at any other time during the period under consideration.

1.1 INEGI's Leading Indicator

The chief difference between INEGI's methodology and that of OECD is the way in which a time-series trend is calculated. INEGI used principal component analysis; broadly speaking, this method can be used to explain a given variable in terms of its main characteristics (principal components). By construction, these components are independent and, when all combined, fully explain the variable under study. As INEGI comments, for time series, the first principal component defines the underlying trend.

INEGI calculated three leading indicators of industrial production, with leads of 3, 7 and 11 months. These indicators covered the period 1986-92, except for the 11-month indicator, which covered 1987-92. Maximum correlation with the corresponding reference series was 0.53 for the 3-month leading indicator, 0.55 for the 7-month indicator and 0.59 for the 11-month indicator.

The indicators obtained subsequent to the published study have not been disseminated by INEGI in regular publications.

1.2 The OECD Leading Indicator

1.2.1 Cycles of the reference series For the OECD, the reference series is still total industrial production, beginning in 1985. The trend was computed using the phase-average trend (PAT) method (see OECD, 1987).

All cycles detected in the industrial production series were also found in the gross domestic product (GDP) series[1], except for a cycle of minor amplitude between January and July 1992.

Industrial production cycles generally lead or are coincident with those of GDP (see Table 1 and Figure 1). This confirms the choice of the industrial production series as the reference series for Mexico. It reflects GDP trends and is available on a monthly basis, in contrast to the GDP series, which is computed quarterly.

---

[1] New methodology based on the 1993 SNA and wider coverage of the manufacturing sector, beginning in 1993. Historical data for years prior to 1993 were reconstructed using ratios between the old and the new data in 1993.

Table 1 Comparison of GDP cycles[a] with those of the reference series

Gross domestic product			Industrial production		
Turning point dates (quarters)		Amplitude	Turning point dates (months)		Amplitude
Peaks	Troughs	% of trend	Peaks	Troughs	% of trend
3/85		+2.8	7/85		+ 5.07
	4/86	-2.22		12/86	- 5.78
4/87		+1.05	9/87		+ 2.78
	3/88	-2.07		7/88	- 3.94
2/91		+2.36	8/90		+ 1.94
				1/92	- 2.60
			7/92		+ 3.04
	2/93	-1.8		6/93	- 2.00
4/94		+3.72	8/94		+ 6.39
	2/95	-5.69		5/95	- 7.10

a) New methodology based on the 1993 SNA and wider coverage of the manufacturing sector, beginning in 1993. Historical data for years prior to 1993 were reconstructed using ratios between the old and the new data in 1993.

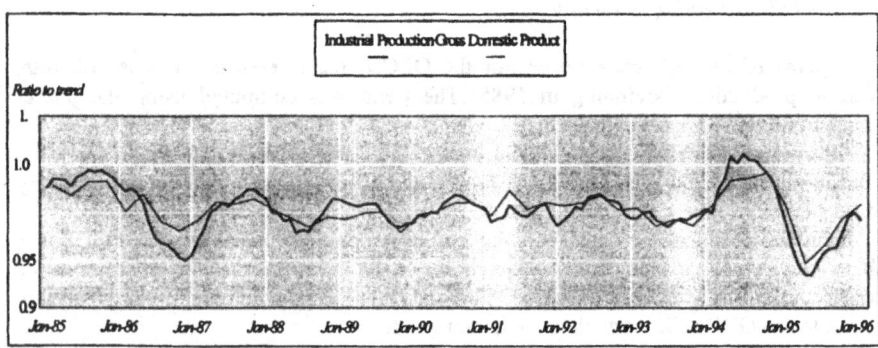

Figure 1 Ratio to trend for GDP[a, b] and the reference series[b]

a) New methodology based on the 1993 SNA and wider coverage of the manufacturing sector, beginning in 1993. Historical data for years prior to 1993 were reconstructed using ratios between the old and the new data in 1993.
b) A series smoothed by an MCD (Months for Cyclical Dominance) moving average. See also OECD, 1987, pp. 38, 42, 75.

Examination of the reference series shows four major periods reflecting the development of the Mexican economy (see particular OECD, 1995).

Between August 1988 and mid-1993, cycles were not very pronounced and had low relative amplitude. This reflected the government's economic policy, which combined a tight rein on public finances with strict monetary policy in order to stabilise inflation at a level near that of Mexico's main economic partners.

After 1993, implementation of economic reforms and an opening up to the outside world (membership of the North American market through NAFTA as of 1 January 1994) were followed by a policy of expansion. The phase between June 1993 and July 1994 was clearly pronounced (with a peak of relative amplitude of 6.4 per cent).

Finally, the severe recession that followed devaluation of the peso on 20 December 1994 was reflected in the industrial production series by a short (nine-month) phase with high amplitude (7 per cent of the trend).

1.2.2 Component series of the leading indicator The component series used to compute the OECD leading indicator were chosen after an examination of 62 different time series, drawn primarily from the "Main Economic Indicators" database, but also from INEGI's *"Banco de datos"* base and the Bank of Mexico's SINIEE database. A diskette version of SINIEE as of 27 February 1996 (containing data to January 1996 at the latest) was used.

A large number of these series were rejected, because they lacked a relevant cyclical profile or because the amplitudes of the cycles they contained were out of proportion to the corresponding cycles of the reference series. The series had to do with the "real" economy (components of industrial production, wages, prices, construction costs, exports, etc., in terms of levels or differentials) or with financial data (the money supply, share prices, official reserves, peso/US dollar exchange rates, federal government deficits, etc.).

Moreover, it was impossible to test the cyclical behaviour of a great many series, either because data were not available over a long enough period (e.g. the yield on *"tesobonos"*[1]) or because they were calculated on an annual basis only (e.g. foreign investment in Mexico).

In the end, seven series were selected:

- *Three net opinion series from the Bank of Mexico's business survey:*
  1. Employment: tendency;
  2. Stocks of finished goods: tendency;
  3. Production: tendency.

These three series relate to business opinion for the month of the survey, as compared with the previous month. It should be noted that the Bank of Mexico also questions businesses about the one-month outlook. The corresponding net opinions are not released, however, and it was not possible to test these data, which would be likely to yield a better lead on cycles of the reference series.

- *Two series of financial rates:*
  1. Average cost to banks of managing deposits in national currency *(costo promedio de captación en moneda nacional,* CPP).
  2. US ten-year interest rates: interest rates on 10-year federal government bonds, as currently published in Main Economic Indicators.

---

[1] Securities indexed to the US dollar.

- The *Real effective exchange rate* calculated by the OECD Economics Department and also published in Main Economic Indicators. This rate is an indicator of competitiveness, which takes into account the relative importance of Mexico's competitors in thirty markets, and the relative importance of those markets (see Durand, Simon, Webb, 1992).

- *A series derived from INEGI's monthly industrial survey:*
  Monthly changes in manufacturing employment. These data are akin to employment tendency in manufacturing (see above), which is a business survey series. Note that the level of manufacturing employment is not relevant.

It should be noted that the US 10-year interest rate series is included from 1990, when its cyclical behaviour began to coincide with the industrial production series. All other series are included from 1985.

1.2.3 Main Results The composite leading indicator of industrial activity has been calculated for the period beginning in 1985. All cycles correspond to those of the reference series with an average lead of 7.1 months. This gap is uniform (averaging four months) over the entire period under consideration, except for 1989-92, when the average lead was 13 months. This difference may be explained by the fact that this period, as stated above, was characterised by an absence of clearly defined cycles. The composite indicator's performance is therefore presented in two different manners in Table 2 below, depending on whether or not the minor cycle of 1989-92 is considered to be missing. The performance is better if the cycle is omitted.

The composite indicator has a maximum correlation of 0.81 with the reference series since 1985 at a four-month lead. Data for the component series of the indicator are available within a month and a half to two months for all series except *Changes in manufacturing employment* and *Employment: tendency*, which take three months to obtain.

An Update of OECD Leading Indicators

Table 2   Characteristics of the chosen leading indicator

	MCD[a]	Availability (months)	Extra (x) or missing (m) cycles	Average leads/lags			Median leads/lags			Standard deviation	Correlation	
				peaks and troughs	peaks	troughs	peaks and troughs	peaks	troughs		Coefficient	Lead
Leading indicator	1	2		7.1	7.5	6.8	5	5	5	5.67	0.81	4
Leading indicator (1 cycle missing)	1	2	1m	4.4	4.0	4.8	4	3	5	2.07	0.81	4
Production: trend	6	2		5.3	5.6	5.0	4	4	1	5.29	0.65	4
Stocks of finished goods: trend[b]	6	2	3m	3.3	4.5	1.0	4	5	1	3.01	-0.38	6
Employment: trend	4	3	2m	4.0	3.7	4.3	4	4	5	1.53	0.66	3
Changes in manufacturing employment	6	3	1m	4.6	5.3	4.0	5	5	5	2.30	0.64	4
Average cost to banks of managing deposits in national currency (CPP)[b]	2	1	2m, 1x	3.8	4.3	3.3	5	5	4	1.60	-0.48	2
Real effective exchange rates	2	2	3m, 1x	2.3	2.3	2.0	3	3	2	4.11	0.55	3
US long-term interest rates (since 1990)[b]	3	1	1m	10.6	10.0	11.0	10	10	11	5.03	-0.86	9

a) A series smoothed by an MCD (Months for Cyclical Dominance) moving average. See also OECD, 1987, pp. 38, 42, 75.
b) Inverse relationship.

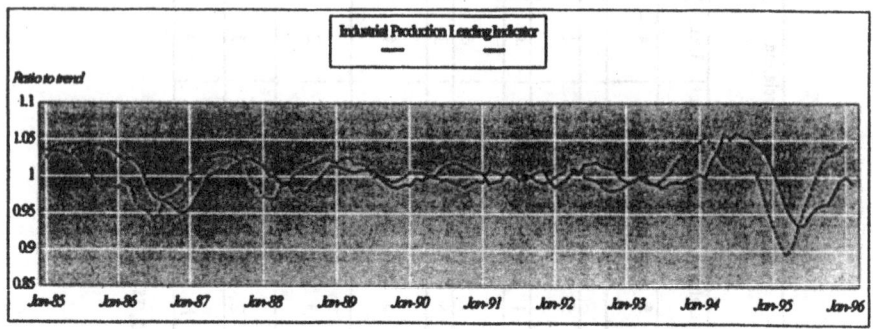

Figure 2   Leading indicator^a and reference series^b, ratio to trend

a) Adjusted to fit the amplitudes of the reference series.
b) A series smoothed by an MCD (Months for Cyclical Dominance) moving average. See also OECD, 1987, pp. 38, 42, 75.

1.2.4 Simulation of the December 1994 recession The composite leading indicator announces the recession with a lead of six months (turning point in February 1994). The indicator was recalculated as it would have been in October 1994, two months after the peak, assuming that, at the time, the databases used for the study had been fully updated through July 1994[1].

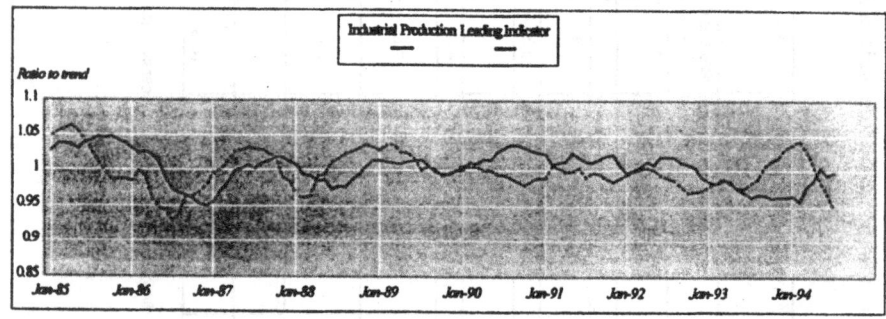

Figure 3   Simulation of the leading indicator^a in October 1994
a) Adjusted to fit the amplitudes of the reference series.

The indicator's ratio to trend had been falling since February 1994, dipping from 1.52 to -1.15 per cent in July. A difference of that amplitude in so short a time had never before been observed over the period under study. This movement was reflected primarily in the financial components: US ten-year interest rates (ratio to trend up sharply since the trough of October 1993: from -14.7 per cent to 15.2 per cent in July 1994), real effective

---

[1] The SINIEE database was not available on diskette until March 1996.

exchange rates (ratio to trend -3.95 per cent in February and -15.53 per cent in July) and average cost to banks of managing deposits in national currency (ratio to trend -13.24 per cent in February and 43.89 per cent in July).

The indicator therefore correctly signals the recession which culminated in May 1995.

Its update and possible publication in *Main Economic Indicators* will depend on the subsequent quality of the updates of its components.

2 United States

The composite leading indicator of industrial production for the United States had two component series that were interrupted and needed to be replaced. As a result, a slightly amended indicator was put in place.

2.1 The Previous Leading Indicator

The leading indicator used until now for the United States in the OECD system was made up of the following nine series:

1. Housing starts;
2. Money supply M2, CPI-deflated (1975 prices);
3. Treasury bill rate;
4. Share prices (Standard & Poor's);
5. Net new orders, durable goods;
6. Average weekly claims for unemployment benefit;
7. Changes in crude materials prices and sensitive prices, smoothed;
8. Changes in credit (business and consumption);
9. Net business formation.

The last two series were suspended as from November 1992 and January 1996 respectively. The quality of updates of the indicator's other components has not deteriorated, and all are still available within less than two months after the reference period.

The OECD's composite indicator for the United States has generally been accurate in anticipating past movements of the reference series, including those in the 1980s, which were not covered in the study carried out for OECD (OECD, 1987). In particular, it has indicated all of the growth cycle's turning points with a lead.

The composite indicator's average lead is six months. In the 1980s, it twice exhibited a very long lead of 20 months for the 1986 trough and 19 months for the 1989 peak. The deviation from the average lead has therefore increased with time, which could impair the indicator's credibility and usefulness.

Table 3 below shows that, at the turning points, industrial production generally anticipates the troughs of the gross domestic product (GDP) cycle and its peaks after 1975.

Table 3   Comparison of GDP cycles with those of the reference series

Gross domestic product			Industrial production		
Turning point dates (quarterly)		Amplitude	Turning point dates (months)		Amplitude
Peaks	Troughs	% of trend	Peaks	Troughs	% of trend
	1/61	-1.89		2/61	-4.56
1/66		+2.39	10/66		+2.95
	4/67	-0.75		7/67	-2.55
1/69		+2.50	3/69		+5.40
	4/70	-3.42		11/70	-7.59
1/73		+4.34	10/73		+8.97
	1/75	-3.64		3/75	-9.81
3/79		+2.17	3/79		+3.83
	4/82	-3.72		12/82	-7.26
2/84		+1.09	7/84		+3.02
	1/87	-1.12		6/86	-2.87
2/89		+1.30	3/89		+2.73
	4/91	-2.47		3/91	-5.79

2.2   The New Indicator

It is proposed to use the series "Contracts and orders for plants and capital equipment" to replace "net business formation" (series No. 9). The two series are similar in that they both signal how businesses read the outlook for future demand. The cyclical conformity of the new series is comparable to that of the other components, as shown in Table 4.

For the moment, it has not been possible to find a replacement for the eighth component series (changes in credit). As it turns out, series that reflect corporate borrowing either exhibit very poor cyclical conformity to the reference, or else they are coincident with or lag the business cycle. It has not been possible to find a series whose cycles lead the reference in this category of indicators.

A detailed study of the respective cyclical performance of each component of the leading indicator since the early 1980s shows that the ability of financial series to anticipate business cycles has deteriorated. M2 money supply at constant prices, for example, no longer exhibits any cyclical pattern at all, whereas interest rates on Treasury bills are no longer in phase with the business cycle. In particular, this is due to changes in financial markets and in economic policies in the 1980s. These components are capable of inducing cycles unrelated to the business cycle of the composite indicator, and it is for this reason that they have been eliminated.

An Update of OECD Leading Indicators

Table 4 Characteristics of the new leading indicator

	MCD[a]	Availability (months)	Extra (x) or missing (m) cycles	Average leads/lags			Median leads/lags			Standard deviation	Correlation	
				peaks and troughs	peaks	troughs	peaks and troughs	peaks	troughs		Coefficient	Lead
Previous leading indicator	1	2		6	8	5	5	7	3	6	0.8	5
New leading indicator	1	2		6	6	5	6	7	4	5	0.8	4
Net new orders, durable goods	3	2		1	2	1	1	3	1	4	0.9	1
Average weekly claims for unemployment benefit	3	2		3	6	1	3	6	1	3	0.9	2
Share prices	2	1	2x	7	6	8	9	8	9	12	0.5	8
Housing starts	3	2	1m	8	11	5	5	8	2	10	0.7	9
Changes in crude materials prices, smoothed;	5	2	1x	4	2	5	4	1	6	13	0.6	8
Contracts and orders for plants and capital equipment	5	2		1	4	-2	1	2	-2	5	0.8	0

a) A series smoothed by an MCD (Months for Cyclical Dominance) moving average. See also OECD, 1987, pp. 38, 42, 75.

The new composite indicator comprises the following six series:
1. Net new orders, durable goods;
2. Average weekly claims for unemployment benefit;
3. Share prices;
4. Housing starts;
5. Changes in crude materials prices, smoothed;
6. Contracts and orders for plants and capital equipment.

Its performance is very similar to that of the previous indicator, as shown in Table 4. The new indicator's lead at turning points is less dispersed, which is reflected in the lower standard deviation of the lead time. However, as with the previous indicator, this one can give false signals which are due to the erratic nature of its components. Legibility of results would be improved if the composite indicator were smoothed further, which is outside the scope of the current methodology.

3 Germany

Data for industrial production in unified Germany are available from January 1991. The new indicator has been made simpler than the previous one. The study shows that components derived from business surveys (relating to the Länder of western Germany) are still performing well, but it also suggests that, as in the United States, certain financial series are losing their ability to lead the industrial production cycle.

3.1 The Previous Leading Indicator

The leading indicator that until now has been used for Germany was developed with the industrial production series for the Federal Republic of Germany ("Western Germany") as a reference series. It was made up of the following nine series:

1. New orders, manufacturing;
2. Business survey: orders inflow or demand, tendency;
3. Business survey: order books, level;
4. Business survey: finished goods stocks, level;
5. Business survey: business climate;
6. Money supply M1 (CPI-deflated);
7. Yield on public-sector bonds;
8. Share prices, industrials;
9. Unit labour cost, mining and manufacturing.

3.1.1 Coverage of component series with regard to reunification[1] The component series now have the following geographical coverage:

---

[1] For further information on the sources and definitions of these series, see *Main Economic Indicators: Sources and Definitions*, OECD, May 1996.

1. New orders, manufacturing: unified Germany from 1991;
2. Business survey: Western Germany;
3. M1 money supply: unified Germany from July 1990; Western Germany prior to then;
4. Yield on public-sector bonds: unified Germany from July 1990; Western Germany prior to then;
5. Share prices: All shares (FWB index), 1990 = 100; prior to January 1993, data are for Western Germany;
6. Unit labour costs: This series refers to Western Germany. It has not been updated by the Federal Statistics Office (*Statistisches Bundesamt*) since December 1994.

3.2 The New Indicator

The industrial production series is seasonally adjusted and provided by the Federal Bank of Germany (*Bundesbank*) on the basis of the raw series calculated by the Federal Statistical Office (*Statistisches Bundesamt*). Data relate to unified Germany as from January 1991, while those referring to Western Germany were linked to current data using the average index of 1991 industrial production for Western Germany.

Table 5 shows that, as a rule, industrial production cycles either anticipate or are coincident with those of gross domestic product. Only the trough of July 1993 has no correspondence with GDP.

Table 5 Comparison of GDP cycles with those of the reference series

Gross domestic product[a]			Industrial production[a]		
Turning point dates (quarters)		Amplitude	Turning point dates (months)		Amplitude
Peaks	Troughs	% of trend	Peaks	Troughs	% of trend
	2/63	-1.49		2/63	-4.73
3/65		+2.84	1/65		+7.65
	3/67	-2.86		5/67	-9.51
2/70		+1.50	5/70		+4.21
	4/71	-1.13		12/71	-4.82
1/73		+2.93	8/73		+6.45
	2/75	-4.28		7/75	-10.59
1/80		+3.86	12/79		+7.87
	4/82	-1.29		11/82	-5.65
1/84		+1.18	11/85		+3.58
	3/89	-2.97		9/87	-4.95
2/91		+8.55	6/91		+8.67
				7/93	-6.43

a) Unified Germany after 1991.

As in the case of the United States, a detailed study of the respective cyclical performance of each component of the leading indicator since the early 1980s shows that the ability of financial series to anticipate business cycles has deteriorated. M1 money supply at constant prices, for example, no longer exhibits any cyclical pattern at all, whereas cycles for yields on public-sector bonds are no longer in phase with the business cycle. Here too, this is due to changes in financial markets and in economic policies in the 1980s. These components are capable of inducing cycles unrelated to the business cycle of the composite indicator, and it is for this reason that they have been eliminated.

The new composite leading indicator for Germany comprises the following six series:

1. New orders, manufacturing;
2. Business survey: order inflow or overall demand trend;
3. Business survey: order books, level;
4. Business survey: finished goods stocks, level;
5. Business survey: business climate;
6. Share prices, all shares (FWB index).

It has not yet been possible to find replacements for the series that have been eliminated or interrupted. Tests to date have not yielded any further improvements to the new indicator.

A comparison of the new indicator's performance with that of the old is summarised in Table 6. The new indicator anticipates all turning points, unlike the old one. It is also more regular in its anticipation, as is shown by the standard deviation of the lead time, which is only half as great.

An Update of OECD Leading Indicators

Table 6 Characteristics of the new leading indicator

	MCD[a]	Availability (months)	Extra (x) or missing (m) cycles	Average leads/lags			Median leads/lags			Standard deviation	Correlation	
				peaks and troughs	peaks	troughs	peaks and troughs	peaks	troughs		Coefficient	Lead
Previous leading indicator	1			6	8	4	6	6	5	6	0.8	8
New leading indicator	1			5	6	4	6	6	4	3	0.8	6
New orders, manufacturing	3	3		5	8	3	6	9	4	4	0.9	3
Business survey: orders or overall demand trend	3	2	1x	7	10	5	7	8	4	6	0.5	9
Business survey: order books, level	1	2		3	5	2	3	6	2	3	0.8	3
Business survey: finished goods stocks[b], level	2	2		4	5	3	3	5	2	3	-0.7	5
Business survey: business climate	1	2		3	4	3	2	4	2	3	0.6	7
Share prices, all shares (FWB index)	2	1		6	6	5	5	6	4	6	0.5	9

a) A series smoothed by an MCD (Months for Cyclical Dominance) moving average. See also OECD, 1987, pp. 38, 42, 75.
b) Inverse relationship.

4 Norway

4.1 The Current Leading Indicator

The composite indicator for Norway, as presented in OECD, 1987, pp. 144-147, is a leading indicator of *manufacturing* production. This restriction vis-à-vis aggregate industrial output stems from the volume of crude oil production, whose cyclical profile is not comparable to that of the reference series. It must be stressed that the reference series is highly volatile, as indicated by its Months for Cyclical Dominance or MCD[1] value of 6. This is due to the fact that Norwegian production is quite specialised (in particular, chemicals and wood).

Initially the composite leading indicator was made up of eleven series:
1. Industrial production, export goods;
2. Stocks of domestic goods;
3. Stocks of export goods;
4. Stocks of imported goods (volume);
5. Crude materials stocks;
6. Production tendency;
7. Inflow of export orders, tendency;
8. Business outlook;
9. Share prices, industrials, Oslo Stock Exchange;
10. Construction costs, dwellings;
11. Value of export goods, excluding ships.

Out of these eleven series, seven are quarterly (series 2-8). Series 6-8 are net percentages of the balance of "positive" over "negative" obtained from the quarterly business survey. Initially, the indicator's median lead (peaks and troughs) was four months, with an average lead of three months and a standard deviation of 3.9 months. The maximum correlation with the reference series was 0.84 at a six-month lead.

Since the leading indicator was established, Statistics Norway has stopped calculating stock data, and series 2-5 have not been updated since the third quarter of 1990. The first component (industrial production, export goods) has not been updated since January 1992. None of these series have been replaced. It must also be pointed out that, over the period available the cycles of construction costs (10) and the value of export goods (11) no longer correspond to those of the reference series since 1986 and 1982 respectively.

For this reason, since 1992 the indicator has been computed using only six of the eleven components; of these six, three (series 6-8) are quarterly.

On average, it now takes about three months to obtain monthly data, just as it generally does for quarterly series from business surveys. However, at the time of writing (June 1996), the most recent data available were from fourth-quarter 1995.[2]

Updates of the composite indicator are entirely dependent on the quarterly data, and five of its components are no longer up-to-date. For this reason, on average it comes out

---

[1] See OECD, 1987, pp. 38, 42 and 75.
[2] Data are taken from Statistics Norway's weekly publication *Ukens statistikk*.

substantially later than most of the other leading indicators computed by the OECD, which are updated an average of three months after the reference period.

When quarterly data become available, data for the composite indicator are updated for three consecutive months. The time lag between the reference period and publication therefore varies between four months, as it was initially, and six months, when there are no updates of quarterly data.

Clearly, then, the quality of the leading indicator for Norway has deteriorated. As it happens, the chronology of turning points for 1983-90 does not correspond to that of the reference series: the reference series' major peak in June 1986 is missing, and the December 1991 trough is not anticipated. The maximum correlation with the reference series is currently 0.60 at a five-month lead.

4.2 The New Indicator

After consultations with the Norway country desk, it was decided to maintain the reference series (manufacturing production) despite its volatility, the exclusion of oil production being deemed justified. Later we shall have more to say about the relevance of the choice of a reference series. Cycles of the reference series that were detected at the time of the initial calculation were confirmed, and cycles after 1986 were updated.

First we compared volume GDP cycles with those of the reference series. Originally, Norwegian GDP data were available only on an annual basis, but since 1978, quarterly figures are now available[1].

Whereas, for many Member countries, GDP cycles either coincide with or lag total industrial production, Table 7 and Figure 4 show that such is not the case for Norway: the correspondence is vague, which is probably due to data from the energy sector (about 20 per cent of annual GDP in value).

Table 7 Comparison of GDP cycles with those of the reference series

Gross domestic product volume			Industrial production (manufacturing)		
Turning point dates (quarters)		Amplitude	Turning point dates (months)		Amplitude
Peaks	Troughs	% of trend	Peaks	Troughs	% of trend
	1/79	-2.78		5/78	-7.32
1/80		4.56	4/80		5.07
	3/82	-4.99		3/83	-13.02
4/87		4.28	6/86		3.98
				(7/88)^a	-3.56
			(9/90)^2		2.2
	2/90	-1.53		12/91	-6.66
1/95		+1.75	5/95		8.23

a) The phase between July 1988 and September 1990, of low amplitude and short duration, was deemed minor and appears in parentheses.

---

[1] The chronological series used for GDP is taken from the Analytical DataBase (ADB), which is managed by the OECD Economics Department.

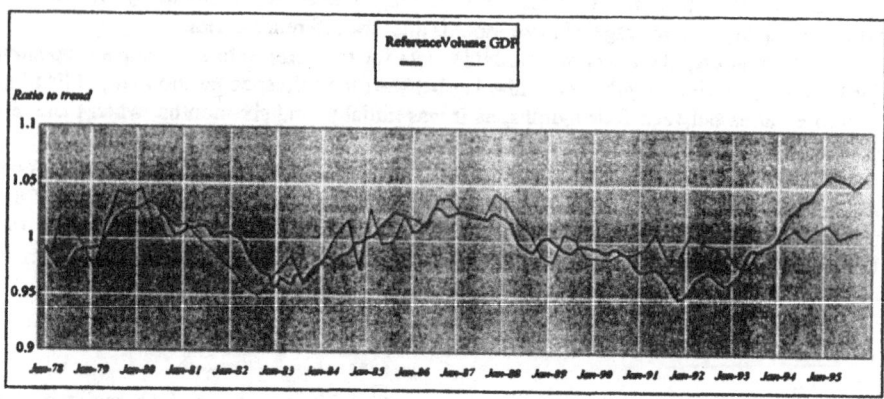

Figure 4   Ratio to trend for GDP^a and the reference series^a

a) A series smoothed by an MCD (Months for Cyclical Dominance) moving average. See also OECD, 1987, pp. 38, 42, 75.

We have been looking for new components with a cyclical profile that anticipates that of the reference series. It should first be pointed out that, at the time of the study (May-June 1996), access to Statistics Norway's data was limited and that a procedure for weekly Internet transfers of the data used by the Main Economic Indicators Division was in preparation.

Examination of the current up-to-date components confirmed the cyclical pertinence of the three quarterly business survey series, and that of share prices, with the updated list of reference series turning points.

Two new series were successfully tested: an international basket of long-term (ten-year) interest rates[1], with the co-operation of the Bank of Norway, and the OECD's leading indicator for Sweden, which still performs satisfactorily. A number of trials on variables dealing with the "real" economy (in particular, total exports, components of industrial production, prices, production and exports of crude oil, in terms of levels or monthly changes) proved unsuccessful.

Virtually all series tested yielded cycles that did not fit exactly with the reference series after the 1986 peak, which was also suggested by the Norway country desk[2]. Each time, there were extra cycles not present in the reference series, in particular between 1983 and 1985 but also in 1987. The composite that was ultimately selected presents two extra phases (peak January 1984-trough March 1985; trough January 1987-peak September 1987), respectively present in four and two of the six chosen components.

---

[1] Drop in oil prices in 1986. See OECD, 1995, p. 70.

Table 8 Characteristics of the new leading indicator

	MCD[a]	Availability (months)	Extra (x) or missing (m) cycles	Start date	Average leads/lags			Median leads/lags			Standard deviation	Correlation	
					peaks and troughs	peaks	troughs	peaks and troughs	peaks	troughs		Coefficient	Lead
Previous leading indicator	1	5	1x,1m	1/71	4.4	6.8	1.3	6	6.5	5	6.11	0.60	5
New leading indicator	2	3	2x	6/74	7.2	9.6	4.3	6	11	6	4.74	0.71	7
International basket of interest rates[b]	1	2	1x,1m	1/78	12.8	9	16.5	15.5	9	16.5	7.27	-0.73	18
Share prices	2	2	2x	1/71	4	7	1	3.5	6	1.5	6.24	0.62	5
OECD leading indicator for Sweden	1	3	1x,1m	1/72	10.3	12.8	7.3	10	13	6	4.80	0.76	8
Business outlook	1Q	3	2x	74Q02	3.8	4.8	2.8	7	8	3	7.80	0.62	6
Production tendency	2Q	3	1x	74Q02	3.5	4.8	2.2	4.5	5	1	3.95	0.58	6
Inflows of export orders, tendency	1Q	3	3x	74Q02	9.2	10.2	8.2	7	11	7	5.37	0.51	6

a) A series smoothed by an MCD (Months for Cyclical Dominance) moving average. See also OECD, 1987, pp. 38, 42, 75.
b) Inverse relationship.

The indicator does not miss any cycle present in the reference series. It announces the recovery that began in 1992 (trough in December 1991), the brief reversal in mid-1995, and it would appear to announce the recovery that was observed thereafter.

It is made up of the following six series and is presented in Table 8:

1. International basket of interest rates;
2. Share prices, industrials (Oslo stock exchange);
3. OECD leading indicator for Sweden;
4. Business outlook;
5. Production tendency;
6. Inflow of export orders, tendency.

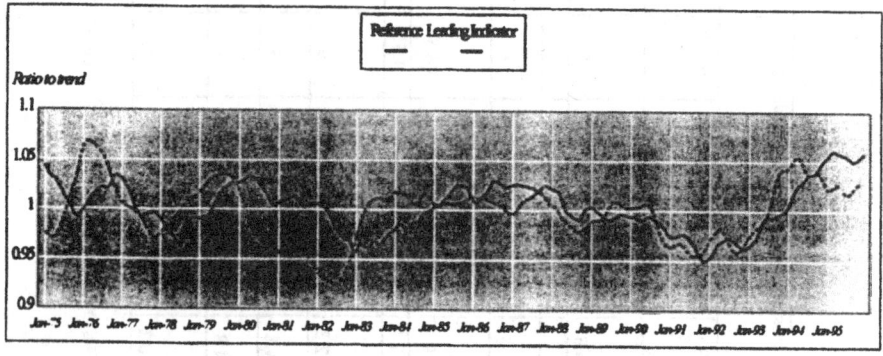

Figure 5 Leading indicator[a] and reference series[b], ratio to trend
a) Adjusted to fit the amplitudes of the reference series.
b) A series smoothed by an MCD (Months for Cyclical Dominance) moving average. See also OECD; 1987, pp. 38, 42, 75.

The composite indicator's MCD[1] value is 2, which underscores its volatility. It is just as dependent on updates of its quarterly components as the previous indicator.

The correlation at a seven-month lead between the composite indicator and the reference series is 0.71 for the whole period. Except for the extra cycles, the new indicator's chronology of turning points fits well with the cycles of the reference series. Moreover, its overall performance is better than that of the current indicator, recalculated to reflect cycles after 1986:

1. The fact that the standard deviation of the new indicator's lead time (4.74) is lower than that of the present indicator (6.11) shows greater regularity in the anticipation of turning points.
2. The new indicator anticipates the major peak of June 1986 (Table 7).

---

[1] See OECD, 1987, pp. 38, 42, 75.

3. The new indicator's lead is uniformly greater than that of the old one, over the entire period, and is more pronounced after 1990: the latest trough, in December 1991, is anticipated five months in advance, whereas the current indicator fails to detect it in time. The latest peak, in May 1995, is anticipated 13 months in advance, versus seven for the current indicator.

The presence of extra cycles in the six composite series may call the reference series into question. Moreover, this series is a volatile one, as stated above. Is industrial production the best choice for ascertaining the business cycle? This issue for debate casts doubt on a past decision of the Secretariat to adopt a single reference series, industrial production, whenever such a series exists.

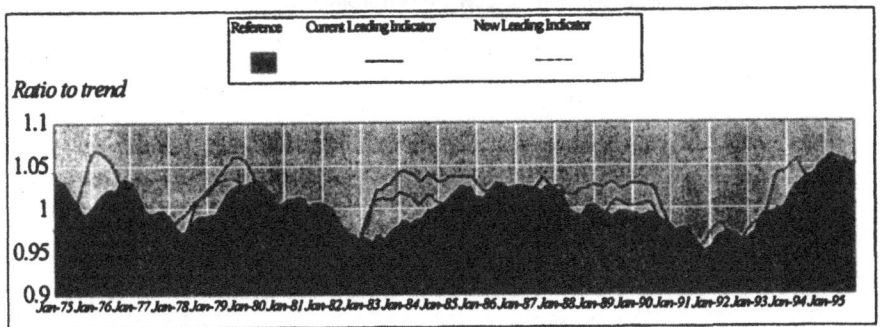

Figure 6 Current[a] and new indicators[a], comparison with the reference series[b], ratio to trend

a) Adjusted to fit the amplitudes of the reference series.
b) A series smoothed by an MCD (Months for Cyclical Dominance) moving average. See also Note No. 11.

5 Conclusions

The four examples studied above suggest a number of conclusions as to how the quality of components has evolved over time. It would appear that monetary series (United States, Germany) no longer anticipate the business cycles of the 1980s and 90s correctly. The use of interest rates yields results of variable quality (adequate for Mexico and Norway over the entire period, mediocre for the United States and Germany). In contrast, surveys of business prospects remain accurate tools for anticipating business cycles.

In addition, the study of Norway illustrates how the choice of a reference series can be a problem for ascertaining cycles. The same problem arises on a more general level for all countries. The leading indicator for the United States, which remains subject to substantial "noise", illustrates the problem of smoothing the composite indicator.

These conclusions could apply across the board for any revision of the leading indicators of other countries, which might take place in 1997 if the Statistics Directorate's resources permit. They are now submitted to members of the working party for their comments.

References

Artis, M.J., Bladen-Howell, R.C. and Zhang, W. (1995), Turning Points in the International Business Cycle: An Analysis of the OECD Leading Indicators for the G-7 Countries, *OECD Economic Studies*, No. 24, first quarter.

Durand, M., Simon, J. and Webb, C. (1992), OECD's Indicators of International Trade and Competitiveness, OECD Economics Department Working Papers, No. 120.

INEGI (1992), *Sistema de Indicadores Adelantados para la Economia Mexicana*.

Nilsson, R. (1987), OECD Leading Indicators, *OECD Economic Studies*, No. 9, Autumn.

OECD (1987), *OECD Leading Indicators and Business Cycles in Member Countries 1960-1985: Sources and Methods*, No. 39, January.

OECD (1995), *OECD Economic Surveys. Mexico*, September.

OECD (1995), OECD *Economic Surveys. Norway*, August.

OECD (1996), Main Economic Indicators: Sources and Definitions, May.

Part II
Timing of Cyclical Turning Points

5 Confidence and the Macroeconomy: A Markov Switching Model

Roy Batchelor

This study examines whether indexes of consumer and business confidence are useful in predicting turning points in the United States and the United Kingdom. Turning points in coincident economic indicator series, and in the confidence indexes, are identified using a two-state Markov switching model, with time-varying transition probabilities. The predictive value of the indexes is assessed by examining whether their turning points consistently lead those in the coincident index, and whether the level of confidence significantly affects the probability that the coincident index will switch states.

The paper can be regarded as an extension of the studies of Moore and Cullity (1989) and Klein and Moore (1991), which analyzed timing relationships between the US business cycle and (respectively) the US Conference Board and University of Michigan consumer confidence indexes, and the US National Association of Purchasing Managers survey of business conditions. We use more recent data, which in itself is of interest because of the key role of consumer confidence in triggering the last US recession (Blanchard, 1993; Hall, 1993). We look at indexes of economic activity and confidence in the UK, which is under-researched relative to their US counterparts. And we use a more formal econometric technique which allows us to test the statistical significance of some of the relationships observed in the data.

The first section of the paper describes the model, and summarizes what we have learnt from its application in the US. The second section introduces the data. The third section analyses timing relationships in the US and the UK, between the state of the economy and the state of consumer and business confidence. The final section discusses implications of the study for empirical modeling, and for the leading indicator properties of confidence indexes.

1 The Markov Switching Model

The Markov model assumes that there are two or more "states" or "regimes" which might characterize the variable we are interested in modeling. For example, GDP growth might be in a "normal" state or in a "recession" state, interest rates might be at "low", "moderate" or "high" levels. The state of the variable at any time is not deterministic, but depends on its previous state and on the probability that the variable will switch states in the current time period. These transition probabilities in turn may be fixed, or may depend on other variables. For example, the probability of GDP growth switching out of recession into the normal state might depend on the length of time the economy has already been in recession - the hypothesis of "duration dependence".

In this paper we use a particular two-regime Markov switching model with time-varying transition probabilities. For variable y_t this model can be written:

$$y_t = S_t \mu_1 + (1 - S_t) \mu_2 + u_t \tag{1}$$

$$u_t \sim \text{i.i.d. } N(0, \sigma^2) \tag{2}$$

$$p_{kt} = \Phi[\alpha_{k0} + \sum_i \alpha_{ki} x_{it-1}], k = 1, 2 \tag{3}$$

where S_t is a variable which takes the value 1 or 0 according as y_t is in state 1 or state 2, μ_1 and μ_2 are the expected values of y in the two states; p_{1t} and p_{2t} are the probabilities that y will persist in state 1 or 2 at time t given that it was in that state at time t-1; the x_{it-1} are variables determining these transition probabilities; and $\Phi[.]$ is the normal cumulative density function, which constrains the probabilities to lie between 0 and 1. The probability of switching from state 1 to state 2 in period t is therefore $(1 - p_{1t})$, and the probability of switching from state 2 to state 1 is $(1 - p_{2t})$. The expected durations of the states at t are consequently $1/(1 - p_{1t})$ and $1/(1 - p_{2t})$ periods respectively.

The parameters α_{ki} measure the impact effects of the values of predetermined variables x_i at time t-1 on the probabilities that y will persist in the same state between t-1 and t. However, because the state of the system is path-dependent, changes in x_{it-1} will have effects beyond period t, and in particular will change the expected duration of the current regime.

The basic structure above can be generalized further. There may be more than two states; Sichel (1993) argues convincingly for a three-state description of the US business cycle. The regime means μ_1 and μ_2 may vary over time (Raymond and Rich, 1997). The residual u_t may follow an autoregressive process (Hamilton, 1989, 1993). The variance σ^2 need not be the same in all states. The density function Φ need not be normal. And so on.

Algorithms for finding maximum likelihood estimates for the parameters of simple and time-varying probability models are discussed in Hamilton (1989, 1990), Diebold, Lee and Weinbach (1994), Kim (1994), Filardo (1994) and Durland and McCurdy (1994).

Given estimates of the parameters $\theta = [\mu_1, \mu_2, \sigma^2, \alpha_{ki}]$, probabilistic inferences can be made about the state of the system at time t. But the exact inferences made will depend crucially on the information set used.

Suppose there are n observations on y_t and the x_{it} available for estimation, and we write the parameter vector conditional on the full sample Ω_n as θ_n, and the parameter vector conditional on sample observations $\Omega_{t-1} = [y_1, y_2, ..., y_{t-1}; x_1, x_2, ..., x_{t-1}]$ up to period t-1 as θ_{t-1}. One possibility is to use the whole data set to estimate the parameters and make inferences about the probability that the variable is in state 1 at time t. This *full-sample smoother* can be written as

$$\pi_t^s = \text{Prob}\{y_t \in \text{State 1} \mid \Omega_n, \theta_n\}, t = 1, 2, ..., n. \tag{4}$$

An alternative is to estimate these probabilities period by period using only data available up to that period. This *recursive filtered estimator* can be written as

$$\pi^r_t = \text{Prob}\{ y_t \in \text{State 1} \mid \Omega_{t-1}, \theta_{t-1} \}, t = 1, 2, ..., n. \tag{5}$$

The full-sample smoothed estimates use all of the observations to interpret the history of the whole time series. The recursive filtered estimator gives an interpretation based only on past data, and in that sense reflects the conditions faced by a forecaster at time t who could not use later observations.

The recursive filter requires very time-consuming iterative computation of the system parameters, and Hamilton (1989) and Kim(1994) propose the compromise statistics Prob$\{ y_t \in \text{State 1} \mid \Omega_{t-1}, \theta_n \}$, which use the full sample to estimate the parameters, but update the probabilities period by period conditional on these parameters and data up to period t only. If the parameters can be assumed stable, this is a convenient procedure, but Lahiri and Wang (1994) show that this assumption is not always warranted in business cycle applications. We use only full-sample and recursive filtered models in this paper.

If the underlying data can be approximated by a two-regime model, all these filters will transform the sample data into visually striking representations of the regimes, by squashing observations which clearly lie in one or other regime close to probabilities of 1 or 0, and highlighting the brief periods when there is a transition from one regime to the other.

The basic two-regime model has been extensively used in empirical analysis of the US business cycle. These applied studies fall into three categories. Some studies take y_t to be the index of the current state of the economy (e.g. real GNP, industrial production, the index of coincident indicators), assume fixed transition probabilities, and use the filter to determine the dates of recessions and recoveries. Examples are Hamilton (1989) and Boldin (1994) on the US, and the cross-country study of Goodwin (1993). The filter mimics closely the NBER dating of the US business cycle and to the extent that it uses only past data, provides more timely signals than conventional heuristic methods, such as that of Bry and Boschan (1971), which are typically based on long centered moving averages.

Other studies assume the state of the economy is already given, for example by the official NBER dating of recessions and recoveries in the US, and take y_t to be a possible predictor of the state of the economy. An example is Lahiri and Wang (1994), who use the Hamilton filter to establish turning points in the US Department of Commerce index of leading indicators, and compare these with the NBER peaks and troughs. By construction, switches in the leading indicators anticipate peaks and troughs in economic activity. But the frequent revisions to the leading indicators series makes their value as genuine ex ante forecasting tools extremely dubious (see Koenig and Emery, 1991; Diebold and Rudebusch, 1991a, b).

Finally, several recent studies have taken y_t to be the current state of the economy, and test the value of various possible determinants x_{it-1} of the transition probabilities. Examples are Filardo (1994), who tests whether leading indicators, interest rates and stock prices affect transition probabilities in a model if US industrial production; Durland and McCurdy (1994), who test whether the duration of recessions and recoveries is important; and Raymond and Rich (1997) who measure the effects of oil price shocks on both transition probabilities and on mean GNP growth rates in recovery and recession.

In this paper we perform all three exercises. First, the full-sample smoother applied to a model with constant transition probabilities is used to identify what in retrospect appear to have been regime shifts in the coincident indicator. Second, the recursive filtered estimator is applied to constant transition probability models of consumer and industrial confidence, to establish whether regime shifts in these series, which could have been identified at the time, consistently anticipate regime shifts in the coincident index. Finally, we apply the recursive filtered estimator to the more general time-varying-probability model of the coincident indicator, to test formally the significance of changes in confidence for changes in the coincident indicator regime. Based on this model, we propose an "early warning" indicator for regime switches, the difference between the recursive conditional probability of being in one regime, and the corresponding full-sample unconditional probability.

2 Data

We use the US Department of Commerce index of Coincident Indicators to track the state of the US economy, and the Office for National Statistics Coincident Indicator for the UK economy. These indexes are somewhat different. The DOC index is based on industrial production, real personal income, manufacturing and trade sales, and nonagricultural employment. The ONS index is based on series for real GDP, industrial production, retail sales, the real value of the monetary base, and capacity utilization and raw materials stocks as reported by the Confederation of British Industry. The ONS series is published with time-varying trends in the components removed, and we also use the trend-removed version of the DOC series. Both series are monthly in the period January 1956 to December 1996.

Our measure of business confidence in the US is the overall index published by the National Association of Purchasing Managers, and our measure of consumer confidence is the index of consumer confidence published by the Conference Board. The NAPM Purchasing Manager's Index is a weighted average of the balances of responses by members of the NAPM to monthly questions about changes in new orders, production, supply deliveries, inventories and employment. It is constructed with the intention that a *high level* of the index means that the economy is *growing fast*. The Conference Board is similarly an average of responses of a panel of households to questions about changes in their past and prospective financial well-being, and the general well-being of the economy. The NAPM survey is available from 1956 onwards (and earlier), while the Conference Board monthly survey starts in April 1969.

The UK business and consumer confidence series are taken from the harmonized surveys coordinated among EU member countries by the European Commission. The business survey data are available since January 1976, and the consumer survey since January 1974. The business surveys ask (mainly manufacturing) firms about past and expected production trends, expected price trends, and current orders and stocks. In the UK, the survey is conducted by the CBI, so some of the responses are incorporated directly into the coincident indicator. The consumer surveys exactly parallel the

Conference Board surveys in constructing the consumer confidence index from the balances of responses to questions about past and future own and general economic conditions, and about the advisability of major durables purchases. Again, if these businesses and households have rational perceptions and expectations, high *levels* of these indexes should be associated with fast economic *growth*.

Figures 1 and 2 show the raw data on US and UK coincident indicators and confidence indexes.

An immediate concern raised by these Figures is that, while in principle changes in the coincident index should be associated with the levels of business and consumer confidence, there are obvious and strong associations between the levels of the coincident indexes and levels of the confidence indexes. The correlation between the US consumer confidence index and the coincident indicator is particularly striking. Consumer confidence was, for example, low in the years 1992-3, when the coincident indicator was below trend but rising. Technically, the confidence indexes are cointegrated with the coincident indicator, but not with its growth rate.

In what follows we therefore look for regime switches not only between periods of low and high growth in the coincident indicators, but also between periods when the indicators were below-trend and above-trend.

While both the levels and differences of the indicator could be argued to be stationary around their means, the levels of the coincident indicators are, almost by definition, serially correlated around their mean values, and in that sense violate equation (2) in our model. The confidence indexes also exhibit varying degrees of serial correlation. One possibility is to introduce an autoregressive process into the model. However, in practice this has two undesirable consequences. First, in some cases it will prevent the model from identifying two separate regimes - the UK coincident indicator is constructed so as to be highly cyclical, for example. Second, it leads to large differences between recursive and smoothed parameter estimators, and hence a high degree of ambiguity in the interpretation of the data. This point was noted by Lahiri and Wang (1994) in their analysis of the US leading indicators, and in the analysis of consumer confidence in Batchelor (1996). Since the attractiveness of the Markov model is the clarity with which it identifies regime changes, in this paper we have overridden these statistical reservations, and applied the simple model (1) - (3). This prevents the model from considering plausible cyclical alternatives to the two-regime description of the data.

3 Empirical Results

Because of their size and number, all Tables and Figures have been collected together at the end of the paper. Table 1 sets out full-sample parameter estimates for two-regime models of the level and growth of the US coincident indicator and the levels of the confidence series, and Table 2 shows corresponding models for the UK. In all cases, there is a satisfactory separation of the high/ fast growth and low/ slow growth means, relative to the standard deviation around these means.

For the level models, the probabilities of staying in state 1 (GOOD) and state 2 (BAD) states are similar, with the BAD state persistence probability only slightly lower. For the US growth rate model, there is a significantly lower probability of staying in the low growth state, reflecting the well-known phenomenon that US recessions tend to be much shorter-lived that expansions. The UK growth rate model shows the exact opposite effect, with the BAD regime more persistent than the GOOD, reflecting the tendency of the UK coincident indicator to show sharp recoveries and long slow declines.

Figures 3 and 4 compare the full-sample-smoothed estimates of the probability that the level/ growth of the indicator was in the high/ fast growth regime month by month, with the filtered probabilities that the confidence indicators were in their GOOD states. The Figures show a clear tendency for both consumer and business confidence to lead the switches between low and high levels of the coincident index. For example, both switched into the BAD state ahead of the indicator in the most recent 1990-4 dip below trend in the US economy, and both recovered ahead of the indicator.

There are some differences in performance between the confidence indexes. In the US, consumer confidence did not dip along with the coincident index in the mid-80s, but it did recover in 1994-5 when the business confidence index was going into decline. In the UK, business confidence failed to decline with the economy in 1985-6, but it did recover in 1993, at the same time as the coincident indicator, but well ahead of consumer confidence.

Table 3 sets out the chronology of switches in these variables for the US, using arbitrary switching points for π^s_t = Prob(GOOD) of 0.9 and 0.1 to identify transitions into and out of GOOD to BAD states. The chronology for the growth rate in the coincident indicator produces results which mirror those on US GNP, with the dates at which the series slips out of the GOOD regime corresponding closely to the NBER dating of business cycle peaks, and the months when it recovers out of the BAD regime closely following the official business cycle troughs. This confirms the value of the model in producing timely signals of recession and recovery. However, there is no clear and consistent timing relation between business confidence and these high/ low growth regimes, and consumer confidence if anything appears to lag the switching points.

In the UK, the model for growth in the coincident indicator does pick up the major recessions of 1980-1 and 1990-1, but there are many switches in the 1980s which do not correspond to any reasonable business cycle chronology, and are not associated with any switches in the confidence indexes.

Tables 4 and 5 carry full-sample estimates of time-varying-probability models for the level and growth in the coincident indicator in the US and UK respectively. The level models confirm that the probability that the coincident index will continue above trend in month t is significantly and positively affected by the level of the consumer confidence and business confidence in month t-1, with business confidence more important when both variables enter the model. Conversely, the probability that the coincident indicator will remain below trend is significantly and negatively affected by consumer confidence, less significantly by business confidence.

A worsening in the level of business confidence is therefore bad news when activity is already high. An improvement in consumer confidence is good news when activity is already low.

It proved impossible to find statistically significant relations between the growth of the coincident indicator and the level of either confidence indicator. Models for coincident indicator growth which relate transition probabilities to lagged growth rates in the confidence indexes do show correctly-signed but barely significant effects. These are not reported in full here, but they are used to compute the switching probabilities and state probabilities discussed below.

Figures 5 and 6 plot for the US what Filardo (1994) terms the marginal contributions of confidence indexes - the difference between the time-varying transition probabilities based on the models of Table 4, and the fixed probabilities from Table 1. Figure 5 shows that there are clear benefits from using confidence indexes to predict switches in the level of the coincident indicator. The main route by which the confidence indexes operate is by changing (reducing) the probability that the coincident indicator will stay above trend, an effect mainly due to movements in business confidence. At some times, for example 1972-3 and 1987-9, consumer confidence has also significantly reduced the probability of staying below trend.

Figure 6 shows no corresponding impact from the confidence indexes on the probability of continuing high growth, but some impact on the probability of continuing low growth in 1980-1 and 1990-1. In spite of the low statistical significance of these models, it appears that on important occasions, notably in 1975, 1980, 1983 and 1991, rising confidence appreciably reduced the probability that the economy will stay in recession. However, these effects are not as large and well-defined as in the levels model.

The results for the UK (not shown) confirm this picture, with the confidence indexes substantially changing the persistence probabilities of above- and below-trend levels of the coincident index, but having small and erratic effects on the probabilities of high and low growth rate regimes.

The upper panels of Figures 7 and 8 compare full-sample smoothed probability estimates of being in the GOOD regime for the level and growth rate of the US coincident indicator, with filtered estimators based on the models of Table 4 in which transition probabilities depend on the confidence indexes. There is a clear benefit in the case of the level model, since the TVP model probabilities turn up and down several months earlier than the simple fixed probabilities model.

The lower panel of the Figures formalizes this early warning property by plotting the difference between the recursively estimated probabilities of being in the GOOD state conditional on the previous month's confidence indexes, as computed from the time-varying parameter models of Table 4, and the unconditional full-sample smoothed estimates of these probabilities based on the simple model of Table 1. In the notation of equations (4) and (5) above, this early warning indicator is

$$\text{Early Warning} = \pi^r_t(\text{TVP}) - \pi^s_t(\text{Simple}) \tag{6}$$

In Figure 7 this index shows desirable characteristics, smoothly rising ahead of the switches from BAD to GOOD regimes for the level of the confidence index, and smoothly falling ahead of switches to the BAD, below-trend, regime. This pattern is observed in almost all cycles. However, in neither the US nor the UK was there any clear signal of the most recent move to above-trend levels of working, which the filters date at around 1993-4.

The lower half of Figure 8 shows no consistent early warnings of the sharp downturns and upturns in the growth of the coincident indicator, confirming that our confidence indexes had little power to predict conventionally defined booms and recessions.

4 Conclusions

The aim of this paper has been to evaluate the usefulness of consumer and business confidence indexes in anticipating turning points in economic activity, using a Markov switching model to provide a sharp and objective criteria by which to determine points at which the relevant data series changed their character.

We have been only partially successful. There do appear to be strong qualitative relations between confidence indexes and the macroeconomy, but not of the kind that was expected, and not of a kind that is necessarily helpful in predicting conventionally defined business cycle peaks and troughs.

Most discussion of the business cycle assumes that it consists of alternate phases of growth and recession. However, high and low levels of consumer and business confidence do not appear to have a consistent timing relationship with switches between these phases.

Instead, high and low levels of consumer and business confidence anticipate switches between above- and below-trend levels of economy activity. High confidence - particularly high consumer confidence - increases the probability that the economy will move sharply from a below-trend to an above-trend level of operation. Low confidence - particularly low business confidence - increases the probability that the economy will move sharply from above to below trend.

In this view of the world, both recovery and recession are short-lived transitional phenomena, rather than persistent states of the economy. This is consistent with the argument of Sichel (1994). who develops a three-regime model of the US economy to capture these patterns. An obvious extension of the present study would be to examine the performance of the confidence indexes in such a model.

Table 1 Simple Markov switching models: United States

| | *Detrended Level:* | | | *Growth:* |
Coefficient:	Coincident Indicator	Consumer Confidence	Business Confidence	Coincident Indicator
GOOD Mean	101.39	102.42	57.7542	0.3228
	(0.09)	(0.84)	(0.42)	(0.02)
BAD Mean	98.37	69.82	46.3338	-0.3077
	(0.10)	(1.28)	(0.56)	(0.05)
Std. Deviation	1.1832	11.12	4.8037	0.2990
	(0.04)	(0.46)	(0.17)	(0.01)
P(Stay GOOD)	0.9649	0.9768	0.9584	0.9712
	(0.08)	(0.09)	(0.08)	(0.08)
P(Stay BAD)	0.9570	0.9585	0.9425	0.8681
	(0.08)	(0.12)	(0.10)	(0.18)
Sample:	1/56-12/96	4/69-12/96	1/56-12/96	1/56-12/96
- Log Likelihood	828.35	1306.84	1523.11	159.93

Note: Figures in parentheses are *standard errors*.

Table 2 Simple Markov switching models: United Kingdom

| | *Detrended Level:* | | | *Growth:* |
Coefficient	Coincident Indicator	Consumer Confidence	Business Confidence	Coincident Indicator
GOOD Mean	103.61	-1.7818	1.2426	0.6112
	(0.19)	(0.72)	(0.81)	(0.05)
BAD Mean	95.52	-17.4521	-28.4040	-0.4400
	(0.21)	(0.58)	(1.40)	(0.04)
Std. Deviation	2.6349	6.2857	10.0617	0.5189
	(0.09)	(22.57)	(0.45)	(.02)
P(Stay in GOOD)	.9693	0.9648	0.9886	0.9281
	(0.08)	(0.12)	(0.12)	(0.09)
P(Stay in BAD)	.9693	0.9735	0.9732	0.9529
	(0.09)	(0.11)	(0.15)	(0.09)
Sample:	1/56-12/96	1/74-12/96	1/76-12/96	1/56-12/96
- Log Likelihood	1221.65	923.2	952.9	437.8

Note: Figures in parentheses are *standard errors*.

Table 3   Chronology of regime switches: United States

Coefficient	Level: Coincident Indicator	Consumer Conf.	Business Conf.	Growth: Coincident Indicator	NBER Pk/Trgh
Out of GOOD	Oct-57		Jun-56	May-57	*Aug-57*
Into BAD	Jan-58		Aug-56	Nov-57	
Out of BAD	Feb-59		Aug-58	Jun-58	*Apr-58*
Into GOOD	Jun-59		Oct-58	Jul-58	
Out of GOOD	Sep-60		Apr-60	Mar-60	*Apr-60*
Into BAD	Jan-61		Jun-60	Dec-60	
Out of BAD	Jan-65		May-61	Feb-61	*Feb-61*
Into GOOD	Dec-65		Jun-61	May-61	
Out of GOOD	May-70	Dec-70	Feb-67	Dec-69	*Dec-69*
Into BAD	Oct-70	Feb-71	Apr-67	Feb-70	
Out of BAD	May-72	Mar-72	Sep-67	Jan-71	*Nov-70*
Into GOOD	Nov-72	May-72	Jan-68	Jan-71	
Out of GOOD	Dec-76	Jan-74	Oct-74	Jan-74	*Nov-73*
Into BAD	Feb-75	Feb-74	Nov-74	Dec-74	
Out of BAD	Apr-77	Jan-76	Oct-75	May-75	*Mar-75*
Into GOOD	Apr-78	Mar-76	Jan-76	Jul-75	
Out of GOOD	Dec-81	Apr-80	Aug-79	Mar-80	*Jan-80*
Into BAD	May-82	May-80	Dec-79	May-80	
Out of BAD	Jan-84	Jun-83	Nov-80	Aug-80	*Jul-80*
Into GOOD	Jun-84	Nov-83	Jun-83	Oct-80	
Out of GOOD	Nov-85		Oct-84	Oct-81	*Jul-81*
Into BAD	Feb-87		Apr-85	Jan-82	
Out of BAD	Mar-87		Sep-86	Nov-82	*Nov-82*
Into GOOD	Apr-88		May-87	Apr-83	
Out of GOOD	Dec-90	Nov-90	Apr-89	Sep-90	*Jul-90*
Into BAD	Apr-91	Nov-90	Aug-89	Dec-90	
Out of BAD	Nov-93	May-94	Mar-92	Mar-91	*Mar-91*
Into GOOD	Nov-94	Aug-94	Feb-93	Jul-91	

Table 4   Time varying probability Markov switching models for US coincident indicator

Coefficient	Consumer Confidence	Business Confidence	Both
GOOD Mean	101.60	101.3736	101.62
BAD Mean	98.26	98.3514	98.27
Std. Deviation	1.19	1.1825	1.1891
P(Stay in GOOD):			
Constant	-2.5332	-11.3547	-11.5540
	(1.34)	(4.17)	(2.32)
Consumer Confidence, t-1	0.0474		0.0329
	(3.07)		(1.53)
Business Confidence, t-1		0.2718	0.2105
		(3.01)	(1.98)
P(Stay in BAD):			
Constant	6.2579	5.4729	8.2186
	(1.93)	(2.01)	(2.34)
Consumer Confidence, t-1	-0.0521		-0.0473
	(2.52))		(2.13)
Business Confidence, t-1		-0.06879	-0.0432
		(1.94)	(0.78)
Sample	4/69-12/96	1/56-12/96	4/69-12/96
-Log Likelihood	552.97	810.89	547.29

Note: Figures in parentheses are *t-statistics*.

Table 5 Time varying probability Markov switching models for UK coincident indicator

Coefficient	Consumer Confidence	Business Confidence	Both
GOOD Mean	103.42	103.48	103.48
BAD Mean	95.55	95.71	95.69
Std. Deviation	2.83	2.84	2.83
P(Stay in GOOD):			
Constant	2.8087	2.4499	2.6236
	(4.49)	(5.57)	(4.41)
Consumer Confidence, t-1	0.0657		0.0197
	(2.07)		(0.53)
Business Confidence, t-1		0.0630	0.0524
		(2.30)	(1.61)
P(Stay in BAD):			
Constant	1.0770	1.6700	0.7952
	(3.18)	(6.90)	(1.74)
Consumer Confidence, t-1	-0.0691		-0.1339
	(2.23)		(2.13)
Business Confidence, t-1		-0.0182	-0.0206
		(1.36)	(0.80)
Sample	1/74-12/96	1/76-12.96	1/76-12.96
Log Likelihood	696.4	632.9	627.9

Note: Figures in parentheses are *t-statistics*.

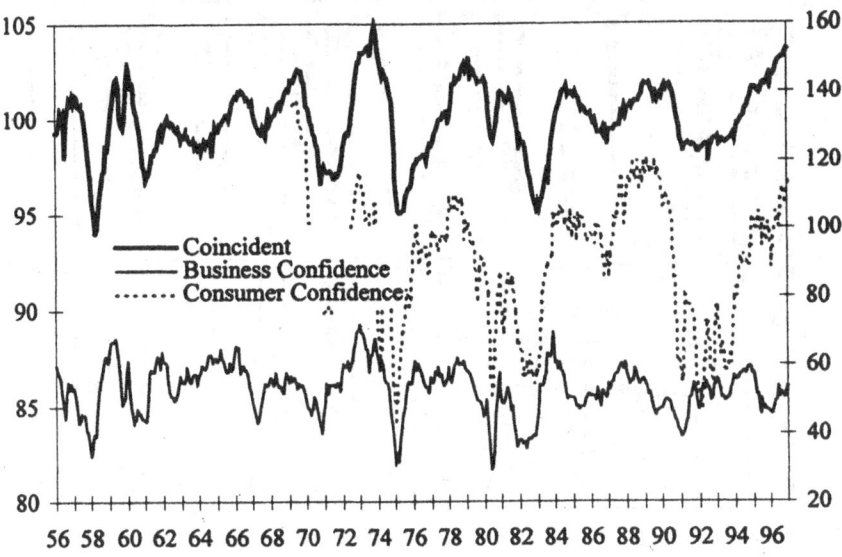

Figure 1 Coincident indicator and confidence indexes: US

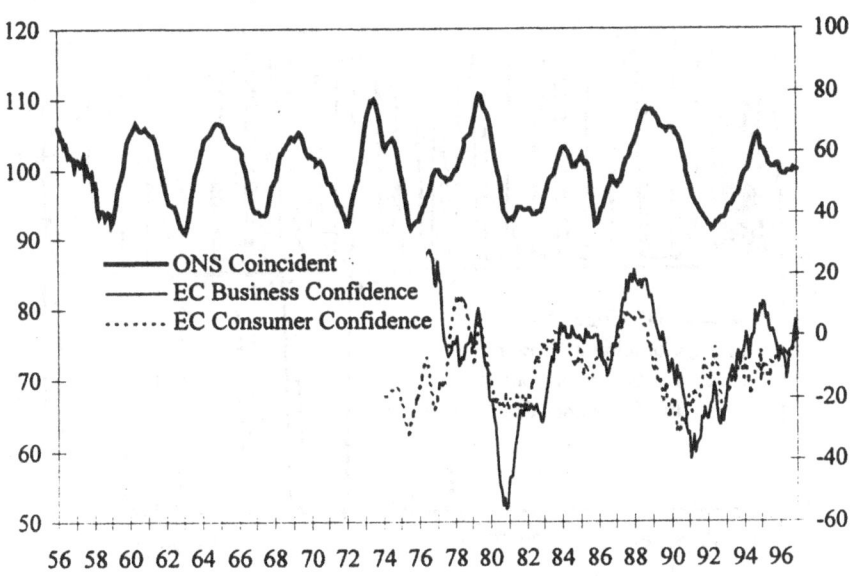

Figure 2 Coincident indicator and confidence indexes: UK

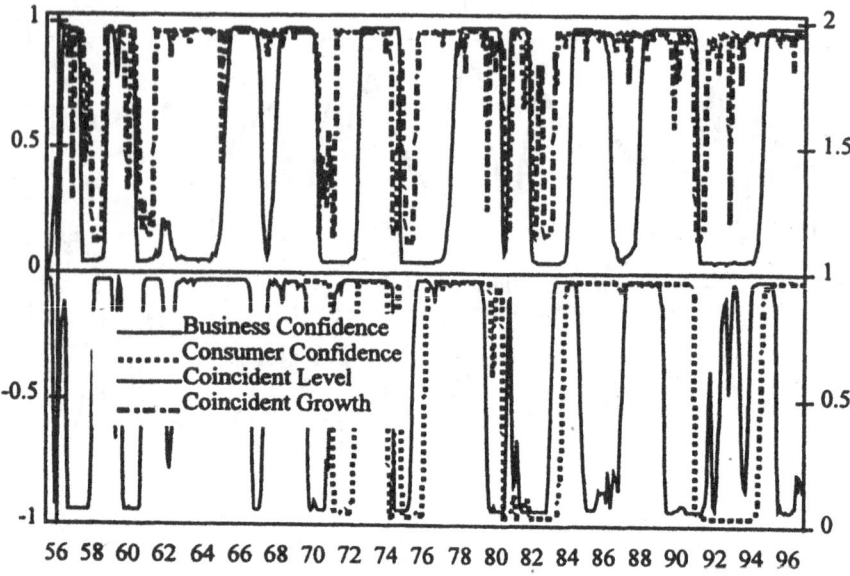

Figure 3 P(GOOD), 2-regime Markov models: US

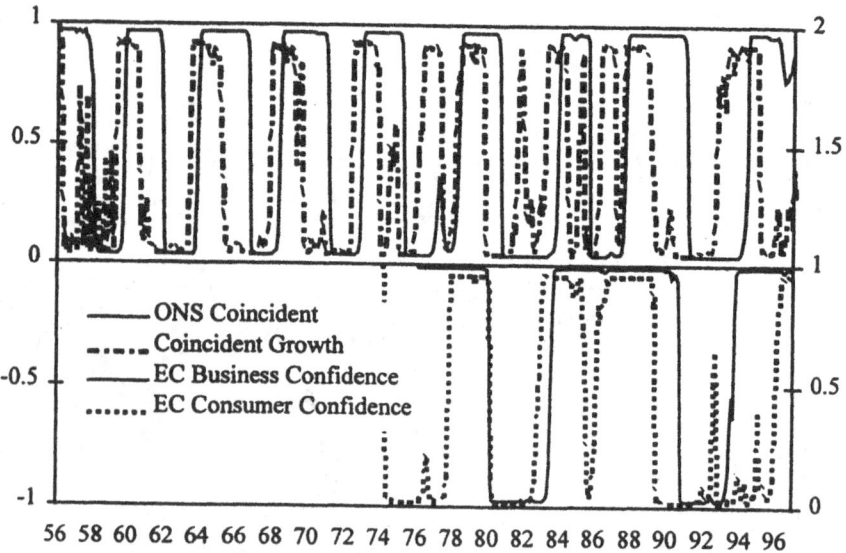

Figure 4 P(GOOD), 2-regime Markov Models: UK

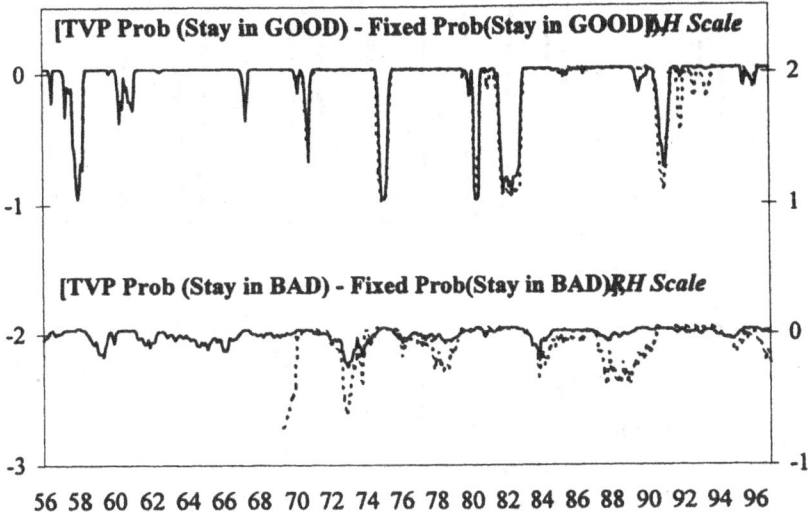

Figure 5 Marginal contribution of confidence indexes to persistence probabilities: US coincident level

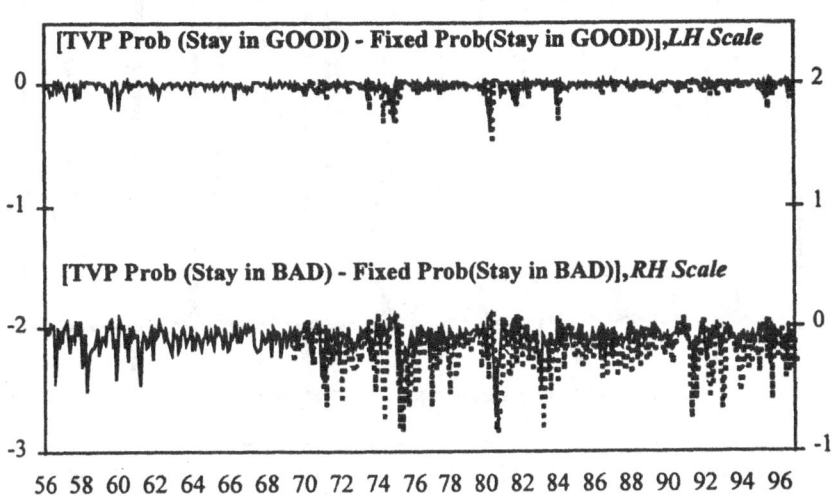

Figure 6 Marginal contribution of confidence indexes to persistence probabilities: US coincident growth

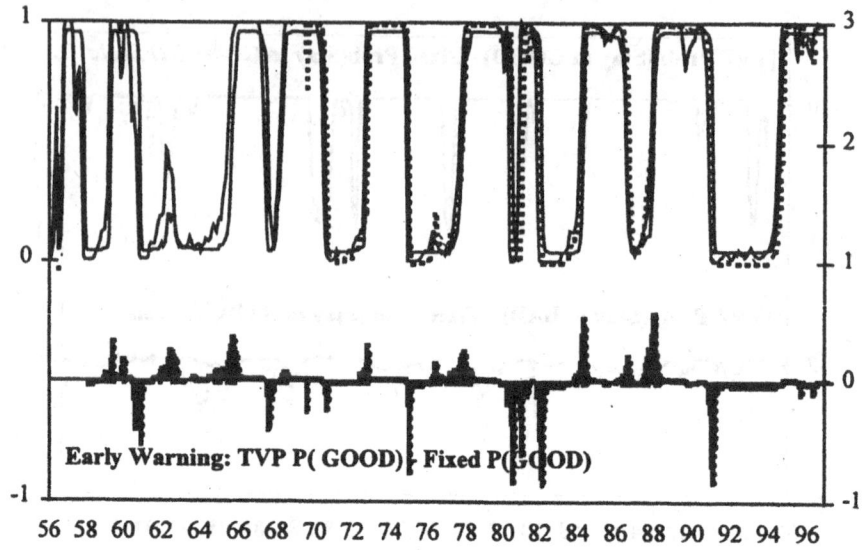

Figure 7 TVP v. simple Markov model of coincident indicator: US

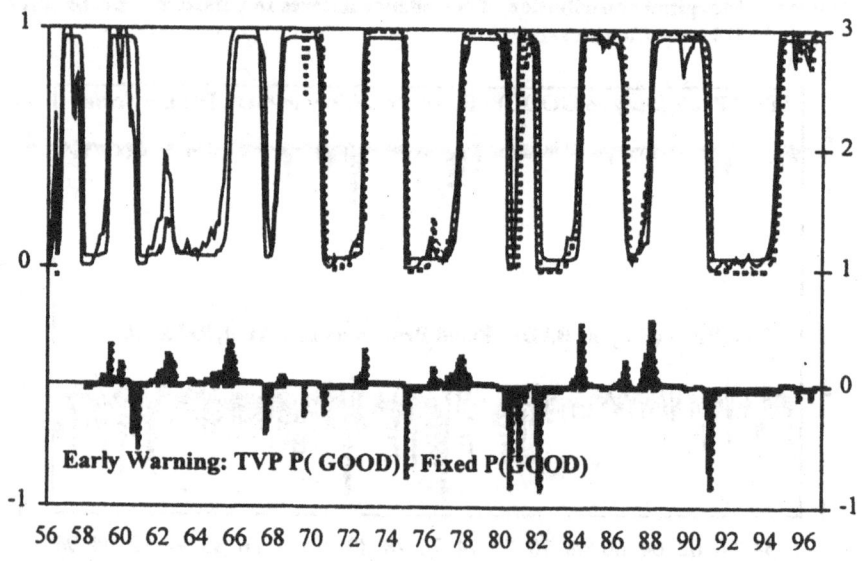

Figure 8 TVP v. simple Markov model of growth in coincident indicator: US

References

Blanchard, O., 1993, Consumption and the recession of 1990-1991, *American Economic Review*, Papers and Proceedings, pp. 270-274.

Boldin, M.D., 1994, Dating turning points in the business cycle, *Journal of Business*, 67, pp. 97-131.

Bry, G. and C. Boschan, 1971, *Cyclical analysis of time series: selected procedures and computer programs*, Technical Paper 20, National Bureau of Economic Research, Columbia University Press.

Diebold, F.X., J.-H. Lee and G.C. Weinbach, 1995, Regime-switching with time-varying transition probabilities, in C. Hargreaves (ed), *Nonstationary time series analysis and cointegration*, Oxford: University Press.

Diebold, F.X. and G.D. Rudebusch, 1991, Turning point prediction with the composite leading index: an ex ante analysis, in K. Lahiri and G.H. Moore (eds), *Leading Economic Indicators: New Approaches and Forecasting Records*, Cambridge University Press.

Durland, J.M. and T.H. McCurdy, 1994, Duration-dependent transitions in a Markov model of US GNP growth, *Journal of Business Economics and Statistics*, 12, pp. 279-288.

Filardo, A.J., 1994, Business-cycle phases and their transitional dynamics, *Journal of Business and Economic Statistics*, 12, pp. 299-308.

Goodwin, T.H., 1993, Business cycle analysis with a Markov switching model, *Journal of Business Economics and Statistics*, 11, pp. 331-339.

Hall, R.E., 1993, Macro theory and the recession of 1990-1991, *American Economic Review*, Papers and Proceedings, pp. 275-279.

Hamilton, J.D., 1989, A new approach to the econometric analysis of nonstationary time series and the business cycle, *Econometrica*, 57, pp. 357-384.

Hamilton, J.D, 1990, Analysis of time series subject to changes in regime, *Journal of Econometrics*, 45, pp. 39-70.

Kim, C.-J., 1994, Dynamic linear models with Markov switching, *Journal of Econometrics*, 60, pp. 1-22.

Klein, P.A. and G.H. Moore, 1991, Purchasing management survey data: their value as leading indicators, in K. Lahiri and G.H. Moore (eds), *Leading Economic Indicators: New Approaches and Forecasting Records*, Cambridge University Press.

Koenig, E.F. and K.M. Emery, 1991, Misleading indicators? Using the composite leading indicators to predict cyclical turning points, *Federal Reserve Bank of Dallas Economic Review*, July, pp. 1-14.

Lahiri, K. and J.G. Wang, 1994, Predicting cyclical turning points with leading index in a Markov switching model, *Journal of Forecasting*, 13(3), pp. 245-263.

Moore, G.H. and J.P. Cullity, 1989, *An evaluation of consumer confidence surveys as leading indicators*, Center for International Business Cycle Research, Columbia Graduate School of Business, Discussion Paper, May, 29pp.

Raymond, J.E. and R. Rich, 1997, Oil and the macroeconomy: a Markov state-switching approach, *Journal of Money, Credit and Banking*.

Sichel, D.E., Inventories and the three phases of the business cycle, *Journal of Business Economics and Statistics*, 12, pp. 269-77.

6 An Alternative Method to Predict the Business Cycle

Georg Goldrian / Birgit Lehne

1 Preliminary Remarks

Adjusting an economic time series to take account of seasonal factors (and possibly also of the number of working days and bad weather)[1] eliminates significant disruptions in the cyclical information it provides. The irregular movements which remain in the seasonally adjusted time series nevertheless shed little light on the cyclical trend. In particular, they do not provide a satisfactory answer to the central question of when a cyclical turning point occurs. The alternative, which involves a direct estimation of the cyclical component, is also associated with a large degree of uncertainty towards the end of the time series. The usual estimation methods provide only a blurred picture of the cyclical component for the section of a time series that is of most interest for short-term economic analysis. It only acquires its final form once additional values are included. It is precisely at the time of an incipient turning point that the information provided by the cyclical component identified is very inaccurate. The reason for this estimation uncertainty lies in the fact that, alongside so-called systematic components such as trend, economic cycle and season, statistical time series also display more or less irregular movements. While the influence of systematic components on the estimation process can be neutralized to some degree, it is not possible to suppress the irregular components towards the end of the time series. The upshot is a lack of clarity of current cyclical information dependent on the relative dynamic (measured against the momentum of the cyclical component) of the irregular movements.

Although the influence of irregular movements cannot be eliminated in so far as the precise course of the cyclical development is looked at, it can be mitigated if the aim is merely to determine whether a cyclical turning point is at hand; determination of this fact is central to economic analysis. The chosen estimation method and the structure of the specific movements of the various series components can provide evidence in this respect.

---

[1] A brief description of adjustment for bad weather within the ASA II seasonal adjustment procedure is given in ifo Discussion paper No. 10, 1993.

2 Procedure for Approximating the Cyclical Development

The estimation method used by the ifo institute adjusts (by regression analysis) predetermined polynomials to series sections of a certain length on a moving basis. For the middle section of the series, each moving regression assigns only one estimated value to the cyclical component (comparable to the calculation of a moving average) whereas, at the beginning and end of the series the development of the estimated polynomial is regarded as cyclical components.

3 Possible Signal of a Cyclical Turning Point

Using a polynomial of a certain degree to represent the cyclical component of the most recent values of a series makes it possible to assess the shape of the curve with regard to the point in time from which a cyclical turning point can be reliably indicated. An example here is an estimation method corresponding to the adaption of a second-degree polynomial (parabola) to 21 values. Our experience has shown this method to be well suited to reconstructing the typical dynamic of cyclical movements within economic time series comprising monthly values. Assuming an average cycle of some five or seven years, its course over a range of 21 values corresponds to that of a parabola. It is only if the *mathematical turning point* of the cycle falls within the range that there is not a perfect fit because a parabola depicts only one flexure. In the neighbourhood of *mathematical turning points*, however, the question of whether there are reliable signs of a cyclical turning point is not as yet generally asked.

The last consecutive (21) values of a series determine the form of the approximated parabola towards the current end and hence the current cyclical information provided by the series. The more or less optically identifiable course is not confirmed until the second-order differences are calculated. Positive second-order differences indicate a lower cyclical turning point (local minimum), while negative ones indicate a higher turning point (local maximum) of the cycle (the second-order differences of a parabola are constant, and their absolute size indicates the degree of the flexure). On the basis of the second-order differences, the change in direction - from the development, determinated through the previous turning point, to the cyclical reversal - can be measured by using the change in the sign. The first signal of a cyclical turning point is provided by the change in the sign as compared with the cyclical estimation made the previous month (corresponding to a change in the curve of the parabola). The only question is how stable the signal is given the relative momentum of the irregular residual component of a time series. Since the range for estimating the parabola shifts by one value when a new value is added, only two of the 21 values change. To that extent, the irregular component of the new value (and of the value which is eliminated at the beginning of the estimation range) must be relatively large in order for there to be a revision of the upswing, i.e. in order to reverse the recorded change in sign.

4 Possibility of Stabilizing the Signal of a Turning Point

The risk of a correction to a turning point which has already been signalled grows, as stated above, with the dispersion of the residual component (relative to the dispersion of the cyclical component). There are therefore two ways of reducing the likelihood of a correction: a threshold can be deduced from the relative dispersion of the residuals which (in addition to the change in sign) must be surpassed by the difference in the second-order differences if it is to be regarded as a significant signal of a turning point. The second possibility is to moderate the irregular movement in advance.

The threshold for the first alternative should be based on the usual variation of the irregular component, e.g. it should be a function of the standard deviation of the residuals σ_r. This means that the threshold must not be set at such a high level that the effect of extremely irregular deviations is also depressed. A compromise must be struck here between an early and still somewhat uncertain signal and later but sounder information. In practice, the goal of empirical economic research ought to be to obtain the earliest possible information, even if this means that an extremely irregular variation the following month, associated, say, with a strike, puts at risk the information thus far obtained concerning a cyclical turning point. Several irregular or cyclical impulses which were moving in the same direction and stemmed from a crisis resulting, for example, from a major oil-price hike would even more strongly indicate the need for a revision of the information.

Let us consider the example of the ifo time series for the business climate in industry, which is nowadays one of the central cyclical indicators for the economic tendency in industry in Germany. It is characterized by a very marked cyclical component and a comparatively weakly dispersed irregular residual component. The conditions for an early and nevertheless reliable determination of the current cyclical trend are correspondingly favourable with the series, in particular as far as the indication of a cyclical turning point is concerned. Figure 1 shows the points in time in the seasonally adjusted climate series at which the cyclical components estimated at those times would have pointed to a cyclical turning point. The threshold developed for this time series seems to be consistent with reality, except that a weakening of the upswing, such as at the end of 1988, is incorrectly interpreted as a turning point. Apart from that, the method would have been reliable and relatively early in indicating cyclical turning points.

4.1 Constructing a Test Threshold

The test threshold used in the example is based on the standard deviation of the test differences. This can be calculated from the differences of the consecutive final values of all smooth components which can be estimated throughout the time series. A quicker way of obtaining this standard deviation rests on the fact that all series transformations, starting with the approximation of the smooth components and up to the calculation of the differences, act as a filter on the time series in question. This filter effect of the individual transformation steps and the overall effect can be clarified with the help of a so-called amplitude function. To this end, one has to imagine a form of spectral analysis where the variance of a time series can be divided into specific frequency bands (see e.g. Granger, 1964 for a description of the spectral analysis of economic time series or - short and easier to grasp: Schips, 1993). These frequency bands are derived in economic time series from the period of oscillation of systematically fluctuating series components such as trend, the business cycle or seasonal variation.[1] According to this spectral analysis method, the variance of irregular components is spread evenly over the possible frequency band from zero to half-cycle per unit of time (in which the series is measured). Provided the sequence of its deviation is random, it is thus superimposed on the entire spectrum of the time series. At these frequencies, the amplitude function of a filter gives a factor by which the relevant amplitude can be multiplied.

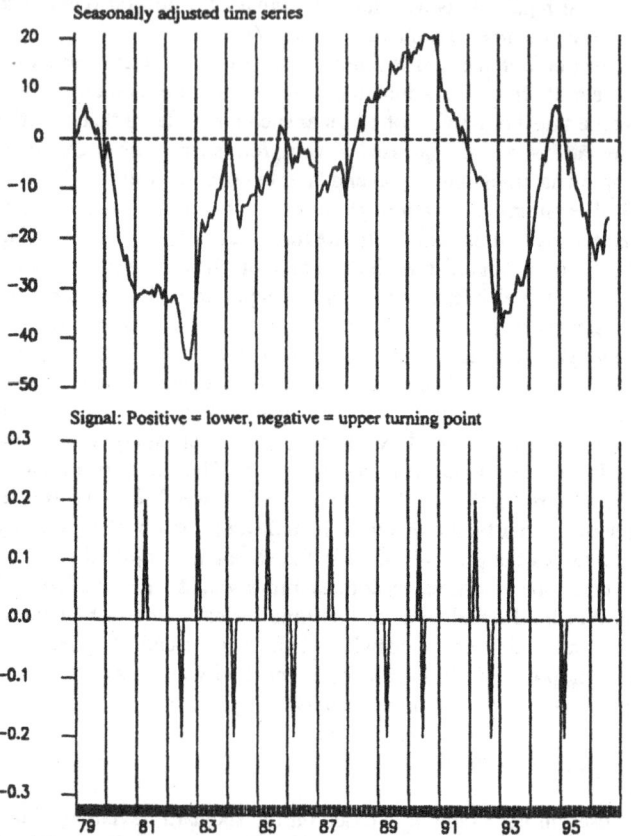

Figure 1 Time of the first reliable signal: Business climate in industry, threshold = 0.04, parabola based on 21 values
Source: ifo business survey, seasonal adjustment and calculations by ifo Institute.

---

[1] The following components of a time series are considered to be cyclical: the trend component, which reflects the long-term movements in an economic aggregate (it is defined as a oscillation lasting more than 5-7 years); the cyclical component of a shorter period than the trend and of a longer period than one year (one year being the period of oscillation of the seasonal component, which is generally repeated very regularly each year). Alongside this fundamental seasonal component, there are also subharmonics with integer multiples of the fundamental frequency; these reflect the deviation of the seasonal movement from a sine function (see e.g. Nerlove, 1979 for the analysis of time series).

Figure 2 shows the amplitude function of the overall effect of all transformations within the time series. It demonstrates very clearly that the suppression is almost complete in those frequency bands belonging to the cyclical series components. Only the irregular movements in the higher frequency band can pass, albeit in a much dampened fashion. This means that the variance of the irregular components determines the threshold and that the suppression effect must be taken into account.

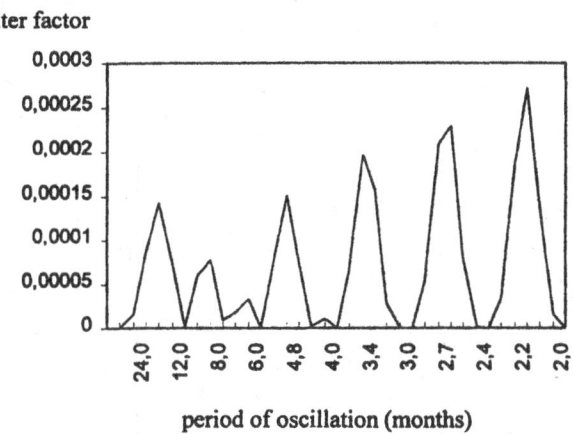

Figure 2   Amplitude function of the overall filter
Source: Calculations by ifo Institute.

An average overall dampening effect of 0.02 can now be derived (over the full frequency band) from the amplitude function, so that the standard deviation of the differences σ_d incorporated in the test can be estimated by the following equation:

$$\sigma_d = 0.02 * \sigma_r.$$

If, taking the normal distribution of purely random irregular residuals, the threshold is set at the interval [$-\sigma_d$, σ_d], only about a third of the test differences can exceed this threshold. These differences are so large that the change in sign is associated with a clear change in direction, which is a rather reliable indicator of a cyclical turning point. This fact and, consequently, the choice of the test interval cannot be underpinned by more objective criteria. A certain latitude remains with regard to determining the interval limits, which, depending on the extent to which the person interpreting the data prepared to take risks, will be more or less narrow. A relatively narrow interval allows the signal to be detected more quickly, with the higher probability that the turning point detected will be subsequently have to be corrected. A broader interval offers greater predictive certainty, but the turning point is detected at a later stage.

Adapting the procedure to deal with the case of a change of sign without sufficient significance creates certain difficulties. The idea is that the compared value should be allowed to stand still until the test difference is sufficiently large.[1] Because of the irregular component, however, the consecutive smooth components do not necessarily change in one direction. The turning point must therefore be identfied as soon as a change in direction occurs, even the test difference has not yet reached the threshold. This ensures that the upper and lower tuning points indicated constantly alternate.

Figure 3 gives the results with a broader test interval (threshold = 0.1). Comparing this figure with Figure 1, we initially find that the result does not react very sensitively to different thresholds. Only on closer inspection is it possible to detect delays in reaction linked to the fact that the threshold in question is not reached.

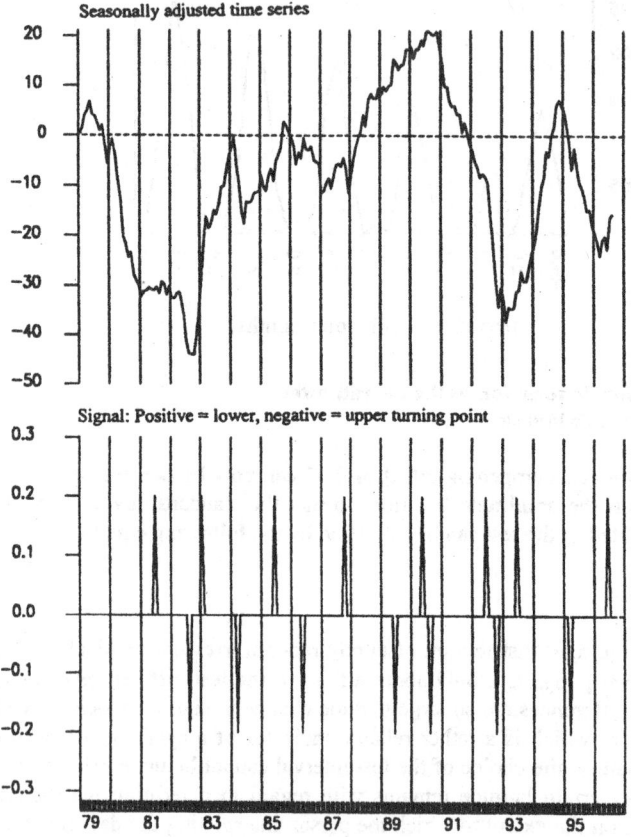

Figure 3 Time of the first reliable signal: Business climate in industry, threshold = 0.1, parabola based on 21 values
Source: ifo business survey, seasonal adjustment and calculations by ifo Institute.

---

[1] This procedure involves a time lag in the detection of a cyclical turning point.

4.2 Alternative Suppression of the Irregular Component

An alternative method of stabilizing the turning point signal is to dispense with any test interval, thereby dampening even further the irregular component. The subjectivity of the procedure here shifts to determination of the degree of damping.

Here, too, the business analyst can determine the actual degree of suppression according to his willingness to take risks. The method differs form the first one described in that it tends, if anything, not to recognize turning points. Experience shows the two methods cannot be applied in such a way as to produce identical results, although a strong suppression of the irregular component generally has the same effect as a broad test interval. Detection of the turning-point signal is delayed in both cases.

The problem with this variant is in selecting the length of the moving average used to estimate the cyclical component according to the relative strength of the irregular component. A small diversion must be made. First, an optimum smoothing of the irregular component is sought. A method for doing this exists; is has been developed to control the seasonal adjustment of time series. This is the so-called MCD measurement, whereby the momentum of the irregular component is measured in terms of the amplitude of the cyclical movement (see Shiskin,1965). Using this measurement - as in, for example, the ASA II seasonal adjustment procedure used by the ifo institute (see Goldrian 1973) - the smoothness of the irregular component in a seasonally adjusted series is optimized in the sense it is reduced to such an extent that reasonably sound cyclical information is obtained. The smoothing process is based on simple moving averages of the residuals, with the number of values incorporated in the averages increasing in line with the relative momentum of the irregular component. The filter effect of this smoothing method is multiplied by the amplitude function of the weighted average in order to estimate the last value of the cyclical component. The length of the moving average (for the approximation of the cyclical component) which filter effect comes closest to the amplitude function obtained (in each case referred to the last value) is then selected. In this way it is possible to indicate a moving average with similar filter characteristics for each MCD value.

The effect of the second variant will now be demonstrated on a time series which has a much larger irregular component than the business climate, namely the time series for new orders in the motor vehicle industry. It is recommended in this case that the irregular component be smoothed using a moving 11-month average. It can be inferred from this that the number of values must be expanded from 21 to 31 values. Figure 4 gives the result obtained. Despite the relatively strong irregular movement of the time series shown in the upper half of the figure, the procedure detects cyclical changes. However, these changes do not, in retrospective, always indicate a cyclical turning point but only a temporary weakening of the upswing or downswing, as occurred, for example, at the end of 1989 / beginning of 1990. To prevent an incorrect assessment, the irregular component must be dampened still further, though this again involves a time lag in the turning-point signal.

Another possibility is to attempt an advance adjustment for extreme deviations, such as occurred in December 1989; this involves suppressing the influence of the extreme values which exists towards the end of the time series. A method exists for this which has proved effective with the ASA II seasonal adjustment procedure. It again involves calculating the standard deviation of the residuals σ_r and establishing the test interval [-2.5 x

σ_r, 2.5 x σ_r] (the factor of 2.5 results from the notion of roughly normally distributed residuals and from the intention to correct only truly extreme values). The residuals lying outside this interval are then reduced to the level of the interval limit. However, towards the end of a series, this adjustment of extreme values functions only imperfectly. At such points, an extreme value influences relatively strongly movements in the approximated cyclical component so that the resulting residual loses some of its magnitude.

4.3 A Proposed Further Improvement

The fact that the method for detecting cyclical turning points also interprets a temporary weakness during an upswing or downswing as a cyclical turning point somewhat impairs the reliability of the signal. To prevent an incorrect interpretation, additional information can be taken into consideration. The representation of the second-order differences of all cyclical components has proved to be relatively helpful in this respect. These are depicted - in the context of the verification of the second stabilization variant for the business climate in industry - in the lower half of Figure 5. As can be clearly seen, the development of the second-order differences serves as a leading indicator of an incipient turning point (they move in the direction of the signal: upwards (or downwards) when a lower (or upper) turning point is imminent). In order to obtain reliable information on the turning point, there must be no erratic movements before the presumed signal (April 1988) occurs (e.g. the period from the end of 1987 to the end of 1988) which might point to a change that does not constitute a genuine turning point. Irrespective of this, immediately after each signal (as occurred, for example, in July 1992) must be payed attention to a change in direction of the second-order differences. In retrospect, such a change indicates a false or premature signal. Weak cyclical fluctuations in the second-order differences point to a phase in which it may be more probable to make incorrect assessments.

To obtain the result represented in Figure 5, the number of values for estimating the cyclical component was increased to 23., instead of setting a threshold. Compared with the first stabilization method (Figure 1), this gives rise to an almost continuous delay in reaction. This enabled the two false signals in 1990 to be eliminated.

5 Conclusion

The special feature of the method for detecting a cyclical turning point is the capability to recognize first signs of a development toward a cyclical upturn or downturn. It can give a more or less reliable signal, dependent on the share of the irregular component on the variance of the seasonally adjusted time series and on the smoothness of the cyclical movement (sinusoidal or abrupt). Interruptions in upward or downward movement can be falsely interpreted as signaling a turning point. To prevent such problems, the business analyst must accept a delay in reaction. However, a later signal provides more reliable information.

The turning point is indicated clearly before its realization, when time series show a nearly sinusoidal cyclical course which is only superimposed by small irregular disturbances. Applying to such time series, the both methods are very efficient. Tests with other time series, in particular with a pronounced irregular component do not entirely confirm the hoped-for reliability. However, the user is able to adapt the method to the extent to which he is prepared to take risks. Here, the differences between both procedures are relatively small. Although it is generally important to detect turning points as early as possible, analysts tend to prefer the second method (i.e. extension of the moving average) because the choice of a threshold is not conclusive. However, it is possible by experimentation to find the threshold allowing the method to indicate a turning point somewhat earlier than is possible with the more straightforward second method. On the other hand, the second variant is the better method to detect turning points in time series with a small irregular component but with abrupt changes in the cyclical development, like the ifo Business Climate. Here is a length of 23 values the first choice.

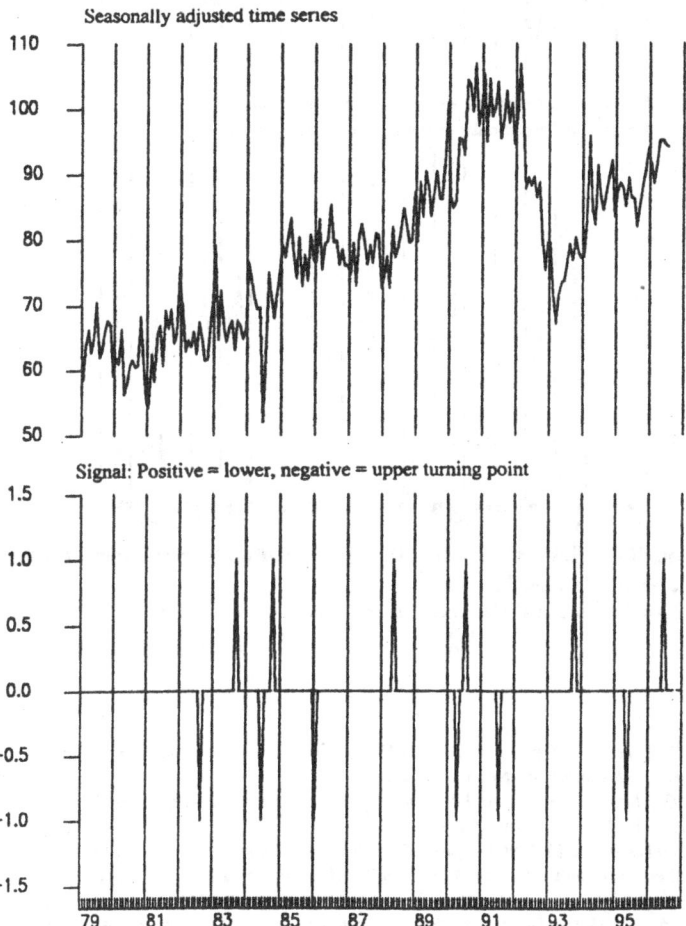

Figure 4 Time of the first reliable signal: New orders in the motor vehicle industry, parabola based on 31 values

Source: Official statistics, seasonal adjustment and calculations by ifo Institute.

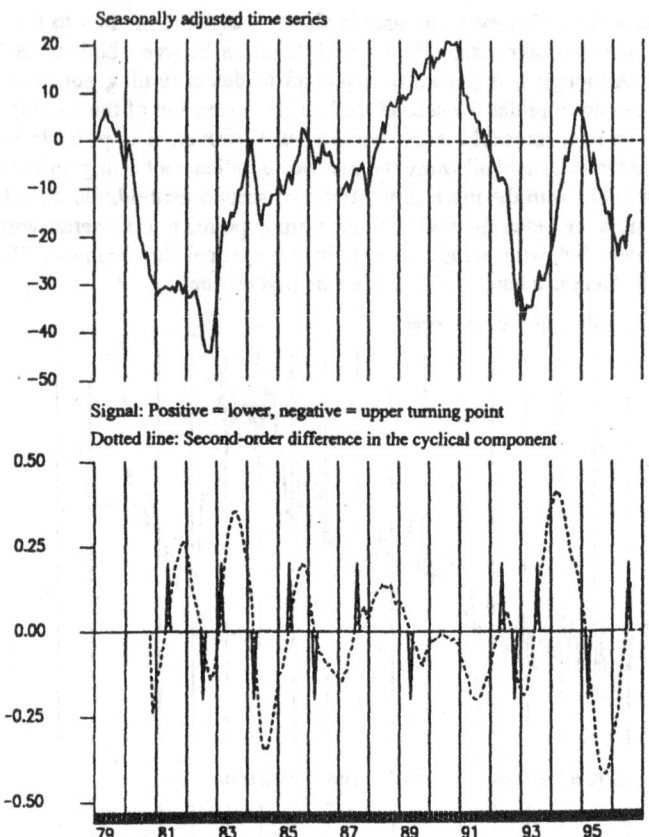

Figure 5 Time of the first reliable signal: Business climate in industry, no threshold, parabola based on 23 values

Source: ifo business survey, seasonal adjustment and calculations by ifo Institute.

References

Goldrian, G. (1973), Eine neue Version des ASA-II-Verfahrens zur Saisonbereinigung von wirtschaftlichen Zeitreihen, *Wirtschaftskonjunktur*, No. 4, Munich.

Goldrian, G. (1993), *Erweiterungen und Verbesserungen des Saisonbe-reinigungsverfahrens ASA-II*, ifo Discussion Paper No. 10, ifo Institute, Munich.

Granger, C.W.J. and Hatanaka, M. (1964), *Spectral Analysis of Economic Time Series*, Princeton.

Nerlove, M., Grether, D.M. and Calvalho, J.OL. (1979), *Analysis of Economic Time Series. A Synthesis*, New York.

Schips, B. and Stier, W. (1993), *Das CENSUS-X-11-Verfahren. Darstellung, Kritik, Alternativen*, Bundesamt für Statistik, Bern.

Shiskin, J., Young, A.H. and Musgrave, J.C. (1965), *The X-11 Variant of the Census Method II, Seasonal Adjustment Program*. US Department of Commerce, Bureau of the Census, Technical Paper No. 15, Washington.

7 The Timing of M-shaped Growth Cycles of the German Economy

Ernst Helmstädter

1 Introduction

To analyse the cyclical behaviour of an economy the economics disciplines apply several methods: theoretic models, econometric tests and also rules of thumb of different types. This paper falls more or less in the last category. It presents a scheme to identify cyclical turning points, which has been used successfully by the author over the last ten years in forecasting the upcoming movements of the growth process of the German economy.

The underlying basic hypothesis presupposes a division of an entire growth cycle into four phases. During the first phase, starting at the lowest point of the foregoing cycle, the growth rate of real GDP increases quickly to a first height. The second phase shows a slowly decreasing growth rate which comes to an end at a medium low point. The third phase brings a new climb of the growth rate and then from the altitude during the fourth phase a fast drop down. Thus, the movement of the GDP growth rates follows a so-called M-form (Helmstädter, 1989). Since the fifties, five cycles of this form with an average length of around 8 years have been observed.

The paper deals specifically with the identification of the respective turning points. It distinguishes between two types of growth rates of the quarterly moving GDP of a one-year time span. The usual growth rate from year to year is called the year-to-year rate (YYR) and the growth rate from quarter to quarter the quarter-to-quarter rate (QQR). The latter is multiplied by 4 to put it on the yearly basis. The use of both growth rates together is the characteristic method to show the cyclical behaviour of the data and specifically to identify the turning points.

2 Quarterly Moving Four Quarter Totals and Two Different Growth Rates

Given a time series of quarterly data x_i (i= 1,2,3, ...t...n-1, n) we build the quarterly moving total of a year's time span by summing up the four elements x_i :

$$\bar{x}_{t.} = \sum_{t-1}^{t+2} x_i \qquad (1)$$

The index t. belongs to the point of time at the end of the t-quarter. That time point lies in the middle of the year, consisting of the four quarters t-1, t, t+1 and t+2.

The YYR in per cent is now defined as follows :

$$YYR_{t.} = \left(\frac{\bar{x}_{t.}}{\bar{x}_{t.-1}} - 1\right)100. \tag{2}$$

The QQR in per cent reads on a year's basis as follows:

$$QQR_{t.} = \left(\frac{\bar{x}_{t.}}{\bar{x}_{t.-1}} - 1\right)400. \tag{3}$$

The QQR behaves much more volatily than the YYR. It shows the irregular and the cyclical swings quite clearly, while the YYR levels out many of them. If the QQR held its value over 4 quarters, the YYR would reach exactly the same value.

The current deviation between YYR and QQR gives us an indicator of the cyclical volatility of a time series. We define the degree of volatility v as follows:

$$V = \frac{\sum_{1}^{n}|QQR_{t.} - YYR_{t.}|}{n}. \tag{4}$$

The degree of volatility is the average absolute difference between the QQR and the YYR in percent.

Incidentally, seasonal swings disturb neither the YYR nor the QQR. They are excluded by the simple method of applying moving four quarter totals.

3 The M Cycles of the German Economy 1950 - 1996

First we describe the growth process of the German economy during the very long time period of 1950 to 1997 by using both of the growth rates YYR and QQR. For the first decade the underlying quarterly data series of the real GDP was estimated by the DIW (Deutsches Institut für Wirtschaftsforschung, Berlin). Since 1960 official quarterly data of the Statistical Office of Germany (Statistisches Bundesamt, Wiesbaden) on the price basis of 1991 have been available. Until 1992 the data refer to West Germany only and since then to all of Germany. We will not discuss here the problems of the changing price basis or of the territorial borders. In either case these changes do not really matter with respect to the shape of the growth process of the total economy. This is even true for the economy of united Germany. Its cyclical behaviour doesn't seem to be much different from that of West Germany. Nonetheless, there will be some remarks on this issue later on.

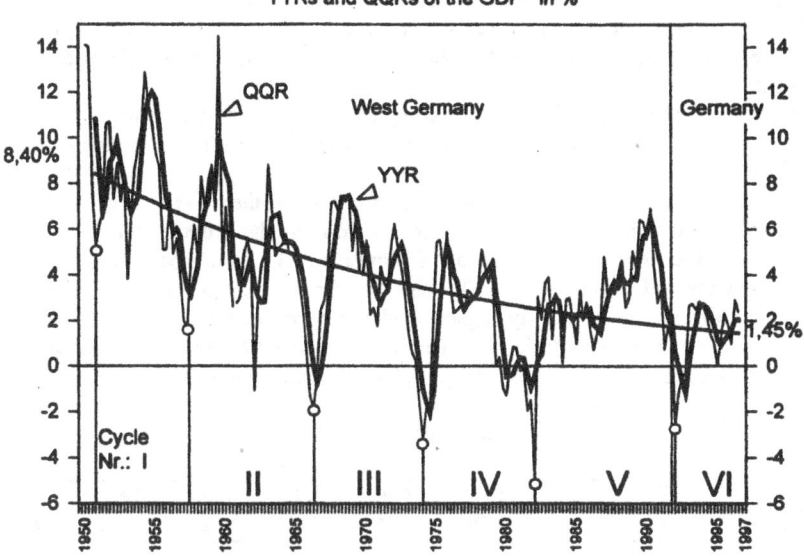

Figure 1 The M cycles of the German economy, 1950-1997

Figure 1 shows the development of the YYRs and QQRs. We see a long-run downward movement of the growth rates and a cyclical volatility around this trend.

To calibrate the M cycles a very simple counting-out rule seems to be worthwhile. The turning points of the cyclical movement are found by using the QQR series. A downward moving phase of the M cycle has ended when, after an extremely low value of the QQR, the two following QQRs are higher. An upward moving phase has ended when, after an extremely high value, the two following QQRs are lower. This counting-out rule has been applied consistently in calibrating the cycles and phases shown in Figure 1. Table 1 shows the length of the phases of the five completed cycles since 1950.

Table 1 Period length of cycles and phases

Cycle	Period Q.Y.-Q.Y.	Cycle	Phase 1	Length in quarters Phase 2	Phase 3	Phase 4
I	2.51 - 3.57	26	4	5	5	12
II	4.57 - 3.66	36	9	10	4	13
II	4.58 - 2.74	31	10	8	5	8
IV	3.74 - 4.81	30	7	5	5	13
V	1.82 - 2.92	42	6	13	16	7
	Average Length	33.0	7.2	8.2	7.0	10.6
VI	3.92 - ?	?	7	5	8?	?

We see that the cycle length as well as the length of the different phases vary somehow. No cycle is the exact replica of another one. There is one extreme length of phase 3 within cycle V. The long duration of this phase was brought about by the German unification boom.

The length of phases 2 and 3 of the uncompleted cycle VI gets near to the average length of the completed five cycles before. Phase 2 was relatively short. Whether phase 3 has already come to its end will be discussed later on.

In spite of the different length of the cycles and phases, there was no difficulty in applying the aforementioned counting-out rule to determine the different turning points. There are only two exceptions. The unification boom showed a double peak. The first one was reached at the end of quarter 1.1990. The QQR dropped down for two periods but turned up again to an insignificantly higher level at the end of quarter 4.1990. Table 2 shows the values of the QQR during that period. The second exception can be seen in figure 6 where a double dip at the beginning of phase 3 has occurred.

Table 2   Double peak during the unification boom

End of quarter	3.89	4.89	1.90	2.90	3.90	4.90	1.91	2.91
QQR in %	5.08	4.33	6.44	6.34	5.63	6.95	4.42	2.76

                        ↑   ↑
                  First peak   Peak turning point

4 Cycle Makers and Signal Givers

So far, we have observed only the GDP time series as the main indicator of the process of cyclical movements. But GDP itself is composed of elements with very different cyclical behaviour. The above defined degree of volatility gives us a useful measure to differentiate between the GDP components with respect to their cyclical patterns. Table 3 shows the degree of volatility as found in the data of West Germany 1960–1994 and Germany 1992–1997.

Table 3   The degree of volatility of the GDP components

GDP components	West Germany 1961-1994	Germany 1992-1997
	Degree of volatility in %	
Private Consumption	0.92	0.86
Public consumption	1.22	0.74
Imports	2.63	2.81
Non-cycle makers	1.30	0.93
Equipment	3.45	3.36
Buildings	3.70	2.92
Exports	5.96	2.91
Cycle makers	2.60	2.52
Total GDP	1.22	0.94

Figure 2 shows the development of the volatility degrees of exports and private consumption from 1961 to 1997. They would reach zero values when the QQR and the YYR are equal for more then four quarters. Near zero values arrive when the QQR crosses the YYR line (see figure 1).

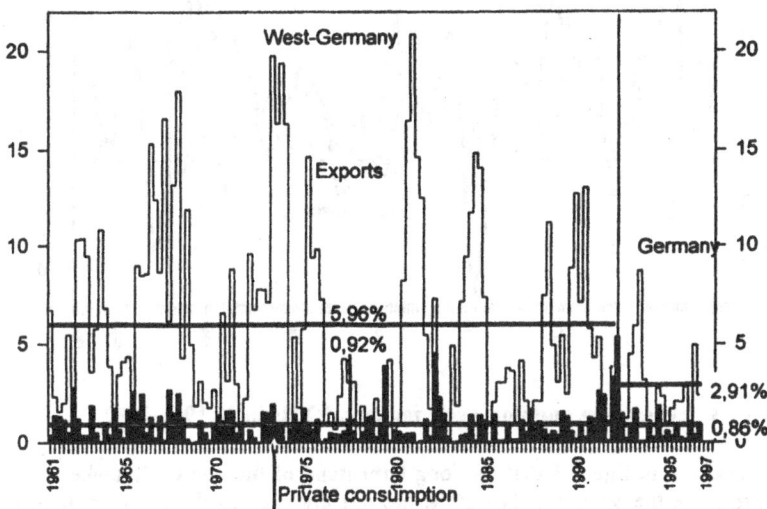

Figure 2   Exports and private consumption, volatility degrees (V) in % 1961-1997

Because of their remarkably high volatility especially during the long period of 1961-1994 we aggregate the components equipment, buildings and exports to the cycle makers and regard the remaining components of the GDP as non-cycle makers. With this aggregation, we gain a deeper insight into the mechanism of cyclical movement.

Figure 3 describes the development of the cyclical components by their YYRs from the sixties until today. The figure also shows, on the basis of these YYRs, a much higher volatility of the cycle makers compared to the non-cycle maker components of GDP. Nevertheless, the non-cycle makers underlie clear cyclical movements as well. They may be characterised as more or less parallel swings. A specific lag structure, one could presume, doesn't seem to prevail.

The contribution of the cycle makers to the GDP has grown during the last decades. At the beginning of the sixties they contributed around 40% to the GDP. This percentage in West Germany reached around 55% in 1994. It amounts to up to 50% in Germany today. The course of the three elements of the cycle makers developed differently: the share of exports has remarkably increased, the share of buildings decreased, and that of equipment remained roughly constant. So one may say that the cyclical movement of the German economy became more and more export-driven.

Social and Structural Change - Consequences for Business Cycle Surveys

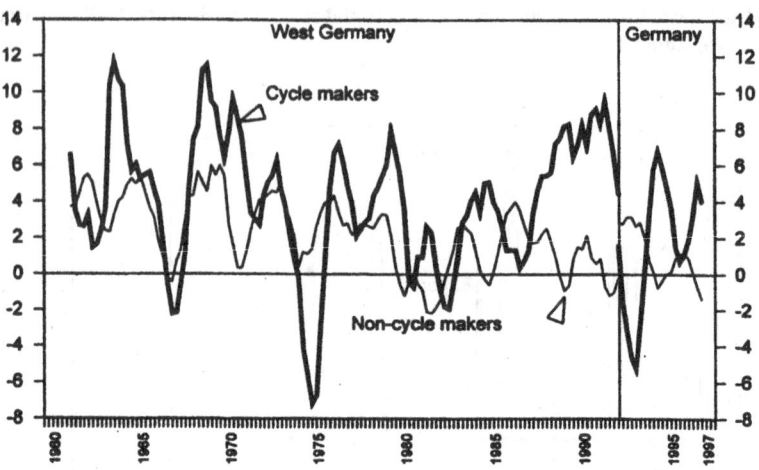

Figure 3 Cycle makers and non-cycle makers, YYRs in % 1961-1997

We also see in figure 3 that the long term trend of the non-cycle makers has been downward since the seventies. The YYR has already reached the negative area. Its last value in figure 3 amounts to -1.41%. The trend of the cycle makers went upward at the beginning eighties but didn't yet really recover after the last recession of 1993 (see also figure 6).

If we now compare the M cycle with the movement of the Ifo Business Climate index (see figure 4) we find an astonishing parallel swing. One would presume that this climate index should show a certain lead to the production path as given by the GDP growth rate.

Another time series in comparison with the M cycle is shown in figure 5. Foreign orders to the manufacturing industry should move clearly ahead of actual production as was the case during the eighties. During the first half of the nineties we observe a more parallel development. If we compare the foreign orders with the development of exports (see the line marked by squares) we see again parallel swings. There is one exception during the early nineties. The leading downswing of orders is followed two years later by exports. The reason may be that the increasing exports from Western Germany to Eastern Germany at the end of 1989 and during 1990 and 1991 are not further included in the foreign order statistics. So we can only say that a special development is in progress.

The Timing of M-shaped Growth Cycles of the German Economy

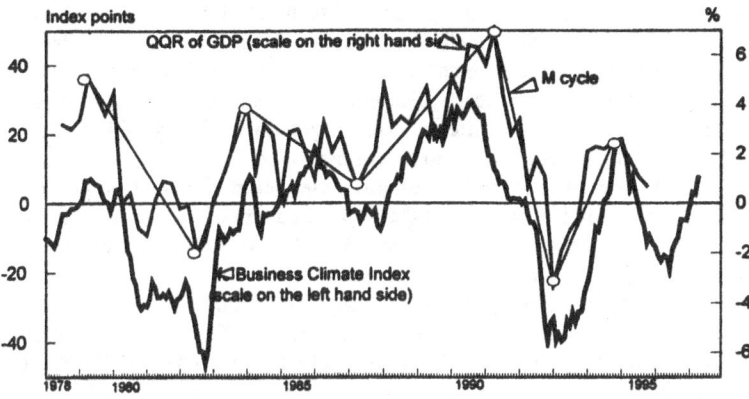

Figure 4 The Ifo business climate index of the manufacturing industry and the M cycle, West Germany 1978-1997

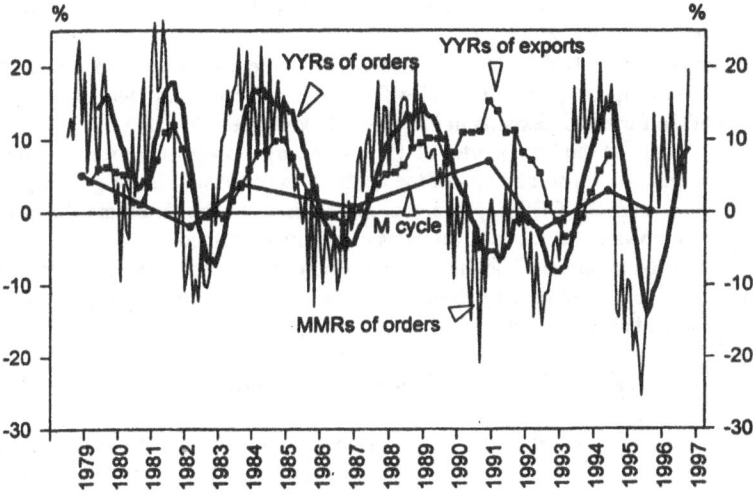

Figure 5 Foreign orders to the manufacturing sector and the M cycle West Germany 1979-1997

5 The Current Situation

It may be of interest to take a look at the current situation to find out what the real advantage can be in using the described method to calibrate the growth cycle. The basic insight we derive is that the cyclical movement doesn't show erratic swings but certain regularities with respect to the length of clearly distinguishable phases. To distinguish the phases, we need nothing else but the two different rates of growth YYR and QQR and the abovementioned simple rule of counting out to determine the peaks and dips. The main mistake made by so many forecasters is the lack of any cycle idea at all. The German forecasting institutes don't take sufficient account of the cyclical pattern of the movements in the medium term of cyclical phases. The author has often criticized this fault. Thus, the medium-term ups and downs are systematically underestimated.

In the middle of 1997, everyone in Germany was looking for the long-awaited upswing. The Ifo Business Climate Index looked friendly. The Kiel institute forecast that the German economy might reach a growth rate of real GDP of 2.7% in 1997 (Handelsblatt, 1997). The RWI institute of Essen was expecting even 2.8% (RWI, 1997). Its forecasts are based on a huge macroeconomic model which takes into consideration the monetary as well as the specific fiscal conditions of the next year.

But according to the national accounts figures published in December 1997 the YYR of GDP only reached 2.04% at the end of the first quarter 1997 as shown in figure 6 (see also table 4). The Council of Economic Experts forecast a YYR for 1997 of 2½% what was also a bit too high.

Let us ask now what can be said about the probable development of 1998 under the viewpoint of the M cycle regularities.

As of the end of 1997 the YYRs and the QQRs of the last quarters appear as shown in table 4 (see also figure 6). There we also find the development of 1998 as forecast by the Council of the Economic Experts in its report of November 1997.

The GDP result of the first quarter of 1997 was very disappointing for seasonal reasons. This brought about a second low of the QQR. This double dip (see figure 6) was the latest available data at the CIRET conference in Helsinki. In the meantime the development again went upward but not so strongly as originally presumed.

The Council of Economic Experts as well as other forecasters have made their forecast for 1998. Table 4 shows the forecast of the Council in quarterly terms, as calculated from the Council's half year figures.

Table 4   The current development of the GDP YYR and QQR in %

	Actual					Forecast by the Council of Economic Experts (quarterly adjusted by the author)				
Quarter	1.96	2.96	3.96	4.96	1.97	2.97	3.97	4.97	1.98	2.98
YYR %	1.13	1.35	1.58	2.04	2.04	2.36	2.59	2.98	2.91	2.83
QQR %	2.34	1.85	0.96	2.92	2.92	2.80	3.15	3.22	2.48	2.46

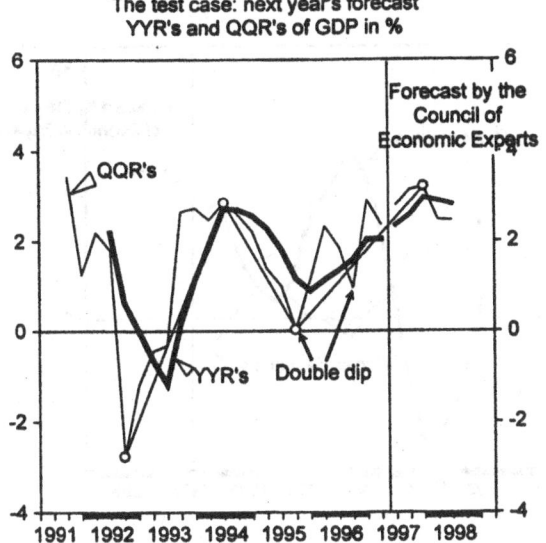

Figure 6 The test case: next year's forecast YYRs and QQRs of GDP in %

If the forecast of the Council turns out to have been realistic, then, seen in the ligtht of the M cycle hypothesis, phase 4 of cycle VI begins at the end of the third quarter of 1997. This point of time lies in the middle of the year's time span of the second quarter of 1997 to the first quarter of 1998. It shows that the upswing during the phase 3 was relatively weak or, to say it more clearly: it did not even happen. The highest value of YYR would just touch the 3% record (see table 4) and would lie quite near to the trend line (the trend is shown in figure 1). The end of phase 3 came to a QQR of 3.22% as compared to 2.73% at the end of phase 1 of cycle VI. It looks as if the German economy was already confronted with the upcoming downswing of phase 4. In either case many new impulses would be needed if phase 3 should turn up to a double peak as we have observed at the end of phase 3 in cycle V.

This pessimistic prognosis finds support in the behavior of the cycle maker and the non-cycle maker component as shown in figure 7. The cycle makers seem to have reached their peak, holding it since five quarters, as the Council forecast. The non-cycle makers have remained in the negative area since the end of the second quarter. Under those conditions there is no economic force to allow a continuation of phase 3 in the current cycle.

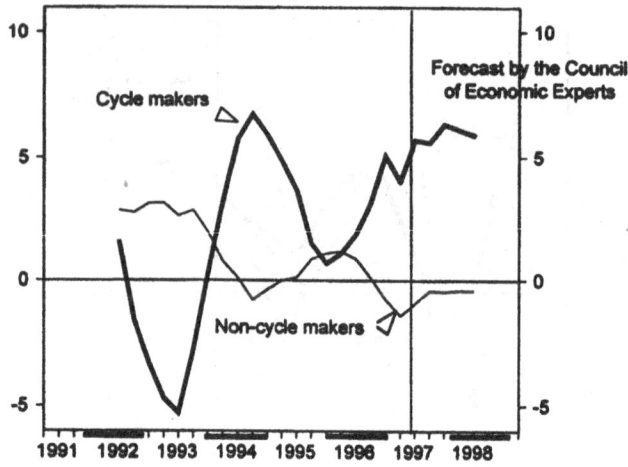

Figure 7 Cycle makers and non-cycle makers today and tomorrow
YYRs of the GDP components in %

6 Conclusions

It was our aim to show that the cyclical swings of the growth process of the German economy are characterized by medium term phases which can be understood as M-shaped. Elisabeth Herwegh (1994) found similar cyclical patterns for the USA and the United Kingdom since the 1980s.

A theoretical explanation for this phenomenon has not yet been found. Some observers understand it as the result of an overlapping of two impulses of a different time patterns like investments in buildings and equipment, and stock investments.

Here, these movements have been regarded as observable regularities. We have attempted to provide a certain taxonomy of the cycle. Especially with respect to the turning points, we have formulated a simple rule of thumb to determine them. Used in practical forecasting, these instruments can help to improve the forecast results. The failures of the forecasters often arise from a too cautious behaviour: the course of upswings as well as the downswings is often underestimated (Helmstädter, 1996). With an understanding of the medium-term cyclical movements, many such mistakes can be avoided.

References

Helmstädter, E. (1989), Die M-Form des Wachstumszyklus, Jahrbücher für Nationalökonomie und Statistik, Band 206/4-5, pp. 383-394.

Helmstädter, E. (1996), Wirtschaftspolitisches Forum. Zur wirtschaftspolitischen Nützlichkeit von Konjunkturprognosen, Zeitschrift für Wirtschaftspolitik, Vol. 45, pp.162-170.

Helmstädter, E. (1997), Der Kurs der deutschen Konjunktur ist derzeit nicht eindeutig, Handelsblatt No. 120, p.6.

Herwegh, E. (1994), Die jüngste Rezession in den Industrieländern im Lichte früherer Zyklen. Eine phänomenologische Betrachtung, RWI-Mitteilungen, Zeitschrift für Wirtschaftsforschung, Vol. 45, No. 2, pp. 127-145.

RWI Rheinisch-Westfälisches Institut für Wirtschaftsforschung (1997), Vierteljährliche Prognose mit dem RWI-Konjunkturmodell 1997-1 bis 1998-4, No. 45.

Sachverständigenrat zur Begutachtung der gesamtwirtschaftlichen Entwicklung (1997), Wachstum, Beschäftigung, Währungsunion – Orientierungen für die Zukunft, Jahresgutachten 1997/98, Stuttgart.

8 Survey on the Timing of Cyclical Turning Points

Rudolf Marty / Bernd Schips

Abstract

In this paper two popular approaches for identifying and predicting cyclical turning points are discussed and surveyed. The first one consists in composite leading indices which are used widely by the OECD for short-term forecasting purposes. The second one deals with the interest rate spread's slope, e.g. the difference between long-term and short-term interest rates. According to various studies this financial variable which is said to be highly sensitive to an economy's future growth prospects can also be used to predict major cyclical turning points. Comparing the prediction performance of these two approaches using data for Switzerland, the USA and Japan shows that composite leading indices as well as interest rate spreads have useful information concerning future growth cycles' turning points.

1 Introduction

Identifying and forecasting cyclical turning points in a country's economy remains a challenging task for researchers in business cycle analyses. Additionally, timely recognition of the impending arrival of a business cycle turning point is also of considerable interest to policy makers and private agents as well. Various approaches to forecast or signal business cycle turning points have been explored and tested. Among them are macroeconometric modelling and leading indicators. As the macroeconometric models are designed mainly to make quantitative medium- and long-term forecasts of the gross domestic product's various components, they are seldom used for short-term prediction of business cycle turning points. Because this paper focuses on the timing of cyclical turning points, the leading indicator approach seems more appropriate for this purpose and is therefore studied more carefully in this paper.

The use of leading indicators for short-term forecasting of business cycle turning points is popular among economists. The OECD for example routinely maintains a system of business cycle indicators pertaining to 22 of its member countries (see e.g. Nilsson, 1987). However, it must be stressed that leading indicators can only be used to forecast qualitatively the economy's output. Moreover, as most leading indicators are subject to major short-term changes that obscure the series' cyclical components, it is hard to identify clearly the indicators' turning points using real time data. Thus, having a procedure for quickly recognising the onset of a turning point in the leading indicator series helps recognising the onset of a turning point in this series; by definition the leading indicator's signal can then be assumed to lead the corresponding turning point in the reference series.

The aim of this paper is to present and test various leading indicator series for the USA, Japan and Switzerland. Among them are the composite leading indices published by the OECD and interest rate spreads, i.e. differences between long-term and short-term interest rates. As these indicators are monthly time series, they are subject to considerable short-run fluctuations. Therefore, what is needed is an appropriate filtering rule that maps changes in these indicators into turning point predictions. In this paper, two different types of procedures are applied to the leading indicator series to detect its major turning points.

This paper is organised as follows. In the next section the system of coincident and leading indicators constructed by the OECD is briefly surveyed. In addition, it is explained shortly how the OECD dates the major cyclical turning points. Next the various leading indicator series are described. Further, the leading indicators' performance in predicting business cycle turning points is surveyed and briefly tested. Finally, this study's most important results are summarised.

2 The OECD's Business Cycle Chronology

The reference chronology of the OECD system of coincident and leading indicators is based upon cyclical movements in the monthly index of industrial production[1] for each country over the period 1961.1 to 1996.11. The chronology itself abstracts from long-run movements in the economy. Instead, it represents fluctuations in the level of economic activity around its long-run trend.[2] Thus, a recession showing up in the reference series does not necessarily indicate an absolute fall in the level of economic activity. Table 2.1 below shows the major cyclical turning points the OECD has identified in the period investigated.

---

[1] Except for Switzerland, the industrial production indices used in this study are monthly series. In Switzerland, the industrial production index is only available as a quarterly series.
[2] The OECD uses a modified phase-average-trend estimation procedure to eliminate the macroeconomic time series' long-run trend.

Table 2.1 The OECD business cycle chronology (major cycles), 61 - 96

Turning Points	Switzerland* Peak ; Trough	USA Peak ; Trough	Japan Peak ; Trough
1st turning point	63/III ; no	61.12 ; 62.12	62.1 ; 62.12
2nd turning point	no ; 68/II	66.10 ; 67.7	64.2 ; 66.2
3rd turning point	70/II ; 72/II	69.3 ; 70.11	70.6 ; 71.12
4th turning point	74/II ; 75/II	73.10 ; 75.3	74.1 ; 75.3
5th turning point	80/I ; 82/IV	79.3 ; 82.12	80.2 ; 82.10
6th turning point	86/III ; 87/II	84.7 ; 86.6	84.10; 87.5
7th turning point	90/I ; 93/II	89.3 ; 91.4	90.10; no

Notes: * : quarterly data ; no : no turning point.
Source: Artis et al. (1995), OECD Economic Studies, No. 24, Paris, p. 128.

3 A Survey of Leading Indicator Series

3.1 The Composite Leading Indices Published by the OECD

For each of its member countries, the OECD calculates a monthly composite leading index. The composite leading indices are constructed as simple averages of macroeconomic time series showing a stable lead with respect to the corresponding reference series. On the one hand, time series included in the composite leading indices are typically based on business surveys due to their timely availability. Among them, series as orders inflow and expectations of future demand are frequently used. On the other hand, the OECD includes various monetary and financial time series (e.g. stock prices, interest rates) in the composite leading indices.[1] In figures 3.1.1 to 3.1.3 the composite leading indices are displayed together with the corresponding reference series (industrial production indices).

---

[1] For a detailed description of the time series included in the various composite leading indices and the way they are constructed see Nilsson (1987).

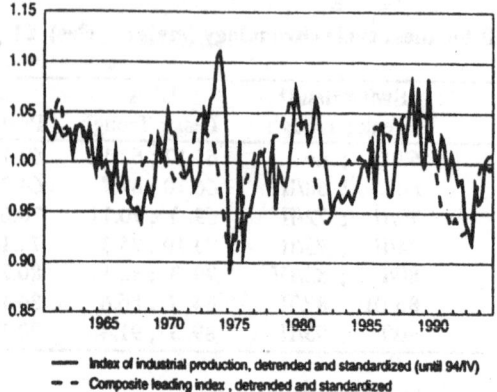

Figure 3.1.1 Industrial production and composite leading index, Switzerland

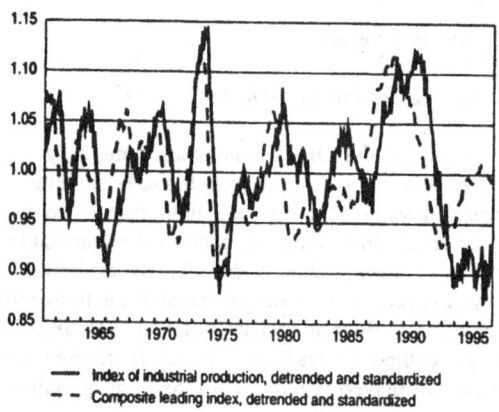

Figure 3.1.2 Industrial production and composite leading index, USA

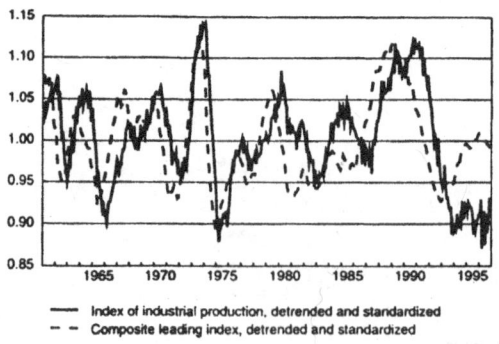

Figure 3.1.3 Industrial production and composite leading index, Japan

3.2 Interest Rate Spreads as Leading Indicators

In recent times the interest rate spread as a predictor of real economic activity has gained increasing attention (see e.g. Hu, 1993 and Estrella and Hardouvelis, 1991). Because the interest rate spread is defined as the difference between a long-term and a short-term interest rate, its main determinants are the central bank's monetary policy stance and the financial market's long-term inflationary expectations. During a boom, the interest rate spread is said to be upward sloping whereas a recession is characterised having a downward sloping interest rate spread. Economically, these empirical findings can be explained on the one hand by shifts in the central bank's monetary policy affecting mainly short-term money market rates. On the other hand changes in the public's inflationary expectations are influencing the interest rate spread by affecting mainly the long-term interest rates. Therefore, as soon as the interest rate spread's slope changes its sign, this can be interpreted as signalling the financial markets' perception of a major cyclical turning point.

In this study, interest rate spreads have to be calculated using long-term and short-term interest rates for the USA, Japan and Switzerland. Constructing the interest rate spread for these countries, it must be kept in mind that until 1974, the Japanese and Swiss central banks were not able to set domestic interest rates completely independent of international interest rates because they pegged their exchange rates against the dollar. Therefore, in these two countries tests of the interest rate spread's prediction accuracy using time series before 1974 must be interpreted carefully.

Because in Switzerland short-term money market rates are available only since the beginning of the nineties, the interest rate spread is calculated using the 3-months eurorates and the yield on confederation bonds. Calculating the US interest rate spread, the yield on 10-year-treasury bonds and the federal funds rate is used. The latter is said to be influenced most directly by the Federal Reserve System's monetary policy actions. Finally, as the Japanese capital market used to be highly regulated until the eighties, short-term interest rates denominated in yen must be chosen carefully. Using the call money market rate and the yield on Japanese government bonds, the interest rate spread can be computed for Japan. Below, plots of these three countries' interest rate spreads' are displayed together with the corresponding reference series (index of industrial production).

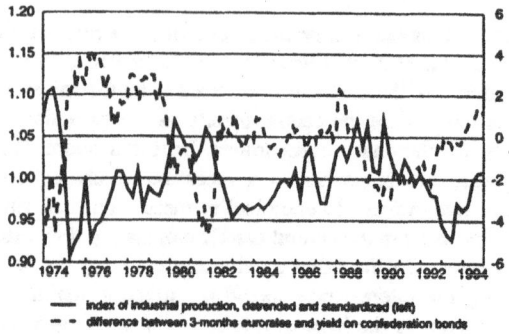

Figure 3.2.1 Industrial production and interest rate spread, Switzerland

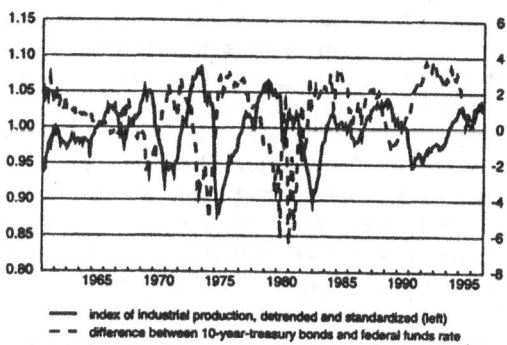

Figure 3.2.2 Industrial production and interest rate spread, USA

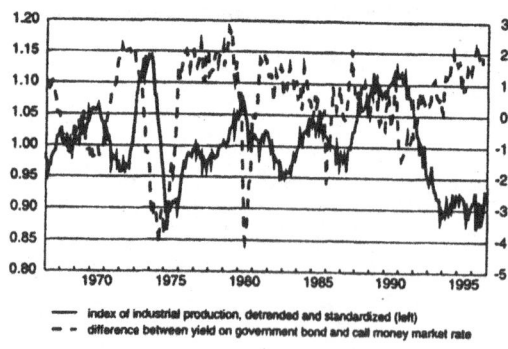

Figure 3.2.3 Industrial production and interest rate spread, Japan

4 Assessing the Leading Indicators' Prediction Accuracy

A crucial issue in evaluating leading indicators as predictors of cyclical turns is the choice of an appropriate filtering rule that may map changes in these indicators into turning point predictions. After all, a leading indicator is only as good as the rule that interprets its movements. In the literature, a number of filtering rules has been suggested. On the one hand, they are simple ad-hoc rules like the one proposed by Vaccara and Zarnowitz (1977). On the other hand, in recent times there has been suggested a number of more sophisticated rules like the one proposed by Neftci (1982). All these empirical rules typically involve trade-offs of accuracy for timeliness and missed signals for false alarms. In the next section, a study using Neftci's procedure to identify the leading indicator's cyclical turning points is discussed.

4.1 Predicting Cyclical Turning Points Using the OECD Leading Indices

The filtering rule proposed by Neftci (1982) has gained increasing attention in recent times. In this framework, the composite leading index is modelled as shifting between two regimes (expansions and recessions). The switch between the two regimes is governed by the outcome of a stochastic process. Further, it is assumed that the analyst cannot observe the two regimes directly but instead he is supposed to be able to make a probabilistic inference about the unobserved underlying regime. Neftci's (1982) non-linear filter permits estimation of the population parameters including conditional probabilities that a cyclical turning point will occur. If these probabilities exceed or fall short of a certain threshold level of statistical confidence, this can be interpreted as spotting a cyclical turning point in the time series studied.[1]

In order to identify the composite leading indices' cyclical turning points, Artis et. al. (1995) have applied the filtering rule proposed by Neftci to the OECD composite leading indices of the G-7 countries to evaluate exactly how well these indices have performed during the last 30 years. In table 4.1.1, these calculations are listed together with an evaluation of the composite leading index computed by the OECD for Switzerland based on our own calculations.[2] There, it can be seen that the OECD composite leading indices' leads are ranging from 4 to 8 months. In addition, the filtering procedure proposed by Neftci and applied to these composite indices only misses one signal and at the same time produces two false signals. Summarising the results in table 4.1.1 it can be concluded that the composite leading indices have performed reasonably well in predicting these countries' growth cycles' turning points during the last thirty years although it must be admitted that the latest cycle's predicted trough in Japan has not yet been materialised.

---

[1] More details about Neftci's non-linear procedure and how it can be applied to a leading indicator series are described in Neftci (1982).

[2] It is assumed that the composite leading indices' leads at cyclical turns should not exceed 24 months.

Table 4.1.1 Turning point prediction using the composite leading indices, 61 - 94

Turning points	Leads (-) and Lags (+) in months					
	Switzerland		USA		Japan	
	Peak	Trough	Peak	Trough	Peak	Trough
1st turning point	1	no	no	no	no	-5
2nd turning point	no	-9	no	-3	-7	-1
3rd turning point	-10	-7	+1	-1	-2	-5
4th turning point	-17	1	-6	0	-1	0
5th turning point	-3	-2	-7	-1	-5	-18
6th turning point	-3	-7	-1	-16	m.s.	-20
7th turning point	-13	-5	-17	+1	-16	f.s.
Average Lead	-7.5	-4.8	-6.0	-6.7	-6.2	-8.2
Number of false signals	1	0	0	0	0	1
Number of missing signals	0	0	0	0	1	0

Notes: "-" denotes leads;
"+" denotes lags ;
"no" denotes no turning point point to be predicted;
"m.s." denotes missing signal; "f.s." denotes false signal.
Source: Artis et al. (1995), OECD Economic Studies, No. 24, Table 5, p. 141.

4.2 Predicting Cyclical Turning Points Using Interest Rate Spreads

Analogous to the procedure in the previous subsection, the interest rate spread's turning points have to be identified in order to access their prediction accuracy. In this subsection, the following simple rule is used.[1] As soon as the interest rate spread changes its sign, this is interpreted as signalling a growth cycle's major turning point. Applying this simple rule to the interest rate spreads' series of Switzerland, the USA and Japan yields a time series consisting of zeros and ones that indicates whether the economy will be in a boom or a recession. In figures 4.2.1 to 4.2.3 these time series are displayed as well as the reference series' growth cycle turning points identified by the OECD.

As can be seen in figures 4.2.1 to 4.2.3 the interest rate spreads are signalling the major cyclical turning points considerably well especially in the case of the USA. However, compared to the composite leading indices provided by the OECD, the interest rate spreads' leads seem to be somewhat shorter. A detailed analysis of the interest rate spreads' prediction accuracy can be found in table 4.2.1 below.

---

[1] Because the Swiss and Japanese interest rate spreads' time series are somewhat shorter than the composite leading indices of Switzerland and Japan, Neftci's procedure is not used in this subsection.

Survey on the Timing of Cyclical Turning Points

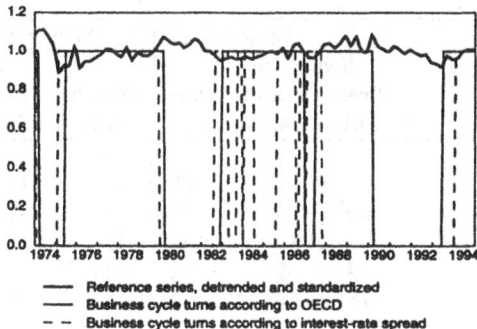

Figure 4.2.1 Interest rate spread as leading indicator, Switzerland

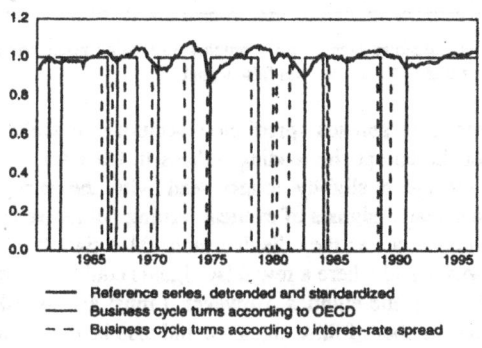

Figure 4.2.2 Interest rate spread as leading indicator, USA

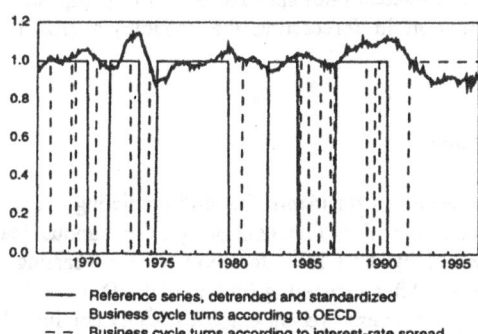

Figure 4.2.3 Interest rate spread as leading indicator, Japan

Table 4.2.1 Turning point prediction using the interest rate spreads

Turning points	Leads (-) and Lags (+) in months		
	Switzerland Peak ; Trough 74.1 - 94.12	USA Peak ; Trough 61.1 - 96.11	Japan Peak ; Trough 67.1 - 96.11
2nd turning point		-5 ; -4	
3rd turning point		-11 ; -6	-11 ; -11
4th turning point	no ; -4	-7 ; -3	-6 ; +6
5th turning point	-2 ; -5	-6 ; -15	+1 ; -21
6th turning point	-5 ; -9	+2 ; +3	+2 ; -13
7th turning point	-15 ; +8	-2 ; -15	-15 ; f.s.
Average Lead	-7.3 ; -2.5	-4.7 ; -6.5	-5.8 ; -9.8
Number of false signals	3 ; 3	1 ; 1	4 ; 4
Number of missing signals	0 ; 0	0 ; 0	0 ; 0

Notes: "-" denotes leads; "+" denotes lags; "no" denotes no turning point point to be predicted; "m.s." denotes missing signal; "f.s." denotes false signal.

Comparing the interest rate spreads' prediction accuracy in table 4.2.1 with the forecasting performance of the composite leading indices in table 4.1.1, it can be stated that the latter have on average a slightly longer lead with the exception of Japan. Moreover, the interest rate spreads' signals of cyclical turning points are less reliable than the composite leading indices' ones as they display more false signals. This can be seen especially in Japan and Switzerland where a few false signals could be detected according to the interest rate spread during the eighties. However it must also be admitted that the interest rate spreads' greater number of false signals could also be due to an inappropriate filtering rule applied to these time series. Using a more sophisticated estimation procedure like the one suggested by Neftci (1982) to detect the interest rate spreads' turning points could well result in a reduction of false signals. Summarising the results in table 4.2.1 and 4.1.1, it can be concluded that interest rates spreads as well as composite leading indices both contain useful information in forecasting the economy's growth cycles' future turning points.

5 Summary and Conclusions

In this paper two popular procedures for identifying and predicting major growth cycles' turning points are discussed. The first one consists of the famous leading indicator approach which is used widely by the OECD for short-term forecasting purposes of its member countries' economies. After explaining how the OECD dates the major cyclical turning points of its member countries, a recent empirical study conducted by Artis et al. (1995) which tests the forecasting performance of these composite leading indices is discussed. Next a leading indicator of economic activity which has become popular only recently is presented. Using the spread between long-term and short-term interest rates for the USA, Japan and Switzerland, it is argued economically that this variable should have predictive power in forecasting future economic activity. Applying a simple rule to these interest rate spreads' time series allows detecting these series' turning points. After having identified this way the leading indicators' major turning points, they can be compared to the OECD growth cycles' turning points of these countries to test the interest rate spreads' forecasting ability. Finally a comparison between the composite leading indices' and the interest rate spreads' predictive performance shows that the leading indices' lead is on average slightly longer. However these results must be interpreted carefully because of the different filtering rules applied to the interest rate spreads and the composite leading indices.

References

Artis M., Bladen-Hovell R. and Zhang W. (1995), Turning points in the international business cycle: An analysis of the OECD leading indicators for the G-7 countries, *OECD Economic Studies*, No. 24, Paris, pp. 125-164.

Estrella A. and Hardouvelis G. (1991), The term structure as a predictor of real economic activity, *Journal of Finance*, 46, pp. 555 - 576.

Hu Z. (1993), The yield curve and real activity, *IMF Staff Papers*, 40, pp. 781 - 806.

Neftci S. (1982), Optimal prediction of cyclical downturns, *Journal of Economic Dynamics and Control*, Vol. 4, pp. 225 - 241.

Nilsson R. (1987), OECD leading indicators, *OECD Economic Studies*, No. 9, Paris, pp. 105 - 146.

Vaccara B. and Zarnowitz V. (1977), How good are the leading indicators?, Proceedings of the Business and Economic Statistics Section, *American Statistical Association*, pp. 41 - 50.

Part III
Firm Behaviour

9 Inflation and Asymmetric Output Adjustments: Tests Using Business Survey Data

Robert A. Buckle / John A. Carlson

Abstract

Using a unique micro data set, we find evidence of output asymmetry that is systematically related to inflation and to price asymmetry. Ordered probit estimates of output and price changes by firms show that output and prices respond asymmetrically to demand shocks. At high inflation there is a greater probability of a fall in output in response to negative demand shocks than a rise in output in response to positive demand shocks. Conversely, at high inflation there is a greater probability of a rise in prices in response to positive shocks than a fall in prices in response to negative shocks. As inflation falls, both output and price asymmetry in response to demand shocks become less pronounced. Strong evidence of price asymmetry in response to cost shocks, however, is not matched by a significant asymmetric output response to cost shocks.

1 Introduction

Recent empirical research has rejuvenated interest in the idea that output responds asymmetrically to monetary shocks. Cover (1988) found that in the USA during the post-WWII period positive shocks to the money supply had no effect on output, whereas negative shocks reduced output. His results have been corroborated by De Long and Summers (1988) and Morgan (1993) using different time periods and measures of monetary shocks, and results from Karras (1996a, 1996b) suggest output asymmetry may be an international phenomenon.

The reasons for output asymmetry remain unclear. They may be due to asymmetries anywhere in the transmission of monetary shocks to output. Asymmetric price adjustment by firms is one possible explanation, but to date the evidence concerning price asymmetry has been mixed. Using data from 38 countries, Karras (1996b) finds no evidence of price asymmetry in response to money supply shocks, whereas studies of the effect on inflation of aggregate output gaps by Laxton, Meredith and Rose (1995) and Turner (1995) imply that money supply shocks are more inflationary as an economy approaches full capacity and less inflationary when an economy approaches low capacity.

The aim of this paper is to test whether output responds asymmetrically to shocks and to evaluate the role of firm pricing behavior. Our approach is different from previous studies in several respects. We use micro-level firm data, evaluate both output and price asymmetry for a common sample of firms, and we evaluate the influence of inflation. The only previous empirical work examining the influence of inflation on output asymmetry is Rhee and Rich (1995) who find the asymmetric relationship between monetary shocks and aggregate output revealed by Cover is influenced by inflation.

We use individual firm data, obtained by a survey of New Zealand manufacturing firms, to estimate a model of output and price change based on a theoretical model of price and output asymmetry developed by Ball and Mankiw (1994). They consider a model in which firms make regularly scheduled price changes and, by paying a menu cost, can also make special adjustments in response to shocks to desired price. The presence of menu costs of price adjustment implies a zone of no-price-change over which shocks to desired price will not result in a change to actual price. Inflation affects the opportunity cost of not changing price and therefore the position of this zone of no-price-change. Asymmetries in the response of prices to shocks therefore arise naturally when there is positive trend inflation and are predicted to be more pronounced at higher rates of inflation.

Ball and Mankiw suggest that a corollary of price asymmetry is output asymmetry. At high inflation prices are predicted to be more responsive to positive shocks than to negative shocks and output more responsive to negative shocks than to positive shocks. As inflation falls these asymmetries are predicted to become less pronounced.

We evaluate output and price asymmetry and the influence of inflation in two ways. Firstly, we estimate the zone of no-price-change and the zone of no-output-change and evaluate how inflation affects the position of these zones. Secondly, we evaluate how the response of prices and output to positive and to negative cost and demand shocks vary with inflation.

We find evidence of output asymmetry and price asymmetry which are systematically related to inflation. Furthermore, in respect of demand shocks, the relative behavior of output and prices is consistent with price asymmetry being an explanation for output asymmetry. However, we also find strong evidence of price asymmetry in response to cost shocks which is not matched by an asymmetric output response to cost shocks.

The remainder of the paper is structured as follows. The second section explains why firm prices and output may respond asymmetrically to shocks and the potential role of inflation in this process. The third section explains the survey data used to test for asymmetry. These tests are based on models of price and output change which were estimated by ordered probit for different inflation regimes. The inflation regimes are also explained in the third section. The fourth section of the paper describes the way we have arranged the survey data, the estimation procedure and the results. The final section presents concluding remarks.

2 A 'Menu-cost' Explanation for Price and Output Asymmetries

Theoretical explanations for asymmetric price adjustment have been developed by Caballero and Engel (1992), Tsiddon (1993), and Ball and Mankiw (1994) who have followed the menu cost approach to modeling price setting by optimizing firms. A feature of their approach is that if it is costly to change price, firms will delay changes until the private benefits outweigh the private costs. If there is general inflation, a firm's real price will automatically fall thereby possibly offsetting a need to lower its nominal price.

The model of price adjustment developed by Ball and Mankiw neatly illustrates this process and suggests why price asymmetry may induce output asymmetry. Their model combines elements of time-contingent pricing, where a firm adjusts prices on a regular time schedule, and state-contingent pricing, where a firm has the option of changing prices whenever economic circumstances warrant a change. If mid-way between regular price changes shocks are large enough, the firm will pay a menu cost and make an additional price change.

Given the rate of general inflation π and a distribution of shocks θ to firms' desired relative price, Ball and Mankiw derive a range for the shocks in which firms will not incur the costs of making an interim price change. Below a lower bound for θ a firm will lower price and above an upper bound a firm will raise price. With zero inflation, this range of inaction is symmetric around zero. With positive inflation, the range shifts so that a higher proportion of firms will incur the menu cost to raise price than will do so to lower price.

Output asymmetry arises as a consequence of price asymmetry. Since the probability of a price rise in response to a positive shock to desired price is greater during high inflation, it follows that during high inflation firms are less likely to raise output in response to positive demand shocks than during low inflation. Similarly, since the probability of a price fall in response to a negative shock is smaller during high inflation, firms are more likely to lower output in response to negative demand shocks during high inflation than during low inflation. As with price asymmetry, output asymmetry is predicted to disappear as inflation approaches zero.

Firms' decisions to change price and output are typically summarized by economists as being influenced by changes in demand or by changes in costs. It is appropriate therefore that we consider the response of prices and output to both cost and demand shocks and evaluate how inflation influences firm reactions to both types of shocks.

3 Survey Data and Inflation Regimes

3.1 Survey Data

The data used to evaluate output and price asymmetry are all categorical consisting of trichotomous responses by New Zealand firms to a survey questionnaire. The individual firm responses are collected by the *Quarterly Survey of Business Opinion* (QSBO) which is managed by the New Zealand Institute of Economic Research (NZIER). The QSBO is similar in style to the 'Business Test' of the IFO Institute für Wirtschaftsforschung, Munich, and there are many other business surveys of this type around the world (see Köhler, 1995).

For many surveys of this type the aggregate proportions of firms reporting for instance increased output, unchanged output, and decreased output, are typically the only data that are available. There are however important features of the NZIER survey which set it apart from most others. The NZIER stores the responses to all questions from every respondent firm and, apart from gradual attrition and increases in the sample in 1986:1

and in 1991:4, the sample of firms surveyed remains the same in each quarter, although not all firms respond in every quarter. The survey also asks firms about the change in their costs which many other surveys do not. Previous studies that have exploited these features to examine firm output and price behavior include Buckle and Meads (1991) and Buckle and Carlson (1996).

These features mean that we can match firm responses to the questions about output and price change with their responses to questions about costs and demand. Moreover, the idea that the probability that increases and decreases in output and prices will vary systematically with inflation can be readily analyzed because we can distinguish between firms that reported increased, decreased, or unchanged output, prices, costs and demand in each quarter. Individual firm data also provide many more observations than would aggregate proportions data.

The NZIER survey involves the distribution to business executives of a standard questionnaire that identifies the firm, its principal activity, location and size, contains a series of questions asking about the firm's operating environment, and a standard question asking executives to report their perceptions of the actual change during the immediate past three months and expected change in the next three months (by reporting 'Up' or 'Same' or 'Down' or 'N/A') for several activity variables.

This paper utilizes responses by manufacturing firms (including builders) to the following questions which have been unchanged throughout the entire sample period and for which individual firm responses are available in every quarter since 1963:3:

"What has been your experience during the past three months in respect of the following":

	1	2	3	4
	Up	Same	Down	N/A
Output				
Average selling prices				
Average costs				
All new orders received				

3.2 Inflation Regimes

New Zealand's annual rate of consumer price (CPI) inflation since 1963 is plotted, at quarterly intervals, in Figure 1. Superimposed on Figure 1 are 10 inflation regimes we selected. Also shown on Figure 1 is the annual rate of underlying inflation which has been the target of monetary policy since the inception of the Reserve Bank of New Zealand Act 1989. Estimates of annual underlying inflation are only available from 1989:4.

The 10 inflation regimes were selected on the basis of New Zealand's annual inflation rate (measured by the percentage change in the price index for quarter t compared to the index for quarter t-4), the timing of the application of a wide-spread set of price and wage controls from 1982 to 1984, the timing of subsequent widespread market deregulation (see Evans, et al, 1996), and the period during which the inflation rate was maintained within the Reserve Bank of New Zealand's target range of 0 to 2 %[1].

4 Ordered Probit Analysis of Firm Output and Price Changes

The responses to the NZIER survey questions are coded as 1 for Up, 2 for Same, and 3 for Down. Occasionally there are missing responses or, for some reason, a firm marks 4 for Not Applicable. All firms with responses other than 1, 2 or 3 were dropped from our sample. We then rescaled the variables by subtracting 2 from every observation and multiplying by -1 so that the variables used in the estimation had the value +1 for Up, 0 for Same and -1 for Down.

To estimate the influence of cost and demand changes on output and price, we chose to use ordered probit regressions (see Carlson and Dunkelburg, 1989, for an example of the application of the ordered probit procedure to business survey data of the type analyzed in this paper). The problem with standard regression procedures, such as ordinary least squares, when dealing with qualitative categories is that one has to assign an arbitrary quantitative value to each category. With ordered probit, this is not an issue. The idea is to maximize the likelihood of observing the actual pattern of responses in each category without regard to its quantitative value.

Let θ_j denote the desired price or output change for firm j and let $x_{1j}, x_{2j}, ... x_{mj}$, be a vector of explanatory variables for firm j. Define

$$\theta_j = b_1 x_{1j} + b_2 x_{2j} + ... + b_m x_{mj} + u_j \qquad (1)$$

where u_j is a standard normal variable. If there are three different ordered outcomes (up, same, down), ordered probit will estimate $b_1, b_2, ..., b_m$ plus two parameters, k_1 and k_2, such that for the following probabilities

Pr(firm j reports up) = Pr ($\theta_j > k_1$)
Pr(firm j reports same) = Pr ($k_1 > \theta_j > k_2$)
Pr(firm j reports down) = Pr ($\theta_j < k_2$)

the parameters chosen will maximize the likelihood of the observed sample over $j = 1, 2, ..., n$ firms (see Greene, 1993 and Stata Corporation, 1995).

4.1 Price Asymmetry and Inflation

For the price change model estimated in this paper, the category in which θ_j falls indicates the predicted change in firm $j's$ own selling price while the $x's$ denote the increases and decreases in costs and demand. The estimated values for k_1 and k_2 determine the size and position of the zone of no-price-change. The model is specified as:

---

[1] More detailed discussion of the features of each regime is contained in Buckle and Carlson (1996).

$$\theta_{jt} = b_1 cup_{jt} + b_2 cdn_{jt} + b_3 dup_{jt} + b_4 ddn_{jt} + u_{jt} \tag{2}$$

where cup_{jt} = cost increase (1 if costs up, 0 otherwise), cdn_{jt} = cost decrease (-1 if costs down, 0 otherwise), dup_{jt} = demand increase, ddn_{jt} = demand decrease, experienced by firm j in quarter t. The expected signs for the coefficients of the price change model are $b_1, b_2, b_3, b_4 > 0$.

The results of the ordered probit estimation for price changes are summarized in Table 1, which contains five panels. The first panel identifies the inflation regime. The second panel shows the number of observations used in the ordered probit estimation and the average annual inflation rate for that regime. The third and fourth panels contain estimates of the coefficients on increases and decreases in costs and on increases and decreases in demand respectively. They also show the estimated chi-square statistic derived to test for equality of the coefficients on cup and cdn and on dup and ddn under the null hypothesis that cup=cdn and dup=ddn, respectively. The fifth panel shows the estimated values for k_1 and k_2 and $(k_1 + k_2)$ which is a convenient way to illustrate whether these cut points are symmetrically distributed, i.e. the same for positive and for negative shocks.

Table 1 therefore contains two types of information that enable us to evaluate the relationship between price asymmetry and the influence of inflation: (i) the relationship between the estimated coefficients on increases and decreases in costs and on increases and decreases in demand across inflation regimes, and (ii) the behavior of the estimated cut points and zone of no-price-change across inflation regimes.

Pervasive evidence of price asymmetry with respect to changes in costs can be seen in the third panel of Table 1. The coefficient on cost increases (cup) is always larger than the coefficient on cost decreases (cdn). Moreover, the difference between the coefficients on cost increases and cost decreases (cp-cdn) tends to be larger at higher rates of inflation. The estimated chi-squared statistic under the null hypothesis of equal coefficients is largest in the highest inflation regimes 4, 5 and 7 and smallest in the lowest inflation regimes 1, 9 and 10. Figure 2 shows a plot of the association between general inflation and (cup-cdn). There is a clear upward slope which is statistically significant.

The fourth panel of Table 1 reports estimates of price responses to demand changes and Figure 2 also shows how the difference between the coefficients on demand increases and demand decreases, (dup-ddn), changes as inflation increases. Once again, there is a clear positive association between general inflation and this difference. Although the relationship is not as strong as it is for (cup-cdn), it is nevertheless statistically significant.

Two features of the coefficients on the demand variables in the price regressions call for further discussion. One is the fact that demand coefficients, while significant, tend to be smaller than the cost coefficients. This should not be interpreted as evidence that firms are more likely to make price changes in response to cost changes than they are in response to demand changes. The reason is that new orders, which we have used as a proxy for demand in the price regressions, appear to reflect real demand changes rather than nominal demand changes. The distribution of changes in new orders is not markedly different in low inflation than in high inflation periods. It generally reflects the phase of the business cycle. As a result in high inflation periods, when nominal demand would be expected to be shifting up and contributing to higher desired price for a large proportion of firms, the demand coefficient in our regressions will understate the influences of demand. Perhaps what is surprising is that the demand coefficients tend to be as significant as they are.

Another feature of the demand coefficients is somewhat more puzzling. At low levels of inflation, firms appear more likely to lower price when new orders are down than they are to raise prices when new orders are up. We had not anticipated this result. One explanation for this phenomenon is consistent with Okun's (1981) hypothesis about customer markets. When demand is up, a cut in orders from existing customers in response to what they view as an unwarranted increase in price may offset the increase in demand. When demand is down, a cut in price may not immediately generate enough new orders to offset the decrease in demand.

The estimated cut point parameters, k_1 and k_2, correspond respectively to the upper and lower bounds of the zone of no-price-change, given the coefficients on the cost and demand variables. Other things equal, lower values of k_1 and k_2 imply that a larger proportion of firms will raise price and a smaller proportion will lower price. We therefore anticipate that the location of these cut points will tend to be lower with a higher general rate of inflation.

The estimated cut points for each inflation regime are shown in the fifth panel of Table 1. The value of k_1 is much closer to the absolute value of k_2 during the lower inflation regimes 1, 2, 3, 6, 8, 9 and 10 than during the higher inflation regimes 4, 5 and 7. This tends to be due to lower values of k_1 during the higher inflation regimes, so that not surprisingly firms are more likely, *ceteris paribus*, to raise price when general inflation is higher.

The relationship between inflation and the mid-point of the zone of no-price-change, measured by $(k_1 + k_2)$, is depicted in the top panel of Figure 3. As can be seen, there is a strong negative relationship between inflation and the mid-point of the no-price-change zone.

4.2 Output Asymmetry and Inflation

One implication of price asymmetry is output asymmetry which is also postulated to be systematically related to inflation. The probability of a price rise in response to a positive shock to desired price is greater during high inflation and, as a consequence, during high inflation firms are less likely to raise output in response to positive demand shocks than during low inflation. Similarly, because the probability of a price fall in response to a negative shock is smaller during high inflation, firms are more likely to lower output in response to negative demand shocks during high inflation than during low inflation.

The primary explanatory variable for a firm's change in output is its change in new orders. However, as we noted in the last section, changes in new orders imperfectly reflect changes in demand, as economists normally view demand. It is possible with use of price change data to modify our demand variable to more closely reflect changes in nominal demand.

If a firm has raised price and reports that new orders are unchanged, the chances are that demand has increased. This is because, with demand a downward sloping function of price, an increase in price should result in a decrease in quantity demanded. If the rate of new orders has not changed, then we may infer that nominal demand has shifted out.

Therefore, for firms which simultaneously reported prices 'Up' and new orders 'Same', we reclassified those observations as demand 'dup' to represent a rise in nominal demand. By a similar logic, for firms that simultaneously reported prices 'Down' and new orders 'Same', we reclassified their demand response as 'ddn' to represent a fall in nominal demand.

We then estimated expression (2) using the modified measures of dup and ddn and using reported changes in output as the dependent variable. The expected coefficients in this output change model are $b_1, b_2 < 0$ (higher costs are expected to lower output, and lower costs to raise output) and $b_3, b_4 > 0$ (higher demand is expected to raise output, and lower demand to lower output).

Although the coefficients on increases and decreases in costs are always significant, as can be seen in the third panel of Table 2, there is little asymmetry in the output response to cost shocks. The coefficient on cost decreases (cdn) is larger than the coefficient on cost increases (cdn) in eight of the ten regimes and this is consistent with the finding that prices are more responsive to cost increases than to cost decreases. But only in regime 4 is this difference statistically significant. In contrast to prices, we find no evidence of significant asymmetry in the response of output to cost shocks and therefore no evidence that inflation affects the relative response of output to cost increases and cost decreases.

There is evidence however of significant asymmetry in the way output responds to demand shocks. Moreover, this asymmetry is systematically related to inflation. The fourth panel of Table 2 reports estimates of output responses to demand changes and Figure 4 shows how the difference between the coefficients on demand increases and demand decreases, (dup-ddn), changes as inflation increases. There is a clear negative and statistically significant association between general inflation and this difference. The negative association between inflation and (dup-ddn) is consistent with the hypothesis that if, as we have found, inflation induces asymmetry in the way prices react to positive and negative demand shocks, a consequence will be asymmetry in the way output responds to positive and negative demand shocks.

The estimated cut point parameters, k_1 and k_2, and the mid-point of the zone for no-output-change, measured by $(k_1 + k_2)$, are shown in the fifth panel of Table 2. In contrast to the situation for prices, the cut points for output do not appear to vary noticeably across inflation regimes. As can be seen in Figure 3, there is not a significant relationship between inflation and the mid-point of the no-output-change zone. It would appear that, after accounting for the impact of reported demand and cost changes, not much else systematically affects changes in output at different rates of inflation.

5 Conclusions

A significant body of recent research has shown that aggregate real output responds asymmetrically to monetary shocks. In a departure from previous procedures used to evaluate output asymmetry, we use micro-level firm data and investigate price asymmetry as a possible explanation for output asymmetry.

We find strong evidence of price asymmetry in response to cost shocks but this is not matched by an asymmetric output response to cost shocks.

For demand shocks, however, we do find clear evidence of both output and price asymmetry systematically related to inflation. At high inflation there is a greater probability of a fall in output in response to negative demand shocks than a rise in output in response to positive demand shocks. Conversely, at high inflation there is a greater probability of a rise in prices in response to positive shocks than a fall in prices in response to negative shocks. As inflation falls, both output and price asymmetry become less pronounced.

We are grateful to Wonchang Jang and Dobrimir Bojilov for excellent research assistance and to the NZ Institute of Economic Research for providing the survey data.

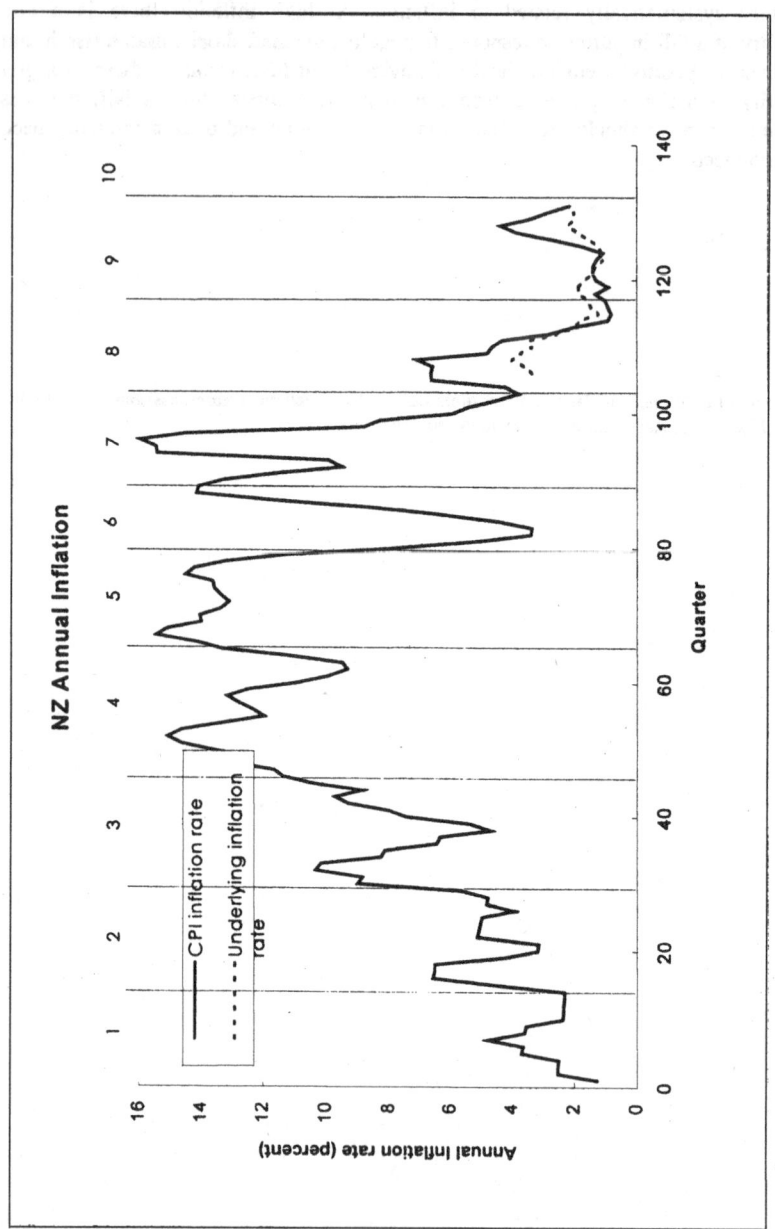

Figure 1 NZ inflation regimes

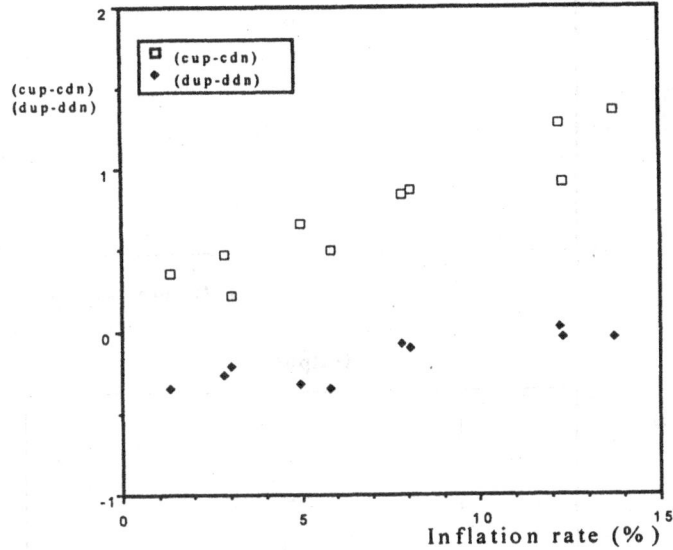

Prices:	$(cup - cdn)_t =$	0.17	+	0.08* $Inflation_t$	$\bar{R}^2 = .85$
		(1.85)		(7.33)	
	$(dup - ddn)_t =$	-0.38*	+	0.03* $Inflation_t$	$\bar{R}^2 = .71$
		(-7.78)		(4.82)	

* denotes significantly different from zero at 5% level; t statistics in parenthesis.

Figure 2 Inflation and differences between coefficients on cost and demand increases and decreases: prices

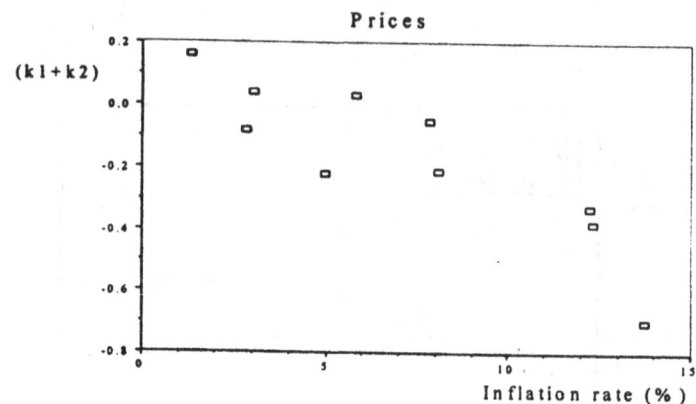

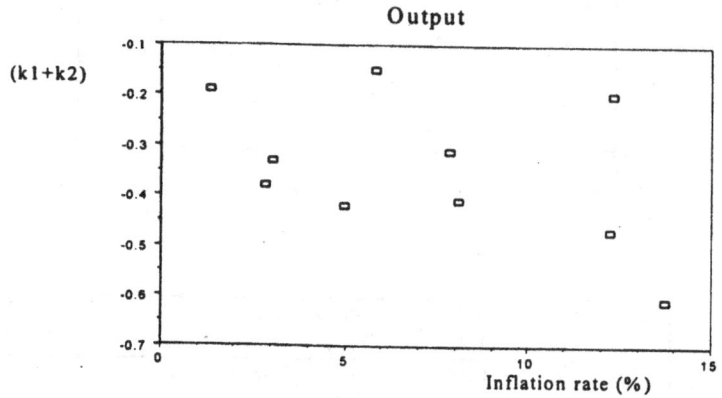

Prices:	$(k_1 + k_2)_t = 0.19^* - 0.05^*$ *Inflation$_t$*	$\bar{R}^2 = .73$
	(2.25) (-5.01)	
Output:	$(k_1 + k_2)_t = -0.24^* - 0.02$ *Inflation$_t$*	$\bar{R}^2 = .11$
	(-2.83) (-1.46)	

* denotes significantly different from zero at 5% level; t statistics in parenthesis.

Figure 3 Inflation and the zones of no-change in prices and output

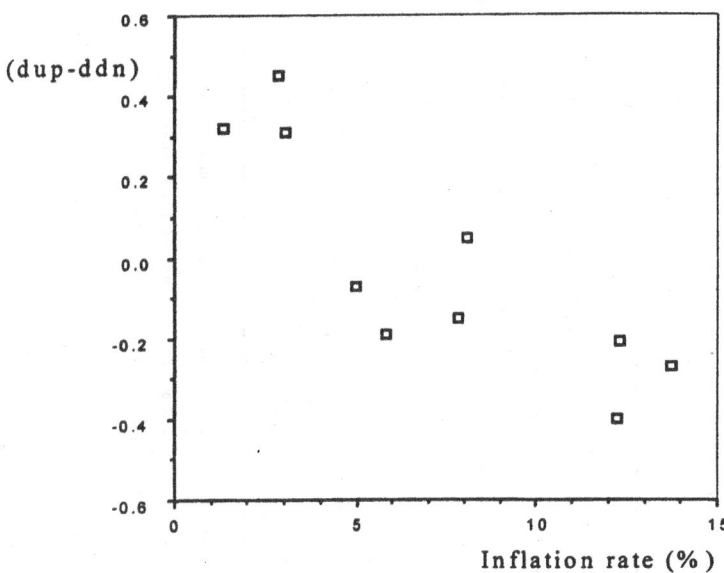

Output:	$(dup - ddn)_t =$ 0.39* - 0.06* $Inflation_t$ (3.80) (-4.56)	$\bar{R}^2 = .68$

* denotes significantly different from zero at 5% level; t statistics in parenthesis

Figure 4   **Inflation and Differences between Coefficients on Demand Increases and Decreases: Output**

Table 1 Ordered probit estimation of price changes

Inflation Regime	Number of Observations	Average annual inflation (%)	cup	cdn	χ_1^2	dup	ddn	χ_1^2	k1	k2	k1 + k2
1	2806	2.85	1.14*	.66*	19.56*	.07	.34*	6.17*	1.24	-1.32	-.08
2	3577	4.96	1.08*	.41*	35.10*	.14*	.46*	12.41*	1.09	-1.31	-.22*
3	3291	8.07	1.11*	.23	21.46*	.10*	.20*	1.14	1.14	-1.35	-.21
4	4062	12.26	1.16*	-.12	55.63*	.14*	.12*	0.11	.74	-1.07	-.33*
5	2519	13.74	1.15*	-.22	41.04*	.16*	.20*	0.15	.47	-1.17	-.70*
6	1433	7.86	.68*	-.17	20.46*	.22*	.30*	0.33	1.14	-1.19	-.05
7	2960	12.34	.96*	.04	54.10*	.24*	.28*	0.15	.63	-1.01	-.38*
8	3135	5.84	.70*	.20*	29.95*	.13*	.48*	15.69*	.88	-.85	.03
9	3375	1.33	.55*	.19*	18.83*	.10*	.45*	16.15*	1.04	-.88	.16*
10	1670	3.02	.57*	.35*	3.35	.11	.32*	3.16	.96	-.92	.04

Notes: n= number of observations; cup=coefficient on cost increase; cdn=coefficient on cost decrease; dup=coefficient on demand increase; ddn=coefficient on demand decrease; k1=cut1; k2=cut2; χ_1^2 =value of chi-square statistic evaluating (cup-cdn) and (dup-ddn) under the null hypothesis cup=cdn and dup=ddn, respectively. * significantly different from zero at 5% level.

Table 2 Ordered probit estimation of output changes

Inflation Regime	Number of Observations	Average annual inflation (%)	cup	cdn	χ_1^2	dup	ddn	χ_1^2	k1	k2	k1 + k2
1	2793	2.85	-.42*	-.59*	2.16	1.28*	.83*	17.09*	.54	-.92	-.38*
2	3552	4.96	-.32*	-.35*	.06	1.17*	1.24*	.40	.53	-.95	-.42*
3	3259	8.07	-.17*	-.53*	3.08	1.01*	.96*	.21	.49	-.90	-.41*
4	4040	12.26	-.17*	-.55*	4.08*	.68*	1.08*	13.46*	.44	-.91	-.47*
5	2509	13.74	-.37*	-.35	.01	.86*	1.13*	3.08	.42	-1.03	-.61*
6	1427	7.86	-.16*	-.59*	3.53	1.12*	1.27*	.90	.56	-.87	-.31*
7	2943	12.34	-.20*	-.22*	.02	.89*	1.10*	3.17	.57	-.77	-.20
8	3116	5.84	-.21*	-.33*	1.31	1.06*	1.25*	3.32	.69	-.84	-.15
9	3346	1.33	-.24*	-.24*	.01	1.44*	1.12*	11.09*	.70	-.89	-.19*
10	1668	3.02	-.24*	-.33*	.92	1.29*	.98*	5.73*	.68	-1.01	-.33*

Notes: n= number of observations; cup=coefficient on cost increase; cdn=coefficient on cost decrease; dup=coefficient on demand increase; ddn=coefficient on demand decrease; k1=cut1; k2=cut2; χ_1^2 =value of chi-square statistic evaluating (cup-cdn) and (dup-ddn) under the null hypothesis cup=cdn and dup=ddn, respectively. *significantly different from zero at 5% level.

References

Ball, L. and Mankiw, N.G. (1994), Asymmetric price adjustment and economic fluctuations, *The Economic Journal*, March, 104, pp. 247 - 261.

Buckle, R.A. and Meads, C.S. (1991), How do firms react to surprising changes to demand? A vector autoregressive analysis using business survey data, *Oxford Bulletin of Economics and Statistics*, 53, November, pp. 451-466.

Buckle, R.A. and Carlson, J.A. (1996), Inflation and asymmetric price adjustment, Victoria University of Wellington Graduate School of Business and Government Administration Working Paper 12/96, Wellington, p. 27.

Caballero, R.J. and Engel, E.M.R.A. (1992), Price rigidities, asymmetries, and output fluctuations, National Bureau of Economic Research Working Paper No. 4091, Cambridge, June, p. 28.

Carlson, J.A. and Dunkelburg, W.C. (1989), Market perceptions and inventory-price-employment plans, *The Review of Economics and Statistics*, 71, May, pp. 318-24.

Cover, J.P. (1988), Asymmetric effects of positive and negative money-supply shocks, University of Alabama, subsequently published in *The Quarterly Journal of Economics*, 107, November, 1992, pp 1261 - 1282.

De Long, J.B. and Summers, L.H. (1988), How does macroeconomic policy affect output?, *Brookings Papers on Economic Activity*, No. 2, pp. 433 - 480.

Evans, L., Grimes, A. and Wilkinson, B. with David Teece (1996), Economic Reform in New Zealand 1984 - 95: The Pursuit of Efficiency, *Journal of Economic Literature*, 34, December, pp. 1856 - 1902.

Greene, W.H. (1993), *Econometric Analysis*, Second edition, New York, MacMillan, p. 791.

Karras, G. (1996a), Are the output effects of monetary policy asymmetric? Evidence from a sample of European countries, *Oxford Bulletin of Economics and Statistics*, 58, No. 2, pp. 267 - 278.

Karras, G. (1996b), Why are the effects of money-supply shocks asymmetric? Convex aggregate supply or 'Pushing-on-a-string'?, *Journal of Macroeconomics*, 18, Fall, No. 4, pp. 605 - 609.

Köhler, A.G. (1995), CIRET International Synoptic Table, Chapter 1.2 in Robert Fildes (ed), *World Index of Economic Forecasts*, Aldershot, Gower, pp 22 - 52.

Laxton, D., Meredith, G. and Rose, D. (1995), Asymmetric effects of economic activity on inflation: evidence and policy implications, *IMF Staff Papers*, 42, No. 2, pp. 344 - 374.

Morgan, D.P. (1993), Asymmetric effects of monetary policy, Federal Reserve Bank of Kansas City *Economic Review*, 78, Second Quarter, pp. 21 - 33.

Okun, A.M. (1981), *Prices and Quantities*, Oxford, Basil Blackwell, p. 367.

Rhee, W. and Rich, R.W. (1995), Inflation and the asymmetric effects of money on output fluctuations, *Journal of Macroeconomics*, 17, Fall, No. 4, pp. 683 - 702.

Stata Corporation (1995), *Stata Statistical Software: Release 4.0*, College Station, Texas.

Tsiddon, D. (1993), The (mis)behavior of the price level, *Review of Economic Studies*, 60, pp. 889 - 902.

Turner, D. (1995), Speed limit and asymmetric effects from the output gap in the major seven countries, *OECD Economic Studies*, 24, No. 1, pp. 57 - 87.

10 Production and Price Flexibility with Stock Adjustment: South African Evidence from Survey Data

Daniël Marais / Eon Smit / Willie J. Conradie

1 Production Smoothing

The production smoothing model incorporating stocks of finished goods and backlogs of unfilled orders has long been the paradigm within which empirical research on stocks and unfilled orders have been conducted. The basic hypothesis embedded in the model is that stocks of finished goods primarily serve to smooth production levels when the firm experiences fluctuating demand and convex cost functions. This is commonly known as the linear-quadratic stock model that was introduced by Holt et al. (1960). Blinder (1981, 1982) introduced the linear-quadratic functions (proposed by Holt et al.) for demand, cost of production and production change, as well as cost of holding stocks into his model which assumes that a firm will optimise net revenue. The conditions under which the optimisation results are obtained from this model are actually considered to be rather weak (see König and Seitz (1991)). Yet, empirical research has since presented evidence that is in sharp contrast to the theoretical model. The production smoothing hypothesis emerging from this model is contradicted in three respects:

1. Variance of production exceeds the variance of sales in most 2-digit industries,
2. Changes in sales and stocks are positively correlated, and
3. Estimated adjustment speeds of partial stock adjustment models turn out to be extremely low.

The partial stock adjustment models are modifications to the traditional linear-quadratic model. They generally allow for an "accelerator" target stock level which supposedly arises from the fact that it is costly for firms to allow stocks to deviate from some fraction of actual or expected sales (see Blanchard (1983), Eichenbaum (1984), West (1986), and Blinder and Maccini (1991)). The manufacturer is presumably keen to adjust stocks back to the "desired" level.

Production smoothing by holding stocks is still a debatable issue. Most of the contributions mentioned above relied on aggregated data analyses to evaluate the particular hypotheses developed from the traditional linear quadratic model in the form presented by Blinder (1981). Blanchard (1983) demonstrated that useful results could be obtained by considering individual industries instead of aggregated data when he relied on data pertaining to the American automobile industry for his evaluation of stock behaviour.

Krane and Braun (1991) followed suit by using disaggregated data from a number of 2-digit industries, and focused on physical products data instead of the dollar-value data. Since the traditional Blinder model was developed as a description of individual firms' decision making and stock behaviour, one would prefer to test the hypotheses on individual firm data. Such data is available in the form of qualitative responses to survey questions, such as that of the Bureau for Economic Research (BER) in South Africa. Some authors did exploit this rich source of information to evaluate their own particular versions of the Blinder model. The first attempt was probably made by Kawasaki et al. (1983), followed by Ottenwaelter and Vuong (1984), König and Seitz (1991), Nerlove et al. (1993), and Etter (1993). In this study the South African situation is explored by utilising the BER survey data and the log-linear model analysis technique. In order to set up the model so that it will be testable on qualitative survey data, the approach of König and Seitz (1991) has been adopted.

The theoretical model of a monopolistic firm which carries stock of finished goods and backlogs of unfilled orders will be developed in Section 2. In Section 3 empirical testing of the model will be discussed and the results, obtained from the log-linear analysis, will be presented. Section 4 contains a summary and brief interpretation of the empirical observations. Finally, the economic implications of the observations will be presented in Section 5.

2 Theoretical Model of the Optimising Firm

A brief outline of a theoretical model of a monopolistic manufacturer carrying stocks of finished goods and unfilled orders will be developed. The main objective is to explore the short-term adjustment behaviour of the manufacturer to cost and demand shocks. In order to permit derivation of an explicit solution, a parametric model is specified as proposed by Carlson (1986) and Blinder (1986).

The manufacturer is assumed to be a value-maximising monopolist. Blinder (1982) demonstrated that the implications of his derived model may also be applicable to a competitive industry but not to a competitive manufacturer, since the latter is a price taker rather than a price setter). The hypothetical monopolistic firm knows its stationary demand curve and, for each period, must select its price and production level before observing its demand shock for that particular period. It does, however, form (rational) expectations of demand shocks. The firm's objective is to select prices, production (output) and stock holding strategy to maximise the expected present value of future profits. The objective may be summarised in the following expression:

$$J'_t = \max E_0 \sum_{t=0}^{\infty} \rho^t [R(X_t, \eta_t) - C(Q_t) - B(N_t)] \tag{1}$$

where E denotes the expected value with information at period 0, and ρ is a discount factor which may be expressed in a more familiar way as $\rho = 1/(1+\rho)$, such that $|\rho| < 1$. $R(X_t, \eta_t)$ denotes the revenue function, $C(Q_t)$ the production cost function, and $B(N_t)$ the cost of carrying stocks of finished goods and unfilled orders. N_t denotes the difference between the number of stock items and unfilled orders and is often referred to as the net stock level. The stochastic term, η_t, to sales, X_t, in the revenue function is discussed in the next section.

2.1 Demand Function

The monopolistic manufacturer is assumed to be facing a linear downward sloping demand curve. The demand curve is assumed linear so that the revenue curve will be quadratic. Linearity would be an approximation over a limited region of any demand curve, which is in line with the approach by Holt et al. (1960). Therefore, the demand curve (with additive stochastic demand shock) is expressed as:

$$X_t = 2(d_0 - dP_t + \eta_t) \qquad (2)$$

where X_t denotes the sales in period t, P_t is the price per unit of its product, d is a positive constant indicating the magnitude of the slope, and η_t is a random demand element, assumed to follow a first order autoregressive process (AR(1)) such that:

$$\eta_t = \omega_d \eta_{t-1} + \varepsilon_t \qquad (3)$$

with $|w_d| \leq 1$ and ε_t is white noise, such that $E[\varepsilon_t] = 0 \ \forall \ t$ and $E[\varepsilon_t \varepsilon_s] = 0 \ \forall \ s \neq t$.

The factor 2 is included in (2) to make d the reciprocal of the slope of the marginal revenue curve, which is determined by partial derivative of total revenue, $P_t X_t$.

Combining the stochastic demand element and the constant, d_0, in (2) yields:

$$X_t = 2d(D_t - P_t) \qquad (4)$$

where D_t now denotes the stochastic demand element.

Expression (4) may be written in expectation format as:

$$X_{t|t+i} = 2d(D_{t|t+i} - P_{t|t+i}) \qquad (5)$$

The revenue function is obtained from the demand function by simply multiplying the expected demand, $X_{t|t+i}$, by the expected price, $P_{t|t+i}$. Thus, a quadratic function in $P_{t|t+i}$ is obtained.

$$X_{t|t+i} P_{t|t+i} = 2d(D_{t|t+i} P_{t|t+i} - P_{t|t+i}^2) \qquad (5a)$$

Expressions (5) and (5a) will be the forms of the demand and revenue functions referred to later in the development of the optimising model.

The marginal revenue function is derived as follows:

$$MR_{t|t+i} = \frac{\partial(XP)_{t|t+i}}{\partial P_{t|t+i}} = 2d(D_{t|t+i} - 2P_{t|t+i}) \qquad (5b)$$

Note that the slope of the marginal revenue curve is twice as steep as that of the demand function.

2.2 Production Cost Function

Similar to the revenue function, the production cost function is also assumed to be quadratic:

$$C(Q_t) = c_0 + c_1 Q_t + \frac{c}{2} Q_t^2 + \frac{\alpha}{2}(Q_t - Q_{t-1})^2 + \mu_t Q_t \tag{6}$$

where Q_t denotes the volume of production in period t, α is the cost associated with the change in production rate (e.g. adjusting resource application), and c_0, c_1 and c are constant cost factors related to the current production rate. Allowing for Ramey's (1991) argument regarding convex and non-convex costs, c_0 and α are assumed to have positive values while c and c_1 may be positive or negative. The random cost element, μ_t, is assumed to follow a first order autoregressive process (AR(1)) such that:

$$\mu_t = \omega_e \mu_{t-1} + \varepsilon_t \tag{7}$$

with $|w_e| \leq 1$ and ε_t is a white noise term, such that $E[\varepsilon_t] = 0 \; \forall \; t$ and $E[\varepsilon_t \varepsilon_s] = 0 \; \forall \; s \neq t$.

The stochastic cost element may be combined with the linear cost term to yield:

$$C(Q_t) = c_0 + C_t Q_t + \frac{c}{2} Q_t^2 + \frac{\alpha}{2}(Q_t - Q_{t-1})^2 \tag{8}$$

Unlike Blinder (1982) C_t is not assumed constant in this case. Since the BER questionnaire features four cost related questions, stochastic cost shocks may be incorporated in the model, i.e. the impact of cost shocks are testable in this study.

Expressed in expectation format, (8) may be written as:

$$C(Q_{t|t+i}) = c_0 + C_{t|t+i} Q_{t|t+i} + \frac{c}{2} Q_{t|t+i}^2 + \frac{\alpha}{2}(Q_{t|t+i} - Q_{t|t-1+i})^2 \tag{9}$$

This will be the form of the production cost function that will be used in further development of the model.

The assumption that production costs follow a quadratic relation with production rate may appear to be unacceptable when considering that production costs are typically expected to be approximated by a third order inverted S-type curve. The full cost curve could, however, be viewed as a simple composition of the two quadratic curves, subject to certain conditions in regard to their respective coefficients. The general cost function may therefore be chosen to be quadratic for both the declining and increasing marginal cost cases. Note that the value of c_1 becomes immaterial in the eventual cost function as expressed in (9) since it is taken up in the stochastic cost shock element, $C_{t|t+i}$.

2.3 Stock Holding Cost Function

Again, since explicit solutions are required for the model, the stock cost function is also assumed quadratic. It is expressed as:

$$B(N_t) = b'_0 + b'_1 H_t + \frac{b}{2} H_t^2 \qquad (10)$$

where b'_0, b'_1 and b should be constants with b'_0, $b > 0$, and H_t is the net stock level at the end of period t. As explained by Holt et al. (1960), intuitively one would prefer to relate the cost to some intermediate net stock level during period t instead of at the beginning or the end of the period. However, averaging stocks over period t will complicate the stock cost function without contributing additional benefits. A relation of costs to stock levels at the end of the period is an equally valid, yet much simpler, approach - the values of b'_0, b'_1 and b will just be different.

The definition of net stock levels warrants some discussion. In order to have a simple relation between output in period t and the stock of finished goods at the end of the period, it is convenient to use the variable, „net stocks", defined as the number of stock items minus the number of unfilled orders. Net stock is increased by production, regardless of whether the product is added to the physical stock of finished goods or sold to decrease the number of unfilled orders. The linear quadratic model places no restriction on the sign of H_t. A negative net stock level would indicate that the number of unfilled orders is larger than that of stocks of finished goods.

It would not make sense for a manufacturer to carry stock of any particular finished product as well as a backlog of unfilled orders for the same product. However, the BER respondents presumably manufacture a variety of products and report on the aggregate. It is therefore perfectly normal for a particular firm to report both stocks and a backlog of unfilled orders at the same time. Incidentally, 85% of the firms normally responding in the BER survey report stocks and unfilled orders simultaneously.

Blinder proposed that H_t be defined as $H_t = N_t - N^*_t$, which would be the deviation of actual net stock, N_t, from the desired level, N^*_t. When considering short-term adjustments to unanticipated fluctuations in demand and costs, the desired level of net stock, N^*_t, is assumed to be stationary and would indicate the level of net stock at which stock holding costs will be minimal. From (10) N^*_t would be assigned the value $N^*_t = -b'_1/b$. Following Holt et al. (1960), N^*_t can be approximated by current sales, X_t. Expression (10) may be revised to:

$$B(N_t) = b_0 + b_1 N_t + \frac{b}{2} N_t^2 \qquad (11)$$

In expectations format (11) is written as:

$$B(N_{t|t+i}) = b_0 + b_1 N_{t|t+i} + \frac{b}{2} N_{t|t+i}^2 \qquad (12)$$

2.4 Optimisation Constraints

The functions defined by (5), (9), and (12) can now be substituted in the objective function (1). The firm selects P_t and Q_t each period before observing η_t and μ_t. Q_t is not available until the end of the period. Thus current sales, X_t, are made out of N_{t-1}, which is inherited from period t-1. Q_t is added to net stock available at the start of period t+1. Therefore Q_t, X_t and N_t are related by the identity:

$$N_t = N_{t-1} - X_t + Q_t \tag{13}$$

In expectation format:

$$N_{t|t+i} - N_{t|t-1+i} = Q_{t|t+i} - X_{t|t+i} \tag{14}$$

Solutions to expression (1) may now be determined by reformulating the objective function as follows:

$$J_t = E_t \sum_{i=0}^{\infty} \rho^i \left[X_{t|t+i} P_{t|t+i} - C(Q_{t|t+i}) - B(N_{t|t+i}) \right. \\ \left. - \lambda_{t|t+i} (N_{t|t+i} - N_{t|t-1+i} - Q_{t|t+i} + X_{t|t+i}) \right] \tag{15}$$

subject to expressions (5), (9) and (12). The LaGrange multiplier, $\lambda_{t|t+i}$, represents the expected shadow price of a marginal unit held in stock. This may be interpreted as the potential net value of the stock item that can be determined by the difference between expected income from selling such a unit in a later period minus the costs involved when carrying it in stock until being sold. This is applicable for both realisation stocks of finished goods and unfilled orders - the latter can be considered to be postponed sales.

Note that the stochastic elements in the demand and cost functions, $D_{t|t+i}$ and $C_{t|t+i}$, are assumed to be identically and independently distributed with current period realisations observed by the manufacturer. While D_t and C_t are known, the manufacturers have to form expectations about all future values of $D_{t|t+i}$ and $C_{t|t+i}$ for i > 0. Since responses to transitory as well as permanent demand and cost shocks are to be evaluated, the formation of expectations regarding $D_{t|t+i}$ and $C_{t|t+i}$ needs to be specified. Following König et al. (1981) and König and Nerlove (1986), the adaptive expectations formation scheme is used. Accordingly, it is proposed that the demand shock be defined as:

$$\Phi D_{t+i} = \omega_d^i \Phi D_t \tag{16}$$

where ΦD_t is the demand shock experienced in period t. A shock is defined as the difference between the expected value and the eventual realisation. Thus:

$$\Phi D_t = D_t - D_{t-1|t}$$

Similarly, it can be shown that:

$$\Phi C_{t+i} = \omega_c^i \Phi C_t \tag{17}$$

Expressions (16) and (17) indicate that when a firm experiences an actual demand or cost shock in period t, and ω_d (or ω_c) $\to 0$, then the firm expects the shock to be transitory. This implies that the future expectations of the demand (or cost) curve will not be revised. However, if ω_d (or ω_c) $\to 1$, then the firm expects the shock to be permanent and that the demand (or cost) curve is shifted. Thus, the parameters w_d and w_c reflect the perceived persistence of the shocks.

2.5 Generation of Solutions

The solutions to (15) require that certain first-order conditions need to be defined. This is achieved by setting the first-order partial differentials of J_t equal to zero. Thus:

$$\frac{\partial J_t}{\partial Q_{t|t+i}} = E_t \rho^i \left[-C_{t|t+i} - cQ_{t|t+i} - \alpha(Q_{t|t+i} - Q_{t|t-1+i}) + \lambda_{t|t+i} \right]$$
$$+ E_t \rho^{i+1} \left[\alpha(Q_{t|t+1+i} - Q_{t|t+i}) \right] = 0$$

which yields:

$$-C_{t|t+i} - \theta Q_{t|t+i} + \alpha Q_{t|t-1+i} + \alpha \rho Q_{t|t+1+i} + \lambda_{t|t+i} = 0 \tag{18}$$

with $\theta = c + \rho + \rho\alpha$

Similarly:

$$\frac{\partial J_t}{\partial P_{t|t+i}} = E_t \rho^i \left[2dD_{t|t+i} - 4dP_{t|t+1} + 2d\lambda_{t|t+i} \right] = 0$$

yielding:

$$D_{t|t+i} - 2P_{t|t+i} + \lambda_{t|t+i} = 0 \tag{19}$$

Furthermore,

$$\frac{\partial J_t}{\partial N_{t|t+i}} = E_t \rho^i \left[-b_1 - bN_{t|t+i} - \lambda_{t|t+i} \right] + E_t \rho^{i+1} \lambda_{t|t+1+i} = 0$$

resulting in:

$$-b_1 - bN_{t|t+i} - \lambda_{t|t+i} + \rho\lambda_{t|t+1+i} = 0 \tag{20}$$

And, lastly:

$$\frac{\partial J_t}{\partial \lambda_{t|t+i}} = E_t \rho^i \left[-N_{t|t+i} + N_{t|t-1+i} + Q_{t|t+i} - 2d(D_{t|t+i} - P_{t|t+i}) \right] = 0$$

which is manipulated into:

$$N_{t|t+i} - N_{t|t-1+i} - Q_{t|t+i} + 2dD_{t|t+i} - 2dP_{t|t+i} = 0 \tag{21}$$

To simplify the notation, the expectation operator has been omitted in expressions (18) through (21).

In order to investigate the impact of demand and cost shocks on the short term adjustments of the monopolistic firm, the first-order conditions can be transformed into a set of equations describing explicitly the firm's responses in terms of the expectational errors of the exogenous variables, ΦD_t and ΦC_t. This can be achieved by generating the shock variables from the general expressions.

Set $i = 0$ and $i = 1$ in expression (18) to yield:

$$-C_t - \theta Q_t + \alpha Q_{t|t-1} + \alpha \rho Q_{t|t+1} + \lambda_t = 0 \tag{22}$$

and

$$-C_{t|t+1} - \theta Q_{t|t+1} + \alpha Q_t + \alpha \rho Q_{t|t+2} + \lambda_{t|t+1} = 0$$

Lagging the last expression by one period:

$$-C_{t-1|t} - \theta Q_{t-1|t} + \alpha Q_{t-1|t-1} + \alpha \rho Q_{t-1|t+1} + \lambda_{t-1|t} = 0 \tag{23}$$

Subtracting (23) from (22) leads to:

$$-\Phi C_t - \theta \Phi Q_t + \alpha \rho \Phi Q_{t+1} + \Phi \lambda_t = 0 \tag{24}$$

where $\Phi C_t = C_t - C_{t-1|t}$ reflects the difference between realised (actual) cost in period t and the cost the manufacturer anticipated in period t-1 for period t. The shocks in output, ΦQ_t, and shadow net stock price, $\Phi \lambda_t$, are defined in the same way. Expressions (19), (20) and (21) are transformed by applying the above procedure to result in:

$$\Phi D_t - 2\Phi P_t + \Phi \lambda_t = 0 \tag{25}$$

$$-b\Phi N_t - \Phi \lambda_t + \rho \Phi \lambda_{t+1} = 0 \tag{26}$$

$$\Phi N_t - \Phi Q_t + 2d\Phi D_t - 2d\Phi P_t = 0 \tag{27}$$

The dynamic process of decision making is described by expressions (24) to (27). The revisions of plans regarding production, pricing and stock holding can now be expressed in terms of the cost and demand shocks. Note that if the firm (entrepreneur) does not receive any new information in period t, all actions in period t, as well those planned for the future, are identical with plans made in the previous period, t-1. All information about the endogenous variables, $Q_{t-1|t}$, $P_{t-1|t}$, $N_{t-1|t}$, and $\lambda_{t-1|t}$ would be fully discounted in the planned values. Therefore, no lagged endogenous variables need to be considered in expressions (24) through (27).

A graphical illustration of the interaction of the various variables is presented in Figures 1 and 2. Figure 1 presents a scenario describing the impact of a one-time positive demand shock, and Figure 2 the impact of a positive cost shock, on production, Q, price, P, sales, X, net stock, N, and the shadow price of net stock, λ. Note that, in both figures, the familiar case of convex total costs, i.e. increasing marginal costs, is presented. The interaction can be presented in a similar way for the case of decreasing or stagnant marginal costs.

The initial conditions in Figure 1 correspond to the plans made in period t-1 to be executed in t. Everything is expected to be in balance - expected sales equal expected production at a level which optimises the marginal revenue at the point where marginal costs equal marginal income. However, in period t the actual stochastic demand element, D_t, turns out to be higher than was expected in the preceding period, $D_{t-1|t}$. The demand shock results in an endogenous increase in the shadow price of net stock, $\Phi\lambda_t$.

In the graphical scenario the shadow price increases to a level where actual production is increased to Q_t while sales increase to X_t, such that the "surprise" change in sales exceeds the "surprise" change in production. It can be shown that this is a special case that will always be true when the cost of production function is convex and b < c, while the demand shock is considered to be transitory.

Assuming, for the moment, that Figure 1 describes a valid scenario, then a rise in shadow price of net stock implies that sales in the stock model will exceed those that will result if the manufacturer does not carry net stock. In the latter case, sales are determined by the intersection between the marginal revenue and marginal cost functions, and sales will equal production at this optimum level.

In Figure 2 the initial conditions again correspond to the plans made in period t-1 for execution in period t. This time, however, actual stochastic demand element, C_t, turns out to be higher in period t than was expected in the preceding period with $C_{t-1|t}$. As in the case of the demand shock, the positive cost shock causes an endogenous increase in the shadow price of net stock, $\Phi\lambda_t$. The resulting decline in production rate exceeds the decrease in sales. Consequently, net stock is reduced.

Assuming that Figures 1 and 2 reflect a true scenario of rising marginal costs, b < c, and the demand and cost shocks are positive and perceived to be transitory, then it is apparent that cost shocks result in a production counter-smoothing effect while net stocks are utilised to smooth production in the case of a demand shock. Note that in the case of a demand shock, the price adjustment appears to be significantly larger than when the manufacturer experiences a cost shock - a net stock decrease in the cost shock case may have a price-smoothing effect. However, the empirical evaluation, further on, rejects this as an illusion due to the specific structure of the graphical representations.

Although the illustrations in Figures 1 and 2 are not universal, they do provide a simple summary of the decision making model described by expressions (24) through (27). However, the firm's responses to the expectational errors in the exogenous variables, D_t and C_t, can also be derived analytically. Substitution of variables in (24) through (27), and utilising expressions (16) and (17), results in the following:

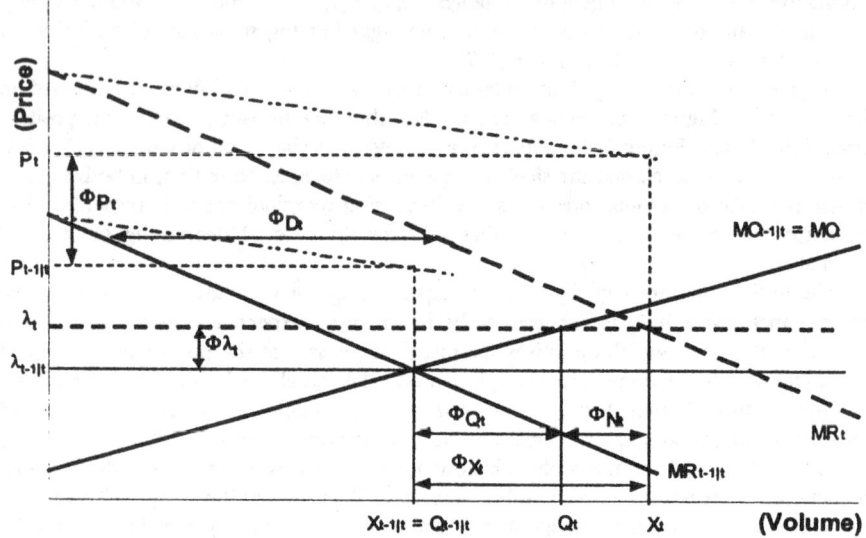

Figure 1   **Effect of demand shock on endogenous variables**

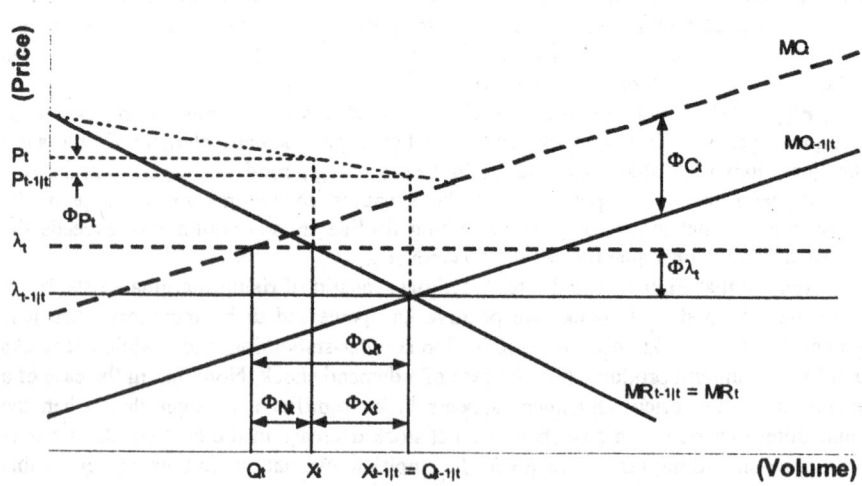

Figure 2   **Effect of cost shock on endogenous variables**

$$\Phi Q_t = \left[\frac{bd}{\upsilon_1 - \upsilon_2\omega_d + \upsilon_3\omega_d^2}\right]\Phi D_t + \left[\frac{\rho\omega_c - bd - 1}{\upsilon_1 - \upsilon_2\omega_c + \upsilon_3\omega_c^2}\right]\Phi C_t \qquad (28)$$

$$\Phi P_t = \frac{1}{2}\left\{\left[1 + \frac{bd(\theta - \rho\alpha\omega_d)}{\upsilon_1 - \upsilon_2\omega_d + \upsilon_3\omega_d^2}\right]\Phi D_t + \left[\frac{b}{\upsilon_1 - \upsilon_2\omega_c + \upsilon_3\omega_c^2}\right]\Phi C_t\right\} \qquad (29)$$

$$\Phi N_t = \left[\frac{-\theta d + \rho d(\alpha + \theta)\omega_d - \rho^2\alpha\omega_d^2}{\upsilon_1 - \upsilon_2\omega_d + \upsilon_3\omega_d^2}\right]\Phi D_t + \left[\frac{\rho\omega_c - 1}{\upsilon_1 - \upsilon_2\omega_c + \upsilon_3\omega_c^2}\right]\Phi C_t \qquad (30)$$

$$\Phi \lambda_t = \left[\frac{bd(\theta - \rho\alpha\omega_d)}{\upsilon_1 - \upsilon_2\omega_d + \upsilon_3\omega_d^2}\right]\Phi D_t + \left[\frac{b}{\upsilon_1 - \upsilon_2\omega_c + \upsilon_3\omega_c^2}\right]\Phi C_t \qquad (31)$$

with

$$\upsilon_1 = b + bd\theta + \theta \qquad (32)$$

$$\upsilon_2 = \rho(\alpha + bd\alpha + \theta) \qquad (33)$$

$$\upsilon_3 = \rho^2\alpha \qquad (34)$$

It is evident from expressions (28) through (31) that if no cost or demand shocks are experienced by the firm, $\Phi D_t = \Phi C_t = 0$, then ΦQ_t, ΦP_t, ΦN_t, and Φl_t will also be zero, implying that plans and realisations are identical. If there are no surprises, there is no need to modify plans.

Evaluating expressions (28) through (31) at $\omega_d = 0$ and $\omega_c = 0$ determines the adjustment of plans when the shocks are considered transitory, while if the firm perceives the shocks to be permanent ($\omega_d = 1$, $\omega_c = 1$) the modifications to plans regarding the endogenous variables will be different. As mentioned above in the discussion of Figures 1 and 2, the magnitude of the change in shadow price of the net stock is crucial when determining what the impacts of ΦD_t and ΦC_t will be on the endogenous variables. The magnitude of the shadow price change is, however, determined by the signs and magnitudes of the coefficients in the revenue, production cost, and stock cost functions. It can be shown that the magnitude of the shadow price of net stock gets larger the more persistent the cost shocks are perceived to be, provided that $c > 0$. It can also be shown that the magnitude of the shadow price of net stock gets larger the more persistent the demand shocks are perceived to be, provided that $\alpha = 0$ and $c > 0$.

3 Empirical Testing of Model

In the form presented by expressions (28) through (31) the model cannot be tested directly on the BER business survey data. Further reformulation is required before it is tested by utilising the log-linear model technique. Since the business survey data is a compilation of responses from individual firms, the model will have to be formulated statistically before it can be considered testable. The BER data also require transformation to accommodate shocks (or "surprises") in certain economic variables. Unfortunately, complete testing of the model is not possible as no measurements of net stock shadow prices are available - neither can it be derived through transformation of available data. Nevertheless, the results obtainable through limited testing of the model should provide a fair amount of insight in the behaviour of entrepreneurs when exposed to exogenous shocks in demand and costs.

3.1 Statistical Formulation of the Model

In order to relate the theoretical model to empirical observations it is necessary to first formulate the model statistically. A series of probabilities relating the endogenous plan changes to the exogenous shocks in demand and costs are constructed. The model in probability format is denoted by enclosing the relevant variables in parentheses, assuming the endogenous variables to be conditioned upon the exogenous shocks. In this case, causality is defined such that the changes in plans are induced by demand and cost shocks, and not the other way around. The model can therefore be expressed as:

$$\Pr[\Phi Q_t | \Phi D_t, \Phi C_t] \tag{35}$$

$$\Pr[\Phi P_t | \Phi D_t, \Phi C_t] \tag{36}$$

$$\Pr[\Phi N_t | \Phi D_t, \Phi C_t] \tag{37}$$

A similar expression can be defined for the change in net stock shadow price. However, as mentioned above, the BER data set does not contain any reference to shadow prices, nor can it be derived. It is therefore omitted from the model in testable format.

The relationship between ΦN_t and ΦD_t, ΦC_t may be checked by observing the following probability as well:

$$\Pr[\Phi X_t, \Phi Q_t | \Phi D_t, \Phi C_t] \tag{38}$$

The evergreen question emerging from the debate between supporters of the Neo-Keynesian disequilibrium and Neo-Classical equilibrium macroeconomics theories concerning the speed of adjustment of prices and output in reaction to demand changes can also be tested empirically. Revisions of planned prices and output in reaction to demand and cost shocks may be tested in the following probability:

$$\Pr[\Phi P_t, \Phi Q_t | \Phi D_t, \Phi C_t] \tag{39}$$

This may be viewed as a statistical reformulation of the addition of expressions (28) and (29). Since this formulation considers only shocks or changes in subsequent periods, and the periods last for a quarter each, it cannot provide a final settlement of the sticky price vs. sticky output issue evolving from the two paradigms in macroeconomic theory. However, it may be interesting to see what sort of support is mustered for the two opposing theories by evaluating the behaviour of individual entrepreneurs when subjected to demand and cost shocks.

3.2 Preparation of the Data

The traditional method of transformation of direct measurements to yield data on shocks entails the setting up of two-dimensional contingency tables that reflect combinational frequencies of the trichotomous responses regarding expectations and realisations of the particular variable. Categorisation of responses on shocks inevitably leads to a reduction in the number of data points available since only firms who respond on specific expectations in a specific period, as well as on the subsequent realisations in the following period, are included in the derived data set. This leads to an increased probability of finding zeroes in the cells of the contingency tables on which the log-linear models are based. Since data availability needs to be maximised, such derivation will be kept to a minimum.

The responses regarding stocks of finished goods and unfilled orders in the BER data set are not available in a simple format as required by the above statistical formulation (37). The questionnaire requests responses to the appraisal of "current stocks of finished goods in relation to expected demand", to which the firm has to respond with "too high", "just sufficient", or "too low". At the same time the firms are requested to respond to realised and expected "unfilled orders in relation to sales", with a selection between "up", "same", or "down". From both these responses the actual appraisals (or changes) of stocks and unfilled orders can be derived, but further manipulation is required to finally derive shocks (or plan changes) in net stock. As mentioned above, this results in a significant loss of data. In addition, only firms who respond to both questions simultaneously in contiguous quarters (periods) can be allowed in the derived data set. This limits data availability even further - for the BER survey data only 48% of the responses satisfy these stringent conditions.

Instead, the relationship expressed in (14) can be used to derive changes in net stock. Most firms report actual and expected changes in sales and production rate. The relation between net stock changes, and production and sales changes can be derived as follows:

For $i = 0$ in (14), we have

$$N_t - N_{t|t-1} = Q_t - X_t \tag{40}$$

Setting $i = 1$ yields

$$N_{t|t+1} - N_t = Q_{t|t+1} - X_{t|t+1}$$

Lagging by one period:

$$N_{t-1|t} - N_{t-1|t-1} = Q_{t-1|t} - X_{t-1|t} \tag{41}$$

Subtracting (41) from (40) leads to

$$\Phi N_t = \Phi Q_t - \Phi X_t \tag{42}$$

The frequency responses for ΦN_t can then be derived as indicated in the following table:

ΦN_t :- ΦX_t

		+	=	-
	+	?	+	+
ΦQ_t	=	-	=	+
	-	-	-	?

The variable ΦN_t is therefore also trichotomous and can be constructed for each individual firm responding to expectations and realisations of sales and production rate in contiguous periods.

The manufacturing industry data set is tested empirically for an economic expansion and a recession phase.

3.3 Tests Results

The unsaturated log-linear model generally provides a sufficient means of analysing the BER business survey data. Thus, the statistics reported here will only reflect the goodness-of-fit of the unsaturated log-linear models with the derived association coefficients based on the bivariate interaction terms in the log-linear models, i.e. the component gamma (γ_c) and α_{11}-coefficients indicating the magnitude and direction of association, and α_{22}-coefficient which reflects the presence or absence of clumping in the no change categories.

The values of the γ_c and α_{11}-coefficients provide only an indication of the relative strength (and direction) of association and are not estimated values for the coefficients of ΦD_t and ΦC_t as derived in expressions (28) through (31). They are rather indirect measures of the relative magnitudes (and signs) of the coefficients in (28) through (31).

The results of the test for shocks (surprises) in production, demand and costs (relating to expression (35)) are presented in Table 1 in the Appendix. The various statistical measures can be compared for the expansion and recession phases. Similarly, the results for shocks in price, demand and costs (relating to expression (36)) are presented in Table 2, and those for shocks in net stock, demand and costs (relating to expression (37)) in Table 3. As a control measure, the interaction of shocks in sales, production, demand and costs (relating to expression (38)) are presented in Tables 4.1 and 4.2, each table reflecting the various statistical measures for one of the economic phases.

In a similar way, the results for the interaction of shocks in price, production, demand and costs (relating to expression (39)) are presented in Tables 5.1 and 5.2.

4 Discussion of Results

4.1 Log-linear Model Fitting

The standard unsaturated log-linear models have been fitted successfully on the BER survey data. In all cases the models provide a good fit to the data (associated probability p > 0,10). It is, therefore, not necessary to include trivariate interaction effects which would improve the goodness-of-fit since it is already at an acceptable level.

4.2 Demand and Cost Shock Independence

The shocks in demand and costs ($\Phi D_t * \Phi C_t$), do not show any evidence of dependency (γ_c and α_{11}-coefficients all have associated probabilities larger than 5%). This is what one would expect since $D_{t|t+i}$ and $C_{t|t+i}$ have been assumed to be identically but independently distributed. Thus, the empirical data generally support the assumption that exogenous demand and cost shocks are independent.

4.3 General Entrepreneurial Behaviour

The coefficients describing the magnitude and direction of bivariate interaction of the respective variables reveal some interesting aspects of entrepreneurial behaviour in view of demand and cost shocks. The magnitudes of association between the variables mentioned above can generally be ranked from very strong to almost non-existent as follows:

$$\underbrace{(\Phi Q_t * \Phi D_t)}_{1,59} > \underbrace{(\Phi P_t * \Phi C_t)}_{0,82} > \underbrace{(\Phi N_t * \Phi D_t)}_{0,35} > \underbrace{(\Phi P_t * \Phi D_t)}_{0,24} > \underbrace{(\Phi Q_t * \Phi C_t)}_{0,06} > \underbrace{(\Phi N_t * \Phi C_t)}_{0,03}$$

The figures below the respective bivariate interactions are typical (absolute) α_{11}-coefficient values indicating the averages for the two economic phases. Only the four highest ranked interactions could yield coefficients with associated probabilities less than 5%.

The quoted α_{11}-values should be viewed with caution, since they were not derived from one single log-linear model accommodating all the variables. These values were estimated from the three separate models described by expressions (35), (36), and (37). Despite the fact that they may not be a true reflection of the magnitudes of association ranked in descending order, the relatively wide differences in the values do provide some indication of the relative strengths. The relative magnitudes of association between ΦP_t, ΦQ_t, ΦD_t and ΦC_t can, however, be confirmed by ranking the bivariate interactions featuring in the log-linear model devised for expression (39). Ranking along descending α_{11}-coefficients for this model yields:

$$\underbrace{(\Phi Q_t * \Phi D_t)}_{1{,}59} > \underbrace{(\Phi P_t * \Phi C_t)}_{0{,}82} > \underbrace{(\Phi P_t * \Phi D_t)}_{0{,}16} > \underbrace{(\Phi Q_t * \Phi C_t)}_{0{,}02}$$

These values, as well as the rank order, clearly confirm those mentioned above, albeit only for these four bivariate interactions.

Expression (38) is meant to act as some sort of a control evaluation of net stock plan revisions described by (37). Ranking of the bivariate interactions of the "control" model yields the following:

$$\underbrace{(\Phi X_t * \Phi D_t)}_{1{,}30} > \underbrace{(\Phi Q_t * \Phi D_t)}_{0{,}73} > \underbrace{(\Phi X_t * \Phi C_t)}_{0{,}08} > \underbrace{(\Phi Q_t * \Phi C_t)}_{0{,}02}$$

The typical α_{11}-values are, again, shown below the respective bivariate interactions. Note that the α_{11}-value for the $(\Phi Q_t * \Phi D_t)$ interaction is significantly smaller than those obtained in the above models. This can be ascribed to the fact that model (38) contains a "foreign" variable in the form of the sales shock, ΦX_t. The absolute values of the α_{11}-coefficients are, however, not that important - here we are more concerned with the relative magnitudes. Model (38) shows that sales are significantly more volatile than production when the manufacturers are faced with demand shocks. When they experience cost shocks, sales and production appear to be equally passive - these plans may be adjusted only slightly. The significant difference between $(\Phi X_t * \Phi D_t)$ and $(\Phi Q_t * \Phi D_t)$ confirms the implication of the above observation that $(\Phi N_t * \Phi D_t)$ is significantly large (and actually negative). Both models (37) and (38) indicate that net stock changes are, to some extent, used to buffer production against demand shocks. However, it is surprising that net stock changes play almost no role when cost shocks occur.

In summary, it is evident that entrepreneurs, when subjected to demand shocks, generally prefer to focus on production plan changes rather than changes in net stock levels or prices to accommodate the shocks. When encountering cost shocks, anticipated prices appear to be adjusted quite readily, but not production or net stock levels.

The above observations are the general and quite obvious. There are, however, finer differences in behaviour which need to be highlighted.

4.4   General Behavioural Differences in the Two Economic Phases

On the whole, the total industry appears to be slightly more responsive to demand shocks in the economic recession phase than in the expansion phase. The larger derived association coefficients indicate a greater propensity to adjust production, net stock plans and prices during the recession phase. This may be attributed to a perception that demand shocks have a more permanent nature during the recession. Added to the assumption that demand shocks in a recession phase generally tend to be negative rather than positive, this rather pessimistic (conservative) perception may be understandable: demand shocks are often negative and (conservatively) expected to last for a considerable period of time - it is therefore wise to prepare for a worse, rather than a better scenario. The conservative approach is maintained during the expansion phase, since entrepreneurs then appear to judge demand shocks as being more of a transitory nature. Positive demand shocks are expected to dominate negative shocks during the expansion phase, but conservatism dictates that it is better to err on the safe side and assume that the shocks are not going to last. Thus, plans are adjusted less often.

Production and net stock adjustments are not associated with cost shocks at a significant level. Therefore, no definite conclusions can be derived from changes in the association coefficients. However, the manufacturing industry does seem to be less willing to adjust prices when confronted with cost shocks, albeit only slightly, during the recession phase. The difference in approach during the expansion and recession phases is, however, less obvious than what is observed for demand shocks. It can possibly be ascribed to a general view that cost shocks affect everybody on an equal basis, regardless of the economic phase and little harm would be done if the cost increases are passed on to consumers. Cost decreases are probably seldom offered to consumers, due to the fact that decreases are rare in an economic environment that has become used to inflation. When cost decreases do occur, they are rather held back to increase profitability and decrease the firm's exposure to inflation, which can erode real income in the long term.

5 Economic Implications of Observations

When viewed against the background of the theoretical economic model derived for the optimising firm, the above empirical observations lead to some interesting conclusions. The following discussion illustrates how the observations precipitate some peculiar values of the coefficients that feature in the demand and cost functions which were assumed to be representative of those experienced by manufacturers in South Africa. Some of the observations even seem to contradict the assumptions on which the competitive monopolistic model is based, and lead one to conclude that the monopolistic model may not be a true representation of the South African manufacturing sector in general.

5.1 The Demand Function

The general reactions of manufacturers in situations where demand shocks are experienced provide some useful information regarding their perception of the demand function. The rank orders of the various bivariate interaction coefficients presented in Section 4.3 indicate that entrepreneurs reveal a very strong propensity to change production plans in view of demand shocks, but almost none when faced by cost shocks. Instead of trying to derive an algebraic conclusion that would fit this observation from expressions (28) through (34), it is simpler to rather utilise the graphical presentations of the theoretical model presented in Figures 1 and 2. Now, big changes in production plans prompted by demand shocks, in addition to almost no plan changes when facing cost shocks, imply that the marginal revenue curve, and therefore the demand curve, is perceived to be almost vertical, i.e. it has a slope approaching negative infinity. In the demand function (2) this would mean that coefficient d approaches zero. Thus, manufacturers generally perceive the demand to be inelastic, i.e. the proportionate change in the output demanded, resulting from a very small proportionate change in price, is very low.

5.2 The Cost Function

The above-mentioned rank orders of bivariate interaction coefficients also indicate that entrepreneurs reveal a reasonably strong propensity to change pricing plans in view of cost shocks, but rather a weak propensity to change when prompted by demand shocks. In Figure 2 this could only be possible if the marginal cost curve is almost flat. The fact that some changes to prices do realise when surprise demand changes are encountered, seem to indicate that the slope of the linear marginal cost curve is not absolutely zero, but slightly positive. Since the slope of the marginal cost curve is determined by $(c + \alpha)$, it means that if there really is a cost associated with deliberate changes in production rate $(\alpha > 0)$, then c should be negative with magnitude approaching that of α.

Ramey (1991) has expounded the implications of a negative c-value in cost function (6) in detail. Contrary to the findings by Ramey, this study indicates that the South African manufacturing firms either perceive their marginal cost functions to be rising, or the cost of changing production rate is overwhelming, to the extent that they operate in a region of convex production costs, despite the fact that c could be negative. This conclusion is supported by the observation that sales in the South African manufacturing industries do appear to fluctuate more than production in view of demand shocks.

The observations in this study would seem to contradict those simulated by Naish (1994) with nearly flat marginal cost curves. However, he distinguishes between demand shocks which are realised before the entrepreneur chooses prices and output, and those that are totally "unanticipated", i.e. not realised in advance. His simulations indicate that production can be significantly more volatile than sales when the manufacturer faces unanticipated demand shocks. He also showed that when demand shocks are anticipated (according to his definition) then stocks do seem to smooth production. This study supports the latter approach that is contradictory to most evidence found in literature. However, the results of this study should be interpreted in view of the fact that the BER respondents have three months in which to react to exogenous shocks. This may be a long enough period to allow for the shocks to realise before plans are adjusted. Thus, the support for production smoothing by net stock changes, despite the fact that the marginal cost curve is almost flat.

5.3 Transitory vs Permanent Shocks

The results offer no substantial evidence to indicate preference for exogenous shocks to be perceived as transitory or permanent. Therefore, it is purely a conjecture to state (above) that demand shocks may be perceived to be more permanent during a recession, and rather transitory during an economic expansion, while cost shocks always seem to be perceived as being permanent. If the above findings, i.e. $d \rightarrow 0$ and $(c + \alpha) \rightarrow 0$, are substituted in expressions (28) through (34), there is no conclusive indication that manufacturers generally perceive the demand and cost shocks to be either transitory, or permanent. The algebraic manipulations always result in some of the coefficients in the stockholding and cost functions having to meet certain conditions, e.g. α must be greater than ρ, for any specific assumption regarding the permanency of exogenous shocks to be true.

5.4 Validity of the Monopolistic Model for the Firm

The monopolistic model of an optimising firm presented in Section 2 is based upon a number of specific assumptions, i.e.

- The firm has a single goal, that of profit maximisation.
- This goal is attained by application of the marginalist principle at the point where marginal cost equals marginal revenue (MC = MR).
- The firm knows with a fair amount of certainty its own demand and cost functions.
- The marginal and average cost functions are U-shaped in both the short term and long term, which implies a single optimum level of output.
- Entry of new firms into the market is blockaded by the monopolistic industries.
- Shocks in exogenous economic factors are allowed to provide for uncertainty in the market.
- Long run profit maximisation is attained by maximisation of profits in each single period since time periods are assumed to be independent, i.e. decisions taken in one period will not affect behaviour in another period. Thus, the rule of MC = MR is applied in each consecutive period.
- The entrepreneur (manufacturer) acts with global rationality, having access to unlimited, costless information and unlimited time to evaluate all possible alternatives to decisions that have to be taken. This is the only way in which sustained maximisation of profit at MC = MR can be possible.

Most of these assumptions pertain to the original marginalistic approach of the Neo-Classical model of firms as monopolies or, as Blinder (1982) pointed out, monopolistic competition. However, a modification to the traditional version has been allowed in the provision for market uncertainty. This is accomplished by recognising that exogenous shocks and subsequent alterations to planned output, pricing and net stock levels do occur in reality.

The Neo-Classical theory of the firm has come under severe attack in literature. A detailed exposition of critique, as well as discussion of the merits of the arguments against and in support of the Neo-Classical theory can be followed in Koutsoyiannis (1979). Several of the results obtained in this study, however, support the critique against the traditional Neo-Classical approach in which firms are viewed as largely monopolies acting in a certain environment. For instance, the fact that allowance has been made for uncertainty in the model presented here, and the strong empirical support found in the BER survey data for shocks in demand, costs, as well as "surprise" changes in output, pricing and net stock levels, indicate that the South African manufacturing industries do not view themselves as isolated monopolists who can dictate markets at will. They realise that adjustment of endogenous economic factors in view of exogenous shocks is vital. Positive and negative demand shocks occur quite often as can be seen from the relative frequencies in the contingency tables for the total industry in the two economic phases:

Expansion Phase :-

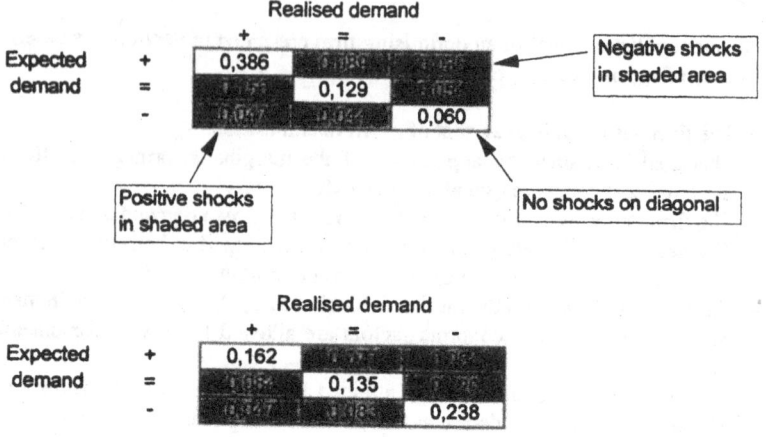

Assuming that the customers of the manufacturing industry do not change significantly in number and preference, the positive and negative shocks indicate surprise impacts due to intervention of competitors. If the amount of competition in the market were negligible, the negative and positive shocks would indicate surprise reactions of customers. Either way, the firms cannot but be well aware of their competitors and customers. Uncertainty in competitor and customer behaviour to implemented price and output changes is, therefore, recognised by the firms. This observation suggests that the South African manufacturing industries, like many other in the world, behave like oligopolists rather than monopolists.

The above conclusions about the demand curves of individual firms being perceived as almost vertical, and the cost curves being almost horizontal, suggest that the demand and cost functions are not really known by the firms. If this is the case, then the manufacturing industry cannot be maximising revenue in the short term by equating marginal cost and marginal revenue (MC = MR). The fact that marginal costs may not be known by the individual manufacturers can probably be ascribed to them being (generally) multi-product firms. Even if the firms did know their marginal cost and marginal revenue curves and they aimed at maximising profits, it would require continuous changes in price in view of demand and cost shocks. This does not appear to be the case, especially when demand shocks are encountered. The observed relatively good association between prices and cost shocks is probably due to cost shocks being perceived as permanent, impacting evenly on all manufacturers in the sector and, thus, not individualised. It is conjectured that prices will also not change significantly when individualised costs (being limited to the particular firm) are encountered, since price changes are generally not considered desirable in view of demand and cost changes. Prices are therefore rather "sticky" despite shocks in demand and (individualised) costs.

All the empirical evidence seems to challenge the characteristics normally associated with a monopolistic Neo-Classical firm. The behaviour of the manufacturing industries in

South Africa rather typify that of oligopolies basing their pricing policies on average costs rather than marginal costs. Koutsoyiannis (1979) describes a "representative" model of average-cost pricing that appears to explain many of the peculiarities of the South African manufacturing industries observed in this study. The average cost pricing model discards the role of demand curves as defined in the monopolistic Neo-Classical model of short-term optimisation. Pricing is rather based on the average variable costs (in a flat region) plus some profit margin for the firm. Short-run costs are presumed to be representative of long-run costs which are actually blurred with uncertainty.

5.5 Implications of Average Cost Pricing

The average cost pricing model evidently accommodates the conclusions regarding the slope of the demand function approaching negative infinity ($d \to 0$), and the almost flat marginal cost curve ($c + \alpha \to 0$). The average cost pricing theory abandons the demand function completely, and works with a saucer-shaped variable cost curve with a flat stretch in the middle. It also seems to provide good arguments to explain "price stickiness" in view of demand shocks, and allows the argument of price increases in view of cost shocks which are normally perceived to affect all firms in the industry. Even the strong association between the observed production plan changes and demand shocks, without affecting price can easily be explained as movements within the normal capacity of the firm (on the flat section of the marginal and variable cost curves). The way in which the functioning of the industry can be "co-ordinated" through tacit collusion or price leadership is also appealing, especially if it results in long-run maximisation of profits (even though profits are very subjectively based on average variable costs at some satisfying level) for all firms in the industry. In short, the empirical evidence of this study supports the theory of average cost pricing much better than the marginalist approach of the monopolistic Neo-Classical theory.

It can be shown that the principle of average cost pricing involves (implicitly) the estimation of the elasticity of demand in the long-run equilibrium, even if it is done subjectively. When applying the rule:

$$P = AVC + GPM$$

such that long-run profits are maximised, firms normally "guess" a gross profit margin which is shown to be related to the elasticity of demand:

$$P = AVC\left(\frac{e}{e-1}\right)$$

where e denotes the demand elasticity, constrained by $|e| > 1$. Average cost pricing therefore does not really abandon the demand function and eventually still optimises the long-run profits by equating MC to MR: the marginalistic approach.

Despite the fact that average cost pricing is not a theory which is different from all the other theories of the firm, the empirical evidence leads to the conclusion that the firms in the South African manufacturing industries apply the principle rule of average cost pricing when optimising their goals.

6 Summary

To summarise, the empirical evidence in this study indicates that:

- The South African manufacturers do not have certain knowledge of their demand and cost functions.
- They are aware of their competitors and customers that can have a definite impact on their business.
- They seem to apply the practice of average cost pricing which emulates the practical implications of a variety of microeconomic theories of the firm.
- Prices do indeed appear to be "sticky" in view of demand shocks, while output is evidently adjusted quite willingly.
- Cost shocks are generally considered to be permanent, or to be factor prices affecting the total industry.
- Net stock changes generally have a production smoothing effect in view of demand shocks - sales are more volatile than production.
- Net stock changes do not play a significant role in production smoothing when the firm is exposed to cost shocks.
- The manufacturing firms are slightly more responsive to demand shocks during a recession than during an expansion phase of the economic cycle - a greater propensity to change production, planned net stock levels, and prices is revealed.

Appendix

Table 1   Surprises in production, demand and costs

	Expansion Phase: 2/86-1/89		Recession Phase: 2/89-4/91	
Goodness-of-fit:-				
LR-ChiSq	4.364		8.421	
Probability	0.823		0.393	
Bivariate Interaction Configuration	$\Phi Q_t * \Phi D_t$	$\Phi Q_t * \Phi C_t$	$\Phi Q_t * \Phi D_t$	$\Phi Q_t * \Phi C_t$
Association Coefficient:				
γ_c	0.9270	0.410	0.9426	0.0613
Probability	0.000	0.471	0.000	0.237
α_{11}	1.5184	0.454	1.6626	0.0669
Probability	0.000	0.478	0.000	0.237
α_{22}	0.7135	0.0027	0.5966	0.0891
Probability	0.000	0.926	0.000	0.0001

Table 2   Surprises in price, demand and costs

	Expansion Phase: 2/86-1/89		Recession Phase: 2/89-4/91	
Goodness-of-fit:-				
LR-ChiSq	7.616		9.822	
Probability	0.472		0.278	
Bivariate Interaction Configuration	$\Phi P_t * \Phi D_t$	$\Phi P_t * \Phi C_t$	$\Phi P_t * \Phi D_t$	$\Phi P_t * \Phi C_t$
Association Coefficient:				
γ_c	0.1906	0.6899	0.2292	0.6615
Probability	0.000	0.471	0.000	0.000
α_{11}	0.2102	0.8311	0.2594	0.7992
Probability	0.000	0.000	0.000	0.000
α_{22}	0.0779	0.4269	0.0282	0.3286
Probability	0.001	0.000	0.185	0.000

Table 3 Surprises in net stock, demand and costs

	Expansion Phase: 2/86-1/89				Recession Phase: 2/89-4/91			
Goodness-of-fit:-								
LR-ChiSq	3.914				5.926			
Probability	0.865				0.656			
Bivariate Interaction Configuration	$\Phi N_t * \Phi D_t$		$\Phi N_t * \Phi C_t$		$\Phi N_t * \Phi D_t$		$\Phi N_t * \Phi C_t$	
Association Coefficient:								
γ_c	-0.2782		0.0127		-0.4274		-0.0733	
Probability	0.000		0.857		0.000		0.245	
α_{11}	-0.2681		0.0145		-0.4318		-0.0836	
Probability	0.000		0.856		0.000		0.247	
α_{22}	0.6736		-0.0154		0.6386		-0.0286	
Probability	0.000		0.682		0.000		0.406	

Table 4.1 Surprises in sales, production, demand and costs

Expansion Phase: 2/86-1/89

Goodness-of-fit:	
LR-ChiSq	47.537
Probability	0.4917

Bivariate Interaction Configuration	$\Phi X_t * \Phi Q_t$	$\Phi X_t * \Phi D_t$	$\Phi X_t * \Phi C_t$	$\Phi Q_t * \Phi D_t$	$\Phi Q_t * \Phi C_t$	$\Phi D_t * \Phi C_t$
Association Coefficients:						
γ_c	0.9113	0.8673	0.417	0.6098	0.0280	-0.0667
Probability	0.000	0.000	0.588	0.000	0.686	0.300
α_{11}	1.4417	1.2511	0.0487	0.7014	0.0310	-0.0757
Probability	0.000	0.000	0.581	0.000	0.688	0.294
α_{22}	0.6348	0.5995	-0.0389	0.3864	0.224	0.0323
Probability	0.000	0.000	0.310	0.000	0.519	0.334

Table 4.2 Surprises in sales, production, demand and costs

Expansion Phase: 2/89-4/91

Goodness-of-fit:
LR-ChiSq   51.049
Probability 0.3547

Bivariate Interaction Configuration	$\Phi X_t * \Phi Q_t$	$\Phi X_t * \Phi D_t$	$\Phi X_t * \Phi C_t$	$\Phi Q_t * \Phi D_t$	$\Phi Q_t * \Phi C_t$	$\Phi D_t * \Phi C_t$
Association Coefficients:						
γ_c	0.9130	0.8867	0.1026	0.6395	0.0085	0.0134
Probability	0.000	0.000	0.120	0.000	0.892	0.818
α_{11}	1.4735	1.3436	0.1172	0.7624	0.0092	0.0153
Probability	0.000	0.000	0.124	0.000	0.892	0.818
α_{22}	0.5500	0.5417	-0.0339	0.3225	0.1044	-0.0294
Probability	0.000	0.000	0.308	0.000	0.001	0.326

Table 5.1 Surprises in price, production, demand and costs

Expansion Phase: 2/86-1/89

Goodness-of-fit:
LR-ChiSq   50.632
Probability 0.3701

Bivariate Interaction Configuration	$\Phi X_t * \Phi Q_t$	$\Phi X_t * \Phi D_t$	$\Phi X_t * \Phi C_t$	$\Phi Q_t * \Phi D_t$	$\Phi Q_t * \Phi C_t$	$\Phi D_t * \Phi C_t$
Association Coefficients:						
γ_c	0.1050	0.1101	0.6896	0.9269	0.0130	-0.0931
Probability	0.077	0.057	0.000	0.000	0.832	0.124
α_{11}	0.1155	0.1229	0.8300	1.5178	0.0143	-0.1051
Probability	0.080	0.058	0.000	0.000	0.838	0.127
α_{22}	0.0683	0.0364	0.4282	0.7137	-0.0279	0.0093
Probability	0.029	0.244	0.000	0.000	0.383	0.771

Table 5.2 Surprises in price, production, demand and costs

Recession Phase: 2/89-4/91

Goodness-of-fit:
LR-ChiSq   56.058
Probability 0.1983

Bivariate Interaction Configuration	$\Phi P_t *\Phi Q_t$	$\Phi P_t *\Phi D_t$	$\Phi P_t *\Phi C_t$	$\Phi Q_t *\Phi D_t$	$\Phi Q_t *\Phi C_t$	$\Phi D_t *\Phi C_t$
Association Coefficients:						
γ_c	0.0723	0.1801	0.6625	0.9434	0.0263	0.0054
Probability	0.152	0.000	0.000	0.000	0.638	0.919
α_{11}	1.0812	0.2024	0.8022	1.6699	0.0287	0.0063
Probability	0.156	0.000	0.000	0.000	0.636	0.919
α_{22}	0.0004	0.0289	0.3231	0.5944	0.0912	-0.0587
Probability	0.989	0.278	0.000	0.000	0.001	0.035

References

Blanchard, O.J. (1983), The Production and Inventory Behaviour of the American Automobile Industry, *Journal of Political Economy*, Vol. 91, No. 3, pp. 365-400.

Blinder, A.S. (1981), Retail Inventory Behavior and Business Fluctuations, *Brookings Papers on Economic Activity*, Vol. 2, pp. 443-520.

Blinder, A.S. (1982), Inventories and Sticky Prices: More on the Microfoundations of Macroeconomics, *American Economic Review*, Vol. 72, No. 3, pp. 334-348.

Blinder, A.S. (1986), Can the Production Smoothing Model of Inventory Behaviour be Saved?, *The Quarterly Journal of Economics*, Vol. 101, No. 3, pp. 431-453.

Blinder, A.S. and Maccini, L.J. (1991), Taking Stock: A Critical Assessment of Recent Research on Inventories, *Journal of Economic Perspectives*, Vol. 5, No. 1, pp. 73-96.

Carlson, J.A. (1986), Stocks, Shocks and Price Output Decisions, *Journal of Macroeconomics*, Summer 1986, Vol. 8, No. 3, pp. 257-277.

Eichenbaum, M. (1984), Rational Expectations and the Smoothing Properties of Inventories of Finished Goods, *Journal of Monetary Economics*, Vol. 14, pp. 71-96.

Eichenbaum, M. (1989), Some Empirical Evidence on the Production Level and Production Cost Smoothing Models of Inventory Investment, *The American Economic Review*, Vol. 79, No. 4, pp. 853-864.

Etter, R. (1993), Inventory Behaviour of Firms at Different Levels of Aggregation, *Paper presented to 21st CIRET Conference*, Stellenbosch, South Africa.

Holt, C.C., Modigliani, F., Muth, J.F. and Simon, H.A. (1960), *Planning Production, Inventories, and Work Force*, Englewood Cliffs, N.J.: Prentice-Hall Inc.

Kawasaki, S., McMillan, J. and Zimmermann, K.F. (1983), Inventories and Price Inflexibility, *Econometrica*, Vol. 51, No. 3, pp. 599-610.

König, H., Nerlove, M. and Oudiz, G. (1981), On the Formation of Price Expectations: An Analysis of Business Test Data by Log-Linear Probability Models, *European Economic Review*, Vol. 16, pp. 103-138.

König, H. and Nerlove, M. (1986), Price Flexibility, Inventory Behaviour, and Production Responses, in W. Heller, R. Storr and D. Starrett (eds), *Equilibrium Analysis: Essays in Honor of Kenneth J Arrow*, Vol. II, pp. 179-218.

König, H. and Seitz, H. (1991), Production and Price Smoothing by Inventory Adjustment?, *Empirical Economics*, Vol. 16, pp. 233-252.

Koutsoyiannis, A. (1979), *Modern Microeconomics*, 2nd ed., London: Macmillan Publishers Ltd.

Krane, S.D. and Braun, S.N. (1991), Production Smoothing Evidence from Physical-Product Data, *Journal of Political Economy*, Vol. 99, No. 3, pp. 558-581.

Naish, H.F. (1984), Production Smoothing in the Linear Quadratic Inventory Model, *The Economic Journal*, Vol. 104, pp. 864-875.

Nerlove, M., Ross, D. and Willson, D. (1993), The Importance of Seasonality in Inventory Models, *Journal of Econometrics*, Vol. 55, pp. 105-128.

Ottenwaelter, B. and Vuong, Q.H. (1984), An Empirical Analysis of Backlog, Inventory, Production, and Price Adjustments: An Application of Recursive Systems of Log-Linear Models, *Journal of Business and Economic Statistics*, Vol. 2, No. 3, pp. 224-234.

Ramey, V.A. (1991), Nonconvex Costs and the Behaviour of Inventories, *Journal of Political Economy*, Vol. 99, No. 2, pp. 306-334.

West, K.D. (1986), A Variance Bounds Test of the Linear Quadratic Inventory Model, *Journal of Political Economy*, Vol. 94, pp. 374-401.

11 Productivity and Prices - Testing the Relationship Using Micro Data

Julian Peters[*]

1 Introduction

This paper undertakes to use micro-data to examine the link between productivity and prices. Theoretically, productivity affects prices through a standard mark-up model. This is the model used here. The markup model includes both demand and supply side factors. It is useful then for this paper to compare the effects of productivity on prices with other shocks. An analysis of this type is important since empirically supply side shocks have become more predominant with the aggregate output-price correlation now negative. A previous stylised business cycle fact was that the correlation was positive.

In empirically estimating the effects of productivity on prices, a two stage estimation procedure is completed. This is required due to data limitations from our unit record data source, the Quarterly Survey of Business Opinion (QSBO). In the specification productivity affects average costs, which then affects prices. Prices are also affected by demand and sectoral prices.

Empirically productivity is found to have a strong negative effect on prices. This occurs with approximately the same strength in every inflation regime and business cycle phase. The affect on prices was measured to be similar in strength to a change in input costs.

The effect of sectoral price changes is significant. The results indicate a very strong propensity for firms to follow price changes of other firms. This propensity to follow is stronger for price decreases than increases.

Following the measurement on how productivity affects prices, we also test whether the pass-through was complete. This is equivalent to analysing whether profit per unit of output is increased. When testing this hypothesis we found strong evidence that profit increased when productivity increased. This indicates that most firms imperfectly adjust prices following a change in productivity.

To close the model an equation for productivity is developed. Although the primary interest has been on shifts of supply curve, it is readily apparent that productivity is highly cyclical. These can be thought of as shifts down an average cost curve. In empirically

---

[*] The New Zealand Institute of Economic Research. Thanks must go to Andrew Coleman, Phil Briggs, and Simon Chapple for helpful comments on earlier drafts, however, all opinions and errors contained in this report remain my own.

estimating productivity this effect was captured. Increasing output leads to higher productivity.

This means that an increase in output has two effects on prices: a demand side effect, and a supply side effect. The supply side effect occurs when increasing output increases productivity, which lowers average cost, which lowers prices. It is apparent that the stronger this supply side effect the more shallow the supply curve would be. We found evidence to suggest that firms supply curves are shallower under low inflation, than higher inflation.

As a final sensitivity this paper shocks both output and productivity (a demand and supply shock). The results for prices depend on the affect of output on prices, or, put another way, the slope of the supply curve. When the supply curve is shallower, as in the low inflation regime, prices fell following the shock to output and productivity, while in higher inflation environments prices rose. We interpret this to mean it is more likely that a negative output-price correlation is observed under conditions of low inflation, than under high inflation.

The paper begins with some theory on prices and productivity. We then outline the desired theoretical specification. Section 3 outlines the unit record data source, the estimateable specification and the estimation technique. Section 4 outlines the results, while Section 5 provides the main interpretation of these results.

2 Background

This paper addresses the relationship between productivity and prices at the firm level. The understanding of this relationship is crucial to explaining key features of empirical work at the aggregate level. Economic theory relating to productivity and prices involves theories regarding the output-price correlation, the determinants of prices and productivity, and issues in productivity growth. The results from the literature - many conflicting - are described below. Following the literature review the approach of this paper is described.

2.1 Price-output Correlation

The price-output correlation debate is relevant to the analysis of productivity because shifts in the supply curve occur due to changes in productivity, or changes in factor prices. When the correlation of output and prices are negative, it gives evidence that supply side shifts are dominant. This paper seeks to quantify the effect on prices of changes in productivity and factors prices.

The growing number of empirical papers that have found a negative correlation between real GDP and the price level led to the establishment of new business cycles models.[1] Known as real business cycle models, these models use productivity changes as the main driving factor for the business cycle. To give further evidence that these are the correct models, these models are calibrated to replicate stylised facts similar to those

---

[1] Kydland and Prescott (1990), Cooley and Ohanian (1991), Backus and Kehoe (1992) and Smith (1992) have established negative correlations.

produced in empirical studies. They believe that these results, particularly the negative correlation of output and prices, show their models are correct and that demand induced theories of the business cycle, which produce a positive output-price correlation, are incorrect.

However, Chanda and Prasad (1994), explain that the demand models of the business cycle do not predict a positive correlation between output and prices, but rather a positive correlation of output and *inflation*. This result was substantiated empirically for all G7 countries. They conclude it is pointless and non-instructive to dismiss economic models of the business cycle on the basis of the output-price level correlation. Further work by Kim (1996), found the same result for Korea and Taiwan.[1]

Another important facet in the price and output correlation is the cyclicality of productivity. Productivity can increase in the pure sense due to a technological innovation. However, it is readily apparent that if firms are quantity constrained, increases in output can lead to increases in productivity. For an individual firm this could mean lower prices are possible. But in aggregate this is unlikely and will usually mean that the aggregate demand curve has a shallow slope.

In this regard the theoretical paper by Mitchell (1994) is important in rectifying the output-price correlation debate. His tenet was that it was ridiculous to assume that only demand *or* supply shocks occur in an economy. It is the case that both shocks occur all the time and his aim was to show that the output-price correlation can turn out to be positive or negative depending on whether; a) demand (supply) shocks are most prevalent, and b) whether the supply (demand) curve has a smaller absolute slope than the demand (supply) curve. In his paper, Mitchell shows that the output-price correlation can be negative if demand shocks are more prevalent, but the supply curve has a smaller absolute slope than demand curve. In economies that show highly procyclical productivity, this result confirms that demand shocks can remain more prevalent, but the output-price correlation can be negative.

2.2 *Determinants of Productivity and Prices*

This section outlines the literature regarding determinants of productivity and prices. The model that this paper is interested in is the causation from productivity to prices. However, literature in the early 1990s found some support for causation from prices to productivity, which we will discuss in brief.

2.2.1 Prices Prices when explained by a normal mark-up model, suggest that productivity lowers prices over time. In most econometric specifications this works though unit labour costs (ULC), and the intercept. The intercept in a price model amounts to trend productivity improvements, while ULC incorporates growth in labour productivity.

---

[1] The results of these two studies hinge on the assumption that inflation is stationary, implying that the price level is I(1). The stationarity of the inflation rate assumption in this study appears crucial to the empirical results on the causation of productivity and inflation addressed in the next section. - I(i) indicates that the series is stationary - has a constant mean and variance - after differencing the series i times.

For instance, the Reserve Bank of New Zealand's single equation models' of core inflation incorporated labour productivity with a highly significant parameter.[1] The inclusion of ULC is equivalent to a test; that changes in wages and changes in labour productivity have the same effect on prices. This test is often thought of as strong, because labour productivity is inherently hard to measure. The Reserve Bank further found a highly significant negative coefficient for the constant in the price equation, indicating negative drift, perhaps caused by productivity.

An issue also arises whether labour productivity is capturing the correct productivity story. Firstly, labour productivity is highly cyclical, due to the inclination to hoard labour. Second; labour productivity could increase if other factors of production increase in proportion. For instance a decrease in the K/L ratio in New Zealand from 1992, due to rising employment, is one of the reasons why New Zealand's labour productivity fell in this period. What is needed is a measure of total factor productivity. Hart (1996) in accounting for growth in UK manufacturing since 1973, shows the diversity of swings in different factor productivities. He shows that the large increase in labour productivity in Britain in the 1980s was offset by changes in other factor productivities. As a result, no Thatcher productivity miracle occurred in the 1980s.

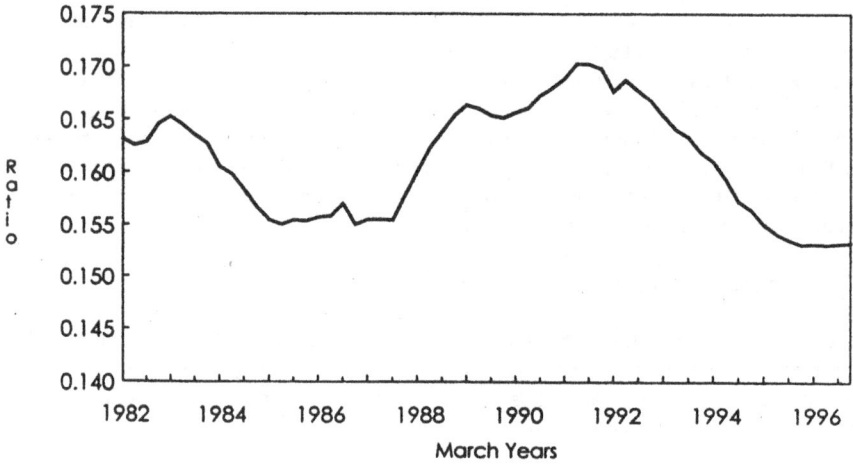

Figure 1   Capital-labour Ratio (K/L)
Source: NZIER.

It is therefore not surprising that empirically ULC is now estimated to be insignificant in explaining inflation.[2] This we believe is more to do with the measurement of productivity than the relationship between productivity and prices itself.

---

[1] See Beaumount, Cassino and Mayes (1994).
[2] See Cozier (1991), Emery and Chang (1996), and Mehra (1991, 1993).

2.2.2 Productivity The popularity of price stability created a wave of research to estimate the merits of low inflation. The overall view in the early 1990s was that low inflation led to higher productivity growth. Higher productivity growth then translated into higher output growth - a good thing.

For instance, Selody (1990), Grimes (1990), and Cozier and Selody (1992), all found that a 1% increase in the rate of inflation would lower productivity growth by around 0.1%. Smyth (1995) found a higher estimate of 0.25% for the German economy.[1] However, more recently this stylised fact has been challenged for developed market economies with low to moderate inflation. Fortin (1993) uses an analysis of 22 OECD countries to conclude that inflation coefficients do not significantly differ from zero. Stanners (1993) attempted unsuccessfully to correlate low inflation and high growth across countries and time. Cameron, Hum, and Simpson (1996) also conclude that no reliable relationship exists.[2]

A paper by Bullard and King (1995), finds that *permanent* changes in inflation have no *permanent* effects on output. They find this result in the context of a structural VAR model similar to Blanchard and Quah (1989). They split a sample of 58 countries into those that have been affected by a permanent shift in the inflation rate and output[3], and those that haven't. Interestingly, only 16 countries satisfied this criteria, while 31 countries had an I(0) inflation series. Of the 16 countries who satisfied the criteria, a permanent output effect given a permanent shock to inflation was not observed. The exceptions were in a very high inflation country that had a negative output result, and certain low inflation counties, which had positive output results, following a positive permanent shock to inflation.

Lastly, an empirical paper by Hamilton (1994) explains real wages, productivity and prices in separate equations for Jamaica. Her specification concerns factors important at the firm level, where productivity occurs. She finds that productivity is affected by capacity utilisation (an output variable), capital intensity, labour intensity, and the import/capital ratio. The fit of the equation is commendable. Her measure of productivity also affects inflation, with the expected negative coefficient.

Overall, the literature has shown that a relationship between productivity and inflation can exist. It is a shame little causation tests have been estimated to find which way round the relationship runs. Recent cross country evidence suggests that the correlation doesn't run from inflation to productivity, at least permanently anyway. The issue of high and low inflation provides some rationale for including inflation regimes in our study. Productivity changes may well be greater at lower levels of inflation.

---

[1] No causation tests have been run on any data that generated these results.

[2] However, they find that productivity growth and inflation did have a relationship. They concluded that this was spurious because inflation was I(1) and productivity growth I(0). However, the relationship makes sense if inflation was I(0). If this was the case, causation tests could have established the direction of causation. Which we believe to be from productivity to prices.

[3] This is the same as a variable being I(1).

3 Theoretical Specification

The objective of this study is to use firm level data to estimate the price transmission mechanism of firms facing changes in demand, costs and productivity. Our main focus is the mechanism by which changes in productivity affect prices and also profits. Below is the theoretical specification used in this study.

$$\text{Price}_i = f(\text{ input prices}_i, \text{demand}_i, \text{productivity}_i, \text{sector prices}_i) \qquad (1)$$

The price equation at the firm level is a standard mark-up model. Prices are set according to input prices, productivity, demand and whether firms in the same sector are raising or lowering prices.

The interest in this specification centres on how changes in productivity affects prices, and in particular how it differs from the effect of input prices.

Demand changes equate to shifts in the demand curve of the firm. If these have a large effect, then this provides evidence that the slope of the firm's supply curve is steep in the short run.

Traditionally demand curves include relative prices of competing goods. If the relative price falls, then we would expect to see an increase in demand. The importance of how other firms in the same sector as firm$_i$ are changing prices, captures this effect. If other firms prices fall, then demand will change at the firm's current prices. This will lead to a propensity for firm$_i$ to change price also. If firm$_i$ doesn't change prices then they will incur a change in output. The more competitive the sector, the larger the shift in demand. Thus changes in prices of other firm's will have a large effect on output, increasing the likelihood of a pricing response will occur.

Another facet of interest is what happens to profits when productivity changes. If productivity changes, what is the inclination of the firm to change price, and what is the effect on profit? Estimation of the following specification will provide an answer to this question.

$$\text{Profit/Output}_i = f(\text{ normal markup}_i, \text{productivity}_i) \qquad (2)$$

Profit per unit is determined by its normal markup and productivity. The markup is the difference between price and average cost for the firm. The stipulation of "normal" recognises that productivity will affect average costs. In this specification, if there is no inclination to increase profit per unit when productivity increases, productivity will be insignificant. Profit per unit of output will carry on being determined by the normal markup.

4 Data

This section outlines the source of the unit record data, other uses of this data, the econometric specification for this study, and lastly properties of the data used across the different cross sections.

4.1 Data Source

The New Zealand Institute of Economic Research (NZIER) has since 1961 surveyed New Zealand firms on their individual performance and short term expectations through the *Quarterly Survey of Business Opinion* (QSBO). Each firm's response since that time is captured on a unit record database. This enables analysis at the individual firm level, improving the accuracy of the results. Appendix A shows the survey questionnaire which has been largely unchanged for 30 years. However, for manufacturing and building firms, a question relating to productivity has been asked only since 1978.

The survey is split into four main sectors of the economy; manufacturing and building, merchants, services and architects. In this study, data from only the manufacturing and building sector is used, since this is the only sector of which the productivity question is asked.

Specifically, each firm is asked whether a variable has improved, remained the same, or deteriorated over the last three months, compared to the previous three months, after allowing for seasonal factors. These variables can be seen in Appendix A and include; the business situation, capacity utilisation, numbers employed, overtime, output, productivity, deliveries in New Zealand, exports, average costs, prices, profitability and stock levels. This information provides a strong basis for in-depth analysis of firm dynamics.

The data itself being in the form - up, the same, and down - means it is; a) ordinal in nature (answers have a natural order), b) able to be aggregated to gain a measure of aggregate *change* at a specified time.

Aggregation of the data can take two forms. First, the data can be represented in net balance form for each survey.[1] This is the simplest transformation. Second, a distribution can be assumed to surround the responses. Two distributions have been used from this type of data in the literature; the normal distribution, as in Carlson and Parkin (1975), and logistic distribution, as in Wren-Lewis (1983). Work at NZIER suggests that all three methods lead to similar results in econometric equations.

4.2 Previous Uses of the Data

The QSBO data is used regularly to indicate how the economy is tracking now and in the future. For this purpose, the net balance response has been a useful description of the aggregate responses of firms to different questions. For instance, the net balance series for the general business situation question has been a reasonably accurate 3 quarter leading indicator of real GDP growth.[2]

Aggregate data in the net balance form has also been used in many econometric specifications at the NZIER and by other researchers.

Recently, the QSBO data has been used for panel econometric estimation. This utilises the unit record nature of the data, where estimation occurs across different cross sections. For instance, Buckle and Carlson (1995), and Buckle, Savage and Peters (1996), break the sample into 10 inflation regimes and into separate sectors.

---

[1] This is obtained as $\frac{(\% \text{ up } - \% \text{ down})}{(100 - \% \text{ N/A})} \times 100$.

[2] See Baird, Fry, and Oliver (1991), and Green and Beaumont (1993).

One further use for the data would be cross sectional time series econometrics, as many respondents have responded consistently to the survey every quarter. This use of the data remains unexploited.

This paper relates to the second use of the data, that is, in estimating cross sectional equations via the ordered probit regression.

4.3 Econometric Specification

In general the theoretical specification described in the previous section cannot be estimated perfectly. This is because of data availability and the type of data we are dealing with. We will describe the impact of each in turn.

4.3.1 Data limitations The theoretical specification for the price equation, included input prices for each firm. In the QSBO questionnaire no input price question is asked. This means that it cannot be explicitly included in the price equation. However, an overall average cost question is asked instead. Unfortunately average costs already include changes in productivity and input prices.

As a solution to this problem, a two stage estimation can be estimated. This explains prices in terms of average costs and average costs in terms of some other variables and productivity. The specifications for prices and average costs are;

$$\text{Price}_i = f(\text{average costs}_i, \text{demand}_i, \text{productivity}_i, \text{sector prices}_i) \qquad (1a)$$

with

$$\text{Average cost}_i = f(\text{input costs}_i, \text{wages}_i, \text{interest rates}_i, \text{productivity}_i) \qquad (3)$$

Since the primary focus of the paper is to analysis the impact of productivity on prices, we leave in the productivity term in the price equation, to see if productivity has any direct effect on prices.

Although input prices are unavailable at the firm level, input costs are available at the sector level. For this we use the producer price index for inputs (PPI), for each sector. This is more imprecise than input prices at the firm level, but is the best measure we have. Likewise, sectoral wages are allocated to each firm.

Average costs are determined by factor prices (wages, intermediate input costs, interest rates), and productivity. We expect that productivity will have a negative effect on average costs.

It is also desirable to analysis the degree to which our productivity variable is cyclical. Since the productivity question is "general" productivity, it does not separate between changes in technological productivity (shifts of the supply curve) and cyclical productivity (shifts down a short run average cost curve). This rationalises why we should seek to derive an expression for productivity also.

Following Hamilton (1994), productivity can be estimated as a function of other variables. For this purpose economic theory is not very useful, as a theory for the determinants of productivity has not been established. As a result, we seek a general specification at the firm level. Productivity is estimated to be dependent on:

$$\text{Productivity}_i = f(\text{output}_i, \text{employment}_i, \text{business climate}_i, \text{capacity utilisation}_i) \qquad (4)$$

When output increases, given stickiness in at least one factor, we expect an increase in productivity will result.[1] The general business situation captures the feel good element in productivity responses. Numbers employed captures the effect on productivity when, everything else constant, labour is changed. Capacity utilisation relates to where the firm is operating on its average cost curve. The closer the firm is to optimal least cost, the smaller the expected productivity gains.

Lastly, the theoretical specification of profit is in terms of profit per unit of output. This is not possible because the QSBO only asks a question related to total profitability. Profit can change if the mark-up changes, or output changes at that mark-up. Mark-up can be thought of as the difference between prices and average costs. The profit equation is now:

$$\text{Profit}_i = f(\text{prices}_i, \text{average costs}_i, \text{output}_i, \text{productivity}_i) \qquad (5)$$

Productivity is still included to see if, allowing for changes in prices and average cost (the mark-up) and output, productivity still affects profitability. If the coefficient on productivity is significant, then firms imperfectly pass through technology improvements into prices.

4.3.2 Estimation technique The nature of the data also dictates the estimation technique. Firstly, the answers to the survey are censored. Respondents will only answer different to "the same" if the variable is greater by an unknown amount. Estimation of censored data calls for a TOBIT estimation. However, this estimation procedure is not appropriate either because the individual data for this study is qualitative - up, down, and the same - and the numerical number given to each response can be given a natural order, the appropriate form for estimation is an ORDERED PROBIT regression (see Madalla (1983)). Below is a brief description of the ordered probit technique.

A "normal" probit estimates the probability that a binomial variable (a variable that takes on a 1 if an event occurs, and a 0 otherwise) will take on a 1. This is estimated via maximum likelihood. In estimation, the likelihood that the prediction, given the values of the independent variables, produce the desired estimate, is maximised.

For the ordered probit, more than two events can occur, with the events having a natural ordering. This creates some auxiliary coefficients that lead to predictions of the events, which, similar to the normal probit, is maximised.

Let y_i be the ith unobserved, dependent variable. Let the independent variables X_{i1} to X_{ik} be represented in the matrix x_i. Assume that:

$$y_i = x_i b_i + u_i$$

---

[1] Hart, R, and Malley, J (1996), find evidence of labour hoarding in Japan, Germany, the UK, and the United States. This they argue provides a justification for the procyclical productivity. Also, our specification has the causation from output to productivity. This view is substantiated from our database. Of the 17,000 observations in our database, - 73% of firms list demand as the factor most inhibiting output, while 18% of firms list supply side factors (materials, labour, or capital). This leads to productivity mainly not to determine output.

where u_i is a standard normal variable. Let z_i be the observed, ordinal dependent variable, which has M possible outcomes: $1, 2,..z_m,...M$. Then y_i is related to z_i, via the set of constants or thresholds (a), where : a_0 = -infinity $< a_1 <......< a_{m-1} < a_m$ = +infinity. Such that:

$$\text{Prob}(y_i = z_m) = \text{Prob}(y_i < a_m) - \text{Prob}(y_i < a_{m-1}) \qquad (6)$$
$$= \text{Prob}(x_i b_i + u_i < a_m) - \text{Prob}(x_i b_i + u_i < a_{m-1})$$
$$= \text{Prob}(u_i < a_m - x_i b_i) - \text{Prob}(u_i < a_{m-1} - x_i b_i)$$

where u_i is normally distributed with a mean 0 and standard deviation of 1. Thus a prediction for the dependent variable on which category or event will occur is made via analysing the probabilities calculated above. A probability is calculated for every category. The category with the highest probability, calculated from the independent variables, is the category predicted by the ordered probit. The maximum likelihood estimation seeks to choose b and a, so that the correct predictions of categories is maximised.

In this study, only three events can occur: up, down and the same. The ordering given to the data is: down = -1, same = 0, up = 1. When this ordering occurs, some authors think that the a's can then be looked at for symmetry purposes. This is not the case. The main reason is that the a's depend on the z's and the X's, thus the distributions of the different X's affect the a's. The a's are primarily there to maximise the likelihood and will vary accordingly.

4.4 Data Properties

This section outlines the aggregate properties of the data used in this study. The data is in up, down, and the same form. Hence, a useful means of describing the data is via the proportion of answers for each variable, for each cross section. The last sub-section shows the aggregate net balance responses of the data over the sample period.

4.4.1 Inflation regimes Table 1 shows the aggregate responses of each variable in each inflation regime. The inflation regimes are those described in Buckle and Carlson (1995). They are summarised as: below 4% pa is treated as low inflation, between 4% and 10% is medium inflation, and above 10% is high inflation. The wage and price freeze in New Zealand in the early 1980s relates to the fixed inflation regime.

The table reveals that output and productivity have increased more often in the low inflation regime, than other regimes. Interestingly, negative price changes have the same frequency in the low inflation regime as under medium inflation, despite average costs decreasing more often in the low inflation regime. Profitability increased most often in the low inflation environment.

4.4.2 Business cycle phases The phases in the business cycle used the turning points identified in Buckle, Kim, and Hall (1992). The phases were chosen by studying the annual percent change of the seasonally adjusted real GDP series. Appendix B shows the different phases identified.

Table 2 shows no surprises regarding what businesses report happened to them during different phases of the business cycle. In the boom phase, firms report output and productivity to increase the most. Price increases occur more frequently during the boom phase, and least frequently in the recession phase. This fact occurs consistently through the different inflation regimes as well.

Table 1   Aggregate responses in each inflation regime

	all		low inflation		med inflation		high inflation		fixed inflation	
	down	up	down	up	down	up	down	up	down	up
output	0.28	0.35	0.22	0.40	0.36	0.27	0.30	0.34	0.30	0.36
productivity	0.16	0.34	0.11	0.40	0.19	0.32	0.18	0.31	0.18	0.32
average cost	0.09	0.53	0.17	0.25	0.12	0.41	0.03	0.78	0.05	0.59
prices	0.12	0.37	0.20	0.18	0.20	0.24	0.04	0.59	0.07	0.24
profit	0.39	0.23	0.31	0.28	0.48	0.18	0.41	0.22	0.46	0.22
input costs	mean	st dev	mean	st dev	mean	st dev	mean	st dev	mean	st dev
qtrly % chg	1.9 %	2.3 %	0.4 %	1.5 %	0.9 %	1.9 %	3.5 %	2.1 %	1.2 %	1.1 %

Table 2   Aggregate responses in each business cycle phase

	boom		downturn		recession		upturn	
	down	up	down	up	down	up	down	up
output	0.20	0.44	0.28	0.32	0.43	0.23	0.26	0.36
productivity	0.13	0.38	0.16	0.31	0.22	0.31	0.15	0.35
average cost	0.08	0.61	0.09	0.49	0.12	0.45	0.09	0.55
price	0.08	0.46	0.15	0.32	0.19	0.27	0.10	0.39
profit	0.32	0.29	0.39	0.21	0.52	0.15	0.38	0.25
input costs	mean	st dev	mean	st dev	mean	st dev	mean	st dev
qtrly % chg	2.2 %	2.3 %	1.4 %	2.0 %	0.8 %	1.6 %	2.8 %	2.6 %

5 Results[1]

This section outlines the results of the econometric estimation. It also highlights differences in each equation that occurred using a reduced cross section, either due to particular inflation regimes or business cycle phases. As a lead in to the main price equation the formulations of average cost and productivity are described first.

5.1 Average Cost and Productivity

5.1.1 Average Cost Following the specification for average cost, the following ordered probit was estimated:

---

[1] All equations were estimated in different regimes and business cycle phases. Appendix C shows the results of these equations. A likelihood ratio test is completed to test statistical significance of the coefficient across business cycle phases or inflation regimes.

$$\text{average cost}_i = 0.163 \text{ input costs}_i + 0.0357 \text{ chg interest}_i - 0.310 \text{ productivity}_i$$
$$\qquad\qquad\quad (45.2) \qquad\qquad\qquad (19.6) \qquad\qquad\quad (22.2)$$

where:
- average costs $_i$, and productivity $_i$ are -1, 0, 1 variables.
- input costs $_i$ is the quarterly percent change of the producer input price for firm i's sector.
- chg interest $_i$ is the quarterly percent change in the base lending rate to businesses.

The major difference between the estimated equation and the original specification is the exclusion of the wage variable. When the wage variable was added, it was found that severe multicollinarity occurred between it and the input cost variable. They were doing the same job. It was decided to estimate two average cost equations. Each equation included the change in the interest rate and productivity, but only input costs or wages, not both. The results of the equations were for the most part identical, so only the average cost equation with input costs is described here.

Productivity and input costs are the major drivers of this equation. A movement from 0 to 1 (an answer from the same to up) for productivity, has the same effect as a 2% decrease in input costs, or an 8% decrease in interest rates (a movement from 11% to 10.1%) over the quarter.

Over the different inflation regimes, all coefficients significantly differ. The pass-through of input costs is insignificant under low and fixed inflation regimes. In the low inflation regime, productivity has the largest effect.

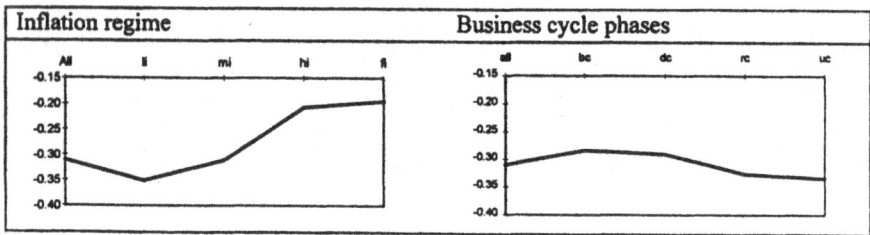

Figure 2   Productivity coefficient

5.1.2 Productivity Following the specification for productivity, the following ordered probit was estimated:

$$\text{productivity} = 1.29 \text{ output}_i - 0.312 \text{ nos employed}_i + 0.0828 \text{ general business situation}_i$$
$$\qquad\qquad\quad (79.7) \qquad\qquad (18.9) \qquad\qquad\qquad (6.3)$$
$$\qquad\qquad\quad -0.0209 \text{ CUBO}_i$$
$$\qquad\qquad\qquad (2.5)$$

where:
- productivity $_i$, output $_i$, nos employed $_i$, and the general business situation $_i$ are -1, 0, 1 variables.
- CUBO $_i$ is an ordered variable, from 0 to 5, indicating how much the firm can increase output *before raising unit costs*. 0 occurs where firms answer not applicable, 1 for firms who can increase output by more than 20%, 2 can increase between 11% to 20%, 3 can

increase between 6% to 10%, 4 can increase between 1% to 5%, and 5 cannot increase output at all.

The results show productivity is strongly procyclical. This indicates that the supply curve of firms are relatively flat. Increases in output lowers productivity, which in turn lowers average costs.

Also, increases in employment lowers productivity. Capacity and the general business situation have the desired signs and are significant. However, their effect is very small compared to output and employment. If capacity utilisation is higher, then productivity is lower - it is harder to squeeze extra gains. Also, a more optimistic business situation in the future is related to higher productivity.

5.2 Price Equation

5.2.1 Original Specification[1] Following the specification for prices, the following ordered probit was estimated:

$$\text{price}_i = 0.511 \text{ average costs}_i + 0.131 \text{ order}_i + 0.0175 \text{ agg price}_i + 0.138 \text{ productivity}_i$$
$$\quad\quad\quad (35.4) \quad\quad\quad\quad\quad (10.2) \quad\quad\quad (51.7) \quad\quad\quad\quad (8.9)$$

where:

- price $_i$, average costs $_i$, orders $_i$, and productivity $_i$ are -1, 0, 1 variables.
- agg price $_i$ is the net balance response of price changes in firm i's sector.

All coefficients are highly significant. Demand is represented by the orders variable. This is consistent with Buckle and Meads (1991), and Buckle and Carlson (1995). Aggregate price change from each firm's own sector is highly significant. This accords with menu cost theory; that the cost of changing price is partly real, and partly customer psychology. If competitors are changing price, then it becomes more acceptable for the firm to change price as well.

Average costs have the strongest influence on the probability of price changes. In the dynamic specification, we found that productivity affects average costs. Thus the inclusion of the productivity variable attempted to capture further marginal affects on price change. The results indicate that there is no negative marginal influence of productivity on prices. In contrast, the results indicate that productivity has a positive impact on price, a perverse result.

We attempted to explain the perverse result by remembering that productivity is highly procyclical. Thus productivity is picking up the impact of output. Higher output, everything else constant, leads to higher prices. To test this hypothesis, output was included into the price equation as well. However, its effect was insignificant, and the productivity term remained positive, although the magnitude of the sign was reduced.

The positive direct marginal impact of productivity on prices may have a coherent explanation. Some degree of productivity might relate to new output. This new output is

---

[1] We estimated equation 1 in the theoretical specification using sectoral input costs as a proxy for firm input prices, however, this was insignificant in all equations across inflation regimes and business cycle phases.

of higher value and can be charged at a higher price, bringing the average price charged by the firm up. However, this explanation is unlikely.

5.2.2 New Specification In an attempt to generate a more coherent price equation we settled on the following equation:

$$\text{price}_i = 0.497 \text{ average costs}_i + 0.102 \text{ order}_i + 0.0175 \text{ agg price}_i + 0.117 \text{ output}_i$$
$$\quad\quad (35.1) \quad\quad\quad\quad\quad (6.1) \quad\quad\quad\quad (51.7) \quad\quad\quad\quad (8.9)$$

where:
- price $_i$, average costs $_i$, orders $_i$, and output $_i$ are -1, 0, 1 variables.
- agg price $_i$ is the net balance response of price changes in firm i's sector.

The second price equation includes output by itself and drops the productivity variable. The equation with both variables rendered output insignificant. This was due to severe multicollinearity between output and productivity, both of which were picking up demand factors. This was confirmed when output was added and productivity excluded. The coefficient on output was significant and around the same level as the productivity term.

The new specification shows that orders alone are an imperfect measure of demand. Although some firms are forward looking enough to use likely future output indicators as demand factors, some firms use current output as a proxy for demand. By including output, we are allowing for both output and orders to affect the price charged by a firm.

Across inflation regimes, the average cost and aggregate price change coefficients vary significantly. The pass-through of costs is highest in the high inflation regime and lowest in the low inflation regime. Under normal Ss pricing rules, when inflation is higher, the trigger point to increase prices, following an increase in cost, is more likely to be reached. Thus prices will increase more often.

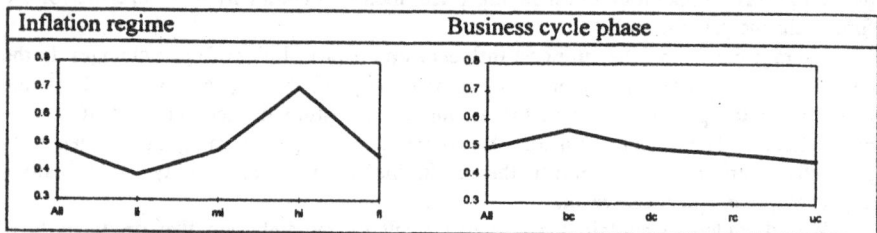

Figure 3 Average cost coefficient

5.3 Profit Equation

Following the specification for profit, the following ordered probit was estimated:

$$\text{profit}_i = 0.709 \text{ prices}_i - 0.616 \text{ average cost}_i + 0.646 \text{ output}_i + 0.342 \text{ productivity}_i$$
$$\quad\quad (45.1) \quad\quad\quad (40.1) \quad\quad\quad\quad (45.8) \quad\quad\quad\quad (20.0)$$

where:
- profit, price $_i$, average costs $_i$, output $_i$, and productivity $_i$ are -1, 0, 1 variables.

The sign for the price, average cost, and output coefficients are as expected. For instance, if price and average costs increase by the same percentage in a markup model, it is expected that the markup has also increased by the same percent. In this model, if firm i indicates that both prices and average costs have increased, then we expect profits to increase. If output increases at the current markup, then expected profits increase also. Expected profit is increased further by increases in productivity.

In the previous results it was shown that productivity changes feed into lower average costs and prices. However, this feed-through is incomplete in nature, as here productivity still contributes positively to profits. If productivity increases, and prices do not fully reflect this, then profits will increase.

Variations of the coefficients across business cycle phases show that the affect of productivity on profit varies significantly. In the boom phase and under high inflation, increases in productivity affect profits the most. In these circumstances higher productivity is past-through to prices the least. Under low inflation increases in productivity have a smaller impact on expected profits.

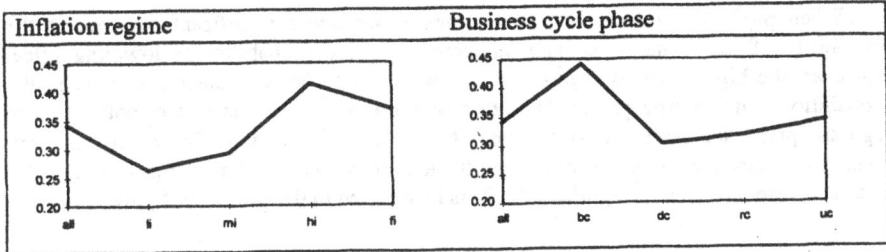

Figure 4 Productivity coefficient

6 Interpretation

6.1 Some Probabilities

Interpretation of ordered probit models need to be completed by looking at changes in the probability of outcomes (up, down or the same) as key independent variables change. In our analysis we also have dynamic interaction between variables. Output affects productivity, which affects average costs, which affects prices. Also, output affects price directly as well.

In this section, we analyse how the probabilities of price changes are affected by productivity, input costs and sectoral prices. To do this we trace through the predicted probabilities of each outcome, and see how the overall price probabilities change. For example, an increase in productivity affects the probability of responses for average costs, which then affects the probability that prices increases.[1]

---

[1] This is formally written as:
Prob(Price = 1|Productivity = 1) = $\sum_{i=1,0,-1}$ (Prob(Avecost = i|Prod = 1) ×(Prob(Price = 1|Avecost = i)

When productivity changes directly and output remains the same, this is similar to technology shock - a shift in the firm's supply curve. Table 3 shows the probabilities of price increases and decreases following a change in productivity.

Table 3   Probabilities of price change when productivity change

Productivity	Probabilities of price increase (1) and decrease (-1)									
	all		boom		recession		low inflation		hi inflation	
	1	-1	1	-1	1	-1	1	-1	1	-1
up	0.34	0.08	0.43	0.05	0.22	0.17	0.14	0.21	0.59	0.03
same	0.37	0.07	0.46	0.04	0.25	0.15	0.16	0.19	0.61	0.03
down	0.39	0.06	0.48	0.04	0.28	0.13	0.17	0.17	0.63	0.02

Note: These probabilities depend on the values assigned to the other independent variables. All variables were assigned the mean from their respective samples.

When productivity increases, all regimes experience a significant decrease in the probability of increasing price and an increase in the probability of lowering price. However, the high inflation regime and the boom phase show a smaller change in the probability of decreasing prices. The reason for this occurrence is that in both of these regimes, price decreases are at the very tail of the distribution. These are not very common occurrences. A large shift along the axis must occur before the probability of a price decrease will change significantly. This is depicted in the following figure.

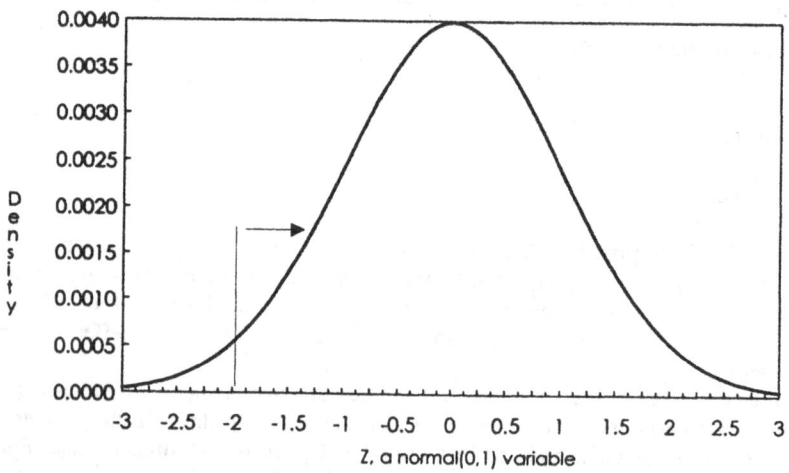

Figure 5   The standard normal distribution

The line in the above standard normal distribution would need to move to the right a long way before the probability of a price decrease changed considerably. This is what is happening in the case of the boom and high inflation regimes.

We can now contrast the productivity results with that of a change in input costs. Table 4 shows the effect of a 2% change in input costs on the probability of price increases and decreases.

Table 4   Probabilities of price change when input costs change

	Probabilities of price increase (1) and decrease (-1)									
	all		boom		recession		low inflation		hi inflation	
Input costs	1	-1	1	-1	1	-1	1	-1	1	-1
2% decrease	0.31	0.10	0.36	0.08	0.22	0.18	0.15	0.19	0.56	0.04
no change	0.34	0.08	0.41	0.06	0.24	0.16	0.16	0.19	0.58	0.04
2% increase	0.37	0.07	0.45	0.04	0.26	0.14	0.16	0.18	0.60	0.03

Note: These probabilities depend on the values assigned to the other independent variables. All variables were assigned the mean from their respective samples.

Input cost changes have a similar effect on the probability of price increases and decreases as productivity changes. The exception is in the low inflation regime. In this regime a 2% change in input costs has a very small effect on prices. This is because input costs are estimated to have a small effect on average costs in this environment, with productivity having a stronger effect. This may occur because in higher inflation regimes input cost increases occur more readily and in larger amounts. Under low inflation, input cost increases are smaller and thus would be treated as insignificant by firms more often. For instance, if firms input costs increased 0.4%, they may answer that average costs have remained the same, even though this is the mean change for input costs under low inflation. Under high inflation, the average input cost change is 3.5%, which is more likely to be responded to as average costs have increased.

The next interest of this paper is to assess how firm's inclination of price changes are affected by how other firms in the same sector are changing prices. Table 5 examines the probability of price changes following a net 50% of firms in the same sector increasing or decreasing price.

The results are quite startling. Firm's are significantly influenced by what other firm's in their same sector are doing. If nothing changes at the representative firm, but a net 50% of firms in their sector decrease price, then the probability the representative firm would decrease price too is 52%. This strong "following" effect occurs more markedly for price decreases than increases. The reason relates to the level of price inertia in the system already. If there is significant positive inflation already, then firm's on the whole would expect to see competitors raising price. This expectation is greater in higher inflation and boom times, leading to a lower inclination to follow increases in these times. Whereas, decreasing prices in this regime is far more unlikely and the need to follow is far greater.

In the low inflation environment, where lowering prices is more normal, the difference between following price increases and decreases is smaller. To reiterate, the amazing aspect about the exceptionally strong propensity to follow occurs when nothing fundamentally has changed to the firm itself.

Table 5   Probabilities of price change when other firms prices change

		Probabilities of price increase (1) and decrease (-1)								
		all		boom		recession		low inflation		hi inflation	
Sector prices		1	-1	1	-1	1	-1	1	-1	1	-1
net decrease	80%	0.03	0.52	0.07	0.31	0.03	0.51	0.02	0.52	0.01	0.71
no change		0.14	0.21	0.13	0.21	0.16	0.21	0.15	0.18	0.09	0.34
net increase	80%	0.42	0.05	0.20	0.13	0.44	0.05	0.46	0.03	0.36	0.08

Note: These probabilities depend on the values assigned to the other independent variables. All variables were assigned the mean from their respective samples.

6.2   Cyclicality of Prices

This section summarises what happens to prices when output changes. Although our primary interest was to quantify what happens when there is a shift in the supply curve, it is readily apparent that our productivity variable is highly cyclical. This means that increases in output have a strong effect on productivity. This can be visualised as a shift down an average cost curve. If the majority of firms have this trait, it implies that the aggregate supply curve is flat. Demand has a smaller effect on prices.

To examine these issues we calculate the probability of price changes given a change in output. Output is demand determined, with over 70% of firms in the sample indicating that they were demand rationed. Thus an increase in output can be thought of as an increase in demand. The calculation for the probability of price changes is more complicated than in the previous section.[1]

The results of calculating these probabilities reveal some very interesting outcomes. Table 6 shows the probabilities of price rises and falls, if output increases, stays the same, or decreases.

In all regimes, prices show a significant procyclical behaviour, with the exception of the low inflation regime. Procyclicality in this case occurs because the probability of a price increase rises, when output increases.

In the low inflation regime, the representative firm shows a very small inclination to raise prices as output rises. i.e. from a decrease (-1) to an increase (1). The reason for this is the higher importance of productivity increases, which occur when output increase, and the low level of average input cost growth in this regime. The latter factor makes average cost more sensitive to the change in productivity.

---

[1] As an example the calculation of the probability price will increase if output increases is as follows:

$$\text{Prob}(\text{Price}=1|\text{Output}=1) = \sum_{j=1,0,-1} \sum_{i=1,0,-1} \text{Prob}(\text{Avecost}=i|\text{Prod}=j) \times \text{Prob}(\text{Prod}=j|\text{Output}=1) \times \text{Prob}(\text{Price}=1|\text{Avecost}=i))$$

Table 6   Probabilities of price change when output change

	Probabilities of price increase (1) and decrease (-1)									
	all		boom		recession		low inflation		hi inflation	
	1	-1	1	-1	1	-1	1	-1	1	-1
output = up	0.39	0.06	0.47	0.04	0.28	0.13	0.16	0.19	0.63	0.03
output = same	0.36	0.07	0.45	0.04	0.25	0.15	0.15	0.19	0.61	0.03
output = down	0.34	0.08	0.44	0.05	0.22	0.17	0.15	0.19	0.58	0.03

Note: These probabilities depend on the values assigned to the other independent variables. All variables were assigned the mean from their respective samples, with the exceptions of: employment and the general business situation which were assigned a zero.

The results also indicate that the aggregate supply curve may be flatter in low inflation environments. This can be imagined as follows. When input costs are rising more often and by a larger amount, as they do under high inflation, the supply curve is moving upward at a rapid rate. This is in comparison to the low inflation regime, where the supply curve is moving up less rapidly. The upshot of this is that if one supply curve was drawn for the economy in the quarter, it would follow that it would have a higher slope under high inflation, compared to low inflation. The following diagram tries to demonstrate this result.

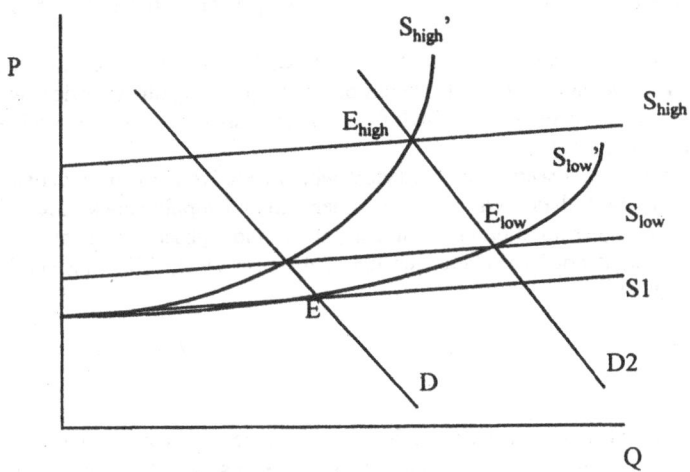

Figure 6   A steeper aggregate supply curve - explained

The initial situation is equilibrium E. Demand increases to D2. However, in that time under high inflation the supply curve has risen to S_{high} and under low inflation the supply curve has risen to S_{low}. The new equilibrium for high inflation is E_{high} and for low inflation is E_{low}. If the movements in the supply curves weren't included in the analysis and only demand, then under high inflation, there is a perception that the aggregate supply curve is steeper than under low inflation.

An interesting sensitivity would be to see what happens when output and productivity changed at the same time. These are a proxy for demand and supply shocks. We include this in table 7 for the entire sample and low inflation. Other tables are contained in Appendix D. The results are in terms of *net probabilities* - which is the probability of a price increase less the probability of a price decrease.

Table 7   Probabilities of price change when productivity and output change

	Net probabilities of price change					
	all output			low inflation output		
Productivity	up	same	down	up	same	down
up	0.31	0.26	0.20	-0.04	-0.07	-0.10
same	0.35	0.30	0.24	0.00	-0.03	-0.06
down	0.39	0.33	0.28	0.04	0.01	-0.02

Note: These probabilities depend on the values assigned to the other independent variables. All variables were assigned the mean from their respective samples, with the exceptions of: employment and the general business situation which were assigned a zero.

Using the full sample, if output and productivity both increase, when previously they had both decreased or stayed the same, net probability increases, an apparent procyclical movement. Thus if demand and supply shocks happen in equal magnitudes, prices will increase.

However, in a low inflation environment, the net probability of a price increase falls. This suggests that when demand and supply shocks occur in equal magnitudes, prices will decrease. This result occurs as the pass-through from output changes to prices is weakest in the low inflation environment.

Overall, the results in this section are consistent with a negative correlation between output and prices in a low inflation environment, if demand and supply shocks occur in similar proportions. In higher inflation environments, across most phases of the business cycle, a procyclical output-price correlation occurs at the firm level, following similar demand and supply shocks.

7 Conclusion

This paper has estimated a transmission mechanism for prices from micro data. The technique used is an ordered probit. This means that the results have to be interpreted taking account of the probability distribution.

The main objective of this paper was to quantify the link between productivity and prices. This can be imagined as a shift of the supply curve. The results indicate that increasing productivity lowers prices significantly. This occurs in all inflation regimes and business cycle phases. This effect on prices was largely similar to a change in input costs. However, both these effects are overwhelmed by the strong "following" inclination of firms. Our results show that if other firms in their same sector either raise or lower prices, then there is a high likelihood that the individual firm will follow also.

In analysing productivity in more depth we found that productivity changes were highly cyclical. This means that increases in output will raise productivity, which as we measured, lowers prices. However, output increases are the result of higher demand. This we estimated to raise prices. The net effect for prices depends on these two effects, which differs according to inflation regime and business cycle phase.

This study finds that in higher inflation environments increases in output are more likely to be associated with price increases than when inflation is lower. Also we find that if productivity and output increase simultaneously, then a decrease in price will occur under the low inflation environment, but an increase in prices will occur in higher inflation environments. Thus in low inflation environments supply side shocks have more effect on prices. This provides a rationale for why negative output-price correlations are now observed, when the previous stylised fact was a positive relationship.

Appendix A Example questionnaire

CONFIDENTIAL
SURVEY OF BUSINESS OPINION

N.Z. INSTITUTE OF ECONOMIC RESEARCH (INC.)
P O BOX 3479 WELLINGTON

No.: 144
Quarter Ending: March 1997

MANUFACTURERS   % of 163 replies

1. Which ONE of the following classifications most closely describes your firm's principal activity?
(Note: Mark only ONE box.)

Consumers' Goods:

Furniture Furnishings	Appliances Electrical goods Electronics	Food Drink Tobacco	Clothing Footwear	Other Household Goods	Building Materials	Other Producers' Materials	Producers' Equipment	Vehicles (incl parts, accessories lubricants and fuels)	Other (please specify)	Building and Construction
4	8	18	6	6	7	3	4	8	31	0

2. How many EMPLOYEES are covered by this return?

1-20	21-50	51-100	101-200	201-500	Over 500
25	13	12	12	26	12

3. In which district is the MAIN PRODUCTION PLANT to which this return relates?

Auckland Northland	Waikato Bay of Plenty	Hawke's Bay East Cape	Taranaki Wanganui	Wellington Manawatu Wairarapa	Nelson West Coast	Canterbury Marlborough	Otago Southland
40	7	4	6	18	2	20	4

4. Do you consider that the general business situation in New Zealand will improve, remain the same, or deteriorate during the NEXT SIX MONTHS?

Improve	Same	Deteriorate	N/A
13	57	29	1

In general, do you find that getting the LABOUR YOU WANT TODAY is easier, the same, or harder than it was THREE MONTHS AGO?

5. Skilled; Specialist

Easier	Same	Harder	N/A
10	60	22	9

6. Unskilled; Semi-skilled

Easier	Same	Harder	N/A
16	75	4	5

7. What SINGLE factor, if any, is most limiting your ability to increase turnover? Shortage of..............

Orders/ Sales	Materials/ Components	Finance	Labour	Capacity	Other
79	6	5	7	6	3

8. Excluding seasonal factors, by how much is it currently practicable for you to increase your production from your EXISTING PLANT AND EQUIPMENT WITHOUT RAISING UNIT COSTS? (Increase per cent)

None	1-5	6-10	11-20	Over 20	N/A
9	11	32	22	23	4

Do you expect the amount of new investment approved for your firm during the NEXT TWELVE MONTHS to be greater/same/less than that approved during the PAST TWELVE MONTHS?

9. ...on Buildings

Greater	Same	Less	N/A
12	40	34	14

10. ...on Fixtures & Fittings, Plant & Equipment

Greater	Same	Less	N/A
23	35	38	3

PAST AND FUTURE TRENDS

What has been your firm's experience during the PAST THREE MONTHS and what changes do you expect in your firm during the NEXT THREE MONTHS in respect of the following (exclude seasonal variations by comparing three month period with the same period a year earlier):

Experienced change PAST three months						Expected change NEXT three months			
1 Up	2 Same	3 Down	4 N/A			1 Up	2 Same	3 Down	4 N/A
15	52	33	0	11 .... Numbers employed 11		11	53	35	1
20	33	44	3	12 .... Overtime worked 12		10	44	42	5
13	64	17	6	13 .... Labour turnover 13		7	70	17	6
19	34	47	1	14 .... All new forward orders received 14		25	50	23	2
21	36	43	0	15 .... Output 15		28	45	26	1
21	53	26	0	16 .... Productivity 16		31	55	13	1
14	39	46	1	17 .... Deliveries in New Zealand 17		26	46	26	3
19	29	24	28	18 .... Export Sales 18		21	35	20	25
31	51	14	3	19 .... Overdue debtors 19		17	63	16	4
23	61	15	1	20 .... Average costs 20		22	55	22	2
10	59	31	0	29 .... Average selling prices 21		15	58	26	1
14	39	47	1	22 .... Profitability 22		24	41	34	1
13	50	31	6	23 .... Stocks-Raw Materials 23		5	53	34	8
24	42	26	8	24 .... Stocks-Finished Goods 24		11	47	33	9

Appendix B Phases of business cycles

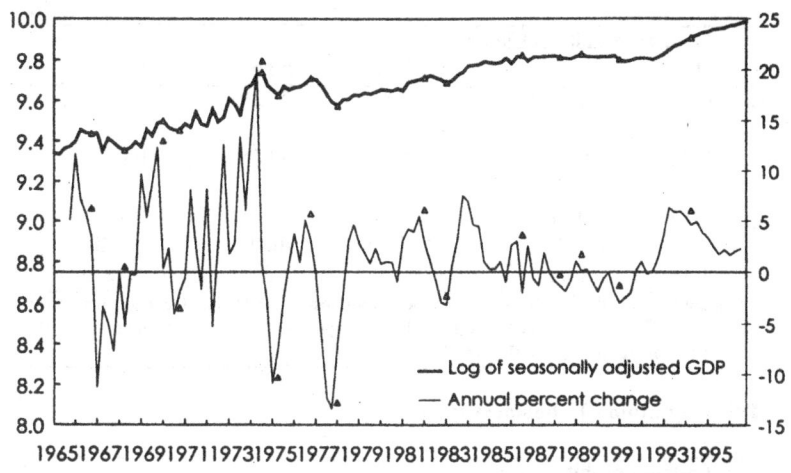

Identified Phases in the Business Cycle December 1996 to December 1996			
Boom	Downturn	Recession	Upturn
Dec66	Mar67 - Jun97	Sep97-Jun68	Sep68-Jun69
Sep69-Mar70	Jun70	Sep70-Dec70	Mar71-Mar73
Jun-73-Sep74	Dec74	Mar75-Jun75	Sep75-Mar76
Jun76-Dec76	Mar77-Jun77	Sep77-Mar78	Jun78-Mar81
Jun81-Mar82	Jun82-Dec82	Dec82-Mar83	Jun83-Mar84
Jun84-Sep86	Dec86-Sep87	Dec87-Jun88	Sep88-Mar89
Jun89	Sep89-Mar90	Jun90-Mar92	Jun92-Sep93
Dec93-Mar95	Jun95-Dec96		

Appendix C Equation coefficients

Table 8 Price equation i) - business cycles

| | Ordered probit coefficients | | | | |
	all	boom	downturn	recession	upturn
average cost	0.51	0.57**	0.53**	0.49**	0.48**
orders	0.13	0.15	0.14	0.17	0.09
aggregate prices	0.02	0.02	0.02	0.02	0.02
productivity	0.14	0.06**	0.23**	0.11**	0.16**
a1	-0.79	-0.79	-0.76	-0.79	-0.84
a2	1.11	1.15	1.10	1.01	1.16

Note: all variables are statistically significant. A likelihood ratio test was completed tesing whether the coefficient parameters differed from over the four cycles. ** signifies statistical difference at the 5% level, * signifies statistical significance at the 10% level.

Table 9   Price equation i) - inflation regimes

	Ordered probit coefficients				
	all	low	medium	high	fixed
average cost	0.51	0.41**	0.50**	0.72**	0.47**
orders	0.13	0.15	0.19	0.08	0.13
aggregate prices	0.02	0.02*	0.02*	0.02*	0.02*
productivity	0.14	0.11	0.17	0.13	0.19
a1	-0.79	-0.89	-0.77	-0.40	-0.98
a2	1.11	1.08	1.01	1.36	1.48

Note: all variables are statistically significant. A likelihood ratio test was completed tesing whether the coefficient parameters differed from over the four cycles. ** signifies statistical difference at the 5% level, * signifies statistical significance at the 10% level.

Table 10   Price equation ii) - business cycles

	Ordered probit coefficients				
	all	boom	downturn	recession	upturn
average cost	0.50	0.57**	0.50**	0.48**	0.45**
orders	0.10	0.12	0.14	0.09	0.08
aggregate prices	0.02	0.02	0.02	0.02	0.02
productivity	0.12	0.09	0.12	0.16	0.11
a1	-0.81	-0.80	-0.79	-0.82	-0.87
a2	1.08	1.15	1.06	0.98	1.12

Note: all variables are statistically significant. A likelihood ratio test was completed tesing whether the coefficient parameters differed from over the four cycles. ** signifies statistical difference at the 5% level, * signifies statistical significance at the 10% level.

Table 11   Price equation ii) - inflation regimes

	Ordered probit coefficients				
	all	low	medium	high	fixed
average cost	0.50	0.39**	0.48**	0.71**	0.46**
orders	0.10	0.15	0.13	0.06	0.07
aggregate prices	0.02	0.02**	0.02*	0.02**	0.02**
productivity	0.12	0.06	0.18	0.10	0.19
a1	-0.81	-0.91	-0.80	-0.42	-1.00
a2	1.08	1.06	0.98	1.34	1.46

Note: all variables are statistically significant. A likelihood ratio test was completed tesing whether the coefficient parameters differed from over the four cycles. ** signifies statistical difference at the 5% level, * signifies statistical significance at the 10% level.

Table 12 Average cost equation - business cycles

	Ordered probit coefficients				
	all	boom	downturn	recession	upturn
input prices	0.16	0.20**	0.18**	0.14**	0.13**
interest rates	0.04	0.02**	0.03**	0.07**	0.06**
productivity	-0.31	-0.28	-0.29	-0.33	-0.33
a1	-1.22	-1.12	-1.22	-1.39	-1.36
a2	0.12	0.13	0.23	0.01	-0.02

Note: all variables are statistically significant. A likelihood ratio test was completed tesing whether the coefficient parameters differed from over the four cycles. ** signifies statistical difference at the 5% level, * signifies statistical significance at the 10% level.

Table 13 Average cost equation - inflation regimes

	Ordered probit coefficients				
	all	low	medium	high	fixed
input prices	0.16	0.01^n**	0.03**	0.08**	0.05^n**
interest rates	0.04	0.02**	0.00^n **	0.03**	0.00^n **
productivity	-0.31	-0.35**	-0.31**	-0.21**	-0.20**
a1	-1.22	-1.09	-1.20	-1.58	-1.67
a2	0.12	0.57	0.23	-0.51	-0.21

Note: all variables are statistically significant unless indicated. A likelihood ratio test was completed tesing whether the coefficient parameters differed from over the four cycles. ** signifies statistical difference at the 5% level, *signifies statistical significance at the 10% level.
N - indicates not significant at 5%.

Table 14 Productivity equation - business cycles

	Ordered probit coefficients				
	all	boom	downturn	recession	upturn
output	1.29	1.45*	1.32*	1.14*	1.30*
numbers employed	-0.31	-0.28**	-0.30**	-0.34**	-0.32**
capacity utilisation	-0.02	0.01	-0.02	-0.07	-0.01
general business	0.08	0.10	0.08	0.07	0.10
a1	-1.33	-1.33	-1.38	-1.29	-1.31
a2	0.65	0.87	0.73	0.36	0.70

Note: all variables are statistically significant. A likelihood ratio test was completed tesing whether the coefficient parameters differed from over the four cycles. ** signifies statistical difference at the 5% level, * signifies statistical significance at the 10% level.

Table 15 Productivity equation - inflation regimes

	Ordered probit coefficients				
	all	low	medium	high	fixed
output	1.29	1.36	1.18	1.29	1.34
numbers employed	-0.31	-0.37**	-0.29**	-0.31**	-0.23**
capacity utilisation	-0.02	-0.04**	-0.04**	0.00**	-0.05**
general business	0.08	0.13**	0.07**	0.03**	-0.07**
a1	-1.33	-1.51	-1.31	-1.22	-1.34
a2	0.65	0.58	0.50	0.78	0.68

Note: all variables are statistically significant. A likelihood ratio test was completed tesing whether the coefficient parameters differed from over the four cycles. ** signifies statistical difference at the 5% level, * signifies statistical significance at the 10% level.

Table 16 Profit equation - business cycles

	Ordered probit coefficients				
	all	boom	downturn	recession	upturn
price	0.71	0.69	0.77	0.65	0.69
average cost	-0.62	-0.59*	-0.69*	-0.56*	-0.66*
output	0.65	0.54**	0.57**	0.67**	0.69**
productivity	0.34	0.44**	0.30**	0.32**	0.34**
a1	-0.35	-0.42	-0.43	-0.18	-0.36
a2	1.00	0.93	0.99	1.15	0.99

Note: all variables are statistically significant. A likelihood ratio test was completed tesing whether the coefficient parameters differed from over the four cycles. ** signifies statistical difference at the 5% level, * signifies statistical significance at the 10% level.

Table 17 Profit equation - inflation regimes

	Ordered probit coefficients				
	all	low	medium	high	fixed
price	0.71	0.81*	0.67*	0.71*	0.85*
average cost	-0.62	-0.57**	-0.50**	-0.64**	-0.76**
output	0.65**	0.69**	0.66**	0.56**	0.77**
productivity	0.34	0.26**	0.29**	0.41**	0.37**
a1	-0.35	-0.52	-0.21	-0.30	-0.31
a2	1.00	0.94	1.09	1.02	0.98

Note: all variables are statistically significant. A likelihood ratio test was completed tesing whether the coefficient parameters differed from over the four cycles. ** signifies statistical difference at the 5% level, * signifies statistical significance at the 10% level.

Appendix D   Probability changes for output and productivity changes

Table 18   Probabilities of price change when productivity and output change

Productivity	Net probability of price change					
	boom cycle output			recession cycle output		
	up	same	down	up	same	down
up	0.41	0.37	0.33	0.14	0.05	-0.03
same	0.45	0.41	0.37	0.19	0.10	0.02
down	0.48	0.44	0.40	0.23	0.15	0.06

Note: These probabilities depend on the values assigned to the other independent variables. All variables were assigned the mean from their respective samples, with the exceptions of: employment and the general business situation who were assigned a zero.

Table 19   Probabilities of price change when productivity and output change

Productivity	Net probabilities of price change					
	high inflation output			low inflation output		
	up	same	down	up	same	down
up	0.60	0.55	0.51	-0.04	-0.07	-0.10
same	0.62	0.58	0.54	0.00	-0.03	-0.06
down	0.64	0.60	0.56	0.04	0.01	-0.02

Note: These probabilities depend on the values assigned to the other independent variables. All variables were assigned the mean from their respective samples, with the exceptions of: employment and the general business situation who were assigned a zero.

References

Backus, D. and Kehoe, P. (1992), International evidence on the historical properties of business cycles, *American Economic Review*, 82, pp. 864-888.

Baird, M., Fry, J. and Oliver, D. (1991), *Economic confidence*. The Treasury of New Zealand Working Paper.

Balke, N. and Wynne, M. (1996), *Supply shocks and the distribution of price changes*, Federal Reserve Bank of Dallas Economic Review, No.1, pp. 10-18.

Blanchard, O. and Quah, D. (1989), The dynamic effects of aggregate demand and supply disturbances, *American Economic Review*, 79, pp. 655-673.

Buckle, R. and Carlson, J. (1996), *Inflation and asymmetric price adjustment*, Victoria University Working Paper.

Buckle, R., Peters, J. and Savage, J. (1996), *Asymmetric price adjustment: an investigation of the merchant and service sectors*, Report to The Treasury. New Zealand Institute of Economic Research.

Bullard, J. and Keating, J. (1995), The long-run relationship between inflation and output in postwar economics, *Journal of Monetary Economics*, No. 36, pp. 477-496.

Cameron, N., Hum, D. and Simpson, W. (1996), Stylized facts and stylized illusions: inflation and productivity revisited, *Canadian Journal of Economics*, 59, No. 1, pp. 152-162.

Carlson, J. and Parkin, M. (1975), Inflation expectations, *Economica*, No. 42, pp. 123-135.

Chanda, B. and Prasad, E. (1994), Are prices countercyclical? Evidence from the G-7, *Journal of Monetary Economics*, 34, pp. 239-257.

Cooley, T. and Ohanian, L. (1991), The cyclical behavior of prices, *Journal of Monetary Economics*, 28, pp. 25-60.

Cozier, B. (1991), *Wage and price dynamics in Canada*, (Ottawa: Bank of Canada Technical Report no. 56).

Cozier, B. and Selody, J. (1992), *Inflation and macroeconomic performance. some cross country evidence* (Ottawa: Bank of Canada Technical Report).

Dowd, K. (1995), Deflating the productivity norm, *Journal of Macroeconomics*, 17, No. 4, pp. 717-732.

Emery, K. and Chang, C. (1996), *Do wagers help predict inflation*. Federal Reserve Bank of Dallas, No. 1, pp. 2-9.

Fortin, P. (1993), The unbearable lightness of zero inflation optimism, *Canadian Business Economics*, 1, pp. 3-18.

Green, A. and Beaumont, C. (1993), *Leading Indicators of Output*, Reserve Bank Bulletin, Vol. 56, No. 2.

Grimes, A. (1990), *The effects of inflation on growth: Some international evidence*. (Reserve Bank of New Zealand).

Hamilton, R. (1994), Analysing real wages, prices and productivity and the effects of state intervention in Caribbean-type economics, *Social and Economic Studies*, 43:1, pp. 1-42.

Hart, P. (1996), Accounting for the economic growth of firms in UK manufacturing since 1973, *Cambridge Journal of Economics*, 20, pp. 225-242.

Hart, R. and Malley, J. (1996), Excess labour and the business cycle: A comparison study of Japan, Germany, the United Kingdom and the United States, *Economica*, No. 66, pp. 325-342.

Kim, K., Buckle, R. and Hall, V. (1994), *Dating the New Zealand Business Cycles*. GSBGM Victoria University, No. 6.

Kim, Y. (1996), *Are prices countercyclical? Evidence from east Asian countries*. Federal Reserve Bank of St Louis, Sept, 69-82.

Kydland, F. and Presscott, E. (1990), Business cycles real facts and a monetary myth, Federal Reserve bank of Minneapolis Quarterly Review, Spring, 1-18.

Mehra, Y. (1991), Wage growth and the inflation process: An empirical note, *American Economic Review*, No. 81, pp. 931-937.

Mehra, Y. (1993), Unit labour costs and the price level, Federal Reserve Bank of Richmond Economic Quarterly, No. 79/4, pp. 35-51.

Mitchell, D. (1994), Business cycle sources and price level-output correlation, *Journal of Macroeconomics*, 16, No. 3, pp. 547-551.

Selody, J. (1990), *The goal of price stability: A review of the issues*. (Ottawa: Bank of Canada Technical Report No. 54).

Smith, R. (1992), The cyclical behavior of prices, *Journal of Money, Credit and Banking*, 24, pp. 413-430.

Smyth, D. (1995), Inflation and total factor productivity in Germany, *Weltwirtschaftliches Archiv*, pp. 403-405.

Stanners, W. (1993), Is inflation an important condition for high growth?, *Cambridge Journal of Economics*, 17, March, pp. 79-107.

Strauss, J. (1996), The cointegrating relationship between productivity, real exchange rates and purchasing power parity, *Journal of Macroeconomics*, 18, No. 2, pp. 299-313.

Wren-Lewis, S. (1985), The quantification of survey data on expectations, *National Institute Economic Review*, No. 113, August, pp. 39-49.

12 Forecasting Models for Demand Series of Private Firms - Using Survey Results and Dynamic Methods of Econometrics

Kurt Stock

1 Purpose of the Study

This report is based on studies that produced demand forecasts for German firms of various sizes, regional orientation and product ranges. The case studies that will be presented in the empirical chapter have two points in common. The time series requested by the commissioners of the studies first require a particular methodological strategy because of their uneven, almost erratic nature. On the request of the firms, the explanatory variables should further include not only time series from the official statistics but also the indicator variables from surveys of the Ifo Institute.

Priority was given to quantitative forecasting models with dynamic econometric estimation methods (Assenmacher 1984, pp. 295-306) and careful statistical and graphical tests. In developing the early warning systems, we tried, where possible, to take new hypotheses on consumption theory (Tichy 1988, pp. 74-267; Westphal 1988, pp. 295-306) as well as market and corporate peculiarities into consideration.

The solution strategy used in this study is based on two proven approaches. In the first (Langhans/Müller 1988) several input series can be weighted together into a demand indicator and finely adjusted using detailed knowledge of the firms and test measures with graphs. A three-stage quantitative-qualitative forecasting method goes a step further (Reiner/Weßner/Wimmer 1991). This method combines traditional quantitative analysis techniques (Box-Jenkins and regression techniques) with qualitative efforts (garnering of expert knowledge). The following methodological principle (K. Stock 1991), which will be explained in more detail, is similar but includes the following extensions.

Qualitative information from Ifo surveys are suitable for portraying both overall and industry assessments and expectations as explanatory time series. Such variables are also indispensable supplements to data from official sources because of their regular early publication dates and the deep industrial disaggregation.

Intensive co-operation of company experts allows us to calculate near-market influencing variables, the detection of special determinants including structural breaks in the target variable, and promotes the acceptance of early indicators.

Of key importance for the quality of estimates and the accuracy of forecasts is a modern, dynamic estimating approach and a testing procedure that combines statistical measures with detailed graphical inspection.

It is nevertheless impossible to take into consideration a sufficient amount of influences that affect company demand as explanatory variables in the forecast equation. A thorough econometric modelling of the remaining systematic residuals (K.Stock 1993) yields a welcome improvement of accuracy.

2 Mathematical Methods

The task led to the choice of a strategy that combines suitable econometric methods including spectral-analytical instruments, correlations and dynamic regressions, as well as modern statistical tests. The entire procedure consists of sequenced blocks. Nearly all analyses were calculated with the SAS software package (SAS Institute 1990, 1991 and 1995). Charts considerably facilitate the decision of which alternative is to be preferred, since they allow quick recognition of details, such as special developments. An overview is found in the flow diagram 'Methods and Tests' and the most important formulas with explanations are in the Annex under 'Mathematical Methods'.

Flow Diagram: Methods and Tests

Purpose of investigation	Method	Test[1)2)]
1. Choice of a suitable filter for <u>transforming the dependent variable</u>	- Requests of the firm - Transfer function - Graphical inspection	N C D
2. <u>Selection and transformation</u> of the <u>explanatory variables</u>	- Experts' knowledge and theoretical economic hypotheses - Serial correlation - Graphical inspection	N C D
3. <u>Lead-lag-analysis</u> ('Selection problem')	- Serial correlation r-coefficient - Graphical inspection - Weighted correlation weighted r-coefficient	N C D

4a. Estimation of fore- casting equations ('Aggregation problem')	Types of dynamic regressions:	White noise -, t-, DW-Test,	N
	- OLS admitting only simple lags ('Base specification')	R^2adj, AIC,	C
	- Successive ARIMA residual models - Simultaneous residual modelling - Almon distributed lag specifications - Transfer function equations	RMSPE from ex- post-forecastings	D

4b. Considering the trend
component
	- Deterministic trend suggested by
	  market experts
	- Stochastic trend
	- Suitable market variable with
	  growth component		

5. Completing checks concerning: Stability of the model structure Forecasting ability	Moving regressions Ex-post-forecastings for different periods	Chow Test RMSPE

[1] Test ist used for: N = necessary condition, C = primary choice, D = final decision.
[2] DW = Durbin-Watson measure, R^2 adj = multiple correlation coefficient adjusted by the degrees of freedom, AIC = Akaike's criterion, RMSPE = root mean square percentage error.

2.1 Transformation of Variables

The demand time-series of the empirical examples provided by the commissioners are irregular, as a rule, and for some periods even erratic. Before they can be used sensibly, they must be smoothed in an appropriate way. The spectral-analytical instrument of transfer functions (Goldrian 1995, König/Wolters 1972) facilitates the pre-selection of suitable filters. The portrayal as a graph let us clearly decide whether the interesting trend and business-cycle components remain almost untouched and the disturbances are furthermore dampened sufficiently (analysis in frequency dimension). The time-dependent depiction of the demand series itself makes final selection easier (analysis in time dimension).

2.2 Correlation Analysis

The forecast goal requires that the explanatory variables are included in the estimating function with sufficiently long leads. It is thus important to determine the optimal temporal distance to the target variable. The conventional method of series correlation is supplemented in the selection phase using a technique by which critical periods for the examination (e.g. intervals around turning points) are emphasized. This weighted correlation measure gives preference in pre-selection to a small number of lead-lag structures. In the last step the dependent and one of the independent variables are compared graphically. In this way the 'optimal' time delay is found for every explanatory variable.

2.3 Dynamic Regressions

The econometric approach most frequently used to process indicator approaches is the ordinary least square method with only simple lags. This base specification is compared to much more refined and dynamic approaches (Harvey 1994 and 1995), which can only be briefly explained here.

With successive ARIMA residual models (Pindyck/Rubinfeld 1991, pp.538-550), the residuals from the causal regressions are subsequently estimated as an independent ARIMA process, since they usually show considerable systematic movement. The structural regression coefficients computed before remain unaffected. By combining the structural and residual parts, a considerably improved adjustment to the dependent variables is achieved in all cases.

Simultaneous estimation procedures allow us to calculate all parameters together. This logical advantage also finds expression in enhanced forecast suitability.

In a further extension, Almon distributed lags take influence of several past periods of one or more explanatory variables into account. A simultaneous modelling of the disturbance term as an autoregressive process is additionally possible.

Transfer function equations were attempted in this report on only a few test calculations for the last example. They are the most complicated type of approach, for which in addition statistical selection is least accessible.

For two of the case studies, the treatment of the long-term components is an additional problem. Three basic trend concepts must be compared. The deterministic company trends are compared with the so-called stochastic trend (H. J. Stock/Watson) and specifications including market variables with growth components. As expected, the last-mentioned concept performs best in the estimates with the second example.

2.4 Testing

The selection of a forecast equation to be recommended to the commissioner must be made with great caution. As necessary conditions, the conventional t- and Durbin-Watson statistics are supplemented by Bartlett's Kolmogorov-Smirnov white noise test. The multiple correlation coefficient, adjusted with regard to the amount of the degrees of freedom and Akaike's information criterion are employed as primary choices. But in accordance with the forecasting goal, the decision is made by using the root mean square percentage error from ex-post forecastings. A closer look at additionally employed test criteria, especially the Box-Jenkins approach related methods (such as autocorrelation plots) is not possible here. Finally, structural consistency must occasionally be tested. Of the variety of tests, moving regressions and a Chow text (A'Walelu et al. 1988) are helpful for this study.

3 Empirical Results for Demand Indicators

The three application examples of the above-mentioned method will be briefly described. The outline is uniform. The description of the problem is followed by the economic hypotheses and the primary methodological goal. The conclusion contains a short appraisal of the results with promising refinements.

3.1 Orders in Western Europe

Incoming orders of an internationally active company on the Western European market is the target variable of the first case study. The dependent series is computed as deviations from weighted moving averages. Forecasts must be made for a highly aggregated variable and additionally with partial indicators for European countries.

The explanatory variables can be seen in Table 1, where it is evident that important influences are incorporated in the forecasting model. The import expectations from the Ifo Institute's Economic Survey International (ESI) and the export expectations in manufacturing from the Ifo Business Survey supplement the exchange-rate variables from the monthly reports of the Bundesbank. Here, valuable information from the commissioners was used since a company's export structure is suitable for weighting the ESI series on the 'present economic situation' that is determined for individual European countries. The numerous tests with additional indicators from international statistics proved to be inferior to the proposed specification (see Equation 2 in Table 2).

The main emphasis in an econometric perspective in this example is the selection of an adequate transformation of the dependent series with the help of transfer functions and the lead-lag examination. Figure 1 underscores that the five-quarter moving averages provide the best filter effects. The instrument of the weighted correlation measure r_w leads in the case of the explanatory variable 'export expectations' to a different optimal lag than when using the simple coefficient r – a result that is confirmed later in the regression analysis. Equation 1b, which is estimated with a simultaneous structure and residual model, is clearly superior to the basis version of ordinary least squares of the statistical examination. These results are seen in Figure 2. In addition, the rising course of the forecasting values correlates well with the overall foreign trade situation (Neumann/Goldrian 1997).

Table 1 Orders received from Western Europe[a] by an international company
- quarterly correlation analyses 1/1986 - 1/1997 -

Explanatory variable	Optimal lag	r[f]	r_w[g]	Source[h]
Production in EC countries[b] 1991 = 100	-3	0.60		EC
Gross domestic product[c] in EC countries 1990 = 100	-3	0.793		MAIN
External value of the DM against the currencies of 18 industrial[c] countries	-4	-0.427		BB
External value of the DM against the currencies of the Ec[c] countries	-3	-0.514		BB
Export expectations[b] in manufacturing industry of Germany	-3/-4	0.64/0.46	0.71/0.73	ifo BS
Judgement about present economic situation[d], overall economy, Western Europe	-3/-4	0.61/0.58	0.69/0.67	ifo ESI
Expected foreign trade volume by the end of the next 6 months, imports[d] Western Europe	-3	0.643		ifo ESI
Market variable[e] for Western Europe	-3	0.682		

a) In current prices, deviations from weighted moving averages.
b) Smoothed by 5-quarter-moving-averages.
c) Differences to preceding year, smoothed.
d) Aggregation across European countries, using weights computed from the company's export structure.
e) Availability of hardware and software in Western Europe, smoothed.
f) Correlation coefficient.
g) Correlation coefficient, important period e.g. turning points emphasised with larger weights.
h) BB = Deutsche Bundesbank, monthly reports, EC = Statistical reports of the European Community, Io BS = Business Surveys of the Ifo Institute, Io ESI = Economic Survey International of the Io Institute, MAIN = Main Economic Indicators, monthly statistical reports of the OECD.

Source: Computations of the author.

Forecasting Models for Demand Series of Private Firms

Table 2   Preferable regressions[a)] for Western Europe demand[b)] / period of analysis 4/1987 –4/1996

Independent[c)] variables	Lags in months	Estimation method	Estimated coefficients							Test statistics		
			b_0	b_1	b_2	b_3	b_4	b_5	b_6	AIC	R^2adj	DW
1a. Equation: Judgement about present economic situation Western-Europe	-4	Ordinary least squares	0.598 (1.0)	1.433 (3.7)	0.261 (3.6)	-0.283 (-2.4)				185.3	0.669	1.6
Export expectations of Germany	-4											
External value of the DM against the currencies of 18 industrial countries	-3											
1b. Equation: Same explanatory variables as in equation 1a.		Simultaneous residual-model	0.764 (1.2)	1.411 (4.5)	0.3 (4.3)	-0.319 (-2.0)	-0.312 (-2.3)	-0.327 (-2.4)	-0.663 (-4.8)	166.5	0.848	2.2
Residuals	-1											
Residuals	-4											
Residuals	-5											
2. Equation: Production in EC countries	-3	Ordinary least squares	-0.835 (-2.4)	0.838 (4.7)	0.2 (4.9)	-0.104 (-1.8)				182.3	0.547	1.3
Export expectations F of Germany	-4											
External value of the DM against the currencies of 18 industrial countries	-3											

a) Explanations: b= estimated regression coefficient, ( ) = t-value, AIC = Akaike's criterion, R^2adj = multiple correlation coefficient adjusted by degrees of freedom, DW = Durbin-Watson-measure.
b) Quarterly deviations from weighted moving averages.
c) Same variable transformation as in Table 1.

Source: Computations of the author.

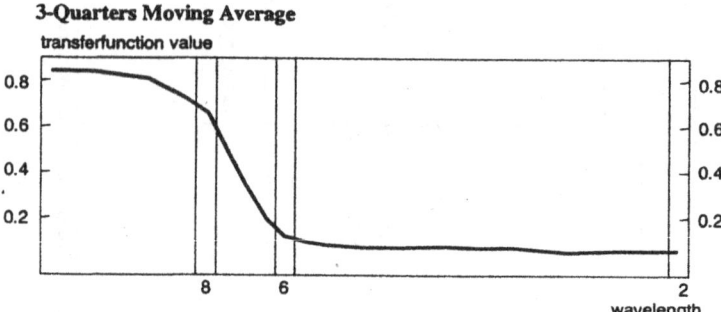

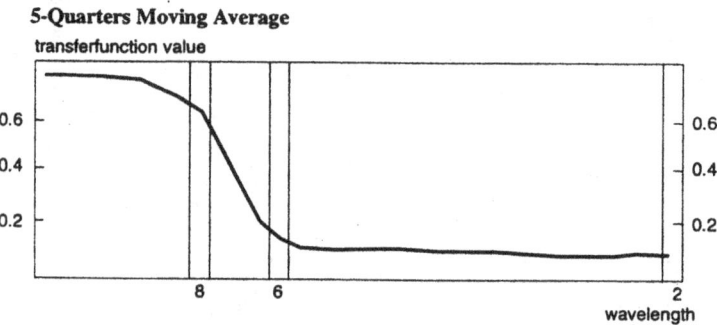

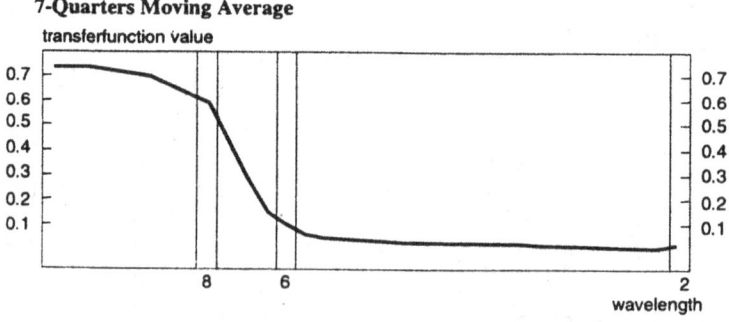

Figure 1   Transformations a) for comparison of alternative smoothing filters / orders received b) from Western Europe

Forecasting Models for Demand Series of Private Firms

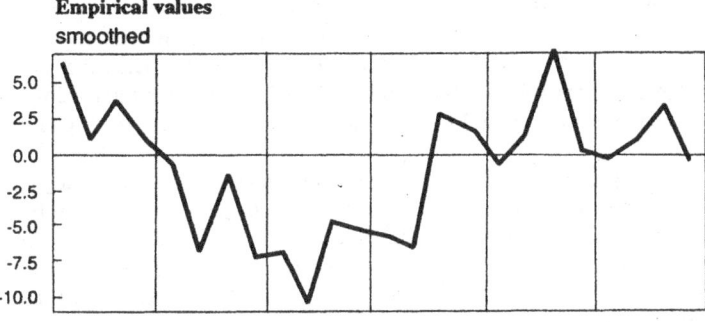

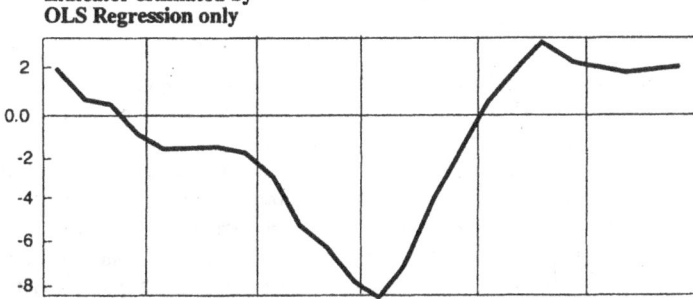

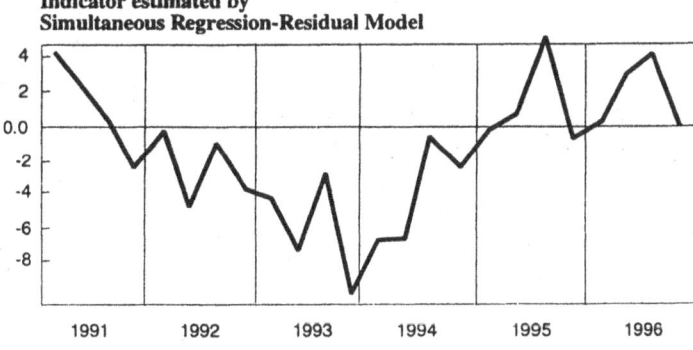

Figure 2 Demand in Western Europe

3.2 Home Demand of a Large Firm

In the second example the target variable is in the form of a smoothed level series. Table 3 also shows the indicators investigated in the correlation analysis and hence also the economic-theoretical hypothesis. Of particular interest is the quantification of the influence exerted by interest-rate policy on company demand. In recent years the yield curve has been a subject of discussion (Lahiri 1997) and preferred for this forecasting system over short-term interest rates - both having about the same estimating quality and forecasting suitability.

In this study of level values a comparison of three trend concepts suggests itself. A series from a company's database that characterizes the market is preferable in every respect to a deterministic presentation of the trend. In this case as well, expert knowledge from companies contributes considerably to an improvement of the forecasting equation. The concept of a stochastic trend (H. J. Stock/Watson 1989) was utilized, but here additional test calculations are necessary. The superiority of modern dynamic models with simultaneous estimations of the error term is seen in Table 3.

3.3 Sales of a Consumer Durable

The commissioning firm in the last example, in contrast to the previously discussed businesses, are active only in the northern German region with a very limited number of products and a small number of similarly sized competitors.

Time series from Ifo Institute surveys were tested as indicators along with construction industry variables and private disposable income. In this case study all the methods explained in more detail in the Annex were used for comparative purposes. In Table 4 the results of the lead-lag analysis, in Table 5 the results of the dynamic estimates, and in Table 6 a test of the forecasting suitability using ex-post pre-estimates over four quarters are shown. The overall favourable estimating accuracy (see Figure 3) leads us to assume in particular a successful ex-ante forecast. Further improvements with dynamic regressions will be endeavoured.

Table 3 Preferable regressions[a] for home demand[b] / period of analysis 6/1987-5/1997

Independent[c] variables	Lags in months	Estimation method	Estimated coefficients				Test statistics	
			b_1	b_2	b_3	b_4	R^2_{adj}	DW
1. Equation:		Ordinary least squares	1037962 (7.8)	-58128 (-2.9)	4088 (2.4)	1,81 (22.3)	0.82	0.6
Stocks of orders in months of production, manufacturing industry	-21							
Short-term interest rate	-12							
Business expectation in manufacturing industry	-15							
Deterministic trend								
2a. Equation:		Simultaneous residual-model[d]	884532 (16.8)	6262 (8.4)	-75368 (-8.6)	18.8 (52.1)	0.967	1,5
Stocks of orders in months of production, manufacturing industry	-21							
Business expectations in manufacturing industry	-15							
Short term interest rate	-12							
Variable for whole market								
2b. Equation:							0.995	2.0
Same explanatory variables as in equation 2a.								
3. Equation:		Almon distributed-lag - with simultaneous error-model[d]	517906 (6.2)	51.6 (3.3)	5.8 (26.5)	-40,1 (-2.6)	0.954	1.9
Stocks of orders in months of production, manufacturing industry	-21							
Variable for whole market	0							
Variable for whole market	-1							
Variable for whole market	-2							
4. Equation:		Variable trend concept					0.998	2.0
univariate ARIMA (1,1,1)-model								

a) Explanations: b = estimated regression coefficient, ( ) = t-value, AIC = Akaike's criterion, R^2_{adj} = multiple correlation coefficient adjusted by degrees of freedom, DW = Durbin-Watson-measure.
b) Smoothed monthly values.
c) All explanatory variables smoothed, interest rates in differences to preceding period.
d) Autoregressive parameters for the residual model are statistically significant but omitted in this table.
Source: Computations of the author.

Table 4 Domestic sales[a] of a consumer durable in Germany
- quarterly correlation analyses beginning with 1/1986 -

Explanatory variable	Smoothing[b]	Optimal lag in quarters	r[c]	Source[d]
1. Construction cost of				
1.1 Renovation	5	-4	0.971	ifo HF
1.2 Hotels and restaurants	5	-3	0.951	ifo HF
2. Disposable income of private households, in constant prices	3	-4	0.983	Stabu
3. Short time workers	5	-4	0.477	BA
4. Credits of private persons	5	-4	0.978	Stabu
5. Business survey-building				
5.1 Housing construction industry and craft, duration of assured production	3	-4	0.928	ifo BS
5.2 Housing construction, duration of assured production	3	-4	0.919	ifo BS
6. Business survey-industry				
6.1 Household plastics, duration of assured production	3	-5	0,816	ifo BS
6.2 Private cars including estate cars, production expectations for 6 months	3	-6	-0.473	ifo BS

a) Quarterly values, smoothed.
b) Number of quarters for moving averages.
c) Correlation coefficient.
d) BA = Bundesanstalt für Arbeit, BB = Deutsche Bundesbank, monthly reports, Ifo BS = business surveys of the Ifo Institute, Ifo HF = housing construction forecast of the Ifo Institute, Stabu = Statistisches Bundesamt.

Source: Computations of the author.

Forecasting Models for Demand Series of Private Firms

Table 5 Preferable regressions[a] for sales[b] of a consumer durable in Germany / period of analysis beginning with 1/1986

Independent[c] variables	Lags in quarters	Estimation method	Estimated coefficients							Test statistics	
			b_1	b_2	b_3	b_4	b_5	b_6	b_7	R^2adj	DW
1a. Equation:		Ordinary least squares	34.9 (2.2)	4868 (6.5)	0.003 (3.2)	968.1 (-3.0)				0.978	1.1
Private disposable income	-5										
Housing construction industry and craft, duration of assured production	-4										
Short time workers	-4										
Construction cost of renovation	-5										
1b. Equation:		Successive residual-model								0.983	1.8
Same explanatory variables as in equation 1a.											
2. Equation:		Simultaneous[d] residual-model	83.4 (5.0)	2951.9 (1.4)	-53.6 (-1.6)	28.3 (1.8)	-0.9 (-9.1)			0,989	2.1
Same explanatory variables as in equation 1a.											
3. Equation:		Almon-distributed-lag-model[e]	4846 (2.9)	-71.9 (-1.7)	34.2 (2.3)	139.2 (4.1)	20.2 (5.0)	-98,9 (-2.7)	-0.4 (-2.4)	0.985	1.4
Housing construction industry and craft, duration of assured production	-4										
Price expectation for plastics	-4										
Construction cost of hotels and restaurants	-5										
Private disposable income	-6										
Private disposable income	-7										
Private disposable income	-8										
Error	-1										

a) Explanations: b= estimated regression coefficient, ( ) = t-value, R^2adj = multiple correlation coefficient adjusted by degrees of freedom, DW = Durbin-Watson-measure. - b) Smoothed quarterly values.
c) Variables are transformed as in table 4.
d) Coefficients belonging to the autoregressive disturbances are statistically significant, but omitted in this table.
e) With a simultaneous autoregressive error model of order 1.

Source: Computations of the author.

Table 6 Forecasting test / sales of a consumer durable in Germany 1990 = 100

Number of quarter	Empirical values	Theoretical values by method			
		OLS	Successive ARMA	Simultan. ARMA	Almon distributed-lag with simultaneous error-model
1	155.4	165.2	159.8	166.7	167.1
2	143.9	161.9	156.8	160.2	160.5
3	146.1	154.2	142.7	159.2	159.4
4	148.4	156.2	143.5	156.3	155.9
1st year	148.5	159.4	150.7	160.6	160.7
Error[a]		7.98	5.12	8.51	8.63
Kolmogorov-Smirnov-test[b]		0.70	0.60	0.43	0.38

a) Root mean square relative percentage error.
b) Statistical measure to check for white noise in disturbance term.
Source: Computations of the author.

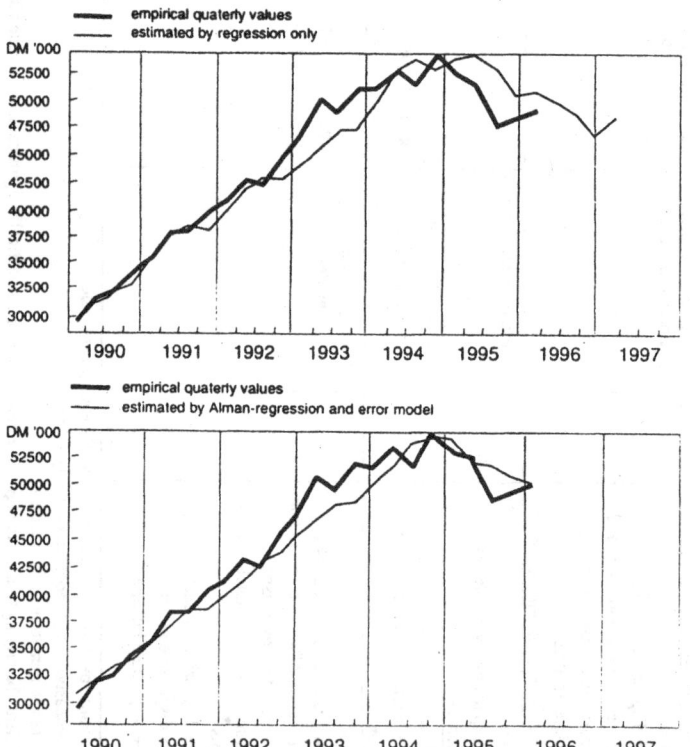

Figure 3 Demand of consumer durables in Germany

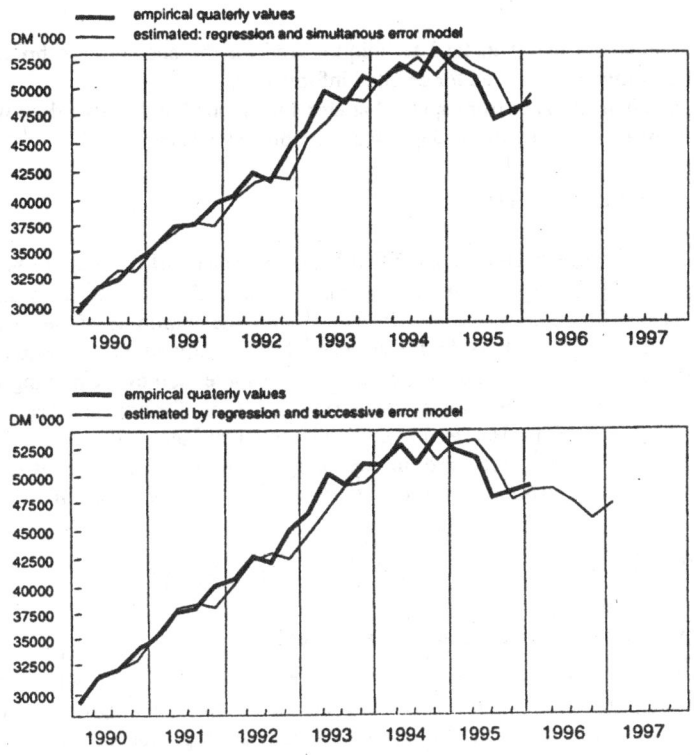

Figure 3 (continued) Demand of consumer durables in Germany

4 Summary and Outlook

The strategy used for gaining forecasting equations proved to be useful. The results discussed in Chapter 3 are summarized below, especially the following three successes:

1. The main influences on company demand were able to be represented with all econometric equations in suitable explanatory variables with statistically significant coefficients.
2. The approaches selected for the forecasts performed well in the tests. The considerable number of usable, independent variables permit the selection of series that have no intercorrelation. Especially the careful modelling of the unexplained movement remaining after causal regressions results in the elimination of disturbing autocorrelations.
3. Especially in the case of tests using ex-post forecasts the suitability of the employed estimation method is particularly clear. We can expect the ex-ante forecasts to be accurate.

Annex: Mathematical Methods

The main econometrical and statistical techniques used for the analyses are briefly described. Sufficient literature is cited for detailed information.

Transfer functions derived from spectral analysis are plotted and enable the final decision between different filters for the dependent variable to be made:

$$TF(\lambda) = S(\lambda, YO) / S(\lambda, YI), \qquad (1)$$

thereby YI denotes the spectrum of input, YO the spectral density of the output series of the filter (e.g. moving averages with varying time periods). The symbol λ means frequency. The transfer function can be explained as a factor the amplitude of the particular input time series component defined by the wavelengths is multiplied with. A value larger than one shows an amplification and smaller than one a suppression of the moving power remaining in the output series after transformation. (For further discussions see König/Wolter 1972; pp. 45-57; Harvey 1992, pp. 235-240; Goldrian 1995.)

Correlation coefficients are tools to find optimal lead-lag-relationships between variables. Especially the *weighted Pearson product-moment correlation coefficient*

$$r^w(XY) = \left(\sum w_i (x_i - \bar{x}_w)(y_i - \bar{y}_w)\right) / \sqrt{\sum w_i (x_i - \bar{x}_w)^2 \sum w_i (y_i - \bar{y}_w)^2}, \qquad (2)$$

is an important decision criterion for preliminary choice.

In this formula $\bar{x}_w = \sum w_i x_i / \sum w_i$ and $\bar{y}_w = \sum w_i y_i / \sum w_i$ are weighted means of the independent or dependent variable and w_i denotes the weights used to emphasize critical periods, e.g. around turning points. It is an important decision criterion (see SAS Institute 1991, pp. 339-346).

Five *types of dynamic regressions* (see especially Chatfield 1991, Hendry 1995 and Palm/Pfann 1993; pp. 182-213) have been selected to estimate demand equations:

1. *Ordinary least squares* with "pure" delay-structures allow for simple time-lags (j) only and don't model the regression residuals (e_t):

$$Y_t = b_0 + \sum_{i=1}^{k} b_i X_{i,t-j} + e_t, \qquad (3.1)$$

with Y_t = dependent variable, $X_{i,t-j}$ = independent variables , b_i = estimated coefficients and b_0 = constant term.

2. *Successive models* of structural and residual parts of the equation (3.1) are analyzed successively. After the regression estimation of the causal part, the resulting disturbances are modelled following a univariate Box-Jenkins approach.

$$e_t = \phi^{-1}(B)\theta(B)n_t, \qquad (3.2)$$

where n_t is a normally distributed error term which may have a different variance from the regression residuals e_t and t = time index. Thereby $\phi(B)$ = moving average operator, $\theta(B)$ = autoregressive operator and B = backshift operator, that is e.g. $Bn_t = n_{t-1}$. This model combines structural economic explanation with a time-series approach for that part of the variance in Y_t not accessible to causal influences. (See Pindyck/Rubinfeld 1991, pp. 538-550 and Judge et al. 1988, pp. 701-719.)

3. *Simultaneous estimation procedure* treat explanatory input series $X_{i,t}$ together with the ARIMA-specification of the disturbances e_t:

$$Y_t = b_0 + \sum_{i=1}^{k} b_i X_{i,t-j_k} + \frac{(1-\theta B)}{(1-\phi B)} e_t \; . \tag{3.3}$$

The only symbol to explain here is j_k = time delay j for the explanatory variable k.
The coefficient of the structural and the time-series part are computed together, in other words considering their interrelationship. (See Harvey 1989, pp. 381-408; Harvey 1994, pp. 229-248 and SAS Institute 1993, pp. 185-253.)

4. *Almon-distributed lag specifications* with or without simultaneous autoregressive error term are an adaptable technique. Only a few parameters for the dynamics in an explanatory variable are to be estimated:

$$Y_t = a + \sum_{i=0}^{p} b_i X_{t-i} + cZ_{t-j} + e_t \; , \tag{3.4.1}$$

and

$$b_i = w_0 + \sum_{k=1}^{j} w_k t_k(i) \; , \tag{3.4.2}$$

where Z_{t-j} = covariate variable with pure delay j, p = lag length, $t_k(i)$ = polynomial of degree k belonging to lag i, w_k = Almon weights. (See Davidson/MacKinnon 1993, pp. 674-676; Hendry 1995, pp. 212-227.)

5. *Transfer-function equations* without feedback loops.
Such a model has to be strongly exogenous. This means, that the explanatory series $X_{i,t}$ ought to be without feedbacks to past values of the dependent variable Y_t.
(See Jäger 1997; Malliaropoulos 1990; Pindyck/Rubinfeld 1971, pp. 337-420 and Singh 1989.)
Following formula can describe this type of dynamic regression:

$$Y_t = b_0 + \sum_i \left(\frac{w_i(B)}{d_i(B)} \right) B^{k_i} X_{i,t} + \frac{\theta(B)}{\phi(B)} e_t \; , \tag{3.5}$$

with symbols: $X_{i,t}$ = input variable, k_i = pure delay for the effect of the ith input series, $w_i(B)/d_i(B)$ = numerator/denominator polynomial of the transfer function for the ith input $X_{i,t}$.

(For software see SAS Institute 1990, 1991 and 1995.)

The concept of „*Variable Trend*" is also called „*Stochastic Trend*" :

$$Y_t = m_{STA} + \sum_i b_i X_{i,t-j} + e_{m/t}$$

$$ST_t = gt + h \quad \sum_i b_i X_{i,t-j} + e_{m/t} \;. \tag{3.6}$$

$$e_{m/t} = d(L)e_t \;.$$

where Y_t = dependent series, ST_t = permanent stochastic trend component, gt = deterministic long-term movement, m_{STA} = smoothed stochastic trend, $e_{m/t}$ = smoothed error term, b_i = estimated coefficients and L = backshift operator, e.g. $L^j X_t = X_{t-j}$. (See Hassler 1996 and Stock/Watson 1988.)

The 'Variable Trend' -also called - 'Stochastic Trend' serves in many situations as a concept to reach a good fit. In this paper it is compared with two other specifications, namely the deterministic long-term component suggested by experts of the firm and trended variables characterizing the market. This new approach enables the econometrician to conceive long-term movements even with breaks in the aggregation phase of indicator analysis. The estimation process has three stages. First univariate ARIMA techniques are applied, then the resulting estimates are smoothed and finally these results are used as an explanatory variable in one of the preceeding types of dynamic regression equations.

The following two statistics for *testing the fit* are shown in the tables of this paper:

Adjusted R^2:

$$R^2_{adj} = 1 - [(T-1)/(T-k)](1 - R^2) \;, \tag{4.1}$$

is a measure for fit which takes the number of explanatory variables k into consideration. (See Harvey 1994, pp. 43.)

Akaike's information criterion is computed as:

$$AIC = -2\ln(L) + 2m \;, \tag{4.2}$$

with L = value of the likelihood function and m = number of free parameters. This decision rule conceives two criteria 'good fit' (L) and 'parsimony' in model parameters (m)' to estimate. Finally the specification with a minimum of AIC is chosen.

Three procedures are used for final discrimination between the remaining 'good' specifications (See Harvey 1994, pp. 181-182 and SAS Institute 1993, pp. 143 - 222.)

First an F-distributed Chow-Test for three time periods (before as well as after the break and total) is proposed to serve as a *check for structural stability* (see A'Walelu et al. 1984):

$$F(k, n_1+n_2-2k) = (A - B - C)(n_1 + n_2 - k) / ((B + C) k), \quad (5.1)$$

with k = number of explanatory variables, n_1 /n_2 = number of periods before/after the supposed time of the break, T = $n_1 + n_2$ total period, A = squared sum of deviations in case of T periods B = ... in case of n_1 periods and C = ... in case of n_2 periods. The equation must be estimated three times with these time periods.

Root mean square percentage error (RMSPE):

$$\text{RMSPE} = \frac{\sum_{t=1}^{T}((Y_t - YH_t)100/Y_t)^2}{T}, \quad (5.2)$$

is the main criterion for testing forecasting ability of the various specifications. Thereby Y_t / YH_t means empirical versus theoretical values of the dependent variable, T denotes the number of periods for analysis. (See Bock/Dietl 1995 and Ogwang 1993, pp. 285-287.)

The statistical measure suggested by Kolmogorov-Smirnov *tests for white noise residuals*. This measure compares the normalized cumulative periodogram F_j and the cumulative distribution function of a uniform-(0,1)-random variable. The formula for the series F_j is:

$$F_j = \frac{\sum_{k=1}^{j} J_k}{\sum_{k=1}^{m} J_k}, \quad (5.3)$$

with j = 1,2,...,m-1 and m = n/2 if the number of observations is even or m = (n-1)/2 if it is odd, furthermore J_k = the periodogram. The test statistic is the maximum absolute difference of F_j and the uniform cumulative distribution function. For m-1 < 100 the null hypothesis that the error series represents white noise is rejected if this statistic exceeds the significance points found in the statistical table belonging to sample size m-1. (For details see SAS Institute 1993, p. 757.)

References

Assenmacher, W. (1984*), Lehrbuch der Konjunkturtheorie*, R. Oldenbourg Verlag, München Wien.

A'Walelu, O., Horn, G.A. and Zwiener, R. (1989), Zu den Stabilitätseigenschaften ausgewählter ökonometrischer Schätzfunktionen, *DIW Vierteljahreshefte zur Wirtschaftsforschung*, 2-3/1989, pp. 214- 236.

Bock, R. and Dietl, W. (1996), Eine Analyse der Zuverlässigkeit des Saisonbereinigungsverfahrens von Winters im Zusammenhang mit klassischen Maßen der Prognosegüte, *GFK, Jahrbuch der Absatz- und Verbrauchsforschung*, 2/1996, pp. 184-196.

Box, G.E.P. and Jenkins, G.M. (1970), *Time Series Analysis: Forecasting and Control*, John Wiley, New York.

Chatfield, C. (1991), A Practical Review of Forecasting Methods, *Allgemeines Statistisches Archiv*, 75/1991, pp. 41-52.

Dankenbring, H. and Missong, M. (1997), GARCH-Effekte auf dem deutschen Aktienmarkt, *Zeitschrift für Betriebswirtschaft*, No. 3, March 1997, pp. 311-331.

Davidson R. and MacKinnon J.G. (1993), *Estimation and Inference in Econometrics*, Oxford University Press, New York, Oxford.

Dormayer, H.-J. (1986), Konjunkturelle Früherkennung und Flexibilität im Produktionsbereich, *ifo Beiträge zur quantitativen Wirtschaftsforschung*, 3, 1986.

Fahrmeir, L. (1991), Zustandsraummodelle: Filtern, Glätten und Prognose dynamischer Systeme, *Allgemeines Statistisches Archiv*, 75/1991, pp. 53-74.

Fuller, W.A. (1976), *Introduction to Statistical Time Series*, John Wiley, New York.

Goldrian, G. (1995), Datenaufbereitung und Zeitreihenzerlegung, in K.H. Oppenländer (ed), *Konjunkturindikatoren*, R. Oldenbourg Verlag, München, Wien, pp. 131-143.

Goldrian, G. (1995), Comment How to Suppress a Lead, *Empirical Economics*, 20/1995, pp. 177-181.

Hannsmann, F. (1990), *Quantitative Betriebswirtschaftslehre: Lehrbuch der modellgestützten Unternehmensplanung*, 3rd edition, R. Oldenbourg Verlag, München.

Harvey, A.C. (1989), *Forecasting, Structural Time Series Models and the Kalman Filter*, Cambridge University Press, Cambridge.

Harvey, A.C. (1994), *Ökonometrische Analyse von Zeitreihen*, 2nd edition, R. Oldenbourg Verlag, München, Wien.

Harvey, A.C. (1995), *Zeitreihenmodelle*, 2nd edition, R. Oldenbourg Verlag, München, Wien.

Hassler, U. (1996), Nonsense Correlations between Time Series with Linear Trends, *Allgemeines Statistisches Archiv*, 80/1996.

Hendry, D.F. (1995), *Dynamic Econometrics, Advanced Texts in Econometrics*, Oxford University Press, New York.

Jäger, U. (1997), Prognosen der kurzfristigen regionalen Beschäftigungsentwicklung unter Anwendung von Transferfunktionsmodellen, *Allgemeines Statistisches Archiv*, 81/1997, pp. 176-192.

Judge, G.G., Griffith, W.E., Hill, Lüdtkepohl, H. and Lee, T.-C. (1985), *The Theory and Practice of Econometrics*, 2nd Edition, John Wiley, New York.

König, H. and Wolters, J. (1972), *Einführung in die Spektralanalyse ökonomischer Zeitreihen*, Verlag Anton Hain, Meisenheim am Glan.

Lahiri, K. (1995), Zinsdifferenzen als neue Frühindikatoren - Theorie und Evidenz, in K.H. Oppenländer (ed), *Konjunkturindikatoren*, R. Oldenbourg Verlag, München, Wien, pp. 216-237.

Langhans, G. and Müller, M. (1988), Anwendungen von Konjunkturtestdaten für Mittelfristprognosen im Investitionsgüterbereich: Erfahrungen in der Praxis, in K.H. Oppenländer and G. Poser (eds), *Handbuch der ifo Umfragen*, Berlin München.

Malliaropoulos, D. (1990), Euro-DM-Depositen und Inflation, *Konjunkturpolitik*, 36, 6/1990, pp. 363-377.

Neumann, F. and Goldrian, G. (1997), Exportkonjunktur bleibt gut, *ifo Schnelldienst*, 19/1997, pp. 19-22.

Ogang, T. (1993), A comparison of the Kernel and ARIMA Estimates of Inflationary Expectations: Some Evidence from Canada, *Empirical Economics*, 18/1993, pp. 281-188.

Oppenländer, K.H. (1995), *Konjunkturindikatoren: Fakten, Analysen, Verwendung*, R. Oldenbourg Verlag, München Wien.

Oppenländer, K.H. and Poser, G. (eds) (1989), *Handbuch der ifo Umfragen*, Duncker & Humblot Verlag, Berlin München.

Palm, C.F. and Pfann, G.A. (1993), Empirical Analysis of Optimal Firm Behaviour: Asymmetric Adjustment in Labour and Capital Demand in the Manufacturing Sector in the Netherlands and the U.K., in H. Schneeweiß and K.F. Zimmermann (eds), *Studies in Applied Econometrics, Contributions for Economics*, Physica-Verlag, Heidelberg.

Palm, C.F. and Vlaar, P.J.G. (1997), Simple Diagnostic Procedures for Modeling Financial Time Series, *Allgemeines Statistisches Archiv*, 81, pp. 85-101.

Pindyck, R.S. and Rubinfeld, D.L. (1991), *Econometric Models and Economic Forecasts*, 3rd Edition, McGraw-Hill, New York.
Priestly, M.B. (1981), *Spectral Analysis and Time Series*, Springer Verlag, New York.
Rall, W. (1997), Strategie für den Weltmarkt, in D. Hahn and B. Taylor (eds), *Strategische Unternehmensplanung - strategische Unternehmensführung: Stand und Entwicklungstendenzen*, 7th edition, Physica-Verlag, Heidelberg, pp. 523-541.
Reiner, M., Weßner, K. and Wimmer, F. (1991), Strategische Prognose von Markt- und Absatzentwicklungen durch kombinierten Einsatz quantitativer und qualitativer Verfahren, *GfK Jahrbuch der Absatz- und Verbrauchsforschung*, 1/1991, Duncher & Humblot, Berlin, pp. 7-87.
Schneeweiß, H. (1990), *Ökonometrie*, 4th edition, 1990, Physica-Verlag, Würzburg.
Singh, H. (1989), Modeling endogenous Monetary Stock Behavior: A simultaneous Transfer Function Approach, *Empirical Economics*, Vol. 14, 1/1989, pp. 291-305.
Stock, J.H. and Watson, M.W. (1988), Variable Trends in Economic Time Series, *Journal of Economic Perspectives*, Volume 2/Number 3, pp. 147-174.
Stock, J.H. and Watson, M.W. (1989), *New Indexes of Coincident and Leading Economic Indicators*, NBER, MIT Press, Cambridge.
Stock. K. (1991), Nachfrageindikatoren als Entscheidungshilfe für die Unternehmensplanung, *ifo Schnelldienst* 6/1991, pp. 11-20.
Stock, K. (1993), Quantitative Frühindikatoren für die betriebliche Absatzentwicklung, *ifo Schnelldienst* 22/1993, pp. 15-19.
SAS Institute Inc. (1990), *SAS/ETS User's Guide*, Version 6, Cary, North Carolina.
SAS Institute Inc. (1991), *SAS/ETS Applications Guide*, Version 6, 1st edition, Cary, North Carolina.
SAS Institute Inc. (1991), *SAS Language and Procedures*: Usage 2, Version 6, 1st edition, pp. 339-346, Cary, North Carolina.
SAS Institute Inc. (1995), *SAS/ETS Software: Time Series Forecasting System*, Version 6, 1st edition, Cary, North Carolina.
Tessaring, I. (1992), Analyse und Prognose industrieller Nachfrageverläufe im In- und Ausland mit Hilfe von Konjunkturtestdaten - Beispiele aus der Praxis der Investitionsgüterindustrie, *CIRET Studien* 44, 1992, pp. 85-132.
Tichy, C. (1988), *Konjunkturpolitik: Quantitative Stabilisierungspolitik bei Unsicherheit*, Springer-Verlag, Berlin, Heidelberg, New York.
Westphal, U. (1988), *Makroökonomik: Theorie, Empirie und Politikanalyse*, Springer-Verlag, Berlin, Heidelberg.
Witte, E. and Senn, J. (1983), Der Werbemarkt der Zukunft - Eine Delphi-Prognose, *Zeitschrift für Betriebswirtschaft*, 53, 1983, pp. 1042 - 1051.

13 Survey Results Relating to Changes in the International Competitiveness of Belgian Manufacturing Enterprises

Jean-Jacques Vanhaelen / Chantal Winter

1 Introduction

In Belgium, a small, open economy, the competitiveness of enterprises has for a long time been closely watched by the country's political and economic decision-making centres. Concern about the competitiveness of Belgian industry in fact led to the "Act for safeguarding the country's competitive position" of 6th January 1989. This law stipulated that intervention should take place as soon as the competitive position was threatened. That was the case, according to the law, when two conditions were fulfilled, namely when market shares on the export markets were lost and when at least one of the other four assessment criteria - labour costs per employee in the private sector, financial charges (interest rates), miscellaneous energy costs and structural elements (business investment and expenditure on scientific research) - showed a negative trend compared with 1987 and with the situation in the main trading partners.[1]

The National Economic Council (NEC), made up of the representatives of the employers' and employees' organisations, published, on the basis of OECD data, before the end of March and the end of September of each year, a report and recommendations about the competitiveness of Belgian enterprises. If the threat to the competitive position was confirmed in the subsequent consultation with the Government, measures had to be taken.

The law gave the Government the necessary means for this. In March 1993 the NEC's report indicated that the competitive position of Belgian industry was worsening: Belgium was losing market shares abroad and wages were rising faster that it was the case with its most important trading partners. Thus, during the period 1987-1993, labour costs per full-time equivalent in enterprises increased on annual average at a faster rate in Belgium than in the three neighbouring countries.

---

[1] For the assessment criteria of export performance, energy costs and structural elements, reference was made to the five most important trading partners (Germany, the Netherlands, France, Great Britain, Italy). For the assessment criteria of labour costs and financial charges, reference was made to the seven most important trading partners (that is, the above-mentioned five countries plus the United States and Japan).

It was at that time that the results of the NBB's quarterly survey on the competitive position of enterprises had been analysed for the first time. The results of this study had been published in an earlier contribution to the CIRET Conference[1].

The finding arrived at in 1993, in accordance with the procedures laid down in the law of 6th January 1989, that a handicap as regards labour costs had developed since 1987, had induced the Government to adjust the movement of wages. The reason for this step was the threat which this differential in labour costs could represent for the competitiveness of Belgian enterprises. But, even more than this concern about a competitive handicap, there had been a gradually growing conviction that such a rapid rise in labour costs, altering the movement of the relative prices of production factors at the expense of the labour factor, was above all detrimental to the development of employment.

The measures adopted in November 1993 included the introduction of a new reference index, for the indexation of wages, allowances, the incomes of members of the liberal professions, directors' fees and rents. The incidence of the change over to this new index, which excludes products regarded as dangerous to health - alcohol, tobacco, petrol and diesel -, whose prices had risen faster, made it possible to cancel out the real rises in wages in 1994. Furthermore, a prohibition against collectively agreed increases had been imposed for 1995 and 1996.

Thanks to these measures, between 1993 and 1996, the rise in labour costs per full-time equivalent was kept below the average, in the three neighbouring countries.

The law of 6th January 1989 did, however, make it possible to react only after a worsening had been observed. That is why this law was replaced by that of 26th July 1996 concerning the promotion of employment and the preventive safeguarding of competitiveness, which includes a preventive mechanism.

This law calls upon the social partners to conclude an inter-trade agreement setting a maximum rise in labour costs in nominal terms which must be complied with in the negotiations for the biennial wage agreements, both at national and sectoral levels, and at enterprise level, and which must not be exceeded, either, in individual agreements. If the social partners fail to reach an agreement, it is up to the Government to fix this maximum.

This figure takes account of the expected rise in labour costs per full-time equivalent, in national currency, in the three main trading partners (Germany, France and the Netherlands), corrected if necessary to take account of the changes in the collectively agreed average annual duration of work. Thus, the new law is an instrument designed to prevent any runaway movements, rather than to try to remedy them after the event. Indexations and scale increases are, however, guaranteed, even if they cause the wage increase to exceed the permitted maximum margin. In the collective negotiations, the social partners may allocate the margin thus defined either to wage increases or to financing measures to promote employment.

Over and above its preventive nature, the law provides for a number of corrective mechanisms. If, nevertheless, the movement of wages in Belgium exceeds that in the

---

[1] De Doncker H. and Vanhaelen J.J. (1994), "The Use of the Capacity Survey to Explain the Behaviour of Entrepreneurs", in Oppenlander K.H. and Poser G. (eds), The Explanatory Power of Business Cycle Surveys, Papers presented at the 21st CIRET Conference, Proceedings, Stellenbosch 1993, Avebury, pp. 133-158.

neighbouring countries, corrections may be made at the end of the first year or the following year, during the wage negotiations, because the law states that the maximum margin can be reduced to the extent of the overstepping observed in the two preceding years.

In view of the renewed interest in this subject, and of the changes which have been made since then in the questionnaire, it has been thought worthwhile to update and supplement the analysis made in 1993. Therefore, after a brief presentation of the Bank's survey, attention will be paid to the survey results relating to competitiveness, at both the macro and micro levels. After that, the link between the survey results and potential indicators of competitiveness will be investigated.

2 Presentation of the NBB Survey on Competitiveness

Since October 1962 the National Bank of Belgium has organised, at the request of the EC and on behalf of the employers' federation VBO (Verbond van Belgische Ondernemingen), a quarterly survey on the utilisation of production capacity in manufacturing industry, which was harmonised at EC level. Since 1985, the capacity survey has also been extended at the request of the VBO to include competitiveness. To this end two questions were added. These related explicitly to competitiveness (in the field of costs and prices) and gave an indication both of the trend in, and the prospects for, competitiveness. More specifically, the questions, which were of a qualitative nature, were formulated as follows in the questionnaire:

Question 58   In the last three months, our competitive position in comparison with foreign producers of this product
☐ improved   ☐ remained unchanged   ☐ worsened

Question 59   In the next three months, our competitive position in comparison with foreign producers of this product will, according to our assessments,
☐ improve   ☐ remain unchanged   ☐ worsen

It must be emphasised that these questions did not at the beginning form part of the harmonised EC survey, as not all the Member States had introduced them. The harmonisation took place later, following a decision adopted by the EC, in 1993, to extend the capacity survey in order to include questions on competitiveness. The questionnaire therefore had to be amended for Belgium.

In view of the results of the analysis carried out in 1993, Question 59 on forecasts was deleted, as it had been found that it did not contain any additional information beyond that obtained by Question 58, concerning the development of competitiveness in the last three months. In other words, as is often the case in qualitative business surveys, the answers did not yield any information of a forecasting nature. Question 58, for its part, in order to comply with the harmonisation criteria issued by the EC, had to be subdivided as follows[1]:

---

[1] A copy of the questionnaire in its present wording is appended hereto.

In the last three months, our competitive position, for this product, has

		improved	remained unchanged	worsened
Question 60	- on the domestic market	☐	☐	☐
Question 61	- on foreign markets (in general)	☐	☐	☐
Question 62	- in countries of the EU	☐	☐	☐
Question 63	- in countries outside the EU	☐	☐	☐

The individual answers are collected by product and by enterprise. They are then globalised at various levels by means of the weighting system described below. Within a product the individual answers are weighted in accordance with the turnover of the responding enterprise. To this end, enterprises mention once per year - in May - their turnover on the internal market, on the one hand, and on the external market, on the other. A breakdown of the turnover between the "European Union" market and the "outside the European Union" market was requested, for the first time, only in May 1997. This means that, up to the present, the weightings for Questions 62 (EU market) and 63 (markets outside the EU) have been made on the basis of total export turnover. For the aggregation of the results by product at the level of sectors, branches and, finally, the economy as a whole, the weights used correspond to the shares of these various categories in the value added of industry (national accounts data). This method of working makes it possible to study the development of the competitive position at the various levels of products, (sub-)sectors, industrial branches and the economy as a whole. The results are presented in the form of net balances, in other words, the difference between the "improved" and "worsened" percentages.

3 Assessment of Competitiveness: Survey Results

3.1 Survey Results Relating to Changes in Global Export Competitiveness

Although a large number of respondents, namely some 70 p.c., always mention an unchanged situation[1] and although the calculated net changes are consequently small in extent, clear movements are nevertheless observable in the results relating to changes in the competitive position on external markets. The period 1985-1997 can be roughly divided into four sub-periods. During the first sub-period (from 1985 to the third quarter of 1988), the competitive position tended to improve. It then worsened until the middle of 1993 and improved again until the end of 1994. The development in the last sub-period is more difficult to discern, because it was affected by major changes in answers, especially in early 1995. This will be discussed in greater detail in section 4.

---

[1] For comparison: the percentage of enterprises which state, in answer to the questions in the monthly survey of manufacturing industry, that the situation has remained unchanged fluctuates around 40 p.c.

Chart 1   Survey results relating to changes in global export competitiveness*

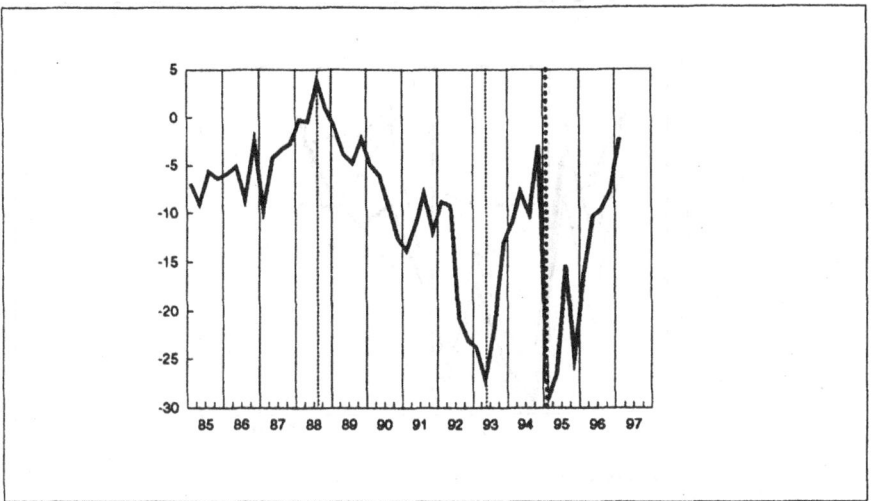

*Net balances of the "improved" and "worsened" percentages, seasonally adjusted data.
Source: NBB.

3.2   Breakdown of Survey Results According to the Destination of Exports (intra- or extra-EC)

The analysis of the results broken down according to the destination of the products sold remains a difficult matter, because of the limited period for which information is available. Thus it has not yet been possible to make an adjustment for seasonal variations. Furthermore, the weighting coefficients used for aggregating the answers by sector while breaking down the results according to export markets are not, as has been seen in section 2, at all precise. However, an attempt to make a more accurate calculation of the weightings, based on the foreign trade statistics, led to practically the same results. Certain trends are however already perceptible.

Thus it has to be said that, on the whole, enterprises do not clearly differentiate, in indicating their competitive position, according to whether their markets are within or outside the European Union, although some sectors, such as wood, non-ferrous metals and construction materials, are an exception. On the whole, no systematic divergence was observed for the period during which the Belgian franc appreciated vis-à-vis the European currencies, while depreciating against the US dollar (and vice versa).

To make a more detailed analysis, however, it would be necessary to have data concerning a longer period. In the following sections, the sectoral analyses will therefore be confined to an examination of the question on a global export competitiveness.

Chart 2 Breakdown of survey results by destination*

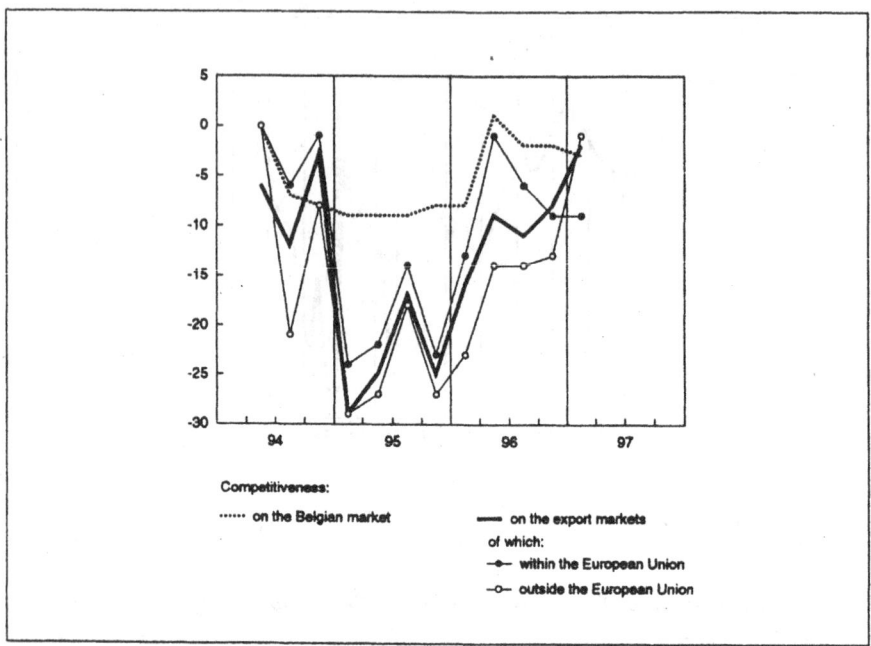

*Net balances of the "improved" and "worsened" percentages, raw data.
Source: NBB.

3.3 Competitiveness on the Domestic Market

As shown on Chart 2 the competitiveness indicator for sales on the Belgian market appears to be appreciably more stable. For this indicator the enterprises which participate in the survey have to assess not only the competition from foreign enterprises which export to Belgium but also the competition on the Belgian market from other Belgian enterprises, most of which also participate in the survey. On balance, the answers from the various categories of Belgian enterprises should in theory tend to offset each other, leaving only competition from abroad. Thus, for the sectors which are relatively little exposed to international competition, this indicator ought to remain practically stable, whereas it would be liable to display greater variations for the sectors which are in competition with foreign enterprises. Overall, this would provide a measure of import competitiveness. As export competitiveness is a function of the same determinants, the survey results should indicate that the two types of competitiveness move more or less parallel with each other. This is indeed the case: the variations - admittedly small - in competitiveness on the Belgian market move in the same direction as the competitive position as regards exports; if the foreign competitors are relatively more competitive, it is logical that this should have a repercussion both on the Belgian market and on the external markets.[1] Some sectors, however, are an exception, as is shown by Chart 4.

Chart 3   Sectoral breakdown of survey results: competitiveness on markets within and outside the EU*

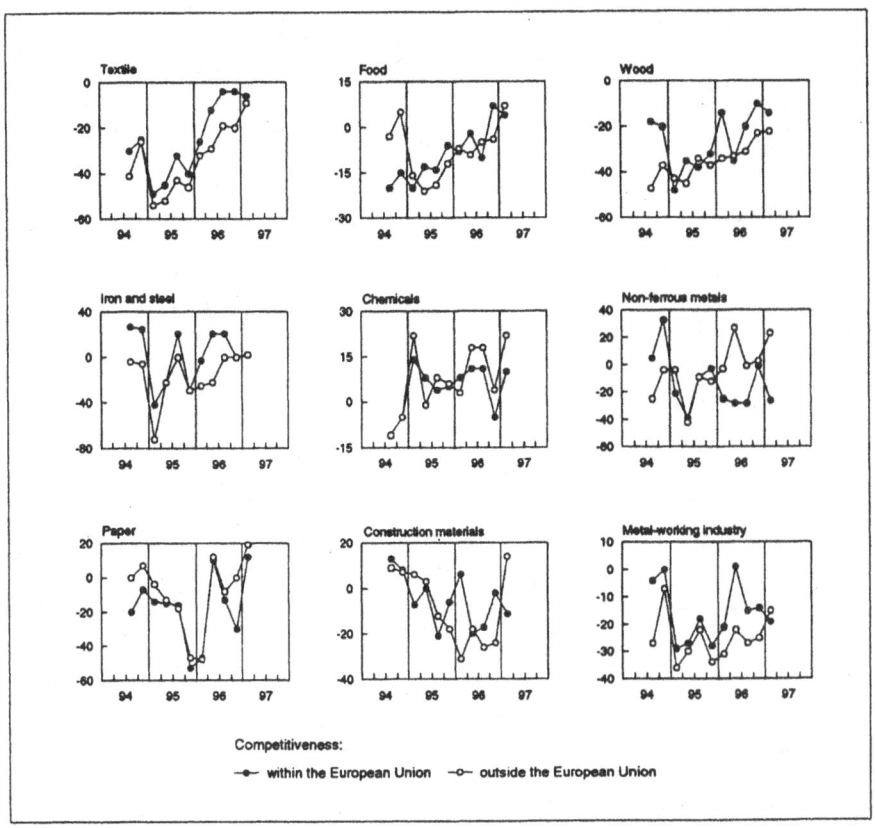

*Net balances of the "improved" and "worsened" percentages, raw data.
Source: NBB.

---

[1] It should be noted that these comparisons were made by changing the weightings for the intra-EC and extra-EC markets respectively, without this having any significant effect on the conclusions.

Chart 4 Sectoral breakdown of survey results: competitiveness on the domestic market and on the export markets*

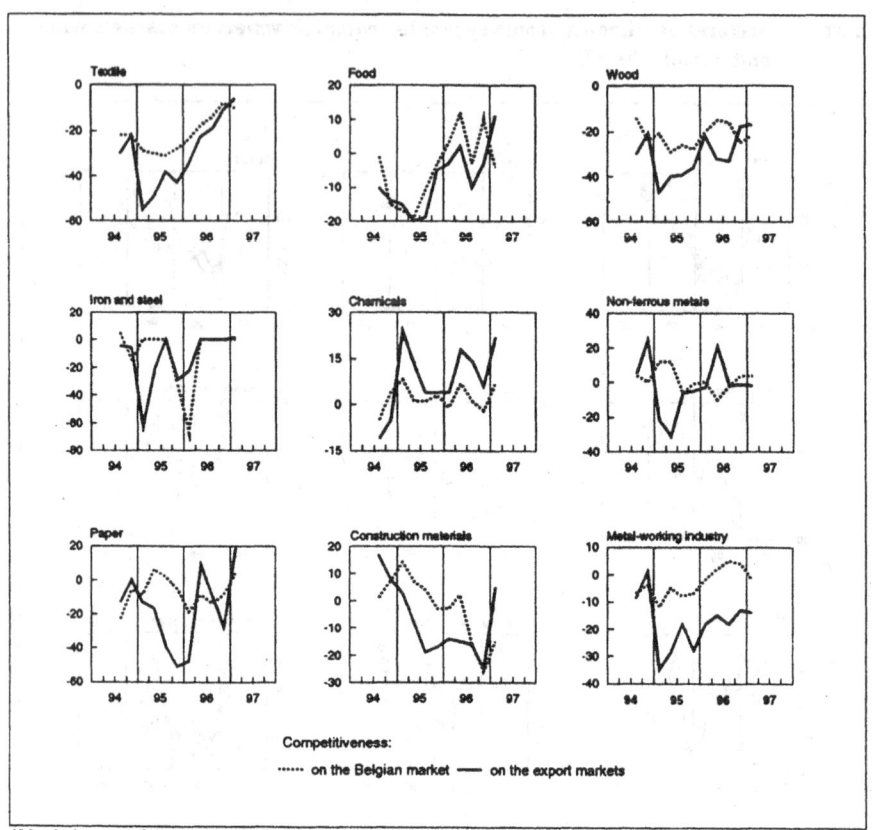

*Net balances of the "improved" and "worsened" percentages, raw data.
Source: NBB.

4 Relationship between the Survey Results and Macroeconomic Competitiveness

In order to gain an idea of the extent to which the information about (price) competitiveness collected via the surveys corresponds to reality, an examination is made of the relationship between the survey results and the statistical data about the competitiveness of Belgian enterprises. The analysis will be restricted to the concept of export competitiveness since survey results relating to import competitiveness are not available before mid 1994.

It is necessary, firstly, to define what we mean by competitiveness and, depending on that, to determine what category of statistical information best reflects the development of competitiveness for a small open economy such as Belgium.

The competitive position defines the cost situation of an enterprise in relation to its competitors' costs. This comparison ought ideally to take account of labour costs, interest charges, the costs of the intermediate inputs, transaction costs and the exchange rate. In practice, the data available for an international comparison are:

- relative export prices;
- export performance;
- relative unit labour costs in a common currency;
- the real effective exchange rate.

None of the concepts gives a true reflection of competitiveness. Thus, the indicators of the relative prices and performance of a country (which are calculated both by the OECD and by the European Commission) depend on its export structure by product. They may therefore be biased when a country, the development of whose competitiveness it is desired to determine, benefits proportionally more from the cyclical phase of its trading partners. The effective exchange rate, corrected to take account of inflation differentials, also provides only partial information: it does not allow full account to be taken of a possible wage moderation which would enable the appreciation of the national currency to be compensated for on the plane of relative costs. Relative unit labour costs avoid the omissions found for the preceding statistics. They do not, however, enable account to be taken of a possible intensification of the capital-intensiveness of an economy, which would have the effect of increasing the relative share of capital costs in the selling price of a product or of causing a decrease in relative unit labour costs without any improvement taking place in competitiveness.

As each of these indicators reflects an aspect of what constitutes the competitiveness of an enterprise, they will all be related to the results of the survey. Special attention will be paid to the movement of labour costs, in so far as they serve as a basis for assessment and prevention under the 1996 law on competitiveness.

First, a correlation analysis shows that the competitiveness indicator derived from the survey tends to be a lagging indicator; it is concomitant only as regards the real effective exchange rate. However, in view of the delay in the publication of the statistical data, it may be assumed that the survey results are at least a quarter ahead of the statistical data. This analysis furthermore shows that the correlation is far from perfect: whatever the indicator used, it is no more than 60 p.c. Thus, there is no exact correspondence, even after the introduction of lags, between the movements of the competitive position for the sub-periods defined in part 3 and the movements of the macroeconomic variables.

Second, it appears that during the recent period, especially since 1992, the volatility of the survey results has increased, without there being any counterpart in the movement of the macroeconomic variables. This great variability might be due to the keener interest shown in the movement of exchange rates since the conclusion of the Treaty of Maastricht, which may have been reflected in an over-reaction by entrepreneurs to movements on the foreign exchange markets. This assumption would make it possible to explain why, between late 1994 and early 1995, entrepreneurs indicated a worsening of their competitiveness which was much greater than the deterioration in the macroeconomic variables. In the first quarter of 1995, several currencies had in fact depreciated greatly against the German mark, chiefly because of the weak US dollar. The franc had, however, remained very close to its central rate vis-à-vis the mark, the guilder and the French franc,[1] so that the real exchange rate had appreciated only very slightly by some 2 p.c. Entrepreneurs appear, however, to have overestimated the effect of this appreciation on their competitive position. A symmetric overreaction followed in the months thereafter when the US dollar appreciated progressively.

Chart 5   Survey results and macroeconomic indicators of competitiveness
(1991=100, seasonally adjusted data)

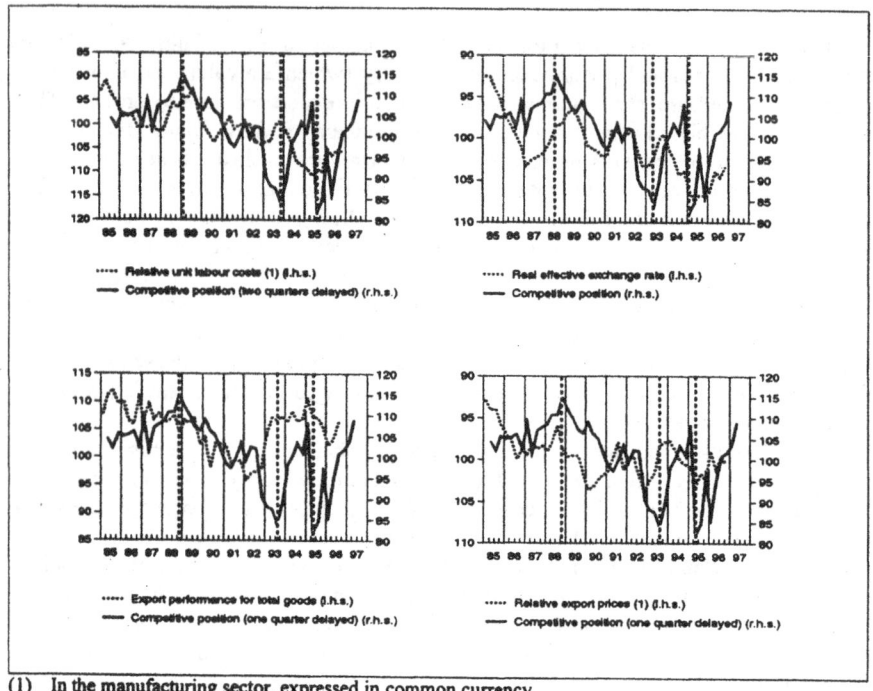

(1) In the manufacturing sector, expressed in common currency.
Sources: NBB, OECD.

All in all when a comparison is made between the levels recorded for the survey before this turbulence on the foreign exchange markets and the present levels, it seems that the movement indicated has been completely cancelled out. Relative exchange rates at the end of 1994 are in fact practically equal to the present rates.

Third, Chart 5 shows that the assessment made by entrepreneurs is not confined to price competitiveness.

For example, relative unit labour costs and the competitive position according to the survey move roughly in line with each other during the first two sub-periods, that is, until the end of 1993. On the other hand, in 1994 and 1995, while relative costs worsened,

---

[1] Which repesent 51 p.c. in terms of foreign trade.

entrepreneurs considered that their competitive position improved. During the most recent period, the two series have again moved parallel. Practically the same phenomenon can be observed for the real effective exchange rate and relative export prices. On the other hand, export performance seems to have been in phase with the answers given by entrepreneurs only since 1993. Entrepreneurs therefore appear to have also included in their assessment an element relating to the volumes sold, which is hardly surprising.

Competitiveness is not, of course, an isolated datum. Just as some elements influence competitiveness, so competitiveness has an effect on other variables. An obvious magnitude which is influenced by competitiveness is activity. The simple argument underlying this relationship is that, when the competitive position improves (or, in other words, the ratio of relative export prices decreases), demand, all other things being equal, increases so that activity is stimulated. The comparison of the results of the survey on the competitive position with those of the monthly survey (indicators of activity and export orders) and of the quarterly survey on the degree of utilisation of production capacities is illustrative in this connection.

Chart 6   Monthly survey results and competitive position*

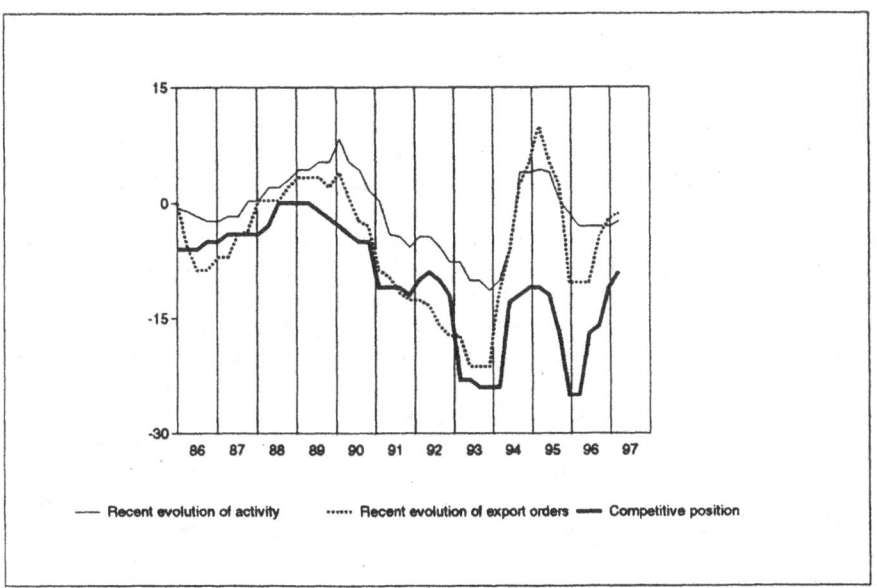

*Net balances of the "improved" and "worsened" percentages, smoothed and seasonally adjusted data.
Source: NBB.

Chart 7 Degree of utilisation of production capacities and competitive position*

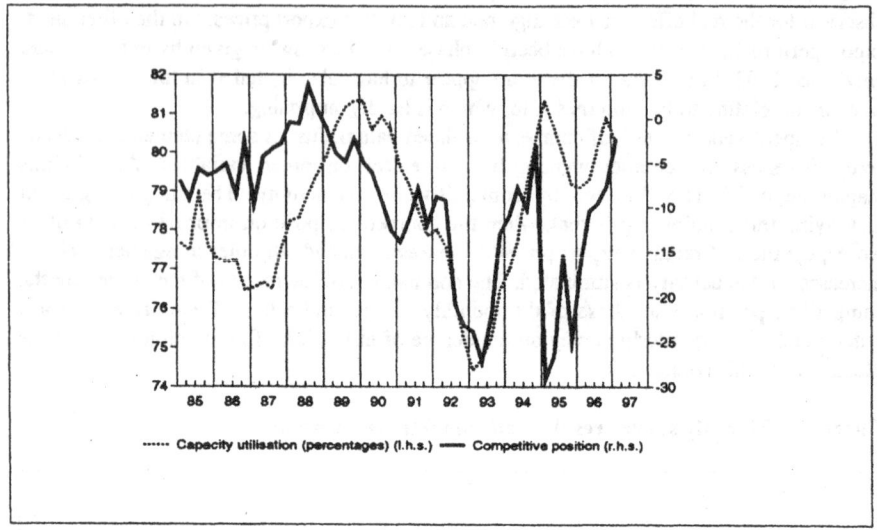

*Seasonally adjusted data.
Source: NBB.

In an earlier analysis the link between the competitive position and the degree of utilisation had already been established. On the basis of the movement of the rate of utilisation and of relative export prices during various sub-periods it had been deduced that relative prices and the utilisation rate were related as assumed: a fall in relative prices is coupled with an increase in the utilisation rate, and vice versa. The period 1989-1990 was, however, an exception to this. But it had been noted that demand from Germany had increased enormously under the influence of unification. Belgium, whose exports are traditionally largely geared to the German market, had taken full advantage of this situation, despite the less favourable relative prices. The divergence which occurred in 1995 is probably attributable to the overreaction to the exchange rates variations which have already been commented upon.

The close correspondence between the various survey results is reassuring in so far as it indicates that entrepreneurs, when they indicate an improvement in their competitiveness, also feel that there is a positive development of the demand reaching them from abroad. This is generally reflected in an improvement in the indicators of export orders. In view of the importance of foreign demand for a small economy such as Belgium, this is also reflected for most sectors in an improvement in the indicators of total activity.

As already mentioned, the results of the competitiveness survey correspond only imperfectly to the macroeconomic variables which are deemed to condition the development of competitiveness. Firstly, competitiveness is a broader concept than that reflected by each of the variables considered separately. Secondly, the statistical series which serve as a reference are of limited quality, especially since the introduction of Intrastat with regard to export prices. Lastly, the replies to the survey probably also incorporate an assessment of demand.

In this connection it is striking to note how closely the results of the competitiveness survey follow the movement of the gross operating surplus before tax of all manufacturing enterprises, that is, an accounting magnitude which reflects both control of all the costs of enterprises and the movement of the demand directed to them.

Chart 8 Gross operating surplus and competitive position

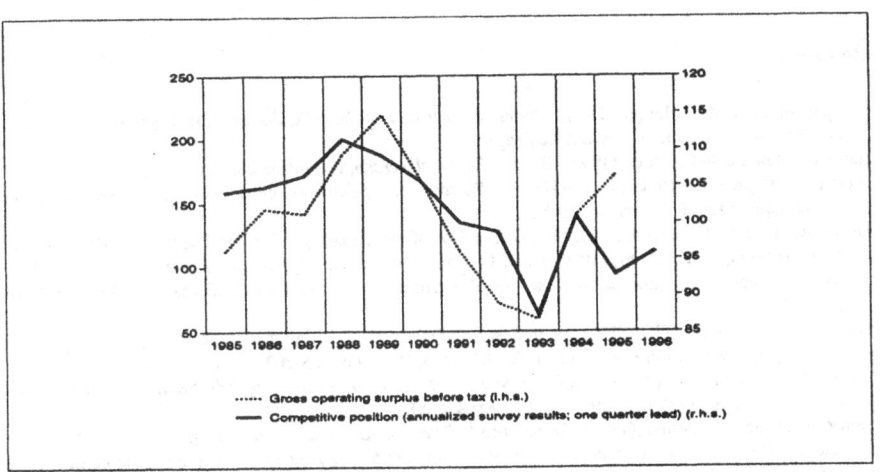

Source: NBB.

5 Conclusion

The main lessons which can be drawn from the analysis can be summarised as follows:

- the profile of the results concerning the competitive position on the domestic market is much more stable than that on the competitive position on the external market, which seems normal in view of the fact that a loss of competitiveness by an enterprise to the benefit of another resident enterprise should, on balance, have a neutral effect on results;

- enterprises do not generally seem able to make a clear-cut distinction between the development of their competitiveness on the European markets, on the one hand, and the markets outside the EC, on the other. In periods of relative stability of exchange rates on the European markets, coupled with major changes in the exchange rate for the dollar, more divergent results for the two markets might have been expected;

- the indicators derived from the competitiveness survey are best correlated with the development of the gross operating surplus before tax of manufacturing enterprises.

With regard to the latter point it therefore seems necessary to be more explicit in the questionnaire. From this viewpoint it might be useful to ask the participants about the origins of the change in the competitive position (labour costs, export prices, other costs, demand, exchange rates). Mention of these determinants would in fact have the advantage of better defining the framework within which entrepreneurs should think when they try to assess their competitiveness. The possibility might also be envisaged of asking enterprises a question on the development of their market shares (increasing, unchanged or decreasing) in order to place greater emphasis on the link between competitiveness and export performance.

References

Banque Nationale de Belgique (1994), *Pertes de parts de marché à l'exportation et amélioration du solde commercial: a paradoxe?*, unpublished paper.

Banque Nationale de Belgique (1997), *Evenwichtswisselkoersen*, unpublished paper.

Banque Nationale de Belgique (1997), La Balance des paiements de l'UEBL en 1996, in *Revue économique*, May, Brussels, pp. 19-24.

De Doncker, H. and Vanhaelen, J.J. (1994), The Use of the Capacity Survey to Explain the Behaviour of Entrepreneurs, in K.H. Oppenländer and G. Poser (eds.), *The Explanatory Power of Business Cycle Surveys*, Papers presented at the 21st CIRET Conference, Proceedings, Stellenbosch 1993, Avebury, pp. 133-158.

Durand, M. and Giorno, C. (1987), Les Indicateurs de Compétitivité internationale: Aspects conceptuels et Evaluation, in *Revue Economique de l'OCDE*, No. 9, Paris, pp. 165-202.

Durand M., Simon J. and Webb, C. (1992), *OECD's Indicators of International Trade and Competitiveness*, Working paper, No. 120, Paris, p. 51.

European Monetary Institute (1997), *Confidence Indicators and Economic Activity*, p. 31.

Loi du 26 juillet 1996 relative à la promotion de l'emploi et à la sauvegarde préventive de la compétitivité [The Law of 26th July 1996 concerning the Promotion of Employment and the Preventive Safeguarding of Competitiveness], Moniteur Belge du 01.08.1996.

National Bank of Belgium, Reports.

Turner P. and Van 't dock J. (1993), *Measuring International Price and Cost Competitiveness*, BIS Economic Papers, No. 39, Basle, p. 149.

Part IV
Financial Indicators

14 The Use of the Interest-Rate-Investment Relationship for Business Cycle Forecast: The Case of the South African Economy

Lorraine Greyling / Gerhardus van Zyl

1 Introduction

South Africa's future security and well-being will largely depend on restructuring and revitalising it's stagnating economy in a manner which addresses the needs of the majority of its people. In his influential work, The Competitive Advantage of Nations, Michael Porter (1990) concludes that the success of an economy lies in the productivity in which a nation's resources are employed. High productivity bestows a "competitive advantage" on domestically based firms, enabling them to outperform their foreign rivals in international markets. At the heart of sustained productivity is the notion of the economy, continually upgrading itself. A nation's firms "must relentlessly improve productivity in existing industries by raising product quality, adding desirable features, improving product technology, or boosting efficiency" (Porter, 1990:6). This upgrading constitutes innovation and investment. Given the severity of the economic crisis which faces South Africa, the belated recognition of the long term significance of investment and productivity is not surprising.

The current interest in the economic implications of investment and productivity as a means of furthering development, represents a return to the precepts of fundamental theories. In the Keynesian economics the accelerator principle of the investment-income relationship was developed. Rising profits in one sector can have the effect of inducing further industrial development. Incomes are earned in one industry and are spent on capital goods, often in linked industries. This may result in what the French economist Perroux has referred to as growth poles, a collection of propellant industries which influence secondary change through multiplier and accelerator effects. There is thus a positive relationship between investment and economic growth, and great emphasis is placed on the way in which increases in output can be achieved through increases in the stock of physical capital. Investment presupposes a willingness to make effort, and a willingness to see present sacrifices in the context of future gains.

This paper will analyse the revival of interest in the dynamics of the investment function and its forecasting potential.

2 Investment and Economic Growth in South Africa

In a simple Keynesian model of a closed economy, investment determines the level of income, employment and economic growth. In this view, investment represents an exogenous expenditure variable and thus a stimulus for economic growth. As a first step the relationship between investment and the economic growth rate must be determined for South Africa. The year-to-year growth in real Gross Domestic Product is taken to represent the fluctuation in economic activity (the business cycle), and the gross domestic fixed investment as an indication of capital accumulation.

Estimates of real GDP are important to businesses to assess the state of the economy and predict the feasibility of current and future investments. A graphical representation of the relationship between real fixed investment and economic activity is provided in figure 1.

The period under investigation is the sixteen years (on a quarterly basis) from 1980:1 - 1996:4. This could be sub-divided into (1) the period of approximately 5 years prior to the implementation of the sanctions and financial boycotts against South Africa; (2) the period 1985 up to 1994; and (3) the period since 1994 with a democratic elected government and therefore easier international relationships.

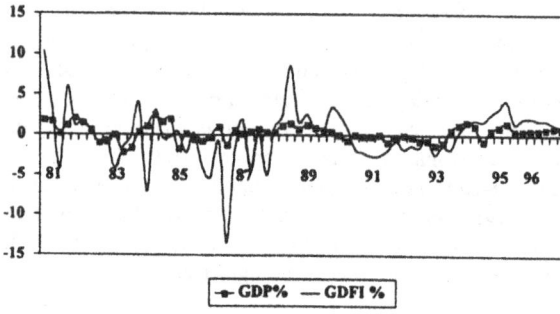

Figure 1 Relationship between economic growth and real fixed investment

The South African economy was characterized from 1980 to 1994 by adverse domestic political developments, exchange rate devaluation, poor macroeconomic performance and a capital flight. Real per capita GDP growth has followed a declining tendency since 1975, employment in the non-agricultural sectors has fallen short of the population growth and real gross domestic fixed investment by the private sector declined constantly until 1994. Another important and devastating effect is that South African investment expenditure is highly dependent on imports of fixed capital stock.

Prior to 1985, the deficit on the current account of the balance of payments was financed, at least partially, by an inflow of foreign capital. In the period preceding 1985 South Africa borrowed heavily abroad and it's foreign debt escalated from 21,3% of GDP in 1980 to a high of 42,9% in 1985. Thereafter it fell to 19,1% in 1990.

The deteriorating balance of payments situation, the poor performance of the economy and political upheaval finally culminated in the debt crisis and an imposition of a debt moratorium in August 1985 and huge capital outflows. A number of policies were introduced as a result of the capital outflow and the balance of payments crisis, such as a dual exchange rate system coupled with exchange control, higher tariff protection and surcharges on imports. Interest rates were increased and it portrayed a highly unstable pattern throughout the 1980's.

In February 1990 South Africa embarked on political reform which lead to a general election in April 1994. Currently South Africa is experiencing political and economic change and policies focused on transition and economic reform.

The model fitting results are summarised in Table 1. The functions were estimated using ordinary least-square regression.

Table 1   Regression results for investment to predict real economic activity in South Africa

Sample	Period	N	Coefficient	t-values	R^2
Whole Period	1980:1-1996:4	68	-0.2117	-3.8884	0.1864
Sub-period 1	1980:1-1985:1	21	0.1195	1.4326	0.0975
Sub-period 2	1985:2-1994:1	36	0.0679	0.8307	0.0198
Sub-period 3	1994:2-1996:4	11	0.4694	21.1420	0.9803

Source: Appendix A.

Table 1 shows that the estimated slope coefficients (with the exception of the whole period) are positive, suggesting that investment is positively related to the growth in real output. The R^2's are rather low (except sub-period 3) and coupled with the t-values for the coefficients lower than 2, indicating that the results are insignificant at the 0,99 percent level of confidence, indicates a poor model fitting. During sub-period 2 (1985:2-1994:1) a very low correlation is experienced between the GDP and GDFI. This is a period characterized by sanctions and financial boycotts against South Africa, and we had to do without any substantial increase in investment.

During sub-period 3 (the current after-election period) a strong positive relationship between economic activity and gross domestic fixed investment is experienced, with a near perfect fit of the model. The readmittance into the international markets and the availability of international trading credit bears on an immediate positive effect on both the output and investment levels, as theoretical expected.

Given the weakness of correlation between investment and economic growth from 1980:1 to 1994:1, an intensive analyses of the determinants of investment is necessary. The volume of investment remains important, not the least because it provides the chief mechanism for embodying technological progress in the productive system.

In contrast with the Keynesian model of a closed economy, a small open and developing economy like South Africa is reliant on imported capital goods and the greater proportion of the productive assets are imported. Hence, in a small economy which imports its capital goods, an increase in investment contributes to immediate balance of payments problems. In the absence of an inflow of foreign capital, as experienced from 1985 till 1994, adjustment to a deficit on the current account of the balance of payments, necessitates that imports decrease and since imports are largely capital goods, adjustments reduce investment.

3 The Determinants of Investment

The determinants of investment in South Africa are varied and included entrepreneurship, the productivity of labour, the marginal efficiency of capital, expectations about the future profitability of particular investment projects, technology and ultimately the availability of resources for investment. On the assumption that all else remain unchanged, a fall in the rate of interest is likely to induce greater investment. Of particular interest for this paper is the cyclical pattern of investment and the term structure of interest rates. During the economic upswing, long-term rates are normally above short-term rates as a result of the greater risk attached to long-term lending. Banks would refrain from increasing lending rates during the early stages of the economic upswing, due to the availability of excess cash reserves. Approaching the peak, and during the initial part of the subsequent economic downswing, short-term rates are, in turn, at higher levels than long-term rates. Banks have now excessively extended credit and have to protect inadequate cash reserves. Short-term and long-term rates are roughly equal at approximately the mid-upswing and mid-downswing phases, which is probably the result of short-term lending rates lagging behind the business cycle more so than long-term rates. An upward sloping yield curve (it is the difference between a long-term and short-term interest rate) is associated with the expectation that the growth of real output in the economy is improving, whilst a downward sloping yield curve represents an expectation of a recession (Nel, 1997:163).

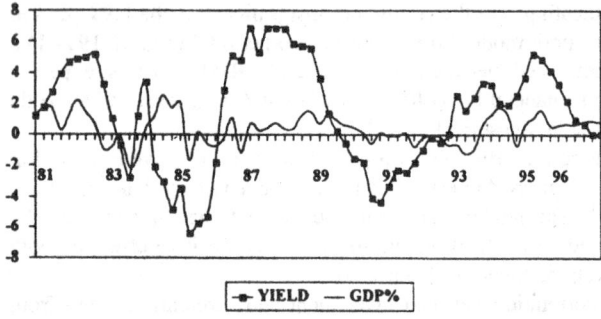

Figure 2   Relationship between yield curve[1] and the business cycle

Figure 2 shows the growth in the GDP and the gap between the long-term stock and the short-term 32 days Notice deposits with clearing banks (the yield curve). It is clear from the visual inspection that a positive yield induces economic activity, (through the possible capital inflow) and that a negative yield corresponds with a downswing in the economy, for example period 1988:1 to 1991:1. The slope of the yield curve in South

---

[1] Yield curve is the difference between a long-term and short-term interest rate.

Africa is positively related to the growth in the real economic activity. The figure also indicates a deterioration of the predictive value of the yield curve since 1994.

Given the cyclical course of the yield curve and the fact that investment is mostly financed by long-term funds, a relationship between real investment and the yield curve must be tested. A positive yield indicates a long-term interest rate higher than the short-term rate, an inflow of capital, and therefore a theoretical positive relationship with real investment is expected.

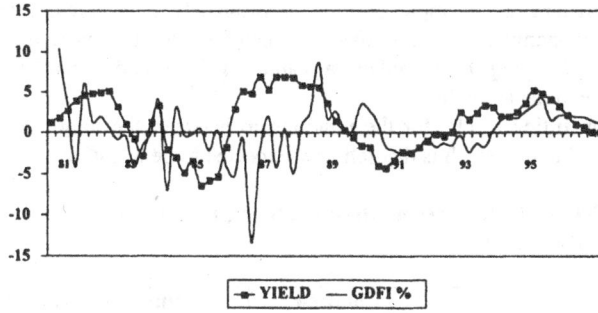

Figure 3   Relationship between yield curve and the fixed investment

Table 2 shows the model fitting results for the relationship between the yield curve and Investment.

Table 2   Regression results for the yield curve to predict real investment in South Africa

Sample	Period	N	Coefficient	T-values	R^2
Whole Period	1980:1-1996:4	68	-724.333	-2.7712	0.1042
Sub-period 1	1980:1-1985:1	21	400.838	2.8054	0.2929
Sub-period 2	1985:2-1994:1	36	-723.462	-4.2688	0.3489
Sub-period 3	1994:2-1996:4	11	-1643.77	-6.2902	0.8147

Source: Appendix C.

The coefficients in Table 2 indicate the expected positive correlation between the yield curve and real investment for only the period 1980:1 - 1985 with the other time periods showing a negative correlation. The relative low R^2's should be carefully interpreted for only one explanatory variable was used. The poor fit appears to be a result of over-simplification in the model-specification. The t-values for all the coefficients are significant. In the whole period sample only 9 per cent of the variation in investment can be explained by the yield curve, while sub-period 3 provided a good fit ($R^2 = 0,8147$).

The model shows a theoretical unacceptable fit, with the exception of sub-period 1. During 1985 the refusal of the international banking community to roll-over debt resulted in the imposition of a debt moratorium by South Africa. The subsequent repayment agreements meant that with access to foreign finance greatly reduced, the interest payments on the long-term debt had to be financed by reduced imports of investment goods and by extremely high domestic long-term interest rates. The coefficient for sub-period 2 is a proof of the unnatural situation in South Africa, with high interest rates, coupled with an outflow of capital, a surplus on the current account of the balance of payments and low and decreasing real investment.

A high interest rate structure, as an input cost, is unfortunately detrimental for investment in a small open economy like South Africa's. Therefore, South Africa has experienced clashing goals of trying to stimulate a capital inflow and financing investment (through restrictive monetary policy).

In table 3 the correlation fitting results for the relationship between the long-term interest rate and investment is shown; which is theoretically expected to be negative.

Table 3   Regression results for the long-term interest rate to predict real Investment in South Africa

Sample	P	N	Coefficient	T-values	R^2
Whole Period	1980:1-1996:4	68	-1596.580	-3.3891	0.1482
Sub-period 1	1980:1-1985:1	21	201.743	0.6165	0.0196
Sub-period 2	1985:2-1994:1	36	1515.793	3.3285	0.2458
Sub-period 3	1994:2-1996:4	11	-454.174	-0.3553	0.0138

The model fitting results have a low statistical significance, with low R^2-values, unacceptable t-values and theoretical unacceptable coefficient slope lines. The regression results show that although high long-term interest rates were experienced in South Africa, positive investment still took place. Theory implies that an increase in the interest rate may result in a reduction in investment, whilst the empirical results in South Africa show absolutely the opposite.

Both the yield curve and the long-term interest rate fail to predict the level of investment in South Africa. Both the variables show an unacceptable theoretical relationship, with poor model fitting results. Hence, when capital goods are imported with the coupling balance of payments problems and offsetting monetary policy, investment is not explained by financial variables.

The Harrod-Domar growth model identifies a dual role for investment - investment that adds to productive capacity while at the same time adding to aggregate demand. Domar sees investment as inextricably linked to growth; if a company invests in more capital goods this may result in the employment of less labour. A growth in productive capacity will gradually cause an increase in unemployment if income fails to grow elsewhere, for example an increase in exports.

Measures of social rates of return on investment by labour are usually calculated using data on the productivity benefits and costs of labour input (remuneration of workers). Productivity benefits are associated with the productivity of the capital goods and the productivity of workers that is enhanced. The productivity of physical capital is enhanced by workers with more work-related knowledge and skills on the operation of production equipment.

Table 4 shows the results of a tested relationship between investment and labour. As an independent variable the cost of labour minus productivity per worker was taken, which results in the yield per worker, which should bear a negative relationship with investment.

Table 4   Regression results for the labour yield to predict real investment in South Africa

Sample	Period	N	Coefficient	T-values	R^2
Whole Period	1980:1-1996:4	68	-366.980	0.0364	0.0457
Sub-period 1	1980:1-1985:1	21	137.136	0.0889	0.09807
Sub-period 2	1985:2-1994:1	36	723.548	0.0813	0.0117
Sub-period 3	1994:2-1996:4	11	1230.240	0.8256	0.8205

Source: Appendix E.

The model fitting results again are rather poor with low R^2-values, economically unacceptable coefficient slope lines and mostly insignificant t-values. The cost and productivity of labour seems to provide no explanation for the level of investment in South Africa.

The determinants of investment were identified as the availability and cost of resources for investment (the yield and long-term interest rate), the productivity and cost of labour and the marginal efficiency of capital. The first two determinants were tested as possible explanatory variables for investment, and both proofed to be rather unsuccessful. As a next approach to this paper the marginal efficiency of capital and the MEC-Investment Relationship for business cycle forecasts will be analyzed.

4 Measurement of the Marginal Efficiency of Capital

Three important causes of economic growth, and the business cycle, are capital accumulation, division of labour and technical progress, whilst economic growth is associated with increasing returns to scale. Increasing returns to scale serve as a functional link between the firm or industry at the micro-economic and economic growth at the macro-economic level. While growth theory upsurged in macro-economic literature, literature continued to lack a firm micro-economic foundation of maximising behaviour and technical progress. A method to calculate and explain economic growth as indigenously determined by increasing returns to scale or by the efficiency of capital, must be developed.

The three methods that were used to estimate the marginal efficiency of capital in the South African manufacturing industry for the sample period 1980-1996 are the Cobb-Douglas production function, the Constant Elasticity of Substitution function and the Transcendental Logarithmic function. The reason why all three methods were used was to identify the function with the highest estimating ability for a specific year in the sample period.

4.1 The Cobb-Douglas Production Function (C-D function)

The theoretically purest and most widely used production function is the C-D function. The logarithmic transformation of the Cobb-Douglas function has the convenient property of linearity. When the function is converted to $L_n Q = L_n A + \delta L_n K + \beta L_n L$, the parameters can be estimated by means of the ordinary least squares method of multiple regression analysis. A "roll-up" estimation technique was implemented. This simply meant that multiple regression were done by adding the next year's data to the sample period (e.g. 1980-1986 then 1980-1987). In this way the tendency of the estimated parameters could be established. In all the multiple C-D regressions that were done, δ and β were between zero and 1 and thus satisfying the theoretical requirements ($0<\delta, \beta<1$).

In all the cases, an increase in one input lead to a decrease in the other one. This implied that the estimated production function met the requirement set by the marginal rate of technical substitution.

4.2 Constant Elasticity of Substitution Function (CES)

The CES function includes the Leontief function where $\sigma = 0$; and the Cobb-Douglas function where $\sigma = 1$; as special cases (Braff, 1969:82). Arrow (1985:92-102) found elasticity of substitution to be typically less than unity, and in some cases of primary production it exceeds unity.

The CES-function that was used can be stated as:

$$Q = [\gamma \Sigma \delta K^{-p} + (1-\delta) L^{-p}]^{-v/p}$$

Where parameter γ increases in this function, output (Q) will increase proportionally, and in that sense γ corresponds with the A-parameter of the Cobb-Douglas function.

Therefore, γ is the efficiency parameter. Parameter v denotes the degree of homogeneity. δ denotes the degree to which the technology is capital intensive. Parameter p is the substitution parameter, and equals $p = (1-\sigma)/\sigma$ (Mororey, 1967:35-38 and Wallis, 1979:68-70).

The CES function can be used where imperfect competition exists, and it satisfied most Neo-Classical criteria. The marginal rate of technical substitution and marginal productivity depend on the input ratio of capital and labour, the capital intensity parameter (δ) and the elasticity of substitution (σ). Non-neutral technological changes are reflected in variations in the capital intensity (δ) and elasticity of substitution (σ) parameters.

In practice the CES function is relatively difficult to fit the data and some of it's parameters are difficult to estimate unless special precautions are taken. The parameters (γ, δ and p) cannot be directly estimated by regression analysis, nor is it possible to linearise the equation by taking logarithms. Estimation of the parameters has to proceed in stages. First estimate p, then δ and lastly γ.

4.3 The Transcendental Logarithmic Function

Christensen and others (1973:28-45) developed a transcendental logarithmic production function (Translog) in which elasticity of substitution can change with output and/or factor proportions. The translog functions do not employ additivity and homogeneity as part of the maintained hypothesis. The approach was to represent the production frontier by functions that are quadratic in the logarithms of the quantities of inputs and outputs. The resulting frontiers permit a greater variety of substitution and transformation patterns than frontiers based on constant elasticity's of substitution and transformations.

The CES equation can be retracted a little to employ linear approximations. J. Kmenta (1967) proposed an approximation by writing the CES function as:

$$\text{Log } Q = \log \gamma - (v/\beta) f(p)$$
where $f(p) = \text{Log } \sum \delta k^{-p} + (1-\delta)L^{-p}$

Neglecting higher order terms, an approximation may be used as:

$$\text{Log } Q = \text{Log } \gamma + v\sigma \log K + v(1-\sigma) \text{lohL} - \tfrac{1}{2}.v p \sigma [\log k/L]^2$$

This is in effect a Cobb-Douglas production function log linear regression. A squared logarithm of the capital-labour ratio is added. The last term indicates a departure from a unit elasticity of substitution.

If the squared term is replaced by an unconstrained quadratic, it forms a transcendental logarithmic production function as:

$$\log Q = a_0 + a_1 \log K + a_2 \log L + a_{11} (\log K)^2 + a_{12} (\log K)(\log L) + a_{22} (\log L)^2$$

(Christensen, 1973:28-45 & Wallis, 1979:76-80).

Where natural logarithms are used $a_0 = \log \gamma$ is the efficiency parameter, parameters a_1 and a_2 are distribution parameters and parameters a_{11}, a_{12} and a_{22} are substitution parameters. This general equation is easy to estimate with multiple regression analysis.

4.4 Estimation Results

Comparing the Cobb-Douglas, CES and Translog estimation ability, it was quite obvious that the Translog function does yield better results. The difference is however small and in only a few cases were the Cobb-Douglas and CES estimates better. Keeping production output values unchanged, and logging the value of capital further improved the results.

An index for the marginal efficiency of capital was constructed from the estimated results. The year 1990 was used as the base year.

Table 5 Marginal efficiency of capital index (1990 = base year)

Year	Index Value	% Change
1980	89,60	-
1981	89,80	0,02
1982	90,15	2,68
1983	92,05	2,11
1984	93,00	1,03
1985	93,65	0,69
1986	94,15	0,53
1987	95,00	0,90
1988	96,45	1,53
1989	97,15	0,73
1990	100,00	2,93
1991	103,15	3,15
1992	108,55	5,24
1993	112,15	3,32
1994	118,05	5,26
1995	126,00	6,73

From the above mentioned table it is clear that the marginal efficiency of capital exhibited a limited upward tendency on average during the 1980's. One should keep in mind that real labour union activity only started in 1986 and that the country was forced into a global sanction situation. It is quite evident that after 1990 (the announcement and implementation of political changes coupled with a very volatile labour market situation) the marginal efficiency of capital did increase dramatically. From several interviews conducted with private sector manufacturers it was pointed out that a high level of automisation was taking place. Capital was increasingly substituted for labour despite relatively strict monetary policy (high interest rates).

The estimation results for the MEC to predict real gross domestic fixed investment in South Africa are presented in table 6.

Table 6 Regression results for the MEC to predict real investment in South Africa

Sample	Period	n	Coefficient	T-values	R^2
Whole Period	1980:1-1996:4	68	-227.700	-3.367	0.1466
Sub-period 1	1980:1-1985:1	21	-732.493	-2.521	0.2507
Sub-period 2	1985:2-1994:1	36	-283.708	-3.128	0.2235
Sub-period 3	1994:2-1996:4	11	535.212	6.827	0.8382

Source: Appendix D.

The coefficients in table 6 are inconsistent with the developed MEC-model and reflects a negative correlation between the marginal efficiency of capital and real investment for the period 1980:1-1994:1. Theoretically this results seem unacceptable with an increase in MEC that would normally induce investment. Given the very unnatural economic period from 1980 to 1994, this contradiction in results may indicate that firms were forced into more output with constant or decreasing levels of fixed investment. The surcharges on imported capital goods, the depreciation of the rand, and high interest rates caused by stringent monetary policy contributed to an increase in the marginal efficiency of capital combined with low levels of investment. Since 1994 an upsurge in investment and marginal efficiency of capital was experienced, and a good fit of the model with a R^2-value of 0.8382 and significant t-values were recorded.

5 Summary

A lack of economic development and growth plus employment opportunities are serious economic problems in South Africa. The obvious question to be asked is whether the conditions identified for successful growth have a theoretical base or whether they stylized facts applicable on a developed country only. Although theoretical studies encourage the understanding of this topical issue of investment, empirical research done in a structured manner could be of great significance and is intended to elucidate what behavioral patterns are mostly likely to occur. The need for growth and higher rates of employment in South Africa necessitates more investment and this hypothesis was empirically tested in this paper.

An in-depth analysis of the relationship of investment and economic activity was done, followed by an analysis of the determinants of investment in South Africa. The traditional determinants of fixed investment in South Africa that are normally used to forecast possible trends in real fixed investment were statistically analysed. The results presented in this paper are not consistent with the Keynesian Investment-Income hypothesis. The findings of the models proof that monetary or financial indicators, as well as the performance of the labour market, were insignificant in predicting the investment level.

A measurement of efficiency of capital was introduced in the paper and its prediction value for fixed investment was tested. The MEC-model proofs to be a useful tool in investment decision-making in the private sector. The results highlight the importance of micro-economic conditions for the macro-economic health of the economy. Efficiency of capital - an aspect often regarded by macro-economists as peripheral is shown to be a critical variable for investment decision.

Appendix A

Regression Analysis: GDP=f(GDFI)

1. Regression (GDP = f(GDFI)) 1980.1-1996.4
Constant   112238.1
Std Err of Y Est   6995.496
R Squared   0.186389
No. of Observations   68
Degrees of Freedom   66

X Coefficient(s)   -0.21165   T-Value   -3.88843
Std Err of Coef.   0.054431

2. Regression (GDP = f(GDFI)) 1980.1-1985.1
Constant   36225.57
Std Err of Y Est   2794.798
R Squared   0.097487
No. of Observations   21
Degrees of Freedom   19

X Coefficient(s)   0.119488   T-Value   1.432598
Std Err of Coef.   0.083407

3. Regression (GDP = f(GDFI)) 1985.2-1994.1
Constant   32521.59
Std Err of Y Est   4165.596
R Squared   0.019896
No. of Observations   36
Degrees of Freedom   34

X Coefficient(s)   0.067888   T-Value   0.83079
Std Err of Coef.   0.081715

4. Regression (GDP = f(GDFI)) 1994.2-1996.4
Constant   -79928.9
Std Err of Y Est   534.8028
R Squared   0.980263
No. of Observations   11
Degrees of Freedom   9

X Coefficient(s)   0.469394   T-Value   21.14204
Std Err of Coef.   0.022202

Appendix B

Regression Analysis: GDFI=f(I)

1. Regression (GDFI = f(I)) 1980.1-1996.4
Constant   80193.02
Std Err of Y Est   7157.653
R Squared   0.148233
No. of Observations   68
Degrees of Freedom   66

X Coefficient(s)   -1596.59   T-Value   -3.38909
Std Err of Coef.   471.095

2. Regression (GDFI = f(I)) 1980.1-1985.1
Constant   63176.28
Std Err of Y Est   2912.882
R Squared   0.019612
No. of Observations   21
Degrees of Freedom   19

X Coefficient(s)   201.7428   T-Value   0.616501
Std Err of Coef.   327.2383

3. Regression (GDFI = f(I)) 1985.2-1994.1
Constant   26747.43
Std Err of Y Est   3654.208
R Squared   0.245769
No. of Observations   36
Degrees of Freedom   34

X Coefficient(s)   1515.794   T-Value   3.328521
Std Err of Coef.   455.3956

4. Regression (GDFI = f(I)) 1994.2-1996.4
Constant   62652.3
Std Err of Y Est   3780.278
R Squared   0.013832
No. of Observations   11
Degrees of Freedom   9

X Coefficient(s)   -454.174   T-Value   -0.35529
Std Err of Coef.   1278.326

Appendix C

Regression Analysis: GDFI=f(Yield)

1. Regression (GDFI = f(Yield)) 1980.1-1996.4
Constant   57116.93
Std Err of Y Est   7340.213
R Squared   0.104229
No. of Observations   68
Degrees of Freedom   66

X Coefficient(s)   -724.333   T-Value   -2.7712
Std Err of Coef.   261.3787

2. Regression (GDFI = f(Yield)) 1980.1-1985.1
Constant   65848.49
Std Err of Y Est   2473.801
R Squared   0.292898
No. of Observations   21
Degrees of Freedom   19

X Coefficient(s)   400.8382   T-Value   2.805397
Std Err of Coef.   142.8811

3. Regression (GDFI = f(Yield)) 1985.2-1994.1
Constant   51930.35
Std Err of Y Est   3395.07
R Squared   0.348949
No. of Observations   36
Degrees of Freedom   34

X Coefficient(s)   -723.463   T-Value   -4.26887
Std Err of Coef.   169.4741

4. Regression (GDFI = f(I)) 1994.2-1996.4
Constant   59335.68
Std Err of Y Est   1638.711
R Squared   0.814686
No. of Observations   11
Degrees of Freedom   9

X Coefficient(s)   -1643.77   T-Value   -6.29017
Std Err of Coef.   261.3245

Appendix D

Regression Analysis: GDFI=f(MEC)

1. Regression (GDFI = f(MEC)) 1980.1-1996.4
Constant   79317.04
Std Err of Y Est   7164.585
R Squared   0.146582
No. of Observations   68
Degrees of Freedom   66

X Coefficient(s)   -227.7   T-Value   -3.36691
Std Err of Coef.   67.62878

2. Regression (GDFI = f(MEC)) 1980.1-1985.1
Constant   132303.4
Std Err of Y Est   2546.606
R Squared   0.250665
No. of Observations   21
Degrees of Freedom   19

X Coefficient(s)   -732.493   T-Value   -2.52107
Std Err of Coef.   290.548

3. Regression (GDFI = f(MEC)) 1985.2-1994.1
Constant   79251.91
Std Err of Y Est   3707.838
R Squared   0.223469
No. of Observations   36
Degrees of Freedom   34

X Coefficient(s)   -283.708   T-Value   -3.12801
Std Err of Coef.   90.69905

4. Regression (GDFI = f(MEC)) 1994.2-1996.4
Constant   -11926.3
Std Err of Y Est   1531.411
R Squared   0.83816
No. of Observations   11
Degrees of Freedom   9

X Coefficient(s)   535.2116   T-Value   6.827176
Std Err of Coef.   78.39428

Appendix E

Regression Analysis: GDFI=f(Labour Yield)

1. Regression (GDFI = f(Labour Yield)) 1980.1-1996.4
Constant   55555.82
Std Err of Y Est   7576.329
R Squared   0.045673
No. of Observations   68
Degrees of Freedom   66

X Coefficient(s)   446.0536   T-Value   1.777262
Std Err of Coef.   250.978

2. Regression (GDFI = f(Labour Yield)) 1980.1-1985.1
Constant   66244
Std Err of Y Est   2793.9
R Squared   0.098067
No. of Observations   21
Degrees of Freedom   19

X Coefficient(s)   -155.983   T-Value   -1.43731
Std Err of Coef.   108.5243

3. Regression (GDFI = f(Labour Yield)) 1985.2-1994.1
Constant   50630.96
Std Err of Y Est   4183.074
R Squared   0.011655
No. of Observations   36
Degrees of Freedom   34

X Coefficient(s)   315.886   T-Value   0.633192
Std Err of Coef.   498.8784

4. Regression (GDFI = f(Labour Yield)) 1994.2-1996.4
Constant   50741.65
Std Err of Y Est   1612.669
R Squared   0.820529
No. of Observations   11
Degrees of Freedom   9

X Coefficient(s)   1361.033   T-Value   6.414624
Std Err of Coef.   212.1766

Appendix F

Regression Analysis: GDFI=f(Labour Cost)

1. Regression (GDFI = f(Labour Cost)) 1980.1-1996.4
Constant   96480.04
Std Err of Y Est   7492.181
R Squared   0.066754
No. of Observations   68
Degrees of Freedom   66

X Coefficient(s)   -402.526   T-Value   -2.17276
Std Err of Coef.   185.2601

2. Regression (GDFI = f(Labour Cost)) 1980.1-1985.1
Constant   50423.52
Std Err of Y Est   2789.931
R Squared   0.100628
No. of Observations   21
Degrees of Freedom   19

X Coefficient(s)   159.7355   T-Value   1.458032
Std Err of Coef.   109.5555

3. Regression (GDFI = f(Labour Cost)) 1985.2-1994.1
Constant   93931.78
Std Err of Y Est   4075.626
R Squared   0.061776
No. of Observations   36
Degrees of Freedom   34

X Coefficient(s)   -432.604   T-Value   -1.49623
Std Err of Coef.   289.1299

4. Regression (GDFI = f(Labour Cost)) 1994.2-1996.4
Constant   -154890
Std Err of Y Est   3172.536
R Squared   0.305429
No. of Observations   11
Degrees of Freedom   9

X Coefficient(s)   1963.091   T-Value   1.989381
Std Err of Coef.   986.7853

References

Arrow, K.J. (1985), Production and capital, Cambridge: Belkrop.
Arrow, K.J., Chenery, H.B., Minhas, B.S. and Solow, R.H. (1961), Capital and labour substitution and economic efficiency, *Review of economics and statistics*, 43, pp. 225-250.
Braff, A.J. (1969), Microeconomic analysis, New York: Wiley.
Browne, G.W. (1943), Production function for South African manufacturing industry, *South African journal of economics*, 11(4), December 1943, pp. 258-268.
Bruwer, M.J. (1994), Estimation of the production function for the motor vehicle industry (Labour input). Unpublished research paper for the motor vehicle research unit at the Rand Afrikaans University.
Christensen, L.R., Jorgenson, D.W. and Lawrence, J.L. (1973), Transcendental logarithmic production frontiers, *Review of economics and statistics*, 55, pp. 28-45.
Cobb, C.W. and Douglas, P.H. (1928), Theory of production, *American economic review*, 23rd supplement, pp.139-65.
Greyling, L. and Schmulow, D. (1996), Monetary policy in the new South Africa: Economic and Political Constraints, *The South African Journal of Economics*, 64(3), pp.175-192.
Heathfield, D.F. (1971), Production functions, London: McMillan.
Kleynhans, E.P.J. (1994), The level of optimalization of the capital and labour input base in the South African motor vehicle industry, Aucklandpark: Rand Afrikaans University. (M.A. dissertation).
Kmenta, J. (1967), On estimation of the CES production function, *International economic review*, 8(2), June 1967, pp. 180-189.
Koutsoyiannis, A. (1977), Theory of econometrics, London: McMillan.
Moroney, J.R. (1967), Cobb-Douglas production functions and returns to scale in U.S. manufacturing industry, *Western economic journal*, pp. 39-51.
Nel, H. (1996), The term structure of interest rates and economic activity in South Africa, *The South African Journal of Economics*, 64(3), pp. 161-174.
Porter, M.E. (1990), The competitive advantage of Nations, London: McMillan.
Van der Schyff, J.P. (1994), Estimation of a production function for the South African motor vehicle industry with special reference to the capital and labour input. Aucklandpark: Rand Afrikaans University (M.Com. research report).
SA Reserve Bank, Quarterly Bulletin. Various.
Van der Walt, J.S. and De Wet, G.L. (1993), The Constraining Effect of limited foreign Capital inflow on the economic growth of South Africa, *South African Journal of Economics*, 61(1), pp. 3-12.
Van Zyl, G. and Kleynhans, E.P.J. (1995), A Cobb-Douglas estimation of labour productivity in the South African motor vehicle industry, *Journal of industrial psychology*. 21(1), pp. 6-9.
Wallis, K.F. (1979), Topics in applied econometrics, Oxford: Basil Blackwell.

15 Economic Policies and Business Cycles in Germany

Willi Leibfritz / Alexander Juchems

Abstract

Many studies have shown that economic policies may have significant impacts on business cycles and they may to some extend be „cycle makers". Hence if it were possible to construct appropriate policy indicators these could be used as leading indicators so that economic forecasting could be improved. Such analysis may also affect policy recommendations. For example economic policies are often blamed for being procyclical i.e. overly expansionary during economic booms and too restrictive during economic downturns. Such policies would increase inflationary pressures during the upswing and unemployment in the downturn. As recessions would be deeper than with more neutral policies, unemployment would not only rise more in the short-term - given problems of hysteresis - employment and growth may also be lower over the long-term.

In the following an attempt is made to construct indicators for monetary conditions and fiscal policies for Germany and to examine the policy mix during the past cycles. It is shown that economic policies had significant effects on economic activity. Furthermore it is a common feature that expansionary fiscal policies are accompanied by restrictive monetary conditions.

1 " Monetary Conditions" as a Single Indicator

There are basically three types of indicators which reflect monetary conditions: 1. indicators of money supply and bank credits, 2. indicators of key interest rates and 3. indicators of exchange rates.

For example an increase in the money supply increases liquidity and may lead to higher demand for goods and services. In Germany, M3 money supply is generally used by the Bundesbank as the indicator for assessing the stance of monetary policy. If the velocity of money supply remains constant or - as was the case in the past - declines by a constant rate a change in growth of money supply leads with a time lag to a change in nominal GDP, if real economic growth remains constant, to a change in the rate of inflation.

In recent years, however, the money supply/GDP relationship became rather unstable in many countries so that the money supply lost it's importance as an intermediate target for monetary policy; many central banks are now using the inflation rate as the direct target without giving much importance to the money supply. While the Bundesbank is still using M3 as an intermediate target for monetary policy it has acknowledged that M3 growth was rather unstable in recent years. It was distorted by various factors, as German reunification, portfolio shifts between the money market and the capital market or foreign deposits, legislation causing high credit demand for construction purposes. Therefore at present German money supply M3 is only a good indicator for future economic activity or inflation if it is adjusted for the various special factors - as far as these are known - are sorted out. Given these difficulties our current indicator for monetary conditions does nor include M3.

Interest rates may also be important indicators for monetary conditions. Higher interest rates reduce the demand for money and credit and increases capital costs. This may reduce demand for goods and services, in particular investment. But higher interest rates may reflect higher inflation expectations. Real interest rates (nominal interest rates less expected inflation) are therefore - in theory - more appropriate for judging the effects of interest rates on the real economy.[1]

In our indicator for monetary conditions we do however, not use the level of interest rates but rather the spread between long and short-term rates (10-year bund yields minus 3-month money market rate). Many empirical studies show that this spread contains useful information for the conduct of monetary policy and may be used as a predictor for economic activity and inflation.[2]

A tighter monetary policy is generally reflected in a smaller spread between long rates and short rates (or even in an inverted yield curve) while monetary easing is reflected in a widening of the spread.

Changes in the real exchange rate may also affect the economic activity (and inflation). Domestic monetary policy may respond to such changes, or it may tolerate exchange rate movements if these are in line with domestic policy targets. The combination of domestic monetary policies - as reflected by the interest rate spread - and the exchange rate may provide a better picture for monetary conditions than the monetary policy variable alone, in particular in an open country like Germany. We therefore use the weighted real exchange rate against Germanys 18 main trading partners as an additional component in our indicator for monetary conditions.

Figure 1 shows the development of the interest rate spread and the real exchange rate since the early 1970s. The time series are smoothed with a Hondrick-Prescott filter. Furthermore a composite indicator for monetary conditions is shown which is a weighted average of the two indicators. The weights are derived form a regression analysis between a business cycle indicator (the ifo business climate) and the two indicators for monetary conditions.[3] All time series are normalised, i.e. their standard deviation has been set to one.

---

[1] The expected inflation rate can be measured only by auxiliary concepts and therefore not very exact. Oftenly the expected inflation rate is approximated by the actual inflation rate. Real interest rates are then calculated by deflating nominal interest rates with actual the inflation rate.

[2] See for example: G.D. Sutton, Is There Excess Comovement of Bond Yields Between Countries?, Bank for International Settlements, Working Papers No. 44, Basle, July 1997, and the literature mentioned there.

[3] The regression function is (t-values in parenteses): IFOBUSINESSCLIMATEINDEX = 92,5 (226,4) + 1,4 (3,4) EXCHANGERATE + 0.9 (2,3) YIELDSPEAD.

Figure 2 shows that this composite indicator for monetary conditions is a relatively good predictor for the ifo business climate. The monetary conditions indicator is generally leading the business climate by around half a year. Only at special events as the oil price shock at the beginning of the 80s or the German reunification in 1990/91 - the fit is interrupted. As economic activity may not only be affected by monetary conditions but by the overall policy mix including fiscal policy we also look for an appropriate indicator for fiscal policies.

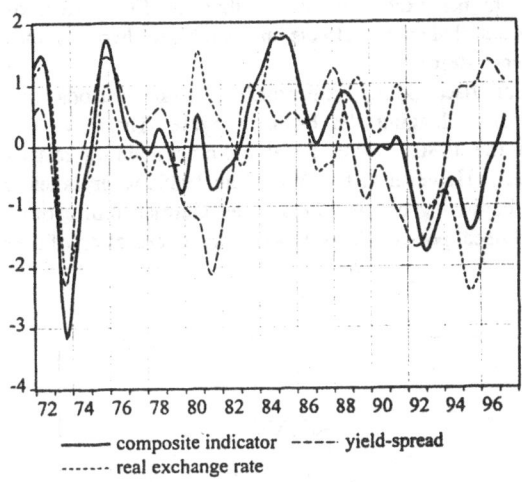

——— composite indicator   ----- yield-spread
------- real exchange rate

Figure 1 Determinants of the monetary conditions indicator (normalised and smoothed time series)

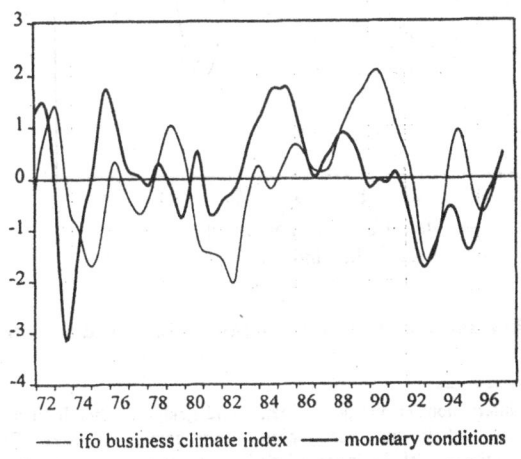

——— ifo business climate index   ——— monetary conditions

Figure 2 Monetary conditions* and the business cycle
*Indicator consisting of the real exchange rate and the yield-spread, normalised and smoothed time series

2 The Fiscal Policy Indicator

Fiscal policy affects economic activity in a rather complex way. It is therefore difficult to assess such effects without using macroeconomic models. The appropriateness of the indicator also depends on the specific question which is asked.[1] Here we use the change of the structural primary deficit (structural budget deficit without interest payments) as a proxy for the impact of discretionary fiscal policy on aggregate demand. While it is possible that a higher budget deficit leads to higher interest rates, more private savings (Ricardo effect) or a higher exchange rate so that the final effect of the deficit is outweighted, such counterbalancing effects are excluded here as they may be less important in the very short-term.

Fig. 3 shows our fiscal-policy indicator.[2] In some periods fiscal policy was procyclical but was often lagging the business cycle. There were also periods of consolidation - as in the 1980s - with fiscal policy remaining restrictive despite an upswing in the economy. However at the end of the 1980s when taxes were cut despite the boom and at the beginning of the 1990s when German unification was to a large extent deficit-financed fiscal policy clearly added to the overheating of the economy.

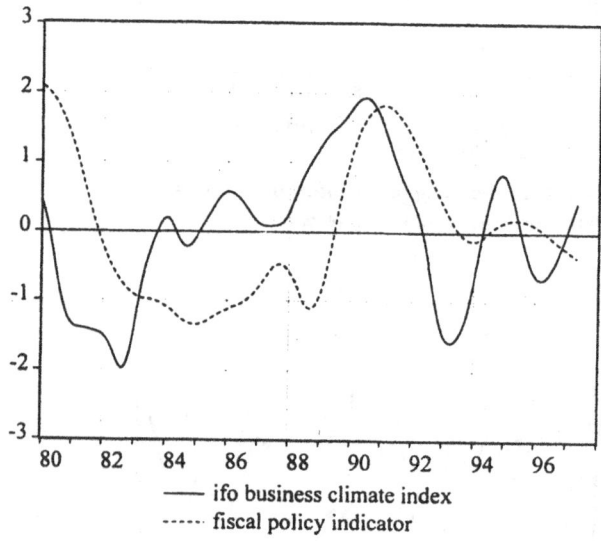

Figure 3 Fiscal policy and the business cycle (normalised and smoothed time series)

---

[1] See also: W. Leibfritz, Internationaler Vergleich finanz- und geldpolitischer Indikatoren (International comparsion of monetary policy and fiscal policy indicators), in: K.H. Oppenländer (ed.), Konjunkturindikatoren (Business Cycle Indicators), Munich, Vienna 1995, pp. 282-297.

[2] The data for this indicator is taken from the OECD, converted from annual values to monthly values by dividing the annual change into 12 similar monthly changes; these changes are then smoothed.

3 The „Overall-policy" Indicator

A composite policy-mix indicator is constructed by weighting the two indicators - monetary conditions and fiscal policies - together. Weights were again derived from regression analysis with respect to the business cycle. The regression function is as following:

IFOBUSINESSCLIMATEINDEX = 93,3 (209,3) + 3,1 (8,4) MONETARY CONDITIONS + 2,7 (6,7) FISCALPOLICY.

The coefficients of the regression indicate that monetary conditions have been on average a somewhat more important indicator for the business cycle than fiscal policy.

The composite policy indicator is shown in Fig. 5. Ot has a relatively close link with the business cycle although it is generally not leading the cycle. On average it is lagging the ifo business climate by three month (see Fig. 6: with a 3-month lag the r^2 is 0.548, higher than with all other leads or lags). It is interesting to note that the ifo business climate is generally leading GDP growth by approximately three month. This implies that the overall policy indicator generally moves in line with GDP growth.

4 Looking at the Policy Mix

Figures 7 and 8 show how the policy mix has changed during the 1980s and 1990s in Germany. It can be seen that whenever fiscal policy is expansionary - as during the early 1990s or the early 1980s - monetary conditions are getting tighter.

In the 1980s the policy-mix was as follows: Fiscal policy became very expansive in 1980; between 1981 and 1985 fiscal policy tightened more and more. Monetary conditions were more restrictive in a direct reaction - in 1981 - to the fiscal expansion. With fiscal consolidation until the year 1985, monetary conditions were eased each year. In the years 1986 and 1987 the policy-mix changed over to tightened monetary conditions (the D-Mark revaluation) while fiscal policy became somewhat more expansionary. In 1988 monetary conditions eased as a reaction to the worldwide expansionary course of monetary policy that followed the October 1987 stock market crash, and also fiscal policy became more expansive. In the next year the policy mix was more restrictive in terms of monetary conditions as well as fiscal policy.

At the beginning of the 1990s fiscal policy was first expansionary due to financing of German unification. It then followed a restrictive course until 1994. In 1995/96 fiscal consolidation was interrupted. Only this year and presumably also next year fiscal consolidation will continue. During the first period of fiscal consolidation until 1993 monetary conditions also became tighter. In 1994 monetary conditions eased. But in 1995 monetary conditions tightened again in particular because of the sharp real appreciation of the exchange rate. Since then monetary conditions eased considerable.

The conclusion is that fiscal policy should consider it's repercussions on monetary conditions. If fiscal policy is overly expansionary it has to pay a high price later and it may be forced to consolidate during recessions. Such policies may have increased cyclical fluctuations in the past.

Social and Structural Change - Consequences for Business Cycle Surveys

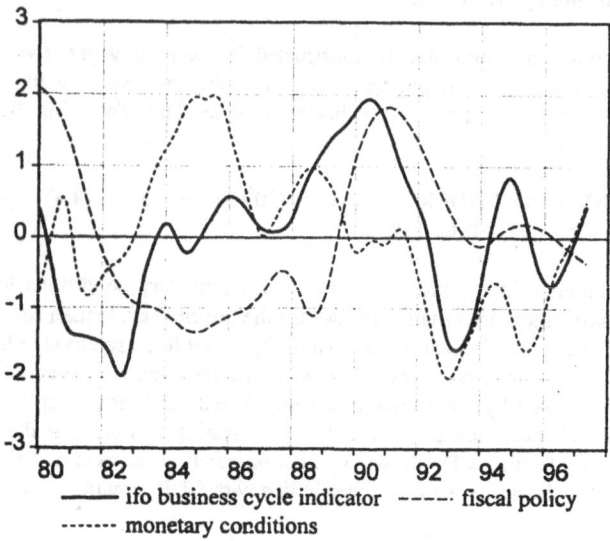

Figure 4 Monetary conditions, fiscal policy and the business cycle (normalised and smoothed time series)

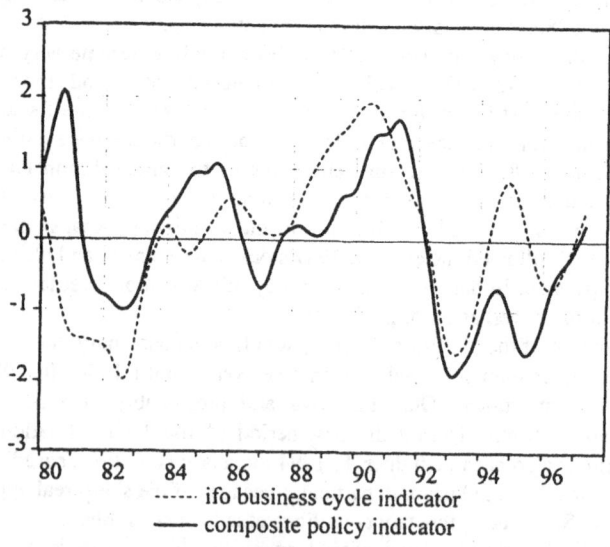

Figure 5 Monetary conditions and fiscal policy as a composite indicator (normalised and smoothed series)

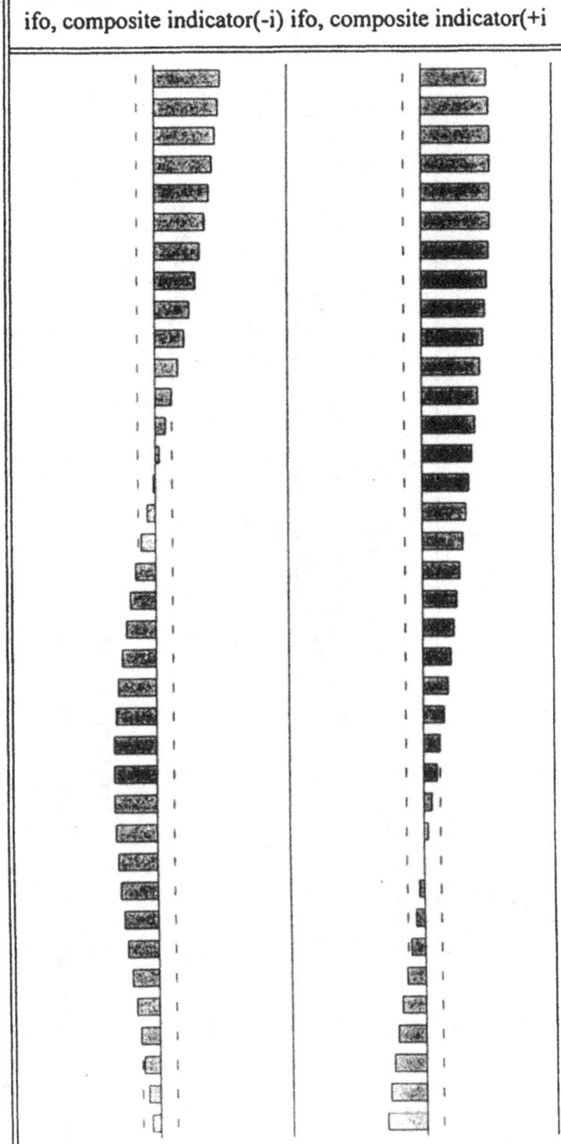

ifo, composite indicator(-i)	ifo, composite indicator(+i)	i	lag	lead
		0	0.5241	0.5241
		1	0.5053	0.5362
		2	0.4830	0.5440
		3	0.4571	0.5475
		4	0.4277	0.5469
		5	0.3951	0.5422
		6	0.3592	0.5336
		7	0.3203	0.5214
		8	0.2785	0.5060
		9	0.2340	0.4876
		10	0.1872	0.4671
		11	0.1385	0.4448
		12	0.0883	0.4215
		13	0.0374	0.3977
		14	-0.0135	0.3738
		15	-0.0635	0.3499
		16	-0.1118	0.3259
		17	-0.1573	0.3016
		18	-0.1993	0.2769
		19	-0.2368	0.2515
		20	-0.2691	0.2251
		21	-0.2954	0.1976
		22	-0.3152	0.1688
		23	-0.3280	0.1386
		24	-0.3337	0.1069
		25	-0.3323	0.0736
		26	-0.3241	0.0390
		27	-0.3098	0.0031
		28	-0.2901	-0.0338
		29	-0.2658	-0.0713
		30	-0.2382	-0.1090
		31	-0.2081	-0.1462
		32	-0.1769	-0.1825
		33	-0.1456	-0.2171
		34	-0.1152	-0.2497
		35	-0.0867	-0.2795
		36	-0.0608	-0.3063

Figure 6   Cross correlogram of the ifo business cycle indicator and the composite indicator

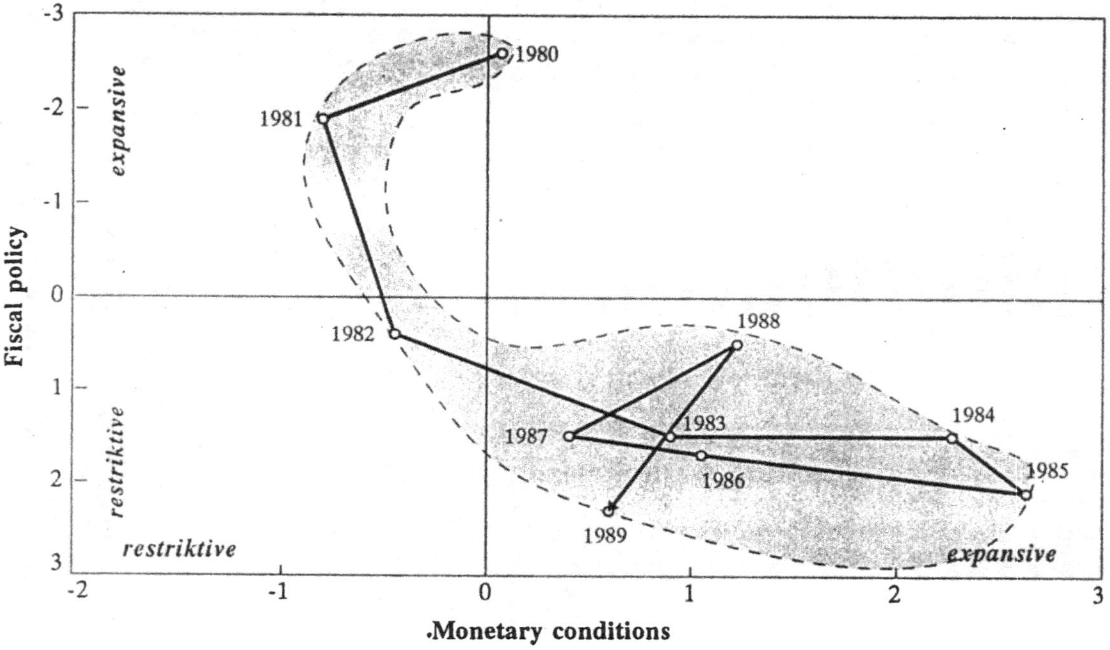

Figure 7 Monetary conditions and fiscal policy in the eighties[1]

1) Fiscal policy measured at the structural primary budget balance; monetary conditions measured at the yield-spread and the real effective exchange rate (normalised).
Source: Deutsche Bundesbank, calculations of the ifo Institute

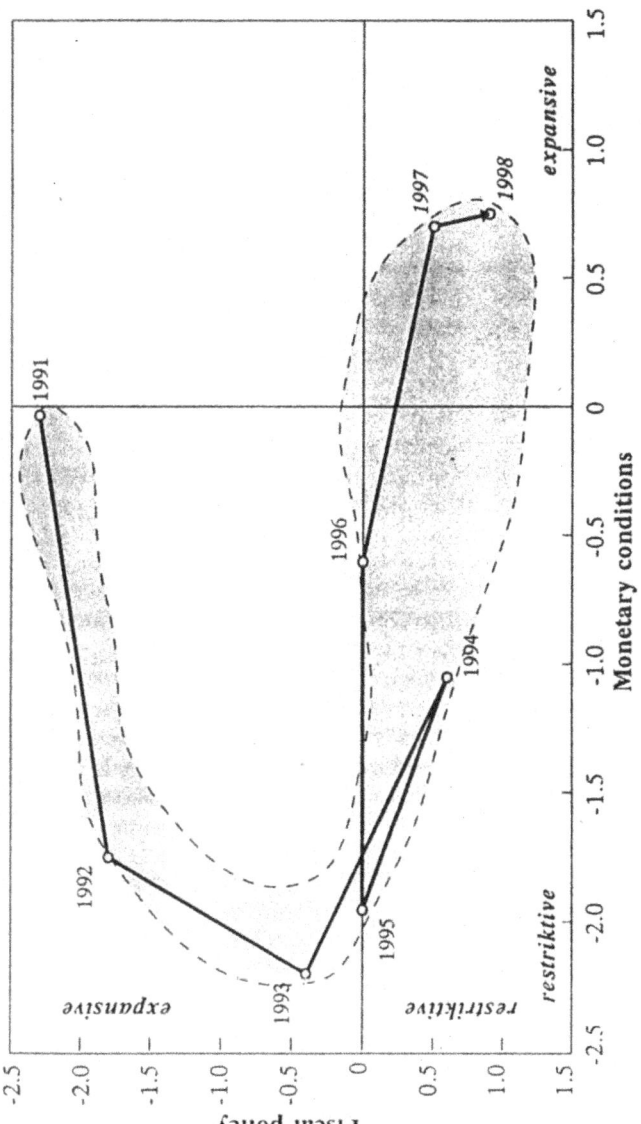

Figure 8 Monetary conditions and fiscal policy in the nineties[1]

1) Fiscal policy measured at the structural primary budget balance; monetary conditions measured at the yield-spread and the real effective exchange rate (normalised).
Source: Deutsche Bundesbank, calculations of the ifo Institute

16 An Index of Leading Indicators on Inflationary Trends and the Business Cycle*

Franz Seitz

1 Introduction

For central banks and other institutions or private professional forecasters it is important to have indicators which can reliably predict price and business cycle trends. For many purposes forecasting their level is probably less important than analysing the basic direction in terms of the trends of inflation and GDP growth and the turning points in their development. Ideally, a leading economic indicator should be able to identify and forecast lasting and substantial changes in the rate of inflation and GDP growth quickly and at an early stage.

To do this, a decision must first be taken on the relevant forecasting horizon. Although inflation is a monetary phenomenon (see the quantity theory and the P*-concept) over the long term, this relationship is supplemented and masked over the short to medium-term by a large number of other factors. It is particularly in phases of higher financial market volatility and economic changes that this period is of interest in monetary policy terms, especially if the adjustments to the long-term equilibrium occur only slowly. The potential influencing factors can be derived from the various inflation theories. Receiving timely notice of the prospective real direction of the economy in terms of growth rates of GDP in the medium-term (one to two years) is also important to a wide variety of decisionmakers (households, firms, policymakers). Here business cycle theories give us hints of the factors that should be included in such a program.

For these reasons, it is usually not possible to concentrate on a single indicator variable.[1] However, in order to facilitate its handling, an *index of leading economic indicators* derived in this way should not contain too many explanatory factors. At the time of the forecast, the partial indicators should ideally be available in order to ensure that the exogenous variables do not have to be forecast, too. In an analysis over a long sample, however, there is the problem that the empirical structures and relationships can change, thus making a *time-dependent* inflation and business cycle explanation necessary. It would be advantageous, therefore, to have an indicator which adjusts adequately to the

---

* I thank K.-H. Toedter from the economics department of the Deutsche Bundesbank for valuable comments.
[1] For a comparison of individual indicators with an index of leading economic indicators for the United States, see Roth (1991). The advantages of such an index for inflation forecasting in the case of Germany and the United States have been emphasised by Juchems et al. (1996) and Garner (1995), respectively.

current circumstances. Accordingly, the index should not consist of a constant set of indicators, but, instead, change in composition over time.

Below, I shall attempt to integrate the points discussed into a single approach. Firstly, the variables considered overall will be explained. In a second step, an inflation and business cycle index, the composition of which can change over time, will be constructed for a given time horizon. This will be followed by a critical evaluation of the index, paying particular attention to the respective partial indicators considered.

2 The Variables Considered

In order to construct an index of leading indicators, it is first of all necessary to determine the *partial indicators* which in principle may influence the relevant development. These variables have to satisfy several criteria. Firstly, there should be a theoretical connection with inflation and GDP growth. Secondly, the data should be available on a monthly basis for inflation in order to obtain a high frequency of inflation forecasts. For GDP I use quarterly data, because GDP is only available on a quarterly basis.[1] And, thirdly, the data should be available as early as possible (see Artis et al. 1995, pp. 1148 f.).

The indicators used can be divided into five groups (see tables 1 and 4): monetary aggregates (M1, M2, M3, central bank money stock), interest rate variables (money market interest rate, capital market interest rate, interest rate spread), price variables (price expectations, producer prices, commodities prices, import prices, external value of the Deutsche Mark, index of share prices), labour market variables (unemployment rate, trends in productivity, unit labour costs, negotiated wage rates) and other real economic variables (inflow of orders in the manufacturing sector and in the consumer goods sector, export expectations, business climate, net output, retail turnover, output gap, disposable income).[2] In general, these variables are then subjected to certain transformations in order to ensure stationarity.[3] Overall, there are 23 and 21 potential leading indicators for price trends and for the growth rate of GDP, respectively. The variables to be explained are the annual change in the consumer price index (even following German unification, this is based on the west German price index) and the annual growth rate of real GDP (with all-German data from the third quarter of 1990 onwards). It is true that the consumer price index shows larger fluctuations than, for example, an index which excludes energy or food and mineral products (see figure 1).[4] This is the index to which the public pays most attention, however, and it probably also plays the most important role in economic decisions and the measurement of purchasing power. In addition, the time series show

---

[1] For an attempt to use monthly data to predict quarterly output in the U.S. see Ingenito and Trehan (1996).
[2] The appropriateness of some of these variables as isolated indicators of the development of inflation has been examined, for example, by Artis et al. (1995), Boughton/Branson (1991), Engsted (1995), Issing (1994), Jorion/Mishkin (1991), Juchems et al. (1995), Papell (1994). For forecasting GDP growth see e.g. Bernard and Gerlach (1996), Goldman Sachs (1993). Composite Leading Indicators are critically discussed, inter alia, in Garner (1995) and Moore et al. (1996).
[3] For the money stocks, for example, two-year growth rates are considered, since the accumulated effects are of importance for inflation. However, as a result of the transformations, the long-term information in the levels is eliminated.
[4] The corresponding standard deviations are 1.80, 1.54 and 1.57. This also shows that the differences are not too big (which is the case, for example, in the USA).

quite similar turning points or inflation cycles. Most of the variables used have been available since the early sixties. Owing to the statistical reorganisation problems in 1995 due to the inclusion of Eastern Germany in some time series and European statistical harmonisation (for that reason, some real variables on a monthly basis are available only up to end of 1994, e.g. retail turnover, unit labour costs) and the possibility of comparing forecast and real inflation trends from 1995 onwards (out-of-sample forecast), only data up to December 1994 are considered for predicting inflation. For GDP growth data until the fourth quarter of 1996 have been used. Here I tried to connect the variables only available until the end of 1994 with the newly constructed ones by the Federal Statistical Office of Germany since 1995.

3 The Construction of the Index

For the indexes to be constructed I propose a strategy for each month or quarter selecting *five* indicator series from a much larger set of candidates. This number is an arbitrary one to a certain extent, but, in my opinion, it represents a fair compromise between transparency and/or manageability, on the one hand, and the utilisation of available information, on the other. With these indexes, the development of inflation and the growth rate of GDP are to be forecast with a lead time of *1 1/2 years*. For periods of less than one year, autoregressive models of various kinds yield quite good results. By contrast, the quantity theory and growth theoretical aspects are based on longer time horizons (see e.g. McCandless and Weber 1995 and Fischer 1993). Thus, it is not the optimum lag length of the various indicators in each case which is being sought (see, for example, Artis et al. 1995), but, rather, the indicator quality over a constant time horizon which is being examined. In this context, the index should contain only variables which are available at the time of the forecast (at least in a provisional form). In order to ensure that its composition can change over time, the following approach is chosen.

For each observation time, a bilateral *correlation coefficient* between the rate of inflation or GDP growth and the indicator series is calculated. These correlation coefficients do not refer to the total observation period, however, but only to the current situation, measured on the basis of the trend over the past four/five years. In order to concentrate on the correlations with the future inflation or GDP growth, each leading indicator is lagged by 18 months or 6 quarters in accordance with the forecasting horizon. Overall, the construction of the index encompasses the following steps:[1]

1. The indicator series are subjected to certain transformations (see tables 1 and 4).[2]

2. The indicator series are lagged by 1½ years.

---

[1] A similar procedure is used by Feldstein and Stock (1996), pp. 7-12 in the case of the indicator properties of different monetary aggregates.
[2] The transformations are undertaken in order to ensure stationarity of the variables. Therefore, the long-run informations in the levels of the time series are neglected. This should be taken into account in the interpretation of the results.

3. Bilateral correlation coefficients between the rate of inflation (growth rate of real GDP) and the lagged indicators are formed over the past 4 (5) years in each case.[1]

4. Standardisation of the indicators (subtraction of the mean and division by the standard deviation, calculated in each case over the past 4 (5) years).

5. The five series with the highest correlation coefficients are included in the indicator.

6. The inflation indicator is brought forward by one month (one quarter) to emphasise the early availability of the data.

In January 1995, for example, the last available inflation figure is calculated from December 1994 to December 1993, and the last observation of the indicator series would be June 1993. A correlation coefficient for January 1995 would therefore relate to rates of inflation between December 1990 and December 1994 and the chosen leading indicator between June 1989 and June 1993. The index always includes the five series with the highest correlation coefficients. However, no simple arithmetic mean has been calculated. Instead, the correlation coefficient concerned determines (as a share in the sum total of the five correlation coefficients), in terms of the strength of the relation, the weight of the individual indicator. An analogous procedure is applied to the growth rate of real GDP.[2]

4 Results

4.1 Inflationary Developments

Figures 2 and 3 juxtapose the rate of inflation and the index of leading indicators.[3] The "smoother" time series shown in figure 3 indicate the relevant 12-month moving averages; these are perhaps better suited for interpreting the trend of inflation. The general price movements are, in principle, indicated quite clearly, although early identification of turning points of inflation is not always possible. This is not surprising, however, since a constant forecasting horizon was assumed for all indicators. From 1995 onwards, the actual price trend can be compared with the price trend predicted by the index, as only data up to the end of 1994 are used.[4] It can be seen from the charts that, initially, the index

---

[1] The longer time horizon taken into account for the real development is due to the a-priori belief that the current situation considered for GDP should be defined in a broader sense than for the inflationary development.

[2] An alternative weighting scheme would be to run a regression with the five indicator series on inflation and GDP, respectively, and to use the coefficients as (optimal) weights.

[3] The following statements remain valid if the inflation rate is calculated from t+12 to t, as it is done, for example, by Webb/Rowe (1995) in their analysis of the turning points of inflation, and if the construction of the index is adjusted accordingly.

[4] If the statistical problems due to European harmonization and the inclusion of the new Laender are eliminated, it is, in fact, possible to forecast a period of 18 months in advance from the end of the series. At the end of 1996 this would imply that the index shows the development of inflation up to mid-1998. With only two full years of the new time series available (1995, 1996) the statistical breaks created are not easy to handle.

of leading indicators and the rate of inflation point downward. From the end of 1995 onward, however, rising rates of inflation are predicted.

In a simple auto-regressive model, taking due account of the assumed time structure, there is a clear improvement in the explanatory value over the entire observation period when the composite indicator is included. The coefficient of determination rises from 0.37 to 0.59. The hypothesis that there is no relationship between the index and the inflation rate can be rejected by means of an F-test at the 1 % level of significance (F=208.7). The AR-model would admittedly, forecast decreasing rates of inflation for 1996. However, the connection between the index and the development of inflation has become looser in the nineties, which is hardly surprising. Whereas, previously, the correlation coefficient in the partial periods considered in table 3 was always higher than 0.5 and even reached 0.72 between 1985 and 1989, it fell in the period between 1990 and 1994 to 0.47. This result is doubtless mainly attributable to developments in the last part of the observation period.

It is also interesting to see which variables have been included in the index over time and thus have a close current connection with the development of inflation. This is shown in tables 2 and 3. It may be seen from these that *M3* has the highest explanatory value over the entire period, whereas retail turnover has the lowest one. M1 and M2, too, come off comparatively favourably. The strengths of M3 becomes apparent mainly from the mid-eighties onwards. In the nineties, capital and money market rates, commodities prices and the index of share prices are represented in the indicator along with M3. The monetary aggregates played a major role in inflation forecasting in all the periods under consideration, whereas it is mainly in the nineties that this has been true of the interest rate variables. The variables which, according to the time-related breakdown in table 3, *never* belong to the five variables with the largest share in the index, are the interest rate spread, sales price expectations, import prices, negotiated wage rates, industrial output and retail turnover. *M3* and the inflow of orders in the manufacturing sector come off best on this share-related analysis. It is also striking that in the seventies as well as between the mid-eighties and the late eighties, no variable has an extreme dominant position, as can be discerned in the other periods under consideration. Especially remarkable in this respect are the index of share prices and the trends in productivity in the sixties,[1] the unemployment rate in the first half of the eighties and the long-term interest rate in the nineties, which in these phases were included in the index in about 90 % of the possible cases. At the end of the sample, the index is composed of M3, the capital market rate and the change in it, the unit labour costs and the inflow of orders in the manufacturing sector. On the basis of the development of the correlation coefficients from month to month, it is in most cases possible to ascertain relatively early whether an indicator series will be included in the index in the near future or will be eliminated from it. It is by no means the case here that the index changes in composition from month to month. Rather, in general, the indicators are included in the index over a longer period of time.

The changes in economic structures since the sixties are clearly reflected in the index. What is chiefly apparent is a tendency towards an increasing importance of *financial*

---

[1] The sixties are not a representative period since, owing to the transformations made, only a few observations are available in many cases.

variables (monetary aggregates, interest rates) for forecasting price trends.[1] Furthermore, it is striking that price trends at the preliminary stages (producer and import prices) tend to play only a subordinate role.

4.2 Growth Rate of Real GDP

In a second step the same procedure is applied to the growth rate of real GDP with quarterly indicators. With quarterly observations the sample ended in the fourth quarter of 1996 and it is possible to forecast until mid 1998. Table 4 shows the potential candidate series considered. The index and GDP growth are compared in figure 4. All in all, the results are not very promising which demonstrates that this kind of analysis is perhaps not very well suited for GDP. But the poor overall performance may also be due to the considered time horizon, the variables taken into account or an incorrect specification of the current circumstances.

Until the mid 1980s the growth trend in GDP is not well captured by the composite indicator. In many cases even the wrong direction is indicated by the index. But in the last ten years the general development is better predicted. In this period there is no variable which extremely dominates the index: The highest share is 71 % for the change in money market interest rates in the nineties. Interest rates and the output gap are relevant indicator variables in nearly every subperiod (see table 6). But from 1985 onwards "external" variables like commodities prices, the external value of the DM and export expectations more and more dominate the index. This may be due to increased foreign competition and globalisation. In the nineties, short-term interest rates, commodities prices and wage rates played the major role in explaining GDP growth. In contrast, M3 in no case enters the index in that period. M1, M2, sales price expectations, the unemployment rate, productivity, unit labor costs, the business climate and disposable income are the variables which in no subperiod belong to the five time series with the largest share in the index.

For 1997/98 the index would forecast declining growth rates of GDP. In 1996, the relevant base period, the main determinants of the index are the inflow of orders in the manufacturing sector, producer prices, long-term interest rates and the change in short-term interest rates. These are responsible for the pessimistic forecast. Especially the declining producer prices in 1996 enter with a high weight.

5 Summary and Conclusions

The indexes proposed in this paper have the advantage that they respond to changed economic conditions by altering their composition. In terms of a regression analysis, this would satisfy the requirement of time-variable coefficients. One problem, however, is that only bilateral relationships are analysed. Consequently, interactions with other variables

---

[1] An investigation of the role of financial variables in forecasting GDP growth and inflation for various countries and the period 1980-1995 is presented in Andersen (1997). He concludes that forecasts could be improved by using information from changes in the yield curve and of movements in exchange rates and other asset prices.

cannot be taken into consideration. It is quite possible that a variable, if considered in isolation, does not show any lead time in relation to inflation, whereas this would be the case if other variables were taken into account. Thus, the significant role played by the interest rate variables in the nineties might decrease in certain circumstances, if the monetary trend, too, were considered in the forecasting equation. Moreover, with the method chosen, it is not possible to indicate any significance level of the influences. However, it is rather difficult to integrate all the variables used here into one regression analytical approach.[1]

The indexes have a theoretical foundation since nearly all the variables used have been derived from inflation and business cycle theories. They are not suitable for a point forecast of inflation or growth, but yield valuable information for analysing the turning points and general trends. As the presented analysis has shown, the used methodology is more appropriate for explaining inflationary trends than for the growth rates of real GDP. The specific role played by some variables (the index of share prices or sales price expectations, for example,) should be evaluated carefully and not be overinterpreted, however. The fixed time-related forecasting horizon of 18 months, on the other hand, could be easily changed to cover other periods.

One further extension of the paper could be to treat rising and falling inflation rates or recessions and booms in an asymmetrical way (see Kim and Yoo 1995). In the present context that could be done, for example, by considering different (optimal) lead times or different indicators for recessionary and expansionary periods.

---

[1] One possibility is dealt with by Stock/Watson (1989), p. 366. VAR models for inflation forecasting, by contrast, perform rather poorly, at least in the case of the United States (see, for example, Webb 1995). One method which might be useful in this context is the analysis of principal components (Quinn and Mawdsley 1996, Cabrero and Delrieu 1996). This approach considers a linear combination of variables which explain as large a part as possible of the variance of the variables. These variables could then be aggregated by means of weighted least squares.

Table 1   Leading indicators considered for inflation

Variable	Start	Transformation
1. Monetary aggregates[1]		
- M1	1960,1	2-year growth rate
- M2	1960,1	2-year growth rate
- M3	1960,1	2-year growth rate
- Central bank money stock (cbm)	1960,1	2-year growth rate
2. Interest rates		
- 3-months money market rate (is)	1960,1	
- ditto, change against previous year (dis)[2]	1961,1	
- Yield on bonds outstanding (il)	1960,1	
- ditto, change against previous year[2] (dil)	1961,1	
- Interest rate spread[3] (spd)	1960,1	
3. Price variables		
- Sales price expectations[4] (pe)	1970,1	12-months moving average
- Producer prices[5] (pp)	1960,1	Annual growth rate
- Import prices (pim)	1960,1	Annual growth rate
- Commodities prices (comp)	1968,1	Annual growth rate
- Weighted external value of the DM (e)[6]	1960,1	12-months moving average of annual growth rate
- Index of share prices[7] (shp)	1960,1	ditto
4. Labour market[8]		
- Unemployment rate[9] (u)	1960,1	Ratio of the current month to moving 5-year average
- Productivity[10] (pro)	1962,1	12-months moving average of annual growth rate
- Unit labour costs[11] (ulc)	1960,1	ditto
- Negotiated wage rates overall economy	1960,1	Annual growth rate
5. Other real economic variables[8]		
- Inflow of orders in the consumer goods industry (ord1)	1960,1	12-months moving average of absolute annual change
- Inflow of orders in the manufacturing sector (ord2)	1960,1	ditto
- Net production in manufacturing (y)	1960,1	Ratio of the current month to 5-year moving average
- Retail turnover (rtu)	1960,1	ditto

1) From June 1990, figures for the all-Germany; 2) Both the level and the change have been examined since it is not clear which variable is stationary. 3) Yield on bonds outstanding minus 3-month rate.
4) Ifo Institute economic test for the manufacturing sector. 5) Industrial products; from July 1990, west German figures have been used, as before. 6) Vis-à-vis 18 industrial nations.
7) Of the Federal Statistical Office. 8) From July 1990, the figures refer to western Germany, as before.
9) In terms of dependent labour force.
10) Production per employment hour ("Beschaeftigtenstunde") (mining and manufacturing sectors).
11) Gross wages and salaries per product unit (mining and manufacturing sectors).

Table 2 Indicators contained in the overall inflation index[1]

Variable	Number of available months	Number of months considered	Percent
M1	372	113	30
M2	372	124	33
M3	372	154	41
cbm	372	82	22
is	396	90	23
dis	384	50	13
il	396	141	36
dil	384	100	26
spd	396	57	14
pe	270	54	20
pp	390	53	14
pim	390	43	11
comp	294	64	22
e	378	87	23
shp	378	109	29
u	342	95	28
pro	354	98	28
ulc	378	119	31
w	390	93	24
ord1	378	75	20
ord2	378	133	35
y	342	4	1
rtu	342	0	0

1) The five indicators most frequently represented in the index, in terms of their share, have been printed in bold type.

Table 3 Indicators contained in the inflation index, in terms of sub periods, in percent[1]

Variable	Sixties	Seventies	1980-84	1985-89	1990-94
M1	37	44	0	**55**	0
M2	19	**35**	**42**	40	32
M3	**54**	27	0	**65**	**72**
cbm	0	27	17	**63**	3
is	14	27	18	18	**38**
dis	23	7	**37**	2	0
il	36	25	3	37	**88**
dil	1	19	32	25	**65**
spd	15	13	18	12	15
pe	(-)	30	12	0	18
pp	4	**33**	0	0	15
pim	4	7	32	5	13
comp	(-)	18	28	7	**35**
e	24	15	32	**43**	8
shp	**92**	10	0	10	**35**
u	0	20	**93**	25	0
pro	**89**	27	27	0	3
ulc	**78**	19	15	23	20
w	20	**41**	**33**	10	0
ord1	4	29	**47**	0	15
ord2	**63**	**42**	15	**60**	23
y	0	3	0	0	0
rtu	0	0	0	0	0

1) The five variables of the respective period most frequently contained in the index, in terms of their share, have been printed in bold type; "x" means that the variable is included in the index in x % of the possible cases.

Table 4   Leading indicators considered for GDP

Variable	Start	Transformation
1. Monetary aggregates[1]		
- M1	1960,1	2-year growth rate
- M2	1960,1	2-year growth rate
- M3	1960,1	2-year growth rate
2. Interest rates		
- 3-months money market rate (is)	1960,1	
- ditto, change against previous year (dis)[2]	1961,1	
- Yield on bonds outstanding (il)	1960,1	
- ditto, change against previous year[2] (dil)	1961,1	
- Interest rate spread[3] (spd)	1960,1	
3. Price variables		
- Sales price expectations[4] (pe)	1970,1	4-quarter moving average
- Producer prices[5] (pp)	1960,1	Annual growth rate
- Commodities prices (comp)	1968,1	Annual growth rate
- Weighted external value of the DM (e)[6]	1960,1	Annual growth rate
4. Labour market[8]		
- Unemployment rate[9] (u)	1960,1	Ratio of the current quarter to moving 5-year average
- Productivity[10] (pro)	1962,1	4-quarter moving average of annual growth rate
- Unit labour costs[11] (ulc)	1960,1	ditto
- Negotiated wage rates overall economy (w)	1960,1	Annual growth rate
5. Other real economic variables		
- Output gap (gap)	1962,1	ratio of real GDP to production potential
- Inflow of orders in the manufacturing sector (ord2)	1960,1	4-quarter moving average of absolute annual change
- Business climate (bc)[12]	1969,1	
- Export expectations (exe)[12]	1970,1	4-quarter moving average
- Disposable income (yd)	1960,1	4-quarter moving average annual growth rate

1) In real terms. From June 1990, figures for all-Germany
2) Both the level and the change have been examined since it is not clear which variable is stationary.
3) Yield on bonds outstanding minus 3-month rate.
4) Ifo Institute business survey for the manufacturing sector.
5) Industrial products; from July 1990, west German figures have been used, as before.
6) Vis-à-vis 18 industrial nations.
7) Of the Federal Statistical Office.
8) From July 1990, the figures refer to western Germany, as before.
9) In terms of dependent labour force.
10) Production per employment hour ("Beschaeftigtenstunde") (mining and manufacturing sectors).
11) Gross wages and salaries per product unit (mining and manufacturing sectors).
12) Reported by the Ifo Institute for Economic Research.

Table 5 Indicators contained in the overall GDP index[1]

Variable	Number of available quarters	Number of quarters considered	Percent
M1	130	14	11
M2	130	30	23
M3	130	21	16
is	138	38	28
dis	134	89	66
il	138	28	20
dil	134	75	56
spd	138	57	22
pe	106	8	8
pp	138	58	42
comp	110	35	32
e	134	20	15
u	128	9	7
pro	130	14	11
ulc	138	25	18
w	134	53	40
gap	134	74	55
ord2	134	23	17
bc	110	5	5
exe	106	12	11
yd	134	24	18

1) The five indicators most frequently represented in the index, in terms of their share, have been printed in bold type.

Table 6 Indicators contained in the GDP index, in terms of sub periods, in percent[1]

Variable	Sixties	Seventies	1980-84	1985-89	1990-96
M1	9	7	0	30	11
M2	23	35	0	30	18
M3	0	35	0	35	0
is	24	42	**50**	0	11
dis	**65**	**67**	**80**	**45**	**71**
il	33	17	30	0	18
dil	**81**	**50**	**100**	**55**	11
spd	13	37	5	30	14
pe	(-)	5	0	0	21
pp	**90**	32	35	10	32
comp	(-)	10	**50**	30	**54**
e	4	2	5	35	36
u	6	0	20	10	7
pro	0	22	0	15	7
ulc	23	17	0	20	25
w	**54**	20	20	**60**	**54**
gap	31	**77**	**55**	**60**	**43**
ord2	**46**	12	0	0	21
bc	(-)	0	15	5	4
exe	(-)	0	0	10	36
yd	35	17	15	20	4

1) The five variables of the respective period most frequently contained in the index, in terms of their share, have been printed in bold type; "x" means that the variable is included in the index in x % of the possible cases.

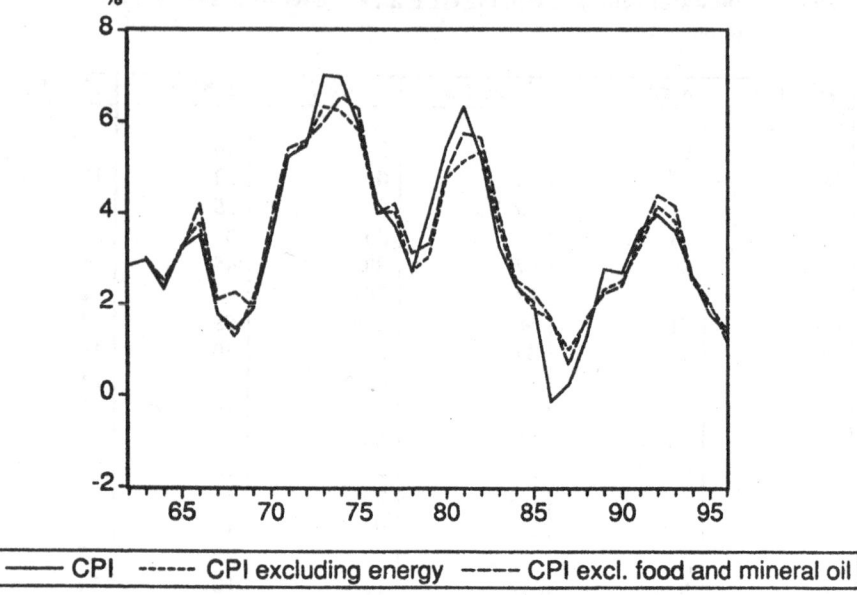

Figure 1 Consumer price index (CPI) in various definitions

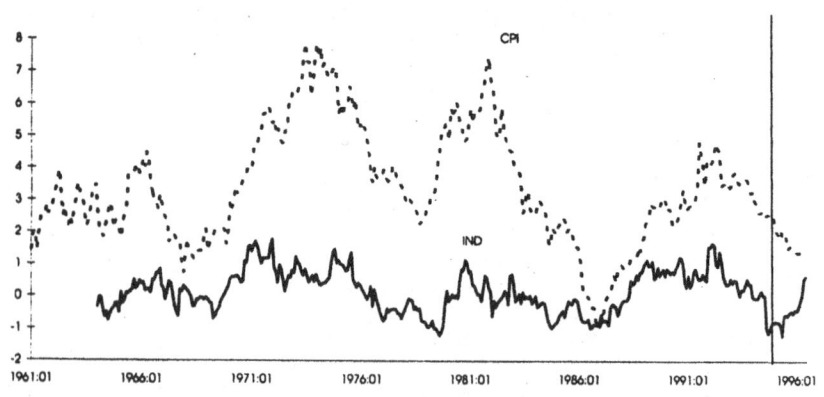

Figure 2 Consumer price index (CPI) and index of leading indicators (IND)[1]
1) The inflation rate is calculated from t to t-12.

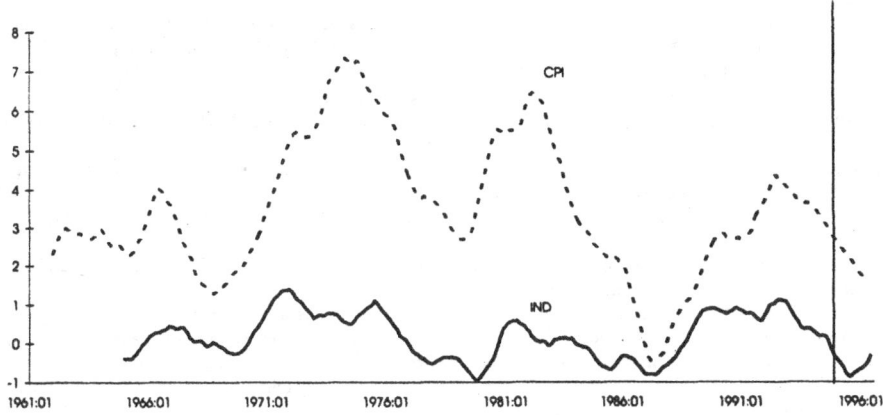

Figure 3   Consumer price index (CPI) and index of leading indicators (IND)[1]
1) 12-month moving average in each case.

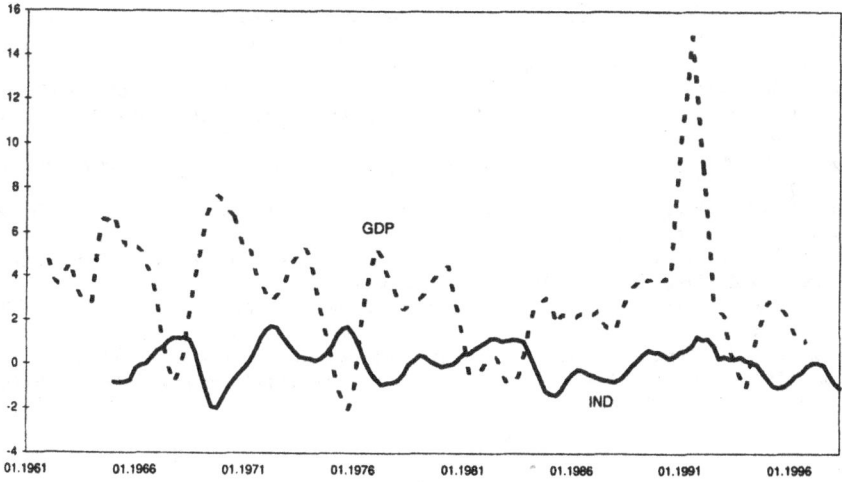

Figure 4   GDP growth (GDP) and index of leading indicators (IND)[1]
1) 4-quarter moving average in each case.

References

Artis, M.J., Bladen-Hovel, R.C., Osborn, D.R., Smith, G. and Zhang, W. (1995), Predicting Turning Points in the UK Inflation Cycle, *The Economic Journal*, Vol. 105, pp. 1145 ff.

Bernard, H. and Gerlach, S. (1996), *Does the Term Structure Predict Recessions?* The International Evidence, BIS Working Paper No. 37, Basle

Boughton, J.M. and Branson, W.H. (1991), Commodity Prices as a Leading Indicator of Inflation, in: Lahiri, K., Moore, G.H. (eds), *Leading Economic Indicators*, Cambridge University Press, pp. 275 ff.

Cabrero, A. and Delrieu, J.C. (1996), *Construction of a Composite Indicator for Predicting Inflation in Spain*, Working Paper No. 9619, Banco de Espana - Servicio de Estudios

Engsted, T. (1995), Does the Long-Term Interest Rate Predict Future Inflation? A Multi-Country Analysis, *Review of Economics and Statistics*, Vol. 77, pp. 42 ff.

Feldstein, M. and Stock, J.H. (1996), Measuring Money Growth when Financial Markets are Changing, *Journal of Monetary Economics*, Vol. 37, pp. 3 ff.

Fischer, S. (1993), The Role of Macroeconomic Factors in Growth, *Journal of Monetary Economics*, Vol. 32, pp. 485 ff.

Garner, C.A. (1995), How Useful are Leading Indicators of Inflation?, *Federal Reserve Bank of Kansas City Economic Review*, second quarter, pp. 5 ff.

Goldman Sachs (1993), *A Liquidity Driven West German Recovery*, Research Note, 8th November

Issing, O. (1994), Zinsstruktur oder Geldmenge? (Yield curve or money stock?) in: Sautter, H. (ed.), *Wirtschaftspolitik in offenen Volkswirtschaften*, Festschrift für Helmut Hesse zum 60. Geburtstag (Economic policy in open economies, Commemorative volume for Helmut Hesse on his 60th birthday), Goettingen, pp. 3 ff.

Ingenito, R. and Trehan, B. (1996), Using Monthly Data to Predict Quarterly Output, *Federal Reserve Bank of San Francisco Economic Review*, No. 3, pp. 3 ff.

Jorion, P. and Mishkin, F. (1991), A Multicountry Comparison of Term-Structure Forecasts at Long Horizons, *Journal of Financial Economics*, Vol. 29, pp. 59 ff.

Juchems, A., Nakajima, S. and Nerb, G. (1996), Indicators for Monetary Policy, in Oppenlaender, K.-H., Poser, G (eds), *Business Cycle Surveys: Forecasting Issues and Methodological Aspects*, Avebury: Aldershot, pp. 395 ff.

Kim, M.-J. and Yoo, J.-S. (1995), New Index of Coincident Indicators: A Multivariate Markov Switching Factor Model Approach, *Journal of Monetary Economics*, Vol. 36, pp. 607 ff.

McCandless Jr., G.T. and Weber, W.E. (1995), Some Monetary Facts, *Federal Reserve Bank of Minneapolis Quarterly Review*, Summer 1995, S. 2-11

Moore, G.M., Cullity, J.P. and Boehm, E.A. (1996), Forecasting Real Gross Domestic Product with Long Leading Indexes: Six Countries, in Helmstaedter, E., Poser, G., Ramser, H.-J. (eds), *Beitraege zur angewandten Wirtschaftsforschung*, Duncker & Humblot: Berlin, pp. 393 ff.

Papell, D.H. (1994), Exchange Rates and Prices: An Empirical Analysis, *International Economic Review*, Vo. 35, pp. 397 ff.

Quinn, T. and Mawdsley, A. (1996), *Forecasting Irish Inflation: A Composite Leading Indicator*, Central Bank of Ireland, Economic Analysis, Research and Publications

Roth, H.L. (1991), Leading Indicators of Inflation, in: Lahiri, K., Moore, G.H. (eds), *Leading Economic Indicators*, Cambridge University Press: Cambridge, pp. 275 ff.

Stock, J.H. and Watson, M.W. (1989), New Indexes of Coincident and Leading Economic Indicators, in: Blanchard, O.J., Fischer, S. (eds), *NBER Macroeconomics Annual*, pp. 351 ff.

Webb, R.H. (1995), Forecasts of Inflation from VAR Models, *Journal of Forecasting*, Vol. 14, pp. 267 ff.

Webb, R.H. and Rowe, T.S. (1995), An Index of Leading Indicators of Inflation, *Federal Reserve Bank of Richmond Economic Quarterly*, Vol. 81/2, pp. 75 ff.

17 Term Structure or Money Growth as Leading Indicator of Inflation: An Empirical Analysis for Germany[*]

Jürgen Wolters

Abstract

The Bundesbank uses a monetary aggregate as an intermediate target in order to control the inflation rate. However, recent empirical studies cast doubt on the stability of this relation, but also suggest that interest rate spreads have strong predictive power for future movements of inflation rates. In this paper the predictive power of several money growth rates and interest rate spreads for the development of inflation rates is analysed. In contrast to other investigations we use frequency domain methods allowing to reveal the relations between the different components of the time series more detailed. All in all there is no strong empirical evidence in favour of the use of leading indicators for predicting inflation.

1 Introduction

In establishing institutional rules for the future European central bank there is a controversy about the financial indicators one should use in the formulation and conduct of monetary policy. Whereas the German Bundesbank prefers monetary aggregates as an intermediate target the Bank of England argues that greater emphasis should be placed on interest rate spreads.[1] There is, however, a general agreement that the ultimate goal of monetary policy should be the control of inflation.

In this paper the predictive power of various money growth rates as well as interest rate spreads for the development of inflation rates in Germany is analysed. Using quarterly data and out-of-sample predictions Kirchgässner and Savioz (1995) found that annual money growth rates are better predictors for inflation than interest rate spreads. On the other hand, Langfeld (1994) shows that the term structure has predictive power for future inflation in Germany. This is in line with the results of Davis and Henry (1994) for Germany with quarterly data from 1974 to 1992.

---

[*] I am grateful to Uwe Hassler and Dieter Nautz, Freie Universität Berlin, for helpful comments. Research of this paper is related to Sonderforschungsbereich 373, Teilprojekt C3, Humboldt-Universität zu Berlin. Financial support by the Deutsche Forschungsgemeinschaft is gratefully acknowledged.

[1] For a broad discussion of the different view points see e.g. Deutsche Bundesbank (1996).

In general papers concerning the quality of different leading indicators have used time domain methods, as regressions, distributed lag approaches, Granger causality tests, out-of-sample predictions, Markov-switching models, vector-autoregressive models, or error correction models if cointegration relations are taken into account.[1] Results of parametric time domain approaches strongly depend on the transformations chosen to create stationary variables, or to eliminate seasonal fluctuations. In contrast, in this paper frequency domain methods are employed.[2] Nonparametric frequency domain approach offers the opportunity to analyse the interdependence of alternative indicators and the inflation rate for different cyclical components, such as short-run, seasonal, business-cycle, and long-run components.[3] This provides a much more detailed analysis of the relations. Moreover, it is not necessary to eliminate e.g. seasonal cycles.

The paper is organized in the following way: In the next section the frequency domain approach is characterized. After that the data and the empirical results are presented. The paper ends with concluding remarks.

2 Frequency Domain Approach

In a bivariate time domain analysis one very often uses the R^2, the coefficient of determination, to judge the importance of different leading indicators. However, as is well known, R^2 is not invariant under linear transformations. On the other hand, coherence which is a measure of determination for each frequency component is invariant under linear transformations. Thus we theoretically obtain the same measures if we use e.g. levels or differences, or if we use annual or monthly differences.

The drawback of the frequency domain approach - like for all nonparametric methods - is that the estimates are not so precise due to the fact that in general one has relatively small degrees of freedom.

The most general linear dynamic relation may be written as (for the following see e.g. Wolters, 1980)

$$y_t = \sum_{j=-\infty}^{\infty} a_j x_{t-j} + u_t, \tag{1}$$

where u_t is a stationary process with zero mean and constant variance independent of x_t. y_t and x_t are stationary stochastic processes having - without loss of generality - zero means. Allowing for leads in x_t means that we allow in (1) for Granger causal relations from y_t to x_t and not only from x_t to y_t.[4] Stationarity of y_t implies that $\sum_{j=-\infty}^{\infty} a_j^2$ is finite.

---

[1] See e.g. Friedman and Kuttner (1992), Davis and Henry (1994), Davis and Fagan (1995), Lahiri (1995), Hagen und Kirchgässner (1996), Estrella and Mishkin (1995), Moersch (1996).
[2] The same approach as in this paper is used in Wolters (1997).
[3] For an introduction to the theory and application of spectral analysis see e.g. König and Wolters (1972).
[4] Such an equation is used by Sims (1972) for testing for causality.

Of course the parameters in equation (1) cannot be estimated in the time domain without introducing additional restrictions.

The transformation in the frequency domain yields

$$f_{xy}(\lambda) = A(\lambda)f_{xx}(\lambda) \qquad (2)$$

$$f_{yy}(\lambda) = |A(\lambda)|^2 f_{xx}(\lambda) + f_{uu}(\lambda) \qquad (3)$$

with

$$A(\lambda) = \sum_{j=-\infty}^{\infty} a_j e^{-i\lambda j}, \ (i^2 = -1).$$

Here $f_{xx}(\lambda)$, $f_{yy}(\lambda)$ and $f_{uu}(\lambda)$ denote the power spectra of x_t, y_t and u_t, respectively. The spectrum describes the cyclical properties of a time series. It gives the relative contribution of distinct cycles to the variance of the process. If a cycle is very important for the variation of a process, the power spectrum will exhibit a peak at the corresponding frequency. The higher and narrower such a peak is, the more important and the more regular is the cycle. For example, if the process is white noise then no particular component dominates and the power spectrum is constant over the frequency range. $f_{xy}(\lambda)$ is the cross spectrum between x_t and y_t at the frequency λ. $A(\lambda)$ may be interpreted as a regression coefficient for each frequency. In analogy to the coefficient of determination in a classical regression one can define a coefficient of determination in the frequency domain for each frequency

$$B(\lambda) = \frac{f_{yy}(\lambda) - f_{uu}(\lambda)}{f_{yy}(\lambda)}, \text{ with } 0 \leq B(\lambda) \leq 1. \qquad (4)$$

Using (2) and (3) leads to

$$B(\lambda) = \frac{|f_{xy}(\lambda)|^2}{f_{xx}(\lambda)f_{yy}(\lambda)} \qquad (5)$$

which is exactly the squared coherence between x_t and y_t.

For each frequency λ, the coherence can be interpreted as a coefficient of determination for the linear relation between corresponding components of x_t and y_t. The crucial advantage of coherence is its invariance to different linear transformations of the two time series x_t and y_t.

One can immediately derive from (1) the lead-lag as well as the causality relations between y_t and x_t. If only coefficients belonging to lagged values of x_t are significant, then x_t leads y_t, i.e. x_t is Granger causal to y_t. Analogously, if only coefficients of future values of x_t are significant, then y_t leads x_t, i.e. y_t is Granger causal to x_t. In case of significant coefficients on leads and lags of x_t a feedback relation between y_t and x_t exists.

Assume that $f_{xy}(\lambda)$ and $f_{xx}(\lambda)$ is given, then one can evaluate the distributed lag coefficients a_j, $j=\ldots-1,0,1,2,\ldots$. Substituting (2) into the definition of the transfer function $A(\lambda)$ yields

$$\sum_{j=-\infty}^{\infty} a_j e^{-i\lambda j} = f_{xy}(\lambda)/f_{xx}(\lambda) .\tag{6}$$

Solving for a_j (see e.g. Wolters, 1973) leads to

$$a_j = \frac{1}{2\pi} \int_{-\pi}^{\pi} \left(f_{xy}(\lambda)/f_{xx}(\lambda)\right) e^{i\lambda j} d\lambda , \; j=\ldots-1,0,1,2,\ldots .\tag{7}$$

With estimated power and cross spectra one gets estimates of the distributed lag coefficients a_j. The spectra may be estimated according to

$$\hat{f}_{xy}(\lambda_j) = \frac{1}{2\pi} \sum_{\tau=-m}^{m} w_m(\tau)\hat{R}_{xy}(\tau)e^{-i\lambda_j \tau} \tag{8}$$

with

$$\lambda_j = \frac{\pi j}{M}, \; j=0,1,2,\ldots,M$$

$$\hat{R}_{xy}(\tau) = \frac{1}{n}\sum_{t=1}^{n-|\tau|}(x_t - \bar{x})(y_{t+\tau} - \bar{y}), \; |\tau|<n ,$$

where $\bar{x}$ and $\bar{y}$ are the empirical means.

For estimating the power spectra y is substituted by x in (8). The number of observations is denoted by n and the truncation point - the number of used covariances - by m . $w_m(.)$ denotes a lag window, which is necessary to get consistent estimates. In order to obtain stable estimates, the ratio m/n should be very low. To get nearly unbiased estimates, however, one must choose a large value for m. In the following a Parzen window is applied. The degrees of freedom are evaluated as (3.71 n)/m for this window.

3 The Data and Empirical Results

The investigation covers the period of monetary targeting by the German Bundesbank thus starting in 1975 and ending due to data availability in 1996. Monthly seasonally unadjusted observations are used. All data are taken from *Monthly Report of the Deutsche Bundesbank*. Growth rates are computed as logarithmic first differences and monthly interest rates in percent as $\left(\sqrt[12]{1+RJ/100}-1\right)\cdot 100$, with RJ the annual interest rate in percent.

The inflation rate is defined as the monthly growth rate of the consumer price index (WP). Monthly growth rates of M1 (WM1), M2 (WM2), and M3 (WM3) are included in the analysis. Six different measures of the term structure are applied. Two definitions of the spread measure the relation between the bond and the money market, RU-R3M and RU-RT, where RU denotes the average yield on bonds in the secondary market, R3M the three-month-money market rate, and RT the day-to-day rate. The remaining four definitions measure different slopes of the bond yield curve. R10-R1 measures the slope of the whole yield curve, R3-R1, the slope of the short end, R8-R3, the slope of the middle range of maturities, and R10-R8 the slope of the long end. Here Rj, j = 1,3,8,10, denotes yields on bonds with j years to maturity.[1]

Investigating whether the term structure helps to predict the future path of inflation most of empirical work is based on the approach introduced by Mishkin (1990).[2] He estimates equations of the following type

$$\pi_t^r - \pi_t^s = \alpha_{r,s} + \beta_{r,s}(i_t^r - i_t^s) + \eta_t^{r,s}, \qquad (9)$$

where $\pi_t^k = \frac{1}{k}(\ln p_{t+k} - \ln p_t)$ is the inflation rate from time t to time $t+k$, i_t^k, $k = 1,2,...$ is the k period nominal interest rate at time t.

Since

$$\pi_t^r - \pi_t^s = \frac{1}{r}\sum_{i=1}^{r} \pi_{t+i}^1 - \frac{1}{n}\sum_{i=1}^{s} \pi_{t+i}^1 \qquad (10)$$

is a weighted sum of lagged one period inflation rates, the dependent variable in equation (9) is a linear transformation of the one period inflation rate. As the coherence in contrast to the R^2 is invariant against linear transformations, the coherence between the monthly inflation rate and the different spreads is a reliable measure of the linear relation between inflation and spreads. Therefore the information content of inflation rates with different time horizons is already reflected in the monthly rate.

First, spectral densities of the different indicators are presented together with the spectral density of the monthly inflation rate. In the following the estimation is performed with a truncation point of m = 60. With n = 264 observations this leads to about 16 degrees of freedom. Variations of the truncation point do not produce different results. For reasons of better comparisons the spectral densities, i.e. the power spectra normalised by the estimated variance of the time series, are drawn in the figures. Figures 1 and 2 show that different interest rate spreads possess in general the same spectral shape. These time series are totally dominated by long-run fluctuations with periods longer than three years, whereas seasonal and short-run cycles do nearly not exist. Note that the sharp peaks

---

[1] RU-R3M, RU-RT, as well as R10-R1 are published by the Bundesbank as different versions of the so-called "Zinsgefälle".

[2] See e.g. Koedijk and Kool (1995) for the United States, Japan, Germany, Switzerland, France, Belgium and the Netherlands (1982 - 1991) or Schich (1996) for Germany. For a very similar approach with UK government bonds see Robertson (1992).

at zero frequency indicate a high positive first order autocorrelation, but do not necessarily imply the non-stationarity of the spreads. In fact, estimating the spectra of the differenced spreads leads to significant dips at zero frequency indicating a clear overdifferentiation.

In contrast to the spreads, the money growth rates behave quite differently. According to their spectral densities in Figure 3 their variations are dominated by seasonal cycles. The most important being the six-months' cycle. The very long-run cycles do not contribute much to the variation of money growth rates. For the inflation rate long-run cycles as well as seasonal cycles are of particular importance.

The strength of the relations between the different indicators and the inflation rate is measured by the different coherences in Figures 4, 5, 6. The horizontal lines show asymptotic 5 (10) percent critical values for the hypothesis that the coherence is zero. These values are taken from Koopmans (1974, Table A9.6). Figure 4 shows that interest rate spreads between the bond and the money market do not show significant relations with the development of the inflation rate. The term structure for the whole bond market R10-R1 is only weakly connected with the inflation rate for very short-run components.

According to the results in Figure 5 the short end of the yield curve exhibits significant influences on the inflation rate for cycles with periods a little bit longer than 6 months. For the middle range of the term structure only the 6-months' component is significant, whereas the long end of the term structure does not contribute to the development of the monthly inflation rate.

The results for the three monthly money growth rates are given in Figure 6. There are significant relations between WM1 and WP at seasonal cycles. Especially for the business cycle range, for annual cycles, and for cycles with a duration of 6 months WM2 and WP are significantly related. The strongest relation between one of the indicators used and the inflation rate is given by the growth rates of M3. We find significant relations not only for short-run and seasonal cycles, but also for cycles with periods of four and more years.

Since the coherences only measure the strength of the relation irrespective of the causality directions one also has to investigate whether indicators with significant relations to the monthly inflation rate do really lead the inflation rate. Estimating the coefficients in the two-sided distributed lag model (1) according to (7) gives this additional information. In estimating (1) in the time domain a maximal number of leads and lags has to be chosen a priori. However, one cannot rule out that the results are sensitive to the maximal values chosen. According to (7) the estimation of a_j in the frequency domain does not depend on the chosen maximal lags or leads. Therefore, in the following the parameters in (1) are estimated in the frequency domain provided the coherence between inflation rate and indicator is significant. All coefficients up to a maximum of 24 leads and lags are computed. But only significant coefficients are presented.

With regard to the six different spreads significant (5 percent) coefficients in (1) are found for R10-R1 only (t-values in parentheses):

$$WP_t = \underset{(2.2)}{0.18}(R10-R1)_{t-2} + \underset{(2.4)}{0.19}(R10-R1)_{t-17} + \hat{u}_t \ . \tag{11}$$

This result shows that the slope of the bond yield curve is a leading indicator for inflation, with a normal yield curve indicating higher and an inverse yield curve indicating lower inflation. But remember that the coherence between R10-R1 and WP exhibits weak significant relations for very short-run cycles only.

With respect to the three money growth rates no significant coefficients in (1) are found for WM1. WM2 shows the following simple lead structure

$$WP_t = \underset{(2.4)}{0.18} WM2_{t-9} + \hat{u}_t \; . \tag{12}$$

Positive (negative) growth rates of M2 today indicate higher (lower) inflation in 9 months.

The relation between inflation and the growth rate of M3 looks much more complicated:

$$\begin{aligned} WP_t = &\underset{(2.2)}{0.16} WM3_t + \underset{(4.9)}{0.35} WM3_{t-2} + \underset{(2.1)}{0.15} WM3_{t-13} \\ &- \underset{(-2.2)}{0.16} WM3_{t+4} + \underset{(2.1)}{0.15} WM3_{t+11} + \hat{u}_t \end{aligned} \tag{13}$$

Besides a highly significant lead of two months there exist non negligible contemporaneous and feedback effects. In the long run the influence of the reverse causality vanishes, because the coefficients of the leading monetary growth rates add up to zero. Such a reverse causal relation from inflation to money growth may be interpreted as the outcome of a reaction function of the Bundesbank. Setting the target value of the annual growth rate of M3 the observed inflation rate plays a role.

4 Conclusion

Six different measures of the term structure and monthly growth rates of three different monetary aggregates are investigated with respect to their predictive power for future movements of inflation rates. Monthly seasonally unadjusted data for the period of monetary targeting in Germany are used.

The bivariate relations between alternative indicators and the monthly inflation rate are analysed in the frequency domain, giving detailed information about the different cyclical movements. Moreover, the coherence - comparable to a coefficient of determination for each frequency - is in contrast to the usual R^2 invariant under linear transformations. That means that the results presented here do not change no matter whether differences or linear seasonal filters such as annual growth rates are used.

The estimated coherences do not show strong relations between the indicators and the inflation rate. This is especially true for all different kinds of the term structure. The monthly growth rate of M3 is the only variable with a relatively strong linkage to the monthly inflation rate. However, it turns out that WM3 is not only a simple leading indicator, but that the movement of WM3 is also influenced by the development of the inflation rate.

To sum up all results it seems that the transmission of monetary policy to inflation is a very complicated process and one cannot only use simple leading indicators or intermediate targets to receive reliable information about these relations.

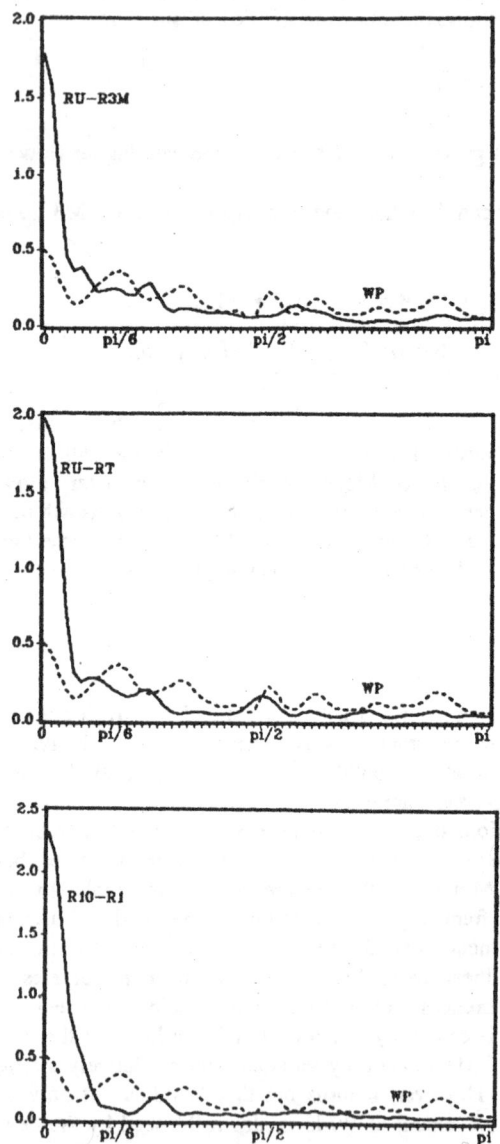

Figure 1   Spectral densities of interest rate spreads and the inflation rate

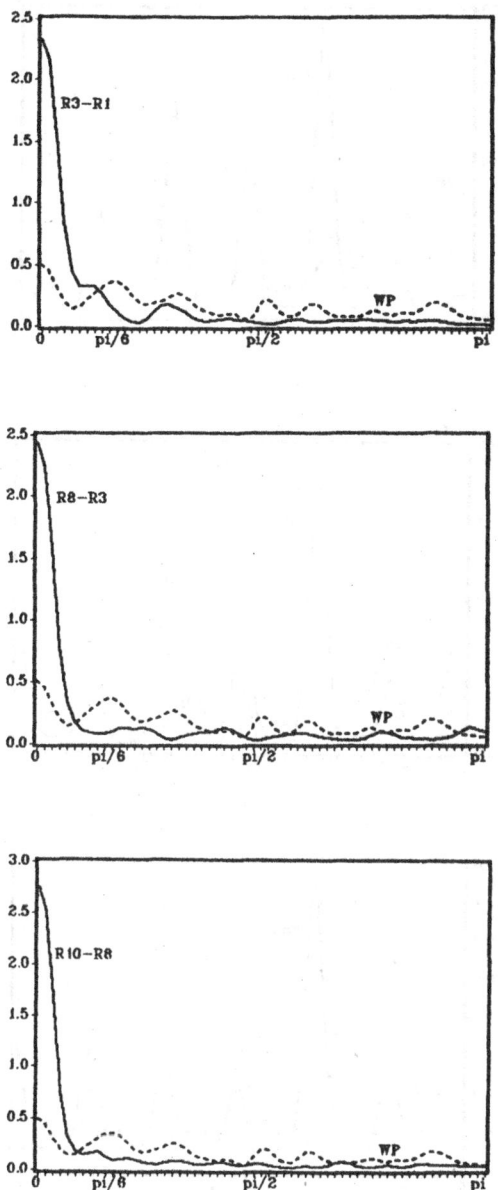

Figure 2 Spectral densities of yield spreads and the inflation rate

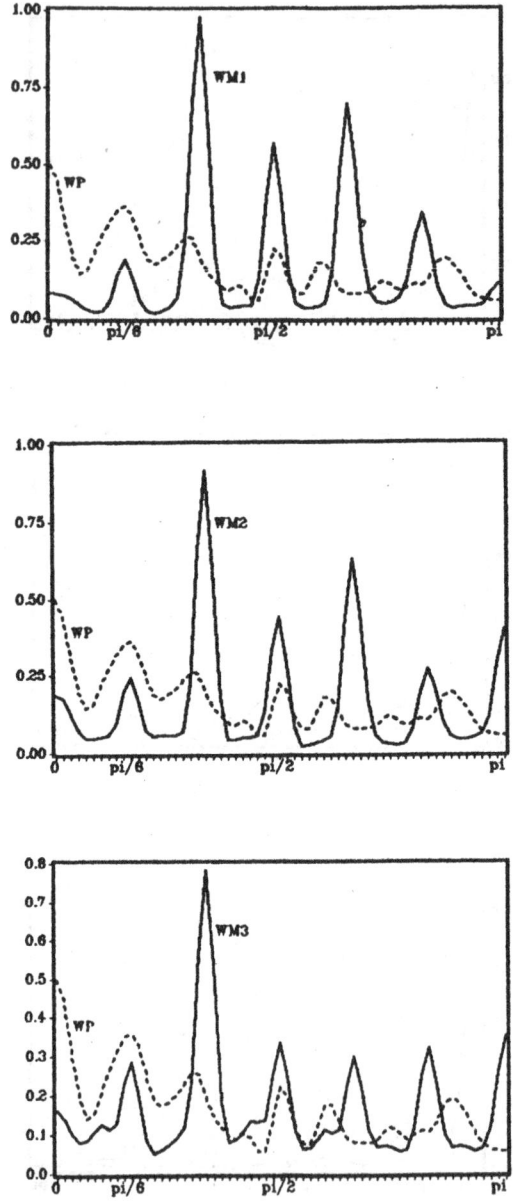

Figure 3 Spectral densities of money growth rates and the inflation rate

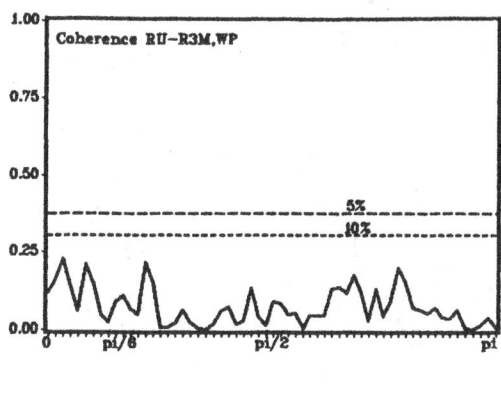

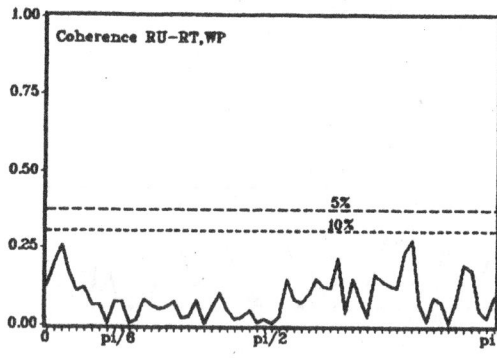

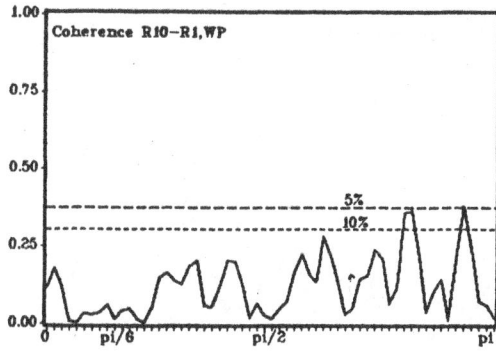

Figure 4   Coherences between interest rate spreads and the inflation rate

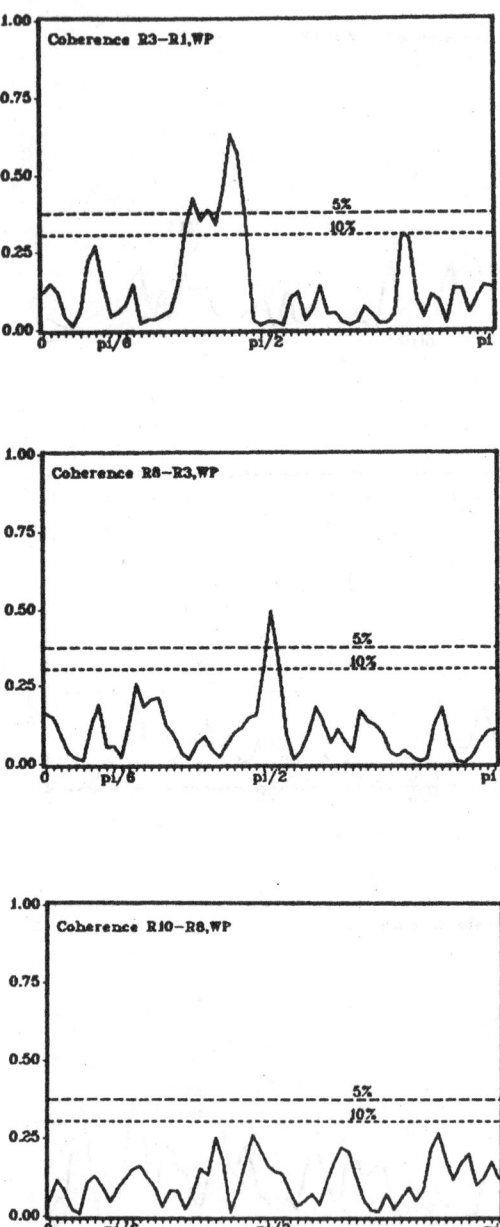

Figure 5   Coherences between yield spreads and the inflation rate

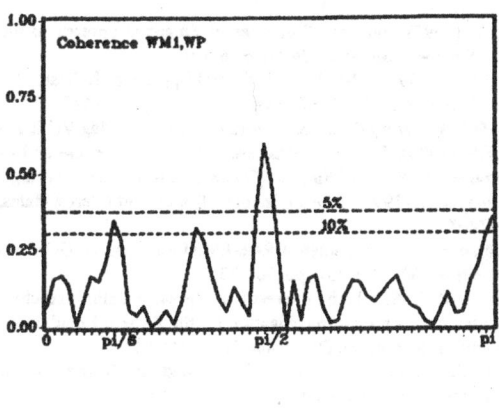

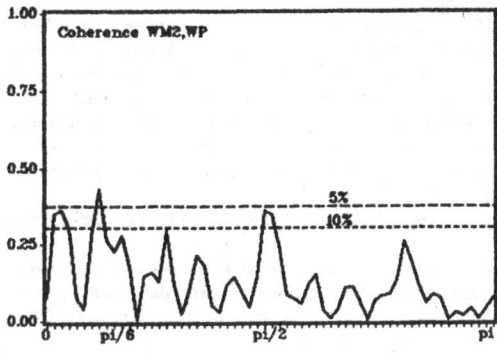

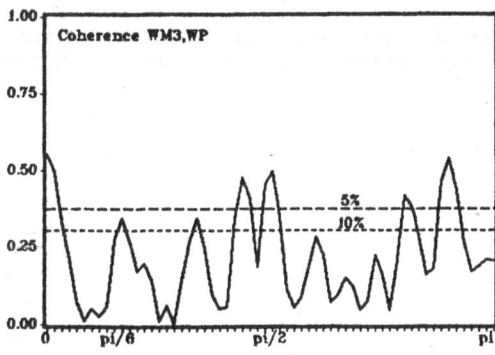

Figure 6   Coherences between money growth rates and the inflation rate

References

Davis, E.Ph. and Fagan, G. (1995), Indicator Properties of Financial Spreads in the EU: Evidence from Aggregate Union Data, *European Monetary Institute*, mimeo.

Davis, E.Ph. and Henry, S.G.B. (1994), The Use of Financial Spreads as Indicator Variables: Evidence for the United Kingdom and Germany, *IMF Staff Papers*, Vol. 41, pp. 517-525.

Deutsche Bundesbank (1996), *Monetary Policy Strategies in Europe*, Verlag Vahlen: München.

Estrella, A. and Mishkin,F.S. (1995), The Term Structure of Interest Rates and its Role in Monetary Policy for the European Central Bank, *National Bureau of Economic Research*, Working Paper Series 5279.

Friedman, B.M. and Kuttner, K.N. (1992), Money, Income, Prices, and Interest Rates, *American Economic Review*, Vol. 82, pp. 472-92.

Hagen, H.M. and Kirchgässner, G. (1996), Interest Rate-Based Forecasts of German Economic Growth: A Note, *Weltwirtschaftliches Archiv*, Vol. 132, pp. 763-73.

Kirchgässner, G. and Savioz, M. (1995), Is the Interest Rate Spread a Valid Predictor for Real and Nominal Economic Developments? An Empirical Investigation for the Federal Republic of Germany, University of St. Gallen, Department of Economics, *Discussion Paper* No. 9510.

Koedijk, K.G. and Kool, C.J.M. (1995), Future Inflation and the Information in International Term Structures, *Empirical Economics*, Vol. 20, pp. 217-42.

König, H. and Wolters, J. (1972), *Einführung in die Spektralanalyse ökonomischer Zeitreihen*, Verlag Anton Hain: Meisenheim am Glan.

Koopmans, L.H. (1974), *The Spectral Analysis of Time Series*, Academic Press: New York and London.

Lahiri, K. (1995), Zinsdifferenzen als neue Frühindikatoren - Theorie und Evidenz, in K.H. Oppenländer (ed), *Konjunkturindikatoren*, R. Oldenbourg Verlag: München Wien, pp. 216-237.

Langfeld, E. (1994), Die Zinsstruktur als Frühindikator für Konjunktur und Preisentwicklung in Deutschland, Paper presented at the Symposium about "Zinsstruktur, Geldpolitik und Wirtschaftsentwicklung", Deutsche Bundesbank, Frankfurt, February 8.

Mishkin, F.S. (1990), What does the Term Stucture Tell us about Future Inflation?, *Journal of Monetary Economics*, Vol. 20, pp. 77-95.

Moersch, M. (1996), Interest Rates or Spreads as Predictors of Real Economic Activity?, *Konjunkturpolitik*, Vol. 42, pp. 40-52.

Robertson, D. (1992), Term Structure Forecasts of Inflation, *Economic Journal*, Vol. 102, pp. 1083-1093.

Schich, S.T. (1996), Alternative Spezifikationen der deutschen Zinsstrukturkurve und ihr Informationsgehalt hinsichtlich der Inflation, Diskussionspapier 8/96, *Volkswirtschaftliche Forschungsgruppe der Deutschen Bundesbank*.

Sims, C.A. (1972), Money, Income, and Causality', *American Economic Review*, Vol. 62, pp. 540-552.

Wolters, J. (1973), *Spektralanalytische Schätzung linearer dynamischer Systeme*, Verlag Anton Hain: Meisenheim am Glan.

Wolters, J. (1980), *Stochastic Dynamic Properties of Linear Econometric Models*, Springer-Verlag: Berlin Heidelberg New York.

Wolters, J. (1997), Zur Beurteilung verschiedener Frühindikatoren für die Produktionsentwicklung, in E. Helmstädter, G. Poser and H.J. Ramser (eds), *Beiträge zur angewandten Wirtschaftsforschung*, Duncker & Humblot: Berlin, pp. 339-361.

Part V
Economic Policy Recommendations

18 Aggregate Demand and Economic Growth: Empirical Evidence from Business Survey Data

Marcella Corsi[*]

> When we turn, however, to the relevant statistics to find some exact measure of the degree of these fluctuations, we find that they are few and unsatisfactory. There is no single set of figures which measures accurately what should be capable of quite precise measurement - namely, the rate at which the community is adding to its investment in fixed capital. The best we can do, therefore, is to take a number of partial indicators and to judge as well as we can from their combined results (J.M.Keynes (1930), *A Treatise on Money*, vol.II, The Royal Economic Society, 1971, p. 87).

1 Introduction

The 1990's have witnessed a revival in economist's interest and hope of explaining aggregate and microeconomic demand behaviour. On the one hand, much attention has been devoted to aggregate investment, viewed as providing hope for future prosperity.[1] On the other hand, much has been written about precautionary saving, linking consumption to future income prospects.[2]

In spite of the abundance of theoretical work, so far there have been few empirical studies focusing on aggregate demand in explaining business cycles and growth performances, especially at EU level.[3] Much attention has been devoted in recent years to EMU problems and less care has been taken of the effects of restrictive policy measures on economic climate and demand.

This paper aims to give a modest contribution in this direction, tracking EU domestic demand from 1985 mainly using simple and composite indicators stemming from the EU-harmonized qualitative surveys results.

Harmonized surveys do present many advantages as sources of economic information, because they allow to study aggregate behaviour on the basis of

---

[*] Financial support from CNR (Contract no.94.02025.CT10) is gratefully acknowledged. Thanks are due to Alessandro Roncaglia for his useful suggestions.
[1] Cf. Caballero (1997).
[2] Cf. Deaton (1991) and Carroll (1994).
[3] Most empirical studies have been complementary to the theoretical work in trying to assess validity of theoretical assumptions. The theoretical emphasis on demand behaviour has scarcely incentivated empirical analysis of demand trends based on new-developed theories, may be because of the increasing complexities of their mathematical form and/or lack of suitable panel data.

microfounded data (at firm and household levels) plus they provide a rapid mean of compiling simple statistics, with the results available before those obtained with traditional statistical methods. Moreover, business surveys provide information in areas not covered by quantitative statistics (e.g., about capacity utilization and stocks of finished goods) and therefore may be considered as complementary to official statistical sources.

The layout of the paper is as follows. Section 2 highlights the main characteristics of the European economy since 1985. Indeed, various events and shocks have shaped the Community economy during the period under consideration: the launching of the Single Market Programme in 1985, the adhesion of Spain and Portugal in 1986, German reunification in 1990, structural factors such as technological change and globalization, and cyclical factors including exchange rate crises.[1] The effects of all these events are only sketched while attention is devoted to comparing EU demand performance within the triad (USA, Japan, EU).

Section 3 clarifies the theoretical framework for the empirical analysis and draws attention both on entrepreneurs' judgement of the relevance of demand as a limit to production and on aggregate demand behaviour as described by a composite demand indicator.

Section 4 presents some findings concerning investment and Section 5 concentrates on consumption and savings.

Section 6 draws some conclusions.

2 The European Economy in the Period 1985-1995

2.1 Macroeconomic Outlook

2.1.1 Between 1985 and 1995 the EU, USA and Japan all almost completed a full economic cycle, from the expansion that had started well before 1985 to the recovery of 1994-95 after the recession of 1992-93 (1990-91 for the USA, see fig.1).

The EU's GDP growth first accelerated between 1986 and 1989, peaking at 4.2% in 1988, and then slowed down between 1989 and 1991 to give way to the 1992/93 crisis, when GDP at 1990 prices decreased 0.6% in 1993. Recovery started in 1994 (quarterly data show the second quarter of 1993), but growth rates in 1994 and 1995 remained under 3%, thus below the ones reached in the preceding expansion. Within the triad, Japan's cycle has moved in phase with the EU, although the expansion peak exceeded 6% in 1988, whilst the 1994 recovery was much weaker than in the EU; Japanese GDP only grew by below 1% over the period 1994-95. The USA, however, only shared the first part of the cycle with the EU. An almost equivalent expansion took place between 1986 and 1989, with US GDP growth reaching almost 4% in 1988, but after 1989 the slowdown was quicker so that the USA went into recession in 1991 before recovering the next year. Furthermore, the USA's recorded growth rates were higher than 3% in 1993 and 1994.

---

[1] Cf. European Commission (1996).

Aggregate Demand and Economic Growth: Empirical Evidence from Business Survey Data

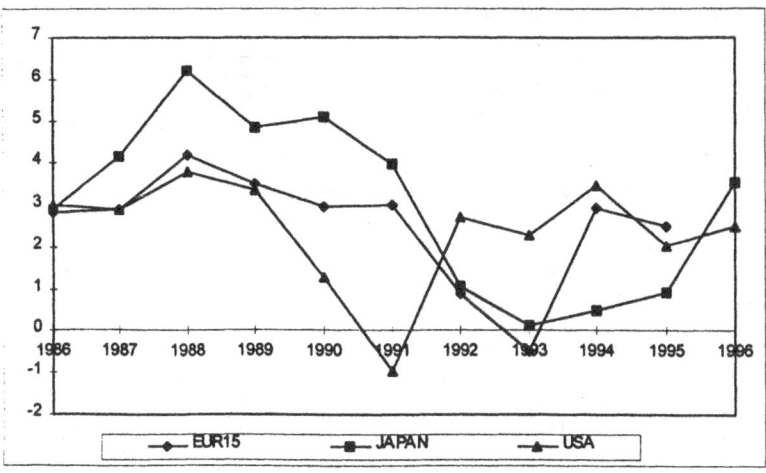

Figure 1   GDP at 1990 prices (EU, USA, Japan)
Source: European Commission Services.

Most Member States' cycles reflect the EU average. However, a number of exceptions are worth mentioning. First, although their cycles moved in line with the EU average, Spain and Portugal recorded higher growth than the EU average over the period 1986-89 (6% in Portugal and 5.6% in Spain in 1987). Secondly, due to the reunification effect, German GDP growth reached its peak in 1990-91 (at over 5%). Third, the UK does not seem to follow the same economic cycle as the EU as a whole, but rather the US one. British GDP growth, after reaching 5% in 1988, fell within two years to -2% in 1991 before quickly recovering during 1993 and 1994 and equalling EU average growth in 1995 (2.4%).

2.1.2 In terms of both GDP and employment the EU's share in the triad steadily decreased between 1985 and 1995. Since the USA's share of the triad's GDP remained quite stable in that period, much of the fall in the EU's share was gained by Japan, though, in employment terms, the USA recorded the highest growth.

In 1995, the European Union (including former East Germany) represented 42% of real GDP (constant 1990 prices) in the triad, as compared with 38.4% for the USA and 19.7% for Japan (see Table 1). The so-called big four (Germany, France, Italy and the United Kingdom) accounted for almost 79% of EU's GDP in the same year, while Spain and Portugal, which acceded in 1986, represented around 9%. In terms of employment, the EU represented 41.9% of total employment in the triad in 1995 (38.4% and 19.7% for the USA and Japan respectively), whilst the big four accounted for 74.6% of the EU's total employment.

Table 1 Employment and real GDP at 1990 prices within the triad

	GDP				Employment			
	1985	1990	1995[1]	1995[2]	1985	1990	1995[1]	1995[2]
B	3.2	3.2	3.2	3.1	2.9	2.8	2.8	2.7
DK	2.3	2.1	2.2	2.1	2.0	2.0	2.0	1.9
D	24.6	24.7	25.2	27.0	21.2	21.0	21.7	25.3
GR	1.5	1.4	1.4	1.3	2.9	2.7	2.9	2.8
E	7.7	8.1	8.1	7.9	8.8	9.5	9.2	8.9
F	19.8	19.7	19.4	18.9	17.1	16.7	17.1	16.4
IRL	0.7	0.7	0.9	0.9	0.9	0.8	0.9	0.9
I	18.2	18.0	17.8	17.3	16.8	16.1	15.3	14.4
L	0.2	0.2	0.2	0.2	0.1	0.1	0.2	0.2
NL	4.7	4.7	4.8	4.7	4.5	4.7	5.1	4.9
P	1.0	1.1	1.1	1.1	3.3	3.3	3.4	3.2
UK	16.1	16.1	15.9	15.5	19.7	20.1	19.5	18.5
EU	100	100	100	100	100	100	100	100
USA	38.9	37.8	38.8	38.4	37.2	37.7	39.0	38.4
J	19.2	20.3	19.9	19.7	19.8	19.7	20.2	19.7
EU	42.0	41.9	41.4	42.0	43.0	42.6	40.9	41.9
Triad	100	100	100	100	100	100	100	100

N.B.: Since the period of reference is 1985-95, thus prior to the accession of Austria, Finland and Sweden, EU=EU12; [1] Without including former East Germany; [2] Including former East Germany.
Source: European Commission services.

Table 2 Domestic demand in the triad as % of GDP

	1985			1995[1]		
	PRC	PC	GFCF	PRC	PC	GFCF
B	62.7	16.6	14.9	63.3	14.3	18.1
DK	54.2	26.7	17.9	54.1	24.1	15.6
D	60.5	13.6	19.5	64.6	12.3	22.2
GR	69.9	15.0	23.2	74.7	14.6	23.3
E	61.9	14.1	17.6	61.6	16.5	21.9
F	59.7	19.0	18.8	60.0	19.1	19.2
IRL	61.5	19.4	18.4	53.0	13.4	15.4
I	58.6	18.3	19.0	59.6	17.1	17.6
L	64.6	13.9	15.4	62.6	13.2	26.4
NL	59.6	15.2	20.2	59.3	13.8	20.1
P	62.5	15.0	21.8	67.4	16.1	28.6
UK	59.0	22.5	17.5	62.7	20.5	17.1
EU	59.9	17.6	18.7	61.9	16.5	19.7
J	58.2	10.2	26.3	58.7	9.5	29.8
USA	66.3	18.2	18.3	66.9	15.9	19.4

N.B.: Since the period of reference is 1985-95, thus prior to the accession of Austria, Finland and Sweden, EU=EU12; [1] Including former East Germany.
Source: European Commission services.

Table 2 compares the components of aggregate demand in the European Union, the USA and Japan. Over the period under consideration, the average rates of public consumption in the EU and USA were broadly comparable (around 16-17%), despite the fact that the public sector is larger in the EU than in the USA. EU and USA have also rather similar rates of investment (18-19%), always considerably below the average investment rate in Japan (always above 26%).

Differences concerning private consumption between the EU and USA are mainly due to differences in the external balances, which have been positive in the EU (and Japan) but negative in the USA over the 1985-95 period.

Direct comparisons between the EU and the other two members of the triad conceal significant heterogeneity among Member States. Diversity within the EU is so large that is practically impossible to find a 'representative' Member State for the EU average. Surprisingly, apart from a higher GFCF rate, which is compensated by a lower external balance, Spain was the country with the highest degree of similarity with the EU average in 1995. The most drastic changes in structure of aggregate demand are found in Germany, Spain and Portugal. These changes relate to reunification and accession. Between 1985 and 1990 private consumption accounted for 60.5% of GDP in Germany (PC 13%, GFCF 20%); in 1995, although public consumption fell by less than 1 percentage point, private consumption and investment rates respectively had jumped by 4 and 2 points, thus reducing the external balance by more than 5 percentage points.

Structural changes in Spain and Portugal were also significant. Both countries saw increases in the relative weight of public consumption and investment at the expense of drastic falls in their external balances. The structural change was particularly sharp in Portugal, where the share of private consumption increased 5 percentage points.

3 Theory and Evidence of Aggregate (Domestic) Demand

3.1 Theoretical Framework

3.1.1 The theory of aggregate demand has been enriched in the 1990s of new interesting insights concerning both investment and consumption.

On the investment side, the traditional *accelerator*-like model, linking investment to the desired level of capital (i.e., to the level of output and the cost of capital) has been partly abandoned because of a change in emphasis from aggregate to microeconomic investment behaviour. Theories of lumpy and irreversible investment have drawn attention on the *path* leading capital stock to its desired level, highlighting the existence of obstacles to investment at the firm level. In brief, such a vast literature on microeconomic investment behaviour stresses that

1. investment occurs when the marginal profitability of capital is substantially above the cost of capital (this is the famous 'reluctance to invest' result);

2. a considerable fraction of a firm's investment is bunched into infrequent and lumpy episodes;[1]
3. aggregate investment is heavily influenced by the degree of synchronization of microeconomic investment spikes.[2]

Moreover, there is now a large body of evidence supporting the view that credit constraints have substantial effects on firm level investment; in other terms, the cumulative evidence seems overwhelmingly in favour of the claim that investment is more easily financed with internal than external funds.[3]

On the consumption side, the Life Cycle Hypothesis (LCH), linking households consumption of non-durable goods to real wealth, current real disposable income and expected real future incomes, has been revised to take into account credit constraints on the part of consumers[4] and consumption of durables. There are several reasons to be interested in durable goods:

1. they are luxuries, thus more procyclical than the non-durable component of total consumer expenditure;
2. they are often (partly) bought on credit, and are therefore more influenced by credit regulations and interest rates;

---

[1] Cf. Doms - Dunne (1993). As reported by Caballero (1997), Doms and Dunne documented investment patterns of 12,000 plants in US manufacturing over the period 1972-1989. For each establishment they constructed a series of the proportion of the total equipment investment (over the 17-year period) made in each year. They found that on average the largest investment episode accounts for more than 25% of the 17-year investment of an establishment and that more than half of the establishments exhibited capital growth close to 50% in a single year. They also noted that the second largest investment spike often came next to the largest investment spike (right before or after) suggesting that both spikes correspond to a single investment episode. As evidence of the macroeconomic relevance of microeconomic lumpiness, Doms and Dunne documented - using data on about 360,000 establishments for Census years 1977 and 1987 - that about 18% of aggregate investment is accounted for by the top 100 projects; as a metric, only 6% of employment is in the top 100 employers, and less than 10% of production occurs in the top 100 producers.

[2] Cf. Gale (1996). Informational problems play an important role in the synchronization mechanism, causing episodes of gradualism during which industry investment can occur at an excessively slow pace, or even collapse altogether. As a matter of fact, information seldom arrives uniformly and comprehensively to every potential investor. Each investor probably holds part of a truth which would be more easily seen if all investors could (or would) pool their information. Actions by others are a partial substitute for information pooling, for they reveal the information of those who have taken actions. Indeed, if investment is irreversible, it may pay to wait for others to act and reveal their information before investing. However, if lumpiness leads to periods of no or little action, information may remain trapped for extended periods of time, and when agents finally act, an avalanche may occur because accumulated private information is suddenly aggregated. These issues are the focus of the literature on 'social learning'.

[3] Cf. Bernanke et al. (1996).

[4] Several works have been devoted to study the impact of financial liberalization on aggregate consumption, especially in the UK. In Britain real consumption grew on average 6.5% on an annual basis between 1986 and 1988; the British boom was probably due to an upward revision in income expectations but was made possible by the financial liberalization of the early 1980s, and found its transmission mechanism mostly in the housing market. Cf. Jappelli - Pagano (1994).

3. they are a long-term investment, i.e. consumers increase their purchases of durable goods when they expect income to grow.[1]

In particular, the relevance of expected future income in determining consumer expenditure has been stressed, for any kind of good, by the theory of precautionary saving which states that the amount of saving (consumption) increases (decreases) in response to an increase in the uncertainty associated to the income generating process.[2] Although determining a proper measure of the degree of income uncertainty is a difficult task, it may be shown that precautionary savings are potentially able to provide simultaneous explanations for the excess smoothness[3] and the excess sensitivity[4] of consumption to unanticipated and anticipated income changes, respectively.[5]

3.1.2 In accordance with the recent developments in the theory of aggregate demand, the most suitable specification of a domestic demand function is as follows:

$$DDEM = f(G, E(G), L, U, W, Y, E(Y), \sigma) \tag{1}$$

with

$$I = f(U, G, E(G), L) \tag{2}$$

and

$$C = f(W, Y, E(Y), L, \sigma) \tag{3}$$

where
G = current profits;
L = liquidity constraint;
U = capacity utilization;
W = real wealth;
Y = disposable income;
σ = uncertainty on future income;[6]
$E()$ = expectation operator.

---

[1] This is particularly relevant if second-hand markets are absent (e.g., electrical appliances) or imperfect (e.g., cars).
[2] Cf. Guiso - Jappelli - Terlizzese (1992).
[3] Cf. Deaton (1986) and Campbell - Deaton (1989).
[4] Cf. Flavin (1981).
[5] Cf. Caballero (1990).
[6] Uncertainty may also play a role in the determination of firm's investment, but the sign and intensity of the investment-uncertainty (on demand) relationship cannot be settled on a purely theoretical ground. Depending on assumptions about the production technology, competition in product markets, the shape of adjustment costs and management attitudes toward risk, increases in uncertainty over the demand for the firm's product and over input costs may have opposite effects on demand. That is why such a link is ignored in this paper and is left as an empirical problem. Cf. Guiso - Parigi (1996) and references.

The investment function states that firms' investment behaviour depends on their own financial means, depending on current profits, and by their possibilities of drawing on bank credit,[1] again influenced by current profits. If current profits determine the possibility of financing investment, the inducement to invest is given by expected profits. Moreover, demand is relevant for firm's investment behaviour insofar as it determines the degree of utilization of their production capacity: this seems the most appropriate expression of that variant of the accelerator principle known as the capital-stock adjustment principle.

The consumption function is based on the LCH enriched with the influence of future income uncertainty and liquidity constraint on consumers' decisions.[2] The effects of increases in wealth, current and expected disposable income are all positive as implied by the LCH, while the effects of L and σ are expected to be negative. No distinction is made between durables and non-durables, although it is acknowledged that it would be advisable, for forecasting purposes, to postulate two separate equations for dealing with consumers' expectations and liquidity constraints; in fact, given that the consumption of durables is more easily postponable, one would expect a stronger effect of a change in consumers' attitude on the expenditure of durables that on non-durables.

3.2 Observable Variables

3.2.1 The EU-harmonized qualitative surveys offer a variety of indicators suitable to track domestic demand in accordance with the theoretical framework described above.

As is known, the EU-harmonized system includes five different surveys: the industry survey, the investment survey, the construction survey, the retail trade survey and the consumer survey.[3] Each of the five surveys provides information concerning some aspects of domestic demand.

1. *Industry Survey*:
   - Demand/order books : present level and future tendency;
   - Stocks of finished goods : present level;
   - Limits to production : present situation;
   - Production Capacity : present situation;
   - Degree of capacity utilization : present level;

2. *Investment Survey*:
   - Investment : future tendency;
   - Type of investment : planned situation;

---

[1] Variations in the availability of bank credit can be measured from the variations in the liquidity of the banking system or total liquidity (primary and secondary). Cf. Sylos Labini (1967).

[2] A similar consumption function has been used to produce real time estimates of consumption expenditure for the Italian economy. Cf. Parigi - Schlitzer (1995).

[3] Cf. European Commission (1991). All variables are quantified by the balance: $f(n_t, t) = 2n_{1t} + 1n_{2t} + 0n_{3t} - 1n_{4t} - 2n_{5t}$. The balance has proved to be a very reliable method for converting qualitative information into quantitative form. EU-harmonized survey data are usually available to the public in this form and composite indicators are calculated aggregating information concerning different variables quantified by the balance and then seasonally adjusted.

- Factors limiting investment : planned situation;

3. *Construction Survey*:
   - Limits to production : present situation;
   - Order books (contracts) : present level and future tendency;

4. *Retail Trade Survey*:
   - Business situation : present situation and future tendency;
   - Stocks : present level;
   - Orders placed with suppliers : future tendency;

5. *Consumer Survey*:
   - Financial situation of household : present situation and future tendency;
   - General economic situation : present situation and future tendency;
   - Major purchases (furniture, etc.) : present situation and future tendency;
   - Household's savings : present situation and future tendency;
   - Financial position of household : present situation;
   - Car purchase : future tendency;
   - House purchase : future tendency;
   - House improvements : future tendency.

The first information which stems from the Industry survey concerns the influence of demand as a limit to production. Question 8 (quarterly) of the harmonized questionnaire includes five answers concerning limits to production: 1) none, 2) insufficient demand, 3) shortage of labour, 4) lack of equipment and 5) other.

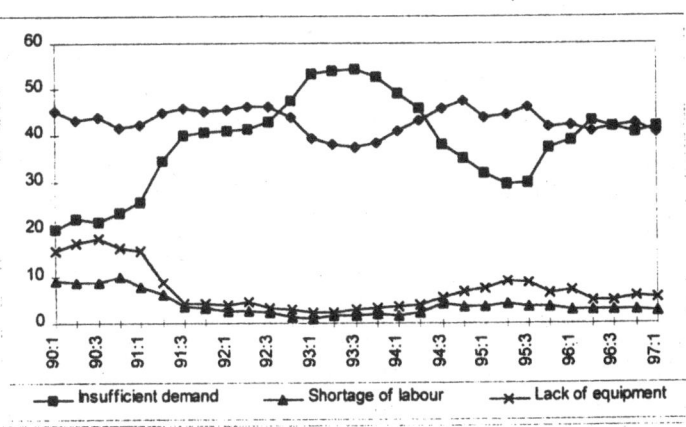

Figure 2   EU - limits to production
Source: European Commission Services.

As figure 2 shows, insufficient demand is by far the most important obstacle to growth in entrepreneurs' view. The survey indicator follows the business cycle described in §2.1 providing updated information for 1996 and the first quarter of 1997. Indeed, it peaked during the 1992/93 recession, slowed down in 1994 and started rising again from the third quarter of 1995. Since then, complaints of a lack of demand for industrial goods have been increasing significantly and no sign of relief has still appeared.

3.2.2 The EU-harmonized qualitative survey data can be aggregated to provide composite information concerning domestic demand. It is possible to calculate four demand indicators (see fig.3).

1. *Industry demand indicator*: it is obtained as the indexed average of the industry survey results concerning order-books and expected new orders, in the context of manufacturing industry.

2. *Construction demand indicator*: it is based on the replies to the question concerning production schedules (order-books) within the construction survey.

3. *Consumer demand indicator*: it is an index calculated from the average of the consumer survey results concerning actual and forecasted purchases of durables by interviewed households.

4. *Demand global indicator*: it collects all the above information as the indexed average of the specific replies.

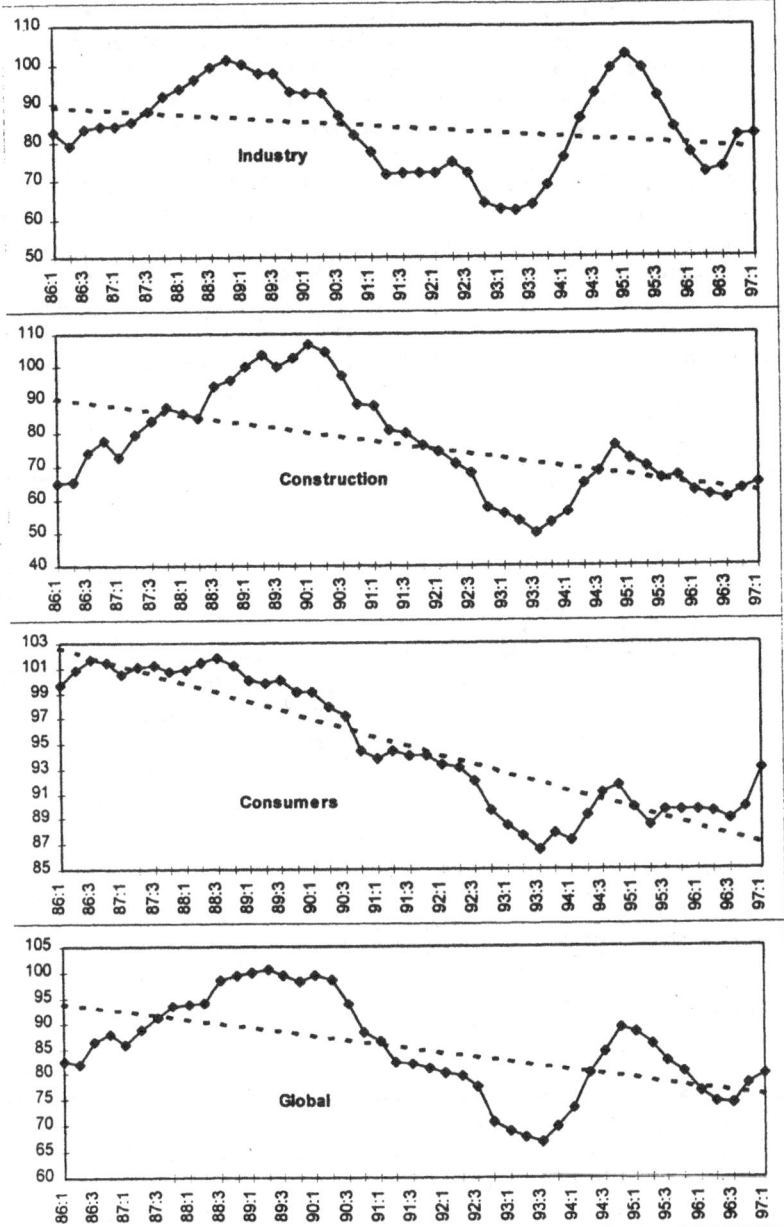

Figure 3 EU - demand indicators
Source: European Commission services.

In particular, the demand global indicator seems to track reasonably well the cyclical behaviour of EU domestic demand, as figure 4 shows. Alike GDP growth, the EU's domestic demand growth first accelerated between 1986 and 1988, peaking at 5.1% in 1988, and then slowed down between 1989 and 1991 to give way to the 1992/93 crisis, when national uses (excluding stocks) at 1990 prices decreased 1.8% in 1993. Recovery started in 1994 (quarterly data show the second quarter of 1993), but growth rates in 1994 and 1995 remained under 3%, thus below the ones reached in the preceding expansion.

The global demand indicator shows a weakening of EU's domestic demand in recent years, which makes recovery still hard to come.

Economic agents started viewing the demand-side of the economy more unfavourably from the first quarter of 1995, mainly because of the worsening of entrepreneurs' assessments of actual and incoming orders.

The industry demand indicator fell in 1995 at the same pace of 1990, when the loss of confidence had been affected by the increasing uncertainties caused by the Gulf War.

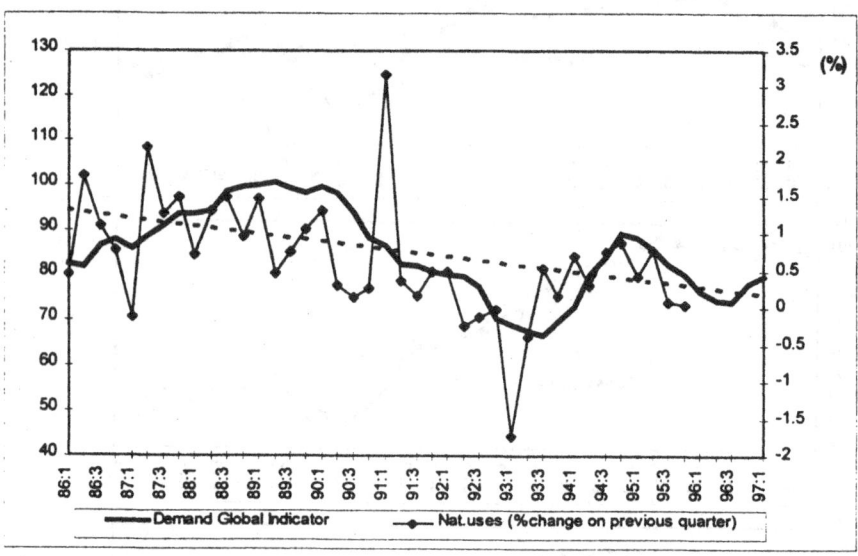

Figure 4   EU - domestic demand
Source: European Commission services.

Demand appears more stable in the construction industry, since 1995. However, order-books have been regarded as more and more inadequate especially in Germany, France and Italy and consequently the trend of activity has declined overall the Community despite some isolated bright spots (e.g., the United Kingdom).

The consumers' demand indicator shows a steady decrease of the demand for durables throughout the most recent period, which confirms the procyclical nature of the products involved. However, there are relevant divergencies among the Member States on account of different households' opinions about their financial situation: the consumer demand indicator has been declining for Italy and France, augmenting for United Kingdom and virtually unchanged for Germany.

4 Investment Trends

4.1 Investment Survey Indicators

The EU-harmonized business survey has a very high information content concerning industrial investment and its determinants.

First of all, the investment survey provides a very good proxy of investment annual growth rates. As figure 5 shows, EU investment growth reached its peak in 1988 (at 8%) and fell within three years to -1% in 1992 (-7% in 1993) before recovering during 1994-95. The survey indicator is obtained by aggregating firms' replies to the October/November questionnaire, which includes a quantitative question about the percentage change in firms' current investment expenditure compared with the previous year (in volume terms).[1] According to entrepreneurs' estimates, investment growth rate dropped significantly in 1996 and survey results confirm the same tendency for 1997. In industrialists' view, the drop of investment has been caused by the weakening of demand and the excess of production capacity, despite the positive effect of the downward trend in interest rates.

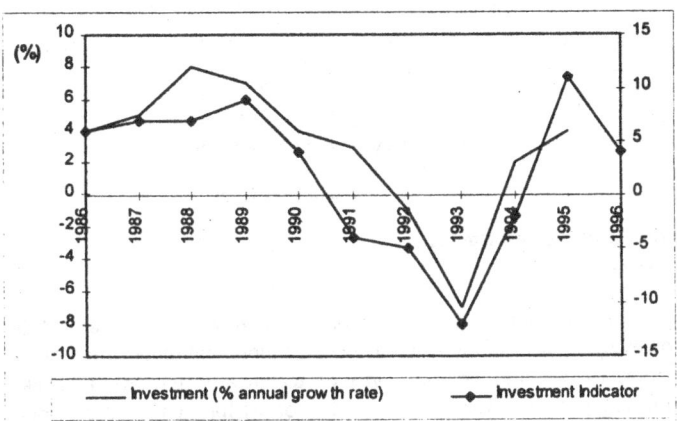

Figure 5 EU - investment trend
Source: European Commission services.

---

[1] As is known, the investment survey in industry is conducted twice a year, in March/April and October/November. The autumn survey yields a fairly good estimate of percentage growth for the current year and gives an idea of the trend of investment for the following year. The spring survey provides the percentage growth for the past year and a preliminary estimate for the current year.

The negative impact of the lack of demand on investment is clearly shown by the investment survey results concerning factors affecting investment, available since 1988. The following factors are considered:

1. *demand*: this relates to the degree of capacity utilization and the sales prospects;
2. *financial resources or expected profits*: this covers the availability of resources for investment and their costs, including the opportunity cost of not using firm's resources for financial purposes.
3. *technical factors*: this concern technical progress, the availability of qualified manpower and their attitude towards new technologies, and the technical conditions set by public authorities before granting investment.
4. *others*: this may include economic policy measures, notably with regard to taxation, as well as many other unspecified factors (i.e., uncertainty) affecting investment.

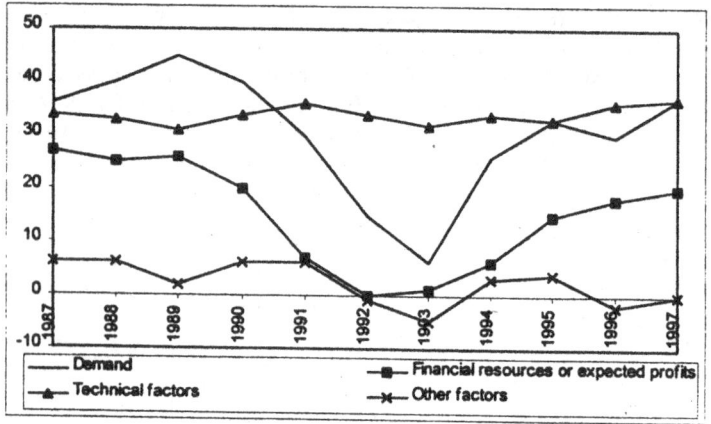

Figure 6   EU - factors limiting investment
Source: European Commission services.

As figure 6 shows, demand and technical factors are the principal reasons behind firms' investment. However, the lack of demand has become more and more important as a limit to investment since 1993, while the importance of technical factors has increased only moderately during recent years. The constant reduction of long-term interest rates has increased in importance as a factor influencing planned investment in recent years; in the firms' opinion, the improved financial conditions and expected profits will have a favourable influence on investment activity also in 1997.

The October/November investment survey also includes, since 1988, questions relating to the purposes of investment, the aim being to assess the impact of investment on the change in production capacity and on productivity.

The suggested motives are:
1. *replacement of worn out capacity*;
2. *extension of production capacity*;

3. *rationalization of production techniques*;
4. *others* (e.g., pollution control, safety).

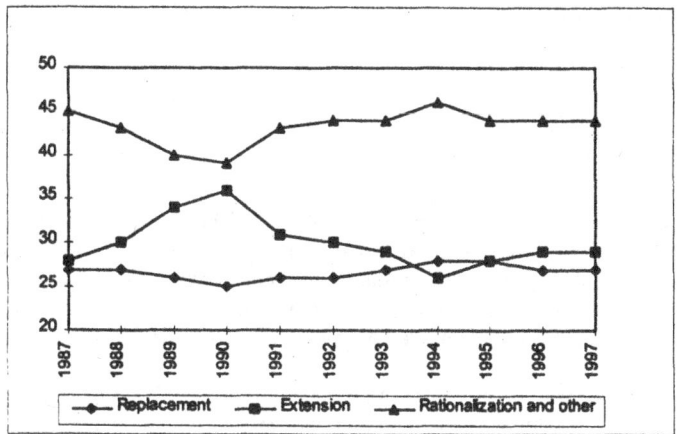

Figure 7   EU - structure of industrial investment
Source: European Commission services.

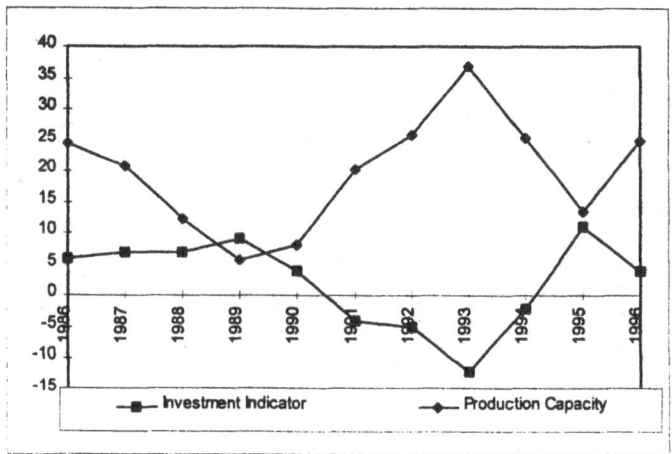

Figure 8   Investment and capacity utilization
Source: European Commission services.

As figure 7 shows, investment expenditure aimed to increase productivity, on the one hand, and to extend firms' production capacity, on the other hand, have inverted their trends since 1990. Due to the weakening of demand, firms' productive capacities have become more and more inadequate to entrepreneurs' production plans, as industry survey results concerning the assessment of capacity utilization[1] highlights (see fig. 8). Consequently, investment aimed to extend production capacity has drastically fallen during the last years and most of investment activity has been turned to increasing productivity and reducing production costs.

5 Consumption

5.1 Consumer Sentiment

It is widely recognized - since the pioneering work of Katona and his colleagues at the Survey Research Center of the University of Michigan[2] - that both the ability to buy (household income) and the willingness to buy (attitude, expectation) determine consumer expenditure, saving and credit.[3] Willingness to buy, also named consumer sentiment, is a function of the evaluation and expectation households have of the economic conditions of the household itself and of the nation.

The EU-harmonized consumer survey deals with consumer sentiment by questioning households about the financial situation of the household, the national economic situation, inflation, unemployment, saving plans and buying intentions for durables, especially cars. Such information is qualitative in nature and is radically different from the one obtainable from households' budget surveys that normally explore the composition of consumer expenditure in terms of goods and the actual behaviour of households about saving.

Indeed, information on consumer sentiment, optimism and pessimism, is useful for the prediction and explanation of aggregate demand of consumer durables and other types of discretionary consumer expenditure.[4] Since in affluent societies a large part of private consumption consists of discretionary and postponable expenditures and the private consumption represents the larger part of the GDP, discretionary expenditures exert a dominant influence on the aggregate economic activity. This way of aggregating results has been first applied to the Michigan Consumer Survey in USA and is now largely diffused all over the world.

As a matter of fact, the cyclical pattern of the Consumer Confidence Indicator tracks reasonably well that of aggregate consumption, as figure 8 shows. The composite indicator seems to proxy households' expectations in future income as well as the degree of subjective uncertainty.[5] Thus, a rise in the Consumer Confidence Indicator implies an improvement in the expectations of future income and/or a decrease in the degree of consumers' subjective uncertainty, which should induce an increase in consumption.

---

[1] Question 9 (quarterly) of the EU-harmonized industry survey questionnaire concerns the assessment of current production capacity in terms of 1) more than sufficient, 2) sufficient, 3) not sufficient. Thus, a positive balance reveals excess capacity and a negative balance means lack of capacity.

[2] Cf. Katona (1951).

[3] Indeed, optimistic consumers tend to save less and to borrow more than pessimistic consumers; thus consumer credit and mortgages tend to increase when consumers are optimistic.

[4] Non-discretionary expenditure concerns the contractual obligations of the households (rent, mortgage, energy, insurance premium etc.) and basic necessities such as food, clothing and transportation which cannot be postponed or cancelled.

[5] Cf. Parigi - Schlitzer (1995).

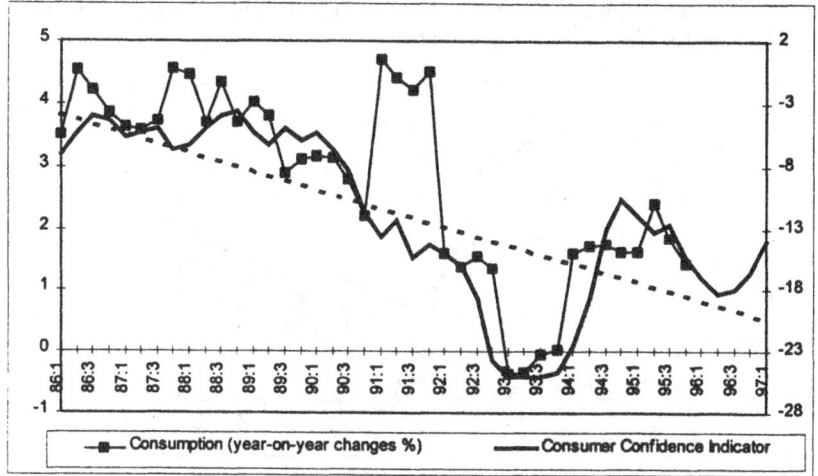

Figure 9   EU - Consumption trend
Source: European Commission services.

The recent pattern of the Consumer Confidence Indicator shows that consumer sentiment is mostly hesitant in the European Union. The evolution of the Consumer Confidence Indicator has been decelerating over the most recent months: since consumers face no better income prospects and are vulnerable to uncertainty, their willingness to spend has decreased. This puts the expected continuation of a sustained expansion of domestic demand in a more vulnerable light.

5.2   Precautionary Saving

The buoyancy of consumption expenditure, which should support the transformation of the present recovery into a sustainable medium-term growth process, seems to be weakened by a cautious behaviour of households. Indeed, consumers expect a rebound in their savings since the beginning of 1994 in virtually all Member States, despite falling interest rates and price expectations.[1]

Given that the assessments of saving intentions undertaken in the past haven proved to be a good indicator of the percentage change in gross savings of households[2], the observed increase in the balance of saving expectations could point to a further increase in households' savings.

The pace of the increase in saving intentions cannot be attributed to better income expectations. Households did not see any change in their recent financial situation and do not expect any significant change in the future. Indeed, high unemployment figures and

---

[1] As is known, rising price expectations by enducing a flight of money into real assets play an important role in the short-term fluctuations of the saving ratio.

[2] Cf. European Economy - Suppl. B, June 1995.

worsening employment expectations, as registered in industry and construction surveys, do depress the hope for wage increases in the future.

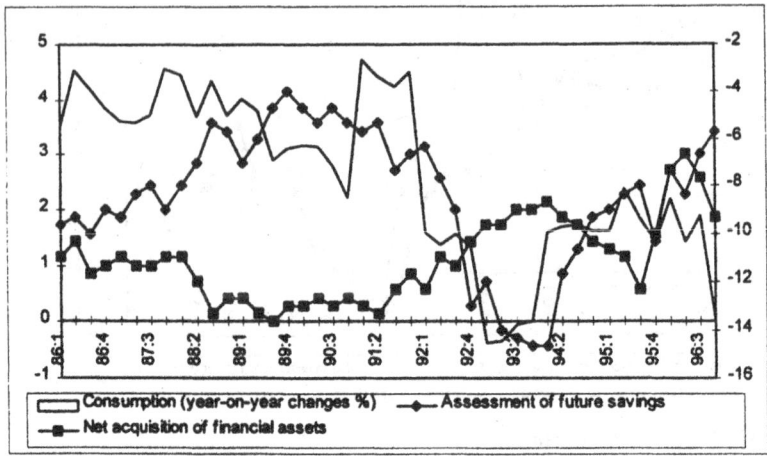

Figure 10 EU - Saving intentions
Source: European Commission services.

The pick-up in the indicator of savings is probably due to financial and political uncertainties which exert a negative impact on the assessment of the general economic situation. Consumer survey indicators concerning both actual and expected general economic situation point downwards since the beginning of 1995. These downward expectations can be explained by different factors. Firstly, the weakening of the US dollar has affected negatively EU economic prospects both in terms of lost competitiveness in appreciating countries and fear of inflationary pressures in depreciating countries. Secondly, expectations reflect the negative impact of economic policy tightening in the Member States towards sounder public finances. Moreover, government changes in several countries might have led to a more cautious attitude towards spending and to higher savings. These forms of precautionary savings can be inferred from the balance of the indicator of net acquisition of financial assets, which indicates a clear tendency towards households saving more.[1]

---

[1] Indeed, dealing with pure subjective variables it is often the case that the balance does not reflect the full information offered by the survey. As far as the financial position of the household is concerned it seems interesting to study individually the two categories "saving" and "making ends meet" since in recession they tend to invert their trends (e.g., this happens both in West Germany and in Italy). Similar considerations might apply to any other variable while working under specific hypotheses: if, for example, it is necessary to calculate a demand indicator for durables, a "probable" subjective variable like households' intentions to buy cars in the next two years might be well considered only in terms of the most positive categories "very likely" and "fairly likely" since any change in their relative percentages of replies might affect directly the overall demand.

6 Conclusive Remarks

The focus of this paper has been on showing the information content of the EU-harmonized qualitative surveys as far as the analysis of domestic demand is concerned. According to the most recent developments of aggregate demand theory, domestic demand can be considered as the driving force of growth and it really matters in identifying the ability of nations to react to recession. Thus, this paper has explored the demand side of the European economy searching for signs of real recovery and/or highlighting obstacles to growth.

It has been shown that EU-harmonized survey data offer a clear view of the relationship between production and demand trends, specifying links between investment and its determinants (expected profits, current demand and technical factors) as well as between consumer durables (the most procyclical component of consumption) and expected income.

In brief, commented data show a disappointing growth trend for the European economy mainly due to lack of domestic demand during most recent years.

According to entrepreneurs' estimates, investment growth rate dropped significantly in 1996 and survey results confirm the same tendency for 1997. In industrialists' view, the drop of investment has been caused by the weakening of demand and the excess of production capacity, despite the positive effect of the downward trend in interest rates.

The recent pattern of the Consumer Confidence Indicator shows that consumer sentiment is mostly hesitant in the European Union. The evolution of the Consumer Confidence Indicator has been decelerating over the most recent months: since consumers face no better income prospects and are vulnerable to uncertainty, their willingness to spend has not increased significantly. Moreover, the buoyancy of consumption expenditure, which should support the transformation of the present recovery into a sustainable medium-term growth process, seems to be weakened by a cautious behaviour of households. Indeed, various indicators show that consumers still expect a rebound in their savings for 1997, despite falling interest rates and price expectations.

Thus, the momentum appears insufficient to prevent unemployment from rising and inadequate for achieving relevant progress with fiscal consolidation. Since better results on these two fronts are crucial to the credibility of the Community's medium-term ambitions, policy makers should revive the EU growth process by adopting measures able to scale up spending and hiring decisions.

References

Bernanke, B. et al. (1996), The Financial Accelerator and the Flight to Quality, *Review of Economics and Statistics*, Vol. 78, pp.1-15.

Caballero, R. (1990), Consumption Puzzle and Precautionary Savings, *Journal of Monetary Economics*, Vol. 23, pp.113-36.

Caballero, R. (1997), Aggregate Investment: A 90's View, in Taylor, J. and Woodford, M. (eds), *Handbook of Macroeconomics*, forthcoming.

Campbell, J.Y. and Deaton, A. (1989) Why Is Consumption So Smooth?, *Review of Economic Studies*, No.56, pp.357-74.

Carroll, C.D. (1994), How Does Future Income Affect Current Consumption?, *Quarterly Journal of Economics*, Vol.109, pp. 111-47.

Deaton, A. (1986) Life-cycle Models of Consumption: Is the Evidence Consistent with the Theory?, *NBER Working Paper*, No.1910.

De aton, A. (1991), Saving and Liquidity Constraints, *Econometrica*, Vol. 59, pp.1221-48.

Doms, M. and Dunne, T. (1993), An Investigation into Capital and Labor Adjustment at the Plant Level, mimeo, Center for Economic Studies, Census Bureau.

European Commission (1991), The System of Business Surveys in the European Community: An Effective and Widely Respected Instrument, *European Economy - Suppl.B*, special edition, July.

European Commission (1996), Economic Evaluation of the Internal Market, *European Economy - Reports and Studies*, No. 4.

Flavin, M.A. (1981), The Adjustment of Consumption to Changing Expectations about Future Income, *Journal of Political Economy*, Vol.8, pp. 974-1009.

Gale, D. (1996), Delay and Cycles, *Review of Economic Studies*, Vol. 63, pp. 169-198.

Guiso, L. and Parigi, G. (1996), Investment and Demand Uncertainty, *Temi di Discussione*, Banca d'Italia, No.289.

Guiso, L., Jappelli,T, and Terlizzese, D. (1992), Earnings Uncertainty and Precautionary Saving, *Journal of Monetary Economics*, Vol. 30, pp.307-37.

Jappelli, T. and Pagano, M. (1994), Saving Growth and Liquidity Constraints, *Quarterly Journal of Economics*, Vol.109, pp.83-110.

Katona, G. (1951), *Psychological Analysis of Economic Behaviour*, McGraw Hill.

Parigi, G. and Schlitzer, G. (1995), Quarterly Forecasts of the Italian Business Cycle by Means of Monthly Economic Indicators, *Journal of Forecasting*, Vol.14, pp.77-158.

Sylos Labini, P. (1967), Prices, Distribution and Investment in Italy, 1951-1966: An Interpretation, *BNL - Quarterly Review*, No. 83, pp. 316-375.

19 Post-Unemployment Wages: Findings Based on the Swiss Labour Force Survey[*]

Monica Curti

1 Introduction, Line of Research

Due to a period of recession, and also to the ever faster pace of technological change which affects society in general and which has a particularly strong impact on the labour market, an increasing number of people are experiencing unemployment in Switzerland. The Federal Office for Industry and Labour, as the body responsible for implementing an active labour market policy, does its best to help the unemployed through vocational training and retraining, targeted temporary employment, and job search programmes. As it is yet too early to evaluate these measures, this paper will limit itself to looking at the short and medium term effects which a period of unemployment has on the wages of those who manage to again find work. Another objective of the research is to find out what factors have a significant impact on the loss of earnings of those who experience a period of unemployment. The findings should allow a detailed analysis of some of the more interesting short-and-medium-term consequences of unemployment, and are to serve as a basis for policy recommendations. The findings should be of particular interest for job counsellors involved in job assistance programmes in the regional placement offices. They will also be of help in any future efforts to reform unemployment insurance.

The empirical conclusions contained in this paper would not have been possible without the new Swiss Labour Force Survey (SLFS) database. The SLFS was carried out for the first time in 1991. No other official or published statistical sources allow analysis in such detail at the micro-level, with cross-sections as well as panel data.

The pattern of this paper is as follows: the next section takes a brief look at studies carried out abroad in this field. The third section explains the procedures, the data and the methods employed. The empirical findings are presented in the fourth section, and evaluated in the fifth. The final section contains a few policy recommendations.

---

[*] The author would particularly like to thank Stefan Wolter of the Federal Office for Industry and Labour for his helpful comments and useful suggestions. Any errors that remain are my own.

2 International Experience

At the beginning of the Nineties, several researchers applied instruments for evaluating active labour market measures to a study of the long-term effects of a period of unemployment on the subsequent wage level. Topel (1990) provides some evidence that long-lasting effects of job loss on annual income are strongly related to prior job tenure. Moreover, he argues that the solidity of the specific human capital is a central factor in determining the extent of the loss of earnings to the displaced workers.[1] Only when workers' skills are entirely general and when the wage reflects accumulated skills might it be possible for the displacement not to have long-term consequences. Jacobson et al. (1993a) studied the development of displaced workers' wages at the end of the period of unemployment, with particular reliance on administrative longitudinal section data. They found that workers with long tenure (six or more years of tenure, at the beginning of 1980) separating from troubled firms suffered long-term losses averaging 25 percent per year. In addition, they found that displaced workers' losses begin to mount even before the separation, and that although they decline with time, they do not entirely disappear. Earnings losses are only slightly age- and gender-related. They recognize that their empirical findings on displaced workers' loss of earnings may not be representative of the losses experienced by workers who do not show strong labour force attachment, or of losses by displaced workers who left Pennsylvania (Jacobson et al., 1993b). However, Stevens (1997) found recently the effects of involuntary job separation to quite persistent, with the wages of displaced workers remaining approximately 9% below their expected levels for six or more years after the displacement. In an attempt to understand why the losses are so persistent, she shows that subsequent displacements are a strong contributing factor.

In Europe, Bacache et al. (1996), using the data of an « Enquête sur l'emploi », tried to find out if a period of unemployment restricts the earnings potential of displaced workers. Ceteris paribus, the wages of those who had held a job in the previous year were 12% higher than the wages of those who had been unemployed in the previous year. If one looks at the years between 1990 and 1994, the amount of the "premium" appears stable. The survey also confirms the American findings that length of service has an influence on the loss of earnings. Whereas employees with less than five years seniority enjoyed wage premiums amounting to about 8% compared to the wages of workers who had been unemployed in the previous year, employees with over 10 years of service benefited from 16% premiums. In order to calculate the earnings loss methodologically, the individual monthly wage (converted to logarithmic scale) has to be reduced to the variables which influence the productivity of the worker. Finally, the wage comparison was completed with a variable which represents the employment status of the worker in the period under consideration.

It is safe to assume that, in view of the difference of economic situation and the nature of labour relations, it would be inappropriate to attempt to apply the results of these studies to Switzerland.

---

[1] Displaced workers : « A displacement is defined as leaving due to a plant or business closing or due to being laid off or fired » (Stevens, 1997, p. 170). It includes virtually all involuntary job separations, with the exception of temporary layoffs and the ending of temporary jobs.

3 Data and Procedures

3.1 Data

This paper examines the effect which unemployment has on the subsequent level of wages. Using the SLFS data, we studied the loss of earnings of a group of workers who after being unemployed in 1994 were reemployed in 1995. We assessed this loss by observing the new wage levels of these workers. Our calculations provide an estimated loss of earnings, being the difference between the wage a worker could expect and the actual wage after unemployment. SLFS data manipulations are performed using the SPSS. Wage regressions are estimated using ordinary least square models with an E-View econometrics programme.

The literature references are either the Panel Study of Income Dynamics (i.e. Ruhm, 1991, Stevens, 1997), the Displaced Workers Survey, or state administrative records (i.e. Jacobson et al.,1993b), which include long wage histories free from the response biases that can arise with interview data. One advantage of the SLFS data used for our assessments is that it has a wider range of characteristics and demographic information, including workers' educational attainments, job histories and job tenure information. Moreover, the data permits us to identify the reasons for unemployment. The rotating nature of the SLFS makes its longitudinal use problematic however. We have therefore employed a statistical technique which makes good use of the main advantage of this sample: the large amount of information available.

The analysis is based on data from a survey of the Swiss Labour Force Survey (SLFS), which is carried out in the second quarter of each year. The 1995 survey gathered data from about 32,000 people. The method of the rotating panel, in which four fifths of the households from the previous year's survey are reinterviewed, makes it possible to conduct limited longitudinal analyses of individual wage histories.

Box 1   The random sample

The empirical analysis relies on microdata from the Swiss Labour Force Survey, SLFS, which the Swiss Federal Statistical Office has carried out in the second quarter of each year since the spring of 1991. The second quarter of 1995 thus marked SLFS's fifth anniversary. The survey serves above all to gather information about the employment structure and employment behaviour of the Swiss resident population, from the age of 15 up. Altogether some 18,000 people are asked to cooperate in the context of SLFS (random sample[1]). Answers provided by the established resident population, i.e. excluding seasonal workers, those on short-term permits, cross-border commuters and asylum seekers, are then weighted and extrapolated to the whole nation. In 1995, between two census years, the random sampling was extended exceptionally to 32,000 people. This increase made it possible for the first time to also carry out assessments on a cantonal basis, as up to 1,000 interviews were carried out in each canton. SLFS makes use of two types of questionnaire, a basic interview type (initial interview) and a panel interview (follow-up questionnaire). *In toto* the random sample consists of one fifth first interviews and fourth fifths follow-up questionnaires. The participating households are thus sounded five years running. The

---

[1] The basic strategy for selecting the addresses is that of random sampling, canton by canton, i.e. by means of computerised selection of the households from the Swiss telephone directory.

SLFS statistics have the advantage of containing sociodemographic data which make it possible to gain a deeper understanding of the day-to-day situation of the respondents (see also BFS, 1996a).

There are however certain problems with these statistics as an unemployment record. To begin with, they only tell us about the employment situation at a given point of the year, the so-called "reference week", i.e. the week which ended immediately before the interview, which is always held in April-June. A brief reentry of the labour market between two interviews would not appear in the statistics. Furthermore, longitudinal analyses relating to unemployment are based on few observations. If for example we wished to study reinsertion in the labour market after a period of unemployment, the possibilities are extremely limited, and it is for this reason that we have restricted the analysis to two years. Having to forego analysis of how wages are affected before unemployment period is of course not the optimal solution.

Our analysis is limited to roughly half of the unemployed[1] in 1994, who in 1995 managed to successfully rejoin the labour market. As Figure 1 shows, more than 40,000 of the almost 140,000 persons who were unemployed in 1994 were unable to make the transition back to a life of employment in the following year.

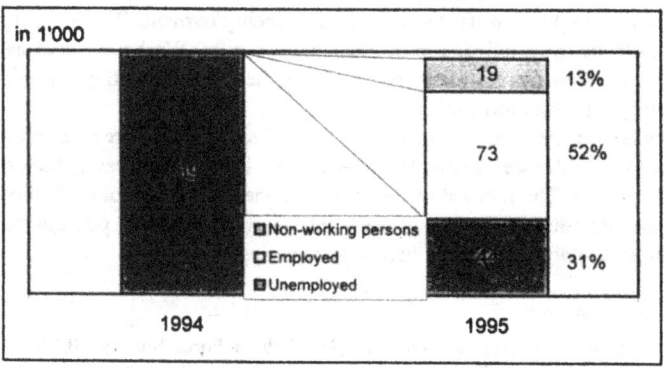

Figure 1 Situation of workers who experienced unemployment

3.2 Those Who Find Reemployment: A Portrait

One thing which the unemployed who manage to rejoin the labour market have in common is their youth. Some 46% of those who found work after being jobless were in the 15-29 age group, whereas just 26% of those already established in the labour market fall into this same age category. Another distinguishing factor of those who qualify as particularly reemployable is their high educational level: the proportion of those who had a university degree was twice as high as can be found in the labour market in general, and

---

[1] Neither conscripts in the Swiss army nor apprentices are counted in the statistics, which are extrapolated with the help of weights for longitudinal data, which in turn are based on the established resident population at the beginning and at the end of the year. The unemployed who have decided to leave Switzerland are thus not included in these statistics.

amounts to 15,4% of those reemployed. It is also interesting to note that almost a quarter of these people had not suffered any lengthy interruption (i.e. more than six months) in their employment "curriculum vitae" over the previous six years or more. Their experience of unemployment has thus been a brief one. As for the duration of unemployment, the data collected shows that more than half of those unemployed in the second quarter of 1994 had been without jobs for less than six months. Reinsertion in the labour market seems to be made easier with the help of very small firms in the manufacturing industries, and the public administration (Table 1).

Table 1   Labour market status in previous year of persons employed in 1995

1994 :	Employed	Unemployed
No. of cases	3198	65
Median age	36	30
Proportion of males	67.8%	72.3%
Swiss	84,1%	72,3%
University education	8.5%	15,4%
Employment with only brief interruption (i.e. not longer than 6 months) : 6+ years	85.2%	24,6%
Very small firm (up to 10 people.)	19.1%	43.1%
Professional position : trainee	0.1%	1.5%
Economic sector III	70.7%	66.2%
Resident in French-speaking Switzerland	41.8%	64.6%
Unempl period * : up to 6 months		55.4%
Unempl. Period * : 7-12 months		24.6%
Unempl period* : 13 months - 2 years		20.0%

*These figures relate to the year 1994.

3.3 Procedures

In the first place we assess the wage function with microdata for those who are not self-employed. This involves a regression formula with hourly wages for the year 1995 as the dependent variable. On the basis of another statistic, the wage structure survey (LSE), which is meant to assess the level and structure of wages for those in employment in Switzerland, the following explanatory variables were used (among others): gender, age category, seniority, nationality, educational level, professional position, size of company (number of employees). The regression model also included (0,1) variables for the particular industrial sector to which the company belongs and the canton of residence of the person concerned. The large size of the random sample, containing over 7,000 individual data, made it possible for us to isolate the factors which influence the hourly wage for the first time. The definitive regression coefficients for individuals who were employed in the years 1994 and 1995 were calculated for use at a later stage. The individual wages for those who were formerly unemployed were also estimated on the basis of this wage function and its characteristics, making it possible to calculate the individual differences between the estimated hourly wages and those actually found. We also managed to identify the factors which influence the differences.

The loss of earnings of workers who have experienced unemployment is formally defined as the difference between the earnings they could have expected if they had not lost their jobs and their actual earnings (for 1995). To make this definition more precise, we let w_i denote the wage of worker i in 1995 and let $D_i=1$ if worker i was unemployed in 1994 (and $D_i=0$ otherwise). The exact formula for the loss is thus:

$$E(w_i \mid D_i=0, F_i) - E(w_i \mid D_i=1, F_i) = E(w_i \mid D_i=0, F_i) - w_{i\,actual} \qquad (1)$$

where F_i is the information available in 1995 and

$$E(w_i \mid D_i=0, F_i) = \alpha + \beta X_i \qquad (2)$$

where X_i is a vector of observed characteristics for the worker and his job.

An alternative and complementary procedure for quantifying the loss of earnings after a period of unemployment involves the use of a dummy variable for the period of unemployment experienced in the previous year. Our procedure takes only a partial random sample into consideration in which those concerned were neither employed nor unemployed in 1994, but were employed in 1995. The coefficient of regression of the dummy variable estimates the average loss of earnings which someone who endured a period of unemployment would have to accept. Formula-wise our specification calls for a wage function in which a period of unemployment in the latter year is also to be taken into consideration by means of a dummy variable (D_i: 0,1) (see equation 3). On the basis of the outcome equation given by evaluation research, in which the wage is used to indicate the success or efficiency of an active measure, we obtain the following model:

$$w_i = \alpha + \beta X_i + \mu D_i + \varepsilon_i \qquad (3)$$

The wage of the person i in 1995 thus depends on economy-related socio-demographic factors (vector X), as well as on the circumstance of whether or not the person under study was unemployed or not (D). The β and the μ give the coefficients of regression, while α is the fixed effect. It is otherwise assumed that all extraneous factors are evenly distributed across all cases in the study.

As evaluation of the wage function plays a major role in the present study, we have taken the year 1995 as our reference point, since the data provides a relatively large partial sample with which we can work.[1] To avoid special circumstances such as those that might arise from a transition to pension rights, our sample takes only employees aged between 15 and 54. The gross hourly wage is a variable dependent on the wage function as we estimate it. The findings for 1995 show that Swiss employees between the ages of 15 and 54 who worked more than 37 hours per week were paid Sfr. 29.80 per hour. As just 4% of all employees in our sample had an hourly wage of over Sfr. 60 and such relatively high

---

[1] A relatively large basic sample is all the more important in view of the fact that a transposition of data across two years is carried out in step two.

levels of remuneration are difficult to assess, these cases have been eliminated from our study.

Box 2   Wage regression
Since the wage data available in Switzerland does not support long longitudinal analysis, our search for an equation for the individual wage is based on a cross section of data, namely that obtained from the SLFS. The dependent variable is the hourly wage of persons not independently employed. The hourly wage is calculated on the basis of the gross annual earned income divided by 52 and by the number of hours in the work week. We have limited our study to persons who work a minimum of 38 hours per week. The common conditioning factors of productivity and wage policy have been adopted as explanatory variables. We have begun by taking into consideration such individual characteristics as gender, age, nationality and educational level and the nature of the job. Also included are such indicators as the professional experience and accumulated, company-specific "human capital" of the employee concerned, such as long years of company service or a long period of employment uninterrupted for more than six months. Such company-specific variables as the size of the firm and its sector of activities are taken into account on the right side of the equation. Finally, we also take into account such geographical variables as the country of origin in the case of foreign workers, and the location concerned. The latter variables should reflect any region-specific wage differences. We have included only four dummy variables, for the three largest Swiss agglomerations (Zurich, Basle and Geneva), as for the canton of Ticino where the wages are particularly low, presumably due to the nearness of Italy and the presence of cross-border commuting workers. The inclusion of the country of origin for foreign workers should serve as a rough indicator as to the linguistic abilities of the person concerned. Apart from age, which is an absolute value on the right side of the equation, the other variables are shown only as values of 0 or 1 (dummy variables). All variables relate to the survey of 1995 (see also BFS, 1996b).

4 Findings

The wage function model can be said to work rather well, since almost 50% of the variance in the standard regression (assuming independence of variables) can be explained by the model ($R^2 \sim =0.45$). Generally speaking, the wages of women are considerably lower than those of men. The authors of the wage structure survey feel that this can be explained by women's overall lack of seniority, the frequency of job interruptions and their overrepresentation in the less well paid occupations. Since we have already taken seniority and job interruption into consideration, the unequal remuneration of men and women is more likely to be due to the predominance of women in secretarial jobs and in the "caring" professions. The jobs particularly associated with women, and in which they are indeed to be found in great numbers, are usually less well paid than typical male jobs. The findings also show clearly that foreigners tend to be less well paid than Swiss. This can be explained by their concentration in mainly low-wage occupations. A tertiary level education on the other hand seems to be a good guarantee for earning a high hourly wage. The positive sign of the coefficient of regression in relation to the educational level, seniority and uninterrupted employment tends to support the assumptions of the human capital theory.

Table 2   Wage function of the employed, in 1995

	Large sample 94: -- 95: employed	Full sample unemployed employed /employed	Employed sample (Reference group) employed employed	Reemployed sample unemployed employed
Sample	7850	3263	3198	65
Mean hourly wage	30.75	32.70	32.90	22.88
Median hourly wage	29.76	31.22	31.33	23.78
Std. Dev.	10.38	10.44	10.38	8.40
Variables:				
Male	3.74*	3.62*	3.71*	3.73*
Age	0.29*	0.31*	0.31*	0.32*
Nationality: Swiss	1.59*	2.03*	1.93*	2.05*
Secondary education	5.63*	5.22*	5.21*	5.17*
Tertiary education	11.84*	11.64*	11.62*	11.63*
Length of service (more than 6 years)	1.30*	1.56*	1.45*	1.42*
Public service	3.53*	2.56*	2.65*	2.87*
employment without any long interruptions (over 6 y)	2.84*	2.89*	2.46*	2.5*
Very small firms (up to 10)	-2.89*	-3.07*	-2.96*	-2.95*
Superior function	2.58*	3.22*	3.17*	3.18*
in company management	2.59*	1.40*	1.40*	1.48**
Economic sector:				
- bank/insurance	3.26*	3.46*	3.47*	3.54*
- transport/communications	1.15*	1.02**	1.08**	1.04**
Zurich canton	2.45*	2.01*	1.98*	2.04*
Geneva canton	2.81*	2.06*	1.99*	2.07*
Basle city, Basle region canton	0.82**	1.04***	1.03***	1.00
Ticino canton	-2.15*	-2.82*	-2.87*	-2.81*
Foreigners from Sri Lanka, Albania, Turkey, the former Yugoslavia	-2.42*	-2.56***	-2.86**	-2.72
Constant	5.72*	5.65*	6.03*	5.78*
Dummy for unemployment (1994)			-5.28*	
R-squared	0.461730	0.449253	0.453648	0.449927
Adjusted R-squared	0.460462	0.446108	0.450353	0.446726
S.E. of regression	7.575411	7.731208	7.701523	7.696755
Durbin-Watson stat	1.952710	1.924379	1.938303	1.932852

* $p \leq 0.01$; ** $0.01 < p \leq 0.05$; *** $0.05 < p \leq 0.10$.

The first important finding is that wages react to even a short period of unemployment. As can be seen in the third column of Table 2, the loss of earnings resulting from a period of unemployment amounts to Sfr. 5.30 on average, or about 16% of the average hourly wage. Secondly, as Figure 2 clearly indicates, more than 70% of those who were employed in 1995 and who had experienced unemployment in the previous year were obliged to accept a loss of earnings, compared to their estimated wage. If we consider only those who suffer a loss of earnings, then the average loss amounts to Sfr. 8.70, corresponding to a third of the average estimated hourly wage. On the other hand, those who in 1995 earned more than was expected enjoyed an average wage gain of Sfr. 3.20 (10% of the median wage).

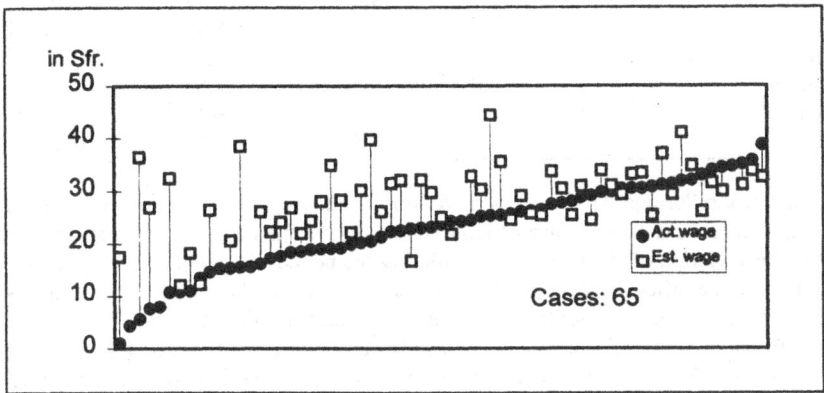

Figure 2 Expected and actual earnings of workers after a period of unemployment

Thirdly, in Table 3 we identify the variables which have a significant influence on the loss of earnings.[1] This shows that Swiss nationals and persons in management positions are the most likely to suffer a loss of earnings in conditions of reemployment. In our view, these findings can be explained in part by the fact that the rates paid to foreign workers are already so low as to make further wage cuts almost impossible, and also in part to the fact that companies are introducing flatter management structures, and that the new jobs are likely to be with smaller firms. It also seems to be the case that people who owe their reinsertion in the world of work to the help of a public administration have to accept a considerable loss of earnings, presumably due to the transformation of temporary employment contracts into more permanent arrangements. Another possible explanation is that the level of remuneration in the public sector, which was formerly higher, has been

---

[1] We have tested the influence of the variables already used for wage regression on the difference between the expected wage and the actual wage, due to the individual and job-related variables. Furthermore we have included in the analysis a few unemployment-related dummy variables, such as the duration of the previous unemployment up to the second quarter of 1994, registration with a public or private employment agency, the reason for leaving the last job, and the person's willingness to move if necessary to a new job location. And we have created two new variables, for the current occupation (in 1996) and current self classification as to economic sector, for the earlier coded occupation and the related economic sector of unemployed person's former company. These represent the possible change of occupation and economic sector with the values 0 and 1.

reduced in line with budget-cutting measures whose effect is restricted to those newly employed in this sector.

Table 3 Comparison

	$E(w_i)$	w_i	$E(w_i) - w_i$
Sample	65	65	65
Mean	28.73	22.88	5.26
Median	29.40	23.78	4.76
Std. Dev.	6.45	8.40	7.93
Maximum	44.38	38.69	30.65
Minimum	12.11	1.09	-6.82
Skewness	-0.31	-0.46	0.88
Probability	0.55	0.27	0.01

Addison and Portugal (1989) show moreover that the length of the intervening period of unemployment is a major cause of reduced earnings in the new job. One explanation might be depreciation of the human capital during the period of unemployment, together with the "stigma effect" of unemployment, and a fall in the reservation wage as unemployment insurance benefits come to an end. According to their findings, a 10% increase in the duration of unemployment will lower the wage in the next job by 0.6%-0.8%. However, they also report evidence of simultaneity between the post-displacement wage and the duration of unemployment. Our own analysis confirms that the length of unemployment does play a role. Strangely however, only the medium length of unemployment of between 7-12 months seems to act as a discriminatory factor, a phenomenon for which there is no apparent explanation.

Moreover Addison and Portugal (1989) find that a change of economic sector or occupation has a major impact on the wage level, amounting to a loss of earnings of 18.1% and 13.5% respectively. Our own analysis however indicates that such changes have no significant influence on the subsequent wage level.

Finally, the actual hourly wage after a period of unemployment was included in the study as an explanatory variable for the loss of earnings. We have come to the conclusion that, ceteris paribus, the lower the actual hourly wage after reemployment, the higher will be the loss of earnings when compared to those who had a job in the previous year. Since the estimated hourly wage is not a significant explanatory variable for the loss of earnings after a period of unemployment, we may exclude the possibility that quantification of the loss of earnings depends on the procedures which we have adopted. It is also interesting and indeed gratifying to note that those who were registered with a public sector employment bureau had a smaller loss of earnings.

Table 4 Factors which influence the difference

Sample	65		
Mean	5.26		
Median	4.76		
Variable:			
Constant			8.74*
Actual post-displacement wage			-1.02*
Nationality : Swiss	4.44*	3.17**	
Male			4.22*
Age			0.26*
Secondary education			8.07*
Tertiary education			14.83*
Public service	9.22*	8.88*	
Superior function			2.96*
in company management	11.83*	13.10*	
Length of unempl: 7-12 months		4.37**	
Registered by public placement offices			-2.11*
R-squared	0.261155	0.325765	0.935298
Adjusted R-squared	0.234768	0.288989	0.926418
S.E . of regression	6.935870	6.685634	2.150758
Durbin-Watson stat	2.269427	2.477024	1.698052

* $p \leq 0.01$; ** $0.01 < p \leq 0.05$; $0.05 < p \leq 0.10$.

5 Conclusions

The main conclusion of our analysis is that workers who have experienced a period of unemployment have to endure a loss of earnings at the time of reemployment: The post-displacement earnings fall below the level such workers could have expected had they not experienced a period of unemployment. The study shows that unemployment insurance benefits paid to unemployed workers only compensate for a portion of the medium-to-long-term losses which result from unemployment.

In our attempt to quantify post-displacement earnings losses we have come to the conclusion that, compared to someone who remained in employment, the average loss of a person who experienced a period of unemployment in the previous year amounted to 16% of the average hourly wage for the full sample. We also found that roughly 70% of those reemployed were affected by a real loss of earnings, amounting to an average of 26% of the average hourly wage. In other words, two thirds of those who were unemployed found their wages in the new position to be between 20% and 30% lower than the insured wage, i.e. it corresponds more or less to the amount paid as unemployment benefit.

Other Swiss studies based on interviews with a representative sample of formerly unemployed persons selected at random have produced similar results. The IPSO study of the quality of reemployment (1995) for example has shown that only one third of those who had been unemployed found themselves earning more in their new jobs. For the vast majority, there was either no change worth mentioning compared to the pre-displacement status quo, or there was a loss of earnings. This confirms our own findings. It should be noted however that these results concern only differences with the wages of the last position prior to the period of unemployment, so that quantification of the earnings loss is not possible. Another interesting aspect of the IPSO study is that it took into consideration the motives for accepting a wage equal to or less than the last one. The most frequently given reason for doing so was simply a desire to "get back to work at long last" (68%). This leads to the conclusion that the experience of unemployment is a burden, to be removed at the first opportunity, even if it means a loss of earnings. Secondly, the IPSO study reaches the conclusion that persons who have others to support are more often forced to take a wage cut than those free of such responsibilities, and are correspondingly less likely to make a wage gain. In the case of those earning high salaries, the outplacement consultant Econova (1996), which specializes mainly in the recruitment of top managers,[1] notes that 18% of its candidates in the year 1996 had to be content with a lower salary in their new positions that they had ever accepted before.

The research of Aeppli et al. (1996) focuses on those unemployed who have come to the end of their unemployment benefit entitlement. This showed that half of those who at the time of the interview had been reemployed were earning just about two thirds less than was the case prior to being displaced. In this context, it is above all the eldest of those who lost their benefit rights, i.e. those over 49 years of age, who had to accept the fact that if they were ever to find work again they would have to accept lower earnings. Roughly a third had to settle for 25% less, while 16% of those in this category had to accept a loss of earnings of 50% and more compared to their pre-displacement wages. Another interesting fact is that 45% of the participating out-of-benefit workers who managed to find reemployment were paid wages below the level of their former unemployment insurance. They thus accepted work which the terms of unemployment insurance define as "unacceptable", i.e. work which pays less than the unemployment benefit.

From a purely methodological point of view it must be pointed out, simple comparisons between wages before and after a period of unemployment are highly questionable for several reasons. To begin with it has been proven, on the basis of longitudinal data from the United States, that wage levels had already begun to fall three years before the period of unemployment in question. And secondly, such comparisons do not take into account growth in wages which takes place without any reference to a period of unemployment (Jacobson et al., 1993). For these reasons we think it makes sense to make comparisons with an econometrically constructed control group.

We were unable to verify whether or not the impact of displacements is merely transitory, i.e. that initially workers might accept unstable positions with low wages and later move on to more secure jobs and better pay.

---

[1] Some 94% of these candidates had salaries of more than Sfr 101,000 p.a., which is far higher than the earnings of any of the former unemployed in our analysis.

6 Assessment from the Economic Policy Point of View

Switzerland has one of the highest ratios for the replacement of unemployment benefit in the world.[1] According to the job search theory, a high level of unemployment benefit should lead to high reservation wages and a reduction in search costs. This leads to a low probability of re-employment[2] and a long period of unemployment. However, the effect of the level of benefit on the post-displacement wage is not clear in theoretical terms, and is also unresolved at the empirical level (see also Maani, 1993). We can assume, that the unemployed person will first try to find a job with a wage above the level of unemployment benefit, which in Switzerland means that the reservation wage would correspond to about 70-80% of the pre-displacement wage. A high benefit replacement ratio level thus increases the duration of unemployment and may explain the large proportion of long-term unemployment (≈30%), which is one cause of the current problem of how to ensure the financing of unemployment insurance. This in turn explains the political pressure for a reduction of benefit, i.e. demands for a decrease of the duration of unemployment benefit eligibility, or in any case a reduction in the benefit replacement ratio. Sheldon (i.e.1996) supports the idea that a policy geared to quick reintegration of the jobless requires a dramatic shortening of the period of benefit entitlement.

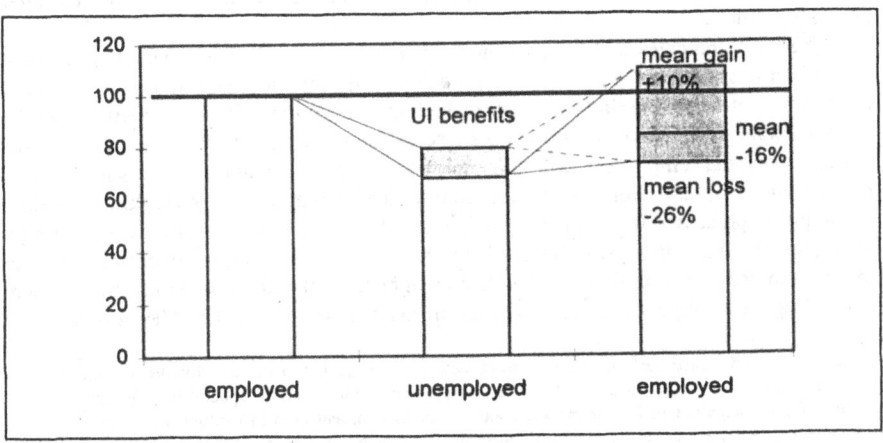

Figure 3   The effect on wages

---

[1] In Switzerland the benefit level takes into account the family situation, and disabilities. Unemployed who are married with dependents to support and/or who have a handicap receive 80 per cent of their last gross wage. Others are entitled to 70 per cent. If the daily allowance exceeds the limit of Sfr. 130 it is reduced by 3%, and if it is exactly Sfr. 130 or less than that amount, it is reduced by 1%. For persons with children to support the reduction is also 1%. Social security contributions are deducted from unemployment benefits, as is income tax which differs from canton to canton .

[2] Maani's (1993) results for New Zealand indicate that a higher unemployment benefit replacement ratio is associated with a lower probability of reemployment, but also leads to a higher post-displacement wage, mainly through a reservation wage effect.

The revised Swiss law on unemployment insurance (AVIG) came into effect in two stages, one in 1996 and the other in 1997. The second stage of the revision requires unemployed persons to actively seek reinsertion in the labour market. The Federal Assembly's idea in making this change was to reduce the average duration of the job-hunting period. The new philosophy aims to shift the emphasis from the passive receiving of benefit, to an active reemployment policy. The new system also gives the unemployed person the right to two years of benefit, amounting to 520 days. The unemployed are obliged to participate in labour market measures, insofar as the canton is able to offer them a training scheme or targeted temporary employment.[1] Moreover, thanks to the creation of 150 new regional placement offices (RAVs)[2] throughout Switzerland, the unemployed are now better supported and advised. The creation of these centres above all means of more professional level of state involvement in helping the jobseeker to find new jobs and in counselling them. This should contribute to a reduction in the length of time between displacement and reemployment. The new creed of "Counselling rather than rubber-stamping" is thus being put into action. Today the regional placement offices have a total staff of 1,850, who among other things are expected to be familiar with post-displacement wage expectations and wage structures, particularly in view of the new tougher ruling on job acceptability. There is thus a great need for better public information in relation to the wage levels that can realistically be expected after unemployment.

The study indicates that the most unemployed persons will face a post-displacement loss of earnings, due in part to lower probability of reemployment and also to a high unemployment benefit replacement ratio which may have the effect of reducing both the accepted wage through adjustments in the reservation wage, and the offered wage in cases where potential employers take unemployment or its duration as a sign of low productivity (stigmatisation) or as a criterion in determining the wage (ranking criterion, in the hiring process[3]). It is extremely important therefore, in view of the relatively high unemployment benefits paid in Switzerland, that those counselling the unemployed try to make them accept the falling wage potential right from the start, so as to prevent them from clinging to wage demands which are in many cases unrealistic. The new law also

---

[1] Those who do not participate in labour market measures are entitled to 150 or 250/400 "normal" days of benefit. Subsequently, up to the end of the two-year entitlement period, special benefits may be paid either for participation in labour market measures or as compensation in cantons which are unable to offer such measures. As of 1.1.1997 eligibility for the maximum number of days no longer depends on how long contributions have been made but rather on the age of the insured person: those who are aged 50 or less may be entitled to up to 150 "normal" benefit days, those aged 50-60 to up to 250 days and those over 60 to up to 400 days.

[2] The duties of the RAV centres can be described as follows:
- Providing the job seeker with counselling and other assistance (As of 1998, employment centres must be in a position to provide each person with a counselling and control session once a month.)
- Keeping regular contacts with employers, obtaining and disseminating information on job vacancies
- Preselection of suitable candidates for vacant positions
- Implementation of active labour market measures with appropriate professional counselling
- Application of the criteria with regard to acceptable employment
  Imposing sanctions, insofar as this is not the responsibility of the cantonal authorities.

[3] Blanchard, Diamond (1994) support the assumption that ranking by duration is important. When firms receive multiple acceptable applications, they tend to hire the worker who has been unemployed for the least amount of time.

uses the intermittent pay rule to this end. In the event that the insured person accepts a new job at a lower wage than the insured earnings (benefit) during the eligibility period, the person will be entitled to compensation for any loss of earnings for days when intermittent pay were obtained. Loss of earnings is taken to mean the difference between the intermittent earnings obtained in the control period, or in any case the minimum normally paid for the type of work in the location in question, and the amount covered by unemployment insurance.[1] It is worth bearing in mind at this point that there is little or not room for manoeuvre with regard to the level of unemployment benefit necessary in Switzerland. This is because of the high cost of living (tax system, rent level, obligatory health insurance, etc.), which is such that even at present there is a rather large number of unemployed who in addition to their employment benefit need social assistance to make ends meet. In this sense, any reduction in the replacement ratio would only shift the burden from the federal government to the cantons and to other forms of social security. Moreover, forced reintegration through low replacement rates would only increase the number of "working poor". The findings of Maani suggest that, due to higher replacement ratios, a lengthy job search period also tends to increase the post-displacement wage level.

A more complete demonstration of the findings would require dynamic analysis with the help of panel data that takes post-displacement wage changes into account, including the possibility of a "catching-up" effect. This has not yet been undertaken. The considerable lack of research in this area is mainly due to the scarcity of available data. Since SLFS data is not particularly suited to longitudinal analysis, the Swiss Federal Office for Industry and Labour has instead ordered a study on wage histories, to be based on administrative data. The first findings are due to be known at the end of this year.

References

Addison, J.T. and Portugal, P. (1989), Job Displacement, Relative Wage Change, and Duration of Unemployment, *Journal of Labor Economics*, Vol. 7, No.3, pp. 281-302.

Aeppli, D., Hotz, C., Hugentobler, V., Theiss, R. (1996), *Die Situation der Ausgesteuerten*, im Auftrag des BIGA, Bern.

Bacache, M., Paserot, R., Peltan, S.(1996), Conséquences du passage par le chômage sur la carrière professionnelle. Analyse économique d'un stigmate, Direction de la Prévision, *Document de travail*, No. 96-11, Déc. 1996.

BFS (1996a), *Die Schweizerische Arbeitskräfteerhebung (SAKE), Konzepte, Methodische Grundlagen, Praktische Ausführung*, Bern.

BFS (1996b), *Die Schweizerische Lohnstrukturerhebung 1994, Kommentierte Ergebnisse und Tabellen*, Bern.

Blanchard, O.J. and Diamond, P.(1994), Ranking, Unemployment Duration, and Wages, *Review of Economic Studies*, Vol. 61, pp. 417-434.

Econova (1996), *Erfahrungszahlen 1996*, Manuskript.

IPSO (1995), *Die Qualität der Wiederbeschäftigung nach Arbeitslosigkeit*, im Auftrag des BIGA, Bern.

Jacobson, L.S., LaLonde, R.J. and Sullivan, D.G.(1993a), Earnings losses of Displaced Workers, *The American Economic Review*, Vol. 83, No.4, pp. 685-709.

---

[1] In our research it was not possible to discover how many formerly unemployed persons had made use of this instrument. Only 49, or 10 of the 65 formerly unemployed persons, had a contract for a new job in 1995, either with or without a time limit.

Jacobson, L.S., LaLonde, R.J. and Sullivan, D.G.(1993b), *The Cost of Worker Dislocation*, W. E. Upjohn Institute for Employment Research, Kalamazoo, Michigan.

Maani, A.A. (1993), Post-Unemployment Wages, the Probability of Re-Employment, and the Unemployment Benefit, *New Zealand Economic Papers*, Vol. 27, No.1, pp. 35-55.

Ruhm, C.J. (1991), Are Workers Permanently Scarred by Job Displacement, *The American Economic Review*, Vol. 81, No.1, pp. 319-324.

Sheldon, G. (1996), *Unemployment and Unemployment Insurance in Switzerland*, Manuscript, University of Basle.

Stevens, A.H. (1997), Persistent Effects of Job Displacement: The Importance of Multiple Job Losses, *Journal of Labor Economics*, Vol. 15, No.1, pp. 165-188.

Topel, R. (1990), Specific Capital and Unemployment: Measuring the Costs and Consequences of Job Loss, *Carnegie-Rochester Conference Series on Public Policy*, Vol. 33, North-Holland, pp. 181-214.

20 A Time Series and Cross Sectional Analysis of Consumer Sentiment and its Components

Detelina Ivanova / Kajal Lahiri[*]

1 Introduction

The Index of Consumer Sentiment (ICS) compiled by the University of Michigan's Survey Research Center (SRC) has often been found to move similar to the business cycle path of the U. S. economy. The 1990-91 recession has been widely attributed to a drop in consumer confidence in the wake of Iraq's invasion of Kuwait.[1] The index has typically led other business cycles as well, and three of its five components are explicitly included in the Conference Board's Index of Leading Economic Indicators.[2] Numerous studies have found the ICS to be helpful in predicting consumption expenditures both on durables and nondurables. However, no definite consensus has emerged as to why measures of consumer sentiment such as the ICS have such explanatory power, or what is it that the index actually captures - consumers' perception of the overall uncertainty in the economy, their optimism or pessimism about future economic conditions, or expectations about personal economic factors (Mishkin 1978). Many studies have investigated the relationship between the ICS and observable macroeconomic variables at the aggregate level using time-series techniques. They find that in normal times a very large proportion of the movement in the ICS can be explained by movements in such economy-wide variables as the inflation and unemployment rates, recession headline news, and the job rating of the existing administration (Lovell 1975, Blood and Phillips 1995). However, in times of unusual aggregate uncertainty econometric models of sentiment seem to break down as sentiment wanders away from the current macroeconomic variables, and a very large proportion of the variation in the index remains unexplained.

It is our view therefore that a proper investigation of why consumer sentiment helps predict consumption should start with a determination of the causes of sentiment at the individual level. This paper is our first attempt to summarize results from an analysis of the five individual ICS components using household data from Michigan's Survey of

---

[*] We thank Jae-Young Kim and Thad Mirer for helpful comments.
[1] See, for example, Throop (1992), Walsh (1993), and Carroll, Fuhrer, and Wilcox (1994).
[2] See Lahiri and Moore (1991) and Zarnowitz (1992).

Consumer Attitudes and Behavior (SCAB). The plan of the paper is as follows: in the next section we describe the design of SCAB and the data we use. We then proceed to analyze the relationships between the five components of ICS in a time series context. We are specifically interested in uncovering relationships of Granger-causality and cointegration among the five components. We find two 'major movers' among these. We then estimate a VAR in the five components and consider impulse responses to unit shocks in the two 'main movers' in the context of this VAR. Given our findings of Granger-causality, contemporaneousness, and cointegration, we then proceed to examine the determinants of each of the five index components in the household data from the SCAB using an ordered logit model. We determine how much of the variation in each component is due to an individual's expectations/perceptions of his own economic conditions, those regarding the economy, and how much is due to personal idiosyncratic factors. We unravel the major determinants of each component.

2 Description of Survey and Data

The ICS was developed by Katona (1951), and the SRC has continued to produce it on a regular basis to measure consumer confidence in the U.S. The ICS has generally led business cycles and in 1989 the Commerce Department specifically included three of its components in the revised Composite Index of Leading Indicators. The SRC's Survey of Consumer Attitudes and Behavior (SCAB), on which the ICS is based, has been conducted quarterly since 1952 and monthly since 1978. The five questions the responses to which are used to construct the ICS are given below, with their respective range of answers:

PerFin-Current
Responses to:
'We are interested in how people are getting along financially these days. Would you say that you (and your family living there) are financially better off or worse off financially than you were a year ago?'
Coded
1 Better Off
3 Same
5 Worse Off

PerFin-Expected
Responses to:
'Now looking ahead - do you think that a year from now you (and your family living there) will be better off financially or worse off, or just about the same as now?'
Coded
1 Better Off
3 Same
5 Worse Off

BusCond-12m
Responses to:

'Now turning to business conditions in the country as a whole - do you think that during the next 12 months we'll have good times financially, or bad times, or what?'
Coded
1 Good times
2 Good with Qualifications
3 Pro-Con
4 Bad with Qualifications
5 Bad times
Responses (1,2) and (4,5) are grouped together for Index construction.
BusCond-5y
Responses to:
'Looking ahead, which would you say is more likely - that in the country as a whole we'll have continuous good times during the next 5 years or so, or that we'll have periods of widespread unemployment or depression, or what?'
Coded
1 Good times
2 Good with Qualifications
3 Pro-Con
4 Bad with Qualifications
5 Bad times
Responses (1,2) and (4,5) are grouped together for Index construction.
BuyCond-Present
Responses to:
'About the big things people buy for their homes - such as furniture, refrigerator, stove, television, and things like that. Generally speaking do you think now is a good or a bad time to buy major household items?'
Coded
1 Good
3 Pro-Con
5 Bad
From the responses to these five questions the so-called component relatives are computed as follows:

(% respondents who answer better/good – % respondents who answer worse/bad) +100

The simple average of the five relatives is then computed to obtain the ICS. For our time series analysis we use monthly data on the ICS and the five component relatives dating from 1978:1 through 1996:12 (228 observations). The data was obtained from the SRC's last available publication on the ICS.

The design of SCAB allows us to extract a lot more information about individual's expectations/perceptions of general and personal economic conditions, as well as personal characteristics than is contained in the five index questions alone. Specifically, there are questions regarding an individual's perception about how the economy has done over the past one year, how the government is doing its job at present, and whether the individual has heard any good or bad 'news' about the general economic and political situation. There are also questions about the individual's expectations about general economic conditions over the next year, about prices, real income, unemployment, and interest rate on borrowing, all with answers in the three-response framework - better/same/worse.

There is also information about the respondent's employment status, education, marital status, sex, race, age, region of residence, and annual income. In short, in addition to responses to the five index questions, we use information on more than 20 other questions to explain responses to each of the component questions at the individual level. We used raw data sets from monthly SCAB from 1978:1 through 1989:1 with six exceptions (1978:10, 1988:4 - 1988:6, 1988:8 and 1988:9) due to errors or omissions in the data sets. This gave us a total of 115 data files combined in one, each raw data file having between 500 and 1,000 observations. Households for which data was missing for at least one question were discarded. This rather time-consuming process left us with a total of 52,506 observations for the final analysis of the household data.

3 Time Series Analysis

As is evident from their definitions, the five questions whose responses form the ICS appear to be interrelated. Respondents are being asked to compare their current personal financial situation to the same one year ago, and then to form an expectation about their financial situation over the one-year horizon. The questions also ask about expected change in general economic conditions over the one-year and the five-year horizons. Finally, there is the question about current buying condition for major household items. Since some studies show that the current conditions component of the index (CIND, questions 1, 5) performs better in some cases than ICS as a whole (Throop 1992), and others have found that the expectations component (questions 2, 3, and 4) is superior as a leading indicator of recessions (Zarnowitz 1992) it is interesting to examine the time-series properties of the five series and their relationships, and more specifically the Granger-causality relationships between the five components. Intuition would suggest that if expectations are on average correct, and if the personal financial situation follows the path of the economy (i.e. improving in boom, deteriorating in recession), then the expectations questions concerning the respondent's financial situation (PerFin-Expected) and business conditions (BusCond-12m) next year would Granger-cause the question concerning the respondent's current personal financial situation. It is less clear whether only personal or only general questions should affect the last question (BuyCond), or how the five-year business outlook question (BusCond-5y) should be related to the rest. Our analysis is also concerned with another major issue in determining why sentiment affects consumption, namely what is it that ICS measures. We would expect that if the five questions in the index indeed measure expectations/perceptions about the economy and the individuals are rational then potentially there will not be any relationship between the five components, since some of them refer to personal, others to general economic conditions, with different horizons. On the other hand, if the five questions measure a single unobservable variable - 'consumer attitude' - then we would expect the five components of the index to be strongly related in terms of Granger-causality and cointegration.

3.1 Stationarity Tests

We first examine the stationarity properties of the five components of the ICS and the ICS itself using only monthly time series data. Plots of historical data on the ICS and its components suggest possible nonstationarity in all series. All of the components and hence the index are restricted to be between 0 and 200 by construction; furthermore, the series exhibit no evidence of time trends, so to test stationarity we have used the augmented Dickey-Fuller test with a constant and no time trend. Standard F-tests of lag-length show the relevant model to be

$$H_0: y_t = \xi \Delta y_{t-1} + y_{t-1} + \varepsilon_t$$
$$H_1: y_t = \xi \Delta y_{t-1} + \alpha + \rho y_{t-1} + \varepsilon_t$$

The hypothesis of unit root presence is accepted at the 5% level for the index and all components except PerFin-Expected, for which it is accepted at the 1% level. The F-statistic for testing the joint null of $\rho = 1$, $\alpha = 0$ exceeds the 5% critical value for all series, and we conclude that the somewhat upward movement in the series over the sample period has been generated by a positive constant component.

Though an investigation of the time series properties of the components is lacking in the literature, research has found no evidence of unit root in the index when quarterly data is used (Carroll et al. 1994). This is in contrast with our findings of a random walk with a drift in our sample of monthly data.[1] This suggests we should adopt appropriate correction for nonstationarity before proceeding with the VAR estimation and the Granger-causality tests.

3.2 Granger-Causality Tests

Since tests of cointegration on any two of the components separately reject the hypothesis of cointegration, we examine the Granger-causality relationships between the variables in a first-difference framework (respective results from regressions in levels are shown in Table 1, but these may be subject to spurious regression faults). We use the following 12-lag autoregressive distributed lag model to test for Granger-Causality relationships:

$$\Delta y_t = \alpha + \beta_1 \Delta y_{t-1} + ... + \beta_{12} \Delta y_{t-12} + \gamma_1 \Delta z_{t-1} + ... + \gamma_{12} \Delta z_{t-12} + \varepsilon_t$$

Results from the F-test of the hypothesis

$$H_0: \gamma_1 = ... = \gamma_{12} = 0$$

are shown in Table 1.

One of the components, BusCond-12m appears to Granger-cause all of the other four components of the index. BusCond-12m in turn is Granger-caused only by PerFin-

---

[1] Our evidence of non-stationarity of ICS is consistent with those in Blood and Phillips (1995) who also used monthly data.

Current. The above suggests that the two variables (expectations about business conditions over the 1 year horizon and the evaluation of present personal financial situation) are perhaps contemporaneously determined. It is interesting that although PerFin-Current Granger-causes BusCond-12m, PerFin-Expected is Granger-caused by BusCond-12m only, but not by the more intuitive candidate PerFin-Current, suggesting that expectations of general economic conditions are a better predictor of the expected financial situation over the 1 year horizon than personal factors. Also it would be one's intuition that PerFin-Expected should Granger-cause PerFin-Current, if respondents' predictions about the overall change in personal financial situation is accurate. It would also be understandable if PerFin-Current Granger-caused PerFin-Expected since the former is expected to be a major item in the information set used to form the latter. However, here we do not find a direct relationship between the two personal questions. BusCond-5y appears to Granger cause PerFin-Current which may be simply a result of the high correlation between BusCond-12m and BusCond-5y, or it may reflect accuracy of 'prediction' over the 5 year horizon such that personal financial situation which is influenced by business conditions, follows the path expected over the 5 year horizon for general business conditions. BuyCond-Present is Granger-caused by both PerFin-Current and BusCond-12m. The latter can be viewed again as accuracy of 'prediction' (evaluation of present buying conditions follows the expectation of general business conditions over the 1 year horizon). Overall, it seems two variables generate the long-run motion of the index - one personal (PerFin-Current) and one general (BusCond-12m).

Since some of these results seem counterintuitive and to avoid the danger of incorrect Granger-causality test results because of omitted information, we examine some of the relationships above in an expanded 3-variable framework. First, since PerFin-Current appeared to be Granger-caused by both BusCond-12m and BusCond-5y, we examine the Granger-causality of BusCond-5y to PerFin-Current in the presence of BusCond-12m. This amounts to testing the restrictions

$$\gamma_1 = ... = \gamma_{12} = 0$$

in the model

$$\Delta y_t = \alpha + \beta_1 \Delta y_{t-1} + ... + \beta_{12} \Delta y_{t-12} + \delta_1 \Delta x_{t-1} + ... + \delta_{12} \Delta x_{t-12} \\ + \gamma_1 \Delta z_{t-1} + ... + \gamma_{12} \Delta z_{t-12} + \varepsilon_t \tag{1}$$

where y_t stands for PerFin-Current, x_t for BusCond-12m, and z_t for BusCond-5y. Results for this and other three-variable Granger-causality tests are shown in Table 2. The F-statistic for testing these restrictions is $0.85 < F_{12, 178, 0.05} = 1.80$, and the asymptotic χ^2 test statistic is $12.31 < \chi^2_{12, 0.05} = 21.0$. Therefore Granger-causality of BusCond-5y to PerFin-Current in the bivariate framework is due to the omission of the more fundamental factor BusCond-12m.

Another finding we explore further is the Granger-causality of PerFin-Current to BusCond-12m. This finding suggests that one-year ahead expectations about business conditions are formed based on past personal financial performance. A more intuitive idea however would be that one-year ahead expectations about personal finances and business conditions are formed simultaneously, and hence one would expect PerFin-Expected to Granger-cause BusCond-12m. Since the bivariate tests did not reveal such relationship, we test the Granger-causality of PerFin-Current to BusCond-12m in the presence of PerFin-Expected. The tests do not reject Granger-causality (see Table 2 for test statistics and critical values) at the 5% level. Hence we conclude that Granger-causality of PerFin-Current to BusCond-12m is not due to the effect of PerFin-Expected being omitted, and that indeed past financial performance at the personal level helps predict one-year ahead business outlook.

Another relationship worth investigating further is the Granger-causality of both PerFin-Current and BusCond-12m to BuyCond. To eliminate the possibility of one of these relationships being due to omitted information we test Granger-causality of PerFin-Current to BuyCond in the presence of BusCond-12m (framework is same as in (1)), with test statistics and critical values shown in Table 2. Granger-causality of PerFin-Current to BuyCond is not rejected. We also test Granger-causality of BusCond-12m to BuyCond in the presence of PerFin-Current with results shown in Table 2 - Granger-causality is not rejected again. PerFin-Current and BusCond-12m each appear to independently Granger-cause BuyCond. This is unexpected, since BuyCond is asked in a general frame of mind and refers to present buying conditions. In this sense it is counterintuitive that it should be caused by a question referring to personal current financial situation. The result implies that, to some extent, consumers generalize about overall macroeconomic condition based on their own personal experience. This is consistent with Linden (1982) who argued that people are indeed sensitive to personal day-to-day economic experiences in forming their perceptions of the state of the economy.

Since both PerFin-Current and BusCond-12m show significance in terms of Granger-causality to the rest of the components of the index and to each other, it makes sense to look at the relationship among the five variables in a VAR framework and study the impulse responses of the five components to unit shocks in each of these two fundamental variables. Before attempting to estimate a VAR in the five components we should check if all five variables are cointegrated. As all of our five components are I(1), in the absence of cointegration VAR in first differences would be consistent. However, as the graphs suggest, there may be some cointegration relationship between all five of the ICS components, due to which they do not drift apart but rather move together over time. If this is the case, then VAR in first differences will not be consistent but an error correction will be in order.

3.3 Cointegration Tests

As neither theory nor intuition provides us with any suggestions about possible cointegration relationships between the five components of the index, we use Johansen's FIML method to test for the number of cointegrating relationships and to estimate the cointegration vector(s).[1] We use the model

$$\Delta y_t = \xi_1 \Delta y_{t-1} + \ldots + \xi_4 \Delta y_{t-4} + \alpha + \xi_0 y_{t-1} + \varepsilon_t \tag{2}$$

---

[1] See Hamilton (1994).

where y_t is a 5x1 vector containing values of the five components in the order in which they were listed previously. Since we did not rule out drifts in any of the components, we do not impose any restrictions on α. Eigenvalues from the Johansen procedure are shown in Table 3. The table also shows Maximum Eigenvalue statistic and Trace statistic along with critical values, and also Maximum Eigenvalue statistic and Trace statistic computed when a small-sample correction of T-nm (m=26, number of coefficients estimated in single equation, and n=5, number of variables in VAR) is used instead of T.

The null of no cointegration is rejected by both tests at the 5% level. The maximum eigenvalue test suggests a single cointegration relationship. The trace test statistic marginally rejects $p \leq 1$ (p is the rank of cointegration, number of cointegrating relationships) and accepts the hypothesis if small-sample correction of T-nm is used. We conclude that one cointegrating relationship exists. The table also shows the cointegration relationship subject to the restriction p=1. The existing cointegration relationship among the five components does not render itself to a straightforward interpretation. However we can take it as evidence in support of the conjecture that the five questions actually measure the same underlying 'attitude' and hence averaging the five components to compute the index is justified.

3.4 VAR in Error-correction Form

The findings of cointegration among the series suggest that the relationship among the five components should be examined in a VAR in error-correction form. The model is same as in (2). In light of the Granger-causality findings in the previous section we used the VAR in error-correction form to estimate impulse responses for 24 months ahead of each of the five components to unit shocks in the two 'fundamental' components - PerFin-Current and BusCond-12m (which we do not present here for lack of space). Although impulse responses to one-standard deviation shocks are more common in the literature, we choose unit shocks since they represent the effect of the change of 1 point in the relative for the fundamental component on each of the five components of the index. We find that an increase by 1 unit in the relative for PerFin-Current leads to increases of magnitude between 0.1 and 0.5 in each of the other four components, with largest magnitudes occurring 1 month (BusCond-12m, PerFin-Expected) to 3 months (BusCond-5y) later. An increase by 1 unit in the relative of BusCond-12m leads to increase of magnitude between 0.2 and 0.4 points in the other four components, with largest magnitudes occurring 1 month (BusCond-5y) to 4 month (BuyCond) later.

The results from the Granger-causality tests and the VAR estimation suggest that a measure based on PerFin-Current and BusCond-12m may be useful (1) as a predictor of the movements of the index itself, and (2) as a leading indicator of the movement in consumption expenditure, used in place of the ICS or the CIND, since one of the criticisms about the performance of the index has been that consumption expenditures react too quickly to changes in the index (within one quarter), so that the lead time to forecast consumption is not sufficient (Kumar et al. 1995).

4 Analysis of Household Data

Our time series findings of strong Granger-causality and cointegration relationships among the five components of the index suggest that they measure essentially the same unobservable variable 'consumer attitude'. This, however, is true with respect to long-run movement of the series. In the short-run important differences in the components series will exist and are worth exploring. In general, we would like to establish the factors that determine individual responses to each of the five component questions. We use various questions from the SCAB asked consistently throughout the sample period to define the variables listed in the appendix. Our goal is to find out 1) how much of the variation in responses to each question can be explained by actual expectations/perceptions about general economic conditions, and how much is due entirely to personal idiosyncrasies, and 2) are all five questions determined by the same factors, as would be the case assuming they all measure the same unobservable phenomenon, or do different factors have different impact on each question.

As outlined previously, respondents to the survey have three choices for answering questions PerFin-Current, PerFin-Expected and BuyCond, and five choices for answering BusCond-12m and BusCond-5y, which were regrouped in three categories when the ICS is computed. We have grouped the responses to these last two questions in the same way in our cross-sectional data analysis. Consider each of the five left-hand side variables in a latent-variable framework. Let y^* be the latent unobservable left-hand side variable, which is the true answer to the question asked in the survey. Let

$$y_i^* = \beta' x_i + \varepsilon_i \qquad (3)$$

with lower values of y_i^* designating higher satisfaction/optimism (as the survey responses are ordered), where the variables included in x_i are listed in the appendix.

Modelling this in an ordered logit framework[1], we observe

$$\begin{aligned} y_i &= 0 &&\text{if} & y_i^* &\leq 0 \\ y_i &= 1 &&\text{if} & 0 &< y_i^* \leq \mu_1 \\ y_i &= 2 &&\text{if} & \mu_1 &< y_i^* \end{aligned}$$

Then $E(y_i^*) = \hat{\beta}' x_i$. Hence, $\beta_j < 0$ would imply variable x_j would induce higher satisfaction/optimism, other things held constant, and vice versa.

The results from estimation of the above model for each component are shown in Tables 4 through 8. One thing to notice right away is that all expectational and perceptional dummy variables that show significance at 5% levels have the intuitively correct signs. For example, GoodNews, GoodGovt, EPrices_Down, EReal_Income_Up, EUnempl_Less are intuitively associated with favourable economic conditions and indeed show up significant and with negative signs in the regression for BusCond-12m. In the

---
[1] See Maddala (1983).

same regression, BadNews, PoorGovt, EPrices_Up, EReal_Income_Down, EUnempl_More, and EInt_Rate_Up are all intuitively associated with adverse economic conditions, and indeed show up significant, with positive signs. This confirms the credibility of the survey data in the sense that on average respondents appear to answer in an expected fashion.

To determine the goodness of fit we use the pseudo-R^2 measure proposed by McKelvey and Zavoina (1975) modified to take into account the logistic distribution of our error term. We estimate model (3) for different specifications of the set of explanatory variables x_i and compare the pseudo-R^2 measure to determine the relative explanatory power of general economic expectations versus personal characteristics. Looking at the goodness of fit measures reported in Table 9, we see that personal variables have greater absolute and incremental explanatory power than general variables for PerFin-Current and PerFin-Expected (both asked in a personal frame of mind), and general variables have greater (incremental) explanatory power than personal variables for the remaining three questions, all asked in a general frame of mind. Quite intuitively, the incremental explanatory power of personal variables for general questions is negligible (between 1% and 3%), but the incremental power of general variables in personal questions is substantial (17% and 6% respectively). This is an important empirical finding.

4.1 'Auxiliary Dummies'

For each of PerFin-Current and BuyCond we have a set of 'auxiliary' dummy variables, defined from answers to questions directly following the one we are trying to explain. These questions are of the form 'Why do you answer better/good (bad/worse) to the question before?', with possible reasons to choose from. We have defined dummies, grouping these reasons in several broad categories, as specified in the appendix. Understandably, these will be highly correlated with the corresponding left-hand side variable. Our purpose however was to determine the relative importance of each category of reasons for the left-hand side variable. We compare the relative impact of each of the right-hand side 'auxiliary' dummies by comparing their marginal effects (we have not reported those here, but as a rough guide they are proportional to the estimated coefficients).

For PerFin-Current the greatest impact on individual responses comes from PFCur_Better_Credit, PFCur_Better_General, PFCur_Better_Income, and PFCur_Worse_Income, in this order of importance. That is, positive changes in personal credit conditions and changes in family income figure most heavily in evaluating the change in personal financial situation. For BuyCond, we have a less intuitive result. The greatest impact comes from BuyCond_Bad_Employment, BuyCond_Bad_Prices, and BuyCond_Good_Credit; that is, negative news concerning employment and prices have the most depressing effect on people's opinion of whether the present is a good time to purchase major household appliances, and positive news concerning credit conditions have the largest positive effect. Blood and Phillips (1995) have recently established the causal effect of recession headline news on sentiment in an elaborate time series framework.[1] Here we are quantifying the effects of a number of different types of news in a cross section context, and find that these effects are very strong.

4.2 Expectational and Perceptional Factors for Individual Questions

'Auxiliary' dummies aside, we can look at the expectations/perception variables which have greatest impact for each question. Those are as follows:

PerFin-Current:
    BusCond_Better_1y_ago, BusCond_Worse_1y_ago
    GoodGovt, BadGovt
    EReal_Income_Up, EReal_Income_Down

PerFin-Expected:
    BusCond_Better_1y_ago, BusCond_Worse_1y_ago
    EReal_Income_Up, EReal_Income_Down

BusCond-12m:
    BusCond_Better_1y_ago, BusCond_Worse_1y_ago
    GoodGovt, BadGovt
    EReal_Income_Up, EReal_Income_Down
    BusCond_Better_1y_ahead, BusCond_Worse_1y_ahead
    EUnempl_Less, EUnempl_More

BusCond-5y:
    BusCond_Worse_1y_ago
    GoodGovt, BadGovt
    EReal_Income_Up, EReal_Income_Down
    BusCond_Better_1y_ahead, BusCond_Worse_1y_ahead
    EUnempl_Less, EUnempl_More
    EPrices_Up, EInt_Rate_Up

BuyCond:
    BusCond_Better_1y_ago, BusCond_Worse_1y_ago
    EPrices_Down
    EInt_Rate_Down

Thus, the common determinants of the two main movers PerFin-Current and BusCond-12m are:
    BusCond_Better_1y_ago, BusCond_Worse_1y_ago
    GoodGovt, BadGovt
    EReal_Income_Up, EReal_Income_Down

---

[1] See also MacKuan et. al. (1992).

Expectations/perceptions depend heavily on individual's perceptions about the performance of the economy over the previous year (4 out of 5 questions). Perception about government performance figures heavily in 3 out of the 5 questions, including the two fundamental movers; that is, popular perception about how the government is doing its job has about as much importance as the actual performance of the economy itself (see Blendon et al. 1997 and Blood and Phillips 1995). Four out of five questions depend on individual's expectations about their real income - two personal and two general questions. It is noteworthy that expectations about prices over the 1-year horizon (EPrices_Up and EPrices_Down) do not have any significance once expectations about the individual's real income are included (with two exceptions).

Another interesting finding is that although determinants of BusCond-12m are also determinants of BusCond-5y, the latter depends on a larger number of expectations variables. In particular, expectations of prices and interest rate on borrowing going up depress the 5-year ahead business outlook, but do not affect the 1-year ahead expectation (although the effect of these is small compared to the rest of the variables). Also, individual's perception of the economy doing bad over the previous year depresses both the 1-year and the 5-year outlook, but the individual's perception of the economy doing well over the same period does not affect the 5-year expectation.

Looking at BuyCond, there are two important things to notice. First, this is the only one of the five questions which does not seem to be affected significantly by the individual's expectations about his personal real income. Second, this is the only variable in which expectations about prices and interest rate on borrowing going down play a major role. This concurs with intuition since prices and interest rate on borrowing would seem to have a direct effect on an individual's decision to buy major household appliances. Furthermore, the effect of these expectations is asymmetric - expectations about prices and interest rate on borrowing going down affect adversely individual's evaluation of present buying conditions, but expectations about prices and interest rate going up do not play a role.

4.3   Effect of Personal Characteristics

A list of variables signifying personal characteristics (all dummy variables except Age) that have explanatory power for each question follows.

PerFin-Current:
    Working, Unemployed, and Age

PerFin-Expected:
    Divorced, Widowed, Separated, Unemployed, Grade_9-11, High_School Some_College, College_Degree, NorthCentral, and NorthEast

BusCond-12m:
    Grade_9-11, High_School, Some_College, and Male

BusCond-5y:
    Grade_9-11, High_School, Some_College, College_Degree, Black, and Male

BuyCond:
Grade_9-11, High_School, Some_College, College_Degree, and Black

Employment status: Dummies signifying individual's employment status (Working, Unemployed) figure heavily in determination of personal questions, but do not seem to affect significantly general business outlook. The Unemployed dummy has opposite effects in the two questions PerFin-Current (depressing) and PerFin-Expected (contributing to a more optimistic expectation); that is, an individual who is unemployed at present is at the worst possible situation (in terms of employment status and personal finances), so comparison of present financial situation to one year ago will be negative, but he will also perceive a higher probability of a positive change in the following year, and hence the dummy would have the opposite effect in PerFin-Expected.

4.3.1 Marital Status The only dummies designating marital status that show any explanatory significance are Divorced, Separated, and Widowed in the regression for PerFin-Expected. All have negative coefficients, meaning they contribute to a more optimistic expectation about personal finances. It seems that dummies designating some sort of personal depressing status significantly contribute to a more optimistic personal financial expectation, possibly simply by contrast with the present situation.

4.3.2 Sex While the sex dummy does not have any effect on the personal questions and the buying conditions question, male respondents appear to give systematically more optimistic responses to questions about 1-year and 5-year ahead business outlook.

4.3.3 Education We have defined four dummies for education: Grade_9-11, High_School, Some_College, and College_Degree. These appear to have significance (in terms of marginal effects of at least .05 in absolute value for at least one of the possible choices) for all questions except PerFin-Current, and to uniformly cause more optimistic responses to those questions, without any particular order of importance among the four dummies. (Some_College indeed seems to have the largest marginal effect in most cases.)

4.3.4 Regional effect Two dummies - NorthCentral and NorthEast - appear significant for determination of PerFin-Expected, both having a depressing effect. This is the so-called 'rust-belt' effect.

5 Conclusions

Based on our econometric analysis we can conclude that over the sample period 01:1978 - 12:1996 ICS and all of its five components seem to follow an $I(1)$ process (random walk with a positive drift). We find two 'major movers' - PerFin-Current and BusCond-12m - among the five index components, which Granger-cause each other and Granger-cause the rest of the components. Strong Granger-causality and cointegration relationships between the five components favor the conjecture that all five index questions, although differently phrased and pertaining to different phenomena, actually measure the same underlying latent variable, which we call 'attitude'. As expected, we find that general economic factors seem to possess high incremental explanatory power for all components, whereas personal factors matter significantly only for components referring to personal economic conditions. The most important general economic factors overall appear to be the individual's perception of how the economy has performed the year before, how government is doing its job at present, and the individual's expectation of personal income relative to prices over the following year.

In order to link these findings with previous research on the subject of sentiment determinants, we need to examine how general economic expectations and perceptions fare in the presence of the actual realized values of the relevant macroeconomic variables. There are common factors affecting all five components, as we would expect if all of them capture the same phenomenon. However, there is an array of factors which figure in some components but not in others, or which seem to have opposite effects on different components. This would suggest that consumer sentiment as measured by the ICS could be potentially very different for subsets of the population determined by such factors. Our next line of research would likely be 1) to determine the significance of expectational dummies when actual lagged values of unemployment, inflation, interest rates, etc. are taken into account, and 2) to compute ICS measures for different subsets of the population and compare their explanatory power with that using the conventional ICS in predicting aggregate consumption expenditures.

Appendix

List of variables (with definitions) used in our household data analysis
Dummy Variables:

PFCur_Better_Income
    1 if Income is cited as a reason why PerFin-Current response is Better
    0 otherwise

PFCur_Better_Prices
    1 if Prices are cited as a reason why PerFin-Current response is Better
    0 otherwise

PFCur_Better_Taxes
    1 if Taxes are cited as a reason why PerFin-Current response is Better
    0 otherwise

PFCur_Better_Credit
    1 if Credit is cited as a reason why PerFin-Current response is Better
    0 otherwise

PFCur_Better_General
1 if General Reasons are cited as a reason why PerFin-Current response is Better
    0 otherwise

PFCur_Better_GovtPolicy
1 if Government Policy is cited as a reason why PerFin-Current response is Better
    0 otherwise

PFCur_Worse_Income
    1 if Income is cited as a reason why PerFin-Current response is Worse
    0 otherwise

PFCur_Worse_Prices
    1 if Prices are cited as a reason why PerFin-Current response is Worse
    0 otherwise

PFCur_Worse_Taxes
    1 if Taxes are cited as a reason why PerFin-Current response is Worse
    0 otherwise

PFCur_Worse_Credit
    1 if Credit is cited as a reason why PerFin-Current response is Worse
    0 otherwise

PFCur_Worse_General
1 if General Reasons are cited as a reason why PerFin-Current response is Worse
    0 otherwise

PFCur_Worse_GovtPolicy
1 if Government Policy is cited as a reason why PerFin-Current response is Worse
    0 otherwise

BusCond_Better_1y_ago
    1 if respondent considers Business Conditions to be Better than 1 year ago.
    0 otherwise

BusCond_Worse_1y_ago
> 1 if respondent considers Business Conditions to be Worse than 1 year ago.
> 0 otherwise

GoodNews
1 if respondent indicates they have heard positive news about the business conditions and the economy as a whole in the past several months.
> 0 otherwise

BadNews
1 if respondent indicates they have heard negative news about the business conditions and the economy as a whole in the past several months.
> 0 otherwise

GoodGovt
> 1 if respondent considers Government to be doing a Good job.
> 0 otherwise.

PoorGovt
> 1 if respondent considers Government to be doing a Poor job.
> 0 otherwise.

BusCond_Better_1y_ahead
> 1 if respondent expects Business Conditions to be Better in 1 year
> 0 otherwise

BusCond_Worse_1y_ahead
> 1 if respondent expects Business Conditions to be Worse in 1 year
> 0 otherwise

EPrices_Up
> 1 if respondent expects Prices to go Up during following 12 months
> 0 otherwise

EPrices_Down
> 1 if respondent expects Prices to go Down during following 12 months
> 0 otherwise

EReal_Income_Up
> 1 if respondent expects Family Income to go Up more than prices
> 0 otherwise

EReal_Income_Down
> 1 if respondent expects Family Income to go Down more than prices
> 0 otherwise

EUnempl_Less
> 1 if respondent expects Less Unemployment during next 12 months
> 0 otherwise

EUnempl_More
> 1 if respondent expects More Unemployment during next 12 months
> 0 otherwise

EInt_Rate_Up
1 if respondent expects Interest Rate on borrowing to go Up during next 12 months
> 0 otherwise

EInt_Rate_Down
1 if respondent expects Interest Rate on borrowing to go Down during next 12 months
    0 otherwise

BuyCond_Good_Prices
    1 if Prices are cited as reason why response to BuyCond-Present is Good
    0 otherwise

BuyCond_Good_Credit
    1 if Credit is cited as reason why response to BuyCond-Present is Good
    0 otherwise

BuyCond_Good_Employment
1 if Employment Conditions are cited as reason why response to BuyCond-Present is Good
    0 otherwise

BuyCond_Bad_Prices
    1 if Prices are cited as reason why response to BuyCond-Present is Bad
    0 otherwise

BuyCond_Bad_Credit
    1 if Credit is cited as reason why response to BuyCond-Present is Bad
    0 otherwise

BuyCond_Bad_Employment
1 if Employment Conditions are cited as reason why response to BuyCond-Present is Bad
    0 otherwise

For the following the dummy takes value of 1 if condition indicated by the name of the variable is present, 0 otherwise:
Married, Divorced, Widowed, Separated, Working, Unemployed, Student, Housewife, Grade_9-11, High_School, Some_College, College_Degree, White, Black, Hispanic, NorthCentral, NorthEast, South, Male.

Continuous Variables:
Age: Respondent's age, divided by 10
AgeSq: Square of Age
Income: Total annual family income for the year preceding survey, divided by 10,000, divided by number of family members and adjusted by CPI (base January 1978).

Table 1 *F*-statistics for testing Granger-causality in a 12-lag autoregressive distributed lag model (levels)*

Independent Variable Dependent Variable	PerFin-Current	PerFin-Expected	BusCond-12m	BusCond-5y	BuyCond
PerFin-Current	-	1.91*	4.55**	3.32**	0.57
PerFin-Expected	1.14	-	3.03**	1.79	1.66
BusCond-12m	1.82*	0.76	-	1.31	1.07
BusCond-5y	1.06	1.69	2.13*	-	1.18
BuyCond	3.29**	2.13*	3.73**	2.16*	-

F-statistics for testing Granger-causality in a 12-lag autoregressive distributed lag model (first differences)

Independent Variable Dependent Variable	PerFin-Current	PerFin-Expected	BusCond-12m	BusCond-5y	BuyCond
PerFin-Current	-	1.11	2.97**	1.96*	1.31
PerFin-Expected	1.23	-	2.82**	1.72	1.77
BusCond-12m	2.12*	0.61	-	1.09	1.13
BusCond-5y	1.12	1.53	1.98*	-	1.52
BuyCond-Present	3.08**	1.5	3.36**	1.64	-

Table 2 Results from trivariate Granger-causality tests

y_t	z_t	x_t	χ^2	5% critical value	F	5% critical value
PerFin-Current	BusCond-5y	BusCond-12m	12.31	21	0.85	1.8
BusCond-12m	PerFin-Current	PerFin-Expected	28.35	21	1.96	1.8
BuyCond	PerFin-Current	BusCond-12m	31.22	21	2.15	1.8
BuyCond	BusCond-12m	PerFin-Current	34.91	21	2.41	1.8

* * denotes rejection of the null at the 5% level,
** denotes rejection of the null at the 1% level.

Table 3 Cointegration tests (Johansen FIML estimation)

Null Hypothesis	Max. Eigenvalue	5% Crit. value	Trace Statistic	5% Crit. value
$p=0$	37.91*	33.50	86.19**	68.50
$p<=1$	26.58	27.10	48.28*	47.20
$p<=2$	9.58	21.00	21.70	29.70
$p<=3$	8.93	14.10	12.12	15.40
$p<=4$	3.19	3.80	3.19	3.80

Using small sample correction T-nm

Null Hypothesis	Max. Eigenvalue	5% Crit. value	Trace Statistic	5% Crit. value
$p=0$	33.66*	33.50	76.53**	68.50
$p<=1$	23.60	27.10	42.87	47.20
$p<=2$	8.50	21.00	19.27	29.70
$p<=3$	7.93	14.10	10.76	15.40
$p<=4$	2.83	3.80	2.83	3.80

Cointegrating vector under constraint $p=1$				
	PerFin-Expected	BusCond-12m	BusCond-5y	BuyCond
PerFin-Current	0.633	1.055	-1.289	0.007

Table 4 Ordered logit model for PerFin-Current, N = 52506

Variable Name	Coef	Standard Error	$z=\beta$/s.e.	p-value	Mean of regressor
Constant	1.353	0.209	6.46	0.00	-
"Auxiliary" Dummies					
PFCur_Better_Income	-4.080	0.109	-37.36	0.00	0.385
PFCur_Better_Prices	-3.155	0.150	-20.97	0.00	0.009
PFCur_Better_Taxes	-3.810	0.347	-10.95	0.00	0.001
PFCur_Better_Credit	-4.691	0.126	-37.03	0.00	0.053
PFCur_Better_General	-4.569	0.129	-35.39	0.00	0.044
PFCur_Better_GovtPolicy	-3.659	0.561	-6.51	0.00	0.000
PFCur_Worse_Income	4.191	0.113	37.02	0.00	0.171
PFCur_Worse_Prices	3.648	0.112	32.28	0.00	0.157
PFCur_Worse_Taxes	4.030	0.138	29.09	0.00	0.017
PFCur_Worse_Credit	3.466	0.172	20.06	0.00	0.005
PFCur_Worse_General	4.024	0.146	27.51	0.00	0.014
PFCur_Worse_GovtPolicy	3.002	0.307	9.74	0.00	0.001
Perceptional Dummies					
BusCond_Better_1y_ago	-0.215	0.044	-4.83	0.00	0.429
BusCond_Worse_1y_ago	0.271	0.042	6.33	0.00	0.468
GoodNews	0.061	0.037	1.61	0.10	0.234
BadNews	-0.006	0.031	-0.21	0.82	0.386

Table 4 (continued)

Variable Name	Coef	Standard Error	z=β/s.e.	p-value	Mean of regressor
Perceptional Dummies					
GoodGovt	-0.214	0.038	-5.50	0.00	0.201
PoorGovt	0.242	0.031	7.79	0.00	0.287
Expectational Dummies					
BusCond_Better_1y_ahead	0.105	0.033	3.10	0.00	0.285
BusCond_Worse_1y_ahead	0.054	0.034	1.56	0.11	0.226
Eprices_Up	-0.021	0.038	-0.57	0.56	0.800
Eprices_Down	-0.145	0.081	-1.78	0.07	0.033
EReal_Income_Up	-0.222	0.041	-5.40	0.00	0.205
EReal_Income_Down	0.357	0.029	12.03	0.00	0.374
Eunempl_Less	0.013	0.040	0.33	0.73	0.177
Eunempl_More	0.080	0.031	2.57	0.01	0.360
Eint_Rate_Up	0.019	0.031	0.62	0.53	0.480
Eint_Rate_Down	0.074	0.038	1.93	0.05	0.213
Personal Characteristics					
Married	-0.020	0.044	-0.45	0.65	0.619
Divorced	0.073	0.059	1.23	0.21	0.098
Widowed	0.075	0.068	1.10	0.26	0.071
Separated	0.260	0.090	2.88	0.00	0.028
Working	-0.108	0.049	-2.19	0.02	0.664
Unemployed	0.237	0.082	2.88	0.00	0.048
Student	0.020	0.066	0.31	0.75	0.071
Housewife	-0.023	0.061	-0.38	0.70	0.095
Grade_9-11	-0.015	0.067	-0.22	0.82	0.114
High_School	-0.044	0.060	0.73	0.46	0.339
Some_College	-0.040	0.062	-0.65	0.51	0.304
College_Degree	0.069	0.066	1.04	0.29	0.189
White	0.073	0.116	0.63	0.52	0.870
Black	0.143	0.125	1.14	0.25	0.083
Hispanic	0.096	0.138	0.69	0.48	0.027
NorthCentral	-0.036	0.039	-0.92	0.35	0.290
NorthEast	-0.020	0.042	-0.49	0.62	0.200
South	-0.069	0.038	-1.79	0.07	0.313
Male	-0.066	0.029	-2.27	0.02	0.470
Age	0.405	0.056	7.18	0.00	4.040
AgeSq	-0.036	0.059	-6.15	0.00	19.000
Income	-0.107	0.019	-5.39	0.00	0.826

Table 5 Ordered logit model for PerFin-expected, N = 52506

Variable Name	Coef	Standard Error	z=β/s.e.	p-value	Mean of regressor
Constant	0.038	0.113	0.34	0.73	-
Perceptional Dummies					
GoodNews	-0.120	0.024	-4.86	0.00	0.234
BadNews	-0.066	0.021	-3.12	0.00	0.386
BusCond_Better_1y_ago	-0.087	0.032	-2.69	0.00	0.429
BusCond_Worse_1y_ago	0.123	0.031	3.88	0.00	0.468
GoodGovt	-0.108	0.025	-4.31	0.00	0.201
PoorGovt	0.212	0.020	10.18	0.00	0.287
Expectational Dummies					
BusCond_Better_1y_ahead	-0.394	0.022	-17.49	0.00	0.285
BusCond_Worse_1y_ahead	0.549	0.023	23.75	0.00	0.226
Eprices_Up	0.028	0.025	1.10	0.27	0.800
Eprices_Down	-0.036	0.053	-0.67	0.49	0.033
Ereal_Income_Up	-1.294	0.025	-50.05	0.00	0.205
Ereal_Income_Down	0.761	0.020	37.00	0.00	0.374
Eunempl_Less	-0.103	0.026	-3.88	0.00	0.177
Eunempl_More	0.173	0.021	8.25	0.00	0.360
Eint_Rate_Up	0.001	0.021	0.05	0.95	0.481
Eint_Rate_Down	-0.023	0.025	-0.92	0.35	0.213
Personal Characteristics					
Married	-0.038	0.027	-1.42	0.15	0.619
Divorced	-0.281	0.037	-7.58	0.00	0.098
Widowed	-0.147	0.048	-3.01	0.00	0.071
Separated	-0.220	0.055	-4.00	0.00	0.028
Working	-0.144	0.036	-3.96	0.00	0.664
Unemployed	-0.363	0.051	-7.01	0.00	0.048
Student	-0.046	0.047	-0.97	0.32	0.071
Housewife	-0.044	0.044	-0.99	0.31	0.095
Grades_9-11	-0.186	0.047	-3.93	0.00	0.114
High_School	-0.149	0.043	-3.43	0.00	0.339
Some_College	-0.277	0.044	-6.21	0.00	0.304
College_Degree	-0.229	0.046	-4.90	0.00	0.189
White	0.034	0.065	0.52	0.59	0.871
Black	-0.131	0.071	-1.83	0.06	0.083
Hispanic	0.072	0.082	0.88	0.37	0.027
NorthCentral	0.188	0.026	7.22	0.00	0.290
NorthEast	0.238	0.028	8.48	0.00	0.200
South	0.070	0.025	2.73	0.00	0.313
Male	0.031	0.019	1.66	0.09	0.470
Age	0.145	0.038	3.82	0.00	4.048
AgeSq	0.008	0.004	2.02	0.04	19.030
Income	-0.001	0.006	-0.21	0.82	0.826

Table 6 Ordered logit model for BusCond-12m, N = 52506

Variable Name	Coef	Standard Error	z=β/s.e.	p-value	Mean of regressor
Constant	0.012	0.126	0.09	0.92	-
Perceptional Dummies					
GoodNews	-0.193	0.030	-6.39	0.00	0.234
BadNews	0.230	0.025	8.88	0.00	0.386
BusCond_Better_1y_ago	-0.651	0.035	-18.33	0.00	0.429
BusCond_Worse_1y_ago	0.954	0.035	27.01	0.00	0.468
GoodGovt	-0.593	0.030	-19.21	0.00	0.201
PoorGovt	0.500	0.026	19.23	0.00	0.287
Expectational Dummies					
BusCond_Better_1y_ahead	-0.753	0.026	-28.66	0.00	0.285
BusCond_Worse_1y_ahead	1.200	0.032	37.27	0.00	0.226
EPrices_Up	0.069	0.030	2.28	0.02	0.800
EPrices_Down	-0.073	0.066	-1.11	0.26	0.033
EReal_Income_Up	-0.257	0.031	-8.28	0.00	0.205
EReal_Income_Down	0.367	0.024	14.83	0.00	0.374
EUnempl_Less	-0.330	0.032	-10.21	0.00	0.177
EUnempl_More	0.697	0.024	27.92	0.00	0.360
EInt_Rate_Up	0.142	0.025	5.48	0.00	0.481
EInt_Rate_Down	0.057	0.031	1.81	0.06	0.213
Personal Characteristics					
Married	-0.082	0.032	-2.55	0.01	0.619
Divorced	-0.039	0.045	-0.87	0.38	0.098
Widowed	0.152	0.057	2.63	0.00	0.071
Separated	0.128	0.070	1.80	0.07	0.028
Working	-0.112	0.042	-2.62	0.00	0.664
Unemployed	-0.015	0.062	-0.25	0.79	0.048
Student	-0.003	0.056	-0.05	0.95	0.071
Housewife	0.040	0.052	0.76	0.44	0.095
Grade_9-11	-0.214	0.056	-3.79	0.00	0.114
High_School	-0.173	0.052	-3.32	0.00	0.339
Some_College	-0.235	0.053	-4.37	0.00	0.304
College_Degree	0.048	0.057	0.83	0.40	0.189
White	0.014	0.082	0.18	0.85	0.871
Black	0.110	0.089	1.23	0.21	0.083
Hispanic	-0.050	0.103	-0.48	0.62	0.027
NorthCentral	0.000	0.032	-0.02	0.98	0.290
NorthEast	0.049	0.035	1.39	0.16	0.200
South	0.007	0.031	0.23	0.81	0.313
Male	-0.265	0.023	-11.08	0.00	0.470
Age	0.007	0.029	0.26	0.79	4.048
AgeSq	-0.007	0.003	-2.10	0.03	19.030
Income	-0.057	0.016	-3.50	0.00	0.826

Table 7   Ordered logit model for BusCond-5y, N = 52506

Variable Name	Coef	Standard Error	z=β/s.e.	p-value	Mean of regressor
Constant	0.888	0.108	8.21	0.00	-
Perceptional Dummies					
GoodNews	-0.107	0.025	-4.23	0.00	0.234
BadNews	0.017	0.023	0.73	0.46	0.386
BusCond_Better_ly_ago	-0.182	0.032	-5.60	0.00	0.429
BusCond_Worse_ly_ago	0.379	0.033	11.48	0.00	0.460
GoodGovt	-0.552	0.024	-22.21	0.00	0.201
PoorGovt	0.497	0.024	20.38	0.00	0.287
Expectational Dummies					
BusCond_Better_ly_ahead	-0.566	0.022	-25.25	0.00	0.285
BusCond_Worse_ly_ahead	0.830	0.029	27.77	0.00	0.226
EPrices_Up	0.239	0.025	9.32	0.00	0.800
EPrices_Down	0.087	0.056	1.54	0.12	0.033
EReal_Income_Up	-0.223	0.025	-8.71	0.00	0.205
EReal_Income_Down	0.340	0.022	15.27	0.00	0.374
EUnempl_Less	-0.349	0.026	-13.14	0.00	0.177
EUnempl_More	0.742	0.023	31.47	0.00	0.360
EInt_Rate_Up	0.220	0.022	9.78	0.00	0.481
EInt_Rate_Down	-0.021	0.026	-0.80	0.42	0.213
Personal Characteristics					
Married	-0.017	0.027	-0.65	0.51	0.619
Divorced	0.025	0.039	0.64	0.52	0.098
Widowed	0.072	0.051	1.39	0.16	0.071
Separated	0.161	0.063	2.55	0.01	0.028
Working	-0.044	0.039	-1.12	0.25	0.664
Unemployed	0.159	0.058	2.72	0.00	0.048
Student	0.054	0.052	1.04	0.29	0.071
Housewife	0.080	0.048	1.65	0.09	0.095
Grade_9-11	-0.293	0.053	-5.51	0.00	0.114
High_School	-0.347	0.049	-7.09	0.00	0.339
Some_College	-0.488	0.050	-9.74	0.00	0.304
College_Degree	-0.416	0.052	-7.86	0.00	0.189
White	-0.005	0.069	-0.07	0.93	0.871
Black	0.302	0.077	3.91	0.00	0.083
Hispanic	0.174	0.089	1.94	0.05	0.027
NorthCentral	0.044	0.028	1.57	0.11	0.290
NorthEast	0.006	0.030	0.21	0.83	0.200
South	0.002	0.027	0.08	0.92	0.313
Male	-0.422	0.020	-20.24	0.00	0.470
Age	0.009	0.021	0.42	0.66	4.048
AgeSq	-0.007	0.002	-2.88	0.00	19.030
Income	-0.126	0.014	-8.96	0.00	0.826

Table 8   Ordered logit model for BuyCond, N = 52506

Variable Name	Coef	Standard Error	z=β/s.e.	p-value	Mean of regressor
Constant	-1.170	0.231	-5.07	0.00	-
"Auxiliary" Dummies					
BuyCond_Good_Prices	-2.830	0.049	-57.66	0.00	0.519
BuyCond_Good_Credit	-3.320	0.137	-24.15	0.00	0.074
BuyCond_Good_Employment	-2.660	0.133	-20.03	0.00	0.043
BuyCond_Bad_Prices	4.190	0.056	74.07	0.00	0.122
BuyCond_Bad_Credit	2.670	0.053	50.24	0.00	0.065
BuyCond_Bad_Employment	4.300	0.076	56.63	0.00	0.069
Perceptional Dummies					
GoodNews	0.070	0.050	1.39	0.16	0.234
BadNews	0.121	0.041	2.93	0.00	0.386
BusCond_Better_1y_ago	-0.244	0.061	-3.97	0.00	0.429
BusCond_Worse_1y_ago	0.229	0.058	3.92	0.00	0.468
GoodGovt	-0.111	0.051	-2.18	0.02	0.201
PoorGovt	0.148	0.040	3.70	0.00	0.287
Expectational Dummies					
BusCond_Better_1y_ahead	0.037	0.045	0.83	0.40	0.285
BusCond_Worse_1y_ahead	0.079	0.044	1.79	0.07	0.226
Eprices_Up	-0.036	0.049	-0.73	0.46	0.800
Eprices_Down	0.298	0.103	2.87	0.00	0.033
Ereal_Income_Up	-0.207	0.050	-4.11	0.00	0.205
Ereal_Income_Down	0.169	0.039	4.27	0.00	0.374
Eunempl_Less	0.100	0.053	1.85	0.06	0.177
Eunempl_More	0.132	0.040	3.29	0.00	0.360
EInt_Rate_Up	-0.030	0.041	-0.73	0.46	0.481
EInt_Rate_Down	0.081	0.048	1.65	0.09	0.213
Personal Characteristics					
Married	-0.038	0.055	-0.69	0.48	0.619
Divorced	-0.024	0.075	-0.32	0.74	0.098
Widowed	0.091	0.090	1.01	0.31	0.071
Separated	0.029	0.114	0.25	0.79	0.028
Working	0.017	0.064	0.27	0.78	0.664
Uneployed	-0.088	0.103	-0.86	0.38	0.048
Student	0.166	0.088	1.88	0.06	0.071
Housewife	0.056	0.081	0.68	0.49	0.095
Grade_9-11	-0.195	0.090	-2.16	0.03	0.114
High_School	-0.210	0.082	-2.56	0.01	0.339
Some_College	-0.248	0.084	-2.93	0.00	0.304
College_Degree	-0.150	0.088	-1.71	0.08	0.189

Table 8 (continued)

Variable Name	Coef	Standard Error	z=β/s.e.	p-value	Mean of regressor
White	0.185	0.146	1.26	0.20	0.871
Black	0.188	0.157	1.19	0.23	0.083
Hispanic	0.085	0.180	0.47	0.63	0.027
NorthCentral	-0.022	0.051	-0.44	0.65	0.290
NorthEast	-0.025	0.054	-0.47	0.63	0.200
South	-0.015	0.049	-0.31	0.75	0.313
Male	-0.027	0.037	-0.71	0.47	0.470
Age	0.115	0.073	1.57	0.11	4.048
AgeSq	-0.009	0.007	-1.22	0.22	19.030
Income	-0.001	0.007	-0.19	0.84	0.826

Table 9 Pseudo-R^2 measures for different model specifications

Left-hand side Variable	Full Model	Personal Variables Only	General Variables Only	General Var. Incremental R^2	Personal Var. Incremental R^2
PerFin-Current	0.83	0.66	0.65	0.17	0.18
PerFin-Expected	0.29	0.23	0.11	0.06	0.18
BusCond-12m	0.49	0.10	0.48	0.39	0.01
BusCond-5y	0.35	0.11	0.32	0.24	0.03
BuyCond	0.74	0.04	0.74	0.69	0.00

References

Blendon, R. J., J. M. Benson, M. Brodie, R. Morin, D. E. Altman, D. Gitterman, M. Brossard, and James, M.(1997), Bridging the Gap Between the public's and Economists' Views of the Economy, *Journal of Economic Perspectives*, 11, No. 3, pp. 105-118.

Blood, D.J. and Phillips, P.C.B. (1995), Recession Headline News, Consumer Sentiment, the State of the Economy, and Presidential Popularity: A Time Series Analysis 1989-1993, *International Journal of Public Opinion*, Vol. 7, No. 1, pp. 2-22.

Carroll, Christopher D., Fuhrer, J., and Wilcox, D., Does Consumer Sentiment Forecast Household Spending? If So, Why?, *American Economic Review*, 84(5), pp.1397-1408.

Fuhrer, J.C. (1993), What Role Does Consumer Sentiment Play in the U.S. Eonomy?, *New England Economic Review*, January/February, pp. 32-44.

Hamilton, J.D., *Time Series Analysis*, Princeton University Press, Princeton, 1994.

Katona, G. (1951), *Psychological Analysis of Economic Behavior*, McGraw-Hill, New York.

Kumar, V., R.P. Leone, and Gaskins, J.N. (1995), Aggregate and Disaggregate Sector Forecasting Using Consumer Confidence Measures, *International Journal of Forecasting*, 11(1995), pp.361-377.

Lahiri, K. and Moore, G.H. (1991), *Leading Economic Indicators: New Approaches and Forecasting Records*. Cambridge University Press, Cambridge, UK.

Linden, F. (1982). The Consumer as Forecaster, *Public Opinion Quarterly*, 45, pp. 353-360.

Lovell, M.C. (1975), Why Was the Consumer Feeling So Sad?, *Brookings Papers on Economic Activity*, 1975:2, pp. 473-479.

MacKuan, M.B., R.S. Erikson., and Stimson, J.A. (1992), Peasants or Bankers? The American Electorate and the U.S. Economy, *American Political Science Review*, 86, 3, 597-611.

McKelvey, R. and Zavoina, W. (1975), Statistical Model for the Analysis of ordinal Level Dependent Variables, Journal of Mathematical Sociology (4), pp. 103-120.

Maddala, G.S. (1983), *Limited Dependent And Qualitative Variables In Econometrics*, Cambridge University Press, Cambridge, UK.

Mishkin, F.S. (1978), Consumer Sentiment and Spending on Durable Goods, *Brookings Papers on Economic Activity*, 1978:1, pp. 17-31.

Throop, A.W., Consumer Sentiment: Its Causes And Effects, *Federal Reserve Bank of San Francisco Economic Review*, 1992, p.35-59.

Walsh, Carl E. (1993), What Caused the 1990-1991 Recession?, *Federal Reserve Bank of San Francisco Economic Review*, 1993(2), pp. 3-48.

Zarnowitz, V. (1992), *Business Cycles: Theory, History, Indicators, and Forecasting*, The University of Chicago Press, Chicago.

21 A Microsimulation Approach for Tax and Social Policy Recommendations in the Federal Republic of Germany[*]

Gerhard Wagenhals

Abstract

Microsimulation modelling of tax-benefit policies based on survey data is used as a tool for policy recommendations in many countries. The purpose of this paper is to present a microsimulation model for Germany which has been used to analyse the effects of tax and benefit reforms on incentives, on the allocation and distribution of resources, and on government revenues. We summarise the model, what it does and how it works, and show, with some examples, the type of results the model produces: How it can be used to augment survey statistics in an explanatory manner, and how the model has been used to assess the impact of changes in the German tax-benefit system, and to support policy formulation.

1 Introduction

1.1 Aims of the Paper

User of survey statistics often want more information. Typically, additional data will not be sufficient. What is needed is a coherent, consistent and integrated approach to augment the survey statistics in an explanatory manner. My paper aims to show that microsimulation models can help to do this, and thus to form a solid basis to assess the impact of policy changes, and to support policy decisions.

This paper introduces a microsimulation model for tax and social policy recommendations in the Federal Republic of Germany, which during recent years has been used for this purpose. The paper is structured as follows. The first section briefly surveys competing tax-benefit microsimulation models for Germany. Section two describes the survey on which the model is based, and what has to be done to augment it in order to make it a data set suitable for tax-benefit simulations. The third section presents a broad picture of what

---

[*] I thank Ulrich Scheurle for his helpful comments, Andy Lawrence for checking my English, Barbara A. Butrica and Johannes Schwarze for providing me with their SAS programs. The German Institute for Economic Research (DIW) in Berlin provided the data of the German Socio-economic Panel. The usual disclaimer applies.

the model does and how it works. Section four gives examples showing how it can be used to augment survey statistics in an explanatory manner and to support policy formulation. The final section provides an overall assessment.

1.2 A Tax-benefit Microsimulation Model

My microsimulation model of the tax-benefit system in Germany (called *GMOD* for the sake of convenience) may be characterised by its following features:
- It is a comprehensive desktop-computer model of the personal tax and benefit system in the Federal Republic of Germany. It is written in GAUSS, a powerful matrix programming language. The program consists of a set of inter-connected procedures, which can be compiled separately. Therefore, it is very easy to adapt the model to changes of the tax or benefit rules, and to run the model on any DOS-, Windows- or Unix-based system.
- It uses survey data to simulate personal and household taxes and social security contributions as well as cash benefits for each responding individual and each household. Given total income and personal characteristics, the model calculates (total, average and marginal) taxes, social security contributions and benefit receipts for any given set of tax-benefit rules. The user may change these rules, and simulate the impact of changes.
- It combines the results for all individuals and households in the survey, calculates the tax-benefit position of individuals and household before and after a reform, and predicts the impact of the tax and benefits changes for the whole German Population (with or without taking behavioural responses into account).
- Tax base is *total* income from all sources. The model accounts for employees' social security contributions, and for the most important benefits. Special rules for East Germany are included, if applicable.
- Weighting factors allow to gross up the individual and household data to obtain population totals.
- Econometrically estimated and tested behavioural relations allow to assess the impact of changes in the tax-benefit system on the allocation and distribution of resources, on work incentives and on the distribution of income and welfare.

In my view, this model is the most comprehensive tax-benefit microsimulation model available in Germany today. It is, of course, not the only microsimulation model for Germany.

1.3 Other German Microsimulation Models

In many countries microsimulation modelling has been established as a helpful tool to assess the impacts of tax and social policy alternatives (see e.g. Citro and Hanushek, 1991, Merz, 1994, Sutherland, 1995, Harding, 1996, or Klevmarken, 1997). In Germany, there have been only a few attempts to model the tax and benefit system comprehensively and based on a representative survey. Table 1.1 lists recent microsimulation models for the German tax-benefit system which have been designed to operate on a survey of individuals and households. Most of these models use data of the German Socio-Economic Panel (see Section two below).

The *Frankfurt Income Tax Simulation model* (FITS) is one of the first approaches to a microsimulation model of the income tax. It was developed in 1986 within the former Special Research Area 3 (Sfb, Sonderforschungsbereich 3), a project funded by the German National Research Foundation (see Spahn et al., 1992, or Hauser et al., 1994, for general surveys).

The FITS model is based on the taxable years 1983-90, until the German National Research Foundation stopped funding the project. FITS presents the regulations of the Income Tax Act in great detail (van Essen et al., 1986), but is characterised by strong assumptions with respect to missing values for certain special expenses and outliers (see Gyárfás, 1993, for a detailed critique). Although social security contributions act as wage taxes under the institutional conditions of the German welfare system, FITS does not model them. Worse, income-tested benefits are assumed to be exogenous in determining income and wages. The 1984 version of the model is very well documented, and FORTRAN77 code is available.

Table 1.1 German tax-benefit microsimulation models

Model	GMOD	FITS	Schwarze	Ifo	RWI	IfW	GMD
Years	1983-99	1983-90	1983-94	1987	1991	1995	?-1999
Survey based	√	√	√	—	√	—	—
Tax system	√	√	√	√	√	√	√
Total tax base	√	√	√	—	—	—	√
Social security contributions	√	—	—	√	√	√	—
Benefit system	√	—	—	√	√	√	—
East Germany	√	—	—	—	√	—	√
Population totals	√	√	—	—	√	—	√
Computer code	√	√	√	—	—	—	—
Behavioural relations	√	√	√	—	—	—	—

1.3.1 Successors of FITS The gap left by the abandonment of the FITS model is partially filled by two offsprings. First, a simplified version of FITS has been continually updated by *Schwarze* (1995) at the German Institute for Economic Research (DIW, Deutsches Institut für Wirtschaftsforschung). His tax program relies on less rigorous assumptions. It calculates household tax burdens up to 1994. SAS computer code is available and easily modified and updated. Tax computations for the East German subsample of the GSOEP are not possible yet, but planned to be available in the near future. The second offspring from the FITS model is *MICSIM*, a general purpose microsimulation model based on the static Sfb 3 microsimulation model, which, however, does not include an updated tax-benefit simulation module (see Merz, 1996, for details on MICSIM).

1.3.2 Non-academic German microsimulation models Three of the leading economic research institutes in Germany, the Institute for Economic Research (IFO) in Munich, the Rhine-Westphalia Institute for Economic Research (RWI) in Essen and the Institute of World Economics (IFW) in Kiel have published small tax-benefit models for Germany relating to just one or two years, respectively. The *IFO* integrated tax-transfer model accounts for the 1987 tax-benefit rules (Nierhaus, 1988). More up-to-date, the *IFW* tax-transfer model (Gern, 1996) is based on the 1995 and 1996 tax-benefit rules. Though in principle both models could be applied to a survey, up to now, they haven't. Instead, the models are used to model the effective tax burdens of "typical" households (see e.g. Leibfritz and Parsche, 1988), ignoring the fact that household characteristics vary widely in the population and that one never knows if and how representative one of the "typical" families is. No population totals are given. Contrary to these models, the *RWI* tax-tansfer model (see Fritzsche and von Löffelholz, 1993, 1994) is based on the GSOEP, although on the 1991 wave only. All "non-academic" microsimulation models describe the transfer section. Unfortunately, they all account for income from paid employment only. Ignoring all other types of income, and disregarding population totals makes them unsuitable to analyse the aggregate revenue effect of tax and benefit reforms.

1.3.3 A model based on a synthetic database Most ministries of finance in industrialised countries nowadays rely on microsimulation models to assess the impact of tax and benefit changes on the allocation and distribution of resources. The German Federal Ministry of Finance (BMF, Bundesministerium der Finanzen) does not. Instead, it uses a group simulation model based on "synthetic" microdata. The model concentrates on taxes, interaction with benefits is not accounted for. Its data base is generated from aggregated structural information which is used for a partial disaggregation. Lietmeyer (1983, 1986) sketches the model, Gyárfás (1990) and Gyárfás, Quinke (1990, 1993) describe the methodology. Galler (1990) strongly criticises this approach because it imputes strong assumptions on the independence of individual attributes which cannot be checked empirically. "This reduces the explanatory power of such data considerably." (op.cit., p. 291). The model is run by a working group at the Gesellschaft für Mathematik und Datenverarbeitung (GMD) in St. Augustin near Bonn. No up to date information on the workings of the GMD model is available. Independent reproduction of the results is impossible. According to private information from government officials, the Federal Ministry of Finance plans to turn to a microsimulation model based on the GSOEP and other data sources during the next few years. This may put public discussion on the impact of tax and benefit reforms on a more rational basis.

1.3.4 Behavioural modelling Like most microsimulation models, my program does not include behavioural equations *routinely*, because behavioural simulation results depend on additional sources of error such as sample variation or specification errors in behavioural relationships. There is, however a series of papers based on my microsimulation model, which additionally rely on econometrically estimated and tested behavioural equations. They analyse, for example the impact of
- the 1984, 1986 and 1990 Tax Reforms Acts on female labour supply and welfare (Wagenhals 1990, 1994),
- income taxation on the intertemporal labour supply of married women (Laisney et al., 1993a),
- alternative reform proposals to increase the tax allowance for the basic level of subsistence according to the 1996 Annual Tax Reform Act (Wagenhals, 1996a),
- a potential removal of the splitting rule (Strøm, Wagenhals, 1991, Wagenhals, 1996b),
- tax and benefit reforms on the labour force participation and welfare dependence of single mothers (Staat, Wagenhals, 1994, Laisney et al. 1993, 1997).

Apart from my model, only the old FITS model (Spahn et al., 1992) and Schwarze (1997) account for behavioural responses. Thus, the German experience confirms Klevmarken's (1997) findings for other countries: behavioural modelling based on microsimulation models is still an academic exercise.

2 The Survey

My microsimulation model is based on the GSOEP, the German Socio-Economic Panel. The GSOEP is a representative longitudinal data set of private households in Germany (see Wagner et al, 1993, for details). It covers data on a wide range of socio-economic personal and household characteristics.

My model uses data on all individuals and households who ever participated in the German Socio-Economic Panel. The first wave was collected in 1984 in West Germany. This sample included 5,921 households with 12,290 adult respondents and additionally 3,936 records of children. Since 1990, an East German subsample is collected. The 1996 sample includes 6,894 households with 13,511 individual interviews and 3,993 records of children.

Although the GSOEP is a very comprehensive dataset, some data important for the modelling of taxes and benefits are missing.

First, some income variables necessary for tax-benefit simulations are not directly available in the original survey. For example, the GSOEP does not include earnings from paid employment. They have to be constructed as the sum of income from different jobs, 13th and 14th month pay, and miscellaneous bonus payments. Fortunately, some constructed variables are included in the Syracuse University PSID-GSOEP equivalent data file (Daly and Butrica, 1994), a data set which can be easily merged with the original GSOEP data set. Whenever applicable, I use these data. (Detailed information on the construction of these data is provided in the GSOEP codebook, see Butrica and Jurkat, 1995.)

Second, often the additional information provided by the PSID-GSOEP equivalent data file is not sufficient. For example, most recent tax reform proposals apply different rates to different sources of income from self-employment. The GSOEP gives only one aggregate figure for self-employment income (not even clearly defined). Therefore I have to split the GSOEP variable "income from self-employment" in its three sources in line with historical statistics published by the German Federal Statistical Office. Unlike all other GSOEP based microsimulation models, my model distinguishes three sources of income from self-employment, namely (1) income from agriculture and forestry, (2) income from trade and business, and (3) income from independent personal services.

A third problem is underreporting of income from non-labour income. To adjust for this, the values of these variables are inflated, respectively. In the case of self-employment income I assume that the understated income is not reported, and therefore tax on it is not collected.

Forth, foreigners and East Germans are deliberately oversampled in the GSOEP. Fortunately, the survey provides weights for each individual and each household which allow the construction of grossed up figures, and which account for over-sampling (see Pischner and Rendtel, 1993, for details). In many applications I use the GSOEP to represent the whole German population. After using the model to calculate taxes and transfers for each household, I combine the results to forecast tax revenues and benefit payments for the entire population, adjusting the survey data to make them representative for the total German population.

Finally, although many of the variables necessary to simulate tax and benefit reforms are available or can be constructed or modified along the lines described above, there are areas where the data is not sufficient, and where I am not able to remedy this. For example, the GSOEP includes limited information on expenditures, savings or assets.

How reliable are the tax and benefit data generated? The reliability of model predictions depends on the quality of the original and derived data. My experience with grossing up the tax and benefit data and comparing the results with aggregate tax and benefit statistics from other sources validate the usefulness of the GSOEP as a database for tax-benefit-policy simulations (see also van Essen, Kassella (1988) and van Essen, Kassella, Landua (1988)). Nevertheless we might ask for the pros and cons of other German surveys as base datasets for tax-policy simulations.

2.1 Other surveys There are three more German surveys which might serve as a basis for a tax-benefit microsimulation model. The German *microcensus* ("Mikrozensus") collected by the Federal Statistical Office is a very comprehensive labour force survey. Unfortunately, it codes income from employment only, and in wide categories. All other types of income in the German Income Tax Act are ignored. The *Einkommens- und Verbrauchsstichprobe* (EVS), also collected by the Federal Statistical Office, is a very expensive cross section survey, with limited information about income and socio-economic background variables. The *IAB-Beschäftigungsstichprobe* (IABS) is a survey made available by the Research Institute of the German Federal Bureau of Labour. It is a random sample of the Employment Register of the Federal Labour Office, a one percent sample of all - but only - persons - in paid employment and covered by the statutory social security system (see Bender et al., 1996, for details). Furthermore, EVS and IABS do not contain information on hours worked, a necessary input e.g. to analyse incentive effects of tax reforms, and they are available up to 1988 (EVS) or 1990 (IABS) only.

2.2 Summing up Although the GSOEP is a very rich survey, it is not designed for tax and social policy simulations and in a number of respects it is deficient: information is missing, I have to adjust old variables and construct new ones, and there are areas of the personal tax and benefit system that I cannot model at all. Given the drawbacks of alternative German surveys, however, the GSOEP is still the best available choice as a database for tax and social policy simulations.

3 Taxes and Benefits

This section describes the coding of my microsimulation model. It neither attempts to survey the German tax-benefit-system (see e.g. OECD, 1996, pp. 51-97) nor to describe its incentive effects on work and welfare (see e.g. Zimmermann, 1993, and OECD, 1996, pp.176-178).

My model takes into account the legal positions starting in the taxable year 1983, and includes tax and benefit rules up to 1999, as well as many reform proposals which have been discussed publicly in recent years. All taxes and benefits are modelled simultaneously, because they are interconnected: Some household pay taxes and receive benefits, some benefits are taxable, other benefits are means-tested and pre- or post-tax incomes and the level of social security contributions are used to assess entitlements to benefits.

The rest of this section describes the core modules of my microsimulation model, which generate income taxes, social security contributions (employees' contributions to old age insurance, health insurance, long-term care insurance, and unemployment insurance), and benefits (social assistance, housing benefits, child benefits).

3.1 Taxes

My model accounts for that part of the income tax law which applies to individuals domiciled or ordinarily resident in Germany and which is regulated in the Income Tax Act ("Einkommensteuergesetz").

Basis of assessment is the sum of seven types of income after offsetting losses which result from the individual type of income and deducting special expenditure and certain other items. According to the Income Tax Act, total gross income is defined as the sum of incomes from (and limited to) the following seven sources:
1. agriculture and forestry,
2. trade and business,
3. independent personal services,
4. paid employment,
5. capital,
6. rent and royalties,
7. miscellaneous income.

3.1.1 Exemptions The model accounts for the fact that, among others, certain receipts are tax-exempt, such as overtime premia for night work, for Sunday and holiday work, and for public or private old-age pensions up to a share of some 30 per cent representing capital gains ("Ertragsanteil"). Social assistance, housing benefits and unemployment assistance are tax-free, as are employers' social insurance payments if they are or rank as statutory requirements.

3.1.2 Deductions The model accounts for allowances for children, elderly persons and for single parents with at least one child living in the household, and for deductible special expenses such as certain social insurance expenses (provident expenditure), insurance premiums, payments to building societies and loan associations, maintenance payments to a divorced or permanently separated spouse. Unless I have more detailed information for the survey, I assume flat-rate allowances. For itemised special expenses due to the need to travel from home to the place of work, I calculate figures for documentary proof. Special rules for civil servants ("Beamte"), retired civil servants and recipients of a full old-age pension are accounted for.

Married couples may opt for separate assessment, special assessment for the tax period in which they were married, or joint assessment with taxation under a splitting rule ("Ehegatten- splitting"). In the latter case, income tax is calculated by applying the income tax schedule on half of the total taxable income of the spouses, and then doubling the resulting tax liability. We assume that all married couples (not permanently separated) opt for the splitting rule.

3.1.3 Tax schedule In 1997, low incomes up to a basic tax allowance for untaxed income ("Grundfreibetrag") of DM 12,095 are tax exempted. In a first income bracket marginal tax rates rise linearly from 25.9 per cent to 33.5 per cent at a taxable income of DM 55,727. In a second income bracket marginal taxes increases again linearly from 33.5 per cent to 53 per cent (excluding a solidarity surcharge of 7.5 per cent) at a taxable income of DM 120,041 after which the marginal tax rate remains constant. For married couples the income limits are doubled. Figure 3.1 shows marginal income tax rates for a married coupled as a function of annual taxable income for the taxable year 1997 and for the taxable year 1999 according to a new tax schedule of a tax reform ("Petersberger Steuervorschläge") proposed on January 22nd, 1997, by the Federal Government (Bundesregierung, 1997).

3.1.4 Entrepreneurial income Since 1994, income from trade and business is taxed differently, with a top marginal tax rate of 47 per cent. The model accounts for this fact. As the GSOEP doesn't give information on the sources of entrepreneurial income, I assume that it is taxed according to the income tax law, not according to the Corporation Tax Law ("Körperschaftsteuer"). For the same reason, I have to disregard local business taxes ("Gewerbesteuer") and local business taxes on profits ("Gewerbekapitalsteuer").

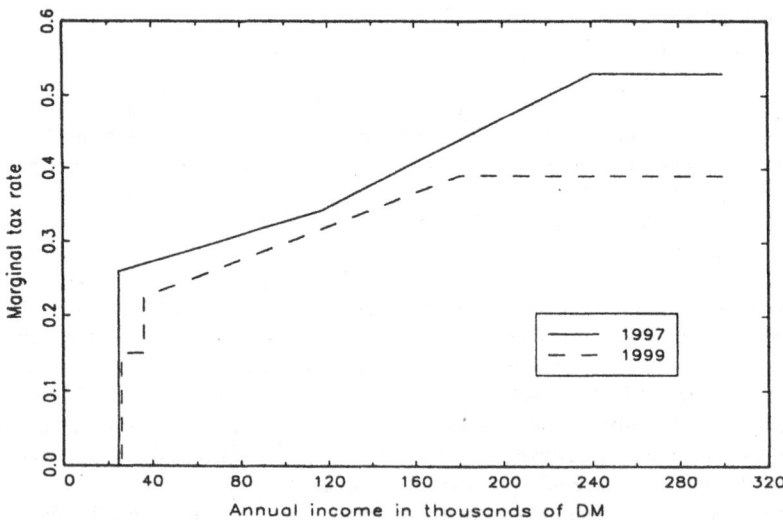

Figure 3.1 Marginal tax rates, 1997 (actual) and 1999 (tax reform proposal)
Note: Joint assessment of a married couple; without income from trade and business, excluding the solidarity tax surcharge.

3.2 Social Security Contributions

In Germany, there exist separate social security systems for different occupational groups. Entitlement to social security is conditional on having paid contributions. Social security contributions are shared by employees and employers (50 per cent each). Contribution rates have been increasing steadily during the last few years and amount to more that 40 per cent of gross wages in 1997. I account for employees' contributions to old age insurance, health insurance, long-term care insurance, and unemployment insurance.

Wage earners and salaried employees with monthly incomes exceeding a casual employment limit (i.e. DM 610 (West) or DM 520 (East) in 1997) are compulsorily insured. Contributions are proportional to gross income up to a contribution assessment limit, then they remain constant. Self-employed individuals and individuals with incomes above the contribution assessment limit may join their own systems. I assume that they join the statutory social security system. Civil servants, retired civil servants and recipients of a full old-age pension are exempted from old age and unemployment insurance.

3.3 Benefits Modelled

Of the benefits, my program models child benefits, housing benefits and social assistance benefits. I first turn to these benefits, then I explain other benefits which could be relevant for some couples, but which are not modelled explicitly up to now. The benefits I model are practically tax free.

3.3.1 Child benefits Ordinarily residents in Germany may claim child benefits ("Kindergeld") for their children living in the Federal Republic. It is paid to one person for each eligible child under 18 years of age. Prolongation to children aged between 18 and 27 is possible for pupils, students and for children registered for occupational training schemes with low incomes. The upper age limit is 27 for children in full-time education or in vocational training if they earn less than DM 2,000 DM per month (in 1997). There is no age limit for children with serious infirmity if their subsistence is not secured by other sources of livelihood. In 1997, child benefits consist in monthly payments of DM 220 for the first and second child, of DM 300 for the third, and DM 350 for the forth child and subsequent children. Since January, 1st, 1996, child benefits are not income-tested any more, but there is an obligatory choice between child benefits and an annual income tax allowance of DM 6,912 per child. Child benefits count as unearned income for social assistance purposes.

3.3.2 Housing benefits Low income families may be entitled to rent subsidies from a housing allowance scheme ("Wohngeld"). Whether housing benefit is paid depends (1) on the family size, (2) on the level of the rent (or housing costs for owner-occupiers), and (3) on "family income", which is derived starting from the sum of gross earnings of all household members, and subtracting of maintenance payments up to a fixed maximum, certain other allowances and of a lump-sum amount between 6 per cent and 30 per cent depending on the amount and type of social security contributions paid by the family members. Housing benefit is granted if the family income does not exceed a certain maximum. It consists in a monthly subsidy for rent or housing costs and depends on housing conditions, age of the apartment, living space and the local level of rents.

3.3.3 Social assistance ("Sozialhilfe") may be claimed by anyone who is in need, i.e. whose income from other sources is below a prescribed minimum if no other means of support are available. (Income limits are given in the Federal Social Assistance Act ("Bundessozialhilfegesetz"). There are two forms of social assistance: (1) assistance in special circumstances ("Hilfe in besonderen Lebenslagen") for persons who are e.g. ill or invalid and who cannot reasonably be expected to help themselves, (2) help for living ("Hilfe zum Lebensunterhalt"), an income support for persons who are not able to earn a living. Anyone poor enough to qualify for help for living is entitled to a basic scale social assistance rate ("Sozialhilferegelsatz"), and to support to meet the costs of accommodation (including heating). Special payments and benefits in kind for special purposes (e.g. assistance to meet exceptional costs of living) are non-recurring subsidies for larger purchases. There availability is up to the discretion of the local social assistance offices.

The level of social assistance benefits depends on the person of the recipients, on their needs, on the family situation, on local conditions and on existing claims to benefits under other benefit schemes. Child benefits and housing benefits count as unearned income. Apart from a small allowance to cover work expenses and part of the rent and heating costs (for details see e.g. Bundesministerium der Finanzen, 1995, pp. 99-101), earnings have to be deducted from the social assistance entitlement. Only child-minding benefits are disregarded when calculating social assistance. In 1997, the basic assistance rate for the head of the household averages DM 530 per month (West) or DM 512 (East). Standard rates for other household members are lower. They depend on age, health, and on whether a child lives in the same household as its single parent. To receive help for living, all available means of support (e.g. unearned income and assets above DM 2,000, or maintenance from the absent parent) have to be exhausted. I model help for living, and disregard non-recurring subsidies in kind.

3.4 Other Benefits

Net disposable family income consists in gross income minus income and social security taxes plus benefits. Apart from child benefits, housing benefits and social assistance, there exist many other benefits which may apply to individuals and households depending on needs, resources, family size and composition, employment status and socio-demographic variables. These other benefits are accounted for in the tax-benefit model, but up to now, they are not modelled explicitly. I mention some of the more important of these benefits (see Laisney et al. (1993a, 1997) for more details).

3.4.1 Unemployment Unemployed persons may qualify for unemployment benefits or unemployment assistance. Unemployment benefit ("Arbeitslosengeld") is a cash benefit payable to every worker who is unemployed, capable of and available for work and who was in insured employment for at least 12 months preceding unemployment. Benefits amount to 60 per cent (or 67 per cent for persons with children) of standardised former earnings net of statutory deductions for employees for a period between six and 32 month, depending on duration of contribution and age. Unemployment assistance

("Arbeitslosenhilfe") provides a cash benefit to unemployed workers who have exhausted their entitlements to unemployment benefits. It amounts up to a maximum of 53 per cent (or 57 per cent for persons with children) of former earnings net of statutory deductions for employees. Furthermore, compulsory short time work is supported by income transfers ("Kurzarbeitergeld").

3.4.2 Maternity All mothers who are gainfully employed in the Federal Republic of Germany are entitled to maternity protection, i.e. to a maternity leave during a time period from six weeks before delivery of a child until eight weeks after, and they may receive means-tested maternity benefits in cash ("Mutterschaftsgeld").

3.4.3 Child-minding All mothers or fathers who provide for and bring up their new-born child themselves and who are not employed full-time are entitled to a child-minding benefit ("Erziehungsgeld") which is paid up to two years after birth. The monthly benefit rate amounts to DM 600 per child. After the first six months benefits are means-tested. They do not count as unearned income for social assistance purposes, housing benefits and unemployment benefits, but maternity benefits are taken into account.

4 Augmenting Survey Statistics and Policy Implications

Public discussion of economic policies is often hampered by the lack of transparency of the tax and benefit system, and by concentrating on isolated cases. Economic theory often can help to clarify the issues, but there are many important points on which theoretical economic models are ambiguous. Recent examples dealing with the impact of social assistance and housing benefits on work incentives include Weeber (1992), Barthel (1994), Siebert, Stähler (1995) or Hubert (1996). While these studies are very valuable, survey based microeconometric studies are needed to reach clearer conclusions.

This section shows the potential of my microsimulation model (1) to enhance survey statistics and (2) to support policy decisions. First, using it as a quick tax-benefit calculator, I calculate marginal effective tax rates for alternative tax-benefit schemes. Second, I show how the model can be used to evaluate policy measures designed to decrease the welfare dependence of single mothers, currently a subject of heated policy controversies in Germany.

4.1 Example: Marginal Effective Tax Rates

Marginal effective tax rates (METRs) combine income and social security tax rates and the rate at which benefits are withdrawn, i.e. they denote the amount that goes to the state in taxes and social security contributions plus withdrawn benefits from an extra Deutsche Mark earned.

Starting from the gross annual income of the husband the model calculates the entitlement to housing benefits and to child benefits, accounting for the number and age of children. Then it derives social assistance benefits taking housing benefits and child benefits into account. Finally, it calculates METRs using gradient methods.

Figure 4.1 shows METRs for the full tax-benefit system in 1997 and in 1999 (reform proposal). It stipulates a family of four living in West Germany: a married couple aged 30 and 34, with two children, aged four and six. If the husband participates, he earns income from employment as a production worker; the mother does not participate in the labour market. Income from other sources of income is not available. Rent and heating costs of the family add up to DM 600 per month.

The two METR schedules shown in Figure 4.1 start with marginal effective tax rates of zero per cent in the very low income range. Earnings are disregarded up to a quarter of the basic social assistance rate. Then, social assistance is gradually withdrawn. First at a rate of 85 per cent, then at a rate of 100 per cent until eligibility for social assistance stops. Jumps in METRs occur with annual incomes between DM 40,000 and DM 100,000 because of changes in social security contributions. Finally, in the top income range, the METRs equal 53 per cent (excluding a solidarity tax surcharge, "Solidaritätszuschlag").

The "standard" figure in the discussion of the current Government tax reform proposal is figure 3.1 which concentrates on pure income tax schedule analysis. Figure 4.1 however additionally accounts for changes in the social security system (changes in contribution rates, contribution assessment limits and casual employment limits in the heath, pension, long term care and unemployment insurance), and in the benefit system (e.g. changes in social assistance rates, housing benefits, and child benefits). For example, it suggests the possibility of unemployment and poverty traps not to be seen when we look at figure 3.1 only.

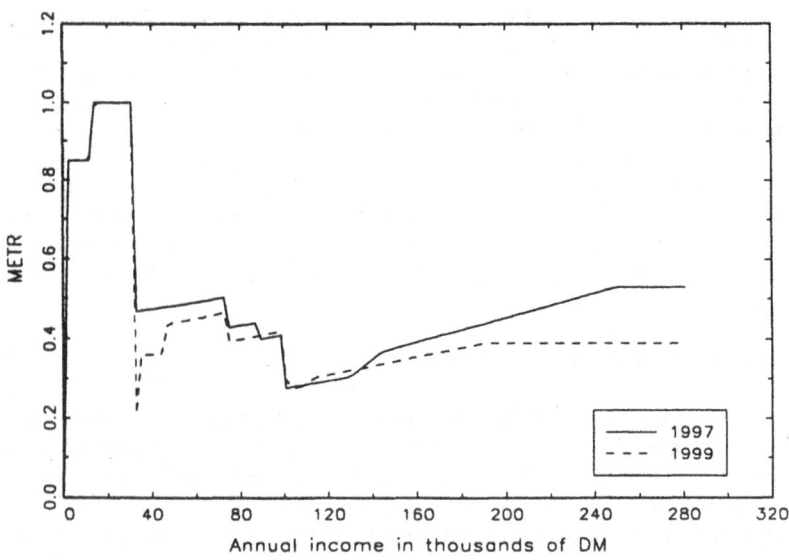

Figure 4.1 Marginal effective tax rates, 1997 (actual) and 1999 (tax reform proposal)
Source: Own calculations. Assumptions: See main text.

Table 4.1 Marginal effective tax rates (METRs) for total work force and single mothers percentage shares, 1997 and 1999 reform proposal

METRs	Total work force		Single mothers	
	1997	*1999*	*1997*	*1999*
above 80 %	5	5	18	17
40 % - 80 %	55	49	33	30
0 % - 40 %	39	46	48	53

Source: Own calculations assuming no behavioural changes. Errors are due to rounding.

Using the model as tax-benefit calculator as described above, I can quickly calculate METRs for any person in the survey, and derive descriptive statistics for the total population. Table 4.1 provides empirical information about the incidence of METRs in Germany, based on 1994 and 1995 survey data, updated to 1997 and 1999, and assuming no behavioural changes. We see that one in twenty persons in the total work force, and one in six single mothers faces a METR of more than 80 per cent. The 1999 tax reform will generally decrease the effective tax burden (see Wagenhals, 1997, for details), but METRs shall be still higher for poor people than for much better off people facing the top rate of income tax.

What does this observation imply for work incentives and welfare dependence? As an example, we discuss the example of single mothers, whose number has increased dramatically during the last two decades in Germany, and which are at a high risk of poverty. (See Staat, Wagenhals, 1996, for a review of studies dealing with the economic behaviour of single mothers.)

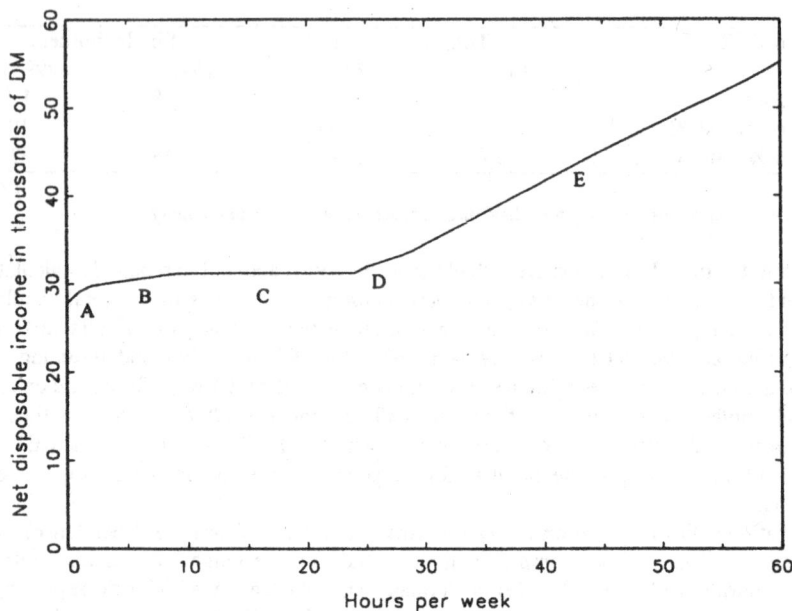

Figure 4.2 Budget set of a single mother, 1997
Source: Own calculations. Assumptions: See main text.

4.2 Example: Work and Welfare of Single Mothers in Germany

4.2.1 A budget set for a single mother Figure 4.2 illustrates the constraints that a single mother typically faces when decides on her labour supply. In this graph we assume a single mother, aged 30, living in West Germany, with her two children, aged four and six. Her only source of earnings is employment in the services sector, her gross hourly labour market wage equals DM 25, and she pays DM 600 in rent and heating. Up to DM 130 per month, an allowance for work expenses leaves her the extra income earned completely (section A). Then there are two segments of the budget constraint where social assistance is withdrawn gradually as earnings rises, first with a withdrawal rate of 85 per cent (section B), then with a 100 percent withdrawal rate (labelled C). This horizontal segment of the budget line, where benefits are reduced *one-to-one* as earnings increase, stretches to almost 25 hours of work. When social assistance entitlements are exhausted, housing benefits may still be claimed. They are also gradually withdrawn with rising income (section D). Only if the single mother works more than 30 hours, the "usual" withdrawal rates of income and social security taxes apply (section E).

The mother facing the budget set shown in Figure 4.2 may be caught in a poverty trap, where the financial reward for increased work hours and effort is quite small or even negative. Because, if we account for fixed costs of work, a single mother can find herself with a reduced income if she accepts low-paid work or a part-time job. In any case she cannot increase net disposable family income more than marginally, unless she can find a full time job. Are there policy measures to help single mothers to overcome this poverty trap and to allow them to keep more of the money they earn? To answer this question as a basis for policy recommendations, the information derived by using the model to augment survey statistics is not sufficient.

4.2.2 Simulation of alternative policy measures To serve as a basis for policy recommendations, my microsimulation model has to be enhanced by an econometrically estimated and validated behavioural model which considers possible behavioural responses to tax and benefit reforms. In concrete terms: changes in METRS might have an impact on economic behaviour, and any study which neglects these second round effects is incomplete.

In a research project funded by the European Union, Staat / Wagenhals (1994), and Laisney / Lechner / Staat / Wagenhals (1993, 1997) use such a model to analyse the impact of alternatives to the current tax-benefit system on the labour supply and welfare dependence of single mothers in Germany based. The econometric part of the model uses a bivariate probit estimator combining GSOEP and microcensus data. Although this approach still has many limitations (e.g. its reduced-form static partial equilibrium character, the neglect of the take-up problem and of fixed costs of work), it has the merit of allowing for non-convexity of the budget set. As I demonstrated above, this is a critical feature of the situation faced by single mothers in Germany.

It is beyond the scope of this paper, to repeat the results of this project in detail. Instead I present the results of one of our simulation experiments, where we ask whether work incentives for single mothers could be improved by decreasing the level of social assistance. Table 4.2 presents our simulation results. On average, a ten per cent reduction of the social assistance basic scale rate could increase the labour force participation probability by some four percentage points. Most single mothers would wish to take a full-time work job, because working part-time only would retain many single mothers in a poverty trap where higher work effort would yield no significant increases in earnings. Only with higher full-time earnings, the discouragingly high marginal effective tax rates diminish somewhat.

Decreasing social assistance benefit rates is only one example for a policy measure designed to increase work incentives for single mothers. Other scenarios show that participation can also be encouraged by ensuring that single mothers can keep more of any extra money they earn by decreasing the benefit withdrawal rate, by providing British-style in-work means-tested benefits or American-style earned-income tax credits.

Table 4.2 Impact of a decrease of social assistance benefits by 10 per cent, (deviations from the observed averages obtained assuming no institutional changes)

Year	Change in average probabilities (in percentage points)		
	non-participation	part-time participation	full-time participation
1984	-3.5	0.4	3.1
1985	-3.9	0.3	3.6
1986	-4.0	0.4	3.7
1987	-4.2	0.5	3.7
1988	-4.1	0.5	3.7
1989	-4.2	0.7	3.5
1990	-4.3	0.9	3.4
Average	-4.0	0.5	3.5

Source: Laisney et al. (1997) and own calculations.

5 Conclusions

This paper has described a microsimulation model of the German personal tax and benefit system, and illustrated part of its repertoire by using it to calculate marginal effective tax rates for individuals, by constructing budget sets for families, and by taking it as a tool to assess the incentive effects of tax-benefit reforms.

The model is continually maintained and supported. This involves revisions and updating, inclusion of new survey data, inclusion of new options and testing of the model. Additional research input is required with regard to the "pure" tax-benefit modelling and with regard to the econometric modelling of individual behavioural responses to taxes and benefits. Apart from the improvement of its behavioural basis, the inclusion of value added and excise taxes is one of the most pressing needs in the further development of the model. However, information on commodity demands is not included in the GSOEP. Therefore, if direct and indirect taxes are to be modelled simultaneously, complementary surveys such as EVS have to be merged, leaving the ground of individual-based behavioural models.

Summing up, I hope to have shown that my survey-based microsimulation model can help to illuminate individual and aggregate impacts of tax and benefit reforms that cannot be caught by a "typical-household" or pure tax schedule analysis. I feel that is a better approach than the one used currently by the German government, which relies on the analysis of population subgroups which are assumed to be homogeneous and which is based on "synthetic" instead of individual data.

Although further refinements of my model are certainly possible, I believe that even in its present form the model is a useful research tool. It has been and will be used for policy evaluation in - and outside academia in an effort to augment survey statistics in an explanatory manner, and to support policy makers in the preparation of their decisions.

References

Barthel, A. (1994), Sozialhilfe behindert Lohndifferenzierung, *Arbeitgeber* 17/46, pp. 573-579
Bender, S., Hilzdegen, J. and Rohwer, G., Rudolph, H. (1996), Die IAB-Beschäftigtenstichprobe 1975-1990, *Beiträge zur Arbeitsmarkt- und Berufsforschung* 197, Nürnberg
Bundesministerium der Finanzen (1995), *Thesen der Einkommensteuer-Kommission zur Freistellung des Existenzminimums ab 1996 und zur Reform der Einkommensteuer*, Schriftenreihe des Bundesministeriums der Finanzen, Heft 55
Bundesregierung (1997), *Reform der Einkommenbesteuerung, Vorschläge der Steuerreform-Kommission vom 22. Januar 1997, „Petersberger Steuervorschläge"*, mimeo, Bonn: Bundespressamt
Butrica, B.A. and Jurkat, D. (1995), *Codebook for PSID-GSOEP Equivalent File 1980-1994*, Center for Policy Research, The Maxwell School, Syracuse NY: Syracuse University
Citro, C.F. and Hanushek, E.A. (eds) (1991), *The Uses of Microsimulation Modelling*, vol. 1, Review and Recommendations, National Academy Press, Washington, D.C.
Daly, M.C. and Butrica, B.A. (1994), *The Syracuse University Panel Study of Income Dynamics and the German Socio-Economic Panel Equivalent Data File*, Cross-National Studies in Ageing Program Project Paper No. 16, Center for Policy Research, The Maxwell School, Syracuse NY: Syracuse University
Fritzsche, B. and von Löffelholz, H.D. (1993), Das RWI-Steuer-Transfer-Modell als Instrument zur Untersuchung verteilungspolitischer Fragestellungen, in U. Heilemann, P. Klemmer, K. Löbbe, *Empirische Wirtschaftsforschung und wirtschaftspolitische Beratung - Willi Lamberts zum 60. Geburtstag*, Untersuchungen des Rheinisch-Westfälischen Instituts für Wirtschaftsforschung, Heft 8, Essen: Rheinisch-Westfälisches Institut für Wirtschaftsforschung
Fritzsche, B. and von Löffelholz, H.D. (1994), Grenzbelastungen der Einkommen durch das Steuer-Transfer-System, eine empirische Analyse für Haushalte von Erwerbstätigen in den neuen und alten Bundesländern, *RWI-Mitteilungen* 45, pp. 235-260
Galler, H.P. (1990), Microsimulation of Tax-Transfer Systems, in J. K. Brunner and H.-G. Petersen (eds), *Simulation Models in Tax and Transfer Policy*, Frankfurt am Main, pp. 279-299
Galler, H.P. (1990,) Politikanalyse mit Mikrosimulationsmodellen - Die Frankfurter Modelle, in R. Hauser et al. (eds), *Mikroanalytische Grundlagen der Gesellschaftspolitik*, Band 1, Ausgewählte Probleme und Lösungsansätze, Berlin, pp. 113-135
Galler, H.P. (1996), Simulation of Pension Reform Proposals: Modelling the Earnings of Couples, in A. Harding (ed) *Microsimulation and Public Policy*, Contributions to Economic Analysis 232, Elsevier: Amsterdam, pp. 293-312
Gern, K.-J. (1996), *Ein Modell zur Simulation des Deutschen Steuer-Transfer-Systems*, Kieler Arbeitspapier Nr. 725, Institut für Weltwirtschaft, Kiel
Gyárfás, G. (1990), *Ein Simulationsmodell der Einkommensbesteuerung auf der Grundlage synthetischer Mikrodaten*, München/Wien.
Gyárfás, G. (1993), Review of Spahn, P.B., Galler H.P., Kaiser H., Kassella T., Merz J., Mikrosimulation in der Steuerpolitik, Heidelberg, 1992, *Finanzarchiv* 50(1), pp.129-133
Gyárfás, G. and Quinke, H. (1990), Methods of Estimating Revenue Effects of Changes in the German Personal Income Tax, in J. K. Brunner and H.-G. Petersen (eds), *Simulation Models in Tax and Transfer Policy*, Frankfurt am Main., pp. 31-50
Gyárfás, G. and Quinke, H. (1993), Ein Verfahren zur Konstruktion synthetischer Mikrodaten aus aggregierten Strukturinformationen, *Allgemeines Statistisches Archiv* 77, pp. 149-165
Gyárfás, G. and Wiesmeth, H. (1993), *Zur Ermittlung der Verteilungswirkung von Steuertarifreformen mit Hilfe der Tarifanalyse*, Diskussionspapier Nr. A-399 des Sonderforschungsbereichs 303, Bonn
Harding, A. (ed) (1996), *Microsimulation and Public Policy*, Contributions to Economic Analysis 232, Elsevier Science B.V., Amsterdam
Hauser, R., Hochmuth U. and Schwarze J. (eds) (1994), *Deutsche Forschungsgemeinschaft: Mikroanalytische Grundlagen der Gesellschaftspolitik: Ergebnisse aus dem gleichnamigen Sonderforschungsbereich an den Universitäten Frankfurt und Mannheim*, Deutsche Forschungsgemeinschaft, Berlin: Akademie-Verlag
Hubert, F. (1996), Zur Reform des Wohngeldes, *Zeitschrift für Wirtschafts- und Sozialwissenschaften* 116(4), pp. 503-530

Klevmarken, N.A. (1997), *Behavioral Modeling in Micro Simulation Models*, unpublished manuscript, Department of Economics, Uppsala University

Laisney, F. and Lechner, M. (1996), Combining Panel Data and Macro Information for the Estimation of a Panel Probit Model, *Zeitschrift für Wirtschafts- und Sozialwissenschaften* 116, pp. 339-358

Laisney, F., Lechner, M., Staat, M. and Wagenhals, G. (1993), *Labour Force and Welfare Participation of Lone Mothers in Germany*, Zentrum für Europäische Wirtschaftsforschung, Discussion Paper no. 93-26

Laisney, F., Lechner, M., Staat, M. and Wagenhals, G. (1997), *Work and Welfare of Single Mothers in Germany*, Diskussionsbeiträge aus dem Institut für Volkswirtschaftslehre, Nr. 141, Universität Hohenheim, Stuttgart

Laisney, F., Lechner, M., van Soest, A.E. and Wagenhals, G. (1993a), A Life Cycle Labour Supply Model With Taxes Estimated on German Panel Data: The Case of Parallel Preferences, *The Economic and Social Review* 24 (4), pp. 335-368

Leibfried, W. and Parsche, R. (1988), *Umverteilung in der Bundesrepublik Deutschland. Das Zusammenwirken von Steuern und Sozialtransfers, Band 1*, Ifo-Institut für Wirtschaftsforschung, München

Lietmeyer, V. (1983), Das Einkommensteuermodell des Bundesministeriums der Finanzen - Aufbau und Anwendungsbeispiele, in J. Bendisch and P. Hoschka (eds), *Möglichkeiten und Grenzen soziöokonomischer Modelle*, GMD-Studien, Nr. 73, pp.7-26

Lietmeyer, V. (1986), Microanalytic Tax Simulation Models in Europe: Development and Experience in the German Federal Ministry of Fincance, in G.H. Orcutt, J. Merz, H. Quincke (eds): *Microanalytic Simulation Models to Support Social and Finance policy*, Amsterdam: North-Holland, pp. 139-152

Merz, J. (1994), *Microsimulation - A Survey of Methods and Applications for Analyzing Economic and Social Policy*, Forschungsinstitut Freie Berufe, Discussion Paper No. 9, Fachbereich Wirtschafts- und Sozialwissenschaften, Universität Lüneburg

Merz, J. (1996), MICSIM: Concept, Developments, and Applications of a PC Microsimulation Model for Research and Teaching, in Troitzsch, K.G., Mueller, U., Gilbert, G.N., and Doran J.E. (eds), *Social Science Microsimulation*, Berlin: Springer-Verlag, pp. 33-65

Nierhaus, W. (1988), *Umverteilung in der Bundesrepublik Deutschland. Das Zusammenwirken von Steuern und Sozialtransfers, Band 2*, Ifo-Institut für Wirtschaftsforschung, München

OECD (1996), *OECD Economic Surveys, Germany*, Paris, OECD

Pischner, R. and Rendtel, U. (1993), *Quer- und Längsschnittgewichtung des Sozio-ökonomischen Panels*, DIW Discussion Paper Nr. 69, German Institute for Economic Research, Berlin

Schwarze, J. (1995), *Simulating German Income and Social Security Tax Payments Using the GSOEP*, CrossNational Studies in Ageing Program Project Paper No. 19, Center for Policy Research, The Maxwell School, Syracuse NY: Syracuse University

Schwarze, J. (1997), *Die Geringfügigkeitsregelung und das Arbeitsangebot verheirateter Frauen - Theoretische Überlegungen, ein ökonometrisches Modell und die Simulation von Reformvorschlägen*, DIW Discussion Paper Nr. 146, German Institute for Economic Research, Berlin

Siebert, H. and Stähler, F. (1995), Sozialtransfer und Arbeitsangebot, *Zeitschrift für Wirtschafts- und Sozialwissenschaften* 115(3), pp. 377-392

Spahn, P.B., Galler H.P., Kaiser H., Kassella T. and Merz, J. (1992), *Mikrosimulation in der Steuerpolitik*, Heidelberg

Staat, M. and Wagenhals, G. (1994), The Labour Supply of German Single Mothers: A Bivariate Probit Model, *Vierteljahreshefte zur Wirtschaftsforschung*, Heft 1/2, pp. 113-118

Staat, M. and Wagenhals, G. (1996), Lone Mothers: A Review, *Journal of Population Economics* 9, pp. 131-140

Strøm, S. and Wagenhals, G. (1991), Female Labour Supply in the Federal Republic of Germany, *Jahrbücher für Nationalökonomie und Statistik* 208(6), pp. 575-595

Sutherland, H. (1995) *Static Microsimulation Models in Europe: A Survey*, Microsimulation Unit Discussion Paper MU9503 (DAE Working Paper 9523), University of Cambridge, Department of Applied Economics

van Essen, U. and Kassella, T. (1988), Die Einkommensangaben im Sozio-ökonomischen Panel des Sonderforschungsbereichs 3 und ihre Relevanz für steuerpolitische Simulationen, in U.-P. Reich (ed), *Aufgaben und Probleme der Einkommensstatistik*, Sonderheft zum Allgemeinen Statistischen Archiv, Heft 26, pp. 133-166 van Essen, U., Kassella, T. and Landua, M. (1986), *Ein Simulationsmodell der Einkommensbesteuerung auf der Basis des Sozio-ökonomischen Panels*, Sonderforschungsbereich 3, Arbeitspapier Nr. 188, Frankfurt and Mannheim

Wagenhals, G. (1990), Einkommensbesteuerung und Frauenerwerbstätigkeit, in B. Felderer (ed): *Bevölkerung und Wirtschaft*, Schriften des Vereins für Socialpolitik, Berlin: Duncker und Humblodt, pp. 473-492

Wagenhals, G. (1994), Income Tax Reform in Germany: A Welfare Analysis, in W. Eichhorn (ed), *Models and Measurement of Welfare and Inequality*, Berlin, Heidelberg, New York: Springer-Verlag, pp. 419-432

Wagenhals, G. (1996a), Auswirkungen des Ehegattensplitting in der Bundesrepublik Deutschland. Ergebnisse einer mikroökonometrischen Analyse, In Seel, B. (ed), *Frauenpolitische Aspekte im Einkommensteuerrecht*, Wiesbaden, pp. 159-183

Wagenhals, G. (1996b), Wohlfahrt und Besteuerung, in Statistisches Bundesamt (ed.) *Wohlfahrtsmessung. Aufgabe der Statistik im gesellschaftlichen Wandel*, Stuttgart: Metzler-Poeschel, pp. 97-120

Wagenhals, G. (1997), Wirkungen der „Großen Steuerreform 1999" auf Arbeitnehmerhaushalte. Eine vergleichende mikroökonometrische Studie der Reformvorschläge der Bundestagsfraktionen, Diskussionsbeiträge aus dem Institut für Volkswirtschaftslehre, Universität Hohenheim, Nr. 144, Stuttgart

Wagner, G., Burkhauser, R. and Behringer, F. (1993), The English Language Public Use File of the German SocioEconomic Panel Study, *Journal of Human Resources* 28, pp. 429-433

Weeber, J. (1992), Vermindert die bestehende Sozialhilfe das Arbeitsangebot, *Konjunkturpolitik* 38(2), pp. 55-68

Zimmermann, K.F. (1993), Labour Responses to Taxes and Benefits in Germany, in Atkinson, A. B. and Mogensen, G. V. (eds), *Welfare and Work Incentives. A North European Perspective*, Oxford: Clarendon Press, pp. 192-240

Part VI
Transition Economies

22 Why do the Russian Enterprises Hoard Labour?

Sergei Aukutsionek / Rostislav Kapeliushnikov

Labour hoarding is one of the salient features of today's Russian economy. This phenomenon is also described by quite a number of other terms, namely «labour surplus», «part-time employment», «overemployment», «labour underutilisation», «intrafirm unemployment», «hidden unemployment» etc. It consists in the fact that enterprises maintain more workers than it is necessary for their operation.

Labour hoarding is inherent in various economic systems. In the market economy it is mostly a cyclical phenomenon and is observed in downward phases of economic cycle when cuts in employment lag behind fall in output. This explains, among other things, the procyclical movement of labour productivity (Hazledine, 1981).

In the centrally planned economy excessive employment is not a short-term but long-term, systemic phenomenon. Socialist enterprises are not interested in economising on any resources including labour (Kornai, 1982, Aukutsionek, 1995). It is not therefore surprising that the Russian economy entered reforms with an enormous excessive employment reaching, by guesses of some experts, one-seventh of the total workforce.

At the start of transition to a market system it was rather unclear how the Russian enterprises would manage their labour surplus. Expectations which prevailed during this initial stage could be summed up as follows. Under new, market conditions even a bigger part of workforce would be in excess than before. At the same time, incentives for hoarding «idle» labour reserves would be undermined and administrative fetters, which could have hampered cuts in employment, would fall away. As a result, the government should be ready for massive labour-shedding and an explosive increase in open unemployment. Such expectations were confirmed by the experience of a number of Central and East European countries that had entered reforms earlier than Russia. For example, in Poland and Eastern Germany transition to market gave impetus to such tendencies.

Russian enterprises, however, behaved differently. They did not hurry to get rid of «idle» labour reserves, that is why on the sixth year of market reforms the Russian economy continues to maintain a significant employment «overhang» (while suffering rather moderately from open unemployment).

Thus there is nothing unusual or outstanding in excessive employment per se. What is unique is rather its scale and persistence. On that score the Russian economy by far outrivals not only mature market ones but transition economies of Central and Eastern Europe too.

Hence it is quite understandable that the issue of overemployment provokes much interest. It poses to researchers of Russia's transition economy a lot of difficult questions:

What is the burden of excessive employment for enterprises? What are economic and social roots of this phenomenon? Can it be solved and in what ways?

The present paper assesses the scale and costs of labour hoarding, its causes and main forms, along with analysing perspectives of solving this problem. A special attention is paid to comparing official indicators of involuntary part-time employment with our survey data.

Surveys of «The Russian Economic Barometer» (REB), which cover monthly around 200 industrial enterprises of major branches and regions across Russia, serve as an empirical base of the paper.[1] The problem of labour hoarding has been consistently studied through REB surveys during the last three years. The present analysis continues and develops approaches suggested in our previous publications (Kapeliushnikov, Aukutsio-nek, 1994 a, Kapeliushnikov, Aukutsionek, 1994 b, Kapeliushnikov, Aukutsionek, 1995).

1 Involuntary Part-time Employment as Mirrored by Official Statistics

Official statistics responded to the increasing accumulation of «idle» labour reserves rather quickly. Since 1993 (the second year of the market reforms) data on involuntary part-time employment has been regularly collected and made public. In 1993 it covered (on annual base) five sectors - industry, construction, transport and communications, personal services and science, and since the next year all the sectors of the economy (in 1994 and 1996 on quarterly and in 1995 on monthly base).

Official statistics focuses on part-time employment in two basic forms - involuntary short-time work and administrative leaves. Official data corrected are presented in Table 1. It shows that during the period under investigation the unemployment rate has been slowly but steadily rising from 5.3 per cent at the beginning of 1993 to 9.3 per cent at the end of 1996. In contrast indicators of involuntary part-time employment experienced irregular fluctuations from quarter to quarter. In 1993-96 on average 2.4 per cent of employees were forced to work on a short-time basis and 1.4 per cent to be on unpaid or partially paid administrative leave.

Both rates changed in a rather narrow range. Administrative leaves were more popular in 1994 whereas short-time work in 1996. The average (incomplete) spell of an administrative leave was equal to 10-11 days in 1995-96.

Involuntary part-time employment became a most widespread phenomenon in four sectors, i.e. industry, transport, construction and science with industry as an indisputable leader.

Figure 1 based on uncorrected official data displays change in using of short-time regime and involuntary leaves in the Russian industry during the last two years. It follows that the 1995 and 1996 did not visibly differ in the portion of employees on administrative leave though it largely fluctuated in time. From 9 per cent to 14 per cent of employees were monthly forced to be on leave. The percentage of short-timers fluctuated around a 10 per cent level in 1995 but sharply jumped in 1996 - almost 1.5 times.

Unfortunately official assessments of involuntary part-time employment have a lot of drawbacks and fail to give an adequate picture of the phenomenon under review. First,

---

[1] The REB surveys are conducted monthly since the end of 1991. Project Director is Sergei Aukutsionek.

data were collected in uneven intervals and presented in non-identical forms. Second, the assessments are formed on a different time basis: when calculating the percentage of short-timers the data as of the end of the month are used (measure of *stock*) while when calculating the percentage of employees on administrative leave the data over the whole month are used (measure of *flow*). Third, the data are collected for only medium-size and large enterprises (with workforce over 200 people).[1] Fourth, they do not give information on how many work hours a partial work day or a partial work week comprise. Fifth, official statistics is blind to such an important feature of labour underutilisation as reduction of efforts on the work place.

Most of these drawbacks can be overcome by using alternative, specially designed indicators being assessed via regular enterprise surveys.

2 Incidence of Labour Surplus: Actual and Anticipated Estimates

We could distinguish two main dimensions of the phenomenon under consideration. First, the *width* of its incidence measured by the frequency of positive answers by respondents to the question whether their enterprises have (or have not) any surplus of workers. Second, the *depth* (or intensity) of labour hoarding measured by the labour utilisation rate. To begin with, let us discuss the first aspect.

The question on existence of labour surplus was put to the respondents first once and later twice a year. By the REB data, in 1995-97 approximately two-thirds of the Russian industrial enterprises have had employees in excess.[2] From January 1995 to January 1997 this ratio grew further - almost by 10 percentage points (See Table 2).

The increase in the percentage of overstaffed enterprises was observed against the background of active cuts in their workforce. Indeed, in 1995-96 the REB respondent enterprises were cutting employment by up to 9-10 per cent per annum. Such a combination of the two processes - quite paradoxical at the first glance - was conditioned by the continuos recession which outperformed labour «shedding».

In the investment goods sector the respondents complained of employment «overhang» a bit more often (66 per cent); they were followed by the respondents from the intermediate goods sector of manufacturing (64 per cent) and by those from consumer goods sector (60 per cent) (data averaged over the two years of observation).

There are no strong effects of the type of ownership (state/non-state) or of wages (lower/higher than the sample average).

By contrast, the difference in enterprise size played quite a significant part. From January 1995 to January 1997 on average the portion of entities with labour surplus was

---

[1] As a result, official data *overestimate* the scale of labour hoarding, first, because they confuse the notions of stocks and flows and, second, because they imply that at small enterprises incidence of short-time regime and administrative leaves is the same as at medium-size and large. Meantime, data corrected by experts of the Working Centre (presented in Table 1) *underestimate* the actual scale of this phenomenon because they imply that small enterprises do not resort to either of these forms of involuntary part-time employment at all.

[2] Similar results were obtained by other researchers who asked the same question (Commander, Liberman, Ugaz, Yemtsov, 1993).

49 per cent among the small (under 200 employees) and 71-76 per cent among the large and largest (500-1000 and over 1000 employees) enterprises.

Along with incidence of *current* labour surplus estimates of *anticipated* overemployment are largely suggestive. The latter are obtained from enterprises' answers to the question on how completely they are staffed as against demand for their products anticipated in 12 months (on a scale: «overstaffed», «normally staffed» and «understaffed»). The breakdown of such forecasts remained symmetric and rather stable throughout 1993-95 (Table 3). For example, in 1994-95 on average there were 27 per cent of enterprises likely to have labour surplus and 20 per cent labour deficit in 12 months. The 1996-97 data testify that gradually this symmetry was being destroyed: the number of enterprises with anticipated labour surplus increased and reached almost 40 per cent.

The comparison of these figures with incidence of *current* labour surplus shows that most of overstaffed enterprises have been, until recently, hoping to tackle this problem not by cutting employment but rather by recovering demand for their products. They have been counting that as yet «idle» labour reserves could be required in near future again. Naturally such optimistic expectations served as a strong brake on reduction of excessive workforce. Only on the turn from 1995 to 1996 enterprises began to adjust their expectations to reality. The number of enterprises with perspective labour surplus reached about two-thirds of the number of currently overstaffed ones.

3 Labour Utilisation: Level and Dynamics

To describe the other aspect of labour hoarding (its depth) we suggested a new aggregate indicator, i.e. the labour utilisation rate analogous to the conventional indicator of capacity utilisation rate (the questions on both were put to respondents monthly). Respondents were asked to assess the current labour utilisation rate at their enterprises in percentage of the level they consider as normal for the month (taking this level for 100 per cent).

Average labour utilisation rate amounted to 75 per cent in 1994, 77 per cent in 1995 and 72 per cent in 1996. Its dynamics (as compared with dynamics of capacity utilisation rate) is shown in Figure 2.

The two utilisation measures have been changing in rather a synchronous manner. For all that, the gap between them has been gradually increasing. Whereas at the beginning of 1994 the personnel was utilised 10 percentage points higher than capacities, in 1995-96 this gap reached 16-20 percentage points. This testifies that it is easier for enterprises to manipulate the number of employees than production capacities.

The breakdown of enterprises by the labour utilisation rate is of a certain interest. Over the three years on average the portion of enterprises where personnel was less then half utilised amounted to 18 per cent, while that of enterprises where it was practically fully or even over-utilised amounted to 38 per cent. Moreover, in the survey period the percentages of these two polar groups - with the labour utilisation rate under 50 per cent and over 90 per cent - tended to change in opposite directions.

The data in Table 4 show that the labour utilisation rate varies little across sectors or status groups. Neither does it directly depend on such a factor as enterprise size. While in 1994 the degree of labour underutilisation was minimum at the smallest enterprises, in 1995-96 it was already large enterprises that were in a more favourable position. The only distinct correlation was revealed between labour utilisation and wages. Indeed, the labour utilisation rate at enterprises with wages higher than the sample average exceeded by 16 percentage points that at enterprises with wages lower than the sample average (84 per cent against 68 per cent). The latter group lagged behind the former by the labour utilisation rate much more than outrivaled it by incidence of labour surplus (cf. Table 2).

On the whole, however, differences between major groups of enterprises observed in labour utilisation rates are relatively small. This proves that incidents of labour surplus and of labour underutilisation occur rather evenly at enterprises of different kinds.

4 What Does Labour Hoarding Mean?

By measuring labour hoarding in the two different ways, we can catch the gist of this phenomenon and try to understand how managers view it. On the one hand, when answering the question on labour surplus a manager simply states its existence without specifying its magnitude. On the other hand, when assessing the labour utilisation rate he or she may not connect it directly with maintenance of excessive workforce (or do it only partially).

In fact, the analysis of survey data readily shows that labour underutilisation and labour surplus are close but not identical things.

At the overstaffed enterprises the labour utilisation rate was assessed as 67 per cent (over the four 1995-97 surveys on average), whereas at those without labour surplus it was 84 per cent. This means that even at those enterprises, whose managers reported having no excessive employees, the actual labour utilisation rate was visibly lower than «normal» 100 per cent.

The problem can be also considered in an inverted form: to what extent does the labour utilisation rate affect managers' answers to the question on labour surplus? Table 5 contains data that shed some light on this issue.

Ranking of the main enterprise groups by the degree of labour underutilisation coincides, as a rule, with their ranking by incidence of overstaffing. Labour hoarding does turn out to occur more frequently in the groups where it is deeper (cf. Table 2 and Table 4).

Although the degree of labour utilisation does affect the recognition of labour surplus, its influence is not absolute. The crucial point, as we could guess, lies closely to the 90 per cent level of labour utilisation. The personnel underusing starts arousing enterprise managers' alarm and is regarded as a real employment «overhang» when the labour utilisation rate falls below this level.[1]

When the deviation of the labour utilisation rate from the normal one is smaller, enterprises mostly do not describe themselves as overstaffed. And even when enterprises of this category recognise existence of labour surplus, we most probably deal with overemployment of some other kind (or origin) than that observed at the enterprises with low labour utilisation. This paradox can be explained at least in two ways.

---

[1] We have the impression that at small enterprises cuts in employment may, in many cases, be fraught with misfires and for this reason their managers try to the utmost to maintain it at the level they consider absolutely necessary. As a result they begin to qualify their personnel as "excessive" under the labour utilisation rate much lower than managers of larger enterprises do.

First, it may take place when one part of the personnel is being utilised superintensively while the other is being underutilised (or is excessive). Second, we can not exclude the situation where some part of the workforce, though being rather highly utilised, is nevertheless regarded as excessive because of producing wasteful products.

The REB data on reasons for wasteful production indirectly confirm the latter hypothesis. Indeed, in 1996 almost one-third of the Russian industrial enterprises with partially wasteful production reported doing it, in the first instance, to engage «idle» workers. Among the reasons for which enterprises maintained wasteful production the engaging of «idle» workers occupied, as a rule, the third or the fourth place, with such factors as unexpected fluctuations of prices and desire to retain the market share usually leading (S. Aukutsionek, 1995).

5 Costs of Labour Hoarding

What is the burden of labour hoarding at the microlevel?

One can judge about this on the basis of answers of overstaffed enterprises' managers to the question on the share of costs connected with labour hoarding in the total production and marketing costs. This question was introduced to the REB questionnaires twice - in July 1996 and January 1997. Labour hoarding costs accounted for 6.3 per cent of the total costs of overstaffed enterprises in the first and 8.2 per cent in the second survey. According to official statistics for the entire population of Russian industrial firms the share of labour costs in their total costs amounts to 22 per cent (Informational bulletin of statistics, 1996). Assuming that it is the same both for overstaffed and other entities we could conclude that *labour hoarding costs on average account for about one-third of total labour costs at enterprises with labour surplus.* (By the way, this corresponds to the labour utilisation rate in this group: the 65 per cent rate means that workforce is one-third underutilised.)

The distribution of labour hoarding costs is not even. At almost every second overstaffed enterprise their share in the total production and marketing costs was from 0 per cent to 4 cent, at almost every third from 4 to 10 per cent and at almost every fourth was over 10 per cent. And only four per cent of overstaffed enterprises incurred no additional costs because of labour surplus.

Table 6 shows how «hoarding» costs vary across different groups of overstaffed enterprises. For example, as the labour utilisation rate diminishes, «hoarding» costs begin to account for a bigger share in the total costs. The estimation of the simplest regressions shows that a 10 per cent fall in the labour utilisation rate (UL) brings about a one percentage point increase on average in the share of «hoarding» costs (HC) (all the coefficients are significant on a one per cent level):

$HC_{7.96}$ 10.57 $0.07 UL_{7.96}$, R^2 0.11 (1a)
$HC_{1.97}$ 16.34 $0.13 UL_{1.97}$, R^2 0.13 (1b)

Table 7 shows how «hoarding» costs are connected with enterprise performance. As could be well expected, they increase along with fall of capacity utilisation and labour utilisation rates. Besides, this increase gives rise to the probability of losses and going bankrupt. Indeed, almost two-thirds of enterprises with an over 10 per cent share of labour hoarding costs are loss-making and almost half of them are likely to go bankrupt in the coming 1-2 years whereas for the polar group without labour surplus this probability is more than twice less.

All this enables us to reject the widespread opinion that overstaffed enterprises practically do not suffer from the burden of overemployment and that for this reason it prevails in the Russian economy.

6 Forms of Labour Hoarding

What is the relationship between the two standard indicators of involuntary part-time employment and how are they related to those studied above? To answer this question let us turn to results of two REB surveys when respondents were invited to report the percentages of their involuntary short-timers and of persons on administrative leave. In May 1995 the first portion amounted to 18 per cent and the second 11 per cent. By November 1996 they were 27 per cent and 10 per cent respectively.[1] At the moment of the first survey 65 per cent of REB respondent enterprises did not resort to short-time regime and at the moment of the second 51 per cent. For involuntary leaves the respective figures were 63 per cent and 57 per cent (Table 8).

These data suggest that the labour utilisation rate corresponds well to conventional measures of involuntary part-time employment. Indeed, the gap between labour utilisation rates at enterprises which did and did not resort to shortened hours reached (over the two surveys on average) 17 percentage points (64 per cent against 81 per cent). An even larger gap - 21 percentage points - was observed between labour utilisation rates at enterprises which did and did not force their workers to be on administrative leave (60 per cent against 81 per cent).

A more detailed classification used in Table 9 enables us to assess the role of alternative forms of involuntary part-time employment. It follows from it that a bit over 10 per cent of enterprises resorted only to short-time regime and practically the same percentage only to administrative leaves and almost one-fourth of the enterprises practised both forms of involuntary part-time employment (data averaged over the two surveys). The labour utilisation rate was maximum at enterprises which practised neither shortened hours nor administrative leaves, and minimum at enterprises which used both. Interestingly, at enterprises which resorted only to administrative leaves the labour utilisation rate was by about 10 percentage points higher than at those which resorted only to short-time regime. Most likely this is so because sending of part of personnel on involuntary leave makes it possible to utilise the rest of it more intensively. At the same time, in respon-

---

[1] Official estimates for the industry as a whole for May 1995: the portion of short-timers - 9.1%, the portion of persons on involuntary leave - 14%. Estimates for December 1996 (in November data were not collected): 16.1% and 14.1% respectively.

dents' opinion, some persons on involuntary leave will never come back to their enterprises and as virtual quitters they cease to impact the labour utilisation level.

Various forms of involuntary part-time employment may perform different functions and be applied at different stages of intrafirm employment crisis.

Reducing intensity of work evidently performs as a mechanism of short-term adjustment and is used by enterprises instead of cutting employment. The case with transfers on short-time work and involuntary leave is more complicated. They may be used, first, to delay dismissals and, second, to perform them in a more «soft», less conflictory form. As is well known, short-time regime and administrative leaves usually imply that wages are severely cut or not paid at all. This creates powerful incentives for workers to quit thus releasing enterprises from costs connected with involuntary lay-offs.

As our data show, administrative leaves serve in a large degree as a «soft» form of employment cuts. Frequently rather than substituting for labour «shedding» they perform it in another form. As a result the annual quit rate was on average by about one-fifth higher at enterprises which resorted to administrative leaves than in the opposite group (17.5 per cent against 14.5 per cent respectively).

The impact of shortened hours is more ambiguous. By results of the May 1995 survey transferring personnel on short-time work rather retarded separations than intensified them. The net outflow of employees from enterprises which used short-time regime was only five per cent against nine per cent in the opposite group. Shortened hours seem to have been used, at the moment, as a means to delay cuts in employment - in the hope for better times. However, results of the November 1996 survey showed another tendency: the short-time regime was increasingly becoming a device for *prompting* workers to quit instead of being a means of delaying employment cuts.

The data of Table 10 demonstrate development of intra-firm employment crisis in the course of accumulation of «idle» labour reserves (this process can be followed by moving over columns of Table 10 from the right to the left).

As the first response of an enterprise to the emergence of employment «overhang», a portion of the personnel is usually transferred on shortened hours (the initial stage). With the deterioration of the situation the number of short-timers increases. However, at a certain point the management starts resorting, in parallel, to involuntary leaves (the intermediate stage). When the situation becomes crucial, the number of short-timers can diminish and that on administrative leave reaches its maximum (the final stage). With the overcoming of the crisis the process develops backwards.

Hence the level of labour underutilisation is not necessarily monotonously related to the portion of involuntary short-timers. When the former is increasing, the latter may decrease due to the fact that from a definite point administrative leaves begin to increasingly substitute for transfers on short-time work.[1] Whereas in 1995 the «turning point» in using short-time regime occurred at the labour utilisation rate of 50-70 per cent, in the more distressing 1996 it shifted to a lower level of 30-50 per cent.

---

[1] Of course, development of intra-firm employment crisis may be strongly influenced by technological constraints. Some technological processes provide few opportunities for introducing shortened hours or for transferring part of personnel on involuntary leave

By contrast, labour underutilisation directly depends on the percentage of persons on involuntary leave: the more numerous are such leaves, the higher is the degree of labour underutilisation.

These conclusions were further confirmed by the results of our econometric analysis. We estimated the simple correlations between the labour utilisation rate (UL) as a dependent variable and the percentage of short-timers (S) or the percentage of persons on involuntary leave (V) as independent ones. Results obtained are as follows (all variables were measured in percentage points):

$$UL_{5.95} = 78.04 - 0.17 S_{5.95}, \quad R^2 = 0.05 \qquad (2a)$$
$$UL_{11.96} = 78.34 - 0.14 S_{11.96}, \quad R^2 = 0.14 \qquad (2b)$$
$$UL_{5.95} = 80.65 - 0.62 V_{5.95}, \quad R^2 = 0.31 \qquad (3a)$$
$$UL_{11.96} = 77.62 - 0.78 V_{11.96}, \quad R^2 = 0.19 \qquad (3b)$$

Regression coefficients in all the equations are significant on a one per cent level, their signs correspond to theoretical expectations. But the character of relationship is rather different.

A one per cent increase in the percentage of short-timers causes a 0.14-0.17 per cent fall of labour utilisation rate on average. The parameters of equations (2a) and (2b) enabled us also to assess the average duration of the shortened hours. It appeared to amount to four-fifths of the standard work week (details are here omitted). In other words, transfers from a five-day week on a four-day prevail.

The equations (3a) and (3b) confirm that the depth of labour hoarding (the degree of labour underutilisation) does directly depend on the percentage of employees on involuntary leave. A one per cent increase in the percentage of persons on such leaves causes a 0.6-0.7 per cent fall in the labour utilisation rate. This suggests that most of workers on involuntary holidays keep ready to hand of managers, so that the latter continue to include such workers in the enterprise workforce (with the utilisation rate equal to zero).

The comparison of indicators characterising different aspects of labour hoarding enables us to make one more, very important conclusion. Assessments of labour utilisation help to record its underusing in cases when conventional indicators do not work. According to the REB data, almost two-thirds of Russian industrial enterprises in May 1995 and half in November 1996 have neither involuntary short-timers, nor workers on administrative leave. Nevertheless, the labour utilisation rate amounted to only 84 per cent on average in this group. Therefore, even when there seemed to be no involuntary part-time employment at all, workforce was substantially underutilised.

Hence we can conclude that non-institutionalised reductions of worktime or work intensity are of no less economic importance than labour hoarding in conventional, institutionalised forms (transferring employees on shortened hours or on administrative leave).

7 Reasons for Labour Hoarding

Why do Russian enterprises delay their getting rid of «idle» employees? What underlies their inclination to labour hoarding? Studies on the Russian labour market discuss a number of reasons for such a behaviour.

1. Social responsibility of the management, concern for those who may have a rough time in case of dismissal (backed, among other things, by managers' fear to be ostracised for their hardheartedness).
2. Managers' belief that demand for their enterprises' products will soon recover and as yet «idle» labour reserves will be needed again.
3. High organisational and monetary costs of labour shedding (severance pay, paperwork etc.).
4. Avoidance of potential conflicts with the workers' collective, reluctance to disturb peaceful social climate at the enterprise.
5. Desire to maintain the enterprise status (director's authority, influence, prestige are often directly determined by the enterprise size).
6. Rigidity of technological processes, fear of technological misfires which could result from rapid labour «shedding».[1]
7. Prohibitions of employment cuts by local, regional or federal authorities.
8. Opposition of trade unions.
9. Opposition of worker shareholders.[2]
10. Avoidance of excess wage tax by transferring unnecessary workers on minimum wages instead of firing them.[3]
11. An opportunity to exert pressure on authorities by threatening with mass dismissals seeking thereby subsidies, credits, privileges etc.
12. Virtual sabotage of employment reduction plans by medium-level managers interested in maintaining and even increasing the size of departments they head.[4]
13. Near costlessness of underutilised workforce for the enterprise.

An attempt to assess these factors' relevance was undertaken in several 1995-97 REB surveys. The results are presented in Table 11. As we see, out of 13 reasons suggested in the questionnaires «social responsibility of the management» is an indisputable leader over the four surveys: on average this reason was marked by 70 per cent of overstaffed enterprises. (It seems to become less popular, although doing it rather slowly.) It is followed by «expected demand recovery» (39 per cent), «high costs of labour shedding» (32 per cent), «avoidance of potential conflicts with the workers' collective» (25 per cent), «desire to maintain the enterprise status» (24 per cent), «technological constraints» (17 per cent). The rating of each of the others does not exceed 4-5 per cent.

---

[1] Note that this explanation can not account for a high percentage of workers engaged in the enterprise social infrastructure which technologically is not linked with the main production lines.

[2] The perception of Russian enterprises as a kind of "close club" being under workers' control and isolated by a rigid wall from external labour market can hardly be right because of the high labour turnover peculiar for them.

[3] As has been estimated each such transfer might give an economy on taxes equal to 36 per cent of minimal wages (Roxburg, Shapiro, 1994). This factor being of much importance, we should here mention that enterprises could avoid this tax in more effective ways, e.g. by remunerating their employees through insurance payments or by opening deposits in their name.

[4] This supposition can be made on the base of results of an interesting research carried out under the supervision of S. Clarke and V. Kabalina and where medium-level managers of several industrial firms were surveyed. Most of the managers interviewed asserted that the number of personnel in their divisions had already reached the critically low mark and could not be further reduced (ISITO, 1996).

Of course, the results obtained should be interpreted with a certain circumspection. Variants of the answers included in the questionnaires have different ethical and emotional complexion. Respondents could have chosen some of the answers simply because the latter suggested more favourable treatment of motives of their conduct. Thus, for example, «social responsibility of the management» sounds very plausible. But its frequency (which is the highest of all) does not necessarily mean that it was really the *most* important for managers and outweighed all the other considerations. An opposite example is «easier access to soft credits and subsidies» which could be hardly ever found in the answers of respondents. At the same time, «the maintenance of the status» which seems very similar in essence was marked by every fourth overstaffed enterprise.

For all the necessary reservations the REB data evidently do not confirm many popular explanations of labour hoarding in the Russian economy. Technological rigidities along with taxation considerations, the prohibitions by authorities and the possibility to blackmail the government by threatening with mass dismissals are certain to play only a secondary part. Then, the REB data support some conclusions of a number of previous studies which have found out that persistence of surplus labour in the Russian industry can not be accounted for by the influence of trade unions or by the opposition of shareholders employed at the enterprise. «Sabotage» from medium-level management, too, can hardly be considered a major obstacle to cuts in employment.

Against this background we can more clearly distinguish the two main reasons for labour hoarding: paternalism and the expectation for the growing demand.

It would be interesting to compare overstaffed firms in transition and mature market economies by their rating of reasons for labour hoarding.

In summer 1996 about 100 Dutch industrial firms were surveyed using the REB questionnaire. 20 per cent of the respondents reported excessive employment as of the time of the survey. Similarly to the Russian sample «social responsibility of the management» appeared to be - though with a smaller lead - the first. It was mentioned in 44 per cent of the cases (Table 11). The ratings of the following reasons are rather close in the two samples: high organisational and monetary costs of labour shedding - 37 per cent in Dutch and 35 per cent in Russian, expected demand recovery - 31 per cent in Dutch and 38 per cent in Russian, desire to maintain the enterprise status - 19 per cent in Dutch and 25 per cent in Russian (for the Russian enterprises averaged data of 1996 are used). The largest difference was observed in the ratings of the following reasons: opposition of trade unions - 38 per cent (this reason was ranked second by the Dutch firms) against 2 per cent; avoidance of conflicts with the workers' collective - 6 per cent against 29 per cent; technological constraints - 31 per cent against 18 per cent.

As we see, the main differences are conditioned by institutional peculiarities of the two economies, while the structures of general economic motives for labour hoarding are very similar. As should be expected, the Dutch managers are less paternalistic in their attitude to employees. Along with this contrary to the widespread opinion the Russian economy does not look more technologically rigid than mature market ones (at least in respect to using of labour). As for the possible reaction of employees, the Dutch managers are more often apprehensive of organised, while the Russians of unorganised opposition. However, in total the employees' pressure (the sum of assessments of items 4, 8 and 9) turns out to be heavier for the Dutch firms that serves as an additional indirect argument against treating Russian enterprises as virtually labour-managed firms.

8 Prospects of Excessive Labour Stock Resolution

The study of various reasons for labour hoarding enables us to put the problem in a more general form. As is easily seen, they can be divided into two large categories, i.e. relating either to maintaining «idle» labour reserves or to «manipulating» the number of employees.

As might be concluded from one of the items of our list labour hoarding results in substantial costs: only 3-5 per cent of overstaffed enterprises report facing no problems caused by maintenance of labour surplus.[1] So we can infer that others do face such problems. Indeed, as was shown above, labour-hoarding costs are quite substantial and presumably reach one-third of total labour costs at overstaffed enterprises.

Other items of our list actually describe different components of costs (both economic and social) to be incurred by an enterprise which takes the way of employment reduction. As follows from data obtained, cuts in employment may arouse ostracism towards enterprise managers by local community, hamper adjustment to possible demand recovery, require substantial monetary costs and much organisational effort, provoke conflicts with the workers' collective, undermine enterprise social status, cause misfires in the technological processes etc. Hence these costs are far from being small too.

However, what does matter in explaining enterprise behaviour in labour market is not absolute magnitudes of costs of the first or the second kind but the *proportion* between them. In the end it is the proportion between «*inequilibrium costs*» (i.e. costs of retaining «idle» employees), on the one hand, and «*adjustment costs*» (i.e. of shedding these employees), on the other hand, that determines the speed of excessive workforce «resolution».

In one of our previous studies we have made an attempt to formalise and assess empirically the relative significance of these costs. For the purpose we have used the simplest dynamic model of labour demand known as the model of partial adjustment in the labour market. Within this model the actual employment at firms approaches desired («optimal») level not immediately but gradually, not in a jump but step by step. That is why (even if no other factors operate) an employment «overhang» is being maintained for some time.[2] The empirical test was based on the data of the 1994-95 surveys. These results enable us to formulate the following conclusions:

1. In spite of numerous peculiarities of Russia's transition economy, the mechanism of partial adjustment is effective in its labour market too. Although we can not assert that employment changes in Russia's industry were conditioned, in the first instance, by the mechanism of its adjustment to the desired level;

---

[1] This result nearly completely coincide with the assessment cited in the discussion on costs of labour hoarding. However, our results differ from assessments of some earlier studies. For example, according to the survey conducted by the World Bank in 1992, maintenance of labour surplus caused no monetary costs for 25 per cent of overstaffed enterprises (Commander, Liberman, Ugaz, Yemtsov, 1993). Probably, these discrepancies mirror actual changes in economic conditions which occurred as the crisis deepened.

[2] See special surveys on this issue: Hazledine, T., 1981, Nickel, J., 1986.

2. According to our estimates costs connected with *firing* a definite number of employees during 1-6 months were 4-8 times bigger than costs connected with *hoarding* an equivalent number of «idle» workers during the same period.

3. The rate of adjustment of the actual employment to desired lay in such a range that if the output became stabilised and the excessive labour stock continued to diminish at the same rate, the process of its «resolution» could take from 1 to 3 years;

9 Concluding Points

Let us summarise main results of our study:

1. Market reforms have not yet resulted in a drastic reduction of employment in Russia's industry. The major part of Russian industrial enterprises suffer from labour over-accumulation. In 1994-96 its magnitude has not diminished.

2. For overstaffed enterprises costs of labour hoarding account for no less than one-third of their total labour costs.

3. The main form of labour hoarding at the Russian enterprises is low labour utilisation. The conventional measures of excessive employment - through the frequency of using shortened work week and involuntary administrative leaves - give a biased picture of this phenomenon visibly underestimating its scale.

4. Among the most widespread reasons for labour hoarding are the paternalistic attitudes of managerial corps often backed by their expectations for the near recovery of demand for their products.

5. The structure of general economic motives for labour hoarding is rather similar in mature and transition market economies The main differences concern institutional specifics of the various countries.

6. The volume, structure and motives of labour hoarding are quite persistent. But this persistence is not a stationary but rather a dynamic phenomenon. It is mainly explained by the near equilibrium between the rate of increasing excessive employment caused by the continuing recession, on the one hand, and the rate of shedding «idle» employees which is observed at most of enterprises, on the other hand.

7. The crucial condition for «resolving» of labour surplus is putting an end to the recession; if it occurs, to recover normal levels of labour utilisation may take not so much time - under 2 or 3 years, as show the quantitative estimates obtained by us.

Table 1 Rates of unemployment and involuntary part-time employment in Russia, 1993-96, %*

	Unemployment rate	Percentage of employees on short-time work	Percentage of employees on unpaid/partially paid involuntary leave
1993			
1 quarter	5.3	1.3	0.5
2 quarter	5.2	1.2	0.5
3 quarter	5.2	1.4	0.7
4 quarter	5.5	2.1	1.2
1994			
1 quarter	6.6	3.5	1.8
2 quarter	7.1	2.4	2.3
3 quarter	7.4	2.4	2.0
4 quarter	7.5	2.6	1.9
1995			
1 quarter	7.7	2.9	1.6
2 quarter	7.8	2.7	1.5
3 quarter	7.9	2.5	1.3
4 quarter	8.2	2.7	1.4
1996			
1 quarter	8.6	3.0	1.6
2 quarter	9.1	-	-
3 quarter	9.2	-	-
4 quarter	9.3	-	-

*Official data corrected by experts of the Working Centre for Economic Reforms under the RF Government. Quarterly figures are averages of monthly totals.
Source: The Russian Economic Trends, various issues.

Table 2 Percentage of enterprises with labour surplus

	1995 (January)	1996 (Average over January and July surveys)	1997 (January)
The whole sample	58	63	67
Sectors of manufacturing			
consumer goods	59	58	63
investment goods	62	66	69
intermediate goods	57	64	71
Status groups [*]			
state enterprises	61	68	58
enterprises of intermediate type	63	60	55
non-state enterprises	58	61	72
Size(number of employees)			
under 200	40	50	56
201-500	57	69	65
501-1000	72	72	83
over 1000	69	66	78
Wages			
lower than the sample average	60	65	64
higher than the sample average	54	62	70

[*]Enterprises were grouped according to their managers' assessment.
Source: Here and below The Russian Economic Barometer's surveys.

Table 3 How enterprises are staffed as against demand for their products anticipated in 12 months (annual average data, % of respondents)

Enterprises are	1993	1994	1995	1996	1997 (February)
overstaffed	21	28	26	37	39
normally staffed	55	52	55	52	51
understaffed	24	20	19	11	10

Table 4   Average annual labour utilisation rate, 1994-96, %

	1994	1995	1996
The whole sample [a]	75	77	72
Sectors of manufacturing			
consumer goods	76	75	71
investment goods	71	76	70
intermediate goods	74	78	75
Status groups [b]			
state enterprises	77	78	78
enterprises of intermediate type	74	76	71
non-state enterprises	75	79	71
Size (number of employees)			
under 200	79	75	70
201-500	74	76	70
501-1000	72	81	75
over 1000	74	80	76
Wages			
lower than the sample average	69	71	64
higher than the sample average	83	85	83

[a] The estimate obtained by averaging labour utilisation rates calculated for different groups may deviate from the sample average because of enterprises not attributed to a certain group. We mean respondents who have not answered to some of the questions (e.g. on enterprise status or on the number of employees).

[b] Enterprises were grouped according to their managers' assessment.

Table 5   The portion of enterprises with labour surplus as depending on the labour utilisation rate (% of respondents in each group)

Survey date	Groups by the labour utilisation rate				
	under 50%	50-70%	70-90%	90-100%	100% and over
1995 (January)	87	82	61	47	22
1996 (average over January and July)	81	78	75	45	27
1997 (January)	76	74	74	53	41

Table 6 Share of labour hoarding costs in the total production and marketing costs by different groups of overstaffed enterprises, % (data averaged over the two surveys of July 1996 and January 1997)

All enterprises with labour surplus	7.3
Sectors of manufacturing	
consumer goods	7.9
investment goods	8.5
intermediate goods	5.9
Status groups [*]	
state enterprises	9.0
enterprises of intermediate type	6.9
non-state enterprises	7.1
Size (number of employees)	
under 200	7.7
201-500	8.2
501-1000	6.7
over 1000	6.2
Wages	
lower than the sample average	8.5
higher than the sample average	5.9
Labour utilisation rate	
under 50%	11.0
50-70%	8.0
70-90%	6.9
90-100%	3.6
100% and over	3.4

[*]Enterprises were grouped according to their managers' assessment.

Table 7 Enterprise performance as depending on the share of labour hoarding costs in the total production and marketing costs (data averaged over the two surveys of July 1996 and January 1997)

	Enterprises without labour surplus	Overstaffed enterprises by the share of labour hoarding costs in the total costs		
		0-4%	4-10%	over 10%
Capacity utilisation rate, %	62	57	45	43
Labour utilisation rate, %	80	79	63	56
Percentage of loss-making enterprises in the past 6 months	31	29	46	65
Percentage of enterprises likely to go bankrupt in the coming 1-2 years	32	36	49	56

Table 8 Using of short-time regime and involuntary leaves by REB respondent enterprises, %

	May 1995			
	The short-time regime		Administrative leaves	
	is used	is not used	are used	are not used
Percentage in the whole sample	35	65	37	63
Capacity utilisation rate	56	64	46	68
Labour utilisation rate	65	80	60	82
Net annual employment change	-5	-9	-13	-4
Average wages as of the survey date (thousand roubles)	275	451	261	465
	November 1996			
	The short-time regime		Administrative leaves	
	is used	is not used	are used	are not used
Percentage in the whole sample	49	51	43	57
Capacity utilisation rate	47	63	44	63
Labour utilisation rate	62	82	60	80
Net annual employment change	-11	-6	-15	-4
Average wages as of the survey date (thousand roubles)	650	852	610	859

Table 9 Labour utilisation rate as depending on use of different forms of involuntary part-time employment, %
(data averaged over May 1995 and November 1996 surveys)

	Groups of enterprises by use of different forms of involuntary part-time employment *			
	S=0, V=0	S=0, V>0	S>0, V=0	S>0, V>0
Percentage of the whole sample	54	11	12	23
Labour utilisation rate	84	73	65	57

*S - the percentage of short-timers, V - the percentage of persons on involuntary leave.

Table 10 Use of short-time regime and involuntary leaves in groups with different labour utilisation rate, % *

Survey date	Indicators of part-time employment	Groups by the labour utilisation rate				
		under 30%	30%-50%	50-70%	70-90%	90-100%	100% and over
1995 (May)	S	26	24	35	16	16	1
	V	47	22	13	6	1	1
1996 (Nov)	S	40	60	28	29	11	4
	V	38	16	11	6	2	2

* S - the percentage of short-timers, V - the percentage of persons on involuntary leave.

Table 11 Reasons for labour hoarding (% of overstaffed enterprises) [a]

Reasons	1995 Jan.	Russian 1996 (average over Jan. and Jul.)	1997 Jan.	Dutch 1996 summer
1. Social responsibility of the management	73	68	70	44
2. Expected demand recovery	40	38	41	31
3. High costs (organisational and monetary) of labour shedding [b]	-	35	27	31 (6) [e]
4. Avoidance of conflicts with the workers' collective	30	27	18	6
5. Desire to maintain the enterprise status	26	25	20	19
6. Technological constraints	15	18	19	31
7. Authorities' counteraction to employment cuts	3	2	2	0
8. Opposition of trade unions	3	2	3	38
9. Opposition of worker shareholders	3	2	3	0
10. Economising on excess wage tax [c]	4	-	-	-
11. Easier access to soft credits, subsidies etc.	1	1	0	0
12. Medium-level managers' counteraction to employment reduction [d]	-	-	5	-
13. No problems with excessive labour	3	4	4	0
14. Other	13	9	8	6

[a] Respondents were asked to choose no more than 3 items.
[b] There was no such an item in the first survey.
[c] The excess wages tax was repealed at the beginning of 1996.
[d] There was no such an item in the previous surveys.
[e] The first figure relates to monetary costs, the figure in parentheses to legal, administrative and paperwork costs.

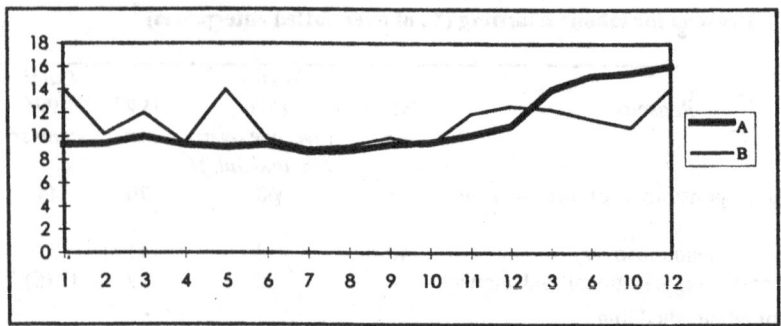

A - The percentage of involuntary short-timers as of the end of the month.
B - The percentage of personnel on administrative leave during the month.

Figure 1 Dynamics of involuntary part-time employment in the Russian industry, 1995-96, % (uncorrected official data)
Source: Publications by RF Goskomstat.

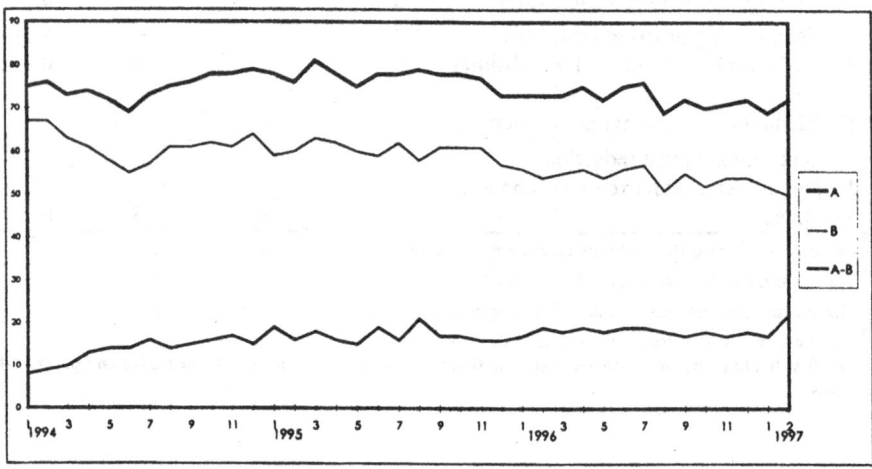

Figure 2 Labour utilisation rate (A) and capacity utilisation rate (B) at RF industrial enterprises (the normal monthly level=100)
Source: The REB surveys.

References

Aukutsionek, S. (1995), *Teoriya perekhoda k rynku (The Theory of Transition to Market)*, Moscow.

Aukutsionek, S. (1995), Wasteful Production in Russian Industry, *The Russian Economic Barometer*, vol.IV, No.4.

Aukutsionek, S. and Kapeliushnikov, R. (1995), Transition in the Russian Labour Market: Enterprises' Behaviour, Selected Papers submitted to the 22nd CIRET Conference in Singapore, 1995, Part II, A.G. Köhler, K.H. Oppenländer, G. Poser (eds), pp.195-212.

Commander, S., Liberman, L., Ugaz, S. and Yemtsov, R. (1993), The Behavior of Russian Firms in 1992: Evidence from a Survey, *World Bank*.

Informatsionnyi statisticheskii byulleten (Informational bulletin of statistics), (1996), No.12, October, p.28.

Hazledine, T., (1981), Employment Functions and the Demand for Labour in the Short Run, *The Economics of the Labour Market*, in Z. Hornstein, J. Grice, A. Webb (eds), Her Majesty's Stationary Office, London.

Kapeliushnikov, R. and Aukutsionek, S. (1994 a), Labour Market in 1993, *The Russian Economic Barometer*, Vol. II, No.1.

Kapeliushnikov, R. and Aukutsionek, S. (1994 b), The Russian Enterprises' Behaviour in the Labour Market: Some Empirical Evidence, Paper presented at IIASA Seminar «Employment and Unemployment in Russia from a Microeconomic Perspective», Laxenburg, Austria, June.

Kapeliushnikov, R. and Aukutsionek, S. (1995), Labour Market in 1994, *The Russian Economic Barometer*, Vol. IV, No.2.

Kornai, J. (1982), A hiány, Közgazdasági és Jogi Könyvkiadó, Budapest, 1982.

Nickell, J. (1986), Dynamic Models of Labour Demand, in O. Ashenfelter and R. Layard (eds), *Handbook of Labour Economics*, Amsterdam, North-Holland, vol.1.

Restrukturirovaniye zanyatosti i formirovaniye lokalnykh rynkov truda v Rossii (Restructuring labour and forming local labour markets in Russia) (1996), Institute for Research in Social Issues of Labour Relations (ISITO), Moscow.

Roxburg, I., Shapiro, J. (1994), Employment-Retention Incentive Effect of the Russian Excess Wages Tax, Paper presented at IIASA Seminar «Employment and Unemployment in Russia from a Microeconomic Perspective», Laxenburg, Austria, June.

23 Business Cycles in Poland

Zbigniew Matkowski

1 Introduction

This paper presents some results of research on cyclical developments in the Polish economy and composite indicators applicable in such an analysis. The research started in 1994 under the project "Synthetic Indicators of Business Activity in Poland", implemented at the Research Institute of Economic Development (RIED), Warsaw School of Economics. The aim was to develop an operational system of composite indicators, based on quantitative and qualitative data, which might be used for analyzing changes in the aggregate economic activity as well as for monitoring purposes. The project was completed in December 1996 and the full account of results of that collective effort appears as a separate book publication (Matkowski, ed., 1997). This paper brings the results of a follow-up study accomplished after the termination of the project.

As early as in the 70's and 80's it became clear (even from the official national income data) that Poland's economy, under the then prevailing property structure and management system, did not develop steadily. On the contrary, its growth record revealed fluctuations quite similar, at least in symptoms, to those observed in the developed market economies, elsewhere known as business vs. growth cycles. Attempts to interpret the facts indicated internal and external factors of instability seen in the centrally planned economy. Growth fluctuations were mainly attributed to the investment cycle and to the five-year period of medium term planning. Some authors also pointed to various institutional and behavioural sources of the changing rate of development as well as to exogenous factors such as business cycles in export markets and the fluctuation in agriculture caused by weather conditions (cf. eg. Kolodko, 1979; Eysymontt and Maciejewski, 1983; Wozniak, 1985).

The deep fall in the Polish economy in 1989-91 combined the features of a typical recession with those of a structural crisis, augmented by the transformation of economic system, reorientation of foreign trade and radical anti-inflationary measures adopted by the governmental stabilization policy. Since 1992, Poland's economy shows a sustained and relatively rapid growth though the chances for keeping up the high growth rate are threatened by multiple problems. With the progress of transformation towards an open market system, the Polish economy will become more and more apt for fluctuations typical of a market economy. This would certainly increase the demand, on the part of both government and business, for a systematic appraisal and forecast of economic activity.

Most empirical analyses of growth cycles in the Polish economy hitherto undertaken relied on yearly national account data. Such attempts, irrespectively of all other merits, do not provide a sufficient framework for business cycle research. What we need in business cycle analysis are monthly or quarterly data. Wherever such data are missing, we should try to fill the gap by proper estimates. This is the approach taken in our research.

Of crucial importance in both historical analysis and in assessment of current tendencies and prospects is the kind of indicator used to describe the cyclical development of economy, i.e. the reference cycle. In particular, a reliable and comprehensive concept of the reference indicator is needed for monitoring systems based on leading indicators.

In earlier studies based on monthly or quarterly data (Kudrycka & Nilsson, 1993-96), business cycles in Poland were usually reconstructed on the basis of industrial production index or a combined index of industrial production and construction. The same indicator served as a reference series for the selection of leading indicators and for evaluation of their performance. In our research on growth cycles in Poland we employ a broader concept of the general indicator of economic activity, based on the monthly data on output of five major sectors, including industry, construction, agriculture, transport and retail trade. We believe that such an indicator, even if still imperfect, gives a good approximation of the cyclical changes in gross domestic product. The same indicator is used as a reference series in our work on composite leading indicators.

The disputes on the virtue and the predictive power of leading indicators have been continued from the earliest days of using this approach to business cycle analysis. Koopmans's attack on this method (1947) has been somewhat mitigated by the tremendous contribution brought by the research on cyclical indicators to the knowledge of business cycles. One can fully agree with the view that "as a practical method of forecasting, the leading indicators cannot be used very effectively or accurately" (Evans, 1969, p. 460). However, much of the same applies as well to all the other methods of short-term business forecasting. After 50 years of a continuous service, the leading indicator approach has by no means exhausted its potential for further development and application (cf. Westlund, 1993).

As early as in the late 70's this author brought nearer to the Polish reader the barometric method, referring to the pioneering works of W.C. Mitchell and A.F. Burns (1946), G.H. Moore (1961) and many other authors and to the experience accumulated in this kind of research in the United States and other Western countries. The time then was not yet ripe for an attempt to apply this method to the analysis of cyclical developments in Poland's economy. Nowadays, thanks to the improvement of statistical data, we can try to apply the leading indicator approach to the analysis of cyclical developments in post-socialist economies.

The paper includes, besides the introduction and conclusion, three points. In paragraph 2 we present our concept of the general indicator of economic activity which is used to reconstruct growth cycles in the Polish economy since 1975; the same indicator is then employed as the reference cycle in the further analysis. Paragraph 3 analyzes cyclical developments in major sectors of economy against the background of the reference cycle. Paragraph 4 brings some results of our work on composite leading indicators for Poland.

2 The Reference Cycle

In order to reconstruct the cyclical movement of national economy over time in the absence of GDP monthly or quarterly statistics, we have developed a synthetic composite indicator GCI (general coincident indicator) based on the available output data. GCI is a weighted average of indices showing the output volumes in five major sectors of economy: 1) industry, 2) construction, 3) agriculture, 4) transport, 5) trade. For industry and construction, activity levels are represented by the production volumes (production sold). For transport, the index is based on the physical volume of freight transports. For trade, it is the volume index of retail sales (at constant prices). For agriculture, we developed a synthetic index of market production based on the procurement of main agricultural products: cereal grains, slaughter animals, and cow milk (one of the versions also includes procurement of potatoes).

The GCI index has been compiled on a monthly basis for the period starting in January 1975, though until 1983 it did not cover trade due to the lack of data on real trade turnover.

Sectoral indicators of activity entering GCI have been transformed into volume indices based on 1992 = 100 and weighted by the yearly shares of the respective sectors in GDP (up to 1989, in gross material product). The resulting GCI index provides quite a representative picture of month-by-month changes in total domestic output. For the years 1975-1989 it covered 80-85% of GMP; for the period from 1990 till now (for which GDP data are available in accord with SNA standards) it covers 60-70% of GDP, so it may be viewed as a good approximation of the change in total national output.

In order to improve the quality of this indicator, we developed several versions of GCI differing more or less in coverage and in some technical details. The version used here has been coded as GCI2D and it is represented in our database by the variable 091. For the period 1975-1982 it covered industry, construction, agriculture and transport, and since 1983 it also includes retail trade.

The alternative solution widely accepted is to use total industrial production as a reference indicator. The latter is however not a good proxy for GDP since it represents merely 30 percent of GDP and it often displays specific cycles not related to the general course of business. Our indicator has the advantage of a much wider coverage.

In order to identify the cyclical movement of the economy over the last two decades GCI time series have been decomposed into four components of dynamics: (a) seasonal fluctuation, (b) irregular random movements, (c) cyclical change, (d) trend. The split into (a), (b) and (c) + (d) was made with help of X11ARIMA, and the division between (c) and (d) with the OECD PAT procedure.

Statistical properties of GCI series and of the estimated ARIMA model (as shown in table 1) seem too be good enough (QCS = 0.59 is much lower than the critical value of 1.00 and squared R = 0.91) to use it both in historical analysis and for 1-year autoregressive forecasts.

These procedures allowed us to reconstruct cyclical development of the Polish economy from 1975 till now. Our GCI reveals two very well pronounced business cycles which had already been present at times of the centrally planned economic system, and which grew in intensity with the transformation into an open market economy. The chronology and the amplitudes of those cycles appear in table 2. Figure 1 shows the behaviour of the GCI index over time; the index is presented in the form of rough data seasonally adjusted time series and trend-cycle. A detailed analysis of the reference cycles has been presented in a separate publication (Matkowski, 1996).

In the period considered, the Polish economy experienced two prolonged and severe recessions. The first recession covered the years 1980-1981; it lasted 23 months and according to our GCI indicator it brought about a decrease of the general economic activity by ca. 30 per cent. The second recession fell onto years 1989-1991; it took 31 months causing a fall in total output by ca 40 per cent.

The depth of those recessions as measured by our GCI monthly index was roughly twice as great as the amplitude suggested by the official GDP data. One explanation of this discrepancy is that national accounts are calculated on a yearly basis whereas our GCI is a monthly index, so it avoids averaging opposite changes in the first and the last year of recession (the same applies to expansion). Another cause is insufficient coverage of the service sector in our reference indicator, a factor that makes it more vulnerable to cyclical movement. Anyway, our reference index turns to be a very sensitive indicator of cyclical changes in the economy.

Both recessions were strongly influenced by political factors and by the change in economic system. They combined the features typical of cyclical downturns and of structural crises. Notwithstanding the complexity of their causes, both recessions launched adjustment processes quite similar to those seen in business cycles. This fact can justify the use of analytical tools developed in the framework of business cycle approach.

The two recessions were separated by a vivid expansion of the eighties, boosted by foreign credits. Two other expansions appear in the beginning and at the end of the analyzed period. Altogether, over the last two decades Poland's economic development has displayed two incomplete growth cycles whose length, depending on the method employed (peak-to-peak or trough-to-through), ranged from 6 to 10 years, with an average of 8.4 years. In addition, some of our GCI versions reveal an extra minor cycle, marked by a weak recession in the first half of 1983, caused by the temporary fall of industrial production, coupled with stagnation in construction and transport. This minor cycle, measured between peaks, lasted about three years.

These estimates have been supported by the results of the spectral analysis of GCI series (Luczynski and Matkowski, 1996) which revealed quite distinct peaks at the frequency interval corresponding to 72-144 month period and a less pronounced peak for 36 months. This would suggest the occurrence of major cycles of the length between 6 and 12 years and minor cycles covering about 3 years.

The above findings show a striking conformity with the long-run pattern of business cycles in the developed market economies, notably in the USA. In the historical record of business cycles in the USA, A.H. Hansen (1941) distinguished minor cycles of the average length of 3,51 years and major cycles of the average length of 8.35 years. In economic theory, the first are often called Kitchin cycles and they are attributed to the change of stocks. The second ones are called Juglar cycles which are related to the fluctuation of fixed investment.

Perhaps, we have found some empirical proof for the hypothesis that fluctuations of the aggregate economic activity resembling business cycles had been present in the Polish economy even at times of the centralized management. With the progress of transformation towards an open market economy these fluctuations may become reinforced and assume a more regular cyclical pattern.

3 Cyclical Movement in Major Sectors

One of the most exciting and least elucidated questions for the economy in transition is the extent of synchronization of cyclical fluctuation among the major sectors of national economy. Are the growth cycles observed in the aggregate economic activity actually diffused? Which sectors are most affected by general economic recessions? Which sectors are the driving force of cyclical movement in the economy and which of them tend to alleviate the size of fluctuation? What is the pattern of specific cycles displayed by individual sectors of economy? In this paper we can only briefly address these important questions.

Table 3 presents statistical characteristics of the time series entering our composite GCI index, reflecting the activity of five major sectors of economy. The time series used to represent the output of individual sectors are regular enough in terms of QCS (≤ 1) and MCD (≤ 6) to allow the analysis of cyclical patterns. Their dynamics is dominated by trend and cycle component (TC) whose contribution ranges from ca. 55 per cent in case of construction and agriculture to 80-90 per cent for industry and for transports. The amount of irregular changes (I) is relatively low; more precisely, this factor is quite negligible in transports but it accounts for more than 10 per cent of the observed change in construction and more then 5 per cent in three other sectors. The relative amount of seasonal movement (S) differs being inversely related to the size of trend and cycle. Industry and transport are least affected by seasonal movement, which represents less than 10 per cent of total variance, while construction and agriculture are heavily influenced by seasonal fluctuation, which accounts for more than 30 per cent of total change. In terms of the F-test, stable seasonality is nevertheless significant at 0.1 per cent level for all sectors.

Correspondence between the cyclical movement of individual sectors and the macroeconomic growth cycle can be judged on the results of cross correlation. Cross-correlation was performed on the detrended, seasonally adjusted and MCD-smoothed time series that can be deemed to represent the pure cyclical component. High correlation observed at minor leads or lags would suggest that the given sector had developed in accord with the reference cycle while low correlation with long leads or lags would indicate that the sector in question is not much susceptible to macroeconomic developments and/or it displays specific cycles unrelated to the general condition of economy.

Table 4 contains the results of cross-correlation between the cyclical components of time series reflecting the activity in major sectors and in the economy as a whole (the latter is represented by our reference indicator). Three sets of results correspond to three alternative methods of trend removal. This is because the common Bry-Boschan routine used to discriminate phase-average-trend (PAT) does not render perfect results when applied to relatively short time series ended by incomplete phases, as was the case in our study. Therefore, apart from the automatic Bry-Boschan routine, denoted here MCDX, we also tried controlled PAT procedure using some preliminary input data on turning points discovered at sight. The respective variant is denoted MCDA. We also tested an auxiliary variant of detrendization MCDR based simply on linear regression. All the alternative variants of sectoral cyclical components were confronted with the MCDA variant of the reference indicator which was found the best fit, not differing much from MCDX.

The results of cross-correlation suggest that industry, construction and transport are well correlated with the reference cycle in most detrending variants while agriculture and trade seem to be less dependent on the course of aggregate economic activity. For trade the correlation is generally weak, and for agriculture it depends on the particular detrending variant. Industry, transport and trade seem to move almost coincidentally with the change of overall economic activity, reaching maximum correlation values at zero lag or slightly later. Construction tends to lead the cyclical movement in the whole economy by 3-6 months while agriculture typically lags behind the changes in the aggregate economic activity by one or two quarters. The correlograms showing the correspondence between agricultural output and general economic activity are quite flat with fuzzy peaks, indicating variable lags.

The chronology of cycles observed in individual sectors, as well as their amplitudes, obviously depend on the identification of trend. The controlled PAT procedure (with preliminary input) allows us to omit minor cycles, as to avoid thereby too variable trends. This procedure has been used to establish the chronology presented in table 6.

Industry, construction and transport have been moving more or less in line with the aggregate economic activity, responding keenly to both recessions. Apart from general economic cycles, industry and construction revealed 1-2 extra specific cycles. Agriculture has also strongly reacted (and contributed) to general recessions but it followed besides its own development pattern; the extremely deep and prolonged fall in agricultural production between 1989 and 1993 was the result of a structural crisis which has not yet been fully overcome. Retail trade, for which the available data enable us to reconstruct the dynamics of real turnover since 1983 only, displays minor trade cycles which distort correlation with the reference cycle.

Table 5 compares the length and depth of recessions in individual sectors. The first column shows the percentage decrease of output between the peak and trough of the reference cycle, and the second column shows the decrease between the start and the end of the respective recession within the sector. Agriculture and transport were most severely hit by the crisis of 1989-91, with the fall in their activity levels by ca. 55 per cent. Industry and construction suffered a drop comparable to the fall in total output as measured by our general index. Retail trade noted a slightly smaller drop and it began to recover much earlier. As a matter of fact, trade and construction, along with the service sector, were the first sectors starting the recovery.

4 Composite Leading Indicator

In search for leading and coincident indicators which might be of use in monitoring the change in current business activity throughout the economy, we analyzed scrupulously, with help of X11ARIMA and OECD PAT programs, over 100 individual time series representing various economic variables of direct interest in this kind of research. Most series were analyzed repeatedly, using updated figures and testing alternative procedures with changing input parameters. This analysis allowed us to discriminate a set of about 60 indicators with well pronounced cyclical changes and a regular pattern of seasonal movement.

Further elimination was based on the MCD criterion (MCD $\leq$ 6) and the selection of leading indicators relied on the comparison of the deseasonalized, MCD-smoothed and detrended time series with the reference cycle. The main criteria applied here were cross-correlation coefficients at various lags, the conformity of the cyclical pattern (the number of missing or extra cycles) and the behavior of the indicator around the reference turning points. As the result, about 20 single indicators have been selected to be used in the composite leading index (CLI). This group includes six or seven indicators of output, two indicators of labour market, two indicators of investment, three variables of the monetary market, one indicator of foreign trade, and four sensitive indicators from the RIED survey data. Table 7 shows the full list of indicators entering alternative CLI formulas, together with their QCS and MCD characteristics and the results of cross-correlation against the reference cycle. (The original list included two other variables: cargo reloaded and credit liabilities of non-financial sector). Table 8 shows the performance of our leading indicators around the reference cycle turning points.

Since our major aim was to develop a CLI formula applicable for monitoring the current level of business activity rather than to attempt at true short-range forecasting, we focused our attention on shorter leading indicators and, in fact, we also accepted some coincident indicators well correlated with the reference cycle. After the last updating (accomplished in April 1997) several indicators originally classified as leading have turned to coincident ones in the sense that the peak correlation coefficient now would appear at zero lead. They have nevertheless been kept on our list because the disappearance of leads might be a temporary technical effect due to the occurrence of a new upper turning point in the movement of several individual variables at the end of the period, not yet reflected by the reference indicator. This is why five or six of our leading indicators are now recorded with zero lead. All the variables entering our composite leading indicators have been brought up to the end of 1996 but their start dates differ according to available data.

In October 1996, at the OECD meeting on leading indicators in Paris, we presented two versions of short lead CLI, denoted CLI3 and CLI4 (Matkowski, 1996). Meanwhile some other formulas have been tested with shorter and longer leads. Here we present a typically short lead formula CLI5A (composed of 13 individual series), a long lead formula CLI8A (6 series), and a mixed formula CLI9A (including 17 series).

All our CLIs are well correlated with the reference cycle (maximum correlation coefficients between 0.87 and 0.91). Both the short and the mixed CLI show, on the average, a very short 1-2-month lead meaning that they are useful first of all for the assessment of current business. Long CLI8A displays a 11-month lead, and it may be more applicable to forecasting, but it has a much narrower coverage and may not be very reliable. Correlation coefficients with the respective leads have been calculated for the whole period and for a shorter period since 1983, covered by most indicators entering the composite index.

The performance of our leading indicators around the reference cycle turning points (as documented by table 8) is less satisfactory, but it seems to improve towards the end of the period, with the progress of economic reforms and the transformation of economic system. The downturn of 1989 as well as the switch to recovery in 1991 were signaled by our CLIs well in advance.

The historical performance of our CLIs and their component indicators is also illustrated by the enclosed graphs. Figure 2 shows some individual leading indicators and the reference series in terms of seasonally adjusted, MCD-smoothed and detrended data, after standardization. Figure 3 shows amplitude-adjusted CLI indicators against the reference cycle.

Since the information lag for most statistical data is typically 1-3 months, we believe that our CLI, even with its short lead, may be a useful tool in evaluating the current level of economic activity.

The procedures used in developing our CLIs follow the OECD methodology of leading indicators, apply the same concepts and technical terms and make use of the same computer programs, so they may be viewed as comparable with the OECD standards. The only major exception is that some shorter time series entering the composite index (denoted with the letter R), for which the PAT program failed to work or rendered doubtful results, have been detrended by linear regression. At the same time, our concept of the reference series GCI is, by and large, original and it seems to be more suitable to the economies in transition.

5 Conclusion

A general composite indicator GCI based on output data from five major sectors of economy has been developed in order to analyze cyclical movements of Poland's economy over time. This indicator, filled with monthly data for the period from January 1975 to December 1996 and decomposed with X11-ARIMA and OECD PAT software, was used to reconstruct the growth cycles seen in the last two decades. During that period the Polish economy experienced two severe recessions of 1980-82 and 1989-91 linked with structural crisis. These fluctuations were strongly affected by political events, structural change and the transformation of economic system. Nevertheless the resulting swings in total output formed two very well pronounced growth cycles which may be analyzed using the methods and procedures commonly applied to business cycle research.

Cyclical changes in the aggregate economic activity have been mainly related to the fluctuation of industrial production, construction and transports. Agriculture was acutely hit by general economic crises but it also displayed a peculiar development pattern. Cyclical developments in retail trade were dominated by specific trade cycles. Economic revival of the last few years was boosted by privatization, rising exports, and a rapid expansion of the service sector.

Leading indicators are one of the methods widely used in evaluating current and future tendencies of economic activity. Three alternative formulas of a composite leading indicator (CLI) for Poland have been presented in the paper and confronted with the reference cycle using the OECD methods and procedures. The results seem to justify the conclusion that we are in possession of a system, based on composite indicator approach, which should be further developed and improved, but which can already be used for the evaluation of aggregate economic activity. While our basic CLI is deliberately confined to the assessment of the current economic activity, the reference composite indicator GCI may well be used for extrapolative 1-year forecasts.

In its first operational use, our monitoring system correctly detected the slowdown of economic growth in 1996 as early as in February, or roughly half a year earlier than most other sources did. At this moment (May 1997) we have an extrapolative forecast of GCI till December 1997 on a monthly basis (including seasonal factor).

In the further research we wish to improve our short-lead CLI and to develop a more legitimate long-lead CLI. New promising indicators will also be tested and included as soon as their time series reach the minimum length required in this research.

Table 1 Statistical properties of the reference series

QCS	MCD	F-test for saisonality		Relative contribution to stationary variance			Average duration of run			Arima forecast		Avg. percentage S.E. in forecast	
		stable	moving	I	S	TC	I	TC	MCD	R^2	χ^2	Last 3 years	Last 1 year
0.59	5	45.2ˣ	0.8	4.0	13.5	81.6	1.5	8.2	3.2	0.91	18%	4.0	3.2

ˣSeasonality present at the 0.1 percent level
QCS is the monitoring and quality control statistics with critical value of 1.00 (QCS<1 is acceptable).

Table 2 Reference cycles

Turning points		Duration	Amplitude	
P	T	months	% change	% of trend
12/79				
	10/81	23	-30.3	-27.0
3/89		89	+26.8	+44.0
	10/91	31	-41.3	-39.9

Table 3 Characteristics of the developments in major sectors

Sector	Start date	QCS	MCD	Relative contribution to stationary variance				F-test for seasonality	
				I	S	TC	Σ	stable	moving
Industry	01/75	0.79	5	6.1	9.2	82.2	97.5	20.3*	2.0
Construction	01/75	0.82	5	11.0	32.6	54.3	97.2	39.3*	3.4
Agriculture	01/75	0.59	6	6.4	35.1	56.8	98.3	67.5*	2.0
Transport	01/75	0.42	3	1.4	7.6	90.3	99.3	52.5*	1.1
Retail trade	01/83	0.68	4	7.4	22.3	60.6	90.3	29.4*	0.6
Economy	01/75	0.59	5	4.0	13.5	81.6	99.1	45.2*	0.8

Table 4 Cross-correlation: major sectors against the reference cycle

Sector	Detrending variants					
	MCDA		MCDX		MCDR	
	Lead (-) or lag (+)	R	Lead (-) or lag (+)	R	Lead (-) or lag (+)	R
Industry	0	0.971	0	0.656	0	0.956
Construction	-3	0.842	-3	0.832	-6	0.645
Agriculture	+6	0.831	+3	0.486	+7	0.854
Transport	+1	0.932	+1	0.938	+1	0.979
Retail trade	+1	0.619	0	0.536	+2	0.669

Table 5 Severity of recessions in major sectors

Sector	Recession 1980-1981			Recession 1989-1991		
	Length (months)	Percentage fall from peak to through of		Length (months)	Percentage fall from peak to through of	
		the reference cycle	the sectoral cycle		the reference cycle	the sectoral cycle
Industry	26	-22.0	-26.3	42	-42.2	-42.5
Construction	30	-29.2	-30.6	21	-35.0	-42.1
Agriculture	35	-29.5	-32.7	59	-36.6	-54.5
Transport	23	-27.2	-36.0	53	-54.6	-56.1
Retail trade	na	na	na	12	-24.0	-38.7
Total (reference cycle)	22	-27.0	x	31	-39.9	x

Business Cycles in Poland

Table 6 Chronology of cycles

Sector	1975	1976	1977	1978	1979	1980	1981	1982	1983	1984	1985	1986	1987	1988	1989	1990	1991	1992	1993	1994	1995
Industry					P 12/79			T 02/82	P 01/83					P 04/88			T 10/91				
Construction						P 01/80	T 09/81		T 09/83					T 06/88	P 01/89	T 10/90			P 07/93	T 01/94	
Agriculture	T 06/75	P 01/76 T 12/76	P 10/78					T 07/82			P 08/85				P 02/89					T 01/94	
Transport						P 02/80		T 01/82						P 02/88							
Retail trade															P 03/89	T 03/90	P 02/91	T 07/92	P 05/93		
Reference cycle					P 12/79		T 10/81								P 03/89		T 10/91	T 07/92	T 12/93		

417

Table 7 Performance characteristics of leading indicators

Code	Indicator	Start date	QCS	MCD	Cross - correlation against reference series			
					the whole period		since 1983	
					lead (-)	R	lead (-)	R
	Selected Leading Indicators							
A001	Industrial Production	01.1975	0.77	5	0	0.969	0	0.972
X003	Food Industry	01.1982	0.69	5	-3	0.642	-3	0.588
A004	Prod Coal	01.1980	1.20	8	-4	0.819	-2	0.922
A005	Crude Petroleum Processing	01.1980	1.72	12	0	0.818	0	0.742
A011	Prod Sawn Wood	01.1980	0.60	5	0	0.981	0	0.925
A015	Labour Productivity	01.1980	0.79	3	0	0.829	0	0.822
A016	Construction	01.1975	0.79	5	-2	0.850	-4	0.837
A029	Imports	01.1983	0.91	6	-12	0.556	-12	0.506
A033G	Investment: Mach & Equip (v. 2)	01.1983	1.41	2	-9	0.545	-10	0.497
A033J	Investment: Mach & Equip (v. 1)	01.1983	0.64	5	0	0.824	0	0.751
A039	Job Advertisements	01.1980	0.60	3	0	0.725	+2	0.822
R041	Issue of Cash	01.1982	0.73	2	0	0.897	-1	0.831
R043	Money Holdings of Households	01.1982	0.92	1	-4	0.820	-4	0.764
A045A	Personal Saving Deposits	01.1982	1.10	1	-3	0.832	-4	0.777
R045A	Personal Saving Deposits	01.1982	1.10	1	-6	0.803	-6	0.750
R060	Ind. Prod. Tendency (BS)	01.1987	0.59	1	-6	0.991	-6	0.903
R061	Ind. Prod. Appr (BS)	01.1987	0.93	4	-6	1.000	-6	0.913
R062	Future Ind. Prod. (BS)	01.1987	0.80	3	-7	0.967	-7	0.881
A069A	Economic Prospects (BS)	01.1987	1.41	3	-5	0.942	-5	0.858
	Composite Leading Indicators							
L105A	CLI5A (13 series: all except A029, A033G, R045A, A039, R061 and R062)	01.1975	0.96	1	-1	0.910	-1	0.908
L108A	CLI8A (6 series: A029, R033G, R045A, R060, R061, R062)	01.1982	0.97	1	-11	0.871	-11	0.812
L109A	CLI9A (17 series: all except A039 and A045A)	01.1975	0.85	1	-2	0.892	-2	0.887
	Reference Series							
C091	GCI2D	01.1975	0.59	5	x	x	x	x

Table 8   Historical performance of leading indicators at turning points

Code	Indicator	Start date	Extra (x) or missing (n) cycles	Leads or lags at turning points			
				P12/79	T10/81	P03/89	T10/91
A001	Industrial Production	01.1975	1x	0	+4	-11	0
X003	Food Industry	01.1982	0	na	na	-2	-7
A004	Prod Coal	01.1980	1x	na	-4	-5	-10
A005	Crude Petroleum Processing	01.1980	2x	na	+2	0	-3
A011	Prod Sawn Wood	01.1980	3x	na	+4	-2	-3
A015	Labour Productivity	01.1980	1x	na	+3	-1	0
A016	Construction	01.1975	2x	0	+9	-2	-12
A029	Imports	01.1983	2x	na	na	-12	-16
A033G	Investment: Mach & Equip (v. 2)	01.1983	2x	na	na	-9	-18
A033J	Investment: Mach & Equip (v. 1)	01.1983	2x	na	na	-8	-15
A039	Job Advertisements	01.1980	1x	na	-11	0	-19
R041	Issue of Cash	01.1982	1x	na	na	-1	-21
R043	Money Holdings of Households	01.1982	0	na	+3	-2	-22
A045A	Personal Saving Deposits	01.1982	1x	na	na	-25	-9
R045A	Personal Saving Deposits	01.1982	0	na	+5	-27	-22
R060	Ind. Prod. Tendency (BS)	01.1987	0	na	na	-24	-20
R061	Ind. Prod. Appr. (BS)	01.1987	0	na	na	-9	-19
R062	Future Ind. Prod. (BS)	01.1987	0	na	na	-26	-20
A069A	Economic Prospects (BS)	01.1987	1x	na	na	-19	-21
L105A	(13 series)	01.1975	0	0	+2	-2	-4
L108A	(6 series)	01.1982	0	na	na	-9	-20
L109A	(17 series)	01.1975	0	0	+2	-2	-5

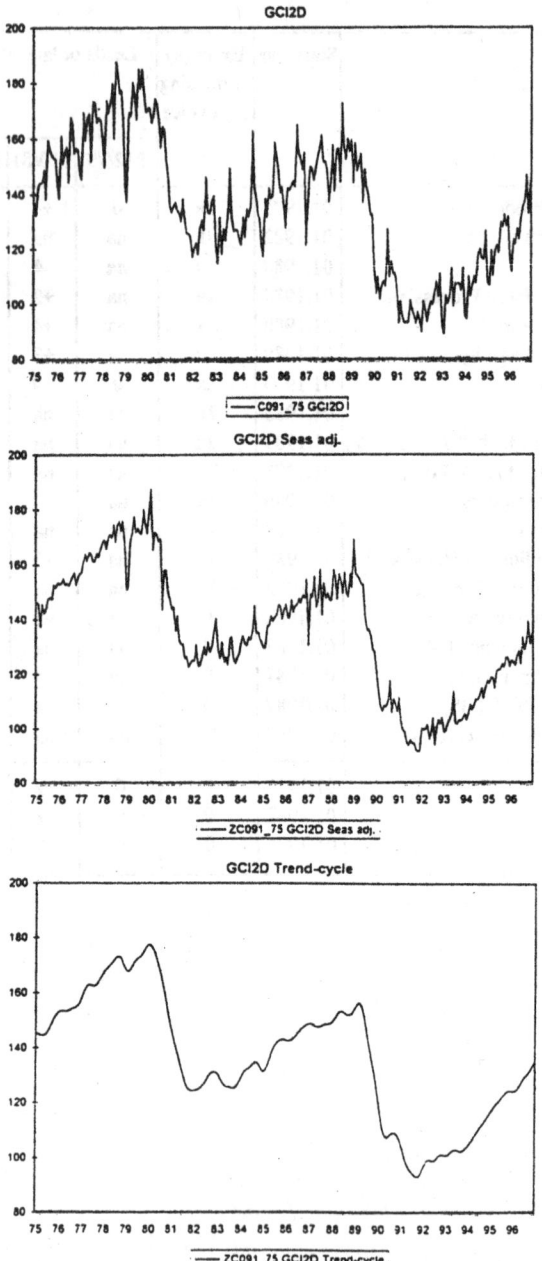

Figure 1

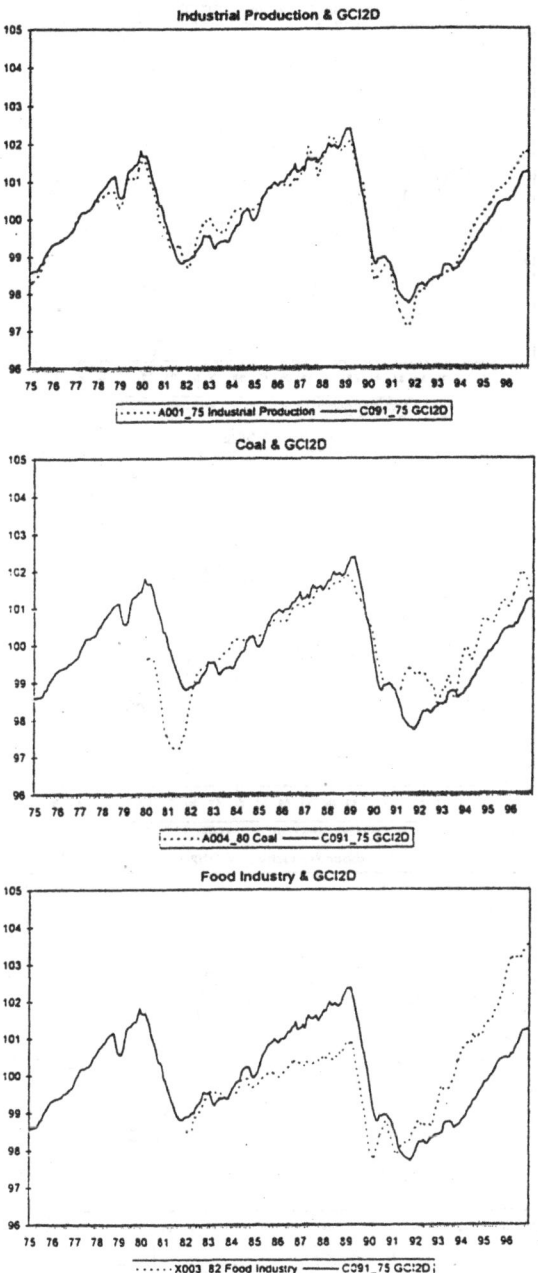

Figure 2a

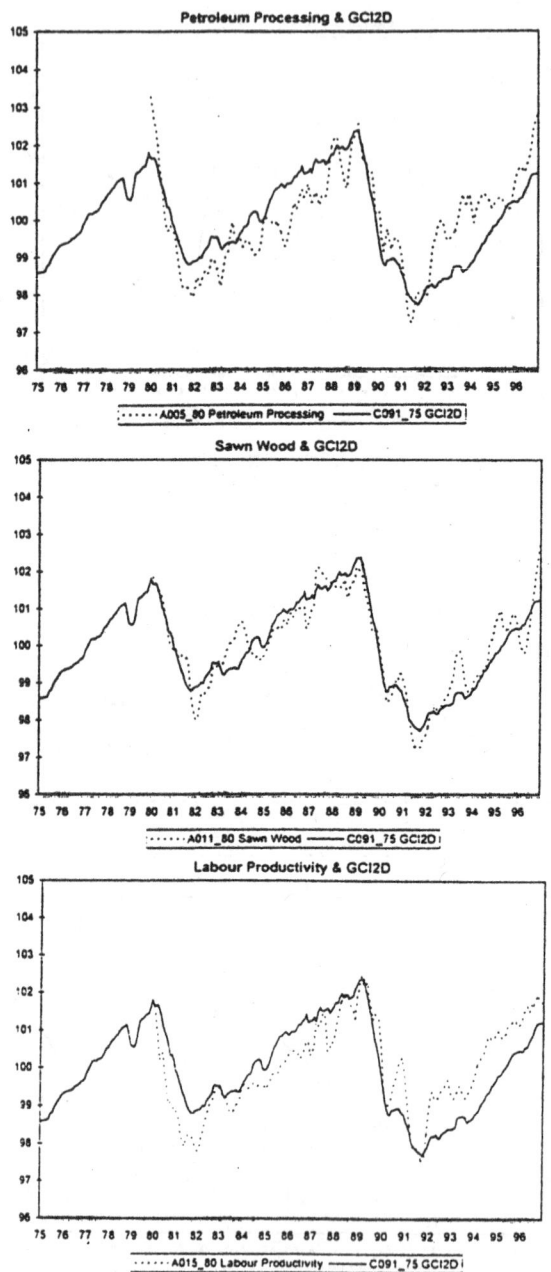

Figure 2b

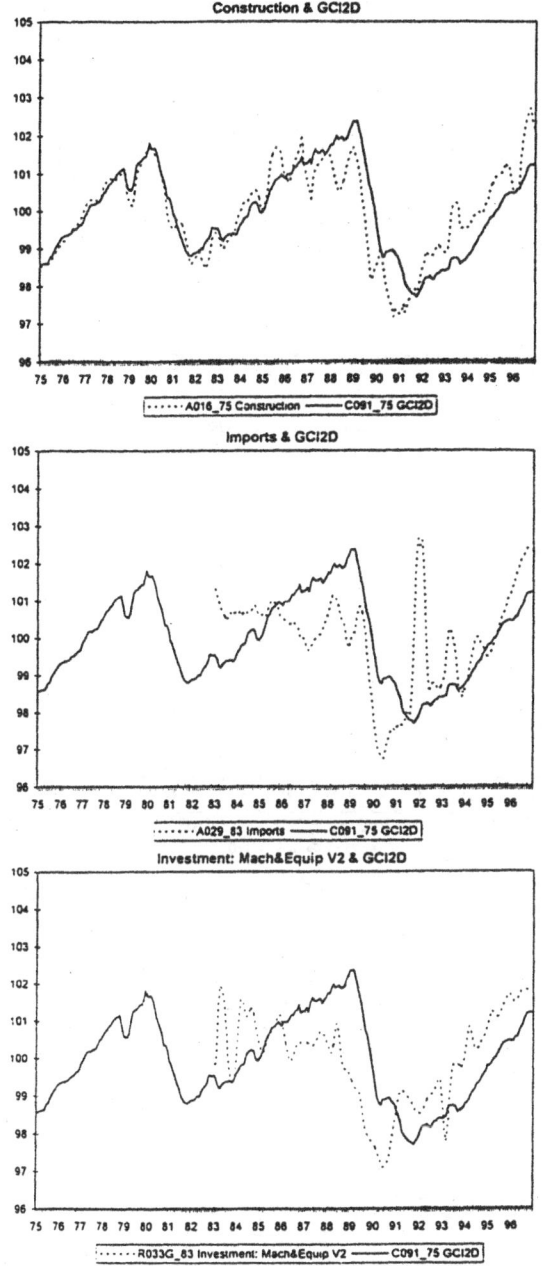

Figure 2c

Social and Structural Change - Consequences for Business Cycle Surveys

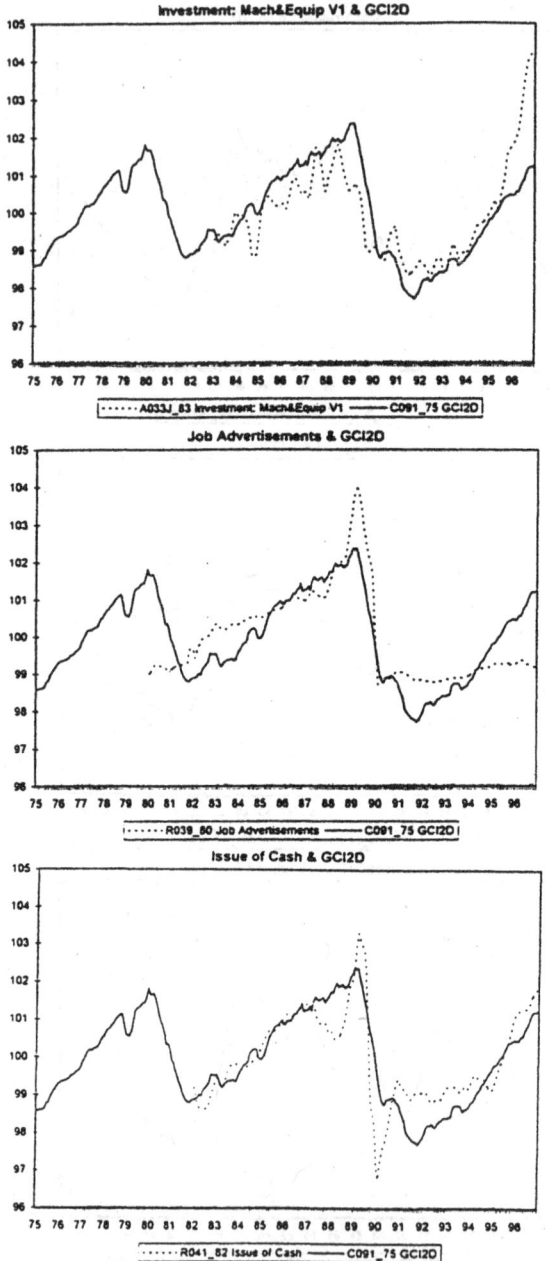

Figure 2d

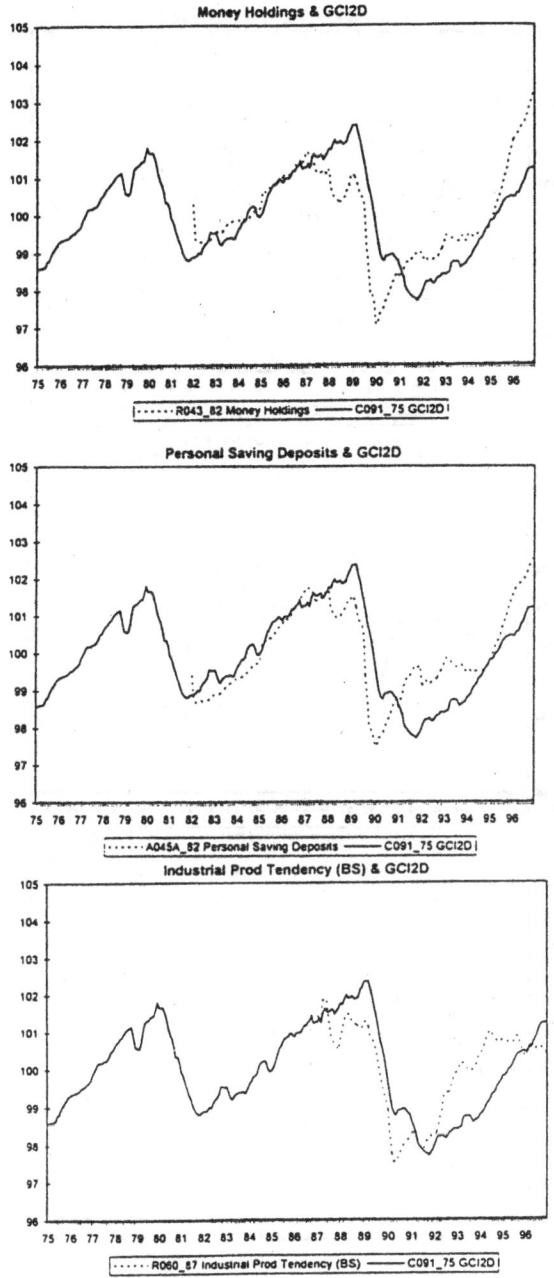

Figure 2e

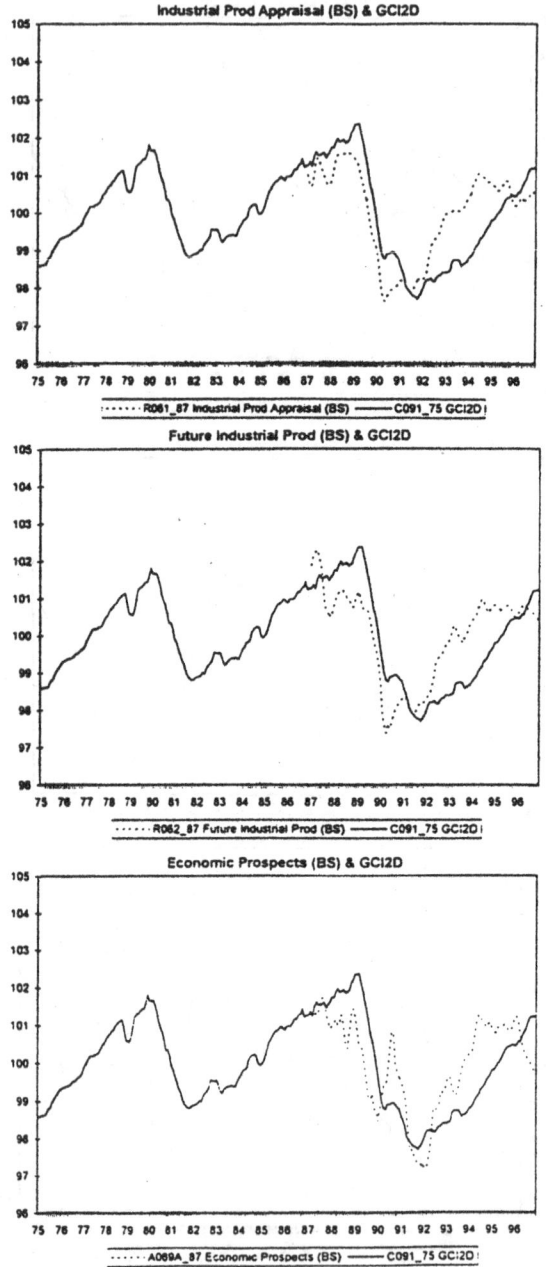

Figure 2f

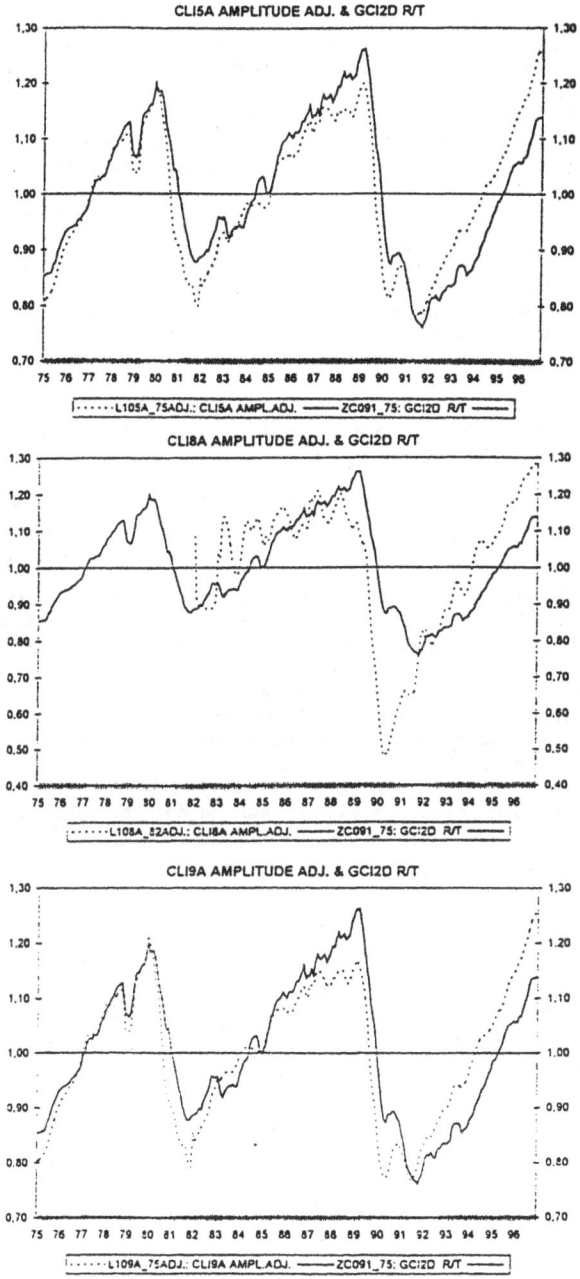

Figure 3

References

Eysymontt, J. and Maciejewski, W. (1983), Kryzysy spoleczno-gospodarcze w Polsce. Ujecie modelowe (Socioeconomic Crises in Poland. A Model Approach), *Ekonomista*, No. 5-6.

Evans, M.K. (1969), *Macroeconomic Activity: Theory, Forecasting and Control. An Econometric Approach*, Harper&Ro, New York.

Hansen, A.H. (1941), *Fiscal Policy and Business Cycle*, New York.

Kolodko, G.W. (1979), Fazy wzrostu gospodarczego w Polsce (Phases of Economic Growth in Poland), *Gospodarka Planowa*, 1975, No. 7-8.

Koopmans, T.C. (1947), Measurement without Theory, *The Review of Economics and Statistics*, No. 2, pp. 161-172.

Kudrycka, I. and Nilsson, R. (1993), Business Cycles in the Period of Transition, *Z Prac Zakladu Badan Statystycznych GUS i PAN*, No. 216, GUS: Warszawa.

Kudrycka, I. and Nilsson, R. (1995), Business Cycles in Poland, *Z Prac Zakladu Badan Statystycznych GUS i PAN*, No. 227, GUS: Warszawa.

Kudrycka, I. and Nilsson, R. (1996), Cyclical Indicators in Poland, in: *Cyclical Indicators in Poland and Hungary*, OECD, Paris.

Luczynski, W. and Matkowski, Z. (1996), Analiza spektralna syntetycznych wskaznikòw koniunktury dla gospodarki polskiej' (Spectral Analysis of the Synthetic Indicators of Business Activity for the Polish Economy), *Zeszyty Koniunktury w Gospodarce Polskiej*, No. 8, Szkola Glòwna Handlowa: Warszawa, p. 101-111.

Matkowski, Z. (1979), *Barometry koniunktury* (Business Cycle Indicators), SGPiS: Warszawa.

Matkowski, Z. (1996), Ogòlny wskaznik koniunktury dla gospodarki polskiej (General Indicator of Business Activity for Poland), *Ekonomista*, No. 1, pp. 23-44.

Matkowski, Z. (1996), Composite Leading Indicators for Poland and the Concept of the Reference Cycle, A contributed paper prepared for the meeting on OECD Leading Indicators: Paris, 17-18th October 1996.

Matkowski, Z. (ed) (1997), *Z prac nad syntetycznymi wskaznikami koniunktur ydla gospo-darki polskiej* (Synthetic Indicators of Business Activity for the Polish Economy), Prace i Materialy Instytutu Rozwoju Gospodarczego, Vol. 51, Szkola Glòwna Handlowa: Warszawa.

Mitchell, W.C. and Burns, A.F. (1946), *Measuring Business Cycles*, NBER: New York.

Moore, G.H. (ed) (1961), *Business Cycle Indicators*, NBER: Princeton.

OECD Leading Indicators and Business Cycles in Member Countries 1960-1985, *Main Economic Indicators. Sources and Methods*, No. 39, OECD: January 1987.

Westlund, A.H. (1993), Business Cycle Forecasting, *Journal of Forecasting*, Vol. 12, pp. 187-196.

Wozniak, M.G. (1985), Zmiennosc stopy wzrostu gospodarczego w krajach socjalistycznych (Variability of the Rate of Economic Growth in Socialist Countries), *Ekonomista*, No. 3.

Part VII
Surveys Covering the Service Sector

24 First Results of the Ifo Business Survey in the Data Processing Services Sector in Western and Eastern Germany

Joachim Gürtler

1 Introduction

The transformation to an information society is the challenge facing Germany on the threshold to the 21st century. Innovations in information and communication technology have provided the technological prerequisites for a previously unimaginable expansion of information and communication (I&C) services and applications. At the same time economic, political and societal trends have increased the need for information in all areas of professional and private life (Hummel and Saul, 1997, p.3).

International sales of information technology (IT) goods and services in 1996 worldwide amounted to nearly DM 2.1 trillion. Europe had a 30% share of this business, with Germany's share at about 8% (see Fig. 1). According to the European Information Technology Observatory (EITO) the I&C world market registered its strongest growth over the past five years of nearly 10% annually. In 1997 growth will continue to be respectable at between 8% and 9%. Above-average growth rates are expected for Latin America and the newly industrializing Southeast Asian economies; I&C growth rates in Europe (+7%) and Japan (+6%) will be below average (EITO, 1997).

2 Ifo Business Survey in Data Processing Services

By the beginning of the new millennium, the I&C industry will be the most important economic factor in Germany. In 1960 Germany had only the rudiments of today's IT industry. Hardware production, of primarily office equipment, lay at DM 1.2 billion and employment stood at 50,000. Software and services were negligible factors. In the meantime domestic production has increased by a factor of 10 to around DM 14 billion, and by a factor of 35 if software and services are included. Employment has increased five-fold. Today about 230,000 people are directly employed in the German I&C industry; indirectly about the same number of jobs have been stimulated in other industries including electronic components, I&C-related services and commerce (Harms and Möller, 1996, p. 1ff, Baukrowitz and Boes, 1997, pp. 13ff.).

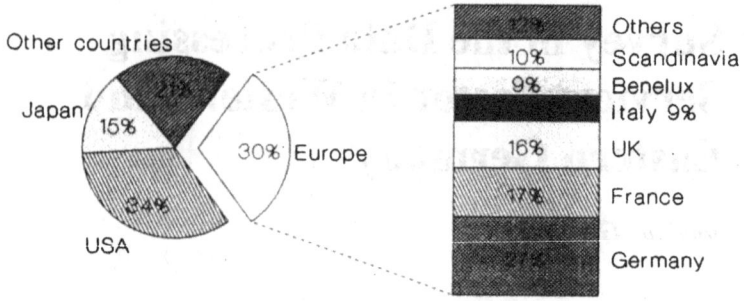

Turnover 1996: DM 2094 billion

Figure 1 Information and communications technologies world market 1996 by regions (in %)
Source: EITO, Diebold 1996.

The market volume for I&C devices, software and services, and telecommunication technology and services should grow by 6% in 1996 to DM 177 billion, according to estimates of the industry's federations. The subsectors software and EDP services also expanded strongly in the past, but the official statistics still contain hardly any data that is suitable for examining the business cycle in this area. According to Diebold, the German market for software and services has grown at an average annual rate of more than 9% (see Fig. 2). In response to the increasing importance of this industry, the Ifo Institute started in 1995 a new survey instrument: the Ifo Business Survey for EDP Services.

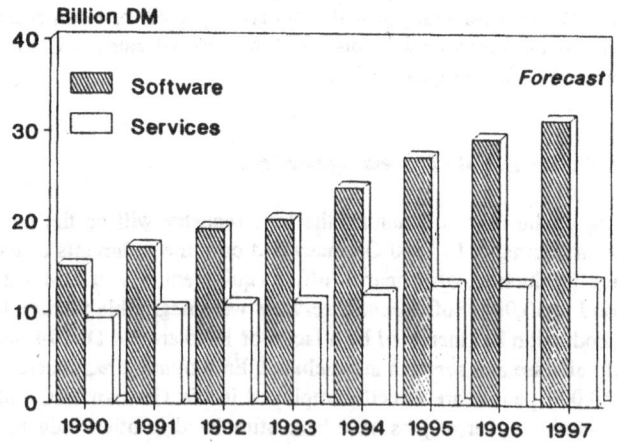

Figure 2 EDP service providers: dynamic turnover growth
Source: Diebold Management Report 1996.

The German software industry continues to be marked by small and medium-sized firms, although concentration is increasing. This is evident not only from company mergers and acquisitions but also from the above-average growth rates of leading firms in this sector. Whereas in 1994, the entire sector grew by 6%, the 25 larger software and service enterprises recorded growth of about one-fifth. This also meant that the small and medium-sized software firms lost considerable market shares to the large, project-oriented businesses and to the large suppliers of standard software. Their share of the entire market volume fell from two-thirds to one-half from 1989 to 1994 (*Computerwoche*, 1996) (see Fig. 3).

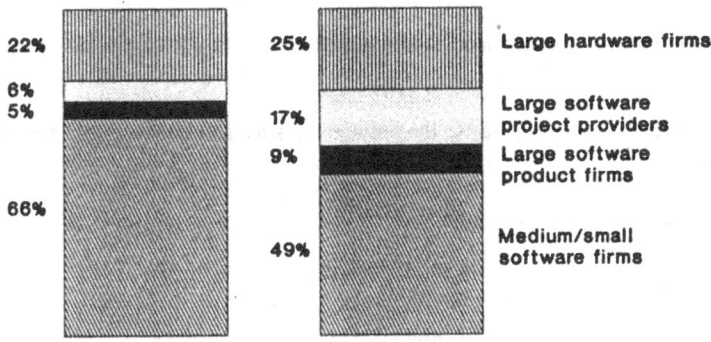

Turnover 1989 (in %)   Turnover 1994 (in %)

Figure 3   EDP service providers: degree of concentration has increased
Source: Diebold, 1996.

2.1 Sub-areas and Question Catalogue

2.1.1 Regions and Sub-areas. The EDP services survey of the Ifo Institute is aimed at enterprises throughout Germany, but results can be separated for east and west Germany. There are no plans at present for an additional regional separation (for the individual federal states).

EDP service providers develop software, advise and train customers, oversee networks and maintain hardware and software. Alongside the general category EDP services, the following six EDP categories are included:

- Consulting and Project Services
- System/network Operations (facilities management, outsourcing)
- Processing and Network Services
- Environmental Services
- Maintenance
- Education and Training

2.1.2 Survey Questions. The Ifo Business Survey primarily contains assessments of business trends, judgements and plans of the enterprises. In contrast to data collected for official statistics, the Ifo Business Survey contains no quantitative data but is based on the qualitative responses of survey participants and asks them to report on trends or give an assessment, not figures. With the help of trend reports, the attempt is made to include both past and future developments, i.e. it is only indicated whether turnover, for example, is higher, about the same or lower than the previous quarter. The assessments are based on the situation prevailing at the time the questionnaire is filled out. In designing the questionnaire we were guided by the harmonized question catalogue of the European Union and also by the results of a trial run to test the questionnaire's practical implementation. The survey takes places four times a year at the end of each quarter (see sample questionnaire in Annex).

The questionnaire asks for assessments on the following:

The change in
- turnover for the present quarter vis-à-vis the previous quarter and the same quarter of the previous year,
- new orders, and
- employment vis-à-vis the previous quarter.

The foreseen change in
- turnover in the coming quarter and
- the business situation for the next two quarters.

Assessments on
- the current business situation and
- order reserves.

In addition, firms are asked about constraints to business activity (from weak demand, labour shortages, financing difficulties, and other causes).

At the end of the first quarter of each year, special questions on the following areas are posed:

- investments,
- hirings,
- availability of skilled labour,
- competition, and
- expansion of business activity.

Comments on how to fill in the questionnaire are limited to the text of the individual questions, with more detailed comments on the reverse side of the questionnaire on how the Ifo Institute defines the individual EDP categories. These comments were extremely helpful in the start-up phase in order to clearly separate the categories from each other.

2.2 Selection, Participation, Weighting and Representation

2.2.1 Selection and Participation.
Although official statistics on the total number of market participants (companies and employees) in the EDP services sector are not available, numbers can be derived from address providers and the turnover tax statistics from the Federal Office of Statistics. In building up the service provider sample, a stratified sample was drawn from the lists of commercial address providers; every quarter nearly 750 businesses receive questionnaires.

Between 300 and 400 firms participated in the first eight surveys in east and west Germany. Considering that the German software and service market is characterized by numerous small and medium-sized firms, the 40% to 50% return rate is quite high. At present the survey panel is not large or stable enough to allow detailed conclusions to be drawn for all EDP categories. However, the present number of participants is sufficient to assess the business cycle trends. In future we plan to expand the panel to 500 firms. For the eighth survey, which was conducted in January 1997, 364 firms participated representing a turnover of nearly DM 21.2 billion. The distribution of the survey participants according to size categories is shown in Table 1.

Table 1   Firms surveyed in EDP service providers

Company size Firms with ... turnover (in DM m)	Firms		Turnover[2]	
	number[1]	in %	in DM m	in %
up to 5	212	58,2	391	1,8
5 - 20	75	20,6	937	4.4
20 - 50	31	8,6	1085	5,1
50 - 100	14	3.8	1050	5.0
100 and more	32	8,8	17730	83,7
Total	364	100,0	21193	100,0

[1] Status: Ifo survey at the end of the 4th quarter, 1996.
[2] Under the assumption of a symmetrical distribution, the mean value for each company-size group was used.

Source: Ifo Business Survey: EDP Service Providers, 1996.

2.2.2 Representativeness.
The survey's representativeness cannot be exactly determined due to the lack of official statistics, but according to the turnover figures regularly published by Diebold, the survey results represent nearly half of the total German market for EDP service providers.[1]

---

[1] In comparison to previous Diebold publications, the segment of software and services is defined more broadly to include smaller firms and service providers: for 1996 this led to a lump-sum additional volume of DM 4.5 billion. The turnover volume in the software and services market in 1996 was DM 42.5 billion.

2.2.3 Weighting. In aggregating the individual responses we made sure that any distortions in the grouping of the survey participants according to company size are adjusted to the distribution of the total number by corresponding correcting factors. To determine the total number of firms, the turnover tax statistics from the Federal Statistical Office have been used. The basis for weighting is business size, for which the firms provide information; currently there are seven categories. Finally the correction is made in such a way that the businesses of a company-size category influence the result only according to the percentage corresponding to their turnover share.

3 Results

3.1 Turnover Growth Weaker in 1996

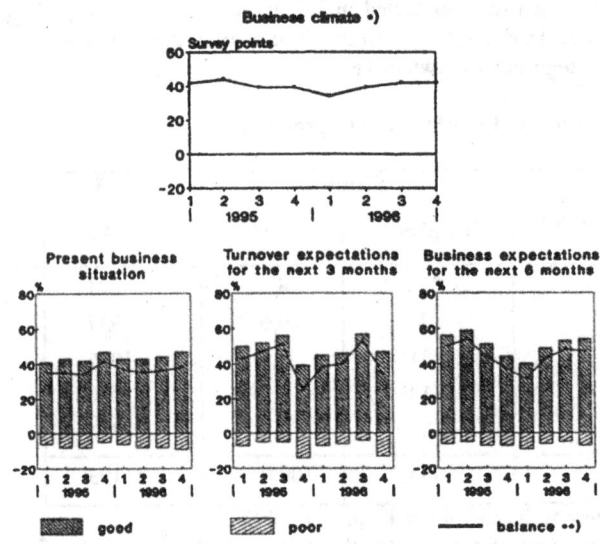

Figure 4   EDP service providers: business optimism increases, 4th quarter 1996
Source: Ifo Business Survey, EDP Service Providers, 1996.

Providers of software and EDP services were very satisfied with business in 1996. Businesses in the sector performed very well, even though turnover growth became less dynamic as the year progressed. Sector turnover in Germany in 1996 expanded by 6% to about DM 42.5 billion according to Diepold (Kröger, 1997, p. 6). Also according to the results of the Ifo survey, the majority of EDP service providers reported a good or very good business situation between October and December, although it was not quite as favourable as in the same quarter of the previous year. Almost half of the queried firms designated the business situation as good, more than two fifths as satisfactory, and only 9% perceived the situation as bad (Fig. 4). Following indications in the previous survey for a further upswing, confidence in the business situation was consolidated. On balance almost every second participant gave a positive response on the business outlook, marking an improvement over the sentiment expressed a year ago.

Also in East Germany, the recovery trends were also visible: strong demand led to considerable improvement in business. The business situation was even more favourable than in west Germany. The hopes for further business revival increased noticeably, as almost every second east German service-sector firm looked confidently into the future.

The pace of demand upturn increased somewhat in the course of 1996 from quarter to quarter, but turnover growth was probably again somewhat flatter in comparison with the corresponding previous-year quarter: in the Ifo survey of December 1995, 51% of the participants reported higher turnover than in the preceding year, but at the end of 1996 it was only around two-fifths. Also vis-à-vis the previous quarter, turnover growth was somewhat less pronounced. The lively activity in incoming orders – above all in the second half-year – influenced judgements of order reserves but did not lead to an enhancement of orders in hand, which were designated by the firms as generally satisfactory. The upswing in turnover should continue for most service providers: more than one-third of EDP service providers expected a plus in the first quarter of 1997, nearly every second firm in the second quarter. A prominent positive factor was that the number of optimists increased vis-à-vis the corresponding preceding-year period (Table 2).

The medium-term growth prospects were also assessed extraordinarily favourably: almost nine in ten EDP service providers planned an expansion of business activity in the following three to five years. Growth impulses are primarily expected from the domestic market. More than two-thirds of the firms plan to expand domestic business activity, nearly one-third in EU markets and almost one-fifth of the firms are planning to expand their business outside the EU. In the next few years, most software must be adjusted to deal with two accounting problems that will affect millions of users and will trigger above-average growth impulses. One of the tasks is associated with the gradual introduction of the single European currency, which will require billing in two currencies during a transition period. The other large task is related to the so-called 'millennium bug': all software with years given in two-digit form must be converted to four digits (*Blick durch die Wirtschaft*, 1997).

The survey participants assessed competitive pressure as extremely high, and it probably increased over the two preceding years. More than two thirds of the EDP service providers assessed competition on domestic markets as 'very strong', nearly two-fifths reported strong competitive pressure within the European Union. The best competitive opportunities from today's perspective go to the large providers of software products since they have succeeded in establishing footholds in all markets – from large enterprises to sole proprietorships. Next are the major hardware manufacturers. Forced by price declines in the core business, most have already completed extensive rationalization projects, have jettisoned ballast, carried out restructuring and have moved into promising areas of business. The great advantage of this group is its extensive customer basis.

Table 2 EDP service providers: business cycle indicators

	1st quart. 1995	2nd quart. 1995	3rd quart. 1995	4th quart. 1995	1st quart. 1996	2nd quart. 1996	3rd quart. 1996	4th quart. 1996
Business climate[1]	+42	+44	+39	+39	+34	+39	+42	+42
Business situation[2]								
- Assessment	+35	+35	+34	+42	+37	+35	+36	+38
- Expectations for 2 quarters	+50	+54	+44	+37	+31	+43	+48	+47
Turnover[2]								
- Trends vis-à-vis previous quarter	+14	+28	+32	+46	+20	+38	+32	+41
- Trends vis-à-vis same quarter last year	+43	+45	+47	+51	+47	+44	+47	+40
- Expectations for the next quarter	+43	+47	+51	+25	+38	+40	+53	+34
Orders[2]								
- Trends vis-à-vis previous quarter	+20	+26	+32	+35	+15	+20	+27	+31
- Current volume of orders (Beurteilung)	•	•	-5	-2	-7	-14	-5	-2
Employment (in %)								
- Trends vis-à-vis previous quarter	+2,1	+2,0	+2,1	+2,0	+2,7	+1,9	+2,0	+1,7
Business constraints (in %)								
- Insufficient demand	28	21	21	20	19	24	23	18
- Lack of skilled labour	16	13	13	17	19	20	19	21
- Financial difficulties	•	•	6	8	10	11	9	9
- Others	13	7		4	5	5	6	3

[1] Average of the present business situation and the expectations for the next two quarters.
[2] Balance: Difference between company responses "increasing" and "decreasing".
Weighting: Turnover concept.

Source: ifo Business survey, EDP Service Providers, 1995, 1996.

Small and medium-sized software firms (SMEs) must take advantage of their on-site presence. Especially these firms must streamline their product range, keep their eyes out for new market segments, and established an individual profile in these segments.

Also in the area of computer-centre services, challenges and opportunities for SMEs go hand-in-hand. The market is growing strongly and offers well-run firms good business opportunities. The driving force is the outsourcing of EDP services. Here Germany has fallen behind in Europe. Whereas in the past EDP users were sceptical of outsourcing, with some good reasons, experts now feel that this has changed considerably in recent years (*Computerwoche*, 1996, pp. 8ff.3.2).

3.2 Modest Employment Growth

EDP services is one of the few sectors in which new jobs are being created, even though employment gains have been modest. According to the survey results, the positive employment effects have displayed some slowdown. In the first quarter of 1996: employment increased by almost 3%, in the second and third quarter by around 2%, but in the last quarter of the year growth was only 1.7%. Especially good employment opportunities have been found in medium-sized service firms, whose personnel increased by almost 4%. Most new jobs went to EDP specialists in the areas of consulting and project services.[1] In east Germany only relatively few new jobs were created, on annual averages, although the situation in the fourth quarter of 1996 was somewhat more favourable. The service firms also plan to create new jobs by the end of 1997. Nearly two-thirds of the firms reported intentions to hire additional staff, primarily for full-time positions.

3.3 Positive Investment Trend

The investment climate is expected to improve. According to the survey results on the investment activities of EDP service providers, on balance one in four firms carried out an investment project last year. Investment activity was particularly prominent in the categories Consulting and Project Services as well as in System/Network Operations. Investment spending for the current year, however, will no longer expand so clearly. On balance nearly 25% of the firms plan to increase their investment budgets, with a slightly above-average investment spending anticipated in the areas of Consulting and Project Services. Most investments will be made by firms in the turnover class of DM 20-50 million. Investment spending in east Germany, however, will be somewhat more moderate.

3.4 Business Constraints

EDP service providers are also regularly asked about factors that hinder business activity. At the end of 1996, more than two-fifths of the firms reported restrictions, which was a smaller number than during the second and third survey quarters. East German firms reported more constraints to their business activity (Fig. 5). The lack of skilled labour was

---

[1] Advice and support in the acquisition of hardware and software, technology and systems consulting, consulting on system security, development of standard, user and system software, system analysis and programming, system integration.

the number one complaint, made by one in five EDP service providers. The larger the firm the more difficult it seems to find suitably qualified staff, and this is particularly the case in the area of consulting and project services. 26% of the survey participants listed this factor as a business constraint. The results of the special survey also confirm this impression: one in ten participants assessed the availability of skilled labour as good, two-thirds as satisfactory, and nearly one in four gave the appraisal "rather insufficient". For nearly one in five firms, turnover growth was hampered by weak demand (west Germany: 16%; east Germany: 41%), with smaller firms experiencing greater difficulties. Financing difficulties still played a major role for one in ten firms, with east German firms reporting more problems in this area: 18% of the east German and 8% of the west German firms reported financing difficulties. Insufficient security, i.e. the inability to use computer software as collateral for secured loans, continued to be the main problem in this area. According to *Blick durch die Wirtschaft*, a large Japanese bank has for the first time accepted computer software as collateral for loans (Odrich, 1995). The Japanese Ministry of Economics is also very interested in the use of software as collateral for loans to improve the economic position of the industry. Other restrictions were reported by only 3% to 5% of the firms and primarily consisted of ruinous competition, purchasing constraints of public organization, insufficient profits, and the lack of prompt invoice settlement.

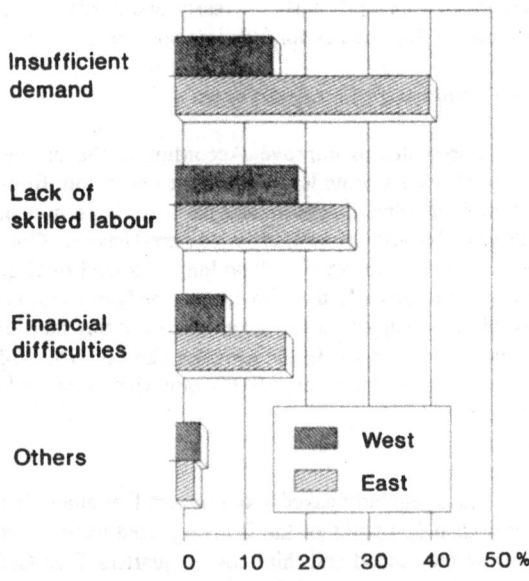

Figure 5   EDP service providers. Higher business constraints in East Germany
Source: Ifo Business Survey, EDP Service Providers, 1997.

3.5 Boom Continues for Consulting and Project Services

The German market for EDP services is characterised by consulting services and the development of standard, user and system software. This area is the largest market segment with a turnover share of more than 60%. According to the survey results, maintenance and training accounted for a 10% turnover share each in 1996. Other categories with turnover shares of about 8% were in System-Network Operations, and Processing and Network Services. Firms in the category Environmental Services had a relatively low turnover share of 4%.

The differences between the EDP categories were considerable. Business in the area of *Consulting and Project Services* was particularly good, with nearly one in two firms reporting a favourable business situation. According to the survey response, demand has risen steadily from quarter to quarter, but turnover has not risen as strongly as in the same period of 1996. The upward trend will continue, according to the participants, with turnover growth showing an accelerating trend. Whereas only 27% of the survey participants of the survey for the fourth quarter of 1995 expected growing turnover, at the end of 1996 it was nearly 40%.

In the area of *System-Network Operations* (facilities management, outsourcing)[1] weak demand characterized the assessments of order reserves and led only to a favourable appraisal of the business situation. Within 12 months the positive judgements of the business situation fell from nearly 40% to 10%, and business prospects were not nearly judged as positively as in previous surveys. The fourth quarter of 1996 brought considerable turnover growth, but firms will have to adjust to considerably lower turnover in the coming months.

After the continuous worsening of the business climate in *Processing and Network Services*[2] the second half of the year seemed to have marked a turning point. A strong demand push led firms to give a renewed less negative assessment of order reserves and a better appraisal of the current business situation. Vis-à-vis the previous-year quarter, the business situation has also improved. In the autumn months, this area experienced growth impulses, with two in five participants reporting higher turnover. The business prospects for the coming half year were assessed confidently, with continuingly positive turnover expectations.

The business situation in *Software Environment Services*[3] was still considered favourable although there was some weakening vis-à-vis the third quarter of 1996. New orders weakened throughout 1996 with a corresponding decline in turnover growth. In comparison to the last quarter of 1995, the share of firms with higher turnover was more than halved. Less confidence was again expressed in business prospects for the first half of 1997, but turnover is still expected to be again somewhat more favourable.

---

[1] Services for assuming EDP tasks for other firms.
[2] Leasing or rentals of computing time, value-added services, data transmission and processing of transmitted data, data compilation.
[3] Services that firms utilized for support in EDP such as customer support in operations and production, software installation, moving and installation of EDP equipment, and precautionary services.

The service enterprises in the category of invoiced *Maintenance*[1] again reported a decline in business activity but still gave a satisfactory appraisal of the business situation.

With growing standardization users require less maintenance than in the "golden age" of mainframe computers. New orders in the survey quarter showed near stagnation, but turnover was slightly higher than the fourth quarter of 1995. Order reserves were frequently assessed as too low. However, more optimism was expressed regarding business prospects; in comparison to the other EDP categories, only modest turnover growth is expected in the near future.

Providers of EDP *Education and Training* services also reported a difficult business situation with an equal number of positive and negative appraisals and a clear slowdown in turnover growth at the end of the year. Assessments of order reserves were influenced by weak demand with one in four firms reporting that order stocks were too low. Their view on the business outlook, nevertheless, was quite confident.

4 Summary

In the Spring of 1995, the Ifo Institute introduced its business survey for EDP service providers. The dearth of official statistics on the rapidly growing EDP sector underscores the urgency for better information. EDP service providers develop software, advise and train customers, compile and process data, oversee networks and maintain hardware and software. It is now possible to follow developments in the entire EDP area from production, to trade and services with the help of timely data. Currently, the time series are still too short for use in business-cycle analysis but they can be of assistance for macroeconomic analysis of the current situation.

German providers of software and EDP services can be very satisfied with the past year. Business in the sector has been very robust even though turnover growth became less dynamic during the course of 1996. According to the results of the Ifo survey conducted in January 1997 the overall optimism among EDP service providers continued with nearly one in two firms reporting a favourable business situation. Confidence in the business outlook solidified. The demand for software and services was still very buoyant, and turnover was even expected to grow further in 1997. The medium-term growth prospects were also assessed very favourably; nearly 90% of the surveyed firms planned to expand their business in the ensuing three to five years.

Recovery is also evident in east Germany with almost all east German service firms expressing confidence on the future.

EDP services was one of the few sectors in which new jobs are being created. The number of employees has risen about 2% per quarter, according to the survey results.

---

[1] Invoiced maintenance service for EDP equipment such as repairs, installation, dismantling, preventative maintenance.

Annex: Questionnaire

ifo Institut
für Wirtschaftsforschung
Abt. Konjunkturumfragen und Investitionsanalysen
Postfach 86 04 60 81631 München

Telefon: (089) 9224-0   bei Rückfragen: Herr Gürtler App. 1242
Telefax: (089) 9224-1463   Herr Lindlbauer App. 1225
            98 53 69

Konjunkturtest
Information und Kommunikation
DV-Dienstleistungen

Ihre Angaben werden streng vertraulich behandelt.
Der gesetzliche Datenschutz ist voll gewährleistet.

DV-Dienstleistungen

Kenn-Nr. →

Nur für Gewichtungszwecke: Die Größenordnung unseres Umsatzes[a] (ohne MWSt.) war im vergangenen Jahr:

    < 1 Mill. DM   50 < 100 Mill. DM
1 < 5 Mill. DM   100 < 500 Mill. DM
5 < 20 Mill. DM   500 und mehr Mill. DM
20 < 50 Mill. DM

Berichtszeitraum: **1. Quartal 1997**

Fragen	DV-Dienst-leistungen (insgesamt)	Consulting + Projekt-Services	System-/ Network Operation (Facilities Management Outsourcing)	Processing und Network Services	Environ-mental Services	Wartung	Ausbildung und Schulung
	72.0	72.1	72.2	72.3	72.4	72.5	72.6

Beurteilung und Entwicklung im Berichtsquartal
Bitte auch die Kästchen der für Sie zutreffenden DV-Sparte(n) ankreuzen!

1) Wir beurteilen unsere Geschäftslage zur Zeit als
    gut
    befriedigend
    schlecht

2) Der Umsatz[a] unserer inländischen Niederlassung war gegenüber dem Vorquartal
    höher
    etwa gleich
    geringer

3) Der Umsatz[a] unserer inländischen Niederlassung war gegenüber dem Vorjahresquartal
    höher
    etwa gleich
    geringer

4) Unser Auftragseingang (wertmäßig in- u. Ausland) ist gegenüber dem Vorquartal
    gestiegen
    gleichgeblieben
    gesunken

5) Unser gegenwärtiges Auftragsvolumen empfinden wir zur Zeit als
    relativ groß
    ausreichend/normal
    zu klein
    Auftr.bestand unüblich

6) Die Zahl der Beschäftigten ist gegenüber dem Vorquartal
    gestiegen um ... %
    gleichgeblieben
    gesunken um ... %

7) Unsere Geschäfts-/Umsatztätigkeit wird z.Zt. behindert
    Ja
    Nein
    Wenn ja, durch: - unzureichende Nachfrage
                      - Mangel an qualif. Fachkräften
                      - Finanzierungsschwierigkeiten
                      - Sonstiges: ....

Pläne und Erwartungen

8) Der Umsatz[a] unserer inländischen Niederlassung wird im nächsten Quartal voraussichtlich
    steigen
    etwa gleichbleiben
    zurückgehen

9) Unsere Geschäftsentwicklung wird in den nächsten 2 Quartalen
    eher günstiger
    etwa gleichbleiben
    eher ungünstiger

Erläuterungen

72.1 Consulting + Projekt-Services
- Beratung und Unterstützung bei der Beschaffung von Hard- und Software
- Technologieberatung
- Beratung über Systemsicherheit
- Systemberatung und technische Beratung (einschl. Durchführbarkeitsstudien über die Implementierung eines Systems sowie Unterstützung bei der Anlaufphase eines neuen Systems)
- Entwicklung von System- und Benutzersoftware (einschl. Vermarktung)
- Entwicklung von Anwendersoftware
- Herstellung von Software-Produkten
- Systemanalyse und Programmierung
- Business Process Engineering
- Kundenindividuelle Software-Entwicklung und Systemimplementierung) Systemintegration

72.2 System-/Network Operation (Facilities Management, Outsourcing)
- Dienstleistungen zum Betreiben und Managen eines kundeneigenen Informationsverarbeitungssystems sowie Dienstleistungen auf anbietereigenen Systemen im Kundenauftrag

72.3 Processing und Network Services
- Leasing oder Vermietung von Rechenzeit (CPU-Zeit) auf dem DV-System an Dritte (im time-sharing Betrieb mit anderen Benutzern)
- Mehrwertdienste
- Datenfernübertragungs- und Datenfernverarbeitungsdienste
- Erfassung der Daten auf Band, Diskette oder einem anderen Träger oder die unmittelbare Eingabe in ein DV-System

72.4 Environmental Services
- Dienstleistungen im Kunden-Rechenzentrum und -Netzwerk oder in einem vom Kunden verantwortlich betriebenen Datenverarbeitungs-System, Host und/oder Netzwerk, wie z.B. Managen, Kundenunterstützung beim Betrieb und bei der Produktion. Ferner Software-Installation, Tuning, Optimierung und SW Support-Services, Performance-Analysen, Design der DV-Einrichtungen, Installation und Umzug von Equipment, Benutzerschulung und -training 'On-the-Job', Netzwerkinstallation und Verkabelung, Helpdesk und jeglicher technischer Support für den Kunden.
- Bereitstellung von Vorsorge-Dienstleistungen, stationäre oder mobile Vorsorge-Rechnerkapazitäten und/oder Backup-Netzwerke. Eingeschlossen sind die folgenden Dienstleistungen: Management und Technologie-Beratung für Vorsorge, Notfallplanung, Design der Notfall-, Backup-, Recovery- und Restart-Lösungen, regelmäßiges Update der Notfall-Pläne und -Prozeduren, die Bereitstellung von Rechnerkapazitäten und Netzwerken für Tests und für Disaster Recovery Services und Restart Services.

72.5 Wartung
- Kostenpflichtige Wartungs-Dienstleistungen für DV-Equipment, wie Reparatur, Installation, Abbau, Problemanalyse, Problemlösung und vorbeugende Wartung.

72.6 Ausbildung und Schulung
- Kostenpflichtige Schulungs- und Trainings-Dienstleistungen, welche im Hause des Anbieters, beim Kunden oder bei Dritten erbracht werden und die dazu benötigten Schulungsunterlagen.

Für eventuelle Rückfragen und   Bearbeiter/in _____   Abt. _____
Versand der Erhebungsergebnisse: Tel.-Nr.: _____   Fax-Nr.: _____

Wir danken für Ihre Mitarbeit!

References

Harms, J. and Möller, G. (1996), Die deutsche IT-Industrie, Entwicklung, Lage Perspektiven, in: BIT-Nachrichten Nr. 68, pp. 1ff.

Hummel, M. and Saul, C. (1997), Beschäftigungspotentiale neuer elektronischer Medien, in: ifo Schnelldienst 3/97, p. 3.

Kröger, C. (1997), IKT-Markt, Ruhiges Fahrwasser, solides Geschäft, in: Diepold Management Report Nr. 1/97, p.6.

Odrich, B. (1995), Im Blick auf Tokio, Software wird als Sicherheit akzeptiert, in: Blick durch die Wirtschaft vom 10. Oktober 1995.

O.V. (1996), Die Informations- und Kommunikationstechnik wächst weiter, in: Frankfurter Allgemeine Zeitung vom 26. November 1996.

O.V. (1996), Die Branche profitiert vom Outsourcing, in: Computerwoche, Extra Nr. 1, vom 16. Februar 1996

O.V. (1997), Software bleibt in Hannover der Schwerpunkt mit der stärksten Ausstellerbeteiligung, in: Blick durch die Wirtschaft vom 24. Februar 1997,

O.V. (1997), Presseinformation, Informationstechnik und Telekommunikation mit stabilem Wachstum, European Information Technology Observatory.

25 Construction of a Confidence Indicator for Retail Trade by the European Commission

Franz-Josef Klein / Guy Lejeune / Anne Roy

1 Introduction

Economic agents' assessments and expectations of the economic situation are summed up, in so-called "confidence indicators", which are made up of the averages of the replies to the main questions in each survey. This is already the case for the business surveys in industry and in construction as well as for the consumer survey. For the business survey in retail trade no confidence indicator has yet been. The main reason for this deficiency is the rather short history of the survey. To make a confidence indicator, one should be able to study the relationship between survey results and a reference variable over a sufficiently long period. The survey in retail trade has been conducted since 1986 (or even longer) in six member countries. For these countries we have over 40 observations on a quarterly basis, which should be enough to make valid statistical inference. We emphasise the country issue because we want the indicator to be *robust and* to be valid for as many countries as possible, not only for Europe as a whole. For every country, the reference variable will be linked to a set of potential indicators, out of which the best performing indicator will be chosen as confidence indicator.

2 Choice of the Countries

For six member countries (Belgium, Germany, France, Italy, the Netherlands and the United Kingdom) we have over 40 observations on a quarterly base. For the other member countries the series are not sufficiently long, the survey started in September 1988 in Spain and later in the other countries. As the four biggest Member Countries were among the early starters, we also have a long enough series for Europe as a whole.

3 Choice of the Reference Variable

The volume of retail sales (RSV) is the logical choice as reference variable. This is the variable that should be traced closely by the indicator. On a monthly basis RSV is very volatile. We will work on a quarterly basis to curb the influence of the volatility. Quarterly private consumption is a less volatile series than RSV. One can compare in

Table 1 the standard deviations of D4C (the percentage change compared to one year ago in private consumption) and D4R (the same change in RSV).

Table 1 **Comparison of volatility between retail sales and private consumption (standard deviations)**

	D4C	D4R	ratio
B	1.23	2.94	2.38
D	1.83	4.06	2.22
F	1.20	1.69	1.41
I	2.19	6.09	2.78
NL	1.23	2.55	2.08
UK	2.82	2.32	0.82
EUR	1.32	1.87	1.41

Retail sales are more volatile in all cases, except for the United Kingdom. Quarterly private consumption is a stable series which has a link with retail sales. Yet there are two good reasons for *not* using this variable in this study:

- it is not the appropriate variable since a large part of private consumption does not go via retail trade: rent, energy, financial services, ...
- choosing an indicator of which the evolution is closely linked to the development of private consumption could simply lead to replicating the consumer confidence indicator as an indicator for retail trade.

4 Choice of the Potential Indicators

We start from the five questions of the survey:

1. We consider our present business (sales) position to be:
   good (+)
   satisfactory (normal for the season) (=)
   bad (-)

2. We consider our present stock to be:
   too small (-)
   adequate (normal for the season) (=)
   too large (+)

3. We expect that our orders placed with suppliers during the next (three) months, excluding purely seasonal variation, will be:
   up (+)
   unchanged (=)
   down (-)

4. Our business trend over the next six months, excluding purely seasonal variations, will:
    improve   (+)
    remain unchanged   (=)
    deteriorate   (-)

5. In the next (three) months, and compared with today, the number of persons we employ will:
    increase   (+)
    remain unchanged   (=)
    decline   (-)

A list of potential indicators, starting from the five balance results[1] of the survey is made. We take linear combinations of the balances, with one up to five elements, imposing equal weights to the elements. Equal weights have also been imposed in making confidence indicators in the other surveys. The simplicity of the *indicator approach* is based on this restriction. The *modelling approach*, on the other hand, is rather complicated: in the BUSY II model, the econometric methods decide on which weights are given to individual balances in order to trace the evolution of macro-economic aggregates. The indicator approach is much simpler, enabling the public to see easily where the indicator values come from.

Restricting the linear combinations by using equal weights yields 31 potential indicators by country. The sign of the results of question 2 (stock assessment) has been inverted throughout this study. In this way an upward movement in the result corresponds to more optimism for each question.

5 Correlation Analysis Methodology

The percentage change in the reference variable, compared to one year ago, is regressed on each potential indicator of the country. It is common practice to transform in this way reference variables, which are in general non-stationary when comparing their evolution with survey results that are stationary in most cases. Taking the change over three or six months (instead of twelve) will in general not alter the picture.

For each country a ranking of the potential indicators according to the correlation coefficient is done. A valid indicator should be ranked high in all seven cases. An indicator is even more valuable if it has a *lead*. Hence the correlation between the potential indicator of quarter t-1 and the reference variable of quarter t is also studied, leading to fourteen cases (seven countries times two).

---

[1] Difference between (+) replies and (-) replies, seasonally adjusted.

6 Results of the Correlation Analysis

Table 2 Results of the correlation analysis: correlations

	Bc	Bl	Dc	Dl	Fc	Fl	UKc	UKl	Ic	Il	NLc	NLl	EUc	EUl
1	0.71	0.59	0.67	0.55	0.44	0.35	0.84	0.76	0.43	0.47	0.64	0.62	0.82	0.80
2	0.47	0.47	0.70	0.69	-0.43	-0.39	0.72	0.73	0.14	0.23	0.46	0.64	0.05	-0.0
3	0.73	0.66	0.57	0.50	0.09	0.01	0.94	0.89	0.30	0.42	0.70	0.73	0.71	0.76
4	0.75	0.76	0.73	0.68	-0.29	-0.49	0.85	0.87	0.32	0.42	0.66	0.77	0.59	0.65
5	0.48	0.40	0.66	0.64	-0.07	-0.38	0.74	0.66	0.31	0.37	0.69	0.67	0.80	0.81
1.2	0.68	0.59	0.70	0.60	0.35	0.25	0.90	0.83	0.42	0.48	0.64	0.66	0.81	0.79
1.3	0.75	0.64	0.64	0.54	0.37	0.28	0.91	0.84	0.38	0.46	0.69	0.70	0.79	0.80
1.4	0.79	0.71	0.71	0.61	0.20	0.03	0.90	0.86	0.39	0.46	0.68	0.73	0.78	0.79
1.5	0.69	0.57	0.69	0.59	0.40	0.25	0.81	0.73	0.41	0.46	0.67	0.65	0.83	0.83
2.3	0.69	0.64	0.65	0.60	-0.24	-0.27	0.94	0.90	0.29	0.41	0.68	0.75	0.69	0.73
2.4	0.69	0.69	0.75	0.71	-0.39	-0.55	0.88	0.89	0.32	0.42	0.65	0.78	0.58	0.62
2.5	0.55	0.51	0.74	0.72	-0.39	-0.51	0.85	0.77	0.29	0.38	0.67	0.73	0.75	0.74
3.4	0.77	0.74	0.67	0.60	-0.17	-0.34	0.93	0.91	0.32	0.42	0.68	0.76	0.67	0.73
3.5	0.68	0.60	0.64	0.57	0.04	-0.12	0.89	0.82	0.32	0.43	0.72	0.74	0.78	0.81
4.5	0.72	0.69	0.74	0.69	-0.27	-0.51	0.88	0.84	0.35	0.44	0.70	0.77	0.74	0.78
1.2.3	0.72	0.64	0.67	0.58	0.30	0.20	0.93	0.87	0.37	0.46	0.69	0.71	0.79	0.80
1.2.4	0.75	0.68	0.72	0.64	0.11	-0.05	0.93	0.89	0.39	0.46	0.68	0.74	0.77	0.78
1.2.5	0.68	0.58	0.71	0.62	0.31	0.16	0.86	0.78	0.40	0.47	0.67	0.68	0.82	0.81
1.3.4	0.79	0.71	0.68	0.58	0.19	0.03	0.92	0.88	0.36	0.45	0.70	0.73	0.77	0.79
1.3.5	0.73	0.62	0.66	0.56	0.34	0.21	0.88	0.80	0.38	0.46	0.70	0.70	0.81	0.82
1.4.5	0.77	0.68	0.72	0.62	0.18	-0.02	0.88	0.82	0.39	0.46	0.69	0.72	0.80	0.81
2.3.4	0.74	0.71	0.70	0.64	-0.29	-0.43	0.93	0.92	0.32	0.43	0.68	0.77	0.66	0.71
2.3.5	0.67	0.61	0.68	0.63	-0.22	-0.35	0.92	0.85	0.32	0.43	0.71	0.75	0.76	0.79
2.4.5	0.69	0.67	0.76	0.71	-0.37	-0.57	0.92	0.88	0.34	0.44	0.69	0.78	0.73	0.76
3.4.5	0.75	0.69	0.69	0.63	-0.17	-0.37	0.92	0.88	0.33	0.43	0.70	0.76	0.74	0.78
1.2.3.4	0.76	0.69	0.69	0.61	0.11	-0.04	0.94	0.90	0.36	0.45	0.69	0.74	0.76	0.78
1.2.3.5	0.71	0.62	0.68	0.60	0.27	0.14	0.90	0.83	0.37	0.46	0.70	0.71	0.81	0.81
1.2.4.5	0.74	0.67	0.73	0.65	0.10	-0.10	0.90	0.85	0.39	0.46	0.69	0.74	0.80	0.80
1.3.4.5	0.77	0.68	0.69	0.60	0.17	-0.01	0.91	0.85	0.37	0.45	0.70	0.73	0.79	0.81
2.3.4.5	0.73	0.69	0.71	0.66	-0.27	-0.46	0.93	0.89	0.33	0.44	0.70	0.77	0.73	0.77
1.2.3.4.5	0.75	0.68	0.70	0.62	0.10	-0.07	0.92	0.87	0.37	0.46	0.70	0.74	0.78	0.80

First row: X y, where X is the country, y is "c" for coincident and "l" for leading
First column: the potential indicator, which is made as a linear combination with equal weights from the questions as listed in Chapter 4.
Other rows and columns: correlation coefficient for the country indicated on the first row, (coincident or leading) between the reference variable (D4R) and the indicator mentioned in the first column.

The level of the results is very different between countries, going from very high levels in the United Kingdom to even negative values in France.

The mass of information shown in Table 2 does not allow the choice of an indicator; one has to see these results only as an input for more sophisticated methods (see Table 3).

Table 3 Results of the correlation analysis: ranking

	SUMSTDC	RANK15	RANK14	RANK13	RANK12	RANK11
1	25	18	16	15	12	8
2	31	30	29	29	31	31
3	28	22	21	25	25	22
4	21	18	16	18	18	15
5	30	28	27	27	26	24
1.2	14	13	16	18	18	15
1.3	15	5	6	4	1	2
1.4	2	5	6	7	3	2
1.5	24	18	16	15	12	8
2.3	27	28	27	27	26	24
2.4	22	22	21	18	18	15
2.5	29	30	29	29	29	28
3.4	20	22	21	18	18	15
3.5	26	27	29	29	29	28
4.5	13	22	21	18	18	15
1.2.3	9	9	6	4	12	8
1.2.4	1	2	2	1	1	1
1.2.5	18	9	6	7	3	2
1.3.4	6	9	11	7	3	2
1.3.5	17	9	11	7	3	8
1.4.5	7	2	2	1	3	2
2.3.4	19	13	16	15	12	15
2.3.5	23	22	21	25	26	28
2.4.5	10	18	21	18	18	22
3.4.5	16	13	11	7	12	8
1.2.3.4	4	5	4	18	18	15
1.2.3.5	11	13	11	7	3	8
1.2.4.5	3	5	6	7	12	8
1.3.4.5	8	4	4	4	3	24
2.3.4.5	12	13	11	7	3	2
1.2.3.4.5	5	1	1	3	3	24

First column: the potential indicator, which is made as a linear combination with equal weights from the questions as listed in Chapter 4.

Second up to seventh column: the results in these columns are rankings of the 31 potential indicators (listed in the first column), according to calculations based on correlation coefficients. Two types of correlations are calculated (on a quarterly base): - between the percentage change in Retail Sales Volume (compared to one year ago) and the potential indicator, coincident in time; - between the percentage change in Retail Sales Volume and the *lagged* potential indicator, to test the leading character of the indicator. Doing these two types of calculations for seven countries yields fourteen cases in which we can test the potential indicators.

Second column: SUMSTDC = ranking according to the sum of standardized correlation coefficients. For each of the fourteen cases, the average and the standard deviation of the correlation coefficients are calculated over the 31 potential indicators. Each correlation coefficient is then standardized by subtracting the average and dividing by the standard deviation. The sum of these coefficients over the fourteen cases is taken. This method selects the indicators which perform well *in all cases*.

Third up to seventh column: RANKXX = rank according to the appearances of the indicator in the top XX of the correlation coefficients. For example, if one looks at the 15 highest correlations out of the 31 potential indicators (RANK15), indicator 1.2.3.4.5 is in the top 15 in twelve out of the fourteen cases and is ranked number one. Indicator 1.2.4 is in the top 15 in eleven cases and is ranked number two.

The RANKXX method has the disadvantage of bringing an arbitrary element into the analysis: the number of top rankings to be used. The numbers presented in Table 3 seem to be the most logical ones: from 15 to 11 out of the 31, requiring the indicator to be in the top half up to the top third of the rankings.

Indicator 1.2.4 has the best result for the first criterion (sum of standardized correlation coefficients) as well as for the other criteria (RANKXX). Thus indicator 1.2.4 (the average of the results for the present business situation, for stocks[1] and for the future business situation) is chosen as confidence indicator for retail trade.

Note that in Annex 2 information is presented which became available after choosing the indicator. This information confirms the relevance of the chosen indicator.

The graphs below show how for each country the chosen indicator (CC.1.2.4, right-hand scale) traces closely the percentage change in the RSV (CC.D4R, left-hand scale).

A special case is however *France*: all potential indicators yield low correlation coefficients. Yet indicator 1.2.4 has good results in relative terms; this is compared to the other potential indicators.

There is probably a problem with the quantitative series for France. Indeed, the correlation between the indicator and the change in RSV rises to 0.51 when the RSV of Eurostat is used.[2] This is a confirmation of the overall goodness of fit of the chosen indicator.[3]

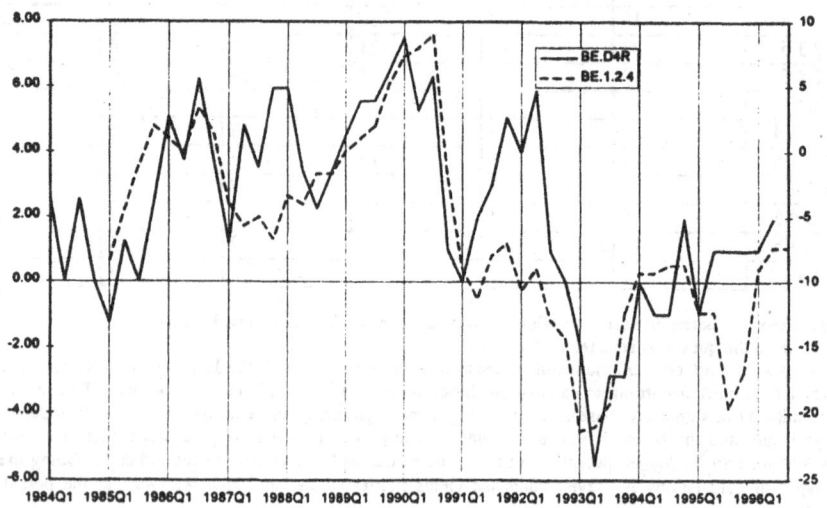

---

[1] With inverted sign.
[2] Calculated over a shorter period: 1989Q1 - 1995Q4.
[3] If one runs the exercise without France, the superiority of the chosen indicator remains.

Construction of a Confidence Indicator for Retail Trade by the European Commission

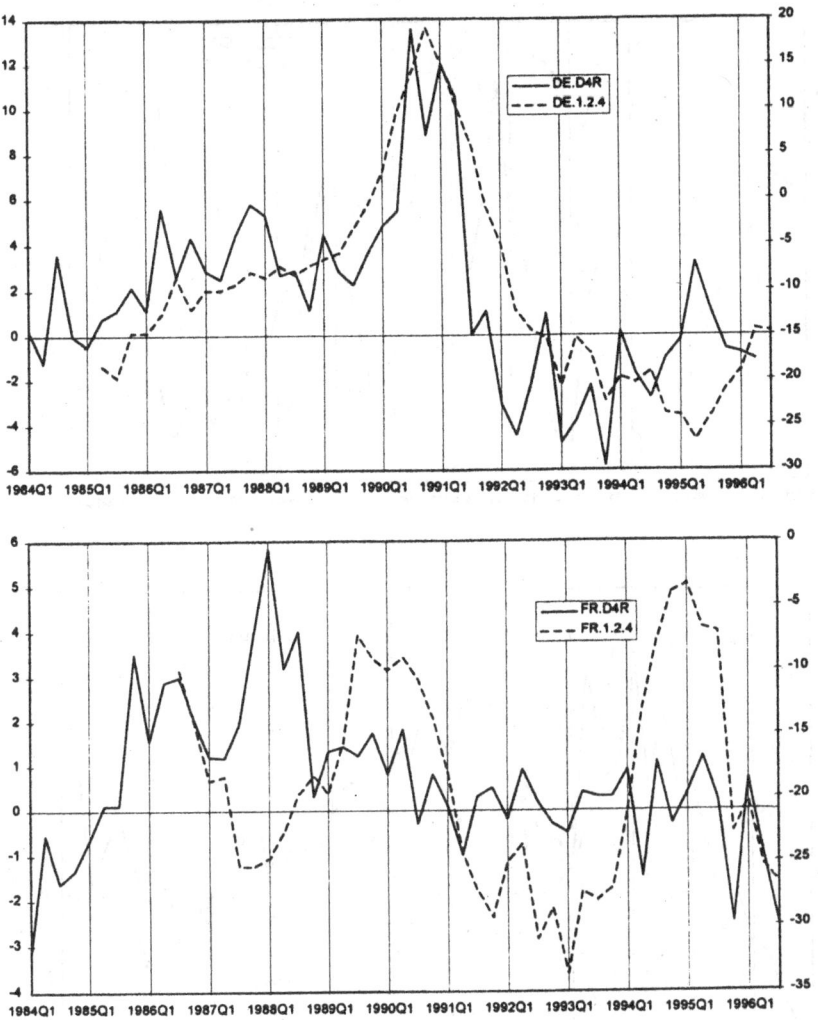

Social and Structural Change - Consequences for Business Cycle Surveys

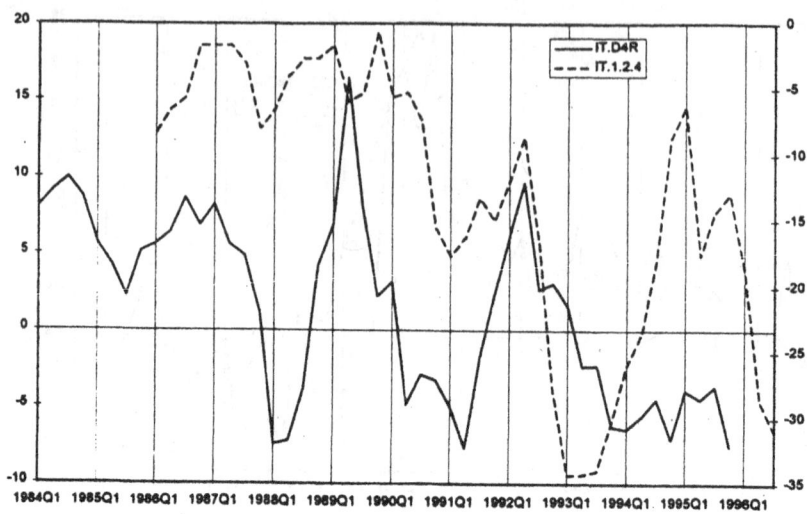

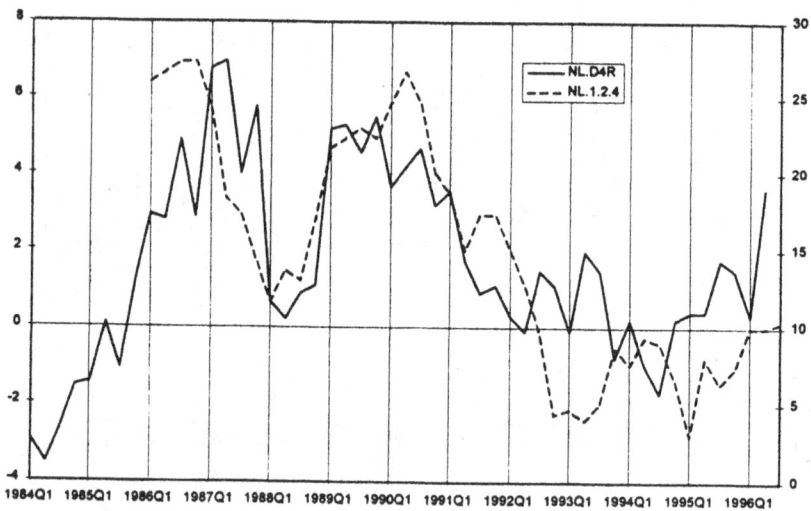

Construction of a Confidence Indicator for Retail Trade by the European Commission

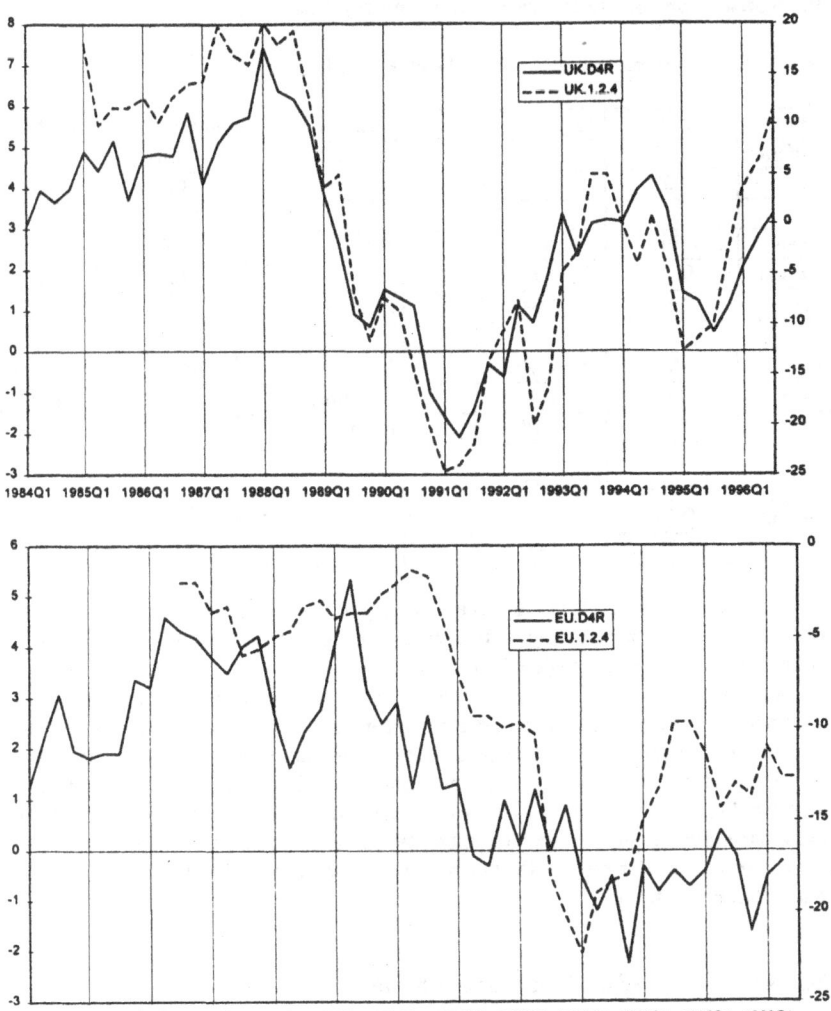

7 The Performance of the Indicator on a Monthly Base

Table 4 Comparison between monthly and quarterly results

Belgium	monthly	quarterly		Netherlands	monthly	quarterly
coincident	0.65	0.75		coincident	0.62	0.68
leading	0.62	0.68		leading	0.59	0.74
Germany	monthly	quarterly		UK	monthly	quarterly
coincident	0.61	0.72		coincident	0.87	0.93
leading	0.63	0.64		leading	0.84	0.89
France	monthly	quarterly		EU	monthly	quarterly
coincident	-0.02	0.11		coincident	0.60	0.77
leading	0.09	-0.05		leading	0.60	0.78
Italy	monthly	quarterly				
coincident	0.31	0.39				
leading	0.32	0.46				

The quarterly results for the seven countries are confirmed in the correlation coefficients between the monthly indicator and the percentage change in the monthly RSV compared to one year ago (Table 4).

Another test would be to apply the new indicator on the countries which are not used in the previous exercise. For Spain and Portugal no RSV is available. Survey results are not available or the series are too short in Austria, Finland, Greece, Ireland, Luxembourg and Sweden. This leaves us with fifteen countries minus six (analysed) minus two (without RSV) minus six (without survey or series too short) = one country: Denmark. Denmark has survey results since November 1989, the correlation between the change in RSV and the indicator is only 0.48, but both series are very volatile. The trends in both series are clearly the same.

8 Comparison with Other Confidence Indicators

In the following, the Retail Confidence Indicator (RCI) is compared with the Industry Confidence Indicator (ICI), the "Building" (Construction) Confidence Indicator (BCI) and the Consumer Confidence Indicator (CCI).

We have calculated volatility measures on monthly data (over the period from January 1986 to October 1996), with the following results:

Table 5 Comparison between confidence indicators

	CCI	ICI	RCI	BCI
number of components	5	3	3	2
LEVEL				
standard deviation	6.87	9.78	5.83	13.02
minimum value	-26	-28	-23	-44
maximum value	3	8	0	4
spread	23	36	23	48
CHANGE (month to month)				
standard deviation	1.38	1.49	2.01	2.64
minimum value	-5	-3	-6	-9
maximum value	4	3	5	7
spread	9	6	11	16

The composition of the CCI explains its low volatility. The *five* components will not necessarily move in the same direction all the time, bringing the global evolution closer to stability. The BCI, which has only two components, is a lot more volatile (see following graph).

Confidence Indicator

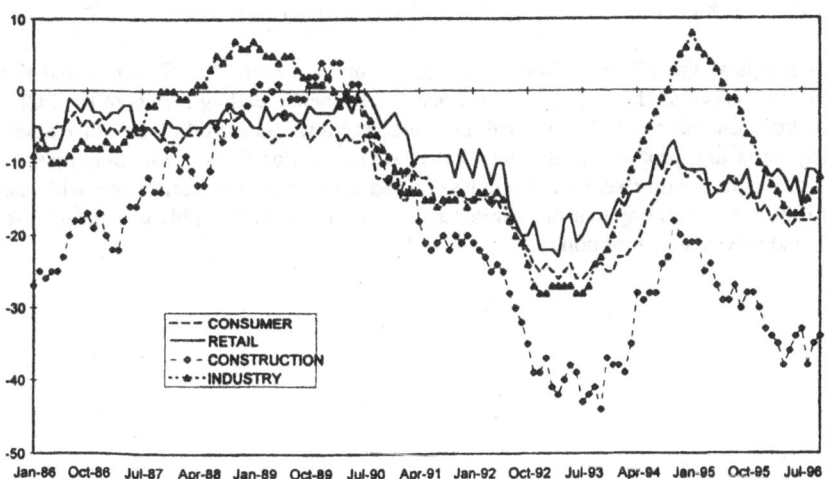

The RCI has a low standard deviation in level: it moves within a narrow range. The RCI has nevertheless a high standard deviation of month-to-month changes; it is not very smooth. These properties are the opposite of the ICI, which does not move inside a narrow range, but which is very smooth. This contrast is very surprising, given the resemblance of RCI and ICI, when looking at their components:

RCI	ICI
present business situation	order-books
stocks	stocks
future business situation	production expectations

9 Relation Between Retail Sales and Private Consumption

In Table 6, the relationship between retail sales and private consumption, for indicators as well as for quantitative statistics, is presented in correlations.

When interpreting these correlations, one should note that they are *coincident*. Yet some indicators are clearly leading:
1) in *Germany*, the CCI seems to have a big lead over D4C. The correlation with the lagged CCI is much higher than the coincident correlation: 0.51 for a lag of one quarter, 0.62 for two, 0.74 for three. The CCI also has a lead over the RCI: 0.49 is the correlation with a lag of one quarter, 0.57 for two, 0.66 for three.
2) in the *Netherlands*, there is also a lead for the CCI over D4C. The correlation with a lagged CCI is higher: 0.54 for a lag of one quarter, 0.51 for two.

For *Belgium*, the *UK* and *Europe*, all correlations are high. For *Germany* and the *Netherlands* this is also the case, taking into account the better leading results of the CCI.

For *Italy*, the three correlations with D4R are very low, compared to the other three. This may point to a problem of the quantitative statistics.[1] For *France*, one may refer to chapter 6, where another series for retail sales had a much higher correlation with the RCI. It is however puzzling that the original series for retail sales is highly correlated with the CCI and private consumption.

---

[1] There are also very important differences between the Eurostat and the OECD quantitative data.

Table 6   Correlations between confidence indicators and quantitative data for retail sales and private consumption

Belgium	CCI	D4C	D4R
D4C	0.84		
D4R	0.69	0.78	
RCI	0.60	0.68	0.75

Germany	CCI	D4C	D4R
D4C	0.40		
D4R	0.63	0.83	
RCI	0.40	0.83	0.72

France	CCI	D4C	D4R
D4C	0.71		
D4R	0.58	0.72	
RCI	0.66	0.42	0.11

Italy	CCI	D4C	D4R
D4C	0.88		
D4R	0.35	0.34	
RCI	0.92	0.89	0.39

Netherlands	CCI	D4C	D4R
D4C	0.43		
D4R	0.65	0.58	
RCI	0.55	0.89	0.39

UK	CCI	D4C	D4R
D4C	0.63		
D4R	0.69	0.90	
RCI	0.78	0.88	0.93

EU	CCI	D4C	D4R
D4C	0.90		
D4R	0.78	0.80	
RCI	0.93	0.87	0.77

10   Conclusion

Indicator 1.2.4 (the average of the results for the present business situation, for stocks[1] and for the future business situation) is chosen as confidence indicator for retail trade.

The relative performance of this indicator is superior to other candidates. The indicator has a lead over retail sales in most countries. This lead should originate in

---

[1] With inverted sign.

question 4 (future business situation). The new retail confidence indicator is published in Supplement B of European Economy from May 1997 on.

Annex 1: Data source

Calculations based on information available on 6 December 1996. Business Survey data are seasonally adjusted by Dainties (data available up to October 1996). For Retail Sales Volume the data from OECD Main Economic Indicators are used. In New Cronos only the period 1988Q1-1995Q4 was available, while OECD had data prior to 1988 and, except for Italy, already for 1996Q2/3 for the countries we are interested in.

Annex 2: Ex-post information

Quantitative and qualitative information which became available after finishing the study in December 1996, clearly confirms the relevance of the chosen indicator as can be seen on following graphs and in a revised Table 4. The additional information is:
- revision of the survey data for Italy[1] and, consequently for Europe;
- alternative quantitative data for France (from the quarterly national accounts);
- quantitative data for Portugal.

Revised version of Table 4   Alternative quantitative data for France, revised survey data for Italy and Europe, quantitative data for Portugal

Belgium	monthly	quarterly		Netherlands	monthly	quarterly
coincident	0.65	0.75		coincident	0.62	0.68
leading	0.62	0.68		leading	0.59	0.74
Germany	monthly	quarterly		UK	monthly	quarterly
coincident	0.61	0.72		coincident	0.87	0.93
leading	0.63	0.64		leading	0.84	0.89
France	monthly	quarterly		EU	monthly	quarterly
coincident	0.33	0.50		coincident	0.57	0.76
leading	0.09	0.33		leading	0.61	0.79
Italy	monthly	quarterly		Portugal	monthly	quarterly
coincident	0.33	0.53		coincident	0.61	0.67
leading	0.43	0.63		leading	0.62	0.73

---

[1] Including the "Large Multiple Shops" in the total, which makes the total more representative.

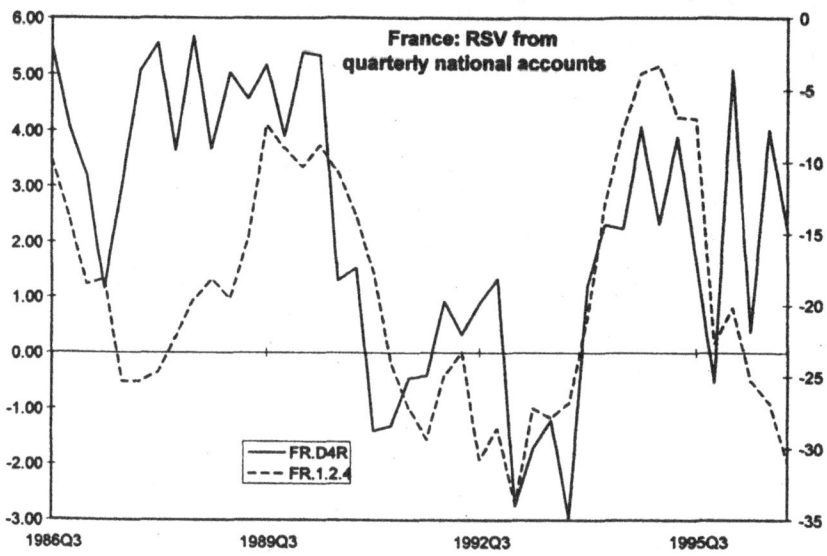

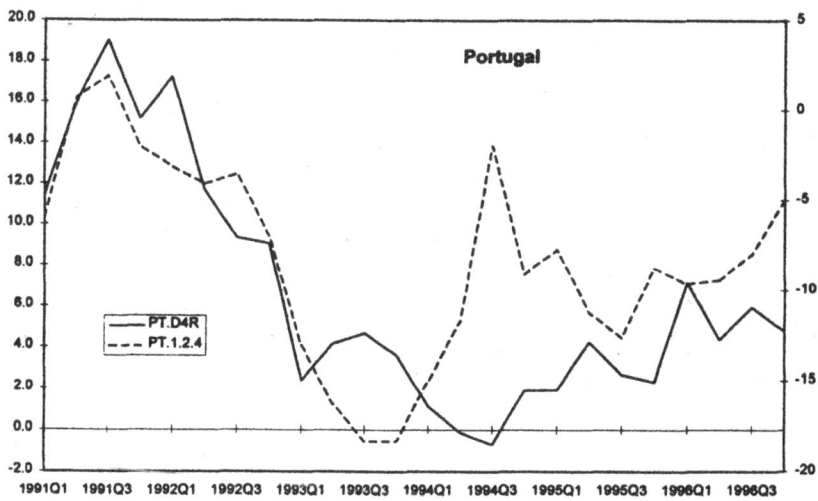

Part VIII
Social and Structural Change

26 Understanding and Measuring the Intangible Economy: Current Status and Suggestions for Further Research

Charles Goldfinger

1 Introduction

This paper addresses the issues of understanding and measuring the key trends which shape the modern economy. We define those trends as the Intangible Economy. Official methods and approaches, whether at the macro-economic or micro-economic levels, are widely acknowledged to be inadequate for its apprehension. Furthermore, it is uncertain whether the current efforts to improve the accuracy of statistical and accounting data will be sufficient to bridge the measurement gap. We believe that there is a need for a substantial and substantive increase in further research. Such research should go beyond methodology and address the questions of qualitative change and of the nature of markets in the economy.

This paper begins by presenting the main elements of the Intangible Economy framework. It then reviews some of the current efforts to apprehend the changing nature of economy. These efforts include proposals to revise the CPI, qualitative change measurements, Intellectual Capital framework and Information Technology mapping. We also survey new approaches in the economic theory such as Increasing Returns and endogenous growth. In the concluding section, we suggest areas for further research. These should include in-depth investigations in the output measurement and the qualitative change as well as more conceptual probing of the dynamics of intangible economy, such its contribution to net growth and asset accumulation, the nature of intangible markets and the economics of abundance.

2 Intangible Economy: A Brief Overview

2.1 *Understanding Economic Change: The Measurement Gap*

That the economy is undergoing a far-reaching, rapid and ubiquitous change is a largely controvertible statement. Knowledge Economy, Digital Economy, Information Society, Third Wave... names for the new economy proliferate to the point of becoming ubiquitous buzzwords. Yet, can we say that we really understand today's economy? Do we agree on its rationale and development path? The answer to those questions is clearly no. The gap between the mainstream measurement systems and the underlying economic reality is growing. The dynamics of measurement systems appear to be governed by a paradox: while our dependence on data is increasing, they are becoming less reliable. According to Zvi Griliches, Harvard Professor and an authority on measurement, the share of economy measured with a degree of accuracy by official statistics has fallen from 50% to 30% between 1947 and 1990 (Griliches, 1995). Weaknesses are the most pronounced in the areas which are most dynamic and trend setting such as services or information technology. In this age of 'information revolution' and 'knowledge economy', measurement systems shed little light on activities where information and knowledge are generated.

The problem goes beyond the weakness of data and the inadequacy of measurement methodologies. One needs to question the relevance of underlying conceptual models and assumptions. The crucial assumptions of national accounts - focus on physical goods production and trade, choice of a nation as the main reference frame, stable sectoral groupings and classifications, neglect of non-material transborder flows - are grounded in a specific vision of the economy, which has not fundamentally changed since Adam Smith's time and which postulates the production of physical goods as the main source of value (Giarini, 1984).

These assumptions and the underlying vision can no longer be considered universally valid (Duncan and Gross, 1995). In recognition of their deficiencies, economists have sought to develop alternative conceptual frameworks. The two best known among these are the service economy and the information economy. They share the same problem. Both terms are well known, to the point of becoming buzzwords. Yet, little progress has been made in making them conceptually more robust and operationally more relevant. They have not gained enough internal consistency and external recognition to provide a credible basis for the development of an alternative measurement framework. As the result, they remain largely on the periphery of mainstream economics and statistics (Goldfinger, 1997).

2.2 Intangible Economy: Three Dimensions

The need for a new conceptual framework for the modern economy remains paramount. Such a framework should build upon the contributions of the service and information economy approaches but should be broader to encompass other significant trends such as the financial markets explosion and development of entertainment industry.

I would like to suggest an alternative framework, based on a single defining trend: the shift from tangible to intangible. The economic landscape of the present and future is no longer shaped by physical flows of material goods and products but by ethereal streams of data, images and symbols. The well-known three stages (Clark, 1940) or three waves (Toffler, 1980) theories of economic evolution can thus be reformulated. At the core of the agricultural economy, there was a relationship between man, nature and natural products. The core relationship of the industrial economy was between man, machine and machine-created artificial objects. The intangible economy is structured around relationships between man, ideas and symbols. The source of economic value and wealth is no longer the production of material goods but the creation and manipulation of intangible content.

The shift to the ethereal is general and long-lasting. It affects all sectors and all aspects of economic life. Intangible inputs account for over 70% of the value added in the car production (Stewart, 1997). Somewhat more surprisingly, 70% of the cost of producing butter are due to intangible factors (Blanc and Breton, 1994). According to Danny Quah, professor at London School of Economics, we live in an 'increasingly weightless economy', where greater and greater share of GDP resides in 'economic commodities that have little or no physical manifestations' (Quah, 1997).

Although information and knowledge are the main vectors of the Intangible economy, they are not the only ones. It is as much an economy of 'useful' information and knowledge as it is of 'wasteful' entertainment and distraction. One of its key features, for instance, is the explosive growth of entertainment activities, comprising toys, sporting goods, VCR equipment, records, books, newspapers and magazines, gambling, amusement parks, home computers, live entertainment and spectator sports. Entertainment is the growth industry of the 1990s. Using Department of Commerce data, Business Week journalists estimated the 1993 US market size of the entertainment industry at $341 billion. In the US, entertainment employs more people than the automobile industry and in 1993, it accounted for 12% of all job creation (Mandel, Landler and Grover, 1994).

The intangible economy is too often seen as a purely technology-driven phenomenon. The new economy is thus seen as the triumph of bits over atoms (Negroponte, 1995). A Canadian consultant, Don Tapscott goes as far to propose a notion of the 'Digital Economy' (Tapscott, 1996). This is a dangerous oversimplification. I do not seek to deny the key contribution of Information Technology (which we will discuss further below) to the advent of the intangible economy but it is important to avoid a fallacy that the intangible economy is technology-determined. While the technological trend toward digitalisation is unmistakable, its economic and business impact remains unclear and the range of potential outcomes is wide open. Moreover, the development of the intangible economy owes at least as much to basic trends in consumer behaviour and in business environment. Shift toward higher relative demand for leisure, information and knowledge is a strong and long-lasting trend in consumer behaviour: for instance, the share of services in household consumption in France has increased from 42% in 1970 to 51% in 1990 (Gadrey, 1992). Business innovations such as brand-driven competition and unbundling of computer hardware and software have been a major dematerialisation factor. The intangible economy is non-deterministic and transcends the opposition between bits and atoms the same way that quantum physics transcends the opposition between particles and waves.

The intangible economy is all around us. Yet, we have great difficulty to apprehend it: by definition, intangible phenomena are elusive. Not limited by physical constraints, they defy attempts to fit them into standard economic categories and taxonomies.

To understand the intangible economy, we propose to approach it from three different perspectives (Goldfinger, 1994):

- Demand perspective: Intangible *artefacts*: final output for consumption.
- Supply perspective: *Intangible assets*, used by firms to establish and maintain their

competitive position and survival. They include: the brand, the intellectual property, the human capital, research and development information and know-how.
- Economic system perspective: *Logic of dematerialisation*: an interrelated set of trends and forces that affect all economic activities, changing the nature of economic transactions and market structures.

2.2.1 Demand: Intangible Artefacts Intangible artefacts include different forms of information and communication, high and low culture, audio-visual media, entertainment and leisure, without forgetting finance, the ultimate intangible.

All artefacts are joint products, combining intangible content with physical support or a set of supports: song with a magnetic tape for an audiocassette; history and a building site for a classical monument. Traditionally, content and support were tightly linked, making them either unique or reproducible on a small-scale only. The development of technologies of storage and replication of content has loosened the links: the same content can now be easily and cheaply replicated and associated with various physical supports. Like a dragon in a fable, artefacts with an identical content appear in various disguises and shapes: a song can be sung live, pressed on a CD or shown as a video-clip. A payment can be made in cash, by cheque, via card or wire transfer. Not only is the cost of replication very low, and getting lower over time, but the replication devices are readily available to the consumer. The dissociation of content and support has led to the proliferation of intangible artefacts in two ways. First, it has lifted capacity constraints limiting a large-scale consumption of intangibles. A theatrical show or a sports game could be only watched by those who could physically attend the theatre or the stadium. Today, television can multiply the number of spectators ad infinitum. One could argue that a stadium attendance and a TV watching of a sport event are two different artefacts, with different consumption, distribution and pricing characteristics. That is precisely the second dimension of proliferation: the same content provides a source for a family of artefacts: a book can be offered as a hardcover, as a paperback, as a CD-ROM or on-line. The ability to generate such families is what makes companies such as Disney successful: each film idea, Aladdin or Lion King, generates not only movies but also videos, park attractions, books, toys and other sources of revenues, thus leveraging the content by a factor of two to four.

The consumption of intangible artefacts displays specific and interrelated properties:

- It is joint (always consumed with other products, tangibles or intangibles).
- It is non-destructive: the same artefact can be consumed repetitively either by a same consumer or by a different one.
- It is non-subtractive (or non-rival): one's consumption does not reduce anyone else's consumption. In other terms, the opportunity cost of sharing is zero.

Intangibles such as information are often presented as a 'public good,' such as fresh air or national defence, whose consumption cannot be limited to a single consumer and therefore is inherently collective (Olson, 1973). We prefer to use the term of a 'shared good.'

Traditionally, the pricing of intangibles was a function of convenience and was based on the support rather than on the content. Thus, the price of a book was determined by its thickness and the printing quality. This pricing largely ignored the content: the price for an excellent book was the same as the price of a bad one.

The advance of dissociation created opportunities for unbundling: content can now be priced separately from the support. Price discrimination, based on the estimated value of content, becomes more common. Commercial on-line services, for instance, differentiate between standard and premium services, which are sold at higher prices. Yet, the bundling has its advantages, in particular the simplicity of administration. It facilitates pricing of composite artefacts, comprising several types of content (multimedia software or amusement parks). It also allows cross-subsidies. In financial services for instance, equity research is bundled into brokerage commissions. Thus, the range of intangibles pricing schemes is getting broader and more complex. Furthermore, depending on the supplier-consumer relationship, different pricing arrangements can apply to apparently similar artefacts. Computer software can be sold as a stand-alone product or it can be bundled with hardware or be distributed as a shareware or freeware over a network (Dyson, 1992, Varian, 1994, 1995). Internet provides a fascinating laboratory of various approaches to pricing through various combinations of selling, sharing and giving away. The debate about the respective merits of those approaches is lively. Some argue that the development of technologies such as metering, which measure the detailed use of a given software, makes feasible fully variable usage-driven pricing (Cox, 1994). Others plead in favour of a fixed access charge, independent of the actual use. Still another group considers that the ease of replication makes content practically free and therefore the only feasible approach is to charge for ancillary services (Dyson, 1995). These approaches should be seen as complementary rather than mutually exclusive.

As pricing of intangibles focuses on content, it highlights its inherent volatility of valuation. Although physical goods also show variation in price, the amplitude of changes is considerably larger for intangible artefacts. Their value is highly time-sensitive and can change dramatically: the same artefact can be valued very differently by the same user - financial information can be worth millions of dollars in the morning and nothing in the afternoon. Economists have grappled with this issue and came up with theoretical solutions. However, their implementation may be costly, due to the need for demand data, thus raising the issue of the trade-off between allocative efficiency and operational cost-effectiveness (Mitchell and Vogelsang, 1991).

Valuation problems result in all likelihood in underestimates of the importance of consumption of intangibles. For instance, if one looks closely at household entertainment expenditures, one can see discrepancies between time spent and monetary outlays. In 1992, each American spent on average 3262 hours consuming different forms of entertainment, close to 9 hours a day (Veronis Suhler, 1994). Of these, the lion's share, close to 5 hours a day, was spent on television and radio, which (excluding cable television and pay-per view) was 'free', funded by advertising, and thus did not show up as consumer expenditures.

2.2.2 Supply The ascent of intangible artefacts is accompanied and stimulated on the supply side by the growing importance of intangible assets.

Statisticians and accountants have long recognised that capital accumulation and asset deployment means more than the acquisition of physical plant and equipment.

At the aggregate level, intangible investment comprises R&D, training, marketing, computer software and services. The French Statistical Institute (INSEE) in its 1992 National Accounts (INSEE, 1993) defines intangible investment as:

> 'Those business expenditures, which develop the production capacity and enhance the value of the firm by creating a capital which could be depreciated or long-term tradable assets.'

Not surprisingly, the share of intangible investment is expanding relative to physical investment. According to INSEE, intangible investment represented 30% of the total investment in 1992 in France and was growing at a quicker rate than fixed assets. Partial evidence suggests that in other countries, such as the UK, the percentage is even higher (OECD, 1992).

At the firm level, the view that the intangible assets are more important to business performance and survival than the physical assets is now conventional wisdom. The acknowledgement of their importance is more than a lip service or a fad. For consumer goods companies, Coca-Cola, Nestle or Danone, brand management is the top priority guiding all their strategies. Brand is also essential for Information Technology companies such as Intel and Compaq, which are spending substantial sums to build it. Leading marketing specialists, such as David Aaker, from University of California at Berkeley, consider brand an integral part of firm's equity (Aaker, 1991). Attempts are often made to quantify this 'brand equity.' An American business monthly, *Financial World*, publishes each year a brands survey, which value them on the basis of their sales, profitability and growth potential. For leading brands such as Coca-Cola or Marlboro, the brand valuation exceeds the total balance sheet of parent companies (Badenhausen, 1996).

Acknowledgement of the importance of intangible assets is not limited to brands. Intellectual property - patents, trademark, technological know-how - is considered as a critical competitive weapon, particularly in software, electronics and biotechnology. The control of intellectual property rights is often a matter of life and death for companies. It is through intellectual property litigation that AMD and Cyrix managed to preserve their foothold in microprocessors, despite Intel's domination. In merger and acquisition transactions, the book value has become largely irrelevant to the company valuation, which is determined primarily by intangible assets (Petersens and Bjurstrom, 1991). Apparently extravagant amount paid for media assets, such as Hollywood studios or newspapers, can be explained by the crucial role attributed to brands, contents and publishing rights in the emerging realm of infotainment, combining information and entertainment (The Economist, 1994).

Intangible assets are difficult to separate, thus violating one of the cardinal rules of traditional asset valuation. First, it is difficult to separate intangible assets from current expenditures. Whether an advertising expenditure can be classified as current expenditure or investment depends on its purpose. Similarly, not all training or software expenditures can be treated as investment.

More importantly, intangible assets often interact with each other, making it difficult to identify their separate contribution. When, in October 1992, Intel decided to give its new microprocessor a recognisable name, Pentium, rather than a number, 80586, it was because it wanted to establish a brand name and simultaneously to reinforce intellectual property protection.

Because intangible assets are, by definition, non-physical, they do not follow the classical progressive depreciation rules. Some assets depreciate very rapidly, others, like a good wine, appreciate with age, stills others follow non-linear and often unpredictable life cycles.

Thus traditional ways of valuing assets cannot be applied.

Aware of the importance of intangible assets, the accounting profession has undertaken efforts to define and to measure them. A well-known accounting firm, Arthur Andersen, gives thus the following definition of intangible assets (Arthur Andersen, 1992):

'...Resources controlled by the enterprise (...) which possess the following attributes:

- non physical in nature
- capable of producing future economic net benefits
- protected legally or through de facto right.'

Arthur Andersen proposes a four part classification of intangible assets: brands, intellectual property, publishing rights and licences.

In light of the shortcomings of cost-based and transaction-based valuation approaches, Andersen recommends another approach, the Discounted Cash Flow (DCF) method which determines the economic value of an asset by looking at its cash generating potential.

Both the four part classification and DCF approach were endorsed by the International Accounting Standards Committee (IASC) in its 1994 *Draft Statement of Principles on Intangible Assets* (IASC, 1994).

This by no means implies that the consensus on intangible assets has been achieved. The DCF method is far from being universally accepted.

More importantly, the proposed classification is far from exhaustive. It excludes what many consider the most critical asset: human capital, the quality of firm's workforce. It also ignores the company culture, its accumulated knowledge (which is often informal and unprotected) and its network of relationships with customers and suppliers.

Thus the issue of accounting treatment of intangible assets remains largely unsettled. Many experts feel that the traditional accounting approaches are inadequate to handle these assets. Their specificity has spurred the emergence of alternative approaches, such as the Intellectual Capital movement, which we will discuss below.

2.2.3 Dematerialisation Logic The impact of the intangible economy is pervasive and ubiquitous and affects all sectors and activities. Intangible economy does not eliminate agriculture or industry. However, its underlying logic affects all economic relationships and profoundly transforms the ways firms and markets are organised and transactions are carried out. The dematerialisation logic is unsettling to the extent that it runs squarely against some of the key tenets of the conventional logic of economics. The conventional logic is concerned with scarcity, the dematerialisation logic with abundance. The former stresses equilibrium, the latter disequilibrium. Phenomena such as obsolescence or redundancy which had been perceived as peripheral and pernicious, are now pivotal and essential, moulding consumption patterns and guiding asset deployment. Instability and volatility become pervasive: market positions and hierarchies change rapidly and dramatically.

The three fundamental features of dematerialisation logic are: (1) abundance, (2) interpenetration and (3) indeterminacy.

(1) Abundance

Intangible economy is structurally abundant. Abundance, of course, is not a new phenomenon. The productive potential of the industrial economy is enormous and clearly exceeds the demand absorption capacity. However, physical goods are subject to physical decay and their consumption marks the beginning of the end of their economic life. Intangible artefacts, on the other hand, are not only extremely cheap to replicate but furthermore are not eliminated through consumption. The intangible economy superimposes on the abundance of production the abundance of accumulation. Contrary to a popular belief, intangible does not automatically signify ephemeral. The lifecycle of popular intangible artefacts is considerably longer than that of material goods: we will forever read Balzac books, listen to Bach music or watch Bergman movies.

Financial systems generate too many transactions, Hollywood, too much entertainment, Internet, too much information. The gap between supply and demand of intangible artefacts is so huge that it has created an 'information overload', also called 'infoglut': 'the inability to absorb the torrential and continuously swelling flood of data, images, messages and transactions' (Tetzeli, 1994). The on-going deregulation of markets for intangibles along with the technological evolution continues to aggravate the overload. For instance, the number of television channels in the European Union has increased from 40 in 1980 to 150 in 1994. Progress in transmission and distribution techniques makes it feasible to increase the number of channels to 500 or even more (Heilemann, 1994). Moreover, the overload is self-perpetuating: to navigate through it we need catalogues, indexes, documentation, whose very proliferation calls for more cross-references, hypertext links and so on. Efficient infoglut management requires more rather than less information. Information about information is a growing business.

Abundance confronts consumers with a dilemma. On the one hand, they want to take advantage of the increased choice of products and artefacts. On the other hand, they seek to minimise the cost of search.

In response to the first objective, new modes of consumption have emerged: zapping, surfing or browsing. They are characterised by a short attention span, latency, high frequency of switching and capriciousness. They blur the distinction between consumption and non-consumption, rendering pricing problems even more intractable.

The expanded range of output makes consumer choice more difficult, by continuously raising the cost of acquiring information about the output. To minimise this cost, the choice is increasingly determined by criteria other than product characteristics such as brand familiarity or mimicking and fashion (Bikchandani and al., 1993, Veblen, 1899). These criteria are discretionary, generating rapid and massive shifts in demand, which are hard to anticipate. The result is an uneasy coexistence of stability, for products and artefacts associated with a strong brand, and volatility for the others. The trend is clearly toward the latter.

Brand and fashion-driven demand forces suppliers to continuously renew their offerings and to actively manage their product portfolio. Product cycle is becoming shorter. Obsolescence is no longer an external constraint, it becomes an instrumental variable. In certain areas, such as personal computers, obsolescence leads to cannibalisation: new products are introduced to replace products that are still successful. Intel and Compaq are particularly skilful in the use of cannibalisation to keep their competitors off balance (Chreiki, 1995, Allen, 1992).

(2) Interpenetration

The intangible economy undermines traditional frontiers and distinctions. Sectoral boundaries are crumbling: previously separate activities of telecommunication, informatics, electronics and audio-visual entertainment are now overlapping. Time-honoured distinctions between work and leisure, home and work-place, intermediate good and final output, consumer and producer, product and service, become blurred. Not only are the boundaries porous and overlaying, they are unstable.

This is not a one-off effect of transition to a new environment but a fundamental trend. The intangible economy does not follow the rules of binary logic of exclusivity but that of fuzzy logic of overlapping (Kosko, 1993).

The interpenetration profoundly changes the nature of the firm and its relationships with the environment. Internal links, between firm and its employees, become weaker; external links, between firms and its suppliers, become stronger. While employees are told to work at home, suppliers are invited to work on premises. Functions traditionally considered as central to the very existence of the firm are now subcontracted or outsourced. This leads to the advent of the 'virtual corporation' (Davidow and Malone, 1992). Nike, leader in sport shoes, does not manufacture any shoes. Nor does Dell, a leading supplier of computers, own any production plant. In the semiconductor industry, many leading firms are 'fabless', concentrating on chip design and subcontracting their production (Rapaport and Halevi, 1991). In computer services, outsourcing is one of the highest growth sectors.

Dematerialisation logic modifies the market power balance and the value chain structure. In the industrial economy, the central position in the value chain was that of final product assembly, while the position of subcontractor was subordinate. Despite the fact that Michelin contributed more to the development of the automobile, by facilitating road travel with maps, signs and guides, than Renault or Citroen, the latter gained greater market power: few people ever buy their cars in function of the brand of its tires. In the intangible economy, a subcontractor often assumes a dominant position. Thus, in personal computers, Intel and Microsoft, are in a considerably stronger position, and are more profitable, than IBM or Compaq, which control final assembly. Their dominance is due to their ability to establish intellectual property rights over key product components, in this instance microprocessor architecture and operating system software.

These changes in the value chain structure reflect a fundamental trend: the weight of the value chain is moving closer to the consumer. This trend has led to the emergence of 'power retailers' such as Wal Mart in the US, Marks and Spencer in the UK, Galleries

Lafayette in France or Ikea in Sweden. They decide which products are put on the scarce real estate of store shelves. They also set prices and become increasingly involved in product design. One visible sign of their increasing power is the development of own-label brands by large retailers. According to Boston Consulting Group estimates (Reid, 1995), own-label brands represent close to 30% of total grocery sales in the UK, 25% in Germany, over 20% in France, and their share is growing.

The transfer of market power does not stop at the check-out counter and frequently crosses the producer-consumer divide. In the personal computer industry, between 1986 and 1991, customers captured 49% of value added, against 31% for software and services suppliers and 20% for equipment manufacturers (McKinsey, 1992).

The intangible economy brings about a momentous change in the relationship between suppliers and consumers - the end of information asymmetry. Today in many businesses, the customer knows as much about products and markets as the supplier. This entails not only substantial end-user price falls, due to the loss of the market power of supplier, but also an unbundling of the production and assembly process, which becomes interactive. The unbundling is particularly apparent in the Information Technology area. Software applications and corporate data networks are often designed and built by customers, using inputs from different suppliers. Of course, they can also be created by suppliers with inputs from customers. 'Make-or-buy' decisions are becoming more prevalent and more convoluted. The nature of competition changes: for computer services suppliers, such as IBM or EDS, their clients are their biggest competitors.

(3) Indeterminacy

The dematerialisation logic is not deterministic. It does not point to a single optimal trajectory. It actually widens the range of choices and alternatives. Instability and volatility which govern the demand for intangibles become pervasive and affect all aspects of the economy, national competitiveness, business hierarchies and market structures, prompting frequent and massive reversals of judgements and opinions.

In the early 1990s, the conventional wisdom was that the competitiveness of the United States was declining and that of Japan, increasing. This was, for instance, the verdict of the widely publicised World Competitiveness Report, compiled by the International Institute for Management Development (IMD) in Lausanne. By 1994, the consensus has changed radically: the US is now considered as having the most competitive economy in the world, while Japan is losing ground (IMD, 1992, IMD, 1996).

The intangible economy is moulded by contradictory cross-currents: globalization and localisation, concentration and fragmentation, vertical integration and horizontal competition. Thus, while the economy is becoming more integrated and more transnational, the political system heads in the opposite directions. The number of new countries has increased in the last fifty years, with twenty having been born between 1989 and 1995. This is what John Naisbitt refers to as a 'Global Paradox.' (Naisbitt, 1994, Alesina and Spolane, 1995).

Contradictory crosscurrents are the strongest in the business area. At times, it appears that the guiding principle of business strategies and economic policy making is the schizophrenia. On the one hand, the competition has never been keener; the fight for market share and shelf space, more brutal; the rivalry between firms, more intense. At the same time, alliances proliferate in all sectors and all areas and management theorists extol the virtues of co-operation and sharing (Badaracco, 1991, Nalebuff and Brandenburger, 1996). This coexistence of competition and co-operation has prompted Ray Noorda, the founder of Novell, the leading provider of networking software, to coin a new term - the 'coopetition'

Nowhere is strategic schizophrenia stronger than in the emerging realm of multimedia. There, at least three radically different approaches coexist: 'oligopolistic convergence', 'oligopolistic specialisation' and 'Internet proliferation'.

The 'oligopolistic convergence' is based on the view that in the new environment, which is being created by the convergence of information, communication and entertainment, economies of scale and vertical integration are the key success factors. Only the biggest companies, controlling various elements of the value chain - programming, distribution, marketing - and all facets of the multimedia spectrum - movies, TV, records, books, computer software...- will survive. When the dust settles, the multimedia domain will be ruled by very few, global, vertically and horizontally integrated players. This approach has provided the rationale for the spectacular media mergers such as Disney-ABC and Time Warner - Turner transactions in August and September 1995.

'Oligopolistic specialisation' also assumes economies of scale and market concentration. Its proponents are sceptical however about the speed and economic viability of convergence. They view vertical integration, whether between hardware and software or between content and distribution, as somewhat of a mixed blessing, hypothetical virtues of synergy being largely counterbalanced by the heavy administrative overhead and persistent conflicts of interest between different businesses. Under this approach, the key success factor is the ability to focus and to concentrate resources on chosen market segments and customer groups. The September 1995 decision by ATT, the perennial paragon of a vertically integrated information company, to split itself into three parts is an example of a strategy guided by oligopolistic specialisation.

The 'Internet proliferation' approach assumes that fragmentation will be the dominant feature of the Information Technology landscape. Wide availability of technology and information maintains low barriers to entry and facilitates unbundling. Networks proliferate and interactivity reigns supreme. This entails a fluid market structure with a high degree of specialisation and segmentation, and a numerous and diversified cast of players. Negroponte sees 'the monopolistic media empires dissolving into an array of cottage industries' (Negroponte, 1995). While the oligopolistic models continue to rule the corporate boardroom, the Internet model has captured imagination of foot soldiers in the Information war trenches, and the interest of fund managers, as evidenced by the success of public offerings of Internet companies such as Netscape in August, 1995, and their (at least initially) astronomical valuation: three Internet upstarts, Raptor Systems, VocalTec and CyberCash, whose combined 1995 revenues were about 5 million dollars had attained an initial market capitalisation of 850 million dollars!

It is difficult to predict which approach will prevail. The empirical evidence is inconclusive. Data can be marshalled to support each approach. Thus, certain segments of Information Technology are utterly dominated by a single supplier: Microsoft and Novell in personal computer software, Intel in microprocessors. Other segments, such as personal computer manufacturing, display a substantial number of players and intense competition. Many specialists point at a strong growth of mergers and acquisitions as evidence of consolidation and concentration. Yet, the robust pace of Initial Public Offerings (IPO), in the US and in the UK in particular, and of venture capital financing indicates a continuing inflow of newcomers. Since the early 1990s, both mergers and acquisitions and IPO activities are at record levels. Furthermore in this area, the past is a very imperfect guide to the future: the shifts in technology and in consumer preferences can be sudden and sweeping, creating threats for existing leaders and opportunities for audacious entrants. The shifts are also hard to predict: very few experts have anticipated the extent, the speed and the impact of the Internet explosion.

Behind the strategic schizophrenia and the inconclusiveness of data lies a more fundamental and structural ambivalence. At the core of the intangible economy, contradictory forces are at work: economies of scale and increasing returns, on the one hand, value shift to the consumer and market upheaval, on the other hand. These forces will continue to coexist and to interact, thus maintaining indeterminacy.

Contrary to the industrial economy, economies of scale in the production of intangible artefacts are limited: adding twice as many programmers to a software development project is unlikely to cut in half its completion time or cost, it may actually double it. However, economies of scale in distribution can be significant, due to a combination of high fixed costs of creating the distribution infrastructure and low variable costs of using it. They are a major vector of the downstream value chain shift. They also constitute the main rationale for the wave of mergers in sectors such as banking, retailing and media, whose prime objective is to create large and ubiquitous distribution networks (Wysocki, 1995).

Scale effects are accentuated by the consumption characteristics of intangible artefacts. The 'bookstore' effect favours a supplier concentration as consumers tend to use a supplier with a largest choice. Sharing leads to network externalities: the value of a given artefact is enhanced by the number of other consumers using it. Large networks tend to grow larger, at the expense of smaller networks. The joint and non-destructive (repetitive) nature of intangibles' consumption entails what Brian Arthur, Stanford professor also affiliated with the Santa Fe Institute and a leading proponent of the increasing returns theory (see below), calls the 'lock-in' effect: once a user is committed to a given technology and accumulates artefacts which depend on it, the cost of switching becomes very high. A supplier who manages to impose his technological standard, whether it is VHS for Matsushita or Windows for Microsoft, locks in consumers and grabs practically a 100% market share. For Brian Arthur, the combination of lock-in effect and increasing returns not only leads to monopolistic concentration but also threatens technological progress. This implies the need for government intervention, such the US Department of Justice restrictions on the activities of Microsoft (Arthur, 1995).

And yet, there are clearly countervailing forces at work. The cardinal one is the shift of the market power to the consumer. Wider availability of information and lower transaction costs eliminate information asymmetry and drastically lowers the search costs. It also reduces the incentive for vertical integration (Huber, 1992). It is the consumer who acquires the integration capability. The rapid pace of technological innovation and the capriciousness of demand limits the 'lock-in' effect and favours the emergence of new product families and market segments, which offers scope for new entrants and for the supplier hierarchy reversal. Ultimately, the reduction of supplier monopoly power comes not from increased competition in the existing segments or from government intervention but from the creation of new markets. So far, the intangible economy has demonstrated an enormous capacity to sustain innovation and to generate new markets. There is no reason to doubt its continuing ability to do so.

3 Current Efforts

Shortcomings of the current economic measurement systems and their underlying conceptual framework are quite widely acknowledged by the statisticians and economists. Broad-ranging and diverse efforts have been undertaken in various countries to improve them and to bring them closer in line with the economic reality. Without pretending to be exhaustive, we can mention several worthwhile efforts. These concern in particular:

At the national macro-economic level
- Measurements of quantitative change and its impact on macroeconomic aggregates such as the price index
- Measurements of national wealth and its impact on the economic performance

At the sectoral level
- Mapping of the Information Technology domain

At the enterprise level
- Measurement of various dimensions of performance
- Capturing of intellectual capital
- Measurement of intangible assets

At the economic theory level
- Increasing returns
- Determinants of economic growth and development
- Weightless economy.

3.1 Qualitative Change and Its Impact

Technical progress and product innovation continuously change the characteristics of the bundle of goods and services consumed by economic agents. The constant quality cannot be assumed, to the contrary economic measurements have to specifically include the impact of technological change, particularly on the consumer price index. The issue has acquired a greater sense of urgency with the implementation of the chain-weight price index methodology for GDP measurement. Unless this methodology is complemented by measures of qualitative change, it may result in a serious underestimation of living standards and productivity. Stakes are extremely high. In 1996, a commission appointed by the US Finance Senate to study the Consumer Price Index, chaired by Michael Boskin and comprising four other prestigious economists, concluded that the US Consumer Price Index has an upward bias estimated at 1.1%, of which 0,6% is due to the underestimate of product quality improvements (Boskin, 1996). The report generated considerable controversy and opposition, to the extent that it is seen as a tool to 'invisibly' cut social benefits and increase taxes, and the implementation of its recommendations is uncertain. Nevertheless, the report's analysis of the factors which contribute to the underestimate of the impact of qualitative product and services improvement on consumers' welfare is rigorous and deserves serious attention. Some economists consider Boskin Commission calculation on the conservative side. For instance, MIT economist, Jerry Hausman analysed the impact of the introduction of the cellular phone and estimated its 1996 net contribution to the customer welfare to be comprised between 24 to 50 billion dollars, corresponding to between 0.3 to 0.6% of the GDP. Yet, the CPI does not include the cellular phone at all (Hausman, 1997).

Statisticians recognise the current shortcomings of CPI in respect of treatment of technological and work diligently to correct them. For instance, French statistical agency, INSEE, introduced in 1990 an index to measure prices for microcomputers and in Spring 1997 it modified it substantially: the number of characteristics taken into account has increased from 12 to 22 for desktop computers, from 16 to 24 for notebook computers, and from 12 to 26 for servers (which soon will be measured separately). This example demonstrates clearly the need to combine the statistical skills with up-to-date technical knowledge.

3.2 National Wealth and Competitiveness

Current national account framework focuses primarily on current production and consumption. It does not adequately address the question of underlying wealth and capital accumulation. This is a difficult topic, which is critically dependent on the conceptual framework adopted: what is wealth, what is productive capital, what are the relative contributions of various types of capital. The traditional economic theory provided only limited answers, to the extent that it focused on accumulation of primary factors such as natural resources, machinery or labour. As we will see below, the theory has become more sophisticated but does not as yet provided a fully satisfactory and empirically robust answer. Attempts to measure national wealth have not proved fully conclusive. World Bank has attempted such measure in 1995 but it proved controversial and was abandoned. Another approach to national wealth is to measure its competitiveness in the global economy. This approach was adopted by two Swiss-based organisations, the World Economic Forum and International Management Development business school, which have been publishing annual competitiveness surveys. These seek to combine objective indicators such as GDP, trade, sectoral mix with subjective assessment of national position by business and opinion leaders (IMD, 1992). In 1996, the two organisations decided to part way, each adopting distinct methodologies, which in turn led to different rankings. While both WEF and IMD rank US as Number One, they disagree about the follow-up countries (WEF, 1997, IMD, 1997). Furthermore, there is a school of thought within the economic profession, of which Paul Krugman, from Stanford is the best known proponent, who argues that the competitiveness is a wrong-headed notion altogether. According to him, only firms compete, nations do not (Krugman, 1997).

3.3 Information Technology

The critical role of Information Technology in the new economy is universally acknowledged by government and business alike. Yet, there are substantive gaps in our understanding of its scope, which makes the measurement of its size and impact quite a laborious and uncertain exercise. The demand of data on Information Technology has led to the emergence of firms specialised in market analysis such as IDC, Forrester Research, or Dataquest. It also led to industry-sponsored or government-sponsored initiatives such as European Information Technology Observatory (EITO) in Europe, which publishes an annual survey of current trends and outlook, using IDC data (EITO, 1996).

The measurement of IT raises non-trivial issues, in particular that of the definition of boundaries. For some, IT includes computer hardware, software and services only. Other add such related industries as semi-conductors and microprocessors for instance. However, an important proportion of semi-conductors remains integrated within end-products such as cars or airplanes. Another question concerns telecommunications, which some consider as a separate domain and others as integral to IT.

In order to define the boundaries of the domain, several mapping projects have been undertaken. For instance, in UK, the Department of Trade Industry has set up the Foresight ITEC (Information technology, electronics and communications) Panel, comprising academics and industry executives with the objective to define a framework for bounding and measuring the domain. In a recent Green Paper, the Science Policy Research Unit of University of Sussex, proposes an eight-segment classification, based on interaction between two axes: products-services and transport-content (SPRU, 1997).

3.4 Measuring Enterprise Performance

Firms live or die by information; they rely on internal and external data to gauge their performance and to make their tactical and strategic decisions. When they are quoted on public equity markets, their value is heavily influenced by the quality of information they provide. Their accounts are closely scrutinised by several official bodies. Shortcomings of the existing accounting framework, particularly their treatment of intangible assets, have been well identified, (Johnston and Kaplan, 1987, Lev, 1996). We have seen above the efforts of professional bodies such as IASC to establish guidelines for such treatment. Although they represent a notable progress relative to the current framework, they do not go far enough. Accordingly, leading specialists of management accounting seek to develop alternative approaches to expand its scope and enhance its relevance.

One approach, which generated considerable business interest, is called 'balanced scorecard.' Developed by a Harvard Business School professor of accounting, Robert Kaplan, and a well-known IT strategy consultant, David Norton, the balanced scorecard seeks to supplement the traditional financial measures of profitability and return on investment with criteria that track performance from three additional and complementary perspectives: customers, internal business processes, and learning and growth (Kaplan and Norton, 1996, 1997). The balanced scorecard thus allows incremental progress, which does not discard the existing measurement system but rather enriches it, by capturing various dimensions of economic performance. Its authors also believe that the scorecard addresses another major deficiency of traditional management systems: their inability to link a company's long-term strategy with its short-term actions.

Kaplan and Norton deal with internal management information. Baruch Lev, New York University professor of accounting, looked at financial reports for outside investors (Lev, 1996). He concluded that the usefulness of these reports have been declining over time. Therefore, he advocates a major overhaul of current financial reporting. Two major proposals he makes are: first, to extensively capitalise intangible investments and, second, to augment historical data-based reports with a forward-looking disclosure system informing investors of the expected consequences of material managerial actions and external events.

A broader approach to intangible assets is proposed by the Intellectual Capital movement. This is an informal international group of business executives, consultants, academics and journalists who share a common belief that the brainpower is the source of real wealth of organisation. Several members of the group published books on the subject in early 1997, thus creating a considerable interest in the topic (Edvinsson and Malone, 1997, Stewart, 1997, Sveiby, 1997). Furthermore, a number of well-known consultancies have set up knowledge management practices. Thus, Intellectual Capital is likely to become a new management fashion in the coming years.

Intellectual capital has been defined by Larry Prusak and David Klein as 'intellectual material that has been formalised, captured and leveraged to produce a higher-value asset '(Stewart, 1997). Hubert Saint-Onge and Leif Edvinsson propose a further typology, based on a division into three parts: Human Capital (which goes home every night), Structural Capital (which is left behind when the staff goes home) and Customer Capital (which is not a property of the organisation). Conceptual framework of intellectual capital is still in its early stages of formulation and remain suggestive rather than rigorous. Nevertheless, it offers considerable promise.

3.5 Economic Theory

One of the frequent criticisms of the classical economic theory is that it does not deal adequately with the questions of growth and qualitative change. In response, the profession has put greater emphasis on these questions. In the recent years, significant new approaches have been developed, which seek to provide alternative models of the growth process. Probably the best known approach is the endogenous growth theory, of which Paul Romer, from Stanford University, is the leading theoretician. The traditional growth models seek to explain growth as function of greater inputs of capital and labour and treat innovation as exogeneous. This led to a considerably discrepancy between theoretical and actual growth rates, the latter being considerably higher than the former. Romer set to develop a more complete model. He integrated two additional variables: scientific knowledge and human capital (Romer, 1986, 1990). In his view, the long-term growth is driven by accumulated knowledge, which is a basic form of capital. However, knowledge has attributes which set it apart from physical capital. It is non-rival (or what we call non-subtractive) and has 'natural externality', it cannot be kept exclusive over the long run, which implies a sharing and progressive diffusion across the economy. Romer also notes that knowledge has a high fixed cost but a low variable cost, which lead to increasing returns in manufacturing. He makes a key distinction between labour and human capital, which in his view is the principal vector of knowledge accumulation and dissemination: "what is important for growth is integration not into an economy with a large number of people but rather into one with a large amount of human capital" (Romer, 1990). The key implication of Romer's theory is the need for public policies to put greater emphasis on human capital and knowledge development rather than the physical capital accumulation.

Another innovative economic approach is the increasing returns theory developed by Brian Arthur. According to him, the modern economy is characterised by a key duality: 'diminishing returns hold sway in the traditional part of the economy. Increasing returns reign in the newer part - the knowledge-based industries (Arthur, 1996).' Increasing returns explain the development dynamics of the high-tech sector, which whose output he defines as 'congealed knowledge with little (physical) resources.' This sector has high upfront costs and low marginal (reproduction) costs. The development costs of an operating system software are in the hundreds of millions of dollars but once the system has been developed, each diskette can produced and distributed for few dollars.

4 What's Next : Suggestions for Further Research

This summary survey shows that there is a considerable work being carried out to understand and to measure the new economy. Nevertheless, in our view there are still significant gaps, which need to be filled, and additional areas which need to be explored. Substantial further research is required, at both conceptual and applied level, addressing both the issues of the broad conceptual framework and specific measurement approaches. In this section, we would like to make some specific suggestions for further research. There is also a strong need to change the ways in which the research on intangible measurement is carried out and in particular to encourage crossing of disciplinary and institutional borders.

4.1 Conceptual Framework

4.1.1 Intangible Markets and Pricing Mechanisms The key issue which needs to be addressed in this domain is this: does the intangible economy substantially modify the basic economic mechanisms of resource allocation and exchange? To what extent the prevalence of non-substractive, non-exclusive assets and artefacts, which generate extensive externalities, fundamentally changes the nature of the pricing mechanisms? Traditional economic theory assumes that intangibles are a marginal phenomenon and the bulk of economic transactions are not significantly affected by externalities. This means that the market price fully reflects both the relative and absolute economic value of goods and factors traded. Therefore market transactions are used as basis for measuring value creation and transfer. These assumptions should be seriously questioned. In today's economy intangible markets are already significantly larger and are growing faster than the markets for tangible output and factors. Significant share of intangible are exchanged through unconventional mechanisms such as barter or third-party payment. They may appear as 'free' exchanges but in fact substantive exchanges of value take place, which are not being captured by conventional measurement approaches. Intangible markets, in particular markets for information, need to be much better understood than there are today.

4.1.2 Demand for Intangibles There is a substantive imbalance between the research effort spent on the supply and demand aspects of the intangible economy. The bulk of work is dedicated to the supply aspects. Endogenous growth and increasing returns approaches, discussed above, deal primarily with intangible assets, the firms and the production rather than with intangible artefacts, the households and consumption. Yet, the demand for intangible artefacts is the key driver of the intangible economy. Due to intangible market characteristics discussed above, its real importance is not well reflected in the classical theory and in the traditional measurement approaches. One approach to capture them is to devise metrics, such as time budgets, which measure actual consumption. In turn such metrics could be used to establish virtual prices and expenditures for 'free' artefacts such as television watching or reading. Time-honoured notions such as the willingness to pay or the consumer surplus need to be critically re-examined from the intangible markets perspective. Finally we need to continue to explore new characteristics of demand such as latency and capriciousness and their impact.

4.1.3 Economics of Abundance Traditional economics focus on scarcity and its impact on resource allocation. Intangible economy is largely driven by abundance of resources and artefacts. We need to understand the nature of economic abundance and its impact on final consumption, resource allocation, industrial structure and market mechanisms.

4.1.4 Economics of the Futile Intangible economy goes beyond information and knowledge. It also encompasses apparently futile activities such as sport and other forms of entertainment. Their economic importance is growing yet their dynamics are not well understood. For instance, how to explain a large increase in sport expenditures (particularly for football and basketball events) ? Is it a simple substitution for existing entertainment? Or is it an addition, generating new revenues and thus contributing to economic growth?

4.1.5 National Balance Sheets Intangible investment and intangible assets contribute in a decisive way to wealth creation and competitiveness at the national level. In order to fully appreciate their contribution, it is necessary to develop new approaches to the measurement of national wealth and to the aggregation of physical and intangible assets.

4.1.6 Nature of the Firm The traditional rationale for the existence of the firm was articulated by Ronald Coase as the minimisation of transaction costs(Coase, 1937, Williamson and Winter, 1993). Is this rationale still valid today? Intangible economy reduced dramatically transaction costs, altered the nature of the markets and enlarged the range of transaction mechanisms, blurring the well-known distinctions between markets, hierarchies and networks. An alternative and broader rationale for the firm needs to be developed, which would stress the brand umbrella, the intellectual property repository and the control of distribution channels as key cohesion factors and functions of the firm.

4.2 Measurement Systems

4.2.1 Self-reflectiveness Measurement data are no longer external, neutral or independent from the facts they calibrate. The intangible economy is highly data-sensitive and intrinsically self-reflective. It continuously monitors and measures its own behaviour. Thus, the publication of economic data triggers rapid and often massive reactions of economic agents. Moreover, these adjust their behaviour not only in reaction to the past data but in anticipation of future data. This kind of attitude may render data less reliable and relevant. Economic and financial measurement system function in conformity with the well-known Heisenberg uncertainty principle, which applies in quantum physics: the very act of observing and measuring changes the measured phenomenon. The new measurement approaches need to explicitly incorporate self-reflectiveness. This means for instance that they recognise and incorporate into their design the multiplicity of users and of user requirements.

4.2.2 Output Measurement The improved understanding of the demand for intangibles entails a greater emphasis on measurement of output of intangible businesses such as financial services and information suppliers. Again, particular emphasis should be given to 'free' (non-directly priced) output. The pioneering work by Griliches and others on techniques such as hedonic regression need to be pursued and amplified (Griliches, 1992). Statistics has to go back to its roots in metrology.

4.2.3 Looking at the Future Traditionally, economic performance measurement systems provided information about the past. Statisticians put a premium on continuity and the comparability of data. Today, comparability becomes more laborious to achieve as goalposts are being continuously moved. More importantly, users want data that signal future trends and performance and help them to cope with rapid and unexpected change. The challenge of economic measurement system is now to provide early warning signals and pinpoint inflection points indicating shifts in major trends.

One of the ways to improve signalling capacity is to rely more on financial markets and its theoretical underpinnings. In particular, option theory offers a promising conceptual approach to the measurement of the economic value of the future (Dixit & Pindyck, 1995).

4.2.4 Evolution or Revolution? The prevailing approach to the economic and financial measurement is incremental. For instance, the balanced scorecard seek to supplement the existing accounting data with non-financial indicators. Yet, the persistence of the gap between the real economy and its image projected by conventional methods may call for more radical approach. Lev for instance believes that the existing accounting framework need to be overhauled to fully take into account the intangibles and their characteristics (Lev, 1996). Clearly, more innovative approaches need to be explored. They should draw on substantive advances made in information sciences and which allow for a fuller treatment of data, which takes into account their heterogeneity and mutual interdependence. Mathematical methods which underlie the concepts of data warehousing and data mining need to be put to contribution by accountants and statisticians.

4.3 Changing Methods: Recognising Diversity

This last point underscores a critical requirement for going forward: need to combine several disciplines and several approaches. The diversity and multiplicity of data sources, treatment methodologies and distribution channels have to be recognised. In an information-based economy, economic measurement systems are fundamentally pluralistic. Ultimately, the multiplicity of systems reflects the underlying multidimensionality of economic phenomena: to understand them, more than one measure or viewpoints are required - a single point needs to be replaced by an array.

The current efforts are adversely affected by conceptual and institutional *fragmentation*. There is not enough formal and informal contacts and interactions across disciplinary and institutional boundaries - between statisticians, economists, financial analysts and accountants - and across public sector/academia/private business divide. Efforts need be made to strengthen the interactions and transform a perceived liability of fragmentation into an asset of diversity.

5 Conclusion: The Centrality of Intangibles

The proposed research agenda may appear overly ambitious. Yet, its scope intends to show the size of the gap between the measurement systems and the underlying reality. If measurement systems are to capture the essence of the economy of today and tomorrow, intangibles have to move from the periphery to the core of these systems. Accountants, economists and statisticians need to undertake a comprehensive appraisal of their business.

References

Aaker, D. (1991), *Managing Brand Equity*, The Free Press: New York.
Alesina A. and Spolane, E. (1995), *On the Number and Size of Nations*, NBER Working Paper no 5050, March.
Allen, M. (1992), Development of a New Line of Low-Cost PCs Shakes Up Compaq, *The Wall Street Journal Europe*, June 16.
Arthur Andersen (1992), *The Valuation of Intangible Assets*, The Economist Intelligence Unit: London.
Arthur, B.W. (1994), *Increasing Returns and Path Dependence in the Economy*, University of Michigan Press, Ann Arbor.
Arthur, B (1995), The More You Sell, the More You Sell, *Wired*, October.
Arthur, B.W. (1996), Increasing Returns and the New World of Business, *Harvard Business Review*, 3
Badenhausen, K. (1996) Blind Faith, *Financial World*, July 8.
Bikchandani, S., Hirshleifer, D. and Welch, I. (1993), *The Blind Leading the Blind: Social Influence, Fads and Information Cascades*, UCLA Working Paper, October.
Blanc, C. and Breton, T. (1994), *Le lièvre et la tortue*, Plon, Paris.
Boskin, M. et al. (1996), *Toward A More Accurate Measure Of The Cost Of Living*, US Senate Finance Committee, Washington, D.C.
Chreiki, E. (1995), Intel: des sauts de puce toujours plus rapprochés, *Le Nouvel Economiste*, December 8.
Clark, C. (1940), *Conditions of Economic Progress*, Macmillan: London.
Clark, K. and Wheelwright, S (eds) (1995), *The Product Development Challenge*, Harvard Business School Press: Cambridge, Mass.

Coase, R. (1937), The Nature of the Firm, *Economica*, 4.
Coase, R. (1974), The Market for Goods and the Market for Ideas, *American Economic Review*, May.
Cox, B (1994), Superdistribution, *Wired*, September.
Curcio, R. and Goodhart, C. (1992), When Support/Resistance Levels Are Broken, Can Profits Be Made ? Evidence From Foreign Exchange Markets, LSE Working Paper.
Davidow, W., and Malone, M. (1992), *The Virtual Corporation*, HarperCollins.
Deschamps, J-Ph. and Ranganath M. (1995), *Product Juggernaut*, Harvard Business School Press: Cambridge, Mass.
Dixit, A. and Pindyck, R. (1995), The Options Approach to Capital Investment, *Harvard Business Review*, 2.
Duncan J. and Gross, A. (1995), *Statistics For the 21st Century*, Irwin Professional Publishing: Chicago.
Dyson, E. (1992), Who pays for data, *Forbes*, February 3.
Dyson, E. (1995), Intellectual Value, *Wired*, July 1995.
Ehrbar, A. (1994), Defying the Odds, *Fortune*, October 17, 1994.
Edvinsson, L. and Malone, M. (1997), *Intellectual Capital: Realizing Your Company's True Value by Finding Its Hidden Roots*, HarperBusiness New York
European Information Technology Observatory (EITO) (1995), *1995 Report*, Frankfort
Franchet, Y. (1996), *Improving the relevance of economic statistics*, Conference on Accuracy, Timeliness and Relevance of Economic Statistics, Washington D.C., September 9-11, 1996
Gadrey, J. (1992), *L'économie des services*, Découverte, Paris
Giarini, O. (1984), The Notion of Economic Value in the Post-Industrial Society: Factors in the Search for New Economic Paradigms, in O. Giarini (ed), *Cycles, Value and Employment*, Pergamon Press: Oxford.
Gilder, G. (1995), From Wires to Waves, *Forbes ASAP Supplement*, June 5, 1995
Goldfinger, C. (1994), *L'utile et le futile, l'économie de l'immatériel*, Editions Odile Jacob, Paris.
Goldfinger, C. (1995), Financial Markets as Information Markets, in CERSI seminar, *Economie de l'Information*, Lyon, May 18-20, 1995.
Goldfinger, C. (1997), Intangible economy and its implications for statistics and statisticians, *International Statistical Review*, August 1997 (forthcoming)
Goldman, K. (1995), Liked the Movie Version? You'll love the Lunch Box, *The Wall Street Journal Europe*, June 21, 1995
Griliches, Z. (ed) (1992), *Output Measurement in the Service Sector*, NBER, The University of Chicago Press: Chicago.
Griliches, Z. (1994), Productivity, R&D and the Data Constraint, Presidential address, American Economic Association, Boston, January 4, *American Economic Review*, Vol. 84, No. 1, March 1994.
Hausman, J.A. (1997), *Cellular Telephones, New Products and CPI*, NBER Working Paper No. 6982, Cambridge, Mass., March.
Hausman, J. A. (1996), Valuation of New Goods under Perfect and Imperfect Competition, in Timothy Bresnahan and Robert J. Gordon (eds), *The Economics Of New Goods*, Chicago, University of Chicago Press.
Heilemann, J. (1994), Feeling for the future, A survey of television, *The Economist*, February 12, 1994.
Huber, P. (1992), The Unbundling of America, *Forbes*, April 13, 1992.
IMD (1992), *1991 World Competitiveness Report*, Lausanne.
IMD (1997), *1996 World Competitiveness Report*, Lausanne.
INSEE (1993), *L'économie française en 1992: rapport sur les comptes de la Nation*, Paris.
International Accounting Standards Committee (IASC) (1994), *Intangible Assets, A Draft Statement of Principles'*, London, January.
Johnson, Th. and Kaplan, R. (1987), Relevance Lost, Rise and Fall of Management Accounting, Harvard Business School Press, Cambridge, Mass.
Kaplan, R. and Norton, D.(1996), Using the Balanced Scorecard as a Strategic Management System, *Harvard Business Review*, 1.
Kaplan, R. and Norton, D.(1997), *The Balanced Scorecard*, Harvard Business Press.
Kosko, B. (1993), *Fuzzy Thinking*, Hyperion, New York.
Krugman, P (1997), *Pop Internationalism*, the MIT Press,
Lev, B. (1996), *The Boundaries of Financial Reporting and How to Extend Them*, University of California, Berkeley: August.

Mandel, M. J., Landler, M. and Grover, R. (1994), The Entertainment Economy, *Business Week*, March 14, 1994.
McKinsey & Co. (1992), *The 1992 Report on The Computer Industry*.
Mitchell, B. and Vogelsang, I. (1991), *Telecommunications Pricing*, Cambridge University Press: Cambridge.
Moore, S. (1995), Glaxo Lab Initiates A High-Speed Chase in the Drugs Industry, *The Wall Street Journal Europe*, December 6.
Nalebuff, B.J. & Brandenburger, A.M,(1996), *Co-opetition*, Currency Doubleday: New York.
Naisbitt, J. (1994), 'Global Paradox', William Morrow & Company, New York
Negroponte, N. (1995), Being Digital, Hodder and Stoughton, London,
OCDE (1992), Technology and The Economy: The Key Relationships, Paris.
Olson, M. (1973), Information as a Public Good, in R.S. Taylor, *Economics of Information Distribution*, State University of New York, Syracuse.
Petersens, F. And Bjurström, J. (1991), Identifying And Analyzing Intangible Assets, *M&A Europe*, septembre-octobre.
Power, C. (1993), Flops, *Business Week*, August 16.
Quah, D. (1997), *Increasingly Weightless Economies*, unpublished paper, London School of Economics, January.
Rapaport, A., and Halevi, S. (1991),The Computerless Computer Company, *Harvard Business Review*, 3.
Reichheld, F. (1996), *The Loyalty Effect*, Harvard Business Press
Reid, M. (1995), Change at the check-out, A survey of retailing, *The Economist*, March 4.
Reuters (1996), Annual Report 1995, London.
Romer, P. (1986), Increasing Returns and Long Run Growth.
Romer, P. (1990), Endogenous Technological Change, *Journal of Political Economy*, 98, October.
Romer, Paul (1994), The Origins of Endogenous Growth, *Journal of Economic Perspectives 8*, Winter.
Science Policy Research Unit (SPRU) (1997), *Green Paper: Mapping and Measuring the Information Technology, Electronics and Communications Sector in the United Kingdom*, University of Sussex, March.
Scholtes, K. (1995), La dynamique de la croissance des marchés de produits dérivés, Faculté des Sciences Economiques et Sociales, Namur, May 5.
Stewart. T. (1997), *Intellectual Capital*, Currency Doubleday: New York.
Stiglitz, J., Joseph (1985), Information and economic analysis: a perspective, *Economic Journal*, 95.
Sveiby, K. H. (1997), *The New Organizational Wealth: Managing and Measuring Knowledge Based Assets*, Berrett-Koehler, San Fransisco.
Tapscott, D. (1995), *The Digital Economy*, McGraw-Hill: New York
The Economist (1994), The price of mogulmania, January 29.
Tetzeli, R. (1994), Surviving Information Overload, *Fortune*, July 14.
Toffler, A. (1980), *Third Wave*, New York
Varian, H. (1995), Pricing Information Goods, May.
Varian, H. (1994), Buying, Renting and Sharing Information Goods, November.
Veblen, T., 1899, *Theory of Leisure Class*, Macmillan and Co. : New York.
Veronis, Suhler (1994), *Communications Industry Forecasts*, New York
Williamson, O. and Winter, S.(ed) (1993), *The Nature of the Firm*, Oxford University Press : New York.
Wooldridge, A. (1995), Big is back. A survey of multinationals, *The Economist*, June 25.
World Economic Forum (WEF) (1997), Global Competitiveness Report.
Wysocki, B. (1995), Improved Distribution, Not Better Production is Key Goal in Mergers, *The Wall Street Journal Europe*, August 31.

27 Analysing the Information Society through Statistics - Problems, Weaknesses and Advantages

Timo Relander

1 Introduction

A major challenge to official statistics today is presented by the statistical description of the information society and all the various phenomena that are related to it. This is not a completely novel challenge in that the problem has been receiving much attention for some time now. However, so far the phenomenon of the information society has remained too big and too complex to grasp, not only for statisticians but for social scientists in general. The challenge of presenting a systematic statistical account of the information society is complicated by the fact that we lack a broader theoretical framework on which to base that account.

National statistical agencies are unfortunately not in the vanguard of developments here. Various information society strategies and programmes are already in full swing. Resources are being allocated in the name of information society policy even though we have still not been able to provide an adequate and systematic statistical description for the assessment of the impacts of that policy. Although the lack of an established statistical description does not in itself preclude the implementation of an information society policy, it certainly adds an element of uncertainty to that policy.

In Finland legislation requires that statistics shall provide as accurate and reliable a picture as possible of society and trends in society. Any new significant phenomena in society must be incorporated into the system of statistical description as early as possible. The information society and all the phenomena related to the information society no doubt represent such a new significant trend in society. During the past couple of years Statistics Finland has been working on a project to create an indicator system for the description of the information society and its development. This is part of our government's national information society strategy.

Statistics on the information society are today largely produced by the private sector; research institutes, private organizations, consultants, business companies etc. have been quicker to respond to the growing need for statistics on the information society than national statistical agencies. However, agencies do still have an important role to play here, and that is to provide for continuity and comparability where the statistics produced do not always meet the highest quality standards.

The phenomenon of the information society is of course basically a matter of definition. Several national statistical agencies and international organizations have their own definitions of the information society or its key elements. However, these have very much been suggested in a tentative manner for the specific purpose of inspiring debate. These problems of definition should be resolved at an international level. If national statistics on the information society do not allow for international comparisons, their use value will be limited indeed.

The job of international organizations is to co-ordinate and develop statistical standards and to promote the adoption of those standards. Both EUROSTAT and the OECD have recently set up working groups to look into ways of developing statistical descriptions of the information society. In addition there are numerous other expert bodies working on related themes.

In Europe there has been an ongoing effort for the past few years at harmonization, motivated primarily by the administrative and political needs of the European Union. However, the importance of global statistical harmonization is also underlined by various market-driven factors, such as the information needs of multinational corporations. The current trend toward the information society is emphatically a global trend, not a development confined to a specific economic area.

2 Technology Provides the Basis for the Information Society

It is a natural choice to look at the phenomenon of the information society from the vantage point of technology and infrastructure. The information society is characterized by an extensive use of information technology and networks, and the technological infrastructure provides a solid basis for the development of the information society. Information and data communications technology is in widespread use throughout the economy and society, not only in the information sector itself. Therefore, a technological approach provides a broader perspective on the information society than do approaches based on products, industries or occupational classifications, for instance.

However, assessment of the impacts of technologies or technological diffusion is notoriously difficult. The technological approach also raises the problem of scale; to what extent should information and data communications technology dominate, to what extent should networks carry information for the label of the information society to be warranted? It is also obvious that a quantitative scale alone is not enough; we need also to assess the quality and the content of the information in the networks.

A recent survey conducted by Statistics Finland suggests that the technical infrastructure in our country is in fairly good shape in view of the needs of the information society. Information technology has been spreading very rapidly in workplaces as well as in households. Relative to population Finland now has a larger number of mobile phones and Internet subscriptions than any other country in the world. Banks, schools, libraries and hospitals also boast a high level of computerization. Consumer prices in telecommunications are markedly lower in Finland than in industrial countries on average, which is due in large part to this industry being opened to free competition at an early stage. The level of education in Finland is also high, on a par with most other industrial countries. The number of new training places in information technology has tripled since the mid-1980s.

The degree of computerization in the workplace and in households may be regarded as a measure of Finland's advanced technological infrastructure. Statistics on internal, structural changes within the group of information technology user also provide important information for purposes of political decision-making related to the information society.

In Finland we have exceptionally long time series on the increasing use of information technology in the workplace. These series indicate that the proportion of wage earners who use information technology in their job has increased from 17 per cent in 1984 to 56 per cent in 1996. In several branches, including administrative and clerical work, virtually all employees have a computer at their desk. However, these figures only provide a rough indication of the trends in development in that the actual use of information technology varies considerably. In many cases classifications also distinguish the core group of information professionals with a theoretical knowledge of information technology; this group comprises no more than a few per cent of all wage earners.

Another important question concerns the links between the diffusion of information technology and employment trends. As well as looking at quantitative trends we should also try to assess the qualitative impacts of information technology in the workplace. In what way are working conditions affected by the introduction of information technology, and what about the nature of work? Are there repercussions for the position of men and women or different age groups, for instance?

The spread of information technology into private households has also continued at a rapid pace. A recent questionnaire survey by Statistics Finland shows that 24% of Finnish households had a PC in November-December 1996. This is 5-6 percentage points up on the figure for 1990. Today one in three people in the age group 10-74 years have access to a computer at home. The hardware in households is fairly new. For instance, the questionnaire indicates that over 40 per cent of the households with a PC have a modem, and almost have CD-ROM.

3 Trends in Household Use of Information Technology

Another trend which highlights the growth of the information society is that household expenditure on information is increasing rapidly. As in other countries the ownership and know-how of information technology in Finland is quite clearly differentiated by age, sex, income level, socio-economic status and other factors. However, these differences have now been reduced to some extent, as have the regional differences in the use of information technology. Our questionnaire survey showed that PCs are most typically purchased by young households without children and by families with teenage children. The likelihood of purchasing a PC increases with rising incomes, but only to a certain level. Home PCs are used most frequently by males aged 10 to 30 years, least by women over 30 years.

It is in other words a rather selective process in which information technology is spreading into Finnish households. There are certain structural trends that are slowing down the spread of information society hardware; one such trend is the declining average size of households. Access to the necessary equipment, software, network connections and training may become a problem. We need to have reliable information on all the relevant trends in development so that we can say when there is enough hardware that it is possible to set up a social service system, for instance, that is based exclusively on computer equipment.

At school, 72 per cent of all children in comprehensive school and upper secondary school used PCs during the autumn term 1996. By far the most common use for the PC, both at school and in households, is for word-processing. The use of modems and the Internet is still comparatively rare.

A good, efficient technical infrastructure does of course provide a solid basis for the development of the information society. However, it does not automatically guarantee that the benefits of technology are put to the best possible use. This also requires a structural adaptation on the part of societies to the requirements of the information society, as well as a change of attitudes on the part of consumers.

It is particularly important to monitor people's attitudes and consumption habits so that the development of the information society can be steered in accordance with consumer needs. In Finland, too, we have had critical voices saying that our information society policy concentrates too heavily on the technical infrastructure and ignores the development of its content. However, attitudes are a major intervening factor in this regard. It is difficult to compete with a more serious subject-matter against pure entertainment. On the other hand, users who are potentially interested in the more serious content of networks and who carry the greatest economic potential are apparently only just beginning to enter network services now.

Statistics Finland has also conducted a questionnaire survey to study the attitudes of citizens towards information and data communications technology and their knowledge of how to use that technology. People in Finland seem to be fairly confident of their ability to cope in the information society. The majority of the respondents do not admit to feeling they have been overwhelmed by the advance of new information technology. The continuing flood of information is not a cause of concern, nor do people fear that new technology threatens their private life.

On the other hand, people do not believe that new information technology can create new jobs. People are also annoyed by the fact that the accent in development is so heavily on the technological side and that much of the equipment is so difficult to use. For instance, over 60 per cent of the respondents were of the opinion that 'new machines are marketed and sold without there being any real use for them'.

4 Economic Impact of the Information Society

As well as from a technological angle the statistical description of the information society can be approached from the vantage-point of business companies, products, industries, occupations and job tasks and more broadly from the vantage-point of cultural change and changes in everyday life.

In Finland economic activity related to the production, handling and distribution of information represented around 12 per cent as a proportion of GDP in 1995. Industrial information technology products accounted for almost 40 per cent of this figure. A total of some 16 000 companies are involved in the information sector, with a combined turnover of almost FIM 120 billion. In addition, Finland is one of the few industrial countries with a surplus in its foreign trade in information technology.

In the light of these figures it is perhaps premature to speak about an information society; for the time being industrial production still accounts for almost three times as large a proportion of GDP than the information sector. However, the rapid growth of the early embryos of the information society in the 1990s certainly deserves our every attention. What is more, these figures are of course highly sensitive to any changes in definitions. It is also possible to assemble broader information clusters around such branches as ADP, telecommunications and the media industry. This is how the United States, for instance, has arrived at much larger proportions for the information society.

The impacts of information and communications technology are perhaps most dramatic of all in the labour market. The rapid advances in these technologies provide business companies and organizations a great opportunity to raise their level of automation, productivity and efficiency. Investment in information technology has indeed become a strategic choice for firms, with a decisive impact on their future business environment. However, it is impossible to measure the overall impacts of technology on employment.

In Finland, the information sector provides employment for almost 200 000 people, accounting for around one-tenth of the country's active labour force. However, during the 1990s employment in this sector has increased for more rapidly than in the national economy as a whole. Furthermore, according to the definition proposed by the OECD in the 1980s, the proportion of people engaged in information occupations of the total active labour force in Finland has risen from 30 per cent in the early 1980s to 44 per cent in 1994. According to a recent questionnaire study about half of the active labour force regard themselves as engaged in one way or another in an information occupation.

5 Need for Revision in Statistical Classification

Statistical systems in society and accounting standards in business firms were originally designed with a view to monitoring traditional commodity production. However, the service sector has continued to expand in recent years, as has the role of immaterial production inputs. The relevance of traditional statistical descriptions has also been called into question by the increasing complexity of households and societies, the trends towards globalization and networking and the accelerating pace of change. Indeed, the statistical classifications we are now using reflect, to a certain extent, outdated economic structures. On the other hand the continuity of time series is of course valuable in itself and speaks in favour of some kind of conservatism in the development of statistical classifications and systems.

One major source of difficulty in statistical classifications is that the boundaries between industries have become increasingly blurred. For instance, technological and commercial developments have led to the convergence of the data communications sector, the manufacture of computers and data communications hardware and closely related industries. Companies with operations in several different branches are known to present a special difficulty for statistical descriptions. The traditional unit of place of business is also poorly suited to the description of the networked information sector, etc.

A good example of how our classifications are becoming outdated is provided by the EU product classification which is now in use in Finland: the CPA comprises over 2500 products, of which traditional commodity production accounts for over 2300, while services account for just over 200. Having said that, it is obviously not always easy to make a clear-cut distinction between commodities and services.

In certain respects things have actually regressed. For instance, the national industrial classification that was adopted in Finland in 1988 identified „data communication" as a separate industry. Following Finland's admission to the European Union, however, we have reverted to the United Nation's global industry classification that is based on the ISIC and that combines the data communications sector with the traditional transport sector. There is also reason to question the classification of statistical agencies under general public administration.

The most urgent needs for revision in statistical classifications apply perhaps to product and industrial classifications. There are also difficulties with occupational classifications, for instance. Current job descriptions (which are used in newspapers' appointments pages, for instance) are increasingly far removed from the international occupational classification currently in use (ISCO).

6 Broad Approach Imperative

Our experience at Statistics Finland clearly underscores the importance of a broad approach to the development of statistical descriptions of the information society. This was also the message of the recent DGINS conference in Helsinki where EU national statistical agencies met to exchange views under the theme of „Information Society and Statistics" (appendix). Many of the delegates at the conference called upon statistical agencies to adopt a more systematic and continuous approach to compiling statistics in the information society and in this way to raise current quality standards. In particular we need to have international cooperation to develop and harmonize statistical classification, definitions and concepts.

Certain elements of the information society are of course covered by various traditional statistics, such as business statistics, R&D statistics, transport and telecommunications statistics, and so on. These provide information that can also be used for the description of the information society - although in many cases this means that the data-material needs to be re-classified and re-processed. However, the assessment of the current stage of development in the information society also requires qualitative criteria. There appears to be a clear demand for barometer-type surveys to systematically monitor consumer attitudes and expectations of the future development of the information society, for instance.

This sort of approach using „softer" indicators can also contribute to the ongoing discussion and increase our knowledge of the mechanism, trends and impacts of the information society. This information is crucially important if the benefits of technology are to be maximized and its adverse effects minimized.

Appendix

General implications of the DGINS-Conference 29 - 30 May 1997

We should proceed in stages, paying attention to the following points:

1. Ascertaining of common data requirements
2. Review and development of existing definitions and classifications:
   - information and communication industries
   - information products
   - occupation and education classifications
   - the need for revising these classifications in light of the demands of the information society
3. Analysis of the present stock of data
4. Development of a list of variables for an IT industry survey and user surveys, and launching of a system of pilot surveys in a system of international co-operation
5. Development of a compendium of methodology for statistics on the information society in close co-operation with research institutes or other non-official statisticians.
6. Development of an indicator system describing the information society/satellite accounts or an analysis corresponding to the SNA 1993 framework
7. Publication of the benchmarks that have been achieved so far
8. Priorities for a strategy aimed at establishing a statistical system for this sector
9. Further development of the legal foundation for statistics on the information society

References

Developing a Finnish Information Society; Decision in Principle, Council of State, Helsinki 1995.
Development of the Information Society: An International Analysis, Spectrum Strategy Consultants, UK, 1996.
Living and Working in the Information Society: People First, 1996. Nurmela, Juha: The Finns and Modern Information Technology, Statistics Finland, Reviews 1997/12.
On the Road to the Finnish Information Society, Statistics Finland, Helsinki 1997.
Proceedings of the 83rd DGINS Conference - May 1997, Eurostat 1997.

28 Social and Structural Change: Challenge and Consequences for Official Statistics

Erich Bader

1 Introduction

For the time being, social statistics is on the defensive. The fact that in social politics conditions are much the same is but little consolation. Single market and currency union demand a concentration on economic politics and economic statistics - both in the European Union and in its individual member states. And the currency union once introduced will require even more rigidity in economic research and economic politics.

The main issue of this meeting is economic research and economic statistics, too. Since there is only one world for all of us, and as we should always remember those who are weaker, I decided to approach this topic from a social statistical point of view, and to concentrate on the borderland of economic and social statistics, a social statistics which is on the defensive. Inadvertently, we slipped into landscape which we did not look forward to some ten years ago. I am not speaking of the seventies - it is a long time since their enthusiastic tune faded away. Presently, the great symphonies of social reporting are played by string quartets in front of a small audience. During the eighties, still, we were able to work on a balanced statistical system more or less appropriately representing a complicated society in its social and economic structures and processes. And now?

Let's try to clarify things: social statistics is *still* on the defensive. Opinions increase that this must change, that we have to break away from the justification pressure we got caught in, sometimes. The recently passed statistical work programme of the EU member states for the next five years already reveals an unmistakable emphasis. This encourages us to reflect upon topics, again, which we used to discuss during the seventies and, afterwards, filed away and almost forgot about.

2 A Look Back

Already, I am plunging into the retrospective view. And although experienced speakers warn from introductions filled with too much history and ancestor-worship: European social statistics has *four great ages* to look back on, and these periods have greatly influenced our professional notions.

During the *first and earliest of these periods*, our profession was established. This starts with the Age of Enlightenment in the late eighteenth century and goes up to

Alphonse Quetelet's 'physique sociale' and his term of the 'homme moyen', the 'middle man', in the fifties of the nineteenth century. It is still deeply touching to realize what passion and what belief in progress must have filled our professional ancestors, when they made use of the instruments of early statistics to explain their population structures and their social situation, to portray their working and housing conditions, living and dying. This *passion for reality* is a characteristic of this early period of our craft.

The *second phase* relates to the two last decades of the nineteenth century, when - after having started in England -"the social question" became a general European problem. Let me remind you of urbanization, of dreadful living conditions, of early industrial working conditions, let us remember the beginning of health and accident insurance systems, of trade unions, of regulations concerning health and safety at work, let us point out the fight for universal suffrage to describe this time. It also reminds us of the term *'labour statistics'* still used for the statistical works of ILO, the International Labour Organization, which goes along with an extended spectrum of social analysis.

A *third phase* were the restless twenties of our century represented in different forms at different places, a creative period with new topics and approaches but often without sufficient means of realization. During these distressed times, a comprehensive earnings and price statistics was developed, for example, and empirical social research started with the use of statistical techniques and graphic methods to visualize these techniques. The exact, almost photographical approach to the observation and description of social behavior goes back to this age.

Many of us have consciously lived to see a *fourth period*: the seventies, the era of the "welfare state", a prime time of social politics, social research and social statistics. We talked about the "resocialization of statistics" then, and Austria was one of the most dynamic participants of the scientific debate. After the failure of those concepts which proved too euphoric to become true, statistics still retained its marked position in social reporting - by publishing its social data handbooks, indicator packages and special surveys. Political social reporting (reports on the situation of women, families, the labour market, etc.) is also based on statistical data. Since the beginning of this century, at the latest, social statistics has belonged to the indispensable informational environment of our societies.

During all these four phases, social statistics takes its impulse from an express value reference. In a progressive position, social statistics accompanies socially desirable developments by observation and documentation. It always contains a bit of a vision, a glimmer of the world how it could be, an 'option for losers'. Frequently, social statistics has been accused of lack of theory, whereas the economic development of theories is pointed out as the basis of economic statistics. Social sciences cannot provide any equivalent; therefore, social statistics is not promoted by a good theory but by the urgency of the issues concerned.

If this is true, social statistics has an - often painful - individual aspect. The inadequacy of theoretical social concepts becomes obvious when we order our macro-data, but it is less noticeable on the micro-level, where the welfare of the individual is in the foreground. There, social statistics must say 'what hurts', must modestly state symptoms without claiming diagnosis or therapy. In contrast to a lot of administrative mass data, social statistics and its surveys portray the human being as an active subject instead of just an object of observation.

3 New Problems

In the coming years, social statistics will be confronted with many old and a number of new problems. I will present some of them and will try to demonstrate our reactions. Let us start with a few slogans standing for certain aspects of social development.

3.1 Employment Society

This key-word is not new and still means that earnings and social positions are distributed mainly through employment and the labour market. For more than a century, employment statistics has been a central area of social statistics, and due to the annual Labour Force Survey and its concepts of measuring employment and unemployment, its position within the European Union is a substantial one. Apart from that, the importance of national statistics taken from employment and unemployment registers to the present labour market politics has not diminished. Contradictions between register-based statistics, which are subject to national law, and the concepts of the Labour Force Survey require an explanation.

For decades, instruments have been supplied which enable constant observation and are sufficient for national and international purposes. Several national surveys support this constant observation by providing additional information. *Deficits* can be found with longitudinal analyses from registers (Who becomes unemployed and how often? Who changes how often his or her employers?), with the registration of precarious working conditions by national registers (additional weekend income, minor part-time work, contract work, etc.), and in the lack of coordination with regard to national surveys.

3.2 Education Society

Education society is another key-word, which has accompanied the expansion of education and training ever since the sixties. The 'educational third' of the curriculum vitae is verified by exact annual data, beginning with nursery and compulsory school up to the area of secondary education, to universities and other post-secondary training institutions. The improved educational qualifications of the population and the employed are confirmed by population censuses, surveys and labour market statistics. *Deficits* are the poor registration of, for example, vocational training courses for adults as well as the fact that educational qualifications may be followed up by cross sections rather than by longitudinal surveys, most of which are biographically oriented.

3.3 Leisure Society

A third term has cropped up since the reduction of working hours during the last decades. In statistics, it has left its traces in the development of culture statistics (and the extension of its responsibilities from 'high culture' to areas as, for example, the use of the media, sports, crafts, etc.), in the installation of tourism surveys, and, last but not least, in the fact that Time Use Surveys have become an indispensable component of official statistics everywhere. Present *deficits* ought to be subdued by the European Time Budget Survey planned for 1997/98 and the expected increase in tourism surveys on the household level according to a 1995 European Union Regulation.

3.4 Consumer Society

An assessment made in the fifties, which statistics has taken into account by the development of regular consumer surveys as well as of additional supplementary surveys. The focus of these surveys has shifted from economic statistics (National Accounts, weighting of consumer price indices) towards social statistics (disparities, questions of distribution!) and - as more and more elements of consumption are leisure activities - goes along with the developments mentioned above. What we are worried about are the costs and troubles such surveys take. *Deficits* may appear if we are not able to realize the presently very ambitious EU programmes in this field.

3.5 The Two-thirds Society

This polemic expression implies the possibility of substantial groups being pushed to the fringe of society and thus made losers by a qualified majority and their ability to assert themselves. To the statistician, this term calls for an increased concentration on questions of distribution. This necessity is expressed by a revival of poverty research, the installation of the European Household Panel and more reports on income issues. *Deficits*, on the other hand, are remarkable; one of them is certainly the lack of comparability with regard to national statistical systems, which are often based on different tax, labour or social laws.

3.6 Grey Society

Demography and population projections are constantly documenting the ageing process of the European society. The slow reaction of many governments to these predictable problems can certainly not be explained by the lack of data. I am quite sure that, in this area, there are *no statistical deficits* to register.

3.7 Single Society

Constant observation and household projections also confirm a decrease in household size and an increase of one-person households, a changed marriage behaviour, and the changes in family structure involved. The by-effects on family relationships, housing or leisure activities require approaches including special evaluations or particular surveys, which are *still lacking* today.

4 Consequences for Social Statistics

At the same time, the mentioned key-words characterize fields of problem that require increasing attention. I will point out some areas which are - in the broadest sense - part of social statistics.

4.1 More Attention to Socio-economic Accounts

In the field of person-related statistics, no framework has yet been created comparable to that of National Accounts in economic statistics. This problem has been discussed ever since the late sixties (as for example, the System of socio-demographic accounts favoured by ECE, for some time) without producing a satisfactory solution. On a medium level, a lot has been done, of course, by social data handbooks, social indicators, standardized surveys, and so on.

Summaries and condensation remain an indispensable necessity in view of the overproduction of individual statistics. With respect to the future, two lines of action seem to be important: in the first place, satellite accounting in monetary units directly affiliated to National Accounts (environmentally adjusted GDP, an evaluation of household work with the help of time budget surveys, etc.); and secondly, patterns of person-related accounting systems in matrix or account form, which are often register-based, process data from different sources by statistical matching and, thus, make movements within the social structure visible (Social accounting, Labour accounting). From these models with the units 'person' or 'working hour', systematic connections to the monetary units of NA are possible. This way, the transition area between population data and economic data can be illustrated much better.

And, to me, this seems to be an important responsibility: to create *inter-disciplinarity* between the individual fields of official statistics. Phenomena produced by the combination of social and economic statistics - which may be observed from a person as well as from a company based angle - become more and more important, and have to be approached on both levels.

Such approaches also force us to concentrate on questions of *common terminology*, which are often forgotten in-between some of the fields of work of official statistics.

4.2 More Attention to Secondary Structures

Many old statistical topics lose their importance or are repressed by new developments. According to population censuses and samples, the increase of part-time farming has diminished the significance of agriculture and forestry as source of living more than corresponds to the economic impact of the agricultural sector. Everywhere secondary gainful activities as well as part-time jobs become more important without their being uniformly recorded. Long-term relationships cannot be captured by population censuses or samples if there are no common lodgings. For quite a long time, temporary residences have had to be included into any analysis of the housing situation (in Austria, they comprise one eighth of the complete housing stock). Even in countries with a population of mixed religious denominations, the socio-cultural characteristic of religion retreats to the background. Social networks and neighbourhood social welfare institutions support social security and perform family care, a work which is difficult to register. A lot remains to be done, there, in the field of surveys and analyses of administrative registers.

4.3 More Attention to Marginalization Processes

Poverty has become an issue again, in the member states of the European Union. Together with the ageing of our society infirmities increase. Precarious forms of employment (seasonal, part-time, weekend and secondary gainful activities, contract work) without sufficient social and legal security are spreading. This is an important issue that surveys will have to consider. The European Household Panel systematically deals with the subject of *poverty*, already, which brings us to the next item:

4.4 More Attention to Questions of Distribution

Distribution conflicts increase when growth declines, and statistics must also accompany this line of social development. From the fifties up to the seventies, the distribution of income and material goods seemed to have evolved rather uniformly, whereas the eighties brought an obvious change in that sphere. Which groups are on top and which are at the bottom of the prosperity scale? Who are the winners and who are the losers of these past years? All these are questions which we must pay attention to again, now, questions which will play an essential role in the surveys and the social reporting of the near future.

4.5 More Attention to Regionalization

The network of European NUTS Regions must, in particular on level NUTS 3, be uniformly provided with data - and this also refers to the social area. If we want to have the same quality of living in different parts of the country, differences must be watched and documented regularly. The development of geographical information systems does not reduce the demand of data on small territories. Regional statistics is no little statistical playhouse but a stage where serious and convincing productions are to be expected from.

4.6 More Attention to Emancipation Processes

Since the last century, social statistics has joined emancipation processes by the supply of data. At present, the emancipation of *women* is of the utmost importance. Apart from the gender breakdown of all person-related tables, it requires particular surveys on female family and employment biographies as well as systematic women-men comparisons in special social reports. Moreover, we must pay attention to the living conditions of ethnic minorities, of disabled persons, of children and the younger generation.

4.7 More Attention to Foreign Populations

High portions of foreigners have become the characteristic of many European populations and have turned into a political quantity. The separate presentation of the most important foreign populations will represent one of the main responsibilities of future official statistics. At present, this already applies to employment statistics, and demography is a similar case - whereas there is a need to catch up in the fields of health, education, housing, equipment and in many other areas of social behaviour which are part of empirical social research, and not of statistics.

4.8 More Attention to New Patterns of Social Differentiation

Gradually, time use has developed into a distinguishing pattern of social groups - and time budget surveys become part of official statistics. The characteristics of the dwelling environment grow more important than the rather uniform interior of flats. Their equipment with expensive home electronics, home computers or handies provides reliable distinguishing features, while car ownership, telephone and colour TV have lost their differentiation value.

4.9 More Attention to Longitudinal Analyses

The true reality every human experience tries to find is not only a condensed extract but also a variety of structures and distributions. In practice, we deal with the real world at different degrees of consistency, closeness and intensity, in statistics. Especially in the area of flows, affluence and poverty, thoroughly exploited grounds and fallows supported by the European Union exist side by side.

Along with cross-sectional surveys, models of stocks and flows should be related to each other on a macro level to illustrate structures and their changes. In a similar way, education, employment, health, migration or family biographies could be documented by surveys, life income and its distribution to the individual periods of life could be computed. This way, demographic approaches are spreading to economic statistics (demography of enterprises). Panel surveys and retrospective surveys develop into characteristic instruments, rise and fall (vertical mobility) become issues of statistics.

That much on some of the winner topics of these years. But there are also loser topics, as the national administration statistics which cannot be adapted. And there are subjects, which will remain wishful thinking in many countries, even at the end of our century, as for example, extensive statistics on land development, property dealing and real estate prices.

5 Consequences for Economic Statistics

Structural changes in economy are, I assume, generally known. Alterations of the social structure, however, also have their impact on economy and economic statistics. Let me, therefore, draw your attention to a number of issues from that part of economic statistics which is closely related to social statistics.

5.1 More Attention to the Service Sector

In almost all countries, economic statistics and business cycle observations concentrate much more on the field of production than on the service area. Anyway, the days are over when movements in industrial production could be used as a first estimate for the development of the whole of national economy. Similar indicators from the service sector are rare: retail trade turnover would be one example, overnight stays in tourism another. In employment, the trend is the reverse: it is easy to corroborate the fact that more and more labour volume of a national economy has been invested into services. Information on the value added produced reaches us only with a great delay. EUROSTAT is just developing a concept of extensive business cycle surveys in the service area. It will not be easy to realize this concept. The production area is much better prepared for statistics than the service sector, which is based on small scale companies, mainly. This takes me to the next item:

5.2 More Attention to the Statistical Capacity of the Business Establishments

Complaints are general about the burden inflicted on the establishments by foreign trade statistics and economic trend statistics, especially in countries where small and medium-sized enterprises are dominant and where many fields require a census to meet the quality standards of EU regulations. I know that every concession in this area must result in a loss of quality. Nevertheless, the introduction of reporting thresholds (which are independent of value added, turnover and employment) for regular surveys seems desirable to me, if there are periodical censuses helping to estimate the missing part.

5.3 More Attention to the Public Sector

The public sector is an important part of the service area. In National Accounts, the value added of the public sector is represented by its costs a high proportion of which is staff expenditure. Employment series for the civil service can, therefore, be treated as economic indicators. This requires the summary of data from various sources (from state, communal, and - in the federal states - provincial bodies as well as from other institutions which are part of the public area). To fulfil this task, only a few countries have a joint government employment statistics; in most countries, this is a macro-operation in the National Accounts framework without much consideration of structural data. Also from the background of an economizing trend in the public area, better structured and better comparable employment data on the public sector seem indispensable.

5.4 More Attention to the Land

Of the three classical production factors land, labour and capital, we know most about labour and not enough about the two others. I do not mention the lack of financial and flow accounts - that would be taking things too far. We must talk about land, however. For the purpose of doing this, we are doubtlessly equipped with a lot of information: on areas, on forms of land use and on ownership from the land register, on cultivation areas and their yields from agricultural statistics, on property dealing and the prices obtained from tax statistics, on possible building land resources from land development (for which, in Austria, the Länder - or provinces - and communes are responsible), on soil quality and emissions from the environmental sector, etc. In Austria, however, there is no data network connecting these pieces of information and, thus, enabling a multi-dimensional presentation of real estate. For decades, experts have tried to realize such a system; now I am counting it among those unfulfilled dreams which will continue to join us into the next century. In spite of all, we must record the fact that land is limited goods, and if we want to treat it carefully and correctly we need better information.

5.5 More Attention to Labour Distinctions

We have already mentioned that second jobs, part-time and contract work, flexible and precarious working conditions are everywhere on the advance, without their being uniformly registered. This area is a classical topic of household samples. Even in economic statistics, the aggregates of employed persons, of wage and labour costs hide a more complex reality, which the existing surveys cannot reveal.

I therefore believe, that the tendency of the Structural Income Survey of the European Union, which will be conducted in Austria in 1997, must be approved, even if, in many cases, it demands too much of the individual establishments with regard to their statistical capacities and, for this reason, cannot provide us with all the business information necessary to deal with the labour issue.

5.6 More Attention to the Structure of Labour Costs

This item is strongly linked to the above item. It need not be pointed out that the total labour costs - the costs of the production factor 'labour' - are of great importance to the competition of EU member countries with third countries as well as of EU member countries with each other. For this reason, I would like to speak a word in favour of the periodical labour cost surveys of the European Union, even if small and medium-sized enterprises are not very well prepared for them.

5.7 More Attention to Regionalization

This is another item which we have already talked about; it must be mentioned once more in economic statistics. The regionalization of National Accounts and of other highly aggregated statistics for the NUTS levels of the European Union has top priority. It is the first step towards the development and financial support of less-favoured regions. Small area evidence of local units of employment, of employment and unemployment, of commuter networks, of transport relations, of emissions, etc., are also important (and take us to the limits of data protection, in particular when concerning the employment and emissions of dominant enterprises). A typical area, which frequently requires data combinations of social and economic statistics, is *market research* (location analyses, labour resources, transport conditions, etc.).

5.8 More Attention to Redistribution Issues

The following remark is a direct continuation of social statistics: a profound treatment of distribution issues on the basis of micro-data from surveys or administration registers requires a macro-economic analysis of redistribution consequences on the national tax, transfer and social security systems. Such studies - as presented by Austrian economists last year - often contain surprising observations: that the biggest part of enormous redistributions of wealth between private and public households has no or very obscure redistributional effects; that measures intending redistribution to the bottom may become ineffective in the course of the years; that many natural budgetary phenomena, as road building expenditure, higher schools and universities, cultural sponsoring or residential building supports cannot be prevented from resulting in redistribution to the top on the part of the users. The redistributional effects of European Union measures remain to be analysed.

6 Conclusions

'Our future is no more what it used to be!' This quotation taken from the Austrian writer Karl Kraus is more than an amusing play on words but seems to anticipate the shadows over our future that developed during the past few years. The main sign cast upon our future seems to be the question mark: great challenges - and less and less financial means to meet them!

These were just a few unsorted and unassuming remarks on the topic, an agglomeration of unfinished ideas. I do not claim to belong to those people who never fail to realize the signs of the times and, therefore, always know what has to be done when. Nevertheless, I have tried to mention a few points where we have not reached our aims and where one could do more, perhaps.

Last but not least, I feel that we should not say good-bye without trying to encourage each other. There is no reason for resignation. Let us remain offensive, even with reduced resources! Act instead of reacting! On qualification, not on expansion we shall place your hopes! Let us not forget the economic side of social statistics, rendering the economic social (or the social economic)! The dialogue between social and economic statistics must intensify! Our predecessors began with statistics by watching human beings and their behaviour, by counting their observations and taking notes of them. We should never stop taking both aspects of statistics seriously, the "human" as well as the "economic" one. I am optimistic, in that respect, because I myself know sufficient people who - amidst their daily work - have not lost their enthusiasm.

29 The European Monetary Union: Challenges and Opportunities for the European Statistical System

Alberto De Michelis / Frank Schönborn

1 Introduction

The Economic and Monetary Union (EMU) is scheduled to begin on 1 January 1999. At the moment, mid-1997, we still do not know which countries will form this union, as the relevant decision will not be taken until Spring 1998. What we *do* know, is that the creation of a huge area in which a single currency - the euro - is used, will affect the organisation and production of statistics in the European Union, in the rest of Europe, and very probably around the globe.

Our objective here is to analyse the situation in Europe after 1999 as we see it in the statistical field. This paper sets out the main strategic thrust of the work that Eurostat, the Statistical Office of the European Communities, together with the future European Central Bank and the national statistical bodies must do in order to meet this challenge. These systemic adjustments also provide golden opportunities for making advances in statistics against the backdrop of the economic globalisation.

The development of the European Statistical System has always been closely related to the deepening and enlargement of the European Community, now European Union. In fact, the statistical activities at the European level have been progressively responding to the growing information requirements emerging from the increasing number of policy tasks to be pursued in the Community framework. Although the extension of statistical achievements was quite gradual, some major development stages deserve to be mentioned.

In 1957, through the Treaty of Rome, the European Economic Community was founded to give post-war Europe an ambitious economic and political perspective of integration. Subsequently, a Statistical Division was created to support the, at that time, rather limited range of EU policies aiming both at the progressive opening of national markets for goods, and at implementing a common agricultural policy. According to these objectives, modest, first attempts were made to gather national data and to produce European aggregates for the major fields of macro economic policies, whereas for the agricultural sector, comprehensive and genuine Community statistics were developed.

After the completion of the customs union during the sixties and in view of the first attempt to create a monetary union at the turn between the sixties and the seventies, great efforts were made to enhance the comprehensiveness and harmonisation of integrated economic accounts and foreign trade statistics. Common standards, classifications and methodologies became important references for the development of national statistics within the European Community. The European System of Economic Accounts: ESA, the general industrial classification of economic activities within the European Communities: NACE and NIMEXE, the nomenclatures of goods for the external trade statistics of the Community are salient examples by which international standards were further developed for their use within the European Community.

The period between 1973 and 1986 was first characterised by several enlargements of the European Communities from 6 to 12 countries and secondly by a progressive liberalisation of national foreign exchange transactions for some Community countries. Whereas the first aspect generally increased the pressure for a higher degree of harmonisation of statistics within the Community, the second one required the countries which dismantled their foreign exchange controls to adapt the collection system for their balance of payments statistics. Statistical information gained through foreign exchange controls, mostly banking records, had to be replaced by specific statistical reporting. It was also during this period, at the beginning of the eighties, that harmonised business tendency surveys were introduced throughout the Community.

A totally new challenge emerged with the Single European Act in 1987 aiming at the completion of the internal Market by the end of 1992. Free circulation of people, goods, services and capital set a milestone in European integration and likewise had considerable repercussions for statistics. A sharply increased demand for more comparable economic, business and also social statistics had again to be met in spite of the loss of essential administrative data sources. The latter particularly refers to the loss of customs statistics for trade between Member Countries. It had to be replaced by a new system collecting directly from enterprises and is partly linked to the administrative system of value added tax returns (INTRASTAT).

2 The Impact of EMU on Statistics

Now, due to the adoption of the Maastricht Treaty in 1993, European monetary unification has become a constitutional objective set up within a fixed time frame. In consequence, a common monetary policy for EU countries (at least for those participating in the single currency) will be defined and implemented by the future European Central Bank. By the same token, with a view to avoiding excessive government deficits, national fiscal policies have become subject to a fairly tight surveillance mechanism at the EU level. Upper limits for both the fiscal deficit and the stock of government debt have been fixed in relation to the GDP.

Before Maastricht, it is true, Member States also had to pursue economic policies ensuring the equilibrium of their overall balance of payments and maintaining confidence in their currencies. A coordination mechanism at EU level was also set in motion. However, the final responsibility and authority for the stance of monetary and fiscal policy remained with the national governments and in the case of insufficient convergence of economic performance of a Member State as compared to the other Member States, the system of fixed exchange rates allowed for exchange rate adjustments, which indeed occurred on several occasions. During the pre-Maastricht era, the essentially nationally oriented monetary, financial and balance of payments statistics were, as a rule, sufficient for pursuing the respective policy and surveillance tasks by national and Community authorities. Due to the EMU, however, this has changed and the impact on the statistical field will be considerable in several respects.

Firstly, on the **demand** side, management of economic and monetary policy at national and EU level will highlight new needs in terms of relevant comprehensive, genuinely consolidated, harmonised and timely data for the different decision levels. However, given the multidimensional objectives of the EU, in the event, the need for genuine EU statistics will comprise virtually all aspects of economic and social life which, according to the treaties, are dealt with in the EU framework.

Due to the creation of the single market in 1992 a number of statistical sources of an administrative nature were abolished; EMU will exacerbate this effect, and statisticians must review and adapt their methodologies and collection systems. This impact on the **production** conditions of statistics will be particularly felt for the bulk of monetary, financial and balance of payments statistics. Until now, these statistics hinged to a large extent on the notion of national territories and borders, and even more importantly, on the differentiation according to national currencies. In consequence, through the creation of a Single Currency area, a number of statistical sources will simply get lost. This mainly concerns transactions between residents of different EMU Member States.

Thirdly, there will be an impact on the **organisation** of the European statistical system. Provision is made under the Treaty on European Union (the Maastricht Treaty) for the European Central Bank, with the assistance of the central banks of the Member States, to collect and compile all the statistics it needs to do its job. That means that alongside with Eurostat there will be another major institution contributing to the development of the European Statistical System. The creation of a single-currency area will quickly push decision-making in the field of economic and monetary policy to a supranational level, and decisions will have to be based on statistical data compiled at the level of the Union and EMU respectively, rather than at Member State level as before. In the light of these developments, Eurostat's role will change: from a body basically responsible for coordinating and harmonising national statistics, it will increasingly have to play a role as producer of statistics at the level of the European Union.

Last, but not least, EMU will effect the **quality** of the statistics that the European statistical system will be led to produce. Like it or not, statistical information will be increasingly used for major policy and administrative decisions. Within the EMU, statistics will become a major tool for the Member States' surveillance mechanisms, and will form a basis for decisions that will affect the whole of the Union. The recent debate on measuring the cost of living in the United States, for instance, should encourage European statisticians to step up their efforts to improve the quality of their statistics, particularly those that will be used as a basis for sensitive political decisions.

3 The Demand for Statistical Information

The transition to a fully fledged Economic and Monetary Union will affect the framework and the efficiency of EU policies to an extent which goes far beyond a strengthened coordination of monetary and fiscal policies as previously mentioned. A look at the general economic EU tasks to be achieved within the Economic and Monetary Union presents good indications of the policy areas to be followed up within the EU framework and consequently, covered by EU statistics. According to the treaties, *common policies shall promote throughout the Community a harmonious and balanced development of economic activities, sustainable and non-inflationary growth respecting the environment, a high degree of convergence of economic performance, a high level of employment and of social protection, the raising of the standards of living and quality of life; and economic and social cohesion and solidarity among Member States.* This concise statement strongly illustrates that the future requirements asked from the European Statistical System in terms of economic, social and environmental statistics will be similar to what constitutes the conventional statistical information of a modern, industrialised economy.

It is worth noting that the respective institutions which have to contribute their due part to the achievements of the common European policy goals are not necessarily institutions acting at the EU level. In accordance with the principle of subsidiarity, only if and in so far as the objectives of the proposed action cannot be sufficiently achieved by the Member States, a Community institution shall take action. Nevertheless, irrespective of the level of the acting institutions - European, national or regional - coherent and comparable statistical information for European policy goals will be needed throughout the whole EU.

As far as transition to EMU is concerned, we cannot talk of demand for really new statistics to cover areas not covered hitherto. However, through the introduction of a single currency, in addition to the internal market, the degree of economic integration will reach a new quality. Therefore, there is a need for much greater comparability, harmonisation and consolidation of existing statistics in order to provide the appropriate information for all decision levels, national and EMU. Both will be an essential feature of the next big decision in Europe. I use the words "in Europe" for good reason, as this requirement will obviously affect not just the Member States of EMU, but also the countries known as the "pre-ins", which, whilst not forming part of the first wave of EMU, might subsequently join, together with countries that wish to become members of the European Union and that will subsequently form part of monetary union. I will give some examples of where harmonisation work will need to be done, and specific data produced more regularly.

The management of monetary policy by the Central Bank will need to be based on a set of short-term indicators produced by each country using the same definitions at very precise and regular intervals. Examples include indicators for supply and demand, production and consumption, the labour market, money supply, etc. Responsibility for producing these indicators will lie with the European System of Central Banks on the one hand and Eurostat with the National Statistical Institutes on the other. It is significant that the International Monetary Fund recently devised a system of statistical indicators for monitoring the economic and monetary policies of all countries at world level. Eurostat's and the future Central Bank's programme of short-term indicators will go well beyond IMF requirements.

The multilateral surveillance reinforced by what is known as a "growth and stability pact", will call for very accurate statistical monitoring country by country. There will be a particular call for harmonisation of quarterly accounts at constant prices, and for the expansion of quarterly harmonised accounts for the general government sector, at least for the main aggregates. The results of the qualitative business tendency surveys will certainly also be an important complement to the quantitative indicators.

On the fiscal level, there is currently provision underway to change over to a common VAT system for using economic accounts, input-output tables and other statistical sources when reallocating VAT receipts between countries. Obviously, this can only be done once fully comparable reference indicators have been established. This will call for specific household consumption surveys on the one hand and harmonisation of final consumption aggregates from the national accounts on the other.

4 The Production of Statistical Data

When the single European market was created in 1992 by eliminating a wide range of barriers to the free movement of people, goods, services and capital between Member States, statisticians had to cope with the disappearance of administrative information that had hitherto been the source of various statistics. EMU will have to deal with a further blow to administrative sources, particularly in the banking sector. This concerns a whole range of balance of payments transactions mainly between different EMU countries such as trade in services, tourism and certain transfers. It is also certain that the banking community is applying strong pressure to limit the burden of statistical declarations needed for the intra-EMU balance of payments.

It is obviously a manageable task to produce balance of payments statistics:

(1) for the EU, as a whole, focusing on the current account and direct investment flows;
(2) for the EMU, as a whole, to comprise all transactions, in the short term, and;
(3) for individual non-EMU countries to be monitored in the pre-in phase to EMU.

However, a conflicting situation occurs if balance of payments statements are, at least partly, to be produced for the individual EMU countries in order to establish their national economic accounts including trade in goods and services, etc.

Due to the General Agreement on Trade of Services (GATS), subsequent to the Uruguay Round, the international trade in services will deserve particular attention. Statistics will have to comprehend both "cross-border trade" and trade through "commercial presence" in the foreign country. In consequence, for all cross-border affairs, the coming years will probably see statisticians having to collect data directly from enterprises, rather than use administrative sources, at least for intra-Union trade

5 Organisation of Statistics

As previously mentioned, provision is made under the Maastricht Treaty for the European Central Bank, with the help of national central banks, to collect and compile all the statistics it needs to do its job. This means that, for the first time in the history of European statistics, a supranational body, the ECB, will have the right to directly produce statistics, the central national banks acting as executives for ECB decisions. No such provision is made for the bulk of other statistics that are not the responsibility of the ECB.

Until now, the relations between Eurostat, a directorate general of the European Commission, and the National Statistical Institutes have been of a different legal nature as in the case of Central Banks. Eurostat's relationship with the National Statistical Institutes has grown in the long process of statistical cooperation. Nevertheless, it is obvious that the transition to EMU enforces the need for a strong central statistical institution acting at EU level which will assume the responsibility of meeting the statistical requirements of the EMU as a whole. This is the natural vocation of Eurostat. On an organisational level however, Eurostat will have to ensure that it is capable of producing EMU statistics which should be more than a simple aggregation of national numbers produced by Member States. Certainly, this task can only be achieved in close cooperation with the national statistical institutes, which have the *in situ* infrastructure and organisational capacity for collecting data.

Comparability, i.e. the strict harmonisation of Member States' statistics will become even more important than in the past. In the event, policy decisions affecting all EU countries will be contingent upon this data. A few examples will show how a new organisation of the European Statistical System will occur in the new EMU environment.

Firstly, for national accounts, it is one thing to combine the financial and non-financial accounts of the Member States to produce accounts for the Union, but it would be quite another to produce them directly (or indirectly via the NSI's and the central banks as collecting bodies). The results of the latter would, in our opinion, be more reliable, more consistent and would be available more rapidly. This would meet a real need, given the importance of national accounts for monitoring the Union's economic and monetary policy. In view of this, it seems obvious to us that the European Central Bank will play the same role in compiling financial accounts as is currently played by most of the national central banks, even if accounts are subsequently revised, supplemented and brought into line with non-financial accounts by the statistical institutes.

The second example is similar; it concerns the Economic and Monetary Union's consumer price index. To some extent, account has already been taken of this in the Union's decisions regarding the harmonisation of consumer price indices. Partially aggregated national data is forwarded to Eurostat by the NSI's, and Eurostat calculates the EMU aggregate. This information for example is relevant for the EMU participation of countries to be decided in Spring 1998.

The third example is of a more general nature. It concerns all surveys or production of indicators whose results are required primarily at EMU level. In our opinion, it is essential for Eurostat to be able to collect the data needed to produce these statistics directly (or indirectly) on its own initiative.

The last example does not concern just Eurostat. It is a topic that must form the subject of close coordination with the European Central Bank: the balance of payments. This data is useful for both trade negotiations and bilateral agreements (the responsibility of Eurostat) and monetary policy (responsibility of the ECB). In all likelihood, and notwithstanding the conflicting situation referred to above, monetary union will mean that, in the long term, we shall no longer need balance of payments figures for individual Member States - all we shall need is the EMU balance of payments. The ECB and

Eurostat, with the assistance of the national institutes (NCB's and NSI's) will play a central role in compiling this data.

6 Data Quality

The quality of statistical information must be guaranteed by a high degree of relevance, reliability; timeliness, objectivity and professional independence. These criteria have always been a central concern of European statisticians. We are convinced that this will become even more important with the transition to EMU. There are two reasons for this:

Firstly, major economic and political decisions will be made at EMU level on the basis of statistics. The quality of these statistics will therefore be crucial for the analysis and the exertion of political pressure. This should not become a subject for political bickering but, like Caesar's wife, must be above suspicion. National and European statistical authorities should thus become guarantors of this quality.

The second reason stems from the novelty of statistics produced directly by Eurostat and the ECB for the EMU. The challenge will be considerable: these statistics will be scrutinised by institutional users and shrewd observers of EMU affairs, economists, research institutes, politicians, etc.

Therefore, continued investments must be made in statistical research, and political authorities should be immediately alerted to the grave risks they run if the qualitative bases of their decision-making instruments is inadequate. We are convinced of the need to provide for closer cooperation between the world of official statistics and research establishments. In terms of the quality of statistics, there is everything to be gained from pooling the ideas and experiences of NSI's, central banks, universities and research centres. To refuse communication between these institutions under the pretext of statistical independence would be unwise and dangerous. EMU represents a golden opportunity to stimulate and deepen this debate.

7 Economic Globalisation

In parallel with the European integration, the process of global integration has gained a strong momentum. Their origins and consequences for the statistics, namely deregulation of international transactions and loss of administrative information, are of a very similar nature. But this time, the problems apply not to transactions between residents of different EU countries, but more generally to transactions between EU countries and the rest of the world. However, the problems are not confined solely to the loss of statistical sources, which in principle could be replaced by developing alternative compiling systems. In addition, the meaning of former concepts of inter-national transactions - transactions between nations - is increasingly put into question by the process of globalisation. We do not really have an "internal" global market, but we have much more than just trade between nations. Trade between affiliated and non-affiliated firms, subcontracting and processing trade are only a few words behind the conventional notion of international trade in goods. This list can easily be extended by the increasing importance of international trade in services, which can take place through very different channels, in addition to the intricate subject of direct investment activities. Reflections have started on what should and could be the subject of statistical records in order to catch the most relevant features of the globalisation process. However, there are a host of conceptual issues, including economic paradigm, as well as the ensuing statistical problems to be cleared. These problems are and can only be tackled by the world community within the appropriate forums - the most important of which are the UN, WTO, IMF, World Bank and the OECD. Eurostat always was and will be a particularly active contributor in these forums attempting to find appropriate statistical solutions. Results coming out of this cooperation concerning for example the statistical methodologies for international trade flows in goods and services; direct investment and other capital flows, have been and will be duly taken into account together with the statistical adjustments with regard to EMU.

8 Conclusions

We have entered a crucial period for statistics in Europe. The strengths and weaknesses, pitfalls and opportunities of European statistics have been systematically analysed during recent congresses and meetings organised by various institutions, as for instance at the 1994 Voorburg conference on the "Long-term Perspectives of International Statistics".

The creation of EMU, for all its intrinsic risks in terms of institutional relations between the Member States, is a golden opportunity to advance statistical knowledge, produce quality data, and make from statistics a reliable, decision-making instrument for political authorities and economic and social operators alike.

More and more tasks were put to the EU level, whilst the framework in which economic activities are to be undertaken approaches a single market and a currency area which is open to meet the international competition in a more and more globalised world.

The current European system must meet these challenges if it is not to fall behind the pace of change of the realities those statistics purport to present. However, as Duncan-Gross put it in their recent book on Statistics in the 21st Century, *truly effective change can only come about if it is informed by a larger vision: a vision that is clear-sighted in its understanding of the current statistical system, bold in its projections of what a more adequate system will look like, and aggressive in its determination to move all affected and interested parties toward making that vision a reality.*

References

Accuracy, timeliness and relevance of economic statistics. Papers and Proceedings of a Conference organized by the International Statistical Institute (ISI), Eurostat (Statistical Office of the European Union) and the Bureau of Economic Analysis (BEA), U.S. Department of Commerce; in Washington, 9-11 September 1996.
Duncan, J.W. and Gross, A.C., Statistics for the 21st Century;
Eurostat: Draft Statistical Programme 1998-2022 (unpublished).
Treaty on European Union (signed in Maastricht 1992).
Treaty establishing the European Community (signed in Rome 1957).